The MICHELIN Guide

New York City

RESTAURANTS

2011

Manufacture française des pneumatiques Michelin

Société en commandite par actions au capital de 304 000 000 EUR
Place des Carmes-Déchaux — 63000 Clermont-Ferrand (France)
R.C.S. Clermont-Fd B 855 200 507

Dépot légal Octobre 2010
Made in Canada
Published in 2010

The MICHELIN Guide
One Parkway South
Greenville, SC 29615 USA
www.michelinguide.com
michelin.guides@us.michelin.com

Dear Reader

We are thrilled to present the sixth edition of our MICHELIN Guide to New York City.

Our dynamic team has spent this year updating our selection to wholly reflect the rich diversity of New York City's restaurants and hotels. As part of our meticulous and highly confidential evaluation process, our inspectors have anonymously and methodically eaten through all five boroughs to compile the finest in each category for your enjoyment. While these inspectors are expertly trained food industry professionals, we remain consumer driven: our goal is to provide comprehensive choices to accommodate your comfort, tastes, and budget. Our inspectors dine, drink, and lodge as 'regular' customers in order to experience and evaluate the same level of service and cuisine you would as a guest.

We have expanded our criteria to reflect some of the more current and unique elements of New York City's dining scene. Don't miss the scrumptious "Small Plates" category, highlighting those establishments with a distinct style of service, setting, and menu; and the further expanded "Under $25" listings which also include a diverse and impressive choice at a very good value.

Additionally, you may now follow our Michelin Inspectors on Twitter @MichelinGuideNY as they chow their way around town. Our anonymous inspectors tweet daily about their unique and entertaining food experiences.

Our company's two founders, Édouard and André Michelin, published the first MICHELIN Guide in 1900, to provide motorists with practical information about where they could service and repair their cars, find quality accommodations, and a good meal. Later in 1926, the star-rating system for outstanding restaurants was introduced, and over the decades we have developed many new improvements to our guides. The local team here in New York enthusiastically carries on these traditions.

We sincerely hope that the MICHELIN Guide will remain your preferred reference to the city's restaurants and hotels.

Contents

Peter L. Wrenn / MICHELIN

John Peden

The Michelin Guide

"This volume was created at the turn of the century and will last at least as long".

This foreword to the very first edition of the MICHELIN Guide, written in 1900, has become famous over the years and the Guide has lived up to the prediction. It is read across the world and the key to its popularity is the consistency in its commitment to its readers, which is based on the following promises.

→ Anonymous Inspections

Our inspectors make anonymous visits to hotels and restaurants to gauge the quality offered to the ordinary customer. They pay their own bill and make no indication of their presence. These visits are supplemented by comprehensive monitoring of information—our readers' comments are one valuable source, and are always taken into consideration.

→ Independence

Our choice of establishments is a completely independent one, made for the benefit of our readers alone. Decisions are discussed by the inspectors and the editor, with the most important decided at the global level. Inclusion in the guide is always free of charge.

→ The Selection

The Guide offers a selection of the best hotels and restaurants in each category of comfort and price. Inclusion in the guides is a commendable award in itself, and defines the establishment among the "best of the best."

How the MICHELIN Guide Works

→ Annual Updates

All practical information, the classifications, and awards, are revised and updated every year to ensure the most reliable information possible.

→ Consistency & Classifications

The criteria for the classifications are the same in all countries covered by the Michelin Guides. Our system is used worldwide and is easy to apply when choosing a restaurant or hotel.

→ The Classifications

We classify our establishments using XXXXX-X and ⌂⌂⌂-⌂ to indicate the level of comfort. The ✿✿✿-✿ specifically designates an award for cuisine, unique from the classification. For hotels and restaurants, a symbol in red suggests a particularly charming spot with unique décor or ambiance.

→ Our Aim

As part of Michelin's ongoing commitment to improving travel and mobility, we do everything possible to make vacations and eating out a pleasure.

How to Use This Guide

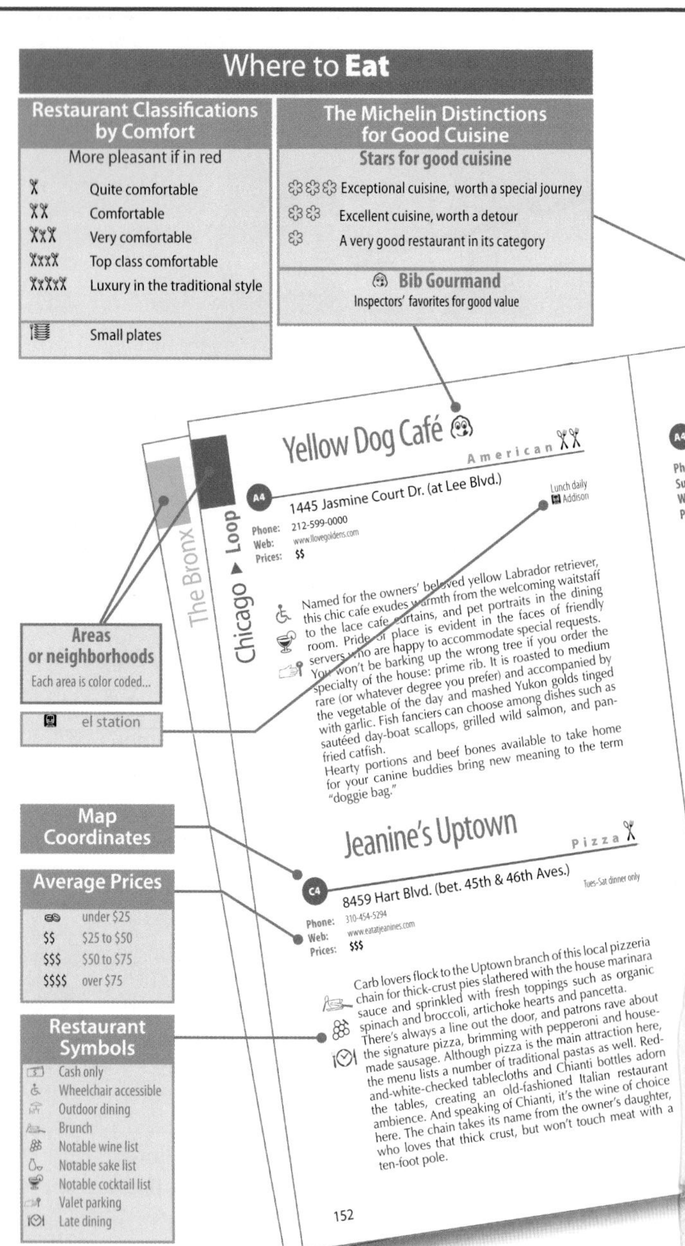

Where to **Stay**

Average Prices	Hotel Symbols	Hotel Classifications by Comfort
Prices do not include applicable taxes	149 rooms — Number of rooms & suites	More pleasant if in red
$ under $200	Wheelchair accessible	Quite comfortable
$$ $200 to $300	Exercise room	Comfortable
$$$ $300 to $400	Spa	Very comfortable
$$$$ over $400	Swimming pool	Top class comfortable
	Conference room	Luxury in the traditional style
Map Coordinates	Pet friendly	

a's Palace

Italian

uther Pl. (at 30th Street)

Dinner daily

5309

8 Av

nyasfabulouspalace.com

Manhattan ▸ Chelsea

David Buffington/Getty Images

Home cooked Italian never tasted so good than at this unpretentious little place. The simple décor claims no big-name designers, and while the Murano glass light fixtures are chic and the velveteen-covered chairs are comfortable, this isn't a restaurant where millions of dollars were spent on the interior.

Instead, food is the focus here. The restaurant's name may not be Italian, but it nonetheless serves some of the best pasta in the city, made fresh in-house. Dishes follow the seasons, thus ravioli may be stuffed with fresh ricotta and herbs in summer, and pumpkin in fall. Most everything is liberally dusted with Parmigiano Reggiano, a favorite ingredient of the chef.

For dessert, you'll have to deliberate between the likes of creamy tiramisu, ricotta cheesecake, and homemade gelato. One thing's for sure: you'll never miss your nonna's cooking when you eat at Sonya's.

153

The Fan Inn

D1

135 Shanghai Street, Oakland

Phone: 650-345-1440 or 888-222-2424
Web: www.superfaninnoakland.com
Prices: $$

45 Rooms
5 Suites

John A. Rizzo/Getty Images

Housed in an Art Deco-era building, the venerable Fan Inn recently underwent a complete facelift. The hotel now fits with the new generation of sleekly understated hotels ering a Zen-inspired aesthetic, despite its 1930s origins. oothing neutral palette runs throughout the property, ctuated with exotic woods, bamboo, and fine fabrics. he lobby, the sultry lounge makes a relaxing place for l-mixed cocktail or a glass of wine.

inens and down pillows cater to your comfort, while een TVs, DVD players with iPod docking stations, eless Internet access satisfy the need for modern s. For business travelers, nightstands convert to ables and credenzas morph into flip-out desks. inter, fax or scanner? It's just a phone call away. est, the hotel will even provide office supplies.

half of the accommodations here are suites, uxury factor ratchets up with marble baths, ting areas, and fully equipped kitchens. inn doesn't have a restaurant, the nearby early everything you could want in terms of dumplings to haute cuisine.

San Francisco ▸ Civic Center

315

Where to Eat

Peter L. Wrenn / MICHELIN

Manhattan

Chelsea

Restaurants in this artsy neighborhood—the hub of New York's gallery scene—feature flavors from around the globe, encompassing everything from French bistros to sushi bars and contemporary Spanish fare. Old World Puerto Rican luncheonettes on and around 9th Avenue—where patrons are accommodated in English or Spanish, and the *café con leche* packs a heady wallop—provide a striking contrast to the mega-hip places that punctuate Chelsea today. For heavenly pizza, try the much-hyped **Company**, home to iconoclast Jim Lahey's blistered and crispy pies. The Chef/owner and founder of **Sullivan Street Bakery**, fires his pizza in a wood-burning oven imported from Modena, and the lines of folks eager to taste them stretch out the door. If that's not hip enough, there's always the scene at **Buddakan**, that tried and trendy temple of modern Asian fare, brought to New York by Philadelphia restaurateur wunderkind Stephen Starr.

In the burgeoning area known as the West Club District, patrons of nightspots like Mansion, Guest House, Home, and Marquee are grateful for all-night restaurants like the **Punjabi Food Junction**, offering a delish self-serve Indian buffet. Also in the open-late category, quintessential New York spot **The Half King** dishes up good all-American grub. Named for an 18th century Seneca Indian chief, Half King also sponsors book readings on Monday nights, thanks to owner and writer Sebastian Junger, author of *The Perfect Storm: A True Story of Men Against the Sea*.

No food-finding excursion to this area would be complete without a visit to the **Chelsea Market**. The 1898 Nabisco factory—where the Oreo cookie was first made in 1912—reopened in 1997 as an urban food market. Interspersed throughout its brick-lined arcades with stores selling flowers, meats, cheeses, artisan-made breads, and other gourmet essentials are cafés, bakeries, and eateries. Drop by to peruse the wares, stock your pantry, and have a bite to eat while you're at it. Treat yourself to organic farm-fresh cuisine and biodynamic wines at **The Green Table** and **The Cleaver Co.** Seafood lovers can pick up a luscious lobster roll or some freshly steamed lobsters at **The Lobster Place**, New York's leading purveyor of these sea creatures. If you have kids in tow, a stop at **L'Arte del Gelato** is a must. Some new welcome additions to the market are **Dickson's Farmstand** for their serious meats and **Lucy's Whey** for cheese. No matter your preference, a trip to the market will nourish you for hours of gallery-hopping on the district's western flank. Upstairs, the Chelsea Market pavilion houses the studios and test kitchens for the Food Network. Once

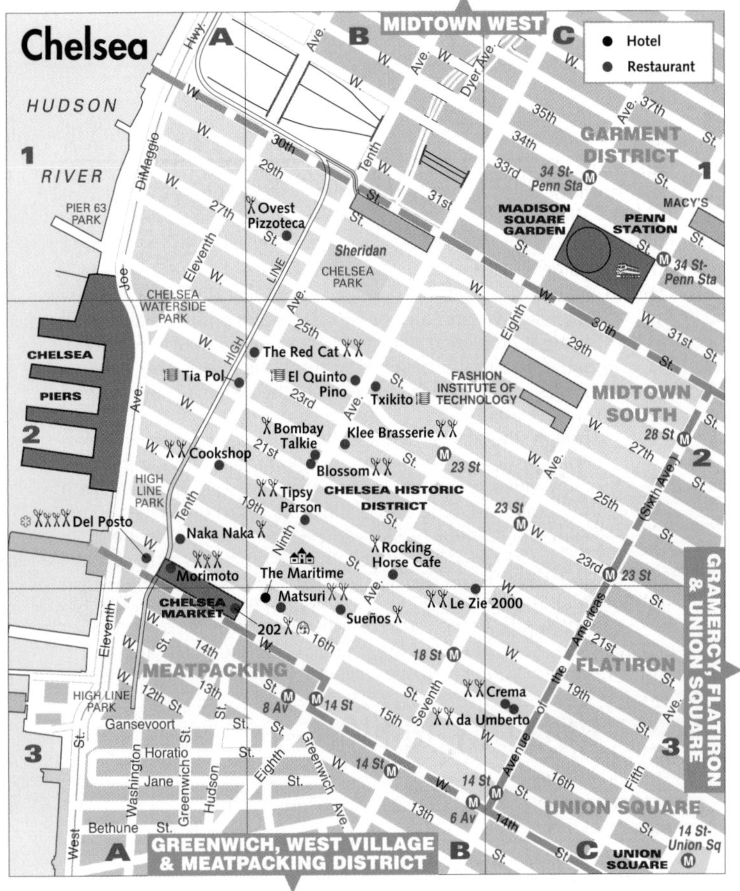

off-limits to the public, these facilities were recently opened for 45-minute tours.

Continue your stroll through Chelsea and follow the meaty scents to **Salumeria Biellese** for some great cured products; and to satisfy your sweet cravings, **La Bergamote Patisserie** is the perfect landing spot. And while in the neighborhood, consider dining with a view of Lady Liberty on one of the dinner cruises that departs from Chelsea Piers, an ever-evolving recreational waterfront area located along the West Side Highway between 17th and 23rd streets. Comprising four historic piers along the Hudson River, the complex now houses state-of-the-art sports facilities, including a spa, ice skating rink, and bowling alley. **Chelsea Brewing Company**, overlooking the Hudson River, is a perfect spot to close your day. Quench your thirst with one of their unique beers like the Checker Cab Blonde Ale.

Blossom

B2 — Vegan XX

187 Ninth Ave. (bet. 21st & 22nd Sts.)

Subway: 23 St (Eighth Ave.)
Phone: 212-627-1144
Web: www.blossomnyc.com
Prices: $$

Lunch Fri – Sun
Dinner nightly

Who says vegan can't be sexy? This charming café hits all the right ambience notes: it's convivial without being loud, intimate without being claustrophobic, and the delicate mirrors and flickering votives offer the space a sultry dose of visual depth.

Though the city's demand for organic, nutritious meals continues to soar, not many restaurants are offering the kind of inventive, dynamic cuisine that Blossom is (along with its Upper East Side sister, Blossom Bistro on First Avenue). Witness a spirited black-eyed pea cake with chipotle aïoli; woodsy strips of grilled seitan over asparagus tips, shiitake mushrooms, and roasted cherry tomatoes, or the vegan Blossom cheesecake, a creamy concoction with an irresistible apricot purée.

Bombay Talkie

B2 — Indian X

189 Ninth Ave. (bet. 21st & 22nd Sts.)

Subway: 23 St (Eighth Ave.)
Phone: 212-242-1900
Web: www.bombaytalkie.com
Prices: $$

Dinner nightly

Located along a charming row of storefronts in Chelsea, the hip Indian restaurant, Bombay Talkie, knows the key to its popularity is in its consistency. Take a seat below the cool murals depicting Bollywood movie stars, and pick your meal off a menu boasting sections like "from the roadside" and "street bites."

Try a plate of *koliwada macchi,* an Indian rest stop staple of crispy fish served with shoe string potatoes; *malai kofta,* dumplings stuffed with cheese and coconut, and bathed in a cashew-yogurt sauce; or *Bomba bhel,* served with wheat flour chips and rice puffs, tossed with a bright lime, mint, onions, and green mango salsa. The double-decker standby offers two stories of seating and a long community table, but reservations are still recommended.

Cookshop

American XX

A2

156 Tenth Ave. (at 20th St.)

Subway: 23 St (Eighth Ave.) Lunch & dinner daily
Phone: 212-924-4440
Web: www.cookshopny.com
Prices: $$

The honest, super-focused menu at Chef Mark Meyer and his wife, Vicki Freeman's, Cookshop, defines a new generation of Manhattan restaurants: with a well-sourced (often local), seasonal menu that rotates faster than Mario Andretti's wheels, but is consistently soulful. Wonderfully al dente garganelli pasta arrives tossed with fresh tomatoes and Grana Padano; while soft, house-smoked Hampshire pork, laced in smoky-vinegary sauce, is tucked into a fresh sesame potato roll with a thump of coleslaw.

The bright, airy space is dotted with green plants and fresh flowers, and by day the big picture windows offer a flood of natural light and visions of the Highline; by night, the space dims and the hip local crowd fills the space with an energetic buzz.

Crema

Mexican XX

C3

111 W. 17th St. (bet. Sixth & Seventh Aves.)

Subway: 18 St Lunch & dinner daily
Phone: 212-691-4477
Web: www.cremarestaurante.com
Prices: $$

Hidden below street level on a Chelsea block dominated by consignment shops, Crema doesn't boast its charms to the world. Rather, this little restaurant relies on Chef Julieta Ballesteros' solid grasp of modern, upscale Mexican cooking to lure them in.

Inside, you'll find a narrow room with smooth, colorful walls, a cactus garden and a bar area sporting lovely glass vats of *agua loca*—a Mexican sangria not to be missed. All the better to wash down a perfectly balanced bowl of cream of corn bobbing with plump crab meat and baby cilantro; a tortilla pie layered with fresh ingredients and tender shredded chicken; or a decadent slice of pecan pie with spiced Mexican eggnog and vanilla ice cream. Come lunchtime, $15.95 scores you an entrée, soup, and side dish.

da Umberto

C3 Italian XX

107 W. 17th St. (bet. Sixth & Seventh Aves.)

Subway: 18 St — Lunch Mon – Fri
Phone: 212-989-0303 — Dinner Mon – Sat
Web: www.daumbertonyc.com
Prices: $$$

"Happy families are all alike," begins Tolstoy's most famous novel, and the same might be said of good Italian food. Not so at da Umberto, which raises the bar with their exacting attention to detail. The payoff for this sort of type-A behavior is creamy, perfectly-cooked risotto; fork-tender rabbit, stewed in a fragrant Sicilian sauce; and seductively sweet ricotta cheesecake, poured into a buttery crust and studded with candied fruit.

Unfortunately, the restaurant's prices are right in step with the sharply dressed businessmen and lunching ladies that fill its sophisticated dining room. And yet, everything is relative—as menu prices across the city have climbed, the questionable numbers gracing da Umberto's menu seem to have returned to market value.

El Quinto Pino

B2 Spanish

401 W. 24th St. (bet. Ninth & Tenth Aves.)

Subway: 23 St (Eighth Ave.) — Dinner nightly
Phone: 212-206-6900
Web: www.elquintopinonyc.com
Prices:

Chelsea has enough tapas joints to give the Barcelona metropolis a run for its money, but El Quinto Pino is a worthy addition that stands out in the crowded landscape. The Lilliputian Pino aims to bring tapas back to its original concept—these are quick snacks rather than sit-down meals. This is an ideal spot to stop and grab a distinctively authentic plate or two and a glass of wine from their blackboard selection.

Despite its lack of traditional table seating, the bar in this warm, narrow, Spanish-tiled space has been mobbed since its debut. Credit goes to the small, creative menu of tapas like deep-fried and perfectly cooked fingers of cod; uni panini, squeezed onto bread slathered with Korean mustard oil; and plates of small, garlicky shrimp.

Del Posto ✿

Italian XXXX

85 Tenth Ave. (bet. 15th & 16th Sts.)

Subway: 14 St - 8 Av
Phone: 212-497-8090
Web: www.delposto.com
Prices: **$$$$**

Lunch Mon – Fri
Dinner nightly

Joe Vaughn

You'd never know it from its Chelsea location and workaday metal awning, but Mario Batali's most ambitious restaurant, hemmed into New York's restaurant row underneath the gorgeous new Highline, is as grand as an opera house—with a sexy, over-the-top theatrical interior fitted out in swirling, wrought-iron balconies and dripping chandeliers.

The rustic Italian menu, carefully rendered under the watchful eye of Executive Chef Mark Ladner, reads deceptively simple, but no: melt-in-your-mouth *carne cruda* reaches ecstatic heights with truffle salsa, nutty porcini shards, and Parmigiano Reggiano; while a perfectly al dente tangle of spaghetti is tossed with scallions, jalapeño, and tender Dungeness crab; and perfectly grilled pork loin finds a heavenly pairing in creamy sunchoke purée dotted with tangy Lambrusco sauce.

This kind of *paradiso* will cost you, but there are ways to lighten the load: sample two or three pastas between your table or hit the solid value lunch menu with three courses at $29. Italian grapehounds will want to linger over Del Posto's neverending wine list, teeming with regional Italian producers and varietals, not to mention an ample Champagne selection.

Klee Brasserie

B2 — Contemporary XX

200 Ninth Ave. (bet. 22nd & 23rd Sts.)

Subway: 23 St (Eighth Ave.) — Lunch Tue – Sun
Phone: 212-633-8033 — Dinner nightly
Web: www.kleebrasserie.com
Prices: $$

It's the little details that make this Chelsea steady stand out from the neighborhood's ample restaurant competition. Guests melt into the soft, toffee-colored banquettes, flanked by bare brick walls and soothing blonde wood, and people-watch from the huge windows that line the façade.

Meanwhile, the sharp-as-a-tack staff quietly slides out plate after plate of Chef Daniel Angerer's innovative cuisine. A velvety bowl of chilled five-color carrot soup arrives lined with crispy dried corn kernels and studded with organic cherry tomatoes, micro chives, and shaved *Idiazábal* cheese; a nutty apple strudel is flanked by a house-made Tahitian vanilla gelato, and paired with crunchy caramelized walnuts, warm apple butter, and a soft, sweet lingonberry sauce.

Le Zie 2000

B3 — Italian XX

172 Seventh Ave. (bet. 20th & 21st Sts.)

Subway: 23 St (Seventh Ave.) — Lunch & dinner daily
Phone: 212-206-8686
Web: www.lezie.com
Prices: $$

Inside this pastel dining room, Le Zie 2000 continues to embody wholesome Italian cuisine. Outside, a small patio remains a fine place to while away the sunny days.

Begin meals in the Venetian tradition by sharing the antipasti sampling—*cicchetti*—which includes several of the region's savory classics and is served with its signature starch, grilled polenta. Among several fine *paste* and heartier *secondi piatti* is the ever-popular Le Zie mac 'n cheese with truffles.

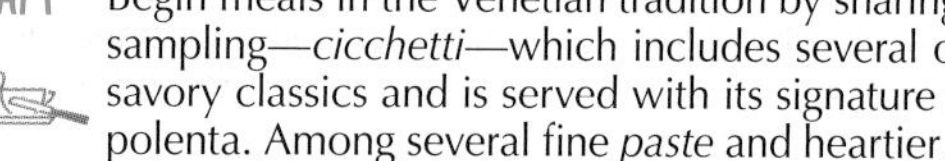

With an entrance on 20th Street, Le Zie features a cute, dimly lit, very comfy back lounge with light tasting and cocktail menus, served by a friendly bartender. All wines from Le Zie's extensive list of some 200 labels representing all of Italy's viticultural regions are available here.

Matsuri

B3 — **Japanese** XX

369 W. 16th St. (bet. Eighth & Ninth Aves.)

Subway: 14 St - 8 Av
Phone: 212-243-6400
Web: www.themaritimehotel.com
Prices: $$

Dinner nightly

Matsuri deserves the hiss of surprise that its jaw-dropping interior provokes—but unlike some Trojan Horses in this town, it has the food to back it up. Step inside the cavernous dining room, with its enormous curved ceiling, extensive sake collection lining the wall, and beautiful misshapen paper lanterns, and soak in the grandeur (the acoustics here rival some of the more prominent concert halls around this city).

When your jaw snaps back into place, settle in for some decadent Japanese fare, which might include a silky, red miso soup, infused with scallion and ginger, and with a single tender claw of lobster floating elegantly in its center; or a fresh young sea bass, deep fried with ponzu-*momiji* sauce.

Morimoto

A2 — **Fusion** XXX

88 Tenth Ave. (at 16th St.)

Subway: 14 St - 8 Av
Phone: 212-989-8883
Web: www.morimotonyc.com
Prices: $$$

Lunch Mon – Fri
Dinner nightly

Located in the super-trendy western nook of Chelsea, Morimoto has been packing them in on nights when even its most famous neighbors are a quarter-full. The draw? A starkly sexy interior with a cuisine bold enough to match it. Sail past Morimoto's billowing curtains and into the sultry cement-and-metal filled space, and you'll be greeted by more beautiful people than you can shake a Blahnik at.

Back on your plate, you'll find upscale Japanese fusion (heavy on the fusion, light on the Japanese) courtesy of the great Masaharu Morimoto. Try the delicate lamb carpaccio, perfectly sliced on the bias and garnished with a creamy lemon-kissed sauce, ginger, and scallions; or curried beef points wrapped in rice paper and breadcrumbs, then tossed in curry.

Naka Naka

A2

Japanese

458 W. 17th St. (at Tenth Ave.)

Subway: 14 St - 8 Av
Phone: 212-929-8544
Web: N/A
Prices: $$$

Dinner Tue – Sun

Like a mouse bucking a tsunami, little Naka Naka has stayed put while everything around it has caved to the ever-changing landscape where Chelsea borders the Meatpacking District. The winning concept of this homespun Japanese restaurant is simple—a small, pretty room tucked into a timeworn tenement building off 10th Avenue, where you'll discover a low-slung, horseshoe-shaped bar and a few well-spaced tables.

Save for the servers kneeling to take your order or ferrying food back and forth, the only commotion in this little haven is on the plate, where you might discover a perfectly-charred Spanish mackerel in sake paste, paired with a fried green horn pepper and roasted cherry tomato; or a fresh lobe of creamy uni, with Japanese pickles and grated radish.

Ovest Pizzoteca

B1

Italian

513 W. 27th St. (bet. 10th & 11th Aves.)

Subway: 23 St (Eighth Ave.)
Phone: 212-967-4392
Web: www.ovestnyc.com
Prices: $$

Lunch & dinner daily

Fine fare is rare in these parts, so Ovest Pizzoteca's (of the lauded Luzzo's) arrival into Chelsea's Club Row stirred up big buzz. Ravenous revelers follow the alluring aromas of pies and panini to this Italian idol—whose wood-and-gas burning oven crackles until first light—much to their delight. Open garage doors cede a glimpse of this mod, chic warehouse with industrial lighting and a wooden ceiling.

Veteran chefs prepare tasty treats like *alici marinate*—deliciously tart anchovies—in vinegar and olive oil; *polpettine* in a shiny tomato purée; *la pizza piccante* made pure with tomato sauce, cherry peppers, and sausage; and *pastiera Napoletana* with berries and vanilla. So let slide the loud crowd and yield to Luzzo's best on this side of the west.

The Red Cat

American 

B2

227 Tenth Ave. (bet. 23rd & 24th Sts.)

Subway: 23 St (Eighth Ave.)
Phone: 212-242-1122
Web: www.redcatrestaurants.com
Prices: $$

Lunch Tue – Sat
Dinner nightly

This clever, cozy, and perpetually hip Jimmy Bradley joint is packed wall-to-wall seven nights a week. And no wonder: with an interior fitted out in rich red banquettes and Moorish light fixtures that radiate warmth in winter and read sultry come summer, a downright sexy cocktail list and scrumptious, always inventive American fare, The Red Cat is what you might call a restaurant triple threat.

Book ahead and you too can get in on dishes like the curried sweet potato soup, served with a dollop of crème fraîche; supremely fresh bluefish, expertly grilled and finished with potatoes, green olives, and pepper salsa; or a warm plum shortcake, bursting with soft quartered plums and topped with maple whipped cream and cinnamon crème anglaise.

Rocking Horse Cafe

Mexican 

B2

182 Eighth Ave. (bet. 19th & 20th Sts.)

Subway: 14 St - 8 Av
Phone: 212-463-9511
Web: www.rockinghorsecafe.com
Prices: $$

Lunch & dinner daily

This easygoing Chelsea standby serves up solid Mexican fare in a vivid, sophisticated dining space fitted out with shimmering blue mosaic tiles, tangerine-colored walls, beet red accents, and creamy jumbo lanterns. At the bar, big mesh containers hold mounds of the house-made tortillas and a cheerful crowd lines the stools, downing seriously good (and strong) margaritas while they wait to be seated.

In the dining room, couples and friends line the tables, tucking into creative spins on Mexican favorites like a marvelous *ensalada de calamares*, spiked with fresh cracked black pepper, cool cilantro, and a lick of crema; a fresh batch of Niman Ranch pork *carnitas*; or a traditional, but irresistible *tres leches con platanos*, strewn with candied pecans.

Sueños

B3 **Mexican**

311 W. 17th St. (bet. Eighth & Ninth Aves.)

Subway: 14 St - 8 Av
Dinner Tue – Sun
Phone: 212-243-1333
Web: www.suenosnyc.com
Prices: $$

Sueños isn't the easiest place to access—you'll need to duck down an alley and walk something like a maritime plank to enter—and its interior won't be winning any design awards anytime soon. But this little Mexican charmer is more than a step above the mom-and-pop ethnic eateries that dot the Latin neighborhoods of East Harlem and Queens.

It's the little touches, like the fresh tortillas being churned out by hand in the rear of the dining room, or the criminally fresh guacamole, made to order with ripe chunks of avocado and bright tomato, and paired with a basket of salty, house-made chips. For dinner, try the empanadas—stuffed with rich, sweet plantain and tart chunks of goat cheese—each warm bite is a delicious study in contrasts.

Tia Pol

A2 **Spanish** 

205 Tenth Ave. (bet. 22nd & 23rd Sts.)

Subway: 23 St (Eighth Ave.)
Lunch Tue – Sun
Dinner nightly
Phone: 212-675-8805
Web: www.tiapol.com
Prices: 

On its surface, this tapas joint of much buzz is nothing more than a narrow, characterless space with a whirring fan and a horse sculpture, tucked behind a steel-patch door on Tenth Avenue.

So why all the fuss? Location, for starters: if you want a good bite along this stretch, the really good eats tend to be super high-end, like Del Posto or Craftsteak. Then there's the clever, affordable Spanish wine list, and the always-buzzing crowd, happily packed around Tia Pol's bar. But mostly, they come for the delicious tapas, a mouthwatering roster that might include tender lamb skewers; seasonal whitebait; cod done every which way but Friday; plus cheese and charcuterie platters loaded with silky hams and garlicky chorizos.

Tipsy Parson

American XX

B2

156 Ninth Ave. (bet. 19th & 20th Sts.)

Subway: 18 St — Lunch & dinner daily
Phone: 212-620-4545
Web: www.tipsyparson.com
Prices: $$

New Yorkers know the small plates drill by heart now: start slow and spend a mint. Tipsy Parson, a jewel in Chelsea compliments of Tasha Gibson and Julie Wallach, is as fine a place to do the dance as ever, with a homey, multi-room layout dressed in flower-fabrics, bric-à-brac, and French doors.

The menu features a nice selection of southern fare, including cheeses from Georgia, Tennessee, Virginia, and South Carolina, an Ambrosia salad (with marshmallows), and buttermilk chive biscuits. Try the deviled eggs and fried pickles, *rumaki*, and oysters; and tender fried Mississippi-farmed catfish aside horseradish and mustard-laced potato salad. Don't miss the apple pie, featuring Northern Spy apples and cinnamon custard, served in a hot cast iron skillet.

202

A3

75 Ninth Ave. (bet. 15th & 16th Sts.)

Subway: 14 St - 8 Av — Lunch & dinner Mon – Sat
Phone: 646-638-1173
Web: N/A
Prices: $$

It's a slightly unsettling concept at first: a lovely café located within—well, interweaved with, to be exact—a chic clothing boutique. But the regulars that flood Chelsea Market's 202 (located inside Nicole Farhi) soon find out that this café is much more than a party trick: it's a delicious afternoon respite from a day of shopping.

Take a seat at one of the beautifully worn, shabby-chic wood tables or find a seat at the surprisingly roomy bar, and tuck into fresh, straightforward market bistro fare like a colorful and luscious lentil, beet, and artichoke salad; a gorgeous tuna burger folded between toasted brioche and topped with guacamole and lime aïoli; or soft ricotta cheesecake, laced with orange and cardamom ice cream.

Txikito

Spanish

240 Ninth Ave. (bet. 24th & 25th Sts.)

Subway: 23 St (Eighth Ave.)
Phone: 212-242-4730
Web: www.txikitonyc.com
Prices: $$

Lunch Tue – Sat
Dinner Tue – Sun

The rise of the tapas movement in the United States is a fascinating one: what began as a concept on loan from Spain—a smattering of small plates paired with alcohol—has gotten so popular that people are willing to shell out as much cash as they would a proper meal.

Good thing the tiny little Txikito offers so many reasons to unload your wallet, with a knowledgeable waitstaff, proper silverware (though fingers and forks are just fine for tapas), and a simple, if slightly grim, décor where Chef Alex Raij, who hails from venerable tapas neighbor, Tia Pol, whips out mouthwatering small plates like meatballs pooled in shellfish broth; and *boquerónes* (marinated white anchovies), smoky eggplant purée, red peppers, and a fan of boiled egg.

Good food without spending a fortune? Look for the Bib Gourmand ☺.

Peter L. Wrenn/MICHELIN

Chinatown & Little Italy

As different as chow mein and chicken cacciatore, these two districts are nonetheless neighbors, though in recent years, their borders have become blurred with Chinatown voraciously gulping up most of Little Italy.

The end of California's Gold Rush brought the arrival of New York's first Chinese in the 1870s. The immigrant influx arrived energetically, setting up garment factories, markets, and restaurants in the quarter, which has inexorably spread into Little Italy and the Lower East Side. It is documented that New York cradles the maximum number of Chinese immigrants in the country and specifically, Queens, followed by Manhattan, holds one of the largest Chinese communities outside Asia. Immigrants from Hong Kong and mainland China (most recently Fujian province) populate the Manhattan Chinatown, each bringing their distinct regional cuisines.

Chowing in Chinatown can be both scrumptious and delightfully affordable. Elbow your way through the crowded streets and find a flurry of food markets, bubble tea cafés, bakeries, and eateries large and small. Feast on freshly pulled noodles; duck into an ice cream parlor for a scoop of avocado or black sesame; or breeze past a market window and spy the crocodile meat and frogs on display (with claws). Haggle over the freshest fish and produce at the storefronts and then sneak under the Manhattan Bridge for a *banh mi*.

Klezmer meets Cantonese at the Egg Rolls and Egg Creams Festival, an annual summer street celebration honoring the neighboring Chinese and Jewish communities of Chinatown and the Lower East Side. Partygoers pack the streets for Chinese New Year (the first full moon after January 19th), with dragons dancing down the avenues accompanied by costumed revelers and fireworks.

The Little Italy of Scorsese's gritty, authentic *Mean Streets* is slowly vanishing into what may now be more aptly called Micro Italy. The onetime stronghold of a large Italian-American population (once spanning from Canal Street north to Houston, and from Lafayette to the Bowery) has dwindled to a mere corridor—Mulberry Street between Canal and Broome streets. Chinatown is quickly devouring Mulberry Street, the main drag and the tenacious heart of the area.

But the spirit of the origins still pulses in century-old, family-run markets, delis, gelato shops, and mom-and-pop trattorias. Established in 1892, **Alleva Dairy** (known for their homemade ricotta) is

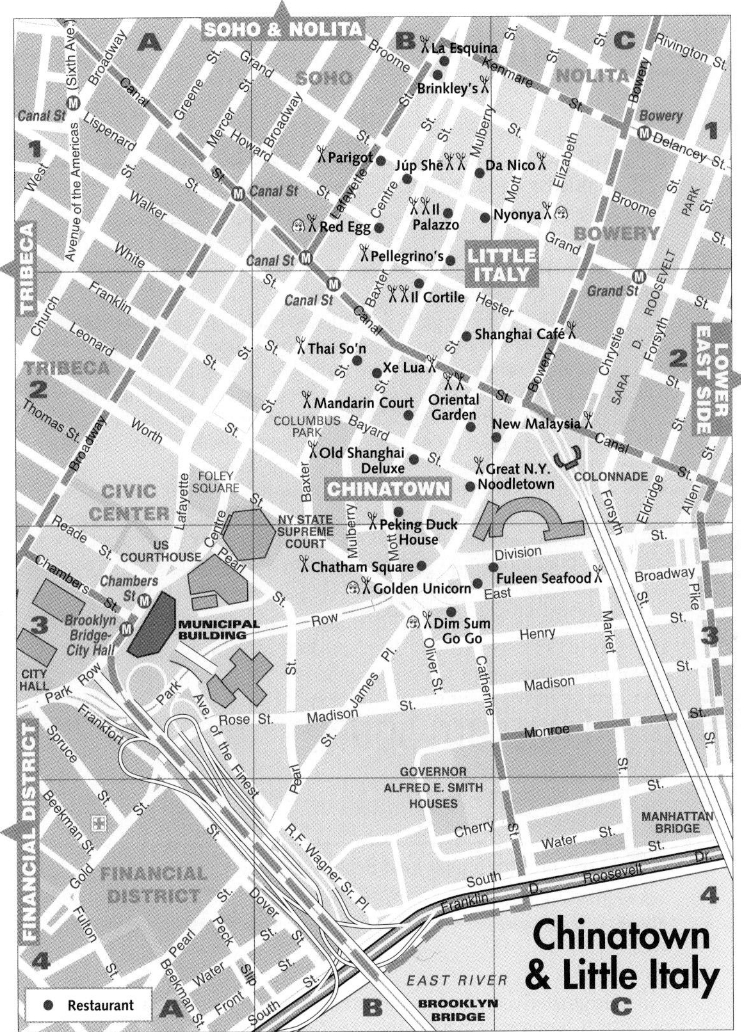

the oldest Italian cheese store in the U.S.; a few doors down at **DiPalo's Fine Foods** find imported *sopressata*, *salumi*, and a medley of wine selections. Renowned for its Italian pastries and strong espresso, devotees frequent the beloved **Ferrara's Bakery and Café** on Grand Street.

On weekends from May to mid-October, Mulberry Street is a pedestrian zone, creating one big alfresco party—the Feast of San Gennaro in September is particularly raucous. While these days you get better Italian food elsewhere, tourists still gather to treasure and bathe in the nostalgia of Mulberry Street.

Brinkley's

B1 Gastropub

406 Broome St. (bet. Centre & Lafayette Sts.)

Subway: Prince St — Lunch & dinner daily
Phone: 212-680-5600
Web: www.brinkleysnyc.com
Prices: $$

Brinkley's, a new gastropub tucked into the old Bar Martignetti space, is turning out to be quite the sleeper hit. Straddling a prime corner of real estate in Nolita, the restaurant (which is still owned by the Martignetti brothers) has good neighbors in nearby shop, Despaña, and the new Crosby Street Hotel; and the space is charmingly weathered, with a sexy, spirited design that reads retro in all the right ways.

British-born Chef Ben Towill mans the kitchen, pushing out a menu that might include sardines mashed into a gorgeous tomato, fennel, and shallot-strewn pulp; noodles of zucchini worked into a gorgeous carbonara, featuring smoky Virginia bacon and a tender poached egg; or a silky, exceptionally tasty pumpkin meringue pie.

Chatham Square

B3 Chinese

6 Chatham Sq. (at East Broadway)

Subway: Canal St (Lafayette St.) — Lunch & dinner daily
Phone: 212-587-8800
Web: N/A
Prices:

Situated on a thriving stretch of the Bowery known as "Chatham Square," this lively, well-priced spot draws a mostly Chinese crowd for its fantastic daytime dim sum and evening classic Cantonese.

Large round tables line the colorful dining space where friendly servers wheel around carts of delicious dumplings, puffs, buns, and soups at lunch. The rolling dim sum show has become a rarity so sidle up next to some strangers at a shared table and indulge in savory steamed dumplings—with at least ten varieties of fillings—or baked turnovers surrounding a savory mound of shredded roast pork. Sticky rice, congee, and dumpling soups provide some warmth. Feeling the funk? Brave the durian puffs—cigar-shaped pastries filled with a funky-fruity custard.

Da Nico

Italian

164 Mulberry St. (bet. Broome & Grand Sts.)

Subway: Canal St (Lafayette St.)
Lunch & dinner daily
Phone: 212-343-1212
Web: www.danicoristorante.com
Prices: $$

Dining here is an Italian-American celebration of garlic, tomatoes, and the traditional flavors typically associated with this culture—and neighborhood. From the coal-fired oven comes a variety of pizzas, all made using a crust recipe that has been passed down through generations of the Luizza family (of the Mulberry Street empire). The ample selection of well-made favorites may include fried calamari, homemade minestrone, and huge portions of pastas. Entrées are likewise copious, from chicken Sorrentino to veal saltimbocca, and everything in between.

Weather permitting, opt to sit on the back patio. This enclosed outdoor terrace nearly doubles the restaurant's seating space and provides a bucolic ambience, removed from the neighborhood commotion.

Dim Sum Go Go

5 East Broadway (at Chatham Sq.)

Subway: Canal St (Lafayette St.)
Lunch & dinner daily
Phone: 212-732-0797
Web: N/A
Prices:

This bright, funky Chinatown spot offers none of those cute little dim sum carts (order from a checklist here), nor, despite the devil-may-care moniker, are there any scantily clad dancers. There is, however, a most excellent selection of dim sum—and loads of it—with over 24 varieties to choose from, even well into the evening. While dim sum is traditionally served at breakfast and lunch, the devoted groups gathering over steamed buns of gogo "hamburgers" or baked roast-pork pies neither mind nor notice this departure from tradition… and paying a bit more for it.

Owner and French-American food writer, Colette Rossant, does not stop with dim sum, but also offers a fabulous yet oft-forgotten Cantonese menu that is something to marvel over and savor.

Fuleen Seafood

C3 — Chinese

11 Division St. (bet. Catherine & Market Sts.)

Subway: Canal St (Lafayette St.) — Lunch & dinner daily
Phone: 212-941-6888
Web: www.fuleenrestaurant.com
Prices:

From their variety of hard- and soft-shell crab dishes to ever-popular snails in black bean sauce or geoduck clams "two different ways," this Cantonese cuisine does impressive things with gourmet ingredients. The large round tables of this upscale Chinatown mainstay are filled with gregarious groups from the local, discerning Chinese community—a testament to its success. Yet all are welcome here, as the polite staff graciously guides you through the menu, making helpful recommendations.

Green vegetable dishes are an essential accompaniment to meals here, perhaps complementing a whole fish, presented raw tableside before being expertly steamed and dressed with ginger and scallions. Landlubbers will unearth plenty of options on the sizeable menu.

Golden Unicorn 

B3 — Chinese

18 East Broadway (at Catherine St.)

Subway: Canal St (Lafayette St.) — Lunch & dinner daily
Phone: 212-941-0911
Web: www.goldenunicornrestaurant.com
Prices: $$

With its rolling carts of dim sum doing outrageous weekend lunch business and multiple stories of both Chinese and Manhattan foodie families gathering around large tables of Cantonese specialties, Golden Unicorn is a quintessential spot for Chinatown cuisine.

True, the décor feels a bit worn, waits are guaranteed at peak dim sum times (11:00 A.M.-2:00 P.M.), and all groups must be on their game to flag the speeding carts, but this perennial favorite is undeniably fun and delicious. Those in-the-know arrive early to avoid crowds and lessen competition for the best selection of roast duck, fried sticky-pork dumplings, steamed bean-curd-skin rolls, and snow-pea-shoot buns.

Evening brings solid Cantonese specialties and nice banquet menus for private rooms.

Great N.Y. Noodletown

Chinese

28 Bowery (at Bayard St.)

Subway: Canal St (Lafayette St.) Lunch & dinner daily
Phone: 212-349-0923
Web: N/A
Prices:

You don't come for the ambience. With its closely-jammed tables, roast ducks hanging in the window, and menus tucked under glass-topped tables, Great N.Y. Noodletown is down-market Chinatown at its drabbest. What you come for is the food—which, served daily from 9:00 - 4.00 A.M.—is not only delicious but remarkably cheap. Who could argue with a big bowl of perfectly roasted duck and tender noodles in a steaming broth for $4?

Best bets include any of the roasted meats served over fluffy rice; and, of course, duck, in all its crispy, fatty succulence. Don't miss the specials located on the table tents, where you'll find irresistible house delights like salt-baked soft shell crab (a must-do when it's in season) and Chinese flowering chive stir-frys.

Il Cortile

Italian

B2

125 Mulberry St. (bet. Canal & Hester Sts.)

Subway: Canal St (Lafayette St) Lunch & dinner daily
Phone: 212-226-6060
Web: www.ilcortile.com
Prices: $$

Beyond this quaint and charming façade lies one of Little Italy's famed mainstays, ever-popular with dreamy-eyed dates seeking the stuff of Billy Joel lyrics. The expansive space does indeed suggest a nostalgic romance, with its series of Mediterranean-themed rooms, though the most celebrated is the pleasant garden atrium (*il cortile* is Italian for "courtyard"), with a glass-paneled ceiling and abundant greenery.

Chef Michael DeGeorgio presents a wide array of familiar starters and entrées, from eggplant rollatini to chicken Francese; as well as a range of pastas, such as *spaghettini puttanesca* or *risotto con Funghi*. More than 30 years of sharing family recipes and bringing men to one bent knee continues to earn Il Cortile a longtime following.

Il Palazzo

B1 — Italian XX

151 Mulberry St. (bet. Grand & Hester Sts.)

Subway: Canal St (Lafayette St.) — Lunch & dinner daily
Phone: 212-343-7000
Web: N/A
Prices: $$

This "palace" on Little Italy's celebrated Mulberry Street rises to every expectation of a good, traditional Italian-American meal. A tuxedo-clad host ushers guests into a long room with stucco walls and linen-draped tables. Beyond, the sunken dining room recalls a winter garden of lush greenery and natural light. Sidewalk seating is lovely and popular among tourists watching tourists.

Old-world dishes reign here, beginning with a basket of focaccia and bowl of Roman egg-drop soup. The classics continue with the likes of *vitello alla pizzaiola* (veal scallopini sautéed with tomato, onions, mustrooms, roasted pepper, and fresh basil); or *gamberoni alla scampi* (jumbo shrimp sautéed in garlic white-wine sauce. Lunchtime frittata specials offer good value.

Júp Shē

B1 — Korean XX

171 Grand St. (at Baxter St.)

Subway: Canal St (Lafayette St.) — Lunch & dinner daily
Phone: 212-343-0090
Web: www.jupshenyc.com
Prices: ⊜

Located on the fringe of Chinatown, this friendly spot delivers a tasty selection of traditional Korean dishes. Nab a seat in the sleek space, where wooden tables, colorful chairs atop tile floors, and red accent walls lend a contemporary feel. Into the spice? We hope so—these fiery dishes aren't toned down for anybody.

Order a plate of *bulgogi duk-bok-ki*—thick noodle sticks, tender chunks of smoky beef, and shaved onion swimming in a spicy-sweet sauce of chili paste and chili oil. The *jae-yook-bokkum,* is another lip smacker: finely sliced strips of tasty pork, cooked up with scallions, garlic, onions, and red chili paste. Service is speedy and straight forward, thus naturally crowded with young professionals and tourists, especially during lunch.

La Esquina

Mexican

B1

106 Kenmare St. (bet. Cleveland Pl. & Lafayette St.)

Subway: Spring St (Lafayette St.) Lunch & dinner daily
Phone: 646-613-7100
Web: www.esquinanyc.com
Prices: $$

Despite the years, this fun and sultry spot remains hip—just ask the doorman checking names at the unmarked entrance to its subterranean brasserie. No one enters without reservations, which are famously difficult to get.

The same kitchen serves its simple yet tremendously bright and flavorful Mexican cuisine throughout three distinct dining areas: the first is a storefront with sidewalk seating, takeout, and creamy café con leche; the second a mellow corner café (no reservations) great for a brunch of *huevos rancheros*; and the almighty third is that stylish (and loud) downstairs spot. All serve the same wonderful tortilla soup.

Still, La Esquina has calmed enough to let the food deservedly take center stage, alongside those signature cocktails.

Mandarin Court

Chinese

B2

61 Mott St. (bet. Bayard & Canal Sts.)

Subway: Canal St (Lafayette St.) Lunch & dinner daily
Phone: 212-608-3838
Web: N/A
Prices: 

Dim sum is not just for weekend brunch anymore. At Mandarin Court, dim sum is served every day from 8:00 A.M. to 4:00 P.M. The presentation is Hong Kong-style; the waitresses roll carts full of dumplings, buns, wontons, and other savories past your table so you can take your pick. There's even sweet dim sum for dessert (egg custard; coconut-flavored gelatin; and sesame balls).

If you're really hungry, try one of the entrées, which include steaming bowls of broth brimming with noodles, vegetables, meat, or seafood. The dining room may not look like much, and it may be a bit noisy with your neighbors a little too close for comfort, but the regulars don't come here for the atmosphere. They're attracted by good Cantonese fare at reasonable prices.

New Malaysia

Malaysian

46-48 Bowery (bet. Bayard & Canal Sts.)

Subway: Canal St (Lafayette St.) Lunch & dinner daily
Phone: 212-964-0284
Web: N/A
Prices:

Hidden in the Chinatown arcade accessed from either Bowery or Elizabeth, New Malaysia is *the* spot to go to in Manhattan for regional Malaysian. Some dishes are better than others, so reserve stomach space for the kitchen's strengths.

Asam laksa is a bowl of soupy, funky heaven, and the fried anchovies are a glorious and addictive could-be bar snack. *Roti canai* comes with a masterful coconut curry so delish you'll want to drink it up; and the fried *belacan* lady finger with shrimp is a complex, haunting stir fry. *Nasi lemak* and *beef rendang* are also killer but don't expect the skinny jeans to fit after all that coconut.

Insulin levels will spike with one of the Malaysian beverages, or colorful sweet shaved ices that bring sugary to a whole new level.

Nyonya

Malaysian 

199 Grand St. (bet. Mott & Mulberry Sts.)

Subway: Canal St (Lafayette St.) Lunch & dinner daily
Phone: 212-334-3669
Web: www.penangusa.com
Prices:

A Malaysian marvel in Manhattan, Nyonya is replete with regulars and City Hall suits. The space, now a bit brighter and larger, retains its Chinatown aesthetic and buzzes with gruff servers. But keep faith, as they hold the keys to some magnificent Malaysian.

Teasing your taste buds is a fluffy oyster omelette anointed with sweet chili sauce. A specialty from the massive menu and perfect for the prudent is beef satay with peanut sauce; while the house special crabs massaged with ground chili and dried shrimp is best for the bodacious.

A bevy of classic beverages gorgeously gratifies Malay faithfuls like *Assam laksa* rich with herbs, lemongrass, noodles, and sardine flakes; and *nasi lemak*, a mélange of coconut rice, chicken, anchovies, veg, and eggs.

Old Shanghai Deluxe

Chinese 

50 Mott St. (at Bayard St.)

Subway: Canal St (Lafayette St.) — Lunch Mon – Fri
Phone: 212-566-4884 — Dinner nightly
Web: N/A
Prices: ⊜

Just off the bustle of Bayard Street in the heart of Chinatown, New Yeah Shanghai offers a taste of its namesake city. Live plants, arched ceilings, and Asian decorative accents lend a cave-like, Pacific Rim feel to this otherwise casual restaurant.

Decision-making may be difficult here, where an extensive menu features Shanghai favorites, dumplings galore, all sorts of noodles, and many daily specials; as well as seasonal items created specifically for holidays throughout the year. The carefully cooked food is served as promptly as it is prepared by the capable staff, and the large portions are ideal for family-style gatherings (with leftovers to go).

New Yeah Shanghai's loyal crowd of regulars, locals, and tourists feel equally at home here.

Oriental Garden

Chinese 

B2

14 Elizabeth St. (bet. Bayard & Canal Sts.)

Subway: Canal St (Lafayette St.) — Lunch & dinner daily
Phone: 212-619-0085
Web: N/A
Prices: ⊜

Located in the bustling heart of Chinatown, Oriental Garden's mid-block location is easily spotted by the large gold lettering on its stone façade. Inside, the slender windows make the dining room feel decidedly tucked away, amid pale walls simply lined with framed Chinese characters and gold dragons. Towards the front, tanks brimming with fish illustrate the expansive menu's orientation toward seafood in dishes like braised abalone with oyster sauce, drunken live prawns, and sautéed cuttlefish with black bean and green pepper.

During the day, there is a hearty selection of dim sum; and you will always find a wide range of stir fries, as well as mounds of delish noodles and vibrant vegetable and tofu dishes.

Parigot

French 

B1

155 Grand St. (at Lafayette St.)

Subway: Canal St (Lafayette St.) Lunch & dinner daily
Phone: 212-274-8859
Web: www.parigotnyc.com
Prices: $$

Straddling a bright corner between Little Italy and SoHo, Parigot works because it does a little bit of everything right. The food is good, but the unending hospitality of Chef/owner Michel Pombet leaves an indelible impression; the cozy bistro atmosphere, covered in black and white nudes, is lovely without being gauche; and the staff is loose and friendly, but efficient.

The restaurant's name is slang for a person born and raised in Paris, and the menu covers said territory by touching all the croque-monsieur-and-ox-tail-terrine bases. Kick things off with a French onion soup, bubbling with hot, stringy cheese over soft chunks of bread; and then move on to a plate of crispy, pan-fried trout in a silky sauce of butter, capers, chives, and tomato.

Peking Duck House

Chinese 

B2

28 Mott St. (bet. Chatham Sq. & Pell St.)

Subway: Canal St (Lafayette St) Lunch & dinner daily
Phone: 212-227-1810
Web: www.pekingduckhousenyc.com
Prices: $$

Only rookies open the menu at Peter Luger steakhouse—and the same ought to apply to any restaurant named after a menu item. So while you may stumble onto a few gems like the fragrant wonton soup, the bird is the word at this group-friendly Chinatown joint.

Despite its boorish name, the Peking Duck House is a touch classier than her Chinatown sisters, with a contemporary polish that won't frighten your Midwestern cousin. Service may slow down at the more elegant midtown location, but both locations wheel out the golden brown duck with proper flare, and carve it into mouthwatering slices. Your job is easy: Fold the freshly carved meat into fresh pancakes, sprinkle with scallion, cucumbers, and a dash of hoisin sauce—then devour.

Pellegrino's

Italian

138 Mulberry St. (bet. Grand & Hester Sts.)

Subway: Canal St (Lafayette St) — Lunch & dinner daily
Phone: 212-226-3177
Web: N/A
Prices: **$$**

On a warm summer day, Pellegrino's quaint sidewalk tables look upon the heart of Little Italy. You will likely find both regulars and tourists frequenting this local mainstay, since the long, narrow dining room is attractive, the umbrella-shaded outdoor tables are inviting, and the service is courteous. Children are welcome at family-friendly Pellegrino's; in fact, half-portions are offered for smaller appetites.

The food stays true to its Italian-American roots with large portions of balanced pasta, meat, and fish selections. Linguini alla Sinatra, the signature dish named for the beloved crooner, teems with lobster, shrimp, mushrooms, and pine nuts in a light red clam sauce. Tasty, classic desserts are likewise a draw to this popular destination.

Red Egg

Chinese 

202 Centre St. (bet. Grand & Hester Sts.)

Subway: Canal St (Lafayette St) — Lunch & dinner daily
Phone: 212-966-1123
Web: www.redeggnyc.com
Prices:

Where are the grandchildren of Chinese immigrants eating? As Chinatown creeps north of Canal, fast approaching micro Italy's turf, a stretch of newer Chinese restaurants angled to a younger crowd arrives. One of the best and brightest is Red Egg, a modish restaurant with an imitation Sex and the City décor: think SoHo-style with lesser cocktails but better food. They even gave the space a face-lift this year; those sexy ladies love their maintenance.

As for the food, by day, there's a massive dim sum menu where you check off boxes until a wealth of goodies start piling up on your table. Dinner features a shorter choice of dim sum, plus a ton of great Chinese options. The Peruvian influence is less apparent now and the focus more Chinese than fusion.

Shanghai Café

B2 **Chinese**

100 Mott St. (bet. Canal & Hester Sts.)

Subway: Canal St (Lafayette St.) Lunch & dinner daily
Phone: 212-966-3988
Web: N/A
Prices: ⚭

Head to this contemporary Chinatown spot when the craving hits for good Shanghai-style cuisine at a fair price. Dumpling assemblers beckon diners in from the front window, assembling the tiny, succulent juicy buns, and adding them to massive steamers. Filled with crabmeat and/or pork, these juicy little jewels explode with flavor in your mouth. A hands-down favorite, "steamed tiny buns," as the menu calls them, appear on nearly every occupied table, sometimes in multiple orders. In addition, the enormous menu cites a decision-defying array of Shanghai classics including cold and hot starters, soups, and seafood and noodle dishes.

Have a taste and you'll agree that Shanghai Café ranks a bun above the usual Chinese fare on this stretch of Mott Street.

Thai So'n

B2 **Vietnamese**

89 Baxter St. (bet. Bayard & Canal Sts.)

Subway: Canal St (Lafayette St.) Lunch & dinner daily
Phone: 212-732-2822
Web: N/A
Prices: ⚭

Even along competitive Baxter Street, Thai So'n is a neighborhood standout for high-quality Vietnamese fare and tremendous value. The atmosphere may feel like a catering hall with minimal focus on comfort, but this does not dissuade the groups and families seeking the huge and authentic Vietnamese menu of fresh, fiery, and flavorful cuisine.

Ignore the Chinese selections (popular with the nearby City Hall crowds) and start with frogs' legs in chili-lemongrass sauce, then go with the *pho*: comforting bowls of rice noodles and delicately sliced raw beef that instantly cook when scalding broth is poured overtop. Garnish this with ample condiments and wash it down with a *tra da chanh* (cold tea with fresh lemonade) for a traditionally delicious experience.

Xe Lua

Vietnamese

86 Mulberry St. (bet. Bayard & Canal Sts.)

Subway: Canal St (Lafayette St) — Lunch & dinner daily
Phone: 212-577-8887
Web: www.xeluanewyork.com
Prices: ⓈⓈ

A cheery orange sign splashed in yellow, blue, and green blazons this lovely spot's name in both English and Vietnamese, while tropical themes outfit the interior in royal blue, bamboo, and a floor-to-ceiling mural of boats, sea, and sky.

The expansive menu features a flavorful assortment of appetizers, stir fries, clay pots, noodles, and rice dishes, with headings like "Porky," "Froggy Style," and "Chicken Little" to express their quirky humor. Dive into one of fourteen varieties of *pho*—these steaming bowls of rice noodle soup are all under seven dollars. Heartier appetites are satisfied with the *pho xe luna*, a massive bowl of noodles, brisket, tendon, tripe, and meatballs swimming in a rich beef broth. The staff is pleasant, quick, and efficient.

The sun is out – let's eat alfresco! Look for 品.

East Village

This storied bohemia is no longer rampant with riots, rockers, and radical zeitgeist, but remains crowned as Manhattan's uncompromising capital of counter-culture. East Villagers may seem tamer now that CBGB is closed, but they are no less creative, casual, and undeniably cool.

The neighborhood's bars and eateries exhibit the same edge, and denizens craving a nightly nosh have plenty to choose from. **Momofuku Bakery & Milk Bar**, turns out a spectrum of delectable baked goods and soft serve ice cream in seasonal flavors like caramel apple and "stuffing" until midnight. Crispy Belgian fries from **Pomme Frites** are heightened by sauces like curry-ketchup and smoked-eggplant mayo. For burgers, **Paul's Palace** may have the best in town. **Crif Dogs**—open until 4:00 A.M. on weekends—deep fries their dogs for the perfect post-pub-crawl snack. Many eateries, cafés, second-hand shops, and vendors line these blocks with specialties from pork (**Porchetta**) to macaroni & cheese (**S'mac**) in a distinctly East Village way. Speaking of cheese, **The Bourgeois Pig** draws celebrities on the "down-low" with its pots of fondue; equally stellar is **Luke's Lobster**, a seafood shack offering the freshest of product directly from Maine. Perhaps most spirited, and in keeping with the kitschy downtown feel, is Japantown—a decidedly down-market and groovier "Harajuku" version of its Midtown East sibling. Along St. Marks Place look for the red paper lanterns of hip yakitori spots like **Taisho**, or smell the *takoyaki* frying and sizzling *okonomiyaki* at **Otafuku**; and explore divey *izakayas* like **Go** or **Village Yokocho**. Among the area's sultry sake dens, few can rival subterranean **Decibel**—serving an outrageous selection of sake and *shochu* in its hideaway setting.

While Japantown may tuck its lounges down a nondescript stairway, everything along the "Curry Row" stretch of East Sixth Street smacks of festivities, with spices as bold as the neon lights that dot the awnings. While these inexpensive spots may cater to NYU students, they also offer a great spread of South Asian food. Still, devout bargain-hunters journey east into Alphabet City, teeming with tasty taquerias, bodegas, and bars.

For a bit of old-world flavor, an afternoon at **Veniero's Pasticceria & Caffè** is in order. Established in 1894, this friendly staple draws long lines (especially around holiday time) for its traditional Italian baked goods. The beloved, family-run **Veselka** has been

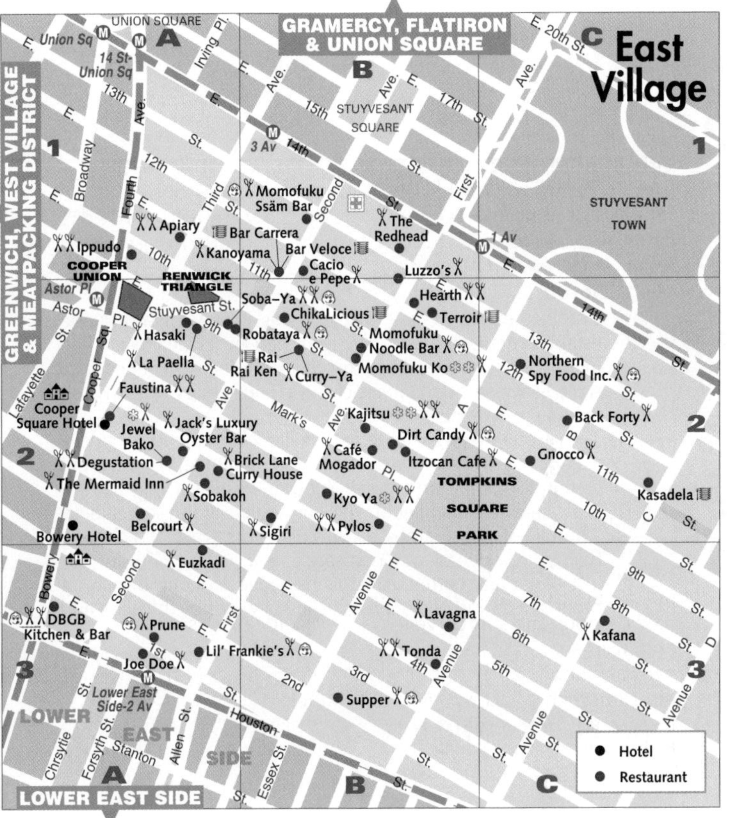

serving Ukrainian treats for over 50 years, representing the area's former Eastern European population. For specialty items, **East Village Cheese** is a premier vendor—find an ample selection here, minus the mark-up of gourmet emporiums.

It goes without saying that liquor flows freely in the East Village. There are an abundance of dive bars, but those with a more urbane palate will be happy that this neighborhood is at the nexus of cutting-edge mixology. **Angel's Share** (hidden in a Japanese restaurant on Stuyvesant Street); **PDT**, or Please Don't Tell (accessed through Crif Dogs); **Death & Co.** on East Sixth Street; and **Mayahuel** (with its south-of-the-border spin) all offer an epicurean approach to cocktail service garnering them accolades.

Whole Foods and Chipotle may have moved in but there's no taking the culinary edge off this vibrant edible quarter with its youthful, international vibe.

Apiary

A1 Contemporary XX

60 Third Ave. (bet. 10th & 11th Sts.)

Subway: 14 St - Union Sq — Dinner nightly
Phone: 212-254-0888
Web: www.apiarynyc.com
Prices: $$

Chef Scott Bryan's new post is at this sleek yet comfortable establishment designed and furnished by Ligne Roset. The intimate and slender dining room is outfitted with generously sized espresso-hued tables, crimson Luca chairs, and modish lighting treatments.

The straightforward menu's skilled production, global accents, and clean presentation are a fitting complement to the contemporary space. Specials display a nod toward seasonality as in a fillet of wild-harvested salmon served atop a bundle of sweet ramps. A bowl of the orzo mac and cheese, bathed in a decadently rich sauce, is a perfect side dish for just about any entrée. Apiary's beverage program displays a broad reach and offers a nice listing of wines by the glass and seasonal cocktails.

Back Forty

C2 Contemporary X

190 Ave. B (at 12th St.)

Subway: 1 Av — Lunch Sat – Sun
Phone: 212-388-1990 — Dinner nightly
Web: www.backfortynyc.com
Prices: $$

Chef/owner Peter Hoffman, also of Savoy, satiates city slickers seeking the country life with this popular tavern's array of fresh-from-the-farm themed preparations. The casual setting evokes heartland charm with its tables topped by brown paper mats that display the menu, walls adorned with found objects and agricultural tools, as well as an inviting backyard dining area.

Snacks and starters, such as pork jowl nuggets with jalapeño jam, are represented alongside seasonal garden side dishes like a cauliflower gratin. A core menu of hearty entrées may include the excellent, succulent braised lamb shank, perfectly manageable in size, slicked with a rich meat jus reduction, then plated with creamy celery root purée and sweet-sour apple chutney.

Bar Carrera

Spanish

175 Second Ave. (bet. 11th & 12th Sts.)

Subway: 1 Av — Dinner nightly
Phone: 212-375-1555
Web: www.barcarrera.com
Prices: 

Perfectly focused and deliciously simple, the owners of beloved Bar Veloce (next door) have erected this culinary temple to Spain. The dark and intimate room brims with regulars, from bankers to scenesters, sipping a lovely selection of Spanish wines and lingering over tapas. With both traditional and modern options, these small plates offer unique authenticity and skill—as in the *albondigas*, simmered so slowly in rich tomato sauce that the meatballs develop deep, savory flavors beyond expectation. A testament to quality is the *jamón serrano*, available in a variety of ages, with each one more decadent and gamey than the last. Chorizo fans will be equally enthused by the offerings.
A second (slightly larger, if less ambient) location is in SoHo.

Bar Veloce

Italian

175 Second Ave. (bet. 11th & 12th Sts.)

Subway: 1 Av — Dinner nightly
Phone: 212-260-3200
Web: www.barveloce.com
Prices: 

Veloce was one of the pioneers in the wine bar craze long before they became repeat cases of banal food and overpriced glasses of wine. A long, stylish strip of spot in the East Village, often marked by a Vespa in front, Veloce makes up for in personality what it lacks in space.
The *vini, aperitivi*, and *digestivi* are mostly Italian and very well-chosen, and the gracious bar team can easily guide you in the right direction. Panini are divine, made with an expert hand on the press, and a select assortment along with some *bruchette* and *formaggi* will happily accompany a few glasses of wine.
Veloce now has locations in Chelsea and SoHo, both with more seating and a few tables in larger spaces but neither with the modern, charismatic charm of the original.

Belcourt

A2

Mediterranean

84 E. 4th St. (at Second Ave.)

Subway: Astor Pl — Lunch & dinner daily
Phone: 212-979-2034
Web: www.belcourtnyc.com
Prices: $$

Brimming with mix-and-match wood furnishings, antique mirror panels, and reclaimed signage, one might be misled to assume that this young and charming neighborhood favorite is from a bygone era. The relaxed look is classic Paris brasserie; the cuisine is anything but.

Chef/partner Matt Hamilton, who sharpened his skills at Five Points and Prune, takes a fresh approach to a seasonally themed menu that sways toward the Mediterranean. Offerings may include a sauce-slurping stew of steamed clams, chewy coarse-ground sausage, and tender white beans all sparked by bold salsa verde; or moist pan-fried Long Island fluke beautifully complemented by a decadent scallion and crème fraîche sauce, garnished with sweet and tender-roasted greenmarket carrots.

Brick Lane Curry House

A2

Indian

306-308 E. 6th St. (bet. First & Second Aves.)

Subway: Astor Pl — Lunch & dinner daily
Phone: 212-979-2900
Web: www.bricklanecurryhouse.com
Prices: $$

Located on Curry Row and named after London's own, Brick Lane is a 6th Street standout featuring numerous influences lifted from across the pond. Beers are available by the half or full pint, an Underground map adorns the wall, and meltingly soft cheddar cheese stuffs the tasty *paratha*.

Despite the Anglo-culinary whimsy, Brick Lane's heart belongs to curry with a selection of fifteen varieties that include Goan, spiked with green chilies and a tangy bite. Prepared with your protein of choice, the selection even includes the *phaal*, said to be so spicy it is accompanied by a disclaimer warning guests of "physical or emotional damage" that may result. However, this may also be a reminder of the thoughtful, friendly, and efficient service staff here.

Cacio e Pepe

Italian

B1

182 Second Ave. (bet. 11th & 12th Sts.)

Subway: 3 Av — Dinner nightly
Phone: 212-505-5931
Web: N/A
Prices: $$

With its low-key temper and genuinely gracious service, this charmingly rustic Italian can be trusted to satisfy. The menu of traditional Roman dishes features a house specialty from which the establishment takes its name: house-made *tonnarelli* tossed with pasta water, olive oil, cracked black pepper, and a plethora of pecorino cheese. Likewise, the kitchen features a number of creative flourishes, such as a starter of bacon-wrapped shrimp in a pool of eggplant purée. Reserve aside, embark on dessert—cannoli filled with lemon-flavored ricotta—and wind up in heaven.

The wine list is short but carefully selected to highlight less-familiar producers in the most notable Italian regions. In warm weather, the backyard garden makes a lovely dining area.

Café Mogador

Moroccan

B2

101 St. Mark's Pl. (bet. First Ave. & Ave. A)

Subway: 1 Av — Lunch & dinner daily
Phone: 212-677-2226
Web: www.cafemogador.com
Prices:

This family-run, neighborhood favorite graciously serves breakfast, lunch, and dinner daily while exuding an inviting coffee-house vibe that spills onto the pleasant sidewalk seating. Moorish lanterns, spice jars, and black-and-white photos of Morocco impart an air of exoticism.

Mediterranean small plates like roasted eggplant with creamy tahini and fresh pita make a fine prelude to the warm and fluffy house specialty: couscous, perhaps offered with vegetables or spicy *merguez*. Traditional, sweet-spicy, slowly simmered, lamb and chicken tagines are moist, tender, and always popular in sauces of apricots and prunes or piquant green *charmoulla*.

Since 1983, reasonable prices and affable service should ensure Café Mogador's continued longevity.

ChikaLicious

Contemporary 

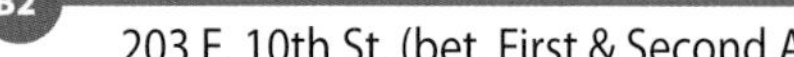

B2

203 E. 10th St. (bet. First & Second Aves.)

Subway: Astor Pl — Dinner nightly
Phone: 212-995-9511
Web: www.chikalicious.com
Prices:

Named for Pastry Chef/owner Chika Tillman, this sweet spot presents an all-encompassing dessert experience that somehow manages to impress without overkill. The chic white space offers counter seating overlooking a lab-clean kitchen where the team prepares elegant jewels that start as butter, sugar, and chocolate. À la carte is offered, but the best way to appreciate this dessert bar is to select the prix-fixe menu. Feasts here may begin with an amuse-bouche of Darjeeling tea gelée with milk sorbet, followed by a mascarpone semifreddo topped with espresso granita, then finish with the pillowy cubes of coconut-marshmallow petits fours.

Dessert Club across the street tempts with cookies, cupcakes, and shaved ice for a grab-and-go fix.

Curry-Ya

Japanese

B2

214 E. 10th St. (bet. First & Second Aves.)

Subway: Astor Pl — Lunch & dinner daily
Phone: 866-602-8779
Web: www.nycurry-ya.com
Prices:

From the co-owner of Soba-Ya, comes this tasty newcomer, specializing in Japan's unique version of curry—*yoshoku*. This culinary icon belongs in the repertoire of Western style dishes that have become a part of the Japanese palate. Characterized by a mild sweetness and restrained heat, Curry-Ya's rich sauce is garnished with pickled vegetables, short grain rice, and is available with a selection of accompaniments like *panko*-crusted Berkshire pork cutlet, organic chicken, and grilled hamburger. The small menu also offers inspiring starters like a salad of *yuba* and snow peas with green olive dressing.

The bright space, warmed by pale pink walls and blonde wood stools, offers seating for 14 at a marble counter set in front of the white tiled kitchen.

DBGB Kitchen & Bar

French

A3

299 Bowery (bet. First & Houston Sts.)

Subway: Lower East Side - 2 Av — Lunch & dinner daily
Phone: 212-933-5300
Web: www.danielnyc.com
Prices: $$

Superstar Chef Daniel Boulud's very popular take on casual, downtown dining features a front windowed café/bar followed by a grey and brown shaded dining room designed to evoke the Bowery's past as a hub for restaurant supplies. Shelves are stocked with dry goods and crockery, while a wraparound exposed kitchen displays gleaming steel surfaces and the bright whites of an eager brigade.

The chef's gilded yet fun, new approach here is clear in everything from matzoh ball soup to rather inventive burgers. The extensive menu also includes the likes of escargot, a very wide and worldly array of house-made sausages, supplemented by fish and meats in classical French preparations. For dessert, ice cream sundaes illustrate the playful spirit here.

Degustation

Spanish

A2

239 E. 5th St. (bet. Second & Third Aves.)

Subway: Astor Pl — Dinner Mon – Sat
Phone: 212-979-1012
Web: N/A
Prices: $$

This discreet and understated East Village tapas bar from Jack and Grace Lamb, also of Jewel Bako next door, bears the chic vibe New Yorkers would expect from this stylish couple. Slate-tiled walls, red leather placemats, and sleek place settings make the dimly lit space feel elegant and intimate. Sushi bar-style seating is arranged on a counter facing the open kitchen, where small plates are artfully prepared by this fresh-faced and well-trained team. Creative offerings may include tiny golden *croquetas* with fine bits of ham and green apple, or wild mushroom salad with lamb bacon.

The knowledgeable, smartly attired staff thoughtfully tends to each guest, often guiding them through the menu and making suggestions from the all-Spanish wine list.

Dirt Candy

B2 Vegetarian 

430 E. 9th St. (bet. First Ave. & Ave. A)

Subway: 1 Av — Dinner Tue – Sat
Phone: 212-228-7732
Web: www.dirtcandynyc.com
Prices: $$

Accommodating less than twenty in a boutique-sized space, Chef/owner Amanda Cohen keeps a watchful eye on each and every diner as she skillfully crafts vegetarian fare from the tiny rear kitchen. Certified by the Green Restaurant Association, the bright room has glass paneled walls and closely packed tables furnished with Arne Jacobsen chairs.

Both devotees and skeptics alike are impressed by this menu of unique items featuring such preparations as portobello mousse with truffle-oil-slicked toast and pickled pear compote; or golden crisped blocks of semi-firm tofu draped with kaffir lime beurre blanc. Yield to temptation with desserts like light and spongy zucchini-ginger cake served à la mode with deliciously smooth cream cheese ice cream.

Euzkadi

A3 Basque 

108 E. 4th St. (bet. First & Second Aves.)

Subway: Lower East Side - 2 Av — Dinner nightly
Phone: 212-982-9788
Web: www.euzkadirestaurant.com
Prices: $$

Haven't heard of Euzkadi? Maybe you've been living in a cave. While some restaurants dish out great food but disappoint in the décor department, this one-of-a-kind place delivers both. With textured, exposed walls painted with prehistoric-style cave drawings, thick, velvet curtains shutting out all sunlight, and soft, low lighting, diners can be cave dwellers—even if just for the evening. This cocoon-like restaurant is a great find, despite its cramped quarters.

Of course, no caveman ever ate this well. The menu covers all the bases of traditional Basque cooking, including tapas and the house specialty, *paella mariscos*. Loaded with fish and shellfish, and redolent of saffron, the paella comes sized for two in a traditional cast-iron pan.

Faustina

A2 Italian XX

25 Cooper Sq. (bet. 5th & 6th Sts.)

Subway: Astor Pl — Lunch & dinner daily
Phone: 212-475-3400
Web: www.faustinanyc.com
Prices: $$

Named after the Roman empress and from Chef Scott Conant, this new dining room at the Cooper Square Hotel gives the chef's Meatpacking District Scarpetta an East Village counterpart. The setup is bright and airy with a muted color scheme and large windows that look out onto an attractively appointed patio area.

Embark this journey with a selection of breads, *salumi*, and cheeses; the *stromboli* is an addictive trifecta—a warm loaf filled with smoked mozzarella and prosciutto. The raw bar includes plates of *crudo*; and the heartier portion of the menu marches the streets of Italy for a contemporary collection of pastas and main courses.

The unique side dishes like the stewed-to-a-silky-pulp eggplant studded with ground pork are of special note.

Gnocco

C2 Italian X 

337 E. 10th St. (bet. Aves. A & B)

Subway: 1 Av — Lunch Sat – Sun
Phone: 212-677-1913 — Dinner nightly
Web: www.gnocco.com
Prices: $$

This quaint Alphabet City Italian is a top local hangout, perfectly suiting the casual, neighborhood vibe. The dining room's rustic charm is accented by rough hewn plank flooring, exposed brick, and large windows that overlook the colorful scenes of Tompkins Square Park. In summer, the shaded back terrace with vine-covered walls and pretty murals is a great place to enjoy the namesake specialty, *gnocco*: crispy, deep-fried pillows of dough served with thin slices of prosciutto di Parma and salami.

Enjoyable homemade pastas, a lengthy listing of thin-crusted pizzas, and heartier main dishes comprise the tasty offerings here, served by an attentive and gracious staff. The fluffy and creamy lemon and mint semifreddo is always a pleasant finish.

Hasaki

Japanese 

210 E. 9th St. (bet. Second & Third Aves.)

Subway: Astor Pl — Lunch Wed – Sun
Phone: 212-473-3327 — Dinner nightly
Web: www.hasakinyc.com
Prices: $$$

Opened in 1984 and still going strong, this unassuming spot on a tree-lined stretch of the East Village is quietly housed just below street level. The dapper dining room has a clean and spare look, with seating available at a number of honey-toned wood tables, or the generously sized counter manned by a personable chef.

Hasaki's longevity is attributed to the high quality of its product. Skillfully prepared, delicately sliced sushi and sashimi share the spotlight with silky noodle soups and crisp tempura, at prices that won't break the bank. The menu is supplemented by a listing of fascinating daily specials that do tend to sell out quickly. Hasaki's "Twilight" menu offered before 6:30 P.M. is cherished, both for its quality and quantity.

Hearth

Mediterranean 

403 E. 12th St. (at First Ave.)

Subway: 1 Av — Dinner nightly
Phone: 646-602-1300
Web: www.restauranthearth.com
Prices: $$$

Simple wooden tables; walls lined with wine glasses and copper pots; a cozy little bar overlooking the kitchen—Hearth's welcoming, candlelit interior sets the stage for the comforting Mediterranean meal to come.

The menu effortlessly skates between old-world classics and seasonal dishes punched up with inspired touches of creativity that work beautifully. Try the spring onion soup, bobbing with rich knobs of sea urchin and tender brioche croutons; fresh Columbia River sturgeon wrapped in crispy prosciutto and paired with ruby-red beets, zingy horseradish, trout eggs, and chervil; or homemade lasagna, fat with fresh ricotta, saffron, and lemon rind. Paired with a gorgeous red plucked off the temptingly descriptive wine list? Mediterranean bliss.

Ippudo

Japanese XX

A1

65 Fourth Ave. (bet. 9th & 10th Sts.)

Subway: 14 St - Union Sq — Lunch & dinner daily
Phone: 212-388-0088
Web: www.ippudo.com/ny
Prices: $$

A wall covered in soup bowls is your clue of what to order at this first stateside outpost of the popular Japanese chain, opened by the renowned "King of Ramen" Shigemi Kawahara. Ramen-hungry diners are given a boisterous welcome from the youthful, energetic staff upon entering; expect the same at the farewell. With most seating arranged at communal oak-topped tables and prominently displayed open kitchen, Ippudo feels laid-back and fun yet sleek. The classic *shiromaru* ramen is a deeply satisfying bowl of rich pork broth and excellent, slender, fresh-made noodles garnished with sliced pork and cabbage.

If left with a bowlful of extra broth, simply tell your server "kae-dama" and for a small charge you'll receive an additional bowl of noodles.

Itzocan Cafe

Mexican 

B2

438 E. 9th St. (bet. First Ave. & Ave. A)

Subway: 1 Av — Lunch & dinner daily
Phone: 212-677-5856
Web: www.itzocanrestaurant.com
Prices: $$

With seating for less than 16, Itzocan is *muy pequeño*, but its menu of bold Mexican fare is certainly big on flavor. Quality ingredients abound in a lunchtime listing of quesadillas and burritos, as well as at dinner when a full menu is offered. The *queso fundido*, a molten cheese dip spiked with poblano peppers and chorizo, is so rich you'll need assistance to finish. The short list of entrées displays dashes of creativity as in the hearty serving of plump, jumbo shrimp sautéed with a flavor-packed sauce of tequila, lime, and *guajillo* chile. Desserts include a cheesecake-dense yogurt flan, dressed with chocolate sauce and candied almond slices.

The predominantly grey interior is brightened with colorfully painted tables and glazed flowerpots.

Jack's Luxury Oyster Bar

A2

Seafood

101 Second Ave. (bet. 5th & 6th Sts.)

Subway: Lower East Side - 2 Av — Dinner Mon – Sat
Phone: 212-253-7848
Web: N/A
Prices: **$$$**

Tucked into a busy Second Avenue block, this oyster bar may be tiny in stature but does not fall short of personality thanks to owners (and namesake) Jack and Grace Lamb. Here, find a tempting raw bar that includes oysters and peel-and-eat shrimp as well as confident cooking in the substantial listing of small plates. These may include creamy duck liver paté capped with port gelée or butter-poached lobster, in addition to a cheese selection and small dessert menu. The dining counter overlooking the open kitchen is a popular seating option, though the cozy wood topped tables up front are also enjoyable.

The intimate space has a romantic glow and distinctly downtown feel, with plaid walls, painted wainscoting, and glass votives all done in red.

Joe Doe

A3

Contemporary

45 E. 1st St. (bet. First & Second Aves.)

Subway: Lower East Side - 2 Av — Lunch Sat – Sun
Phone: 212-780-0262 — Dinner Tue – Sun
Web: www.chefjoedoe.com
Prices: **$$**

The intimate setting of this East Village newcomer from Chef/partner Joe Dobias has an appealing ruggedness to its quaint ambience. Exposed brick and vintage décor strewn throughout complement the assortment of dark wood chairs and salvaged church pews. Seating is bolstered by the bar that doubles as a comfortable dining counter.

The chef's concise, highly enjoyable menu emerges from the closet-sized open kitchen and displays a vibrant personality. These inspired creations may include a sea scallop cured in Veev (*acai* berry-based spirit) and garnished with jalapeño mayonnaise; or braised *cabrito* (goat) sauced with tortilla soup. Save room for dessert: the sundae of vanilla ice cream, chocolate chip-studded banana bread, and "bananas Foster" sauce.

Jewel Bako ✿

Japanese

A2

239 E. 5th St. (bet. Second & Third Aves.)

Subway: Astor Pl — Dinner Mon – Sat
Phone: 212-979-1012
Web: N/A
Prices: $$$

Swee Phuah

Hidden behind an unassuming façade in New York's East Village, Jack and Grace Lamb's beautiful, gilded sushi den, Jewel Bako, wrote the rules on how the East Village does high-end sushi. Should it surprise you then, if you still have to wait a bit to score seats at this ever-packed restaurant? The talented husband-and-wife team seems to know their audience well enough. Odds are they'll wait, or head across the street to Jack's Luxury Oyster Bar, another one of the couple's wildly successful ventures.

As jammed as the place stays, you'll still find a smooth operation led by an understated, but incredibly sharp, service staff, and a kitchen with an extremely talented roster of sushi chefs who somehow manage to throw plenty of love, attention, and detail into every bite.

Sushi and sashimi dominate the menu, where you might find a bright assortment of sashimi featuring paper-thin slices of ruby red tuna, melt-in-your-mouth squares of fatty tuna, rich, dense Japanese sea bass, or gleaming, silvery mackerel; a mouthwatering selection of mushrooms cooked *en papillote* in sake and yuzu; or chocolate shortbread cookies stuffed with green tea ice cream and garnished with roasted almonds.

Kafana

Eastern European

116 Ave. C (bet. 7th & 8th Sts.)

Subway: 1 Av
Phone: 212-353-8000
Web: www.kafananyc.com
Prices: $$

Lunch Sat – Sun
Dinner nightly

Translating to "café" in Serbian, Kafana has a heartwarming ambience that beckons one to stay for a while. Exposed brick walls decorated with mirrors, vintage photographs, rough-hewn wood tables topped with votives and flowers, and boldly patterned banquettes outfit the intimate space, attended by a genuinely friendly staff. In one corner sits the small bar, with a charmingly low-tech antique cash register.
Kafana offers worldly diners an exotic cuisine not often found in Manhattan. The list of hearty Serbian specialties includes a phyllo pie filled with cow's milk feta and spinach, grilled meats, or slow-cooked stews prepared with large, tender white beans perfumed with garlic and paprika, topped with slices of smoky peasant sausage.

Kanoyama

Japanese

175 Second Ave. (at 11th St.)

Subway: 3 Av
Phone: 212-777-5266
Web: www.kanoyama.com
Prices: $$

Dinner nightly

Positive energy emanates from this tiny sushi spot where the amiable young staff caters to a clientele that is fanatical about their nigiri, sashimi, and maki—everything here is both reliable and impressive. Take a seat at the counter for a view of the chefs' amazing knife work and warm banter to fully appreciate petite Kanoyama's chill, downtown feel.
Daily fish specials display incredible variety and the menu supplements with even more choice, which may be best represented in the highlighted chef's recommendations. Kanoyama offers good value considering the quality, but that buttery toro or creamy uni can add up quickly.
Reservations are not accepted on Friday and Saturday nights, but there are plenty of lively bars nearby to ease the wait.

Kajitsu ✿✿

Japanese XX

B2

414 E. 9th St. (bet. First Ave. & Ave. A)

Subway: 1 Av Dinner Tue – Sun
Phone: 212-228-4873
Web: www.kajitsunyc.com
Prices: **$$$**

Kajitsu

Welcome to Kajitsu. No meat, no fish—no problem. Even your most staunch carnivore will be licking their chops at this superb Japanese restaurant specializing in Shojin cuisine, the most pristine vegetarian cooking developed in the temples of Zen Buddhism. Burrowed beneath a few discreetly marked steps along buzzing 9th Street, a shoji screen leads to a serene, wood-soaked room bathed in natural light with traditional Zen, minimalist décor right down to the seasonal incense.

After a ten year stint in Kyoto at *kaiseki* temple Kitcho, Chef Masato Nishihara brings his understanding of the guiding principles of the ancient tradition west, spinning fresh, in-season vegetables, grains, and noodles into nightly 4- or 8-course productions that might include a smoky bowl of red miso soup bobbing with tender, grilled eggplant; a whole spaghetti squash filled with a spring vegetable soup served over crisp tempura; nutty, homemade soba noodles; or sticky basil and white bean *mochi* with azuki bean paste. As is the tradition, foamy *matcha* and sugary sweets complete every meal.

The recommended sake pairings offered with each menu are an excellent way to sample interesting pours at a good value.

Kasadela

C2

647 E. 11th St. (bet. Aves. B & C)

Subway: 1 Av — Dinner nightly
Phone: 212-777-1582
Web: www.kasadela.com
Prices: ⊜

This simply furnished, low-key *izakaya* offers an array of traditional Japanese snacks best washed down with an iced cold beer or sake; just remember that here, your glass of sake can be embellished with gold leaf for a small fee, said to promote better health.

Located in Alphabet City, the space is often quieter early in the evening and stays open late enough to satisfy the cravings of the neighborhood's nocturnal scenesters. Patrons arrive here seeking honest, good-valued satisfaction, in the likes of creamy and smooth Japanese-style potato salad; addictively sweet and salty glazed chicken wings; or the classic fare of *tori kawa*: charred skewers of rich chicken skin. Finish with a crème caramel that would do any talented pastry chef proud.

La Paella

Spanish

A2

214 E. 9th St. (bet. Second & Third Aves.)

Subway: Astor Pl — Lunch & dinner daily
Phone: 212-598-4321
Web: www.lapaellanyc.com
Prices: $$

On a street known for Asian dining spots, La Paella recalls the charm of an old-world Iberian inn with rustic furnishings, wooden ceiling beams draped with bundles of dried flowers, and wrought iron accents. A fresco of a picador on the parchment-colored wall completes the scene. Ideal for groups (though often crowded with them), the menu encourages sharing with its sizable tapas offering as well as the house specialty: paella, sized for two or more. Several variations of this namesake dish include the Basque, with chorizo, chicken, and clams over saffron-scented rice.

The cozy, dimly lit space makes it a delicious date spot for couples enjoying a bottle of Spanish wine, immune to the spirited sounds of sangria-fueled merrymaking.

Kyo Ya ✿

Japanese XX

B2

94 E. 7th St. (bet First Ave. & Ave. A)

Subway: Astor Pl — Dinner Tue – Sun
Phone: 212-982-4140
Web: N/A
Prices: $$$

Kyo Ya

Like so many exquisite culinary temples in this town, Kyo Ya doesn't look like much from the outside. Tucked into the basement of a homely residential building in the East Village's blossoming den of Japanese joints, you'll have to duck down the unmarked slate steps that lead to the restaurant on faith alone.

Once inside, you'll find a surprisingly elegant, wood-kissed atmosphere, smartly dressed in clean, Zen lines that—despite the obvious spatial confines—manages to exude a light, sexy air. But more importantly, you'll find Chef Chikara Sono's mouthwatering *kaiseki,* a series of haute cuisine small plates traditionally served with Japanese tea.

You'll want to plan ahead as the chef's tasting menu here requires two days notice, but it's well worth the forethought: a walk with the master might reveal simmered Kyo ya snapper Chazuke; slow-grilled duck Magret sporting a perfectly crispy caramelized skin with Mongolian salt and paired with a delicious dipping sauce; or soft, milky yuba and fresh uni (Yoshino-style) in a gorgeous crystal clear sauce. Drop-ins, don't despair: the à la carte menu is no-miss, with a wealth of rotating, seasonal goodies.

Lavagna

Italian

B3

545 E. 5th St. (bet. Aves. A & B)

Subway: Lower East Side - 2 Av
Phone: 212-979-1005
Web: www.lavagnanyc.com
Prices: $$

Lunch Sat – Sun
Dinner nightly

The steady stream of regulars frequenting this very popular and charmingly low-key trattoria is immediately evident at Lavagna. The gracious staff often greets guests by name, though this same courteous attention is given to first-time visitors. The warm service is enhanced by the cozy dining room, featuring a visible kitchen, wood-topped bar, framed mirrors, pressed-tin ceiling, and white linen-covered tables glowing in the candlelight.

The Italian menu includes a concise listing of *pizzette*, perhaps topped with roasted wild mushrooms, Fontina, and white truffle oil, fired in the wood-burning oven. Fresh pastas, *secondi*, and excellent desserts complete the offerings. Sunday nights feature a reasonably priced three-course set menu from 5:00-7:00 P.M.

Lil' Frankie's

Italian 

A3

19 First Ave. (bet. 1st & 2nd Sts.)

Subway: Lower East Side - 2 Av
Phone: 212-420-4900
Web: www.lilfrankies.com
Prices:

Lunch & dinner daily

Dinnertime always seems like a party at this offshoot of the ever-popular Frank, featuring a greenery-adorned dining room and a bar area lovingly nicknamed after owner Frank Prisinzano's father, "Big Cheech." The classic East Village space is furnished with a combination of wood and marble-topped tables, colorful benches, and brick walls with black-and-white portraits, fashioning a shabby-chic backdrop.

Cooked to crispy perfection in a wood-burning oven, Naples-style pizza, with toppings like homemade sausage and wild fennel, star on the menu. Equally impressive is the lineup of antipasto and pastas, handmade with the freshest ingredients.

Come with a crowd or expect to wait, reservations are accepted only for parties of six or more.

Luzzo's

Pizza 

B1

211-13 First Ave. (bet. 12th & 13th Sts.)

Subway: 1 Av — Lunch Tue – Sun
Phone: 212-473-7447 — Dinner nightly
Web: N/A
Prices:

Luzzo's is easily spotted by its long line of hungry faces patiently waiting to score a table, especially on a Friday night when the rustic setting of rough-hewn plank flooring and exposed brick adorned with copper cookware can suddenly feel like an NYU dining hall.

Despite the masses, this consistently top-rated pizzeria is a fun night out. Its Naples-born owner and noted *pizzaiolo* does things his own way to produce a stellar pie while defying some of the strict mandates set by the Neapolitan-pizza politburo, most notably baking his pizzas in a mix of wood *and* coal. The results are delectable, as in the pizza *diavolo*—crusty, puffy, and tender with a hint of smoke; topped with tomato, creamy mozzarella, and salty-spicy slices of hearty salami.

The Mermaid Inn

Seafood

A2

96 Second Ave. (bet. 5th & 6th Sts.)

Subway: Astor Pl — Dinner nightly
Phone: 212-674-5870
Web: www.themermaidnyc.com
Prices: $$

When schedules and seasons don't inspire a trip to the Cape, The Mermaid Inn offers a polished yet comfortably rustic take on those familiar sea-sprayed fish shacks. Dark wood furnishings, walls decorated with nautical maps, and a quaint backyard dining area give the setting an undeniable charm. The concise menu begins with a first-rate raw bar and continues with deftly prepared offerings like P.E.I. mussels steamed in an aromatic broth, or the lobster sandwich served on a grilled bun. Their addictive crunchy, golden, Old Bay fries are an essential side dish. A complimentary demitasse of creamy pudding ends things sweetly.

Two additional Manhattan locations (in Greenwich Village and the Upper West Side) continue to spread the wealth.

Momofuku Ko ✿✿

B2 **Contemporary** 

163 First Ave. (bet. 10th & 11th Sts.)

Subway: 1 Av
Phone: 212-777-7773
Web: www.momofuku.com
Prices: **$$$$**

Lunch Fri – Sun
Dinner nightly

Noah Kalina

It's still no cakewalk to get into the restaurant that pushed David Chang into iconic chef territory: reservations can only be made a week in advance by logging onto their website at 10:00 A.M., and the restaurant's 12 backless stools fill up quick. Once you do snag a seat, there is no formal service, no menu to choose from, and you'll have to present your confirmation email at the door like you're catching the redeye to Kathmandu.

Is it worth the fuss? Yes—for not only has the delightfully irreverent Chang gifted New York's elite culinary scene with a rare egalitarian process, but this multi-course extravaganza is a relative steal at around a hundred bucks a pop.

And then there's the food. A sense-jogging trip through the strange hollows of David Chang's mind is like extreme dinner theater: witness a dish of top-notch foie gras, grated like falling snow over a sweet mélange of lychee, Riesling gelée, and pine nut brittle; tawny, perfectly seared Muscovy duck breast paired with mustard greens, honey-braised turnips, and a beautiful country pâté; or a distinctive, quivering panna cotta studded with salty pretzel and matched with root beer sorbet, mustard gelée, and rye bread crumbs.

Momofuku Noodle Bar

Asian

B2

171 First Ave. (bet. 10th & 11th Sts.)

Subway: 1 Av
Lunch & dinner daily
Phone: 212-777-7773
Web: www.momofuku.com
Prices:

This is the spot that launched Chef David Chang's ascent into celebrity chef-dom. The ever-popular destination, and its hoards of hungry fans, may reside in bigger digs now, but this restaurant is still a "lucky peach" (the name's Japanese translation). Momofuku's gutsy menu is fashioned with Asian street food in mind. Steamed buns of chicken, shiitake, and pork are offered alongside generous bowls of chewy ramen in rich, dark, subtly flavored pork broth. For a fun group event, try the order-in-advance fried chicken feast complete with two styles of bird and garden-fresh accompaniments.

Whether sitting at the counter or communal tables, join the devotees slurping noodles elbow-to-elbow and watching the chefs' sleight of hand in the open kitchen.

Momofuku Ssäm Bar

Contemporary

B1

207 Second Ave. (at 13th St.)

Subway: 3 Av
Lunch & dinner daily
Phone: 212-777-7773
Web: www.momofuku.com
Prices: $$

Restless Chef David Chang somehow always manages to wow the taste buds of even the most jaded foodies. At this culinary playground, he offers an exuberant contemporary menu so far-reaching that it somehow all makes sense. Rest assured, this kitchen only serves dishes—and cocktails—that they themselves find delicious.

The signature steamed pork buns remain a draw, but raw bar items like cracked Jonah crab claws and Southern smoked hams are likewise praiseworthy. Seasonal dishes cater to the familiar, while offbeat choices like Sichuan beef tendon entertain more daring diners. Famed mad-scientist desserts have included the likes of beet and lime ganache.

Loud and crowded, the chicly minimalist space is perpetually mobbed by a sophisticated clientele.

Northern Spy Food Co.

American

511 E. 12th St. (bet. Aves. A & B)

Subway: 1 Av | Lunch & dinner daily
Phone: 212-228-5100
Web: www.northernspyfoodco.com
Prices:

Chef Nathan Q. Foot has cooked extensively in San Francisco, but now displays the fuss-free sensibilities for which that city is renowned in this market-driven menu highlighting the finest producers in the Northeast and Mid-Atlantic.

Espousing a country store vibe, this charming all-day café is framed by reclaimed hickory flooring, a wood-slat banquette painted robin's-egg blue, and tables made of salvaged bowling alley lanes filled with diners eagerly enjoying the likes of kale salad studded with artisanal cheddar, roasted kabocha squash, and lemon vinaigrette.

Sample the daily preparation of pastured pork—perhaps rendered into a stew and served with pan-fried mascarpone gnocchi, followed by a slice of apple pie dressed with almond *semifreddo*.

Prune

Contemporary

54 E. 1st St. (bet. First & Second Aves.)

Subway: Lower East Side - 2 Av | Lunch & dinner daily
Phone: 212-677-6221
Web: www.prunerestaurant.com
Prices: $$

Packed with simple furnishings and attended to by a friendly, laid-back staff, the popularity of this endearing breadbox of a restaurant never seems to fade. On a warm day when the front doors open, few Manhattan restaurants can match its ambiance. From her tight kitchen in back, Chef/owner Gabrielle Hamilton has impressed serious diners since 1999. The deceptively modest menu changes often but the chef's signature style shines through in items that are fuss-free yet display an undeniable level of skill and talent. A meal here may feature a crisp-skinned fillet of Tasmanian sea trout set atop a bundle of frisée and crowned by a dollop of perfect homemade mayonnaise; or a creamy, sweet/tart lime custard graced with crumbly oatmeal shortbread.

Pylos

Greek XX

B2

128 E. 7th St. (bet. First Ave. & Ave. A)

Subway: Astor Pl
Phone: 212-473-0220
Web: www.pylosrestaurant.com
Prices: $$

Lunch Wed – Sun
Dinner nightly

Taking its name from the Greek translation of "made from clay," this contemporary taverna features a ceiling canopy of suspended terra-cotta pots and white-washed walls with lapis-blue insets. The restrained décor produces a chic Mediterranean vibe that perfectly suits its lusty, home-style, deliciously refined cuisine—courtesy of noted Greek food authority Diane Kochilas.

Moussaka, a classic Greek comfort favorite, is beautifully presented here as a dome filled with layers of browned meat and silky eggplant, encrusted in slender potato slices, finished with layer of golden-browned béchamel. Sides may include *spanakorizo*, wilted spinach rice flecked with feta crumbles; while custard-filled phyllo drenched in mountain honey ends things sweetly.

Rai Rai Ken

B2

214 E. 10th St. (bet. First & Second Aves.)

Subway: Astor Pl
Phone: 212-477-7030
Web: N/A
Prices:

Lunch & dinner daily

This sliver of a spot specializes in slurp-inducing, soul-satisfying ramen that stands out among the city's recent proliferation. The setting is barebones and unembellished: 14 low stools are situated at the busy counter overlooking a narrow kitchen lined with bubbling pots. Besides the caddies of chopsticks and paper napkins, there's just room enough for a deep brimming bowl at each setting.

The menu shines in its concise listing of near-addictive, complex broth variations such as *shio*, *shoyu*, miso, and curry. Each is chock-full of garnishes, like fishcakes or roasted pork, and nests of fresh, springy noodles. Before leaving, be sure to grab a business card; Rai Rai Ken rewards frequent diners with a complimentary bowlful after ten visits.

The Redhead

Gastropub

B1

349 E. 13th St. (bet. First & Second Aves.)

Subway: 1 Av

Dinner Mon – Sat

Phone: 212-533-6212

Web: www.theredheadnyc.com

Prices: $$

This lil' ole East Village charmer lures an ardent following nightly with its stocked bar, substantial list of well-poured libations, and distinctly Southern appeal. Stop here for a creative cocktail, best enjoyed with the near-addictive bacon-peanut brittle, because this menu reminds us that "everything is better with bacon." Then, continue on to the rear dining area with exposed brick walls and a red velvet banquette. Everything here is done simply, radiating a warm, laid-back charm.

The menu's Southern accent is appetizingly evident in the kitchen's preparations that feature low country shrimp, pan-seared trout, and buttermilk fried chicken served with cornbread. The tasty dessert menu of puddings, tarts, and cakes cleverly unites "gastro" and "pub."

Robataya 

Japanese

A2

231 E. 9th St. (bet. Second & Third Aves.)

Subway: Astor Pl

Dinner Tue – Sun

Phone: 212-979-9674

Web: www.robataya-ny.com

Prices: $$

This latest (and such fun) venture from restaurateur Bon Yagi features a front room with a 26-seat counter lined with salivating diners and platters of ultra-fresh vegetables, fish, and meats to be grilled and served by a paddle-wielding team of chefs perched behind the counter.

The *robatayaki* menu offers up heaps of flavorfully grilled dishes, from silky eggplant to sheets of dried sardines, seasoned with imported salt, brushed with soy or teriyaki, or dressed with miso. The menu is supported by cold, warm, and seasonal appetizers; fried dishes like *yuba gyoza*; and iron pots of steamed rice (*kamameshi*) topped with snow crab meat are among the options.

Table seating is available in the rear dining room for those who prefer a more tranquil experience.

Sigiri

Sri Lankan

B2

91 First Ave. (bet. 5th & 6th Sts.)

Subway: 1 Av — Lunch & dinner daily
Phone: 212-614-9333
Web: www.sigirinyc.com
Prices:

For a delicious taste of something different, round the corner of 6th Street to First Avenue, and climb to Sigiri's small second floor dining room. This humble Sri Lankan establishment stands above its neighbors for wonderfully prepared, intriguingly fragrant cuisine that needs neither a colorful light display nor boisterous greeter. Instead, the warm and sedate room features sienna walls and simple tables with bright cloths.

Specialties are numerous and may include *string hopper kotthu*, a stir-fry of impossibly thin and fluffy rice noodles tossed with eggs, chicken, and vegetables, accompanied by a cup of coconut gravy; or spoon-tender chunks of eggplant *moju*, spiced with dried red chili. In lieu of alcohol, fruit cordials or apple-iced tea is offered.

Sobakoh

Japanese 

A2

309 E. 5th St. (bet. First & Second Aves.)

Subway: Lower East Side - 2 Av — Lunch Fri – Sun
Phone: 212-254-2244 — Dinner nightly
Web: N/A
Prices:

Before entering Sobakoh, stop for a minute to appreciate Chef Hiromi Takahashi, sequestered to his temperature- and humidity-controlled glass booth, forming layers of organically grown buckwheat flour dough into first-rate noodles. This ritual is performed several times daily by the smiling chef and is the foundation of the seasonally arranged offerings at this Japan-meets-East Village soba spot.

Service can be sluggish, so start with a classic Japanese snack, like the refreshing daikon salad dressed with yuzu, wasabi, and bonito flakes, while waiting for your bowlful of *uni ikura soba*—chilled buckwheat noodles heaped with creamy sea urchin and plump salmon roe.

The inexpensive prix-fixe menu offered nightly is even cheaper before 7:00 P.M.

Soba-Ya

Japanese

A2

229 E. 9th St. (bet. Second & Third Aves.)

Subway: Astor Pl — Lunch & dinner daily
Phone: 212-533-6966
Web: www.sobaya-nyc.com
Prices:

In a neighborhood replete with tempting Japanese dining options, Soba-Ya has been sating noodle cravings with awesome buckwheat soba and hearty udon—all homemade daily—for more than a decade. Enterprising co-owner Bon Yagi, also of Curry-Ya, favors authenticity over flash in his establishments, and this popular soba spot fashioning a traditional Japanese aesthetic is no exception.

Sit among the largely Japanese lunchtime clientele to savor and slurp cold, refreshing soba attractively served in a red-black bento box neatly stocked with the likes of dashi-poached vegetables, fresh and deliciously glazed salmon, or crisp shrimp tempura. Complete this meal with a pot of hot broth added to your remaining soy-based dipping sauce for a warming finish.

Supper

Italian 

B3

156 E. 2nd St. (bet. Aves. A & B)

Subway: 1 Av — Lunch & dinner daily
Phone: 212-477-7600
Web: www.supperrestaurant.com
Prices: $$

Supper has a truly convivial vibe that seems impossibly effortless. The front room is creatively thrown together around the blazing open kitchen, while the back dining room offers cozier seating and urbane rusticity amid exposed brick, vintage family photos, and blown glass chandeliers.

Impressive, classic Italian cooking is Supper's specialty as in a panzanella of perfectly grilled bread moistened by a chilled garlicky dressing and tossed with chunks of tomato and *cavolo nero*; or their excellent tagliatelle Bolognese, a heaping bowl of silky strands clinging to a rich and hearty sauce of finely ground meat with a spark of acidity and touch of sweetness.

Reservations are not accepted, so while away the wait at lovely sibling, Sugo Bar, next door.

Terroir

Italian 

B2

413 E. 12th St. (bet. First Ave. & Ave. A)

Subway: Astor Pl
Web: www.wineisterroir.com
Prices: $$

Dinner nightly

This cozy little 24-seat nook with exposed brick walls, raised communal seating, and habit of being packed by 7:00 P.M. ought to be the prototype of all NYC wine bars. Then again, nothing less should be expected of Marco Canora and Paul Grieco—the partners behind Hearth. While the city may be overrun with wine bars, few are accompanying their lengthy lists with such unfussy, strictly Italian, solidly enjoyable snacks.

Those lucky enough to snag a seat will find a clever lineup of by-the-glass choices and simply delicious small plates. The amusing (if cheeky) menu sections include "we love salad!" which may feature frisée with duck confit, gorgonzola, and shallots; or "the best panini in all of New York City!" with roast pork, rapini, and garlic aïoli.

Tonda

Italian 

B3

235 E. 4th St. (bet. Aves. A & B)

Subway: Lower East Side - 2 Av
Phone: 212-254-2900
Web: www.tondapzza.com
Prices: $$

Lunch Sat – Sun
Dinner nightly

Serving up delectable, wood-fired goodness, Tonda's pizza holds its own among the spate of Neapolitan-style offerings flourishing about town. Sixteen varieties are offered, but there is nothing quite like a humble classic: the *margherita* is nicely crisped and faintly smoky, layered with thick marinara, and creamy, fresh mozzarella beneath a dusting of dried oregano. Additionally, there are snacks, small plates, and a short list of entrées and pastas such as the *pasta alla Tonda*—orecchiette in rich pine nut pesto, complimented by broccoli rabe and wild mushrooms.

The open yet intimate setting tempts with a pizza station upfront and contemporary interior that pops with ebony-stained wood furnishings set against whitewashed walls and subway tiles.

Financial District

Widely considered the financial center of the world, the southern tip of Manhattan is flooded by hard-driving Wall Street types. When it's time to eat, they love a hefty steak, especially when expense accounts are paying the bill. And though expense accounts may be shrinking these days, bigger is still better at stalwarts like **Delmonicos**, which opened in 1837 as America's first fine-dining restaurant. The restaurant that introduced diners to now-classic dishes such as eggs Benedict, lobster Newburg, and baked Alaska, continues to pack 'em in for the signature Angus boneless ribeye, aka the Delmonico steak.

New is replacing old as the publicly owned Tin Building and New Market Building—home to the former Fulton Fish Market—house tenants in the form of **The New Amsterdam Market**, a seasonal marketplace where butchers, grocers, fishmongers, artisan cheese producers, and other vendors hope to create a regional food system. With a stated mission "to reinvent the public market as a civic institution in the City of New York," this non-profit organization dedicates itself to promoting sustainable agriculture and regionally sourced food, while offering space for independent purveyors to sell on behalf of farmers and producers. Check their website, www.newamsterdampublic.org for market dates.

One of the district's largest tourist draws, South Street Seaport is surrounded by eateries from family-friendly Irish pubs to the historic **Fraunces Tavern**. Innkeeper Samuel Fraunces purchased this three-story, 18th century brick mansion at the corner of Pearl and Broad streets in 1762.

The Financial District has traditionally catered to power-lunchers by day and business travelers by night. However, that's all changing as the area becomes increasingly residential. What you will discover is a smorgasbord of bars, restaurants, and food services catering to the locals. These blossoming culinary gems incite buttoned-up Wall Street suits to loosen their collars and chill out over a plate of steak frites at **Les Halles Downtown**—the brasserie affiliated with bad boy chef and Travel Channel celebrity Anthony Bourdain.

Front Street has attracted a surprising spate of Italian eateries counting **Il Brigante**, with its dough-spinning *pizzaiolo* who belongs to the United States Pizza Team, among their number. Another newbie, **Barbarini Alimentari** raises the bar with gourmet groceries and an equally upscale menu of Italian fare.

The ultimate in express lunch, New York's famous food-carts are hugely popular in the Financial District. For a quick

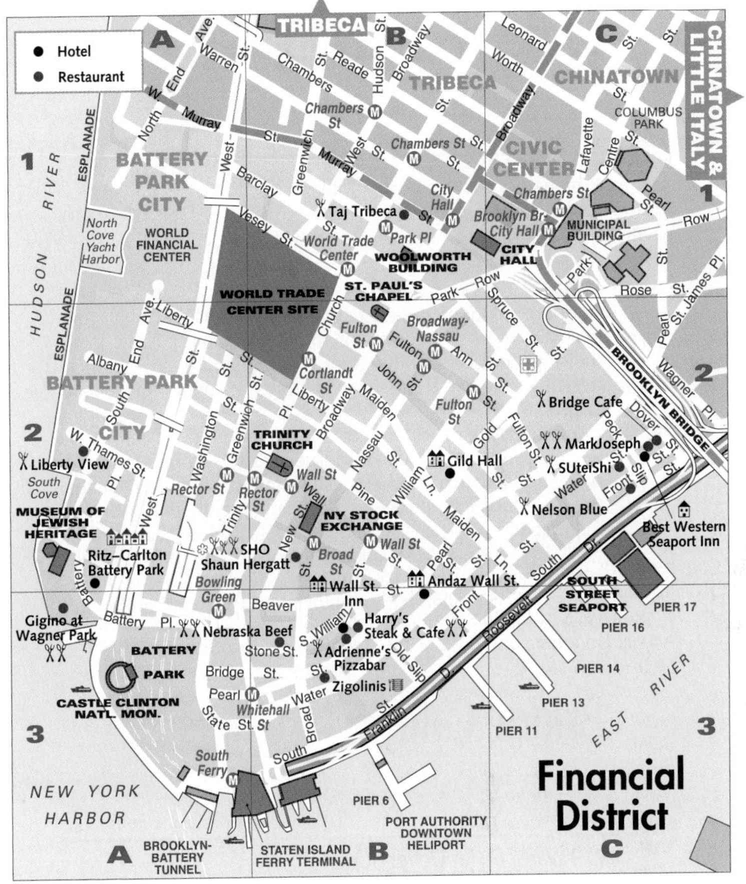

nosh at a bargain price, follow your nose to **Alan's Falafel Cart** on Cedar Street. Then for something sweet, head to **Financier Patisserie** on charming cobblestoned Stone Street, one of the narrow, sinuous streets laid out in the 17th century by New York's Dutch settlers. Wash it all down with an espresso at **Zibetto's** on Fulton Street.

Despite the economic downturn, restaurants downtown are as busy as ever, with former Wall Street wonders drowning their worries in martinis and Manhattans, and reviewing their portfolios over burgers and beer. Events such as the Stone Street Oyster Festival, sponsored by the same folks who operate Financier Patisserie and Ulysses pub, play to the area's strengths. What better way to lift spirits and celebrate the local Blue Point harvest in September than by slurping oysters and swilling libations outdoors on Stone Street?

Adrienne's Pizzabar

B3 — Pizza

54 Stone St. (bet. Coenties Alley & S. William St.)

Subway: Bowling Green — Lunch & dinner daily
Phone: 212-248-3838
Web: www.adriennespizzabar.com
Prices:

At noon, Adrienne's is abuzz with hordes of Financial District business types hungering for their delectable pizzas. With their thin crusts, slightly chunky sauce, and fresh toppings, these pies are a true classic on all fronts (except for the square shape).

Come evening, the restaurant calms and the servers are more engaging as diners slow to appreciate the smoky-grey oak paneling and many other custom-made, upscale touches. Outdoor tables along Stone Street are equally enjoyable, as the neighborhood charmingly reinvents itself for dinner. This is also when the menu adds a list of heartier baked dishes such as lasagna; as well as irresistible desserts, like the made-to-order éclair, filled with chocolate pastry cream and a thin layer of Nutella.

Bridge Cafe

American

C2

279 Water St. (at Dover St.)

Subway: Brooklyn Bridge - City Hall — Lunch Sun – Fri, Dinner nightly
Phone: 212-227-3344
Web: www.bridgecafenyc.com
Prices: $$

Set along the touristy cobblestoned street that is today's Water Street, the Bridge Cafe—which claims to be New York's oldest drinking establishment—was standing here when the area was better known for brothels and saloons than J. Crew and Banana Republic.

And so if the food is simply good, but not heroic, at this Manhattan mainstay, one can let a few details slide—especially for brown liquor enthusiasts looking to cruise the restaurant's extensive list of bourbons, malts, and Scotches. The menu lists some refreshingly light fare like a soft shell crab BLT; grilled wild Pacific salmon; and avocado and watercress salad. But a spot-on buffalo burger, topped with chili, bacon, and pepper jack on a chipotle aïoli-slathered bun really hits the spot.

Gigino at Wagner Park

Italian XX

A3

20 Battery Pl. (in Wagner Park)

Subway: Bowling Green
Lunch & dinner daily
Phone: 212-528-2228
Web: www.gigino-wagnerpark.com
Prices: $$

Impress your buddies after an afternoon romp to Ellis Island with this Southern Italian gem, and you'll be hailed a genius. Harbor views abound at this relaxing Italian restaurant, tucked into the ground floor of a wedge-shaped building in the Financial District's far-flung Wagner Park, but you'll want to call ahead to reserve a seat on the outdoor terrace. If you don't score them, you'll find a fairly soothing oasis inside as well, with a creamy white dining room dancing in blinking lights from the harbor.

Kick dinner off with a rich lentil soup flooded with tender braised escarole, diced tomato, and sweet onion; and then move on to a silky braised lamb shank served with a white bean and mint risotto; and bread pudding with rum and vanilla sauce.

Harry's Steak & Cafe

American XX

B3

1 Hanover Sq. (bet. Pearl & Stone Sts.)

Subway: Wall St (William St.)
Lunch & dinner Mon – Sat
Phone: 212-785-9200
Web: www.harrysnyc.com
Prices: $$

Mornings may begin with a bell, but Wall Street's powerbrokers ring in its end at Harry's Steak & Cafe. A beloved watering hole for decades, this Wall Street institution was reincarnated into two distinct spaces: a café and a steakhouse. Handsome and clubby with a gleaming black walnut bar and copper ceilings, the Cafe defines relaxed elegance, while the more serious Steakhouse feels secreted away with a sophisticated intimacy.

Beef is what's on tap at Harry's, so expect old-fashioned boys' club dining and precise service. The more casual Cafe menu features a few deep-pocketed riffs on American favorites like the Kobe hot dog (only on Wall Street), while the Steakhouse focuses on classics preparations of its excellent quality, rich, and juicy beef.

Liberty View

A2 **Chinese**

21 South End Ave. (below W. Thames St.)

Subway: Rector St (Greenwich St.) — Lunch & dinner daily
Phone: 212-786-1888
Web: www.libertyviewrestaurant.com
Prices: $$

You'll probably get better Chinese food in Chinatown but you aren't going to get this gorgeous peep show of the Hudson River, Ellis Island, and the Statue of Liberty. This upscale Chinese restaurant holds true to its name, offering killer views of the original gray lady from its prime ground floor location (with outdoor seating) at the tip of Battery Park City.

So how's the grub? It pays to be choosy—the chef is from Shanghai, which offers a clue as to the direction you might want to take. No one would kick the lo mein out of bed for eating crackers, but the crab and pork soup dumplings are a better bet. And despite sounding heavy by design, the Shanghai-fried rice, diced with Chinese sausage, shrimp, and peas, is perfectly delicate and sweet.

MarkJoseph

C2 **Steakhouse** 

261 Water St. (bet. Peck Slip & Dover St.)

Subway: Fulton St — Lunch Mon – Fri
Phone: 212-277-0020 — Dinner Mon – Sat
Web: www.markjosephsteakhouse.com
Prices: $$$

Rising from the shadows of the Brooklyn Bridge in the South Street Seaport Historic District, MarkJoseph's caters to both Wall Street wunderkinds and tourists with deep pockets. The cozy dining room is a notch above the standard steakhouse design, with art-glass vases and pastoral photographs of the wine country adding sleek notes.

At lunch, regulars devour hearty half-pound burgers (though a turkey variety is also offered). At dinnertime, prime dry-aged Porterhouse, sized for two to four, takes center stage. Classic accompaniments may include crisp salads, seafood cocktails, and sides like creamed spinach. The wine list offers a nice choice of hefty varietals, as well as some interesting old-world selections to accompany that bone-in ribsteak.

Nebraska Beef

Steakhouse

B3

15 Stone St. (bet. Broad & Whitehall Sts.)

Subway: Bowling Green
Lunch & dinner Mon – Fri
Phone: 212-952-0620
Web: www.nebraskasteakhousenyc.com
Prices: $$$

It's easy to miss the door that marks the entrance to this beloved Financial District watering hole-cum-steakhouse (look for the red and gold sign out front), but not the raucous happy hour crowd that floods the narrow bar leading to the restaurant. Smile and squeeze through, though, and you'll find a much calmer scene on the flip side: A dark, wood-paneled dining room with a clubby, in-the-know vibe.

This is one Wall Street oasis where the recession's on hold—the martinis flow free, the garlic bread melts in your mouth, and the hand-picked, 28-day, dry-aged ribeye still arrives sizzling, perfectly charred, and juicy as sin. If you're short on time or looking for lunch options, you can also grab a steak sandwich, Caesar salad, or burger on the fly.

Nelson Blue

New Zealand

C2

233-235 Front St. (at Peck Slip)

Subway: Fulton St
Lunch & dinner daily
Phone: 212-346-9090
Web: www.nelsonblue.com
Prices: $$

Straddling the corner of Front Street and Peck Slip near the South Street Seaport, in an area dominated by pubs, old bars, and restaurants, Nelson Blue makes for a stunning detour from the usual haunts, with hand-crafted artifacts like a Maori war canoe; a handsome oval bar; and a long communal wood table.

The food is touch and go, but when the New Zealand menu works, it works. Try the excellent curried lamb pot pie, chock-a-block with silky lamb and weaved with a rich sauce perfect for folding into the buttery mashed potatoes; then finish with a moist slice of chocolate truffle cake, served warm with a scoop of ice cream gently melting over it. Knocked down with a cold draft on a lazy midweek afternoon? A simple pleasure that bears repeating.

SHO Shaun Hergatt ✿

B2 **Contemporary** XXX

40 Broad St. (bet. Beaver St. & Exchange Pl.)

Subway: Broad St
Phone: 212-809-3993
Web: www.shoshaunhergatt.com
Prices: $$$

Lunch Mon – Fri
Dinner Mon – Sat

Lucy Schaeffer

Opened in the summer of 2009, this welcome addition to the Financial District arrives courtesy of Chef Shaun Hergatt, a talented Aussie and stone cold veteran of the Ritz-Carlton's legendary Dining Room restaurants. At his newest venture, Hergatt plays off his classical training, pulling notes from his Australian heritage and infusing a wealth of Asian accents (think kaffir lime, galangal, and lychee) into his contemporary cooking.

It can be a little tricky to find the place—tucked into the second floor of The Setai tower which rests along a section of Broad Street closed to traffic—but when you do, the rewards are rich. The sleek, enormous space features an infinity pool, a wine gallery, and a smattering of private dining rooms, each one more impeccably appointed than the next.

The restaurant serves breakfast, lunch, and dinner—the last available in a $69 three-course prix-fixe option that might include a beautifully arranged seafood salad composed of chilled baby octopus, bay scallops, diced lobster tail, and tender uni; or succulent rounds of rabbit loin cooked sous-vide and dressed table-side with a creamy, pale beige sauce flavored with Picholine olives.

SUteiShi

Japanese 

C2

24 Peck Slip (at Front St.)

Subway: Fulton St

Phone: 212-766-2344

Web: www.suteishi.com

Prices: $$

Lunch Mon – Fri
Dinner nightly

In a neighborhood starved for good eats, this relative newcomer makes the grade. Make no mistake: it's not mind-blowing sushi you'll find here, but guests who stick to the inventive rolls or lunchtime bento boxes will be rewarded with a very good meal in a welcoming atmosphere.

Make your way into SUteiShi's sleek, red lacquer-accented dining room and you'll find a sushi bar with a wood-weaved backdrop, a few bonsai plants and the requisite "Hello Kitty" porcelain doll. Don't miss the *ikura* wrapped with King salmon and topped with bright salmon roe; the super-fresh uni; or the strangely appealing black sesame brulée that reads more like a pudding, and arrives accompanied by two sesame wafers, bright slices of strawberries and ripe blueberries.

Taj Tribeca

Indian 

B1

18 Murray St. (bet. Broadway & Church St.)

Subway: Chambers St (West Broadway)

Phone: 212-608-5555

Web: www.tajtribeca.com

Prices: $$

Lunch & dinner daily

Set along one of the more culinary-challenged strips of lower Manhattan, just east of City Hall, Taj Tribeca is a nearly new Indian restaurant with a superb (albeit tiny) bar, exposed brick walls, and mile-high ceilings.

With such lovely design at play, one begins to wonder if the food could be elevated too—and the good news is that it is. Sure, they have the requisite lunch buffet (New Yorkers might picket without it), but the regular à la carte offerings remain ambitious and fresh. Try the compelling Goan shrimp curry headlining pitch-perfect heat and spice, shot with cool coconut milk, and served with fluffy basmati rice topped with perfectly caramelized fried onions. Save room for the warm carrot pudding, fragrant with green cardamom and clove.

Zigolinis

B3

Italian 

66 Pearl St. (at Coenties Slip)

Subway: Wall St (William St.) Lunch & dinner Mon – Sat
Phone: 212-425-3127
Web: www.zigolinis.com
Prices: $$

With its lovely chandeliers, silk fabric, and stylish filament bulbs, this sexy downtown restaurant is a breath of fresh air among the staid options that usually line the Financial District dining scene. The owners know they're leaning towards a good thing: they recently opened a casual Zigolinis, this one a Neapolitan pizzeria, in the vibrant Hell's Kitchen.

The New American small plates menu is broad and appealing, with dishes like plump Maine diver scallops wrapped in pancetta and drizzled with a heady, porcini-infused olive oil, then set over a fluffy bed of cauliflower and Parmesan purée; or a gorgeous trio of grilled New Zealand rack of lamb, paired with fluffy couscous studded with dried cranberries, toasted pine nuts, and crumbled goat cheese.

Look for our symbol 🍶, spotlighting restaurants with a notable sake list.

Jeanine C. Hart/MICHELIN

Gramercy, Flatiron & Union Square

Gramercy Park, anchoring its namesake neighborhood, is steeped in history, old-world beauty, and tranquility; but its extreme exclusivity is the stuff of legends among life-long New Yorkers, few of whom have set foot on its pretty yet private paths. This may be where tourists have an advantage, because outside of the residents whose home address faces the square, Gramercy Park Hotel guests are among the few permitted entrance. The staff accompanies guests to the daunting cast-iron gate, allows them in, and reminds them of the number to call when they wish to be let out again, perhaps to explore this lovely enclave filled with charming cafés and beautiful brownstones.

Still this is New York, so walk a few blocks in any direction to discover the neighborhoods' diverse offerings. North of the park find Gramercy's very own "Curry Hill" with an authentic array of satisfying, budget-friendly restaurants. Food enthusiasts should visit **Kalustyan's**—a spice-scented emporium specializing in a mind-boggling wealth of exotic products ranging from orange blossom water, to thirty varieties of dried whole chilies.

A few blocks to the west, find the very open, tranquil, and welcoming Madison Square Park, which boasts its own unique history and vibe. This was the home of the city's first community Christmas tree in 1912, the original location of Madison Square Garden arena, and site of New York's very first baseball club, the Knickerbockers of 1845. It is therefore only fitting that greeting park visitors is the original and scrumptious **Shake Shack**, serving its signature upscale fast food to a legion of followers from an ivy-covered kiosk. Burgers and Chicago-style dogs are always popular, but the house-made creamy custard has its cultish followers checking the online "custard calendar" weekly for their favorite flavors, like red-velvet or salted caramel. Barbecue fans should time their visits here with the Big Apple Barbecue Block Party held in June. This weekend-long event features celebrity pit masters displaying and serving their talents to throngs of hungry aficionados.

However, this neighborhood's most famous, familiar, and remarkable feature is actually its namesake building, the Flatiron. Measuring an impossibly narrow six feet across at its acute northern edge, the view of this 22-story landmark has been immortalized on countless films, shows, and postcards.

Nearby Union Square may be known as an historic downtown park with playgrounds and tiered plazas that occasionally host political protests and rallies, but today the square is best known for its year-round **Greenmarket**. Despite the

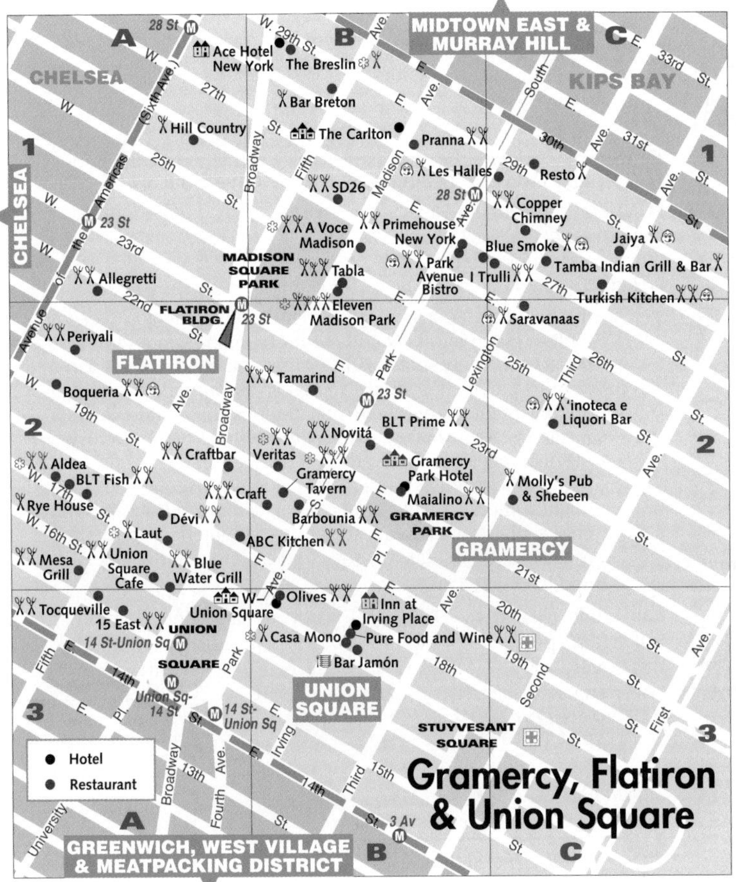

park's ongoing renovations, its beautiful array of seasonal produce, baked goods, fresh meat, seafood, dairy, plants, and flowers are still available every Monday, Wednesday, Friday, and Saturday. Early in the day, it is not uncommon to spot chefs dressed in their whites selecting the day's supplies. During Christmastime, the Union Square Holiday Market features stalls of candles, shirts, knit caps, and decorations for gift shopping in a festive atmosphere.

Beyond the market's borders, find a nice bottle of wine to complement that farm-to-table meal from the comprehensive **Union Square Wines and Spirits**, or the regionally-specific **Italian Wine Merchants**. Further testament to Union Square's reputation as the center of Manhattan food shopping is the presence of **Whole Foods** and the city's very first **Trader Joe's**, all within blocks of one another.

ABC Kitchen

Contemporary XX

A2

35 E. 18th St. (bet. Broadway & Park Ave. South)

Subway: 14 St - Union Sq — Lunch & dinner daily
Phone: 212-475-5829
Web: www.abckitchennyc.net
Prices: **$$**

Super busy, super chef, Jean-George Vongerichten weaves a bit of green into his rich tapestry of dining venues with his invigorating new spot at ABC Carpet and Home. Rooted in a farm-to-table ethos, diners sup on an assortment of seasonal and consciously procured preparations that feature market inspired small plates; wood-fired whole wheat crusted pizzas; and straightforward entrées like seared Arctic char with garlic crumbs and emerald bright broccoli rabe. One might forecast a faux farmhouse backdrop, but instead the chic setting showcases a white washed interior warmed by reclaimed ceiling beams, soy candles; and a trademark ABC touch—chandeliers.

The restaurant's furnishings and handmade service pieces are available for purchase online.

Allegretti

Mediterranean XX

A1

46 W. 22nd St. (bet. Fifth & Sixth Aves.)

Subway: 23 St (Broadway) — Lunch Mon – Fri
Phone: 212-206-0555 — Dinner Mon – Sat
Web: www.allegrettinyc.com
Prices: **$$$**

Chef Alain Allegretti's solo venture has a confidently understated mien where light wood flooring, navy-blue furnishings, and pale walls hung with mirrored panels frame the good-looking crowd enjoying this French-Mediterranean inspired menu. The chef's native Provence is fully explored in flavorful preparations like leek fondant accompanied by a breaded poached egg and sauce *gribiche*; chestnut purée-filled *cappelletti* with tender, flavorful duck ragout; and John Dory accompanied by octopus and shrimp in fennel-saffron broth.

The setting and cuisine are complemented by an impressively focused, smartly dressed service team. The chef's charm and personality extend beyond the menu, into the simply elegant dining room, where he enjoys checking on his patrons.

Aldea ✿

Mediterranean XX

A2

31 W. 17th St. (bet. Fifth & Sixth Aves.)

Subway: 14 St - 6 Av
Phone: 212-675-7223
Web: www.aldearestaurant.com
Prices: $$

Lunch Mon – Fri
Dinner Mon – Sat

Jerry Errico

It may take a village to raise a child, but—in New York at least—it takes George Mendes to raise a village. The talented Portuguese-American chef bounced around the kitchens of some impressive chefs (including David Bouley, Alain Ducasse, and Kurt Gutenbrunner) before opening this intimate Flatiron restaurant, the name of which means village in Portuguese.

The training more than paid off. Step inside the contemporary dining room and you'll find a lovely, sun-bleached coastal setting and a chef's counter (solo diner's welcome) set so closely to the kitchen you feel like you could touch the chefs toiling just beyond the glass partition.

Mendes' menu is small but focused, with a killer charcuterie plate that may feature foie gras terrine and *presunto*, a dry-cured Portuguese ham, and a chef's menu that will only set you back $75. Try the fresh sea urchin on toast, laced with cauliflower cream, sea lettuce, lime, and shiso leaf; smoky baby cuttlefish, expertly scored and laced with a foamy coconut curry; perfectly seared Chatham cod over just-shelled cranberry beans and fresh fava; or the dreamy *sonhos* donut holes filled with spiced chocolate, concord grape jam, and apple cider caramel.

A Voce Madison ✿

B1 — Italian XX

41 Madison Ave. (entrance on 26th St.)

Subway: 28 St (Park Ave. South) — Lunch Mon – Fri
Phone: 212-545-8555 — Dinner nightly
Web: www.avocerestaurant.com
Prices: $$$

Evan Sung

A Voce means "word of mouth" in Italian and the beat on this modern, upscale Italian restaurant is that its food still has the chops to back up the many accolades it's piled up during its short tenure. Much of the credit goes to the very talented Missy Robbins, who left her Executive Chef post at Chicago's esteemed Spiaggia to take the wheel a few years back, bringing her own formidable bag of tricks to the kitchen's regional Italian cooking.

Sashaying into deeper pockets of the peninsula, Robbins turns out deliciously restrained yet immaculate treats like pan-roasted mackerel laced with excellent olive oil and paired with pristine Satsuma mandarin, slivered fennel, capers, and toasted pistachios; or plump, perfectly cooked *raviolini* stuffed with tender chicken liver and foie gras, and bathed in a light olive oil sauce with juniper and nutty *radicchio di Treviso.*

The décor still packs the requisite slick-and-hip city punch, with a gorgeous, ornately-carved dark wood door leading to a cool interior where diners linger over the impressive Italian-dominated wine list. Unfortunately, the service can read a bit too casual at times—hopefully that's due for a shift change sometime soon.

Barbounia

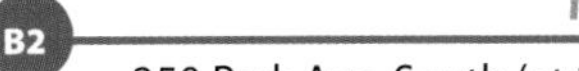

B2 — Mediterranean XX

250 Park Ave. South (at 20th St.)

Subway: 23 St (Park Ave. South) — Lunch & dinner daily
Phone: 212-995-0242
Web: www.barbounia.com
Prices: **$$**

Favored by the nearby business crowd and residents alike, this sprawling space boasts exotic touches throughout. Fat columns and arched openings abate the room's scale, while pillow-lined banquettes, a knobby-wood communal table, and open kitchen equipped with a wood-burning oven allude to the menu's rustic Mediterranean theme.

A recent chef change has resulted in a revamped menu that continues to serve the sunny flavors of the region. Start with the selection of spreads accompanied by a slab of addictive, freshly baked flatbread. Then branch out to explore a tempting array of meze, oven-roasted whole fish, or house specialties like lamb terracotta—a stew perfumed with sweet spices, covered with a crusty bread lid, and baked in an earthenware dish.

Bar Breton

B1 — French X

254 Fifth Ave. (bet. 28th & 29th Sts.)

Subway: 28 St (Broadway) — Lunch & dinner daily
Phone: 212-213-4999
Web: www.chefpiano.com/bar-breton
Prices: **$$**

Chef Cyril Renaud's latest venture is a culinary love letter to the cuisine of his native Brittany. Highlights here include a hearty listing of organic buckwheat crêpes (galettes) filled with the likes of blue cheese, Anjou pear, and honey pecans; or even served as a "lasagna" of crab meat and Parmesan. The attractively presented regular menu offerings are augmented by a rotating selection of daily specials and entrées. Everything here clearly displays the touch of a talented professional, as in the perfectly rosy slices of velvety duck breast.

Open for lunch and dinner daily in an unassuming location, this informal brasserie features a petite, zinc-topped bar serving draught beers and ciders, as well as a casually adorned dining room in back.

Bar Jamón

Spanish 

B3

125 E. 17th St. (at Irving Pl.)

Subway: 14 St - Union Sq — Lunch Sat – Sun
Phone: 212-253-2773 — Dinner nightly
Web: www.barjamonnyc.com
Prices: $$

A nibble at Bar Jamón (little sister of Casa Mono's next door), with its brilliant by-the-glass selection of Spanish wines and small plates, may convince you that Chef Andy Nusser is the unsung hero of the Batali empire. Though the restaurant is the size of a closet, everything is done deliciously and with panache.

This mouthwatering menu so creatively and famously breaks the tired tapas mold that arrival more than 15 minutes past opening almost guarantees a wait (stick to weekend off-hours). Specialties focus on luscious slices of ham from Spain's famed *pata negra* (black hoofed) pigs; cheese with an array of condiments like quince or tomato jam; and peppery, paprika-infused house chorizo. A *cuarto* from the impressive wine list is de rigueur.

BLT Fish

Seafood

A2

21 W. 17th St. (bet. Fifth & Sixth Aves.)

Subway: 14 St - 6 Av — Lunch Mon – Fri
Phone: 212-691-8888 — Dinner nightly
Web: www.bltfish.com
Prices: $$$

BLT Fish presents two options to hungry seafood fans. On the ground floor, the Fish Shack offers an extensive raw bar, beachfront-worthy lobster rolls, and fish and chips. Or, choose the upstairs dining room that bears all the hallmarks of BLT's casual elegance: dark wood furnishings, mocha color schemes, and a wine list to be pondered. There's more! The sightly space is equipped with a glass roof and white-tiled open kitchen.

Exceptionally fresh shellfish or line-caught, hand-cut fish may be simply brushed with olive oil and grilled; but the menu also boasts more ingenious offerings, like the semi-smoked King salmon with avocado hollandaise. Thoughtful extras throughout the meal enhance the experience.

Lunch is served daily at the Fish Shack.

BLT Prime

Steakhouse XX

B2

111 E. 22nd St. (bet. Lexington Ave. & Park Ave. South)

Subway: 23 St (Park Ave. South) — Dinner nightly
Phone: 212-995-8500
Web: www.bltprime.com
Prices: $$$

Though this city offers a world of dining options, it still savors its meat and potatoes. Here at BLT Prime, cuts of USDA prime and certified Black Angus are dry-aged in house, fancifully presented sizzling hot in a cast iron pan, and topped with a slowly melting sheen of herbed butter. The menu is designed to allow diners to further adorn their steaks with an array of homemade sauces, like béarnaise or "3 mustard," and the hearty listing of sides that elevate the humble potato into the likes of Parmesan gnocchi. The Gruyère popovers start meals with a warm and tasty welcome.

The handsome room and bar area, popular with local after-work crowds, are done in rich tones of butterscotch and mocha, and furnished with sleek zebrawood tables.

Blue Smoke

American X

B1

116 E. 27th St. (bet. Lexington Ave. & Park Ave. South)

Subway: 28 St (Park Ave. South) — Lunch & dinner daily
Phone: 212-447-7733
Web: www.bluesmoke.com
Prices: $$

Blue Smoke proves that jazz and barbecue are a winning combination, where hickory and applewood flavor the "low and slow" smoked meats in a real barbeque pit.

The proof lies in the ravishing rib sampler—think baby backs, spareribs, and beef ribs. Other decadent delights include the Blue Smoke burger and chipotle chicken wings with a dollop of blue cheese. Although absurd, try to save room for the classic sides and old-fashioned desserts, like banana cream pie. The wine list features small producers and is impressive for a barbecue joint.

Families and groups are suited to upstairs dining, but the same food can be enjoyed downstairs at Jazz Standard, accompanied by live music. Owner Danny Meyer stamps the restaurant with his signature of gracious service.

Blue Water Grill

Contemporary XX

A2·3

31 Union Sq. West (at 16th St.)

Subway: 14 St - Union Sq — Lunch & dinner daily
Phone: 212-675-9500
Web: www.brguestrestaurants.com
Prices: $$

Facing the Union Square Greenmarket, perennially popular Blue Water Grill is housed in a former, century-old bank, whose grand rooms now bustle with eager guests and a well-trained service team. Still, it retains a stately air with its soaring molded ceiling, gleaming marble, and windows overlooking the terraced dining area, ideal for warmer weather.

The crowd-pleasing menu focuses on seafood, but offers something for everyone. Highlights include a raw bar and sushi or maki selections, as well as fish entrées, simply grilled or accented with international flavors, as in big eye tuna with miso-black garlic vinaigrette. Find live jazz nightly in the downstairs lounge; or private group dining in the Vault Room, a former repository for gold bullion.

Boqueria

Spanish XX

A2

53 W. 19th St. (bet. Fifth & Sixth Aves.)

Subway: 18 St (Seventh Ave.) — Lunch & dinner daily
Phone: 212-255-4160
Web: www.boquerianyc.com
Prices: $$

This hip, upscale tapas restaurant pays homage to the little bars and restaurants that surround the legendary *Mercat de la Boqueria* in Barcelona. The nearby shopping isn't quite the same (think middlebrow department stores like Old Navy and TJ Maxx), but a long lunch at Boqueria—with its communal tables, cozy leather banquettes, and polished good looks—should deliver you to Europe, if only for a spell.

The menu is as long as it is tasty—try the baguette slices topped with fried quail egg and chorizo; dates stuffed with almonds and Valdeon cheese, wrapped in crispy bacon; tender lamb meatballs puddled in a savory tomato sauce and laced with creamy sheep's milk cheese; or a piping hot *cazuela* filled with Mahon cheese and chorizo.

The Breslin ✿

Gastropub

16 W. 29th St. (at Broadway)

Subway: 28 St (Broadway) — Lunch & dinner daily
Phone: 212-679-1939
Web: www.thebreslin.com
Prices: $$

Myriam Babin

After a wham-bam-that-didn't-work-so-well-ma'am turn with seafood at her and partner Ken Friedman's ill-fated venture, John Dory, the celebrated British chef, April Bloomfield is back in her gastropub wheelhouse—and better than ever.

Tucked into the ground level of the Ace Hotel, The Breslin is a bit more obviously hip than Bloomfield's popular sister venture, The Spotted Pig, but anyone who's ever teetered on a stool at this West Village pearl will appreciate how roomy the new space is. Still, with a strict no reservations policy (hotel guests can at least call down at the start of service), the place crowds quickly with a young, lively cluster ordering hand-crafted cocktails from the bar.

Kick things off with a chilled skate and potato terrine layered with bright julienned cucumber, a hint of horseradish, and creamy aïoli; and then move on (if you dare) to the deep-fried pig's foot for two, stuffed with pig's feet sausage, and served with a mound of Brussels sprout leaves and roasted *cipollini* onions finished with a stunning pan sauce. End the affair with a bittersweet chocolate tart dusted with Maldon salt, and paired with a lick of caramel and a cool scoop of banana ice cream.

Casa Mono ✿

Spanish

B3

52 Irving Pl. (at 17th St.)

Subway: 14 St - Union Sq
Lunch & dinner daily
Phone: 212-253-2773
Web: www.casamononyc.com
Prices: $$

Casa Mono

When the weather's right and Casa Mono's enormous glass doors swing out over one of the loveliest corners in Manhattan, Woody Harrelson himself couldn't resist the sizzle and smell of meat cooked *a la plancha* and pleasant thump of music floating onto Irving Place.

Andy Nusser knows how to throw a party. It's probably why big-time partners like Mario Batali and Joseph Bastianich helped him create this rustic Spanish charmer. Lovely though it may be, the interior can read a bit cramped; the kind of place where the bar might prove more comfortable than the Lilliputian tables. A trifling inconvenience, nonetheless, when that ruby-red glass of Spanish wine hits your palm, and those Spanish small plates of *jamón Ibérico,* stuffed piquillo peppers, and *bacalao croquetas* start flying out of the kitchen.

Dinner might kick off with a tangle of saffron-stained angel hair pasta studded with chorizo, sea beans, and cherrystone clams, then laced with a creamy aïoli; then move on to fork-tender goat confit, served over silky stalks of rainbow Swiss chard and topped with a cool, creamy dollop of black olive goat cheese. Finished with a warm square of fudgy, flourless chocolate torta? Perfecto.

Copper Chimney

Indian

126 E. 28th St. (bet. Lexington Ave. & Park Ave. South)

Subway: 28 St (Park Ave. South) — Lunch & dinner daily
Phone: 212-213-5742
Web: www.copperchimneynyc.com
Prices:

This attractive and sleek dining room with hip décor and a fun vibe impresses with Northern and Southern Indian fare that stands well above the array of local options. The appetizer selection may include lovely *malai kofta*, perfectly browned and simmered in a delicious, creamy saffron sauce. Main courses incorporate a wide range of traditional ingredients, while emphasizing refined preparation and elegant presentation. Non-meat eaters will be happy with the ample selection of flavorful vegetarian items. Delicately puffed *kulcha*, served hot and dusted with cilantro and mint, is a great foil to any rich, leftover sauces (and the best way to sop them up).

The contemporary setting is further enhanced by a second floor lounge area.

Craft

American 

43 E. 19th St. (bet. Broadway & Park Ave. South)

Subway: 14 St - Union Sq — Dinner nightly
Phone: 212-780-0880
Web: www.craftrestaurant.com
Prices: **$$$$**

As host of the popular Bravo reality show, *Top Chef*, Tom Colicchio is a Hollywood natural. But years ago, he shot to fame on his home turf—the New York food scene—by ushering in a new, albeit simple, way of thinking about haute cuisine: let fresh, local, organic ingredients do the work, and let customers design their own plates. At Craft, diners can tailor their meals ingredient by ingredient to suit them perfectly, choosing from a basic lineup of seafood, charcuterie, roasted meats, salad, or vegetables. That they can do it in a beautiful Flatiron space with leather-paneled walls, brick-covered columns, and dramatic filament bulbs dripping from the ceiling, takes the cake.

Speaking of, don't miss the to-die-for desserts.

Craftbar

Contemporary XX

A2

900 Broadway (bet. 19th & 20th Sts.)

Subway: 14 St - Union Sq — Lunch & dinner daily
Phone: 212-461-4300
Web: www.craftrestaurant.com
Prices: $$

Craftbar offers a toned-down setting and simpler menu structure than at Chef Tom Colicchio's first-born, Craft (here entrées are already assigned accompaniments). The lofty space, with paper-topped tables and exposed duct work, portrays the casual elegance expected from the acclaimed chef.

Modern American style with Mediterranean flair and focus on seasonality typify Craftbar's menu, which is conventionally arranged by course, but also features a selection of tidbits like oysters, cheeses, and charcuterie. Dishes may include rich and rosy chicken liver pâté topped with deep purple port wine gelée, or fillet of daurade with baby turnips appetizingly browned in savory truffle honey.

Revel in the boundless wine list, with many selections by the glass.

Dévi

Indian XX

A2

8 E. 18th St. (bet. Broadway & Fifth Ave.)

Subway: 14 St - Union Sq — Lunch Mon – Fri
Phone: 212-691-1300 — Dinner nightly
Web: www.devinyc.com
Prices: $$

One of Manhattan's most alluring Indian restaurants, Dévi is awash in warm colors, rich jewel-toned fabrics, and exotic wood carvings. Founder and cookbook author Suvir Saran has new hands in the kitchen in Chef Walter D'Rosario.

The divine menu continues to proffer a creative range of deftly prepared regional specialties and diners are invited to compose their own tasting menu of two to four courses. Lunch offers good value with house favorites such as crispy fried spinach and lentil cakes with sweet-sour tamarind paste; *aloo saag*, a spiced and silky combination of spinach and potato dotted with chicken; and a sweet and milky lemon trio for dessert.

Business diners appreciate the swift service, while those seeking a leisurely pace may feel rushed.

Eleven Madison Park ✿

Contemporary XXXX

B1

11 Madison Ave. (at 24th St.)

Subway: 23 St (Park Ave. South) Lunch Mon – Fri
Phone: 212-889-0905 Dinner Mon – Sat
Web: www.elevenmadisonpark.com
Prices: **$$$**

Robyn Lehr

You may heart the Big Apple, but New York, from the Bronx to the Battery, hearts Eleven Madison Park. What's not to love? Beautiful environs, breathtaking food. Heck, if you go at lunch, you'll even find a sweet bill—$28 lets you choose your own 2-course tasting menu.

Nestled into the beloved MetLife Insurance tower overlooking Madison Square Park, Danny Meyer's most elegant restaurant is flat-out gorgeous—with jumbo windows flooding natural light into a dining room with soaring 30-foot ceilings, glossy marble floors, ethereally pale walls, and white linens broken up by the occasional pop of fresh flowers.

Back in the kitchen, Swiss chef Daniel Humm spins impeccably fresh, seasonal ingredients and small farm meats into creative contemporary fare like a pristine Colorado lamb loin, cooked to juicy perfection and paired with one-bite delicacies like tender lamb ravioli and crispy sweet bread; or perfectly poached Nova Scotia lobster tail served in a pool of decadent Meyer lemon and *piment d'espelette* beurre blanc. Don't miss the excellent wine list—an impressive international songbook offering more than 80 half bottles and over 30 bottles of sparkling wines and bubbly.

15 East

Japanese

15 E. 15th St. (bet. Fifth Ave. & Union Sq. West)

Subway: 14 St - Union Sq — Lunch Mon – Fri
Phone: 212-647-0015 — Dinner Mon – Sat
Web: www.15eastrestaurant.com
Prices: $$$

Chef Masato Shimizu apprenticed in Japan for seven years before making his way to the Big Apple—a training you'll be thanking the sweet heavens for the minute you eyeball a gorgeous ceramic tile of his supremely fresh sashimi. Tucked into a charming four-story building overlooking 15th Street, just steps from Union Square, this modest little sushi den boasts a beautifully detailed interior decked out in gauzy white curtains, lush gray walls, and dangling geometric lanterns.

But what really matters is on your plate: tender braised octopus dusted with salt; Santa Barbara sea urchin served in its spiny shell and topped with shiso leaf; melt-in-your-mouth toro; delicate squid ribbons with lemon zest; and perfectly fried whole shrimp tempura.

Hill Country

Barbecue

30 W. 26th St. (bet. Broadway & Sixth Ave.)

Subway: 28 St (Sixth Ave.) — Lunch & dinner daily
Phone: 212-255-4544
Web: www.hillcountryny.com
Prices: $$

This Texas-size roadhouse has won over the hearts and stomachs of smoked brisket deprived New Yorkers. Always a rollicking good time, Hill Country's food stations, dispensing some of NY's best barbecue and country fare, set it above the booming competition.

After honing his skills at Blue Smoke, Chef and Pit Master Pete Daversa now fuels Hill Country's massive smokers with cords of oak to recreate a truly Texan Hill Country experience. Grab Flintstone-size ribs by the pound, sausages by the link, stamp your meal ticket, and head to the trimmings counter for home-style sides. Then, settle in for some live country music, making this a festive spot for groups and families.

Those seeking a more subdued setting can order takeout or delivery.

Gramercy Tavern 

Contemporary XXX

B2

42 E. 20th St. (bet. Broadway & Park Ave. South)

Subway: 23 St (Park Ave. South) Lunch & dinner daily
Phone: 212-477-0777
Web: www.gramercytavern.com
Prices: **$$$**

Gramercy Tavern

It's best to think of restaurants in terms of cat years. So what does it mean that Danny Meyer's celebrated Gramercy Tavern is still going strong after sixteen years in the turn-and-burn hysteria that is the Manhattan dining circuit?

It means that this cat is doing something right. Try killer ambience—think dramatic wood beams, charming period portraits, and heavenly smells of drifting wood-smoke—and gorgeous, straightforward American fare compliments of Chef Michael Anthony, who earned his greenmarket stripes at the two Blue Hill restaurants before taking the Tavern's reigns a few years ago.

The menu weaves to the season but remains diligently inspired with dishes like an exquisite pork croquette, its meltingly tender interior laced with a hint of creamy sauce, then fried to crunchy perfection and set atop a thin, smooth mound of potato purée and chopped braised greens; lightly smoked arctic char topped with butter-basted Savoy cabbage shavings and puddled in a lemony broth floating with sweet, tiny mussels and sunchokes dusted with nutty black sesame seeds; or an ethereally light kiwi sorbet sundae shot with decadent white chocolate sauce and macadamia nut cookie crumble.

'inoteca e Liquori Bar

Italian

323 Third Ave. (at 24th St.)

Subway: 23 St (Park Ave. South) — Lunch & dinner daily
Phone: 212-683-3035
Web: www.inotecanyc.com
Prices: $$

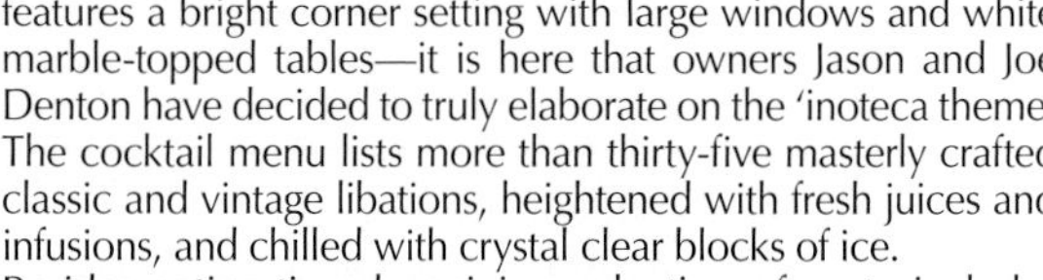

Dressier than her downtown sister, 'inoteca e Liquori Bar brings a beloved menu of small plates to Gramercy. Awash in a warm glow, the chic space is decorated with an earthy rainbow of marble slabs paneling one side of the room. The bar features a bright corner setting with large windows and white marble-topped tables—it is here that owners Jason and Joe Denton have decided to truly elaborate on the 'inoteca theme. The cocktail menu lists more than thirty-five masterly crafted classic and vintage libations, heightened with fresh juices and infusions, and chilled with crystal clear blocks of ice.

Besides antipasti and panini, a selection of pasta includes a decadent baked rigatoni with creamy cauliflower and the crunch of herbed breadcrumbs.

I Trulli

Italian

122 E. 27th St. (bet. Lexington Ave. & Park Ave. South)

Subway: 28 St (Park Ave. South) — Lunch Mon – Fri
Phone: 212-481-7372 — Dinner nightly
Web: www.itrulli.com
Prices: $$$

Equal parts dining room and *enoteca*, the charming I Trulli has been going strong for 15 years. From the roaring fireplace to the breezy outdoor garden, this place oozes warmth and the ambience is chic country comfort. Every detail including the domed white walls and oven is designed to recall the distinctive architecture of the region's *trullo*, or stacked-stone homes.

I Trulli celebrates the wine and food of Southern Italy's Puglia region. The wine bar has a terrific selection of all-Italian wines and a tempting taste of small dishes, while the dining room focuses on heartier selections, handmade pastas, and regional specialties such as *fave e cicoria*.

Desserts show off the chef's proud roots as a pastry artist and provide a strong, and sweet, finish.

Jaiya

Thai

C1

396 Third Ave. (bet. 28th & 29th Sts.)

Subway: 28 St (Park Ave. South) Lunch & dinner daily
Phone: 212-889-1330
Web: www.jaiya.com
Prices:

After twenty years in the same location, this beloved spicy stalwart now has been revitalized with a slicker look. The furnishings may now feature deep-hued woods, dark tables, padded beige walls, and a contemporary bar. Still, rest assured that the vast, budget-friendly menu remains as delicious as ever.

Start with a hot and crisp spring roll filled with glass noodles and bean sprouts while considering the proteins for customizing Jaiya's heaping stir-fried dishes fragrant with basil, garlic, and Kaffir lime. Curry listings encourage the same liberty, highlighting a host of creamy coconut curries, spiced with chilies and sweet with fresh basil, filled with the likes of succulent shrimp and fresh tilapia, accompanied by a cone of hot sticky rice.

Les Halles

French 

C1

411 Park Ave. South (bet. 28th & 29th Sts.)

Subway: 28 St (Park Ave. South) Lunch & dinner daily
Phone: 212-679-4111
Web: www.leshalles.net
Prices: $$

Everyone's favorite bad boy chef, Anthony Bourdain, may have put this beloved brasserie (his alma mater) on the map, but the simple, unfussy French cooking is the true draw. This is the rare spot renowned for skillfully knowing how to leave French classics untouched, unmodernized, and absolutely delicious. The timeless brasseries menu may start the day with breakfast "Parisien" of brioche French toast, and end with a hearty cassoulet accompanied by a selection from the budget-friendly wine list.

After 8:00 P.M, the lights go down, music goes up, and hip yet unpretentious crowds really begin to pour into this perennial favorite, housed in a century-old building. Tiny tables and tight seating put the outdoor tables in high demand during warm weather.

Laut ✿

Asian

A2

15 E. 17th St. (bet. Broadway & Fifth Ave.)

Subway: 14 St - Union Sq
Lunch & dinner Mon – Sat
Phone: 212-206-8989
Web: www.lautnyc.com
Prices: **$$**

Roy Samadi/Laut

From the husband-and-wife duo behind Union Square's popular Mizu Sushi comes Laut, a hot Malaysian joint that's already turned more than a few critics' heads. Set down a nondescript street off of Union Square, Laut is simple and elegant, with red exposed brick; beautifully rendered flowers drawn in colorful chalk; and walls painted with languid scenes from some distant, dreamy otherworld.

Though not all of Chef Kathy Wong's presentations are considered traditionally Malaysian, it's certainly where newcomers will want to kick things off—the chef's devotion to the country's complex cuisine absolutely shines, and each and every bite is a revelation.

Don't miss the *pasembur*, a cold salad featuring a host of goodies like Chinese turnips, prawn fritters, stinky tofu, cashews, and boiled egg; *roti telur*, a thin, almost translucent pancake filled with fresh eggs, scallions, and paper thin mushrooms, lightly fried and paired with a spicy coconut milk chicken curry; or the *Assam laksa*, a mind-blowing and tempting tamarind soup bobbing with all kinds of ingredients like lemongrass fish flakes, pineapple chunks, Vietnamese mint, prawn sauce, explosive chillies, and a fragrant flower bud.

Maialino

Italian

2 Lexington Ave. (at 21st St.)

Subway: 23 St (Park Ave South) — Lunch & dinner daily
Phone: 212-777-2410
Web: www.maialinonyc.com
Prices: $$

Danny Meyer's reworking of the Gramercy Park Hotel's dining venue has rendered a chicly casual Italian spot with a rustic theme conceived by the Rockwell Group. Accessed by a separate street entrance, the expanse up front is bright and lively with plenty of counter seating at the bar; while the back area, with its glossy dark wood accents, is furnished with tables dressed in blue and white checked tablecloths.

An alumnus of Babbo and Gramercy Tavern rules the kitchen; and the Roman trattoria menu offers a selection of salami and antipasti. This is followed by pastas symbolic of the region such as an excellent *tonnarelli cacio e pepe*, and a short list of hearty *secondi* that includes crispy fried suckling pig's foot with braised lentils.

Mesa Grill

Southwestern

102 Fifth Ave. (bet. 15th & 16th Sts.)

Subway: 14 St - Union Sq — Lunch & dinner daily
Phone: 212-807-7400
Web: www.mesagrill.com
Prices: $$$

Responsible for launching Chef Bobby Flay to cookbook and Food Network stardom, Mesa Grill still buzzes nightly even after two decades of service—a particularly impressive achievement in this fickle city. The lofty room, colored with Southwest accents, sees its share of tourists hoping to catch a glimpse of the famous celebrity chef and native Manhattanite; but even if the chef is absent, a glass-walled kitchen entertains with views of his team putting a creative spin on Southwest cuisine.

Flay's trademark style results in a solid menu of vibrant preparations that can include a roasted garlic shrimp tamale; grilled mahi mahi with refreshing pineapple and onion salsa alongside creamy roasted poblano rice; or a moist, toasted-coconut layer cake.

Molly's Pub & Shebeen

Gastropub

287 Third Ave. (bet. 22nd & 23rd Sts.)

Subway: 23 St (Park Ave. South) — Lunch & dinner daily
Phone: 212-889-3361
Web: www.mollysshebeen.com
Prices: ¢¢

Since 1964, Molly's has been hailed as New York's most traditional pub. Even its white stucco façade against dark wood beams and carved wooden sign conjure Ireland. Inside, low ceilings, dark walls, and sawdust floors are warmed by the wood-burning fireplace—a toasty spot to defrost any winter chills.

The pub (or *shebeen*, which is an illicit drinking establishment) draws everyone from twenty-somethings to seasoned regulars, minus the boisterous happy-hour set. An ideal watering hole for a pint and an awesome burger, Molly's also serves pub sausages with mashed potatoes, corned beef and cabbage, and shepherd's pie.

Waits are likely here, but the bar staff will take good care of you, and the friendly regulars usually have a few good stories to share.

Novitá

Italian

102 E. 22nd St. (bet. Lexington Ave. & Park Ave. South)

Subway: 23 St (Park Ave South) — Lunch Mon – Fri
Phone: 212-677-2222 — Dinner nightly
Web: www.novitanyc.com
Prices: $$

For a solid Italian meal in Gramercy, this sweet little trattoria is worth wandering into. Tucked just below street level, along quiet 22nd Street, Novitá is delightfully unpretentious given its tony zip code, with a pretty, straightforward décor featuring sunny yellow walls, wide windows, and beautiful fresh flowers strewn about the room.

Ditto on the food. The daily specials can be pricey (be sure to ask in advance) but are lovely additions to a regular menu that might reveal crimson red tuna, fried in paper-thin pastry and served with a silky mayo and balsamic reduction; perfectly roasted Australian rack of lamb with sautéed baby spinach and garlic; or a soft square of *millefoglie* sporting rich vanilla cream and fresh sprigs of mint.

Olives

Contemporary XX

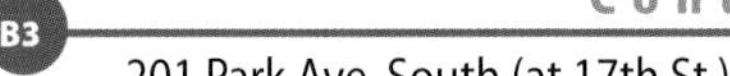

B3

201 Park Ave. South (at 17th St.)

Subway: 14 St - Union Sq — Lunch & dinner daily
Phone: 212-353-8345
Web: www.toddenglish.com
Prices: $$$

Despite the usual disdain for the large, commercial dining affairs, Chef Todd English's Olives restaurant, located on the first floor of the W Hotel-Union Square, offers a serious culinary experience.

The contemporary setting is divided into a popular lounge area and high-ceilinged dining room with comfortable furnishings and warm colors. The ample space is equipped with an open kitchen fronted by a curved dining counter.

English's rendering of Mediterranean cuisine is on display in items like escargot flatbread with Montrachet goat cheese; king crab pappardelle with preserved lemon; and lamb Porterhouse with pistachio vinaigrette.

The prix-fixe lunch menu emphasizes ingredients sourced from the nearby greenmarket and is certainly meritable.

Park Avenue Bistro

French XX

B1

377 Park Ave South (bet. 26th & 27th Sts.)

Subway: 28 St (Park Ave. South) — Lunch Mon – Fri
Phone: 212-689-1360 — Dinner Mon – Sat
Web: www.parkavenuebistronyc.com
Prices: $$

Classic bistro favorites are the strength of this cheerful and immaculately shiny spot. Affable service and walls brightened by the artwork of emerging artists lighten the hearty and soulful mood of the menu, as does the petite section of outdoor dining set on this bustling thoroughfare.

The impressively prepared, classic menu may include a salad of crisp and bitter frisée tumbled with shredded bits of duck confit and crisp bacon; or fork-tender coq au vin bathed with a mouth-coating wine reduction with traditional garnishes set atop a mound of creamy mashed potatoes. Follow these fine examples of Park Avenue Bistro's time-honored cuisine with a tart of thinly sliced apples atop butter-drenched puff pastry with a scoop of vanilla bean ice cream.

Periyali

A2 — **Greek** XX

35 W. 20th St. (bet. Fifth & Sixth Aves.)

Subway: 23 St (Sixth Ave.) — Lunch Mon – Fri
Phone: 212-463-7890 — Dinner nightly
Web: www.periyali.com
Prices: $$$

In a city that prides itself on offering what's new and what's next, the owners of Periyali deserve credit for their sincere dedication to what works—serving their brand of lovely Greek fare in a sophisticated setting since 1987. The freshly done interior's white-washed walls, billowing swathes of fabric, and shimmering fish-shaped accents transport diners to a light and breezy Mediterranean locale.

The gracious staff attends to a crowd of devoted regulars who know that the strength of Periyali's kitchen is in such solid and tempting preparations as oven-cooked *gigante* beans brightened with fresh thyme; skillfully charred yet tender marinated octopus; and hearty rabbit stew cloaked in a rich sauce redolent of tomato, red wine, and vibrant herbs.

Pranna

B1 — **Asian** XX

79 Madison Ave. (at 28th St.)

Subway: 28 St (Park Ave. South) — Dinner nightly
Phone: 212-696-5700
Web: www.prannarestaurant.com
Prices: $$

Pranna offers exotic cuisine in a soaring, glitzy, three-level setting. Dark bamboo flooring, metallic tile work, and a rich scheme of brown and gold embellish the lounge areas. The stately dining room, awash in ivory and grey, offers a more formal experience.

Served family-style, the attractive dishes of Pranna's new chef, Keith Kornfeld, are influenced by his time spent working in Southeast Asia. Pranna's extensive menu features tempting preparations—from the tandoor, jumbo prawns dressed with spicy tomato chutney; from the wok, flash-fried hangar steak; and hand-pounded curries including pumpkin, long beans, and tofu in *massaman* curry; .

Groups seeking seclusion can enjoy Pranna's tasty cuisine in a number of private dining rooms.

Primehouse New York

Steakhouse XX

B1

381 Park Ave. South (at 27th St.)

Subway: 28 St (Park Ave. South) Lunch & dinner daily
Phone: 212-824-2600
Web: www.brguestrestaurants.com
Prices: **$$$**

A glossy and grand ambience sets this steakhouse apart from the recognizable herd of traditionalists. Here, chic multi-room spaces sport walls covered in pale marble and ebony tiles, sleek furnishings, and an impressively stocked smoke-glass-walled wine cellar. However, style does not trump substance.

The focus remains on well-prepared cuts of prime Black Angus beef from Creekstone Farms, KY, aged in-house. Many non-steak options include "ocean meats" or raw bar combinations like the "East Meets West" coastal oyster selection. Attentive servers wheel trolleys throughout the room, ladling soups and preparing Caesar salads tableside. Remember to save room for the very tempting dessert offerings.

The sexy bar lounge is a top stop for after-work cocktails.

Pure Food and Wine

Vegan XX

B3

54 Irving Pl. (bet. 17th & 18th Sts.)

Subway: 14 St - Union Sq Lunch & dinner daily
Phone: 212-477-1010
Web: www.purefoodandwine.com
Prices: **$$**

Carnivores beware: this restaurant's name means what it says. A disciple of the raw-food movement, Pure Food and Wine serves only raw vegan dishes. This means that to preserve vitamins, enzymes, minerals, and flavors in the food, nothing is heated above 118°F.

Dishes like a compressed heirloom tomato, fennel, and avocado salad, or a Lapsang-smoked Portabello mushroom with caper potato salad don't just taste good, they're good for you—especially if you buy into the purported health benefits. Regardless, the kitchen uses only the freshest organic produce and there is no sense of deprivation with desserts like a deceptively decadent non-dairy ice cream sundae.

During the summer, seating spills out to the backyard dining space ringed with greenery.

Resto

C1 **Contemporary**

111 E. 29th St. (bet. Lexington Ave. & Park Ave. South)

Subway: 28 St (Park Ave. South) Lunch & dinner daily
Phone: 212-685-5585
Web: www.restonyc.com
Prices: $$

Sporting a less distinctly Belgian accent than when it first opened, Resto's comfortable dining room beckons to a steady stream of Gramercy residents who find this chicly spare and friendly spot the perfect setting to unwind at day's end or while away an afternoon.

Moules frites is still a specialty, dessert highlights include a Belgian chocolate tasting, and the marble bar's Belgian-focused beer list remains extensive. Yet Resto's highly enjoyable menu now represents a globally inspired array ranging from shrimp and grits to savory house-made lamb and feta sausage on a bed of wilted Swiss chard. The frites remain killer—golden brown, crispy tender, perfectly salted, made even more outrageously delicious when paired with a flavor-spiked mayonnaise.

Rye House

A2 **American** 

11 W. 17 St. (bet. Fifth & Sixth Aves.)

Subway: 14 St (Sixth Ave.) Lunch & dinner daily
Phone: 212-255-7260
Web: www.ryehousenyc.com
Prices: $$

As its name would suggest, Rye House offers a tavern-inspired look and easy-going vibe fueled by an impressive selection of amber liquor. The front bar provides a comfortable perch from which to sip a mint julep or single-malt Scotch, but those who wish to dine sacrifice the bar's ambience for the back area's greater comfort and enjoy the kitchen's concise and enjoyably prepared selection of playful pub grub.

The small plate offerings include the likes of crunchy and well-seasoned fried dill pickle slices, Sloppy Joe sliders, and drunken mussels bathed in Belgian-style ale. The list of entrées may be short but items such as roasted chicken dressed with spoonbread, braised greens, and buttermilk-enriched jus prove this is food to be savored.

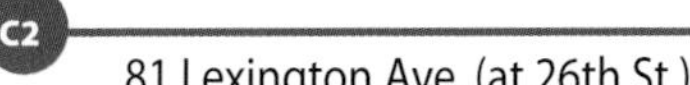

Saravanaas

Indian

C2

81 Lexington Ave. (at 26th St.)

Subway: 28 St (Park Ave. South) Lunch & dinner daily
Phone: 212-679-0204
Web: www.saravanabhavan.com
Prices:

Set smack in the midst of Curry Hill, Saravanaas stands out with its simple, clean contemporary décor. Pastel-hued walls, colorful votives, and gleaming aluminum serving pieces brighten the newly enlarged dining room.

The menu embraces a contemporary reflection of time-honored Southern Indian dishes. *Thalis*, a selection of different foods served with appropriate condiments, come in small or large sizes for a set price. *Dosas*, made with rice and lentils, are a specialty here. You can order these wonderfully thin pancakes plain or with your choice of vegetarian fillings. The *dosas* are so enormous, it's easy to make a meal of just one—for less than $10. And the veggie fillings are so tasty and satisfying, you'll never miss the meat.

SD26

Italian

B1

19 E. 26th St. (bet. Fifth & Madison Aves.)

Subway: 28 St (Park Ave. South) Lunch Mon – Fri
Phone: 212-265-5959 Dinner nightly
Web: www.sd26ny.com
Prices: $$

Located just off Madison Square Park, Tony May's follow-up to San Domenico, his well-known Central Park South restaurant that shuttered in 2008, is designed for major impact—with a 14,000 square foot space boasting a cocktail bar, upstairs dining area, jumbo salumeria station, and private wine cellar.

A far cry from the subdued aesthetic of his old place, May now offers a perfectly contemporary dining experience. Change has also come to the kitchen, where the former chef de cuisine has recently taken charge and sends forth pleasing plates such as plump *raviolini* filled with silky sea urchin and tossed in a spicy cherry tomato ragù pocked with fresh, barely-cooked scallop slices; or perfectly caramelized squab and fresh lentils laid over sautéed escarole.

Tabla

B1 — Contemporary XXX

11 Madison Ave. (at 25th St.)

Subway: 23 St (Park Ave. South) — Lunch Mon – Sat
Phone: 212-889-0667 — Dinner nightly
Web: www.tablany.com
Prices: $$

Housed in a stunning two-story dining room just steps from Madison Square Park, Danny Meyer's much loved upscale Indian restaurant got a quick menu makeover in December 2009, when it nixed its casual downstairs Bread Bar and lowered the prices on its haute upstairs fare in favor of a more moderate menu throughout.

The result is as delicious as ever, with longstanding chef, partner and Mumbai native, Floyd Cardoz, whipping up contemporary Indian cuisine steeped in local, seasonal produce, like a tangy chilled cucumber yogurt soup bobbing with bits of cucumber and a chiffonade of basil; or tender grilled fish cake, wrapped in banana leaf and flecked with fresh lime leaf, basil, and cilantro, paired with braised daikon and sautéed Swiss chard.

Tamarind

B2 — Indian XXX

41-43 E. 22nd St. (bet. Broadway & Park Ave. South)

Subway: 23 St (Park Ave. South) — Lunch & dinner daily
Phone: 212-674-7400
Web: www.tamarinde22.com
Prices: $$

At Tamarind, regional Indian cuisine is tempered by an elegant ambience featuring courteous, polished service, and an upscale, urban space.

The hefty menu offers a virtual tour through the flavors of Goa, Punjab, Madras, and Calcutta. Airy breads, aromatic tandoori dishes, piquant curries, and delectable vegetarian specialties are prepared by an ardent brigade of cooks who combine both familiar and unconventional flavors as in the rosemary naan. A peek inside the dining room's glassed-in kitchen is sure to stimulate your taste buds. Lunchtime offers a reasonable fixed-price menu.

For a casual bite, try the petite Tea Room located next door for its lighter fare of sandwiches, pastries, and Indian specialties, with a recommended tea pairing.

Tamba Indian Grill & Bar

Indian

C1

103 Lexington Ave. (bet. 27th & 28th Sts.)

Subway: 28 St (Park Ave. South)
Lunch & dinner daily
Phone: 212-481-9100
Web: www.tambagrillandbar.com
Prices: $$

The Maliks are back in biz proffering an expo of eats at Curry Hill's Tamba. Hindi for copper, Tamba soars above nearby *desi* diners with its thoughtful service and thrilling flavors. Done in brick and pearl, the refitted space radiates warmth as gaggles hover over the big buffet; so plop into a banquette and let the owners spoil you.

As glorious and glossy as the copper vessels that carry them, are freshly baked naan shined with butter and garlic; deliciously crisp *keema samosas* with lamb, cumin, and chilled coriander chutney; pepper mutton fried with onions and fragrant spices; *saag paneer*, homemade cheese cooked in spinach and herbs; and lemon rice with toasted mustard seeds and curry leaves divulge the depth and diversity of Indian cuisine.

Tocqueville

Contemporary

A3

1 E. 15th St. (bet. Fifth Ave. & Union Sq. West)

Subway: 14 St - Union Sq
Lunch & dinner Mon – Sat
Phone: 212-647-1515
Web: www.tocquevillerestaurant.com
Prices: $$

Lovingly run by proprietors Chef Marco A. Moreira and his wife Jo-Ann Makovitsky, Tocqueville offers a creative approach to seasonal cuisine in a stately dining room located just one block from the Union Square Greenmarket. During the summer months, the restaurant's three course greenmarket menu showcases its bounty at both lunch and dinner. Celebrate each season with the likes of green garlic velouté or house-made gnocchi with a tousle of wilted Swiss chard and grated ricotta *salata*. The 300-label wine list features selections from little-known regions around the world as well as a number of sakes.

Lush fabrics, vintage mirrors, and bold art fashion an elegant décor—a soothing respite in which to enjoy this roster of inspired creations.

Turkish Kitchen

Turkish XX

C1

386 Third Ave. (bet. 27th & 28th Sts.)

Subway: 28 St (Park Ave. South) — Lunch Sun – Fri
Phone: 212-679-6633 — Dinner nightly
Web: www.turkishkitchen.com
Prices: ⊜

This longtime neighborhood fixture is a worthy destination for unique Turkish cuisine. The attractive setting is accented with jewel tones of ruby and sapphire, enhanced by an air of formality from the proper yet personable service team. At the bar, colorfully filled martini glasses stand at the ready for the festivities to begin.

The bountiful appetizer selection makes for a tasty starting point with dishes like pan-fried zucchini pancakes and *manti*, savory beef-filled dumplings served with yogurt sauce. Well-prepared meat and seafood entrées follow suit with fresh flavors. At lunch, Turkish Kitchen offers a reasonably priced four-course prixe-fixe, and on weekends, the buffet brunch adds pastries and omelets to the tasty delights.

Union Square Cafe

American XX

A2

21 E. 16th St. (bet. Fifth Ave. & Union Sq. West)

Subway: 14 St - Union Sq — Lunch & dinner daily
Phone: 212-243-4020
Web: www.unionsquarecafe.com
Prices: $$$

With comfortable bistro décor, winning service, and excellent modern American cooking, Union Square Cafe is both inviting and refined. Since 1985, New Yorkers have held a special place in their hearts for this institution that launched the careers of restaurateur Danny Meyer and Chef/partner Michael Romano.

Today, tables may be more likely to be populated by tourists than local foodies, but a seat at the bar is just as welcoming as the staff is gracious. Arrive here before the crowds for a great burger or a three-course meal and sampling of wines by the glass. The nearby greenmarket figures largely into the planning of the menu that is supplemented by daily and weekly specials.

The tremendous wine list is diverse, special, and reasonably priced.

Veritas ✿

Contemporary XX

B2

43 E. 20th St. (bet. Broadway & Park Ave. South)

Subway: 23 St (Park Ave. South) Dinner Mon – Sat
Phone: 212-353-3700
Web: www.veritas-nyc.com
Prices: $$$$

Veritas

Make your way past the beautiful gated gardens of Gramercy Park, and you'll find a stately gray stone building set along East 20th Street. Only a tiny "V" marks the entrance, but don't mistake this humble façade for mediocrity within—this is Veritas, a beautiful, upscale restaurant and a grapehound's dream come true, with literally thousands of bottles from all regions of the world lining the restaurant's shelves.

There are rare vintages galore, many of which arrive courtesy of private collector, Park B. Smith and carry steep price tags—but oenophile's looking to shoot low should find bottles reasonable enough to help them relax into Veritas' soft, elegant banquettes, letting the room's pale walls, polished wood panels, and soft lighting envelope them for the night.

Chef Grégory Pugin worked extensively with Joël Robuchon before making his way to Veritas, and he brings the legendary chef's perfectionism to his rotating mix of prix-fixe and seasonal menus. Dinner might begin with exquisitely fresh jumbo lump crab and sea urchin, studded with fennel and laced with lemongrass velouté; and then move on to a heavenly bouillabaisse, bobbing with pristine fish and caramelized vegetables.

Greenwich, West Village & Meatpacking District

Artistic, poetic, and edgy: these ideals are the Village's identity. Thank the Beat Generation for this, because fifty years later, many still seek out this neighborhood for its beloved street cafés brimming with struggling artists, philosophical meanderings, and revolutionary convictions. Perhaps due to the prominence of NYU, local residents still embrace the liberal, intellectual, bohemian spirit that, in many ways, is the heart of this city.

Nevertheless, the belly of this area is equally worthy of attention and praise; even the humble **Peanut Butter and Co. Sandwich Shop** flaunts its creative side with peanut-buttery concoctions like the Elvis, which is grilled with bananas and honey (bacon is optional). Or, pick up a jar to-go, flavored with the likes of maple syrup, white chocolate, or chili powder. Nearby, **Mamoun's** has been feeding NYU students some of the best falafel in town for generations; topping one with their killer hot sauce is a must. In Washington Square Park, savvy students and foodies stand shoulder-to-shoulder in line for **N.Y. Dosas**, wrapped in delicate rice and lentil flour crêpes, served with character and flair.

Bleecker Street

Peer into the assortment of old-time Italian bakeries and shops along Bleecker Street, where **Faicco's Pork Store** has been offering its specialties for over 100 years—take home a sampling of their fresh and perfectly seasoned sausages or a tray of *arancini* (fried risotto balls), though etiquette dictates that one must be eaten warm, before leaving the store. Yet the neighborhood's most noteworthy storefront may be **Murray's Cheese Shop**. This is Manhattan's definitive cheesemonger, run by a deeply informed staff, happy to initiate hungry neophytes into the art and understanding of their countless varieties (enthusiasts note that classes are also available, exploring the meaning of terroir or cheese-pairing fundamentals).

If seeking a more lowbrow spot, try **Dirty Bird** for fried or rotisserie chicken. Rest assured that these birds are locally sourced from an Amish farm, and are free-range, vegetarian fed, and antibiotic free—all necessary qualifications for any self-respecting takeout joint in downtown bohemia. Of course, no Village jaunt is complete without pizza—with some of the finest to be found coal-fired and crisp, only by the pie, at the original **John's**. For a quick slice, stop by **Joe's** for traditional thin-crust, or **Famous Ray's**, but be prepared to use a fork here. A visit to **Cones** is equally enticing, where uniquely textured Argentine ice cream is available in both expected and unforeseen flavor combinations.

West Village

For a nearly royal treat, stop by **Tea and Sympathy**, offering tea-time snacks or full Sunday dinners of roast beef and Yorkshire pudding. The storefront also sells prized English wares, ranging from teas to pots to jars of clotted cream.

No matter where you grab your picnic, one of the best places to enjoy it is Hudson River Park, watching the urban vista of roller skaters, marathoners, and an ever-colorful parade of passersby, set against a backdrop of departing cruise ships and the setting sun. Pier 45 is a particularly lovely spot, decorated with benches and patches of grass at the end of Christopher Street, across the Westside Highway.

The influential James Beard Foundation sits in the historic 12th Street townhouse that was once home to the illustrious food writer. While strolling back through chic boutiques and camera-ready brownstones, peek down quaint Perry Street for yet another *very* NY moment: a glimpse at where Carrie Bradshaw (of *Sex and the City*) "lived." Then, let the overpowering aromas of butter and sugar lead you to **Magnolia Bakery**. Filled with pretty little pastel-flowered cupcakes and prettier couples donning Jimmy Choo shoes, this is the Village's official date night finale. Another sweet spot is **Li-Lac**, dispensing chocolate-covered treats and nostalgic confections since 1923.

One of the West Village's most celebrated landmarks may be the **Corner Bistro**, whose pub fare has been at the heart of the "Best Burger in Town" debate for decades. Its long mahogany bar, cheap beers, and great jukebox complete this perfectly laid back (and perennially crowded) scene. Another "bar's bar" incarnate that strives to embody everything a cheap beer and retro juke hope to effuse is the **Rusty Knot**. Kick back, hang out, and grab some Po' boys or pickled eggs to go with that pint. For a more refined late-night scene, expert mixologists can be found creatively pouring "long drinks and fancy cocktails" at **Employees Only**. Likewise, bartenders approach celebrity status at **Little Branch**, where an encyclopedic understanding of the craft brings dizzying and delectable results.

Meatpacking District

Further north is an area known as the Meatpacking District. Just a short decade ago, its cobblestoned streets were so desolate that only the savviest young Manhattanites knew that its empty warehouses held the city's edgiest clubs. Young hipsters take note: the Meatpacking has already arrived, repopulated, and regrouped with seas of sleekly designed lounges serving pricey cocktails to the fashionable minions, as if in defiance of these cautious times. Luxury hotels have risen, and storied bistros so infamously festive that they once defined the neighborhood have fallen. Completing this picture is the High Line, an abandoned 1934 elevated railway that is now transformed into a 19-block long park.

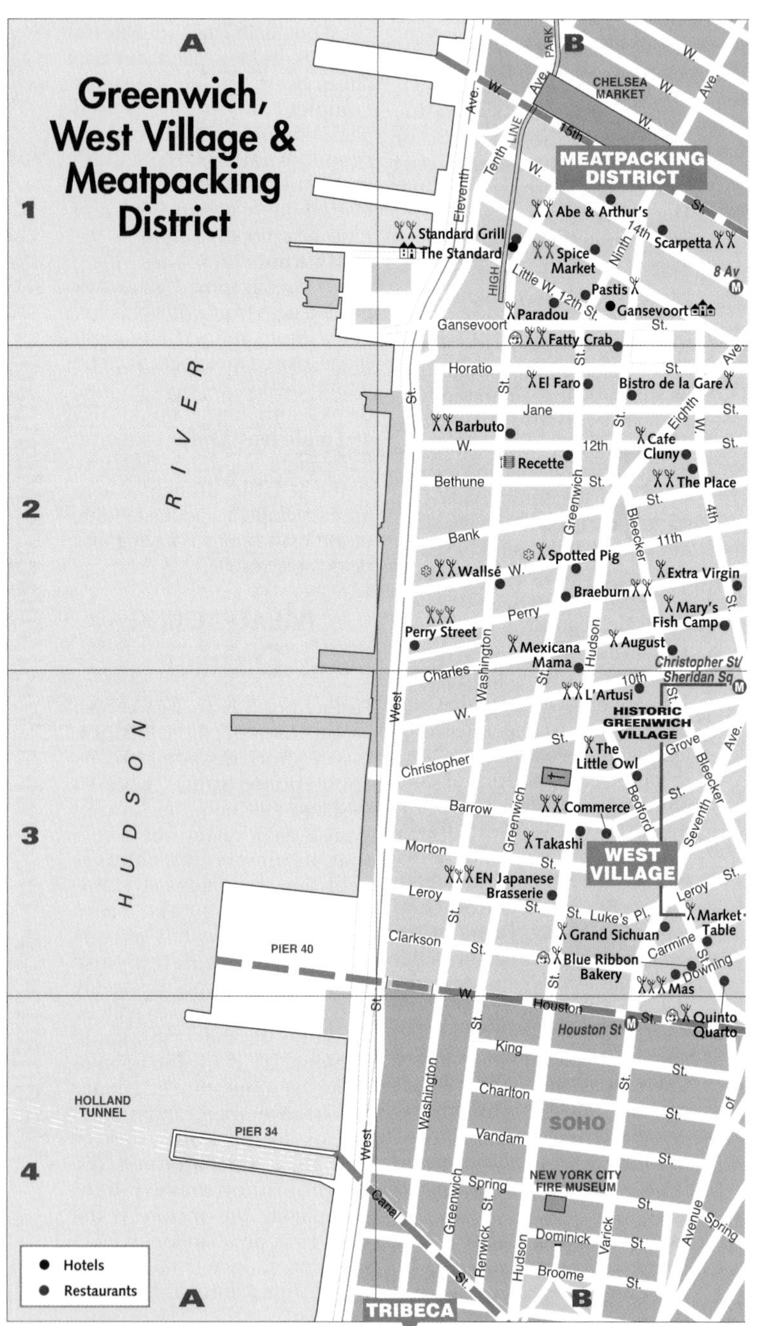

Greenwich, West Village & Meatpacking District
MEATPACKING DISTRICT
CHELSEA MARKET
HISTORIC GREENWICH VILLAGE
WEST VILLAGE
SOHO
TRIBECA
HUDSON RIVER
PIER 40
PIER 34
HOLLAND TUNNEL
NEW YORK CITY FIRE MUSEUM
Abe & Arthur's
Standard Grill
The Standard
Scarpetta
Spice Market
Pastis
Gansevoort
Paradou
Fatty Crab
El Faro
Bistro de la Gare
Barbuto
Cafe Cluny
Recette
The Place
Spotted Pig
Wallsé
Extra Virgin
Braeburn
Mary's Fish Camp
Perry Street
Mexicana Mama
August
L'Artusi
The Little Owl
Commerce
Takashi
EN Japanese Brasserie
Market Table
Grand Sichuan
Blue Ribbon Bakery
Mas
Quinto Quarto
8 Av
Christopher St/ Sheridan Sq
Houston St
Hotels
Restaurants

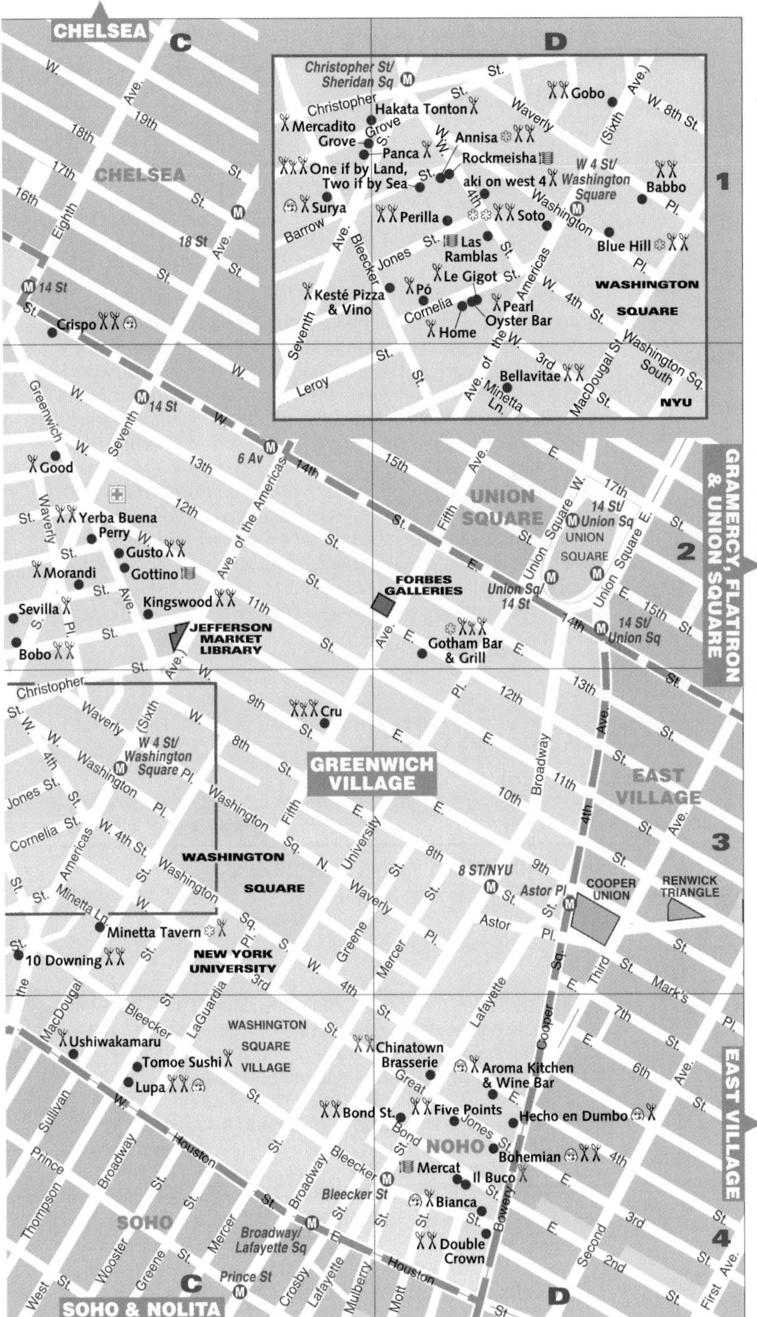

CHELSEA
C
D
Christopher St/ Sheridan Sq
Hakata Tonton
Mercadito Grove
Panca
Annisa
Rockmeisha
One if by Land, Two if by Sea
aki on west 4
W 4 St/ Washington Square
Gobo
Babbo
Surya
Perilla
Soto
Blue Hill
Las Ramblas
Le Gigot
Kesté Pizza & Vino
Pó
Pearl Oyster Bar
Home
Bellavitae
WASHINGTON SQUARE
NYU
1
CHELSEA
18 St
14 St
Crispo
14 St
6 Av
Good
Yerba Buena Perry
Gusto
Morandi
Gottino
Kingswood
Sevilla
Bobo
JEFFERSON MARKET LIBRARY
UNION SQUARE
14 St/ Union Sq
FORBES GALLERIES
Union Sq/ 14 St
14 St/ Union Sq
Gotham Bar & Grill
GRAMERCY, FLATIRON & UNION SQUARE
2
Cru
GREENWICH VILLAGE
W 4 St/ Washington Square
EAST VILLAGE
WASHINGTON SQUARE
8 ST/NYU
Astor Pl
COOPER UNION
RENWICK TRIANGLE
3
Minetta Tavern
10 Downing
NEW YORK UNIVERSITY
WASHINGTON SQUARE VILLAGE
Ushiwakamaru
Tomoe Sushi
Lupa
Chinatown Brasserie
Aroma Kitchen & Wine Bar
Bond St.
Five Points
Hecho en Dumbo
NOHO
Bohemian
Mercat
Il Buco
Bleecker St
Bianca
Broadway/ Lafayette Sq
Double Crown
SOHO
Prince St
4
EAST VILLAGE
SOHO & NOLITA

Abe & Arthur's

American

B1

409 W. 14th St. (bet. Ninth & Tenth Aves.)

Subway: 14 St - 8 Av — Lunch Sun
Phone: 646-289-3930 — Dinner nightly
Web: www.abeandarthurs.com
Prices: **$$$**

Housed in a former nightclub, this serious Meatpacking newcomer offers an enjoyably prepared menu that is both creative and hearty. The front bar sports a sexy dark wood and glossy tiled look, while the high-ceilinged rear dining room is tastefully appointed with creamy tan leather seating, parchment ceiling pendants, and backlit scrims adorned with graffiti-like imagery.

Steaks are a popular option here, procured from Creekstone Farms, embellished with myriad sauces and sides. Starters include the likes of tuna tartare tacos, served as a mound of diced tuna scattered with crunchy mini-tortilla shells for a do-it-yourself aesthetic; non-steak entrée options may include seared sea scallops with crisped foie gras and cauliflower-almond purée.

aki on west 4

Japanese

D1

181 W. 4th St. (bet. Sixth & Seventh Aves.)

Subway: W 4 St - Wash Sq — Dinner nightly
Phone: 212-989-5440
Web: N/A
Prices: **$$**

Set in a red-brick row house, Aki's tiny dining room feels like an intimate parlor. Add to this a warm, polite staff and a menu that displays a distinct personality, and it is easy to see why this spot continues to attract a loyal following.

Chef/owner Siggy Nakanishi once served as private chef to the Japanese Ambassador to Jamaica and his menu reflects a sweet and sunny personality. Daily specials are presented as a tabletop photo display; the chef's menu offers a selection of creative preparations that may include the eel napoleon appetizer composed of panko-crusted tofu, delicate eel tempura, and pumpkin purée. Other dishes include finely prepared sushi and rolls, as in the Jamaica roll, stuffed with jerk chicken and hearts of palm, of course.

Annisa ✿

Contemporary XX

D1

13 Barrow St. (bet. Seventh Ave. South & W. 4th St.)

Subway: Christopher St - Sheridan Sq — Dinner nightly
Phone: 212-741-6699
Web: www.annisarestaurant.com
Prices: $$$

Annisa

Annisa means "women" in Arabic, and this serene, stylish restaurant, tucked into a quaint, tree-lined street in the West Village, does indeed pack a pretty punch. The newly redesigned interior stars sheer, billowing drapes; sunset-colored fabric wall panels; pale blonde wood accents; and big, glossy windows facing the street.

Chef/owner Anita Lo creates an ever-changing, globally-infused menu that draws as much on her culinary days in France as it does from her travels and Chinese-American heritage.

Bold ingredients from Asia—miso, tofu, and soybean—and afar are treated with delicacy and wind their way through a contemporary menu that might feature ruby-red steak tartare, flecked with herbs and Japanese *tonburi* seeds, and set atop bright white Asian pear; grilled, flaky halibut served with bacon-miso sauce, tender, glazed radishes, and a small bundle of micro-greens flecked with crispy bacon bits; or creamy poppy seed bread pudding nestled in a pool of silky lemon curd sprinkled with crunchy poppy seeds. An international wine list boasts scores of labels, many of them hailing from female vintners or vineyards owned by women, as well as a healthy by-the-glass selection.

Aroma Kitchen & Wine Bar 

D4 Italian

36 E. 4th St. (bet. Bowery & Lafayette St.)

Subway: Bleecker St — Dinner nightly
Phone: 212-375-0100
Web: www.aromanyc.com
Prices: $$

This welcoming spot, tucked away on the edge of Greenwich Village, radiates an amiable vibe thanks to hospitable owners Alexandra Degiorgio and Vito Polosa. Simply decorated with a warm and rustic aesthetic, the focal point of the intimate, street-level dining room is a dark-wood dining counter. In warmer weather, the room opens onto the sidewalk, providing additional real estate to alleviate the throng of enthusiastic regulars.

This wine bar offers a substantial menu of small plates and appetizers along with expertly prepared pastas and tempting desserts. Available on Mondays only, the chef's five-course tasting menu is a delicious way to start the week.

The unique and fairly priced wine list contains many varietals rarely found outside Italy.

August

B2 European

359 Bleecker St. (bet. Charles & 10th Sts.)

Subway: Christopher St - Sheridan Sq — Lunch & dinner daily
Phone: 212-929-8727
Web: www.augustny.com
Prices: $$

This charming establishment located on a boutique-lined stretch of Bleecker Street has the cozy spirit of a rustic trattoria. Distressed walls, wood plank flooring, and simple furnishings are complemented by the appetizing aromas wafting from the wood-burning oven. From here, temptations emerge such as a *tarte flambé* topped with a layer of creamy melted onions and smoky lardons, or oven-roasted whole fish. Brunch may feature a variety of baked eggs *en cocotte,* or cast-iron German pancake.

The young staff is decorously laid back yet courteous in this small dining room, augmented by additional seating in the graceful glassed-in back patio. Despite August's plebeian air, don't be surprised to see a celebrity discreetly ducking in for a bite.

Babbo

Italian XX

D1

110 Waverly Pl. (bet. MacDougal St. & Sixth Ave.)

Subway: W 4 St - Wash Sq — Dinner nightly
Phone: 212-777-0303
Web: www.babbonyc.com
Prices: $$$

Considered one of the toughest reservations to get in this city, Mario Batali's flagship restaurant manages to please everyone from out-of-towners to downtown foodies. Whether due to the intimate townhouse setting or the kitchen's inventive spin on rustic Italian fare, Babbo is perpetually packed. However, celebrity chef-gazing is improbable, since *He Who Wears The Orange Crocs* is more likely to be at a public appearance than behind the scenes here.

The menu changes seasonally, but focuses on his trademark Italian creations. Offerings may include Chianti-stained paparadelle with wild boar ragù or whole grilled branzino with radicchio in pancetta and lemon-oregano jam. Silky and sublime panna cotta infused with saffron ends meals with refined beauty.

Barbuto

Italian XX

B2

775 Washington St. (at 12th St.)

Subway: 14 St - 8 Av — Lunch & dinner daily
Phone: 212-924-9700
Web: www.barbutonyc.com
Prices: $$

Those who wax poetic on the virtues of the perfect roast chicken need look no farther. Located on a quiet stretch of the West Village just steps from MePa, Chef Jonathan Waxman's Barbuto plays up its locale and industrial bones with concrete flooring, painted-over brick walls, and garage doors that open up to create an atmospheric indoor/outdoor vibe.

Still, that chicken is what best expresses Barbuto's refined simplicity—the roasted bird has a coarse pepper-freckled auburn skin and tender ivory flesh moist with flavorful juices, further enhanced by a splash of bright and briny salsa verde. This dish is admirably supported by the likes of grilled octopus salad with fennel and pink grapefruit or a cookie-like chocolate hazelnut *crostata*.

Bianca 

Italian

D4

5 Bleecker St. (bet. Bowery & Elizabeth St.)

Subway: Bleecker St — Dinner nightly
Phone: 212-260-4666
Web: www.biancanyc.com
Prices: $$

Curtained windows lead the way to this charming, unassuming spot, perfect for a date or catching up with friends. Wood plank flooring and walls covered with tile and wallpaper are lined with shelves displaying delicate floral-trimmed china. An open kitchen is tucked in the cozy back. Candlelit tables are set with blue-striped kitchen towels to be used as napkins; Bianca's casual personality extends through to its cuisine.

Grilled radicchio and prosciutto dusted with grated pecorino cheese; homemade tagliatelle with wild mushrooms and fresh herbs; and chocolate chip-studded tiramisu remind guests that simplicity is always satisfying.

Generous portions and a moderately priced Italian-focused wine list naturally result in a large following.

Bistro de la Gare

Mediterranean

B2

626 Hudson St. (bet. Horatio & Jane Sts.)

Subway: 14 St - 8 Av — Lunch & Dinner Tue – Sun
Phone: 212-242-4420
Web: www.bistrodelagarenyc.com
Prices: $$

Equally talented and no less charming are Chef/owners Maryann Terillo and Elisa Sarno who have created a wonderfully low-key neighborhood bistro that exudes the aura of an old favorite even though it is new to the scene. The quaint room is simply done with tan walls hung with sepia photography, and is furnished with wooden chairs and white paper-topped tables. Like the décor, the menu follows suit lending a simplistic approach to a listing that boasts Mediterranean influences.

Starters include the likes of blistered-skin grilled sardines with warm cannellini bean salad; entrées may offer a roasted baby chicken cloaked with walnut crumbs; and desserts feature a slice of olive oil cake decked in a compote of plumped raisins and dried figs.

Blue Ribbon Bakery

Contemporary

B3

35 Downing St. (at Bedford St.)

Subway: Houston St — Lunch & dinner daily
Phone: 212-337-0404
Web: www.blueribbonrestaurants.com
Prices: $$

The story of this classic New York bistro begins with an abandoned, old-world brick oven that brothers Eric and Bruce Bromberg discovered in the basement of a bodega. This sparked an idea for a bakery, so they hired a master craftsman to rebuild it and in 1998 opened Blue Ribbon Bakery. Today, the downstairs space is carved into charming, exposed-brick rooms; the street-level windows offer a lovely West Village view; and the bar has a casual, jovial vibe.
House-baked breads star on excellent lunchtime sandwiches like the Blue Ruben, but the dinner menu is as extensive as it is impressive, with offerings that range from steamed lobster to fried chicken. Each dish here is prepared with outstanding ingredients, rich flavor, and great skill.

Bobo

Contemporary

C2

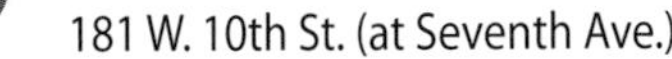

181 W. 10th St. (at Seventh Ave.)

Subway: Christopher St - Sheridan Sq — Lunch Sat – Sun, Dinner nightly
Phone: 212-488-2626
Web: www.bobonyc.com
Prices: $$

Tucked into a gorgeous West Village brownstone meant to invoke a dreamy Parisian apartment, the sexy, relaxed Bobo is built to inspire coos. Make your way through the first floor bar area and you'll find a second floor dining room awash in dark wood, pale blue walls, and whitewashed brick, stuffed with eclectic charms like gilded mirrors and beaded lighting. Chef Patrick Connolly lends a light, seasonally focused touch to Bobo's menu, with dishes like a novel BLT that arrives as a butter lettuce cup filled with tenderly roasted Berkshire pork, mayonnaise, slow cooked tomato, and toasted bread crumbs; or roasted salmon with mushroom broth, served with plump white cannelini beans and baby carrots, then topped with slivers of fried shiitake.

Blue Hill ✿

D1 **American** XX

75 Washington Pl. (bet. Sixth Ave. & Washington Sq. Park)

Subway: W 4 St - Wash Sq — Dinner nightly
Phone: 212-539-1776
Web: www.bluehillnyc.com
Prices: $$$

Thomas Schauer/Blue Hill

Ask any New Yorker what's on their dining wish list, and you're guaranteed to hear Blue Hill again and again. But if near-unanimous local obsession doesn't impress you, then maybe this will: when President Obama flew First Lady Michelle into the Big Apple for a theater date back in 2009, you can bet your seasonal goodies he chose Chef Dan Barber's decade-plus pioneer of the organic-farm-to-urban-table movement, Blue Hill.

Barber takes time to forge personal relationships with neighboring farmers, resulting in a tightly-knit network of small farms to cull ingredients from, all located within a 250-mile radius of the city. One of them is Stone Barns, a biodynamic farm in Pocantico Hills where you'll find a second outpost of Blue Hill.

Back here in the city, you can sample Barber's local, seasonal products in an elegant storybook townhouse near Washington Square. Dinner might include soft pillows of Swiss chard and ricotta ravioli, laced with crispy roasted kale and toasted hazelnuts; sweet and silky Tamsworth pork from Flying Pigs Farm, paired with creamy shelled beans, meaty shiitake mushrooms, and curry; or soft chestnut cake with creamy coconut and *fromage blanc* sorbet.

Bohemian

Japanese

D4

57 Great Jones St. (bet. Bowery & Lafayette St.)

Subway: Bleecker St
Dinner nightly
Phone: 212-388-1070
Web: www.playearth.jp
Prices: $$

This intriguing dining den is secreted away down an unmarked hallway and fronted by a thick glass door. Despite the stealth locale, the staff couldn't be more welcoming or courteous as they attend to diners amid polished concrete floors, white walls, and mid-century furnishings in emerald green, turquoise, and cognac—in a space that once served as a studio for artist Jean-Michel Basquiat.

Bohemian's bill of fare features snacks and small plates such as a decadent mushroom croquette topped with uni. However, the true highlight is the exceptional *washugyu* from Japanese Premium Beef offered in several guises—as a sashimi of short rib, steak of the day, or as luscious mini-burgers dressed with lettuce, slow roasted tomato, and pecorino on tender brioche.

Bond Street

Japanese

D4

6 Bond St. (bet. Broadway & Lafayette St.)

Subway: Bleecker St
Dinner nightly
Phone: 212-777-2500
Web: www.bondstrestaurant.com
Prices: $$$$

There is no name to mark the three-story brownstone that houses dark and swanky Bond Street—only a brown dot on a banner. And so the scene is set: Always stylish, always hopping, Bond Street is where moneyed trendsters find high-end sushi that looks as beautiful as it tastes. Here, pudding-sweet uni is attractively served in a purple shell, then laced with a necklace of diced cucumber and crowned with a golden leaf. Painstakingly beautiful presentations here are as likely to drop some jaws as they are to flash some bling. However, as many "oohs" and "aahs" are bound to follow the first bite of this delicious and inventive cuisine.

As expected, deep pockets are de rigueur, with appetizers that start at $16 and prices rising steeply from there.

Braeburn

B2 **American** XX

117 Perry St. (at Greenwich St.)

Subway: Christopher St - Sheridan Sq
Phone: 212-255-0696
Web: www.braeburnrestaurant.com
Prices: $$

Lunch Sun
Dinner nightly

It's the kind of Village location you see in the movies. Straddling a quaint, tree-lined corner where Perry meets Greenwich Street, with big, glossy windows to let the sun in, a gorgeous rustic-chic interior, and reclaimed tobacco shed wood accents, Braeburn is sitting about as pretty as they come.

The food holds as many charms, with Chef Brian Bistrong spinning freshly-sourced American ingredients into dishes like an amuse-bouche of tender lobster salad laced with tarragon and piled onto fresh brioche toast; hand-cut black pepper fettuccine strewn with blistered cherry tomatoes, preserved lemon, and sheep's milk ricotta; or Rhode Island skate paired with a cool cucumber salad, red onion "a la plume," breakfast radish, mustard seeds, and chili.

Cafe Cluny

B2 **American** 

284 W. 12th St. (at W. 4th St.)

Subway: 14 St - 8 Av
Phone: 212-255-6900
Web: www.cafecluny.com
Prices: $$

Lunch & dinner daily

With its winsome glow, this quintessential neighborhood restaurant sprinkles Village chic throughout its comfortable multi-room interior. Walls are lined with caricatures of regular celebrities and a wall installation of shadowy bird cutouts comes alive in the candlelit space—the popular corner-set bar continues this motif with a bird-themed diorama alongside mounted antlers. Still attracting a devoted following, the service is affable and able.

Open daily from 8:00 A.M until midnight, the kitchen continually churns out dishes with a classic touch. In the morning, homemade granola or poached eggs with short rib hash keeps you going until it's time to refuel with choice delicacies like pan-roasted Arctic char with braised lentils or coq au vin.

Chinatown Brasserie

Chinese XX

D4

380 Lafayette St. (at Great Jones St.)

Subway: Bleecker St — Lunch & dinner daily
Phone: 212-533-7000
Web: www.chinatownbrasserie.com
Prices: $$

You'll think you've died and gone to dim sum heaven at Chinatown Brasserie, a dreamy little spot that says to heck with the usual tea time rules. Here, the Chinese small plates—along with a wealth of Cantonese specialties and fusion fare—are served all day long in a chic downtown space featuring floor-to-ceiling silk curtains, oversize lanterns, and a sexy downstairs mod lounge replete with koi pond. Have kids? Check out the family-friendly brunch.

The playful, but polished, modern dim sum menu might reveal tender, translucent steamed shrimp and snow pea dumplings; ethereally light and silky roast pork buns; crispy, curry-laced black bass and avocado tarts; or warm, fluffy pillows of custard *bao* topped with a crunchy swirl of sugar.

Commerce

Contemporary XX

B3

50 Commerce St. (near Barrow St.)

Subway: Christopher St - Sheridan Sq — Lunch Sat – Sun, Dinner nightly
Phone: 212-524-2301
Web: www.commercerestaurant.com
Prices: $$

Nestled into a tiny, curving West Village alleyway so utterly charming that much of the city pales in comparison—Commerce surely landed one of Manhattan's sweetest locations. Inside, this former speakeasy's quarters are a bit cramped (the building dates back to the early 1900s), but once the very accommodating staff sets a basket of warm, freshly-baked bread upon the Lilliputian table, everything is suddenly right with the world.

Chef Harold Moore's menu focuses on both seasonal and global inspiration. Offerings may include a rich and rustic ragù of "odd things" like oxtail, trotters, and tripe with hand-rolled orecchiette; or lush duck and foie gras rillettes terrine, served with a quenelle of black cherry and shallot jam.

Crispo 

Italian XX

C1

240 W. 14th St. (bet. Seventh & Eighth Aves.)

Subway: 14 St (Seventh Ave.) — Lunch Sun
Phone: 212-229-1818 — Dinner nightly
Web: www.crisporestaurant.com
Prices: $$

Its convenient 14th Street address may help draw crowds, but Chef/owner Frank Crispo's impressive Northern Italian fare is what keeps fans returning again and again. The large room fills up easily and is effortlessly comfortable with attentive service in a rustic ambiance punctuated by filament light bulbs, mahogany panels, and vintage tile work.

The menu begins with a lengthy listing of small plates starring prosciutto, carved in the dining room on the chef's antique Berkel slicers, as well as daily specials like grilled artichokes glossed with a lemony butter sauce. Pastas are expertly prepared and may include a silky twirl of fettucine topped with sweet and plump head-on prawn scampi. For dessert, panna cotta is a voluptuous experience.

Cru

Contemporary 

C3

24 Fifth Ave. (at 9th St.)

Subway: 8 St - NYU — Dinner Mon – Sat
Phone: 212-529-1700
Web: www.cru-nyc.com
Prices: $$$

From the moment you enter Cru's graceful, clubby lair, a peaceful sort of calm washes over you. Of course, the vino helps—straddling a quiet corner of the Village two blocks north of Washington Square Park, Cru is home to one of the most impressive wine lists in the city. Thousands of bottles are drawn from owner Roy Welland's private collection, and value-hunters will find some great deals lurking among the thick leather tomes.

Chef Todd Macdonald's contemporary, classically-rooted menu spins to the season, but might include a fresh tangle of tagliatelle dotted with plump, sautéed wild mushrooms and showered in soft, grated Parmesan; or a tender roulade of skate punctuated by lemon-brown butter, veal tongue remoulade, and earthy beluga lentils.

Double Crown

Fusion

D4

316 Bowery (at Bleecker St.)

Subway: Bleecker St
Phone: 212-254-0350
Web: www.doublecrown-nyc.com
Prices: $$$

Lunch Sat – Sun
Dinner nightly

Just when you were thinking—where the heck are all the British colonialism-meets-Far East restaurants in this town? Chef Brad Farmerie, who designed Public's menu, takes the wheel at this deliriously popular new Village restaurant, which aims to tap into the strange in-between cuisine created after Britain invaded Far Eastern countries like India and Singapore in the 19th century.

With a bizarre dada interior (think clocks caged behind metal wall screens and armless mannequins) and a young, sexy crowd with money to burn, the scene tends to trump the food. Still, a few standouts remain: try a plate of tender, gamey lamb meatballs studded with creamy cashews, bobbing in a sweet-and-tart tomato stew, and paired with a fat stack of onion rings.

El Faro

Spanish

B2

823 Greenwich St. (at Horatio St.)

Subway: 14 St - 8 Av
Phone: 212-929-8210
Web: www.elfaronyc.com
Prices: $$

Lunch & dinner Tue – Sun

Still straddling its original West Village corner spot, El Faro has seen a lot of neighbors come and go since they opened in 1927. Upheld by loyal local regulars and big, celebratory parties, some foodies overlook the dearth of traditional Spanish places left in a city being taken over by tapas joints. So hey, if you have to put up with a bit of crumbling décor and salty service for Spanish seafood this good, then so be it.

The menu boasts an endless lineup of garlicky classics, but the two things not to miss are the paella (in any of its delicious variations), and any dish offered in El Faro's lip-smacking green sauce. Most of the entrées come with a bright green salad sporting a house dressing so addictive they now sell it by the bottle.

EN Japanese Brasserie

B3 — **Japanese** ✗✗✗

435 Hudson St. (at Leroy St.)

Subway: Houston St
Phone: 212-647-9196
Web: www.enjb.com
Prices: $$$

Lunch Mon – Sat
Dinner nightly

Industrial chic meets Tokyo mod in this *izakaya* hot spot with soaring heights, warm tones, brick walls, and regal fittings. EN's open kitchen pays homage to authentic Japanese palates, but also reveals ingenuity in its own inventions.

This West Village favorite draws a swank set with its sophisticated fare. Diners sip from the thorough sake selection and await specialties like house-made tofu skin (*yuba*) or perhaps the chef's *kaiseki* menu starring a Kyoto-style seaweed or lobster tempura with plum salt. Fresh, succulent sashimi and hot treats like delicate crab *chawanmushi* or beautifully marbled Kobe short ribs grilled over a hot stone are menu highlights. End meals with an earthy-sweet soup bobbing with rice dough, red beans, and green tea ice cream.

Extra Virgin

Mediterranean 

259 W. 4th St. (at Perry St.)

Subway: Christopher St - Sheridan Sq
Phone: 212-691-9359
Web: www.extravirginrestaurant.com
Prices: $$

Lunch Tue – Sun
Dinner nightly

Co-owned by two Queens natives, this invitingly laid-back spot sits on an idyllic tree-lined corner. There are touches of rusticity throughout the space, with rough-hewn wood tables, exposed brick walls, and framed mirrors; the vibe here is as chill and enjoyable during days as evenings.

Extra Virgin's Mediterranean menu offers crowd-pleasing fare like a starter salad of warm pistachio and breadcrumb-crusted goat cheese with roasted beets, generously showered with crisp, julienned Granny Smith apple. The kitchen's seriousness is evident in touches like the addition of bright and flavorful sweet peas, roasted yellow peppers, and black olives to the rigatoni with sausage; or the apple tart paired with sour cream ice cream and warmed dark caramel sauce.

Fatty Crab

Malaysian XX

B2

643 Hudson St. (bet. Gansevoort & Horatio Sts.)

Subway: 14 St - 8 Av — Lunch & dinner daily
Phone: 212-352-3592
Web: www.fattycrab.com
Prices: $$

Zak Pelaccio's signature dish could be made with mung beans, and it would still knock the socks off the uninitiated. As it is, the namesake dish at Fatty Crab, a creative Malaysian small plates joint tucked into a cozy storefront in the Meatpacking District, is made with mouthwatering chunks of Dungeness crab, bobbing in a rich, messy chili sauce that is part sweet, part savory—and wholly freaking amazing.

The front patio and small dining room, filled with a few-too-many dark wood tables, fill up fast so arrive early for dinner (a second location on the Upper West Side takes reservations); or swing by for a late afternoon lunch and you'll not only have the place mostly to yourself, but one heck of a deal in the $19 prix-fixe lunch.

Five Points

American XX

D4

31 Great Jones St. (bet. Bowery & Lafayette St.)

Subway: Bleecker St — Lunch & dinner daily
Phone: 212-253-5700
Web: www.fivepointsrestaurant.com
Prices: $$

The pulse of Chef Marc Meyer's first success continues to beat as strongly as when it opened a decade ago. This neighborhood favorite blends relaxed ambience, polished service, and seasonally focused fare with a near-Californian sensibility that is utterly irresistible to its nightly stream of food-savvy sophisticates.

Beyond the energetic bar is a quieter back dining room anchored by a tree trunk bedecked with greenery and surrounded by brown-paper-topped tables. After ordering from a menu that boasts local, seasonal ingredients, a welcoming bread basket paired with homemade pickles winks at Chef Meyer's take on urbane rusticity. Offerings may go on to include fresh ham redolent of cloves, served with local peach relish and creamed collards.

Gobo

D1 **Vegetarian** XX

401 Sixth Ave. (bet. 8th St. & Waverly Pl.)

Subway: W 4 St - Wash Sq
Phone: 212-255-3902
Web: www.goborestaurant.com
Prices: ⊜

Lunch & dinner daily

With its nourishing global vegetarian cuisine and peaceful Zen-inspired décor, Gobo offers a tasty and tranquil timeout from Manhattan's bustle. Muted tones and warm wood accents dominate the airy dining room that is attended by a suitably laidback staff.

Gobo's inexpensive menu of "food for the five senses" begins with healthy beverages like freshly squeezed juices and soy milk-based smoothies as well as organic wines. Ambitious starters easily tempt without pushing the vegetarian envelope in the likes of *roti canai* and homemade hummus. Larger plates offer an appetizing Asian influence in satisfying and flavorful vegetable protein dishes such as the healthful stir-fry of ginger-marinated seitan with lightly sautéed kale and steamed rice.

Good

C2 **American** X

89 Greenwich Ave. (bet. Bank & 12th Sts.)

Subway: 14 St - 8 Av
Phone: 212-691-8080
Web: www.goodrestaurantnyc.com
Prices: $$

Lunch Tue – Sun
Dinner nightly

This Village mainstay lives up to its simply stated name by offering a pleasantly familiar appeal and a comforting menu that features a sprinkling of global influences to the American menu of Chef/owner Steven Picker—romaine salad with *ricotta salata* and green goddess dressing; house-smoked pulled pork with crisp polenta; and macaroni and cheese spiced with green chilies topped with a tortilla crumb crust.

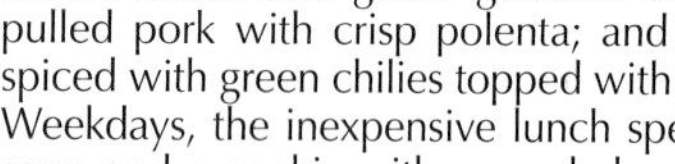

Weekdays, the inexpensive lunch special includes a cup of soup and a cookie with any salad or sandwich and brunch features the likes of a breakfast burrito filled with house-made chorizo, and banana cream cheese stuffed French toast. Good's "brunch punch" or "morning martini" flavored with chilled espresso gets the weekend off to a rosy start.

Gottino

Italian

C2

52 Greenwich Ave. (bet. Charles & Perry Sts.)

Subway: Christopher St - Sheridan Sq — Lunch & dinner daily
Phone: 212-633-2590
Web: www.ilovegottino.com
Prices:

This charming *enoteca* offers a lovely setting to sit and savor a glass of wine and a snack (or three). Intimate and sophisticated, the space uses knobby wood, exposed brick, and a marble dining counter to conjure that requisite chic rusticity that draws the Village crowds. Still, the setting is genuinely welcoming and warm, with baskets of nuts strewn throughout for guests to enjoy while perusing the blackboard listing of wine specials.

Chef Jody Williams offers a slender, thoughtful menu of small plates which gracefully emerge from a white-tiled work space doubling as the bar. The likes of creamy, house-cured *baccala* and delicate *crespelle* filled with prosciutto and fontina are featured alongside a selection of meats, cheeses, and pastas.

Grand Sichuan

Chinese

B3

15 Seventh Ave. South (bet. Camine & Leroy Sts.)

Subway: Houston St — Lunch & dinner daily
Phone: 212-645-0222
Web: www.thegrandsichuan.com
Prices:

This latest outpost of the well-run chain strives to offer a more healthy Chinese option in this Sichuan-focused menu. The enjoyable, delicious fare includes excellent shredded chicken with sour cabbage; chewy *dan dan* noodles layered with spicy minced pork; and a mouthwatering braised whole fish with hot bean sauce. In addition to the expansive "American Chinese," "Classic Sichuan," and "Latest" sections of menu offerings, dining here features a thoughtful touch—both small- and large-sized portions are offered, allowing guests to feast without fear of over doing it.

The pleasant room may be restrained in its décor, but boasts large windows overlooking a stretch of Seventh Avenue and is graciously attended to by the polite, uniformed staff.

Gotham Bar and Grill ✿

Contemporary 

D2

12 E. 12th St. (bet. Fifth Ave. & University Pl.)

Subway: 14 St - Union Sq
Phone: 212-620-4020
Web: www.gothambarandgrill.com
Prices: $$$

Lunch Mon – Fri
Dinner nightly

Gotham Bar and Grill

Consider Gotham's tuna tartare: a soft, ruby red pile of diced yellowfin tuna kissed with ginger-soy vinaigrette and ringed in crunchy Japanese cucumber. Simple but perfect, the restaurant's popular starter is often imitated but rarely duplicated—and the same could be said of the restaurant itself, a 25 year-old Village mainstay set along thumping East 12th Street.

Chef Alfred Portale, who helped put New American cuisine on the map, is to thank for the blueprint. The man has a gift for spinning seasonal products into art: witness a wickedly fresh black sea bass ceviche in radish-jalapeño-cucumber broth, layered with hearts of palm, grapefruit, daikon, and watermelon; tender miso-marinated black cod with sticky rice and roasted shiitake mushrooms in a zesty lemongrass-ginger sauce; or a spot-on warm fig tart Tatin served with Sicilian pistachios, mulberry jam, and a creamy scoop of sweet cream ice cream.

Should you find yourself wandering by come happy hour, you'll find a buzzing bar scene soaking in the live jazz. Come by earlier, and you'll catch the three-course lunch paired with wine—not only a great bargain, but a positively Carrie Bradshaw way to while away an afternoon.

Gusto

Italian XX

C2

60 Greenwich Ave. (at Perry St.)

Subway: 14 St (Seventh Ave.) — Lunch & dinner daily
Phone: 212-924-8000
Web: www.gustonyc.com
Prices: **$$**

Although Gusto's kitchen has been a revolving door of notable talent, this sleek and sexy Village trattoria continues to impress. The menu balances warm antipasti, such as the surprisingly light seafood *fritto misto*, with enticing house-made pastas, like organic spinach and ricotta dumplings in sage butter. Equally pleasing is the simply yet beautifully prepared risotto, perhaps made with the straightforward flavors of lemon and fresh basil. If offered, the luscious, mauve-colored fig gelato, powerful with the flavor of ripe fruit, is not to be missed—especially when enjoying the ample sidewalk seating on a warm evening.

The neatly plated food suits the tailored interior's whitewashed walls, velvet banquettes, crystal chandelier, and Missoni bar stools.

Hakata Tonton

Japanese 

D1

61 Grove St. (bet. Bleecker St. & Seventh Ave.)

Subway: Christopher St - Sheridan Sq — Dinner nightly
Phone: 212-242-3699
Web: www.tontonnyc.com
Prices: **$$**

A new cuisine has taken root in New York. Enter this tiny red and yellow dining room to be educated in this other facet of the Japanese culinary repertoire: *tonsoku* (pigs' feet, ears, and the like).

Varied *tonsoku* dishes may include a luxurious slow roasted pork, or *oreilles du cochon*—French in name only—which are an explosion of crunchy, cool, creamy, sweet, sticky, and vinegary flavors. Truer to its Italian roots, *Tonsoku* carbonara is made with smoky bacon and is a good choice for wary newbies. A "rare cheesecake" of piped cheese and sour cream is a very smart and completely delicious take on the traditional dessert.

The plain-Jane décor sits in stark contrast to the rich and porky fare that diners will come rushing back for.

Hecho en Dumbo

D4 **Mexican**            

354 Bowery (bet. 4th & Great Jones Sts.)

Subway: Bleecker St — Lunch & dinner daily
Phone: 212-937-4245
Web: www.hechoendumbo.com
Prices: $$

Adios DUMBO, this Mexico City-style spot has now taken up residence in Manhattan. The room sports an edgy downtown vibe with reclaimed wood and mismatched chairs; a back dining counter offers diners a view of the kitchen led by Mexico City native Daniel Mena.

Antojitos (small plates) and contemporary fare shape the made-from-scratch menu built around house-made tortillas, *bolillo* bread, and *queso Oaxaca*. Tasty bites may include *pescadillas*: fried turnovers of crispy tortilla filled with shredded tilapia, diced onion, and chilies. The *molletas* is (for lack of a better reference) the ultimate Mexican version of grilled cheese, served toasted and open-faced, topped with black bean purée, *queso* Chihuahua, and crumbles of homemade pork-belly chorizo.

Home

D1 **Contemporary**

20 Cornelia St. (bet. Bleecker & W. 4th Sts.)

Subway: W 4 St - Wash Sq — Lunch & dinner daily
Phone: 212-243-9579
Web: www.homerestaurantnyc.com
Prices: $$

The menu's tagline promises "farm-to-table" fare, and stays true to this philosophy with seasonal cuisine offered as small and large plates in a charming setting. With a focus on comfort, preparations may include the likes of grilled trout with lentils, macaroni and cheese with overnight tomatoes, and butterscotch pudding topped with lightly whipped cream. The wine list focuses on local producers and appropriately includes several labels from Barbara and David Shinn's current endeavour, Shinn Estate Vineyards, the couple who opened Home back in 1993.

This pleasant, slender space features a small bar upfront, colorful artwork hung on white painted brick walls, denim-blue banquettes, and a discreet open kitchen tucked into the back.

Il Buco

Italian

D4

47 Bond St. (bet. Bowery & Lafayette St.)

Subway: Bleecker St — Lunch Mon – Sat
Phone: 212-533-1932 — Dinner nightly
Web: www.ilbuco.com
Prices: $$

Il Buco offers guests the idyllic Tuscan farmhouse fantasy without leaving Manhattan. This artist's studio-cum-restaurant shines with sunny charm and quirky warmth through chicly rustic tables, wood floors, copper plates, and antiques.

However, with delightful service, an extraordinary sommelier, and superlative market-driven Italian cuisine, Il Buco does not rely on looks alone. The chef is a stickler for quality, and the product-focused menu celebrates the seasons, as in an amazingly simple salad of crisp and earthy Tuscan black kale with anchovy vinaigrette. Plentiful appetizers are followed by homemade pastas and daily-changing entrées, such as pan-fried prawns with Sicilian sea salt, a hint of rosemary, and delicious kick of hot pepper.

Kesté Pizza & Vino

Pizza 

D1

271 Bleecker St. (bet. Cornelia & Jones Sts.)

Subway: W 4 St - Wash Sq — Lunch & dinner daily
Phone: 212-243-1500
Web: www.kestepizzeria.com
Prices:

Co-owner Roberto Caporuscio was born and raised near Naples, is a former mozzarella producer, and is the current American-chapter president of the *Associazione Pizzaiuoli Napoletani*. When it comes to creating authentic Neopolitan-style pizza, he knows what he's doing.

A list of salads are offered as a starting point for the main event—distinctively charred, crusty, tender pies scented with wood smoke and baked on a layer of volcanic stone. Fashioned from mostly imported ingredients (flour, tomatoes, cheese, and olive oil) there are eighteen varieties of pizza with a specific combination of toppings (the menu states no changes allowed). The *salsiccia* is crowned with local basil and sweet, meaty crumbles procured from across the street at Faicco's.

Kingswood

C2 Contemporary XX

121 W. 10th St. (bet. Greenwich & Sixth Aves.)

Subway: 14 St (Seventh Ave.) Lunch Sat – Sun
Phone: 212-645-0044 Dinner nightly
Web: www.kingswoodnyc.com
Prices: $$

Kingswood's mirthful spirit is evident from the moment you step inside. The inviting bar is habitually packed by a good-humored crowd, while beyond, the dining room is abuzz with its own sleek rusticity and warmth. Bathed in a flattering glow, diners sit in long communal tables and caramel-leather banquettes set against a softly lit glass-walled installation and votive candles.

The contemporary menu displays boldly flavored accents while paying homage to its owner's native Australia, as in the house burger with cheddar and sweet chili sauce, Goan fish curry, and beer battered fish and chips. Here, surf and turf may mean crisp-skinned salt cod and fork-tender pork cheeks dressed in a dark reduction of meaty jus with creamy, smoked mashed potatoes.

L'Artusi

B3 Italian XX

228 W. 10th St. (bet. Bleecker & Hudson Sts.)

Subway: Christopher St - Sheridan Sq Dinner nightly
Phone: 212-255-5757
Web: www.lartusi.com
Prices: $$

L'Artusi's façade may be demure, but this attractive dining room offers a buzz-worthy vibe to accompany an upscale rendition of Italian-rooted fare, anchored by small plates. The large space, done in gray and ivory, offers three dining counters, table service, and a quieter mezzanine dining area. An open kitchen adds to the lively air.

The impressive, all-Italian wine list, complete with maps, is laid out with a gravitas that demands attention. The well-versed staff is pleased to suggest the best pairings to compliment the mushroom bruschetta slathered with *Robiola*, or the dense and chewy *cavatelli* studded with black kale and "rice beans." A perfect finale is the airy coconut semifreddo set atop almond cake and drizzled with dark chocolate sauce.

Las Ramblas

Spanish

D1

170 W. 4th St. (bet. Cornelia & Jones Sts.)

Subway: Christopher St - Sheridan Sq — Lunch Sat – Sun
Phone: 646-415-7924 — Dinner nightly
Web: www.lasramblasnyc.com
Prices: ⊜

Serving quality tapas packed with flavor, Las Ramblas' small yet imaginative space complements its cuisine. The restaurant, named for Barcelona's historic commercial thoroughfare, also impresses with its smooth, well-informed, and impeccably timed service.

Pleasantly while away time in this beautifully compact bar, where attention to detail is evident in flower arrangements balancing on a tiny shelf; the water fountain embedded in a brick wall; and a banquette that cozies up against the front windows.

This traditional bar food makes a satisfying meal. Go in groups to fully explore the menu. Such small plates as *patatas bravas* (garlicky potatoes with aïoli) and grilled sardines *en escabeche*, arrive on an array of colorful crockery and delicate porcelain.

Le Gigot

D1

18 Cornelia St. (bet. Bleecker & W. 4th Sts.)

Subway: W 4 St - Wash Sq — Lunch & dinner Tue – Sun
Phone: 212-627-3737
Web: www.legigotrestaurant.com
Prices: $$

Looking perfectly at home on its quaint tree-lined street, Le Gigot is quietly and confidently alluring. The petite bistro boasts personable yet polished service, inlaid wood flooring, olive-colored velvet banquettes, and butter-yellow walls hung with blackboards displaying the day's specials, such as lobster salad or bœuf Bourguignon. This intimate setting is a perfect match for the classic French fare.

The salad of endive, apple, and Roquefort, studded with toasted walnuts and dressed with sweet vinaigrette hinting of mustard seed, is simplicity at its most delicious. The duck confit, with its velvety rich meat cloaked with fabulously crisped skin and a bubbling, golden block of potato and celery root gratin, is one of the best in the city.

The Little Owl

B3 — Contemporary

90 Bedford St. (at Grove St.)

Subway: Christopher St - Sheridan Sq — Lunch & dinner daily
Phone: 212-741-4695
Web: www.thelittleowlnyc.com
Prices: **$$**

Perched on a winsome corner of the West Village, Chef Joey Campanaro's Little Owl continues to hold a dear place in the hearts of diners near and far who appreciate that simple food and great food can be one in the same. The broccoli soup—a pure, silky purée enriched with a trace of cream and crowned by a crouton of bubbling, aged cheddar—is among the best examples of this.

The small corner room is quaint and despite this establishment's popularity, the service team is completely attitude-free. The wee kitchen is on display, and the focused crew turns out a rousing roster of preparations that bear an affinity for Mediterranean cuisine such as seared cod with *bagna cauda* vinaigrette, and gravy meatball sliders, a hands-down house specialty.

Lupa 

C4 — Italian

170 Thompson St. (bet. Bleecker & Houston Sts.)

Subway: W 4 St - Wash Sq — Lunch & dinner daily
Phone: 212-982-5089
Web: www.luparestaurant.com
Prices: **$$**

Behind Lupa is a league of culinary maestros who have been shaping Italian dining in New York City since its 1999 opening. While the consistently good food is the main reason why this Roman trattoria continues to attract masses, Lupa's casual excellence and convivial attitude also contribute to its appeal.

Stop at the bar for a carafe of vino from the all-Italian wine list and snack of house-made specialties that feature prominently on the menu, as in the baccala, speck, or preserved tuna. Then, move on to a focused selection of delicious pastas, impressively simple entrées, and daily specials, like rabbit sausages.

Closely arranged wooden tables, a ceramic tile floor, and sienna-toned plaster walls bestow warmth on this buzzing dining room.

Market Table

American

54 Carmine St. (at Bedford St.)

Subway: W 4 St - Wash Sq — Lunch & dinner daily
Phone: 212-255-2100
Web: www.markettablenyc.com
Prices: $$

It appears that together, owner Joey Campanaro (of The Little Owl) and Chef Mikey Price can do no wrong here, with their fresh, unpretentious menu, fantastic staff, and rustic décor to match.

Straddling a bright West Village corner, Market Table is a comfortable yet sophisticated restaurant, with reclaimed beams and hardwood floors, serving American and Italian-American dishes with some welcomed surprises. This is the rare menu that manages to balance the familiar with the exciting. Dishes may range from gnocchi with perfectly braised lamb, aromatics, and escarole to seared halibut with butternut squash risotto.

Desserts are a highlight, especially the moist and outrageously rich chocolate polka-dot cheesecake, paired with an excellent espresso.

Mary's Fish Camp

Seafood

64 Charles St. (at W. 4th St.)

Subway: Christopher St - Sheridan Sq — Lunch & dinner Mon – Sat
Phone: 646-486-2185
Web: www.marysfishcamp.com
Prices: $$

Mary Redding opened this tiny Florida-style fish shack in a West Village brownstone in 2000 and has been enjoying wild success ever since. Her ever-debated lobster rolls are among the city's finest examples, overflowing with succulent chunks of meat, slathered in mayonnaise and piled on a buttery hotdog bun—messy but are definitely worth it! Yet this small spot features an extensive menu that goes well beyond, with particular focus on Key West cuisine, such as conch fritters, and the bounty of New England waters. Accompaniments like Old Bay fries and regional desserts reflect American flair with homespun simplicity.

Bear in mind that only seafood is served here, reservations are not accepted, and the counter couldn't be better for solo dining.

Mas

Contemporary 

39 Downing St. (bet. Bedford & Varick Sts.)

Subway: Houston St — Dinner nightly
Phone: 212-255-1790
Web: www.masfarmhouse.com
Prices: $$$

Set along a charming street in the West Village, Mas is hidden behind a planked exterior shot with a few slivers of window and a discreetly carved wood disk bearing its name. Inside, you'll find an intimate little spot reminiscent of a Provençal farmhouse, with weathered wood beams, a long communal table, and a bar built out of piled sandstone.

C.I.A. trained chef, Galen Zamarra, who honed his skills working David Bouley's kitchen, pays homage to his finely sourced ingredients by producing delicious, unfussy seasonal fare. Dinner might kick off with freshly seared tuna in warm vinegar reduction, topped with crispy fried leeks and a touch of fresh mache; and end with a warm apple confit, paired with toasted rye cake and creamy cinnamon ice cream.

Mercadito Grove

Mexican 

100 Seventh Ave. South (at Grove St.)

Subway: Christopher St - Sheridan Sq — Lunch & dinner daily
Phone: 212-647-0830
Web: www.mercaditorestaurants.com
Prices: $$

Largest in the Mercadito chainlet, Grove has a devoted following filling its pastel-painted chairs and corner sidewalk dining area nightly. Starters range from a small list of fresh ceviches to flautas filled with chicken and black beans. The tacos, prepared from homemade tortillas, are certainly recommended as are any of the *platos fuertes* that make up the menu's concise selection, like the shrimp-filled enchiladas *rojas*, draped with a creamy, tangy, sweet sauce seasoned with *guajillo* and *arbol* chiles.

In the East Village, Mercadito Cantina serves a mouthwatering menu of tacos and guacamoles daily for lunch and dinner. Hungry night owls should note that all three of their locations offer an all-you-can eat taco special late in the evening.

Mercat

Spanish

D4

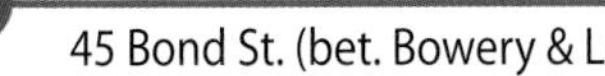

45 Bond St. (bet. Bowery & Lafayette St.)

Subway: Bleecker St — Dinner nightly
Phone: 212-529-8600
Web: www.mercatnyc.com
Prices: $$

Brick walls, white subway tiles, and plank wood flooring line this hip restaurant and tapas den, whose name translates to "market" in Catalan. Owner Jaime Reixach hails from Barcelona, and the two American chefs he hired have both spent extensive time in the area, giving the cooking an authentic leg up on the endless string of Spanish tapas bars that have popped up across the city in recent years.

But don't take our word for it. Taste for yourself in decadent little plates like, cold octopus salad with salsa verde; deep fried artichokes with fennel aïoli; and *fideua negrea amb allioli*—noodles topped with spicy and succulent squid and black ink.

The Spanish wine list sports cavas, sherries, and seasonal sangrías.

Mexicana Mama

Mexican

B2

525 Hudson St. (bet. Charles & 10th Sts.)

Subway: Christopher St - Sheridan Sq — Lunch & dinner Tue – Sun
Phone: 212-924-4119
Web: N/A
Prices: ⚭

Cute and charming, Mexican Mama showcases the homespun flavors of the Mexican kitchen. The space, painted deep blue, barely seats 20 and is so small that a trip to the bathroom necessitates a walk through the open kitchen for an up close and personal view of the crew at work, where everything looks tidy and tempting.

A blackboard announces the day's mouthwatering specials, such as apricot and chipotle-glazed chicken or coconut-marinated fish. The printed menu offers the likes of grilled corn slathered with chipotle mayonnaise and a showering of *cojito* cheese; or *queso flameado*—molten cheese topped with spicy Mexican chorizo and thin strips of roasted poblano pepper, attractively presented with fresh tortillas for a delicious and fun make-your-own feast.

Morandi

Italian

C2

211 Waverly Pl. (bet. Charles St. & Seventh Ave. South)

Subway: 14 St (Seventh Ave.) — Lunch & dinner daily
Phone: 212-627-7575
Web: www.morandiny.com
Prices: $$$

At Morandi, Keith McNally recalls Tuscany with all its glorious clichés, creating both an Italian cantina and farmhouse, with antique-tiled floors, weather-beaten wood, Italian-speaking waiters, and shelves of straw-covered Chianti bottles. The menu, too, respects its rustic Italian roots, from its baskets of sweet pastries at breakfast, lunches of grilled panini, and dinner offerings of hearty, house-made pastas. Daily specials indicate the clear talent at the head of this kitchen, and may feature traditional osso buco, lasagna, or veal Milanese.

This is a neighborhood hot spot, populated by those who know Gucci better than gnocchi, but this genuine Italian comfort food is focused, no nonsense, and does not miss a stiletto-heeled step.

One if by Land, Two if by Sea

Contemporary

D1

17 Barrow St. (bet. Seventh Ave. South & W. 4th St.)

Subway: Christopher St - Sheridan Sq — Lunch Sun
Phone: 212-255-8649 — Dinner nightly
Web: www.oneifbyland.com
Prices: $$$

Step out of the urban mêlée and into this pretty 18th century carriage house, and you just might forget you're in Manhattan. There's a reason One if by Land, Two if by Sea has been a question-popping kind of place for over thirty years—the beautiful brick building oozes old-world sophistication with its flickering fireplaces, glittering chandeliers, and elegant service. Did we mention the live piano? Sigh.

The menu, carefully executed by executive chef, Andrew Matthews, is a thoroughly modern affair, and might unveil gorgeous, ruby-red tuna *crudo* with crunchy sea beans, American caviar, wasabi foam, and Karachi cream; or a perfectly juicy roasted leg of lamb with saffron gnocchi, wild ramps, fiddlehead ferns, fava beans, and fried mint.

Minetta Tavern 

Gastropub

113 MacDougal St. (at Minetta Ln.)

Subway: W 4 St - Wash Sq

Phone: 212-475-3850

Web: www.minettatavernny.com

Prices: $$$

Lunch Sat – Sun
Dinner nightly

Ngoc Minh Ngo

'Twas the name on everyone's lips in the spring of '09, when at the height of its popularity it was harder to get into this Keith McNally bistro than a Michael Jackson concert circa '83. These days, you'll still want to make advance reservations, but odds are a little better, you can snag a random seat at off-hours.

More good news: once you do make it into this lair of cool, you'll find a charming, knowledgeable waitstaff; a dedicated kitchen; and an irresistibly fun atmosphere in the newly revamped space. The building dates back to 1937 and the designers were clever enough to leave the good stuff—black-and-white checkered floors and funny old wall caricatures—intact when they took over.

The gastropub menu turns out spot-on versions of the bistro staples, and the burger, steak, and soufflé are popular for good reason. But why stop there when the kitchen is pushing out all kinds of delicious goodies like an elegant watercress soup bobbing with freshly poached oysters and a dollop of caviar; or break-the-calorie-bank Berkshire pig's trotter, fried to juicy perfection, then paired with Dijon mustard, lentils studded with carrot, celery, and leek, and a refreshing herb salad.

Panca

Peruvian

92 Seventh Ave. South (bet. Bleecker & Grove Sts.)

Subway: Christopher St - Sheridan Sq — Lunch Thu – Sun
Phone: 212-488-3900 — Dinner nightly
Web: N/A
Prices: $$

The exciting flavors of Peru are served in a contemporary space with cool citron walls, a stacked-stone fronted bar lined with bottles of *pisco*, and a sidewalk dining area set along the hubbub of Seventh Avenue.

Discreetly tucked into the dining room's corner is the ceviche station, where ocean-fresh seafood is given a bold dressing up—the *tiradito mixte* is a sampling of sashimi-style ceviche sparked with tart lime juice, chopped garlic, and slivers of red chilies. Cooked options include hearty soups like *aguadito de pollo* (cilantro-flavored chicken soup stocked with yucca and potato, served as an entrée). Specialties like grilled skirt steak with *tacu tacu* (a mixture of mashed beans and rice vibrant with *aji amarillo*) assure no one leaves hungry.

Paradou

French

8 Little W. 12th St. (bet. Greenwich & Washington Sts.)

Subway: 14 St - 8 Av — Lunch Fri – Sun
Phone: 212-463-8345 — Dinner nightly
Web: www.paradounyc.com
Prices: $$

Paradou offers a bit of Provence and a welcome respite from the spate of gargantuan, over-the-top-posh restaurants populating the Meatpacking District. Here, a casual yet energetic crowd shares a carefree French spirit while relaxing over crisp glasses of champagne and bowls of plump mussels *du jour* or traditional bouillabaisse.

The whimsical covered "magical garden" tent offers winter enchantment with heat lamps warming the space during colder evenings, but comes down in spring and summer. Enjoy unlimited champagne cocktails, truly al fresco, during their weekend brunch. Live music and "Paradou Happenings" are scheduled regularly.

The all-French wine list offers some reasonably priced selections to complement the classic and rustic bistro menu.

Pastis

B1

Subway: 14 St - 8 Av
Lunch & dinner daily
Phone: 212-929-4844
Web: www.pastisny.com
Prices: $$

This lovingly recreated bistro is the first success story of the Meatpacking District, then a nascent neighborhood. Even now, it remains a trendy and popular place that is just as much fun during the day as evening, squeezing in a fashionable (and often famous) flock from breakfast through dinner. Inside, the timeless bistro décor (decorative mirrors, long zinc bar, walls lined with vintage Pastis ads) has that hip, informal charm so difficult to replicate; outside, the sidewalk seating was designed with Bellini-sipping and sunshine in mind.

The menu is good and satisfying, focusing on neighborhood favorites, like steak *frites*. The cocktail list, as expected, leans heavily on the anise-flavored aperitif from which the restaurant takes its name.

Pearl Oyster Bar

Seafood

D1

18 Cornelia St. (bet. Bleecker & W. 4th Sts.)

Subway: W 4 St - Wash Sq
Lunch Mon – Fri
Phone: 212-691-8211
Dinner Mon – Sat
Web: www.pearloysterbar.com
Prices: $$

In 1997, Chef/owner Rebecca Charles opened Pearl Oyster Bar in memory of her grandmother and the childhood summers they spent in Maine. Today, she serves a slice of New England to the heart of Manhattan; though many imitations and variations can be found, Pearl is a NY classic. This beloved eatery has a small dining room, a counter handling a brisk business for shellfish aficionados, an accompanying cookbook, and long lines out the door.

The classic New England menu offers small and large plates of pristine seafood as well as their hallowed lobster roll. Try this with one of their carefully selected wines or beers on tap.

Pearl is a true, tried American restaurant, so don't even try to end meals with an espresso (the chef refuses to serve it).

Perilla

Contemporary XX

D1

9 Jones St. (bet. Bleecker & W. 4th Sts.)

Subway: W 4 St - Wash Sq — Lunch Sat – Sun
Phone: 212-929-6868 — Dinner nightly
Web: www.perillanyc.com
Prices: $$

This casually elegant Village fave, with its unaffected vibe, showcases the talents of partners Chef Harold Dieterle and General Manager Alicia Nosenzo. He is a CIA graduate and premier winner of the reality television hit "Top Chef"; and she is a San Francisco native who has honed her front of the house skills at impressive establishments on both coasts.

Up-front is an inviting bar and the rear dining room, with its zebrawood tables and warm lighting, is attended to by an eager staff, forthcoming with suggestions on the seasonally respectful menu. Reflecting global influences, the chef spices a beautifully prepared snapper *crudo* with pickled radish and *tom yum* broth, and transforms game hen into bacon-wrapped roulades sauced with pomegranate molasses.

Perry Street

Contemporary XXX

B2

176 Perry St. (at West St.)

Subway: Christopher St - Sheridan Sq — Lunch & dinner daily
Phone: 212-352-1900
Web: www.jean-georges.com
Prices: $$$

The stylish young professionals that frequent Jean-Georges Vongerichten's Perry Street set the casual-but-sexy tone for the restaurant, with guests arriving in everything from tailored suits to designer jeans. Look closely around the minimalist dining room—bathed in light from the picture windows, and simply dotted with polished wood tables and supple leather banquettes—and you might even spot a celebrity or two.

Jean-George's son, Cedric, the maestro behind Perry Street's globe-trotting menu, pulls inspiration from America, Europe, and Asia to craft dishes like crêpe-wrapped crab dumplings laced with sweet chili-garlic sauce and paired with sugar snap peas and cilantro shoots; or silky Arctic char and white asparagus spears with tangy basil vinaigrette.

The Place

Contemporary

310 W. 4th St. (bet. Bank & 12th Sts.)

Subway: 14 St - 8 Av
Phone: 212-924-2711
Web: www.theplaceny.com
Prices: $$

Lunch Sat – Sun
Dinner nightly

Tucked deep into the West Village, The Place is the kind of cozy, grotto-style dining that makes people want to up and move to the big city. Rendezvous-like, guests duck below street level to find a small bar with lots of flickering votive candles and a few tables with a view of the bustling sidewalk. Wander back a bit, and you'll find low, rustic beams, and white tablecloth seating; behind that, two outdoor terraces beckon in summer.

Even the food seems designed to comfort, like a piping hot roasted tomato soup, drizzled with chive oil, and pocked with pecorino-baked croutons; or seared duck mu shu pancakes, drizzled with sweet tamarind. With a kitchen that employs only fresh, organic ingredients, diners are taken on a surprising gastronomic tour.

Pó

Italian 

31 Cornelia St. (bet. Bleecker & W. 4th Sts.)

Subway: W 4 St - Wash Sq
Phone: 212-645-2189
Web: www.porestaurant.com
Prices: $$

Lunch Wed – Sun
Dinner nightly

It's no wonder reservations at this longtime neighborhood favorite still fill up a week in advance. A devoted following is attracted to tiny, narrow Pó's understated yet sophisticated ambience, well-run front of the house, and its pleasing Italian fare. Regulars fill the tiny, narrow space at lunch, while the dimly lit dinners host a cozy and romantic crowd.

The satisfying menu may include marinated fresh anchovies with leeks and toasted barley, or white bean ravioli with balsamic brown-butter sauce. End meals perfectly with their surprisingly light desserts, or *formaggi* provided by the noted cheese shop, cheekily named "Stinky Brooklyn." Tasting menus are offered at both lunch and dinner.

Quinto Quarto

Italian

B3

14 Bedford St. (bet. Downing & Houston Sts.)

Subway: Houston St — Lunch & dinner daily
Phone: 212-675-9080
Web: www.quintoquarto.com
Prices:

This newly opened *"osteria Romana"* is named after a neighborhood that once served as Rome's Meatpacking District. Its enticingly rustic menu is served in an intimate setting that beams warmth; the dark-wood furnishings, exposed brick walls, and friendly service offer a charmingly heavy Italian accent.

The adept kitchen paves the way to the Eternal City with a listing of regional specialties that include a luscious *bucatini all'amatriciana*, a tangle of perfectly cooked strands dressed with carrot and onion sweetened tomato sauce, bacon, and pecorino cheese. Entrées may include roasted bone-in pieces of tender rabbit wildly fragrant with rosemary, sage, and accompanied by crisped potatoes. Dessert offers a short listing of jam-filled *crostatas*.

Recette

328 W. 12th St. (at Greenwich St.)

Subway: 14 St - 8 Av — Lunch Sat – Sun, Dinner nightly
Phone: 212-414-3000
Web: www.recettenyc.com
Prices: $$

This neighborhood may be well-endowed with impressive eats, but this intimate newcomer is a welcome addition. Set on a quaint tree-lined corner, the setting is tastefully adorned with sage green walls and dark wood furnishings.

Focusing on small plates, Recette's menu offers globally-inspired creations, thereby illustrating a talented and skilled kitchen. Take for example the salt cod fritters—dense rounds of preserved fish encased in feather light batter served atop crumbled lamb sausage ragù and dressed with curry aïoli. Other preparations include braised pork belly lacquered with sherry caramel and dressed with a quenelle of piquillo pepper and Marcona almond *romesco*. Desserts are equally rousing, evident in a whimsical ice cream "club" sandwich.

Rockmeisha

Japanese

11 Barrow St. (bet. Seventh Ave. South & W. 4th St.)

Subway: Christopher St - Sheridan Sq — Dinner Tue – Sun
Phone: 212-675-7775
Web: N/A
Prices: $$

New York City's fascination with *izakaya*—those fabulous little Japanese drinking joints where they take the small plates as seriously as they do the sake—has reached a fever pitch. Enter Rockmeisha: an intimate little West Village restaurant where kitschy memorabilia (think poison warning signs) and curious little cartoon drawings line the walls.

Regional specialties are the way to go on Rockmeisha's menu, especially those hailing from Kyūshū, a large island in Japan and the chef's hometown. The house is known for its ramen, and a thick tangle of noodles flown in from Hakata and laced with barbecued pork easily backs that claim. Items like deep bowls of barbecued beef; fluffy leek omelettes; and succulent yakitori pork skewers round out the menu.

Scarpetta

Italian XX

355 W. 14th St. (bet. Eighth & Ninth Aves.)

Subway: 14 St - 8 Av — Dinner nightly
Phone: 212-691-0555
Web: www.scarpettanyc.com
Prices: $$$$

In a town where location is everything, it takes critically-acclaimed Chef Scott Conant to pull this one off. Stuffed between a diner and a comedy club on bustling West 14th Street, Scarpetta is in a strange place to merit attention from serious eaters—yet they come in droves for the wickedly good food, the impeccable service, and clever wine list.

If you're in the mood to people-watch, grab a seat in the stylish bar area; or retreat back to the slick, pretty dining room, where dinner might unveil a beautiful pile of fresh cavatelli chock-a-block with juicy braised rabbit, tender peas, ripe tomatoes, and creamy pecorino; or oven-roasted halibut wrapped in crispy lardo and surrounded by a seasonal succotash of fiddlehead ferns, fava beans, and ramps.

Sevilla

Spanish X

62 Charles St. (at W. 4th St.)

Subway: Christopher St - Sheridan Sq — Lunch & dinner daily
Phone: 212-929-3189
Web: www.sevillarestaurantandbar.com
Prices: $$

With a long and colorful history since first opening its doors in 1941, charmingly nostalgic Sevilla remains a rarity among Manhattan's dining scene. The roaming menu harks back to traditional Spanish fare, heaping and hearty; the kind enjoyed long before our commonplace exposure to the cuisine became focused on small plates.

The majority of Sevilla's reasonably priced dishes are built around simply prepared seafood and chicken dressed with a number of primary sauces featuring almond, garlic, wine, and the prominent green sauce—parsley-packed and punched with garlic. Starters include the *ajo* soup, a clear chicken broth infused with the nutty essence of roasted garlic and enriched with egg; the smooth, classic flan is a fitting finale.

Spice Market

Asian XX

B1

403 W. 13th St. (at Ninth Ave.)

Subway: 14 St - 8 Av — Lunch & dinner daily
Phone: 212-675-2322
Web: www.spicemarketnewyork.com
Prices: $$

Now a Meatpacking mainstay, Spice Market continues to attract the area's well-dressed, fun-loving scenesters, who come here regularly to graze on Chef Jean-Georges Vongerichten's culinary romp through Asian street food.

This 12,000 square-foot former warehouse realized by Jacques Garcia sexes up marketplace stalls with deep shades of red, violet, and gold; a large teak pagoda takes center stage, while wooden arches divide the seating areas. Enjoy the visual feast of this lively, colorful, and very successful spot that now claims outposts from Istanbul to Qatar.

The Chef's skill and trademark style is evident in vibrant dishes of deeply flavorful spiced chicken samosas with cilantro yogurt or elegantly modernized bowls of coconut-rich *laksa*.

Soto ✿✿

Japanese XX

D1

357 Sixth Ave. (bet. Washington Pl. & W. 4th St.)

Subway: W 4 St - Wash Sq — Dinner Mon – Sat
Phone: 212-414-3088
Web: N/A
Prices: $$$

Soto

If it weren't for its stark white exterior set against a backdrop of tattoo parlors along a rather grungy stretch of Sixth Avenue, this subtle, unmarked Japanese charmer would be easy to miss. Its quiet existence underscores its status as one of the city's hidden treasures. Inside it's Zen personified. White walls, light wood, and slate fashion a textbook representation of clean, Japanese interior design. There are tables, but those-in-the-know nab a counter seat to view the culinary ballet performed by Chef Sotohiro Kosugi and his assistants. Enthusiasm for this spot may verge on hero worship, but after a few bites, it's easy to see why.

Order the omakase to sample the seasonally influenced work of the chef, who has an affinity for uni, featured in numerous creations. From *goma* tofu and geoduck clam salad with daikon and shiso, to minute-steamed *tai* with ginger-scallion oil and scallop, shiso, and fluke *agedashi*, dishes are meticulously prepared with a delicate and fascinating balance of flavors.

Note that sushi is a sleeper here. The chef sources fantastic fish from near and far and though he's better-known for his dishes, he expertly prepares nigiri from *shima aji* to *mirugai*.

Standard Grill

Contemporary XX

B1

848 Washington St. (bet. Little W. 12th & 13th Sts.)

Subway: 14 St - 8 Av — Lunch & dinner daily
Phone: 212-645-4100
Web: www.thestandardgrill.com
Prices: $$

Perched beneath phase one of the Highline in the hip Standard hotel, the Standard Grill offers myriad options to this crowd-drawing neighborhood. There is sidewalk seating, and a bright, airy front lounge, but the knockout dining room that bears the shine of boutique hotelier André Balazs is clearly the draw, with red leather furnishings, an ivory-tiled ceiling, and floors whimsically covered with pennies. The open kitchen is fronted by white-washed brick and has glossy teal blue walls.

Chef Dan Silverman has prepared a delicious, contemporary menu of straightforward, very fine meals from breakfast through dinner. Offerings may include a grilled organic pork chop with spiced salt, or a comforting lemon curd dressed blueberry galette.

Surya

Indian

302 Bleecker St. (bet. Grove St. & Seventh Ave. South)

Subway: Christopher St - Sheridan Sq — Lunch & dinner daily
Phone: 212-807-7770
Web: www.suryany.com
Prices: $$

The sun truly does shine upon this reliably enjoyable little West Village restaurant, whose name means "sun" in Tamil. During warm weather, tables in the small garden are charming, while vibrant colors fashion a sleek and very attractive interior, attended by a superb kitchen and service staff. Surya's menu boasts an array of regional Indian fare that runs the gamut of spices, fresh herbs, and tangy flavors, with focused selections to please both vegetarians and meat lovers alike. The blistered naan and Tandoor dishes are highly recommended here, as well as specialties like *meen kolambu* (fillet of grouper with tamarind and cayenne sauce).

Budget-conscious diners should be sure to take advantage of the reasonable daily lunch buffet.

Spotted Pig ✿

Gastropub

B2

314 W. 11th St. (at Greenwich St.)

Subway: Christopher St - Sheridan Sq — Lunch & dinner daily
Phone: 212-620-0393
Web: www.thespottedpig.com
Prices: **$$**

Melissa Hom

Welcome to the gastropub that started it all. Before bar food became the city's new It Cuisine, the Spotted Pig was packing them in nightly for Chef April Bloomfield's one-of-a-kind upscale gastrofare. And if the food alone didn't seal the deal, the authentic good looks of this Greenwich Village charmer, with its perfectly worn wood floors, exposed polished copper pipes, and red brick archway, certainly did.

Here's the caveat: most nights of the week, you'll still find an insanely long wait time—and once you do get piped into a table, you may find yourself precariously teetering on a stool, hunched over a Lilliputian table. No matter. Go on an off-hour (before 8:00 P.M. or lunch hour is ideal), command a cozy seat at the bar, and you'll be fine.

Classic bar snacks like deviled eggs and devils on horseback get elevated to heavenly planes, and dishes like the *gnudi*—Bloomfield's inimitable naked sheep's milk ricotta dumplings—and Roquefort burger are must-do's on the Manhattan culinary circuit. Specials rotate nightly and never fail to impress—tender soft pork cheeks arrive over freshly grilled country bread in a gorgeous reduced meat jus. Sounds simple, but no: heaven.

Takashi

Japanese 

B3

456 Hudson St. (bet. Barrow & Morton Sts.)

Subway: Christopher St - Sheridan Sq — Dinner Tue – Sun
Phone: 212-414-2929
Web: www.takashinyc.com
Prices: $$

This Korean-style Japanese newcomer is all about beef, raw and cooked, with cuts of *horumon* (the Japanese term for offal) calling out to all carnivores—especially the adventurous ones. Takashi serves the likes of cow's liver, heart, sweetbreads, and tongue presented as slices of the tip, middle, and back for a full experience. These tabletop grill offerings arrive either seasoned with salt, garlic, and sesame oil; or marinated in a special sauce which evokes the Japanese-born chef's Korean heritage. Ribeye and *kalbi* pleases diners seeking the familiar.

The contemporary room features a counter facing the personable crew as well as table seating arranged against a wall bearing whimsical instructions and illustrations on blackboard painted walls.

10 Downing

Contemporary XX

C3

10 Downing St. (bet. Bleecker & Hudson Sts.)

Subway: Houston St — Lunch & dinner daily
Phone: 212-255-0300
Web: www.10downingnyc.com
Prices: $$

This popular downtown hot spot has seen a few changes in recent years, including the departure of Chef Jason Neroni and consulting chef, Katy Sparks—a kitchen overhaul that left San Francisco alum, Chef Jonathan Leiva, manning the ship. Meanwhile, all the regulars want to know is if the food still rocks, the décor's still cheeky and the vibe's just right?

The answer is decidedly yes. Fitted out with upside-down antlers, a white marble-topped bar, and French doors that swing open come summer, 10 Downing's menu is built around a collection of small plates, appetizers, and sides; along with a selection of seasonal entrées like tender lemon-and herb-roasted chicken, accompanied by a bundle of fresh arugula, golden raisins, and grilled radicchio.

Tomoe Sushi

Japanese

172 Thompson St. (bet. Bleecker & Houston Sts.)

Subway: Spring St (Sixth Ave.) — Lunch Tue – Sat
Phone: 212-777-9346 — Dinner nightly
Web: N/A
Prices: ⚭

Tomoe focuses on value and quality rather than soigné appearances. Its tile floor has been dulled by a steady stream of sushi aficionados, the simple furnishings aren't conducive to leisurely meals, and the décor is limited to hand-drawn signs displaying specials. Still, regulars enthuse over these supple morsels prepared by the efficient team behind the counter and presented by swift, casual servers.

Characterized by pieces that err on the side of heft, this sushi has a foundation of rich, thickly cut slices of fish, minimal embellishment, and fine technique. The kitchen also prepares a long list of cooked dishes that display a creative hand, as in steamed buns filled with teriyaki-brushed silken tofu, pickled garlic, and a dollop of mayonnaise.

Ushiwakamaru

Japanese 

136 W. Houston St. (bet. MacDougal & Sullivan Sts.)

Subway: B'way - Lafayette St — Dinner nightly
Phone: 212-228-4181
Web: N/A
Prices: $$$$

Manhattan's sushiphiles rejoice for a taste of Chef Hideo Kuribara's outrageously fresh creations. Most nights of the week, the small and casual spot is packed with its loyal Japanese clientele, ordering drinks from kimono-clad waitresses and watching the kitchen staff hold court at the sushi bar. Some of the area's highest quality fish is the true draw here; while the local set is very content to sit down to a platter of buttery toro, true foodies are ordering the outstanding uni and *ikura*, piece by piece. Their good selection of sake is the perfect complement to a meal here.

Inside its one-room basement location, this lively and loud downtown favorite is dressed in white linen and soothing blonde wood tones. Just remember to book ahead.

Yerba Buena Perry

Latin American 

1 Perry St. (at Greenwich Ave.)

Subway: 14 St (Seventh Ave.)

Dinner nightly

Phone: 212-620-0808

Web: www.ybnyc.com

Prices: **$$**

Tucked into the ground floor of a red brick building along Perry Street, Yerba Buena Perry bleeds New York—it's sultry, cozy, and lively, with a fashionable décor that doesn't try too hard. A sleek, long bar and white leather banquettes set the black-and-white decorative theme; and a great mixed crowd from all walks of life arrives to soak it in.

Kick things off with crispy Manchego-and-spinach empanadas in a *chicha morada* and dried fig vinaigrette showered in crumbled *cojita* cheese; and then move on to blue-cornmeal-crusted calamari tossed in a syrupy tamarind vinaigrette with grape tomatoes and tender fried plantains; or miso- and chile-glazed cod, paired with a Peruvian corn purée and a chili-pomegranate sauce pocked with pomegranate seeds.

Hotels and restaurants change every year, so change your Michelin Guide every year!

Wallsé ✿

Austrian XX

B2

344 W. 11th St. (at Washington St.)

Subway: Christopher St - Sheridan Sq
Phone: 212-352-2300
Web: www.wallse.com
Prices: $$$

Lunch Sat – Sun
Dinner nightly

Wallsé

Chef Kurt Gutenbrunner's popular Wallsé calls a sweet little snatch of Greenwich Village home, and the walk up to this sun-drenched restaurant—filled with winding, old-world cobblestoned streets and storybook brownstones—puts a smile on even the most harried city kid. Spirits crank up another notch once you step inside the gorgeously-appointed space, its minimalist walls dressed with the chef's own art.

But sunny good looks and neighborhood charisma alone don't create as loyal a following as Wallsé has. What really catapults this restaurant into the upper echelon is Gutenbrunner's masterful, but decidedly unfussy, cuisine.

Named for the Austrian town the chef was born in, Wallsé offers a creative culinary tour of the country. A potato pancake topped with sweet, fresh lobster tail and fragrant spices is rendered golden at the edges, and laced with crème fraîche and orange segments; while pan-seared bass is sauced in black truffle cream and presented on a bed of house-made sauerkraut, its vermicelli-thin strands tangled with caraway and cardamom. Save room for one of the divine desserts, like the *apfelstreusel* garnished with a quenelle of salted caramel ice cream.

Harlem, Morningside & Washington Heights

Flanked by Riverside and Morningside parks and home to stately Columbia University, Morningside Heights is a lovely quarter of the city, and known for some of the best breakfast spots around. Sandwich shops and eateries line these avenues, where quick, inexpensive meals are a collegiate necessity. Resident academics and Ivy leaguers are found darting to and from class or lounging at the **Hungarian Pastry Shop** with a sweet and cup of tea. Considered a landmark, this old-world bakery has been open for more than three decades and is a focal point for students and gatherings. Across the street, Saint John the Divine, a gorgeous Gothic revival and a formidable presence on Amsterdam Avenue offers beauty, history, and wonderful community outreach programs. Special occasions call for an evening at Butler Hall's **Terrace In the Sky**. Rather than be misled by the plain building in which it's housed, prepare yourself for the expansive views of the city and fine continental fare. In the summer, enjoy a drink in the breeze on the alluring outdoor terrace.

To the north is Harlem—a true feast for the stomach and soul. Fifth Avenue divides the neighborhood into two very unique areas: West Harlem, an epicenter of African-American culture; and East Harlem, a diverse Latin quarter affectionately known as "El Barrio."

West Harlem still retains a kind of sassy edge as it gives way to slow, welcomed gentrification—one of its most visible borders is at **Fairway**, a Tri-State area staple that lures shoppers off the West Side Highway for their mind boggling offerings and

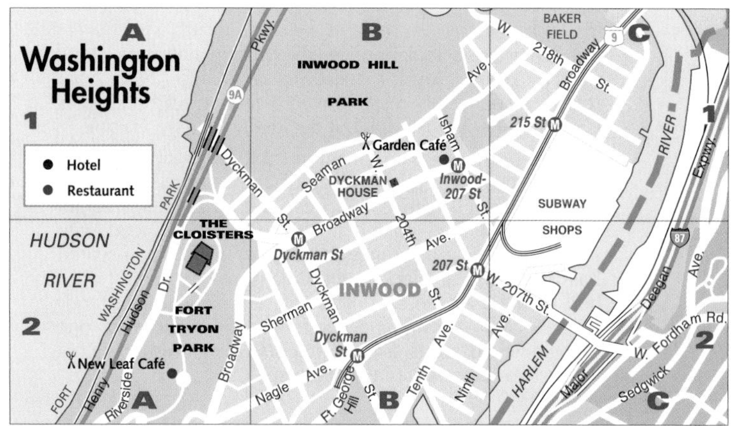

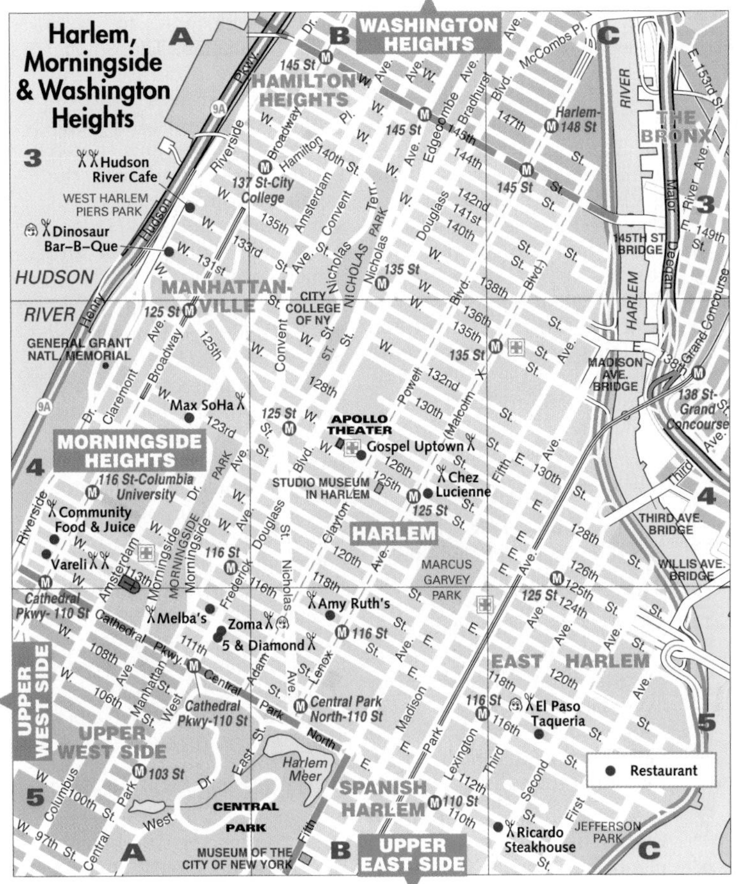

sensational produce. For a taste of the area's history, sift through the impressive literary collection at The Schomburg Center for Research in Black Culture on Lenox Avenue, or spend a sunny afternoon among the quaint row houses in the historic districts of Sugar Hill and Hamilton Heights. In the evening, slip into famed 60-year old **Lenox Lounge** for jazz and drinks and grab a seat at one of the banquettes. Harlem Week is an annual festival that features art, music, and food each August. While there, cool off with a cone of red velvet cake ice cream if the natural ice cream stand is around.

Food factors heavily into Harlem culture—both east and west of Fifth Avenue—and the choices are as diverse as the neighborhood itself. From Mexican to Caribbean to West African, the culinary delights abound. Locals line up around the block at **Famous**

Fish Market for deep-fried faves such as fish and chips or baskets of crispy shrimp. To further indulge your fried foods fantasy, entrée **Charles** for Chef Charles Gabriel's acclaimed buffet and sinfully divine fried chicken. For dangerously spiced Senegalese food, head to **Afrika Kine** restaurant; or shop around **Darou Salam Market** for West African groceries. **Carrot Top Pastries** entices locals with sweet potato pies, while **Raw Soul**, a health-focused Harlem spot, offers a menu of vegan "living foods" and ongoing cooking classes designed to educate seekers of well-being. **The DEN** (Dining Entertainment and Nightlife), a buzzing restaurant and lounge with a downtown feel, is worth a visit for the menu titles alone. Few can resist these feasts of "Slapsumbadi Shrimp" or "Weezies Crabcakes." Then, head to the bar for a "Lick Ya Lips" cocktail and night of live rhythm and blues.

In East Harlem, visit **Itzocan Bistro** for a unique brunch menu and a great selection of pastries. **Amor Cubano**'s *lechon* is savored amidst a vibrant atmosphere of live Cuban music. For Caribbean delights stop into **Sisters**; or peruse the taco trucks and taquerias along the Little Mexico strip of East 116th Street in the heart of one of New York's many Mexican communities.

A remnant of the former Italian population of East Harlem, **Rao's** is a New York institution. Run out of a small basement and frequented by the likes of Donald Trump and Nicole Kidman, Rao's is one of the most difficult tables to get in all of Manhattan. The original patrons have exclusive rights to a seat here and hand off their reservations like rent-controlled apartments. Better try to get in good with the owner if you can. **Patsy's** is still holding strong in Harlem, burning it's coal oven and sometimes its pizza.

The diverse Washington Heights offers a plethora of food choices from trucks to charming restaurants, perfect for the late-night crowd. The Tony award-winning musical *In The Heights* pays loving tribute to the energetic, ebullient Washington Heights neighborhood where Dominican and Puerto Rican communities have taken root. Latin beats blast through the air and bright, refreshing Puerto Rican piragua carts can be found on almost every corner selling shaved ice soaked in a rainbow of tropical flavors. Try *jugos naturales*—juices made from cane sugar and fresh fruits like pineapple and orange—for a healthy treat. Great fish markets and butcher shops dot the streets, and less than ten bucks will get you a delicious plate of *pernil* with rice and beans at any number of eateries. Duck into **La Rosa Fine Foods**, a wonderful Latin gourmet market, for fresh fish, meat, and produce; or **Nelly's Bakery** for a creamy cup of *café con leche* and a *guayaba con queso* (guava and cheese pastry).

Piper's Kilt, a standing relic in Inwood, represents the former Irish and German population of the area. Settle into a booth at the lively "**Kilt**" with some Irish nachos and a perfect pint.

Amy Ruth's

Southern

B5

113 W. 116th St. (at Lenox Ave.)

Subway: 116 St (Lenox Ave.) Lunch & dinner daily
Phone: 212-280-8779
Web: www.amyruthsharlem.com
Prices: ⊗

This famed two-level eatery in Harlem has been going strong for over ten years, and on any given night you'll find a fun mix of locals, tourists, and some of the most influential leaders of the community flanking Amy Ruth's round, blonde wood tables, tucking into fabulous Southern fare and soaking up the friendly service.

Named for the owner's grandmother, half the fun at Amy Ruth's is in the names of the dishes. On Tuesdays, you can dig into "The Atty. Marvin Pettus", a dish of old-fashioned chicken and dumplings; mainstays include the Ludracris (fried chicken wings), the Carl S. Redding (scrumptious waffles), or the fairly new President Barack Obama (fried, smothered, baked, or barbecue chicken). Cash only, so hit the ATM in advance.

Chez Lucienne

French

B4

308 Lenox Ave. (bet. 125th & 126th Sts.)

Subway: 125 St (Lenox Ave.) Lunch & dinner daily
Phone: 212-289-5555
Web: www.chezlucienne.com
Prices: $$

French drifts between patron and staff at this refreshing addition to Central Harlem, overlooking historic Lenox Avenue. Turquoise banquettes and brick walls line the lovely, narrow space, where servers don the typical Parisian bistro uniform (black bowties, white aprons) and present well-made French fare from the semi-open kitchen.

The menu focuses on the homey simplicity inherent to great food, as in the *pâté de maison*, wonderfully textured and served with a sweet reduction and delicate chutney. The talented founders, Jerome Bougherdani and Chef Matthew Tivy (both of Daniel), have created a classic bistro in an unlikely area—and are succeeding. Note the location is very convenient to the subway, which is sure to draw foodies from across the city.

Community Food & Juice

A4 **American** 

2893 Broadway (bet. 112th & 113th Sts.)

Subway: Cathedral Pkwy/110 St (Broadway) Lunch & dinner daily
Phone: 212-665-2800
Web: www.communityrestaurant.com
Prices: $$

Community Food and Juice might be the most exciting place to arrive in this pocket of Morningside Heights yet. Not just because the highly sustainable, locally-sourced food is spectacular, or because the owners arrive via the lauded Clinton Street Baking Company—but because the homey vibe makes you want to come back every night of the week. Unfortunately, so does the rest of the neighborhood—and most nights, you'll find a healthy wait for a table (they don't take reservations). Your reward for all that patience? A piping hot, homespun matzo ball chicken soup dancing with tender carrots, celery, and fragrant herbs; a pan-seared Vietnamese chicken sandwich done *bahn mi*-style; or rich butterscotch pudding sporting a smooth dollop of whipped cream.

Dinosaur Bar-B-Que 

A3 **Barbecue** 

646 W. 131st St. (at Twelfth Ave.)

Subway: 125 St (Broadway) Lunch & dinner daily
Phone: 212-694-1777
Web: www.dinosaurbarbque.com
Prices: $$

The sumptuous smell of smoking meat carries beyond the block, beckoning barbecue lovers for miles. Reports claim that a move may be in the works, but until that happens, the current space will remain open. With a roadhouse-style vibe, this upbeat, unpretentious eatery sports a casual, family-friendly setting with large tables, a lively bar, and fantastic food. Dinosaur Bar-B-Que's monstrous menu demands a colossal appetite—options are as delicious as they are plentiful.

For a starter, try the Jumbo BBQ chicken wings, smoked in-house, and doused with your choice of sauce (go for the Wango Tango), complete with bleu cheese dressing. Next, order up the ribs and half chicken combo served with honey hush cornbread and a choice of two sides.

El Paso Taqueria 

Mexican

237 E. 116th St. (bet. Second & Third Aves.)

Subway: 116 St (Lexington Ave.) — Lunch & dinner daily
Phone: 212-860-4875
Web: www.elpasotaqueria.com
Prices: 

Sweet tacos! After a long-standing Mexican food drought, New York City is finally—happily—awash in the stuff. And does it come as any surprise that one of the more notable places in town is located deep in the heart of Spanish Harlem?

Housed along demographically diverse 116th Street, El Paso Taqueria has a nice lineup of Poblano standards (the dedicated owner, who is often on-site, is from Puebla, Mexico), with a menu that might feature *tamales oaxaqueños*, a plate of warm fluffy corn tamales filled with sweet chicken, tender corn masa, and topped with *salsa de chile pasilla* and soft cheese; or melt-in-your-mouth New Zealand lamb cooked in a maguey leaf and served simmering in a brick-red sauce chile sauce. Save room for the killer sangrias.

5 & Diamond

Contemporary

2072 Frederick Douglass Blvd. (bet. 112th & 113th Sts.)

Subway: Cathedral Pkwy/110 St (Central Park West) — Lunch Sat – Sun, Dinner Tue – Sun
Phone: 646-684-4662
Web: N/A
Prices: $$

The current chef, David Santos (with stints at Per Se and Bouley), arrives with the intention to transform an erstwhile hardware shop into a snug, 35-seat sensation—a fantastic addition to Harlem's burgeoning restaurant scene. The simple space is minimally decorated, tiny, and lacks privacy, but offers a sumptuous Mediterranean-meets-Southern cuisine that is sure to please.

Try the chef's tasting menu filled with thoughtful and delicious pairings, as in the dark, rich uni deeply redolent of the sea, with hamachi and grapefruit atop a crunchy pork rind; grilled *seppia*, smoky-sweet with poppy-piquillo pepper sauce; and perfectly roasted skate, buttery yet balanced by sharp arugula. The cheesecake, neither heavy nor overly sweet, is a near-explosion of tarragon and grapefruit flavors.

Garden Café

Contemporary 

B1

4961 Broadway (bet. 207 & Isham Sts.)

Subway: Inwood - 207 St — Lunch & dinner daily
Phone: 212-544-9480
Web: www.gardencafenyc.com
Prices: $$

A chocolate-brown awning dips over this sweet Inwood favorite, where a charming vibe and broad, contemporary menu that leans heavily on Latin American staples keep locals cheery. Inside, bare bistro tables and leather banquettes sit against golden-hued walls, while sultry jazz soothes the air.
Sit in the quaint outdoor garden and savor the special sangria and dark-grain breadbasket with tasty olive tapenade, but beware that dishes here are deliciously oversized. Peruse the daily specials or simply start with the likes of flavorful corn tortilla soup before delving into the perfectly charred stuffed poblano—bursting with tender shrimp simmered in peppers and chorizo, served with Spanish rice, black beans, *pico de gallo*, and fresh corn tortillas.

Gospel Uptown

Southern 

B4

2110 Seventh Ave. (bet. 125th & 126th Sts.)

Subway: 125 St (Lenox Ave.) — Lunch Sat – Sun
Phone: 212-280-2110 — Dinner nightly
Web: www.gospeluptown.com
Prices: $$

What happens when you combine a gorgeous entertainment space with killer soul fusion food and top-flight talent? Very good things—especially if you place that puppy uptown in Harlem, which is experiencing a heady second renaissance. Follow the red carpet into Gospel Uptown, a new restaurant-cum-jazz hall and who knows what you'll find: Melba Moore and Gloria Gaynor might perform one night; the next morning might feature gospel open-mic.
The young, talented kitchen staff marries traditional Southern food with outside influences, resulting in dishes like Louisiana crab cake set over sweet potato and fennel salad; perfectly seared Cajun tuna over curried fried plantains and micro-greens; or moist red velvet cake with ginger-pecan ice cream.

Hudson River Cafe

American

A3

697 W. 133rd St. (at Twelfth Ave.)

Subway: 125 St (Broadway)
Phone: 212-491-9111
Web: www.hudsonrivercafe.com
Prices: $$

Lunch Sun
Dinner nightly

Though it brought high-end dining to an otherwise casual food hood, fun is still the main point at Hudson River Cafe—a Harlem eatery tucked beneath the unique arched steel underpass of Riverside Drive, with wickedly strong cocktails, live music pouring out of the doors on weekends, and bold American flavors.

Try the delicate empanadas to start, then move on to the delicious Harlem paella, bursting with juicy chorizo, Serrano ham, chicken, smoky duck, wild mushrooms, and truffle oil; and finish with a warm tropical carrot dessert loaded with spicy cinnamon and raisins, then topped with an excellent coconut ice cream. One note going in: lest you get too caught up in the fun and food to see your check clearly, an automatic tip is added to all bills.

Max SoHa

Italian

A4

1274 Amsterdam Ave. (at 123rd St.)

Subway: 125 St (Broadway)
Phone: 212-531-2221
Web: www.maxsoha.com
Prices: $$

Lunch & dinner daily

Locals seeking an unpretentious touch of neighborhood familiarity—especially amid Columbia University's rapid expansion through Morningside Heights—need look no further than Max SoHa. The warm, rustic interior, clad in weathered woods, exposed brick, and colorful ceramics, purrs with coziness and fashions an idyllic atmosphere for comforting Italian fare.

Menu highlights include the well-made, simple, and satisfying pastas and *risotti*, while equally delicious daily specials can be found posted on two chalkboards hanging near the kitchen and bar. On a sunny day, grab a sidewalk table, order a glass from the lovely, affordable Italian wine selection, and enjoy the cacophony of intermingling languages and discourse in this area swarming with change.

Melba's

A5 Southern

300 W. 114th St. (at Frederick Douglass Blvd.)

Subway: 116 St (Frederick Douglass Blvd.)
Phone: 212-864-7777
Web: www.melbasrestaurant.com
Prices: $$

Lunch Sat – Sun
Dinner nightly

This popular Morningside Heights joint stays elbow-to-elbow most nights of the week despite small digs, loud music, and a molasses staff. In fact, that's all part of the charm for the regulars that crowd into Melba's to eat, drink, and listen to music.

Set along a rapidly gentrifying street pocked with as many cutesy storefronts as West African mom-and-pop eateries, Melba's bleeds cozy-chic, with custom chandeliers, plush banquettes, and exposed brick. The Southern comfort menu is decadent all around—velvety catfish strips with chipotle mayo are paired with an eggnog waffle lathered in piping-hot strawberry butter; and a heartbreakingly moist coconut layer cake is infused with butter cream and dusted with coconut flakes.

New Leaf Café

A2 American

1 Margaret Corbin Dr. (in Fort Tryon Park)

Subway: 190 St
Phone: 212-568-5323
Web: www.newleafrestaurant.com
Prices: $$

Lunch & dinner Tue – Sun

Plumb in the heart of bucolic Fort Tyron Park stands the gorgeous stone edifice that houses New Leaf Café. Built in the 1930s and revitalized in 2001 by the New York Restoration Project, the cottage-like structure flaunts a vintage charm with its arched-brick doorways and windows, shaded by a bevy of lush trees. The interior is as enchanting with dark woods, stone walls, and seasonal artwork outfitting the amber-lit rooms; picturesque views of the verdant surroundings add to the allure.

Fresh, carefully sourced ingredients make for a wonderful menu of seasonal dishes. Savor the fantastically flavorful free-range chicken: moist on the inside, crisp on the outside—perfect. To end, the brioche bread pudding with homemade rum raisin ice cream is a must.

Ricardo Steakhouse

Steakhouse

C5

2145 Second Ave. (bet. 110th & 111th Sts.)

Subway: 110 St (Lexington Ave.) Dinner nightly
Phone: 212-289-5895
Web: www.ricardosteakhouse.com
Prices: $$

In recent years, this East Harlem favorite has become a local hangout among the upscale condo set moving into the neighborhood. One peek inside, and it's certainly easy to see why—weather permitting, there's a cute garden to graze in out back, and inside, you'll find a cozy, exposed brick interior flickering with honeyed light from the votive candles.

True to its moniker, red meat is the name of the game at Ricardo's—a Porterhouse for one arrives perfectly seared, and is paired with a combo of bright *chimichurri* and peppery hot oil. If you can wrangle someone into sharing, kick things off with the Ricardo tasting platter—a smorgasbord of plump steak empanadas, expertly-charred calamari, tender crab cake, and butter-kissed Clams Casino.

Vareli

Mediterranean

A4

2869 Broadway (bet. 111th & 112th Sts.)

Subway: Cathedral Pkwy/110 St (Broadway) Dinner nightly
Phone: 212-678-8585
Web: www.varelinyc.com
Prices: $$

Stuffed into the foodie wasteland that surrounds Columbia University, one step into this gorgeous little restaurant and you know you're onto something good. With its barrel-shaped ceilings, polished copper bar, and lovely upstairs dining room replete with Japanese rock water wall, this Morningside looker is young—but exceptionally clever.

Owner George Zoitas ushers in superb ingredients from his nearby market—then lets Israeli chef, Amitzur Mor (who worked at Bouley), spin them into lip-smacking Mediterranean fare like tender grilled octopus, laced with *labneh* yogurt and tossed with chickpeas, Moroccan olives, and serrano peppers; or a juicy, sumac-rubbed pork chop paired with grilled Swiss chard, roasted artichokes, and preserved lemon.

Zoma 

A5 — Ethiopian 

2084 Frederick Douglass Blvd. (at 113th St.)

Subway: 116th (Frederick Douglass Blvd.)
Phone: 212-662-0620
Web: www.zomanyc.com
Prices: ⓈⓈ

Lunch Sat – Sun
Dinner nightly

In terms of Ethiopian joints, this popular Harlem restaurant cuts a particularly cool, sophisticated figure with its spare white interior and beautiful exotic relics. The food is even classier, with ample, delicious portions hovering near the $16 mark—and the mixed crowd of neighborhood locals and budget-minded gourmands are happy to wait their turn for a stab at authentic meat dishes like *doro wett* (a chicken stew redolent with spices and made fiery from berbere).

For two or more, an ideal meal might be a plate of fish or meat, paired with the outstanding vegetarian combination. Mopped up with the tangy, moist *injera* (which doubles as a spoon to scoop the food from the plate to your mouth), and washed down with a sweet glass of honey wine—the result is pure African bliss.

Remember, stars (✿✿✿…✿) are awarded for cuisine only! Elements such as service and décor are not a factor.

Peter L. Wrenn/MICHELIN

Lower East Side

Clockwise from the north, this neighborhood is bounded by Houston Street, the East River, Pike Street, and the Bowery. While it has proudly retained the personality of its first wave of hard-working settlers, the area has embraced a steady change to its landscape brought on by artsy entrepreneurs lured to these formerly overlooked parts. A mostly low-lying neighborhood, with the exception of a few high-rise apartments, towering reminders of a recent real estate boom, the Lower East Side feels village-like in its stature with a palpable creative spirit.

Eastern European Influence

Before checking out the scene as it looks today, visit the Lower East Side Tenement Museum for a glimpse of the past. This restored structure dates back to 1863 and depicts what life was like for the swells of immigrant families, primarily Eastern European Jews that settled here in the early part of the last century fleeing famine and war, making this neighborhood the most densely populated area in the country. For a taste of yore, head to **Russ & Daughters** on Houston Street. Opened in 1914, this beloved institution is a nosher's dream famous for its selection of smoked fish and all things delicious known as "appetizing."

Orchard Street

Orchard Street, long the retail heart of this nabe was once dominated by the garment trade with stores selling fabrics and notions. Tailors remain in the area, offering inexpensive while-you-wait service; but boutiques selling handmade jewelry, designer skateboards, and handcrafted denim have also moved in. Shoppers looking to cool their heels should drop by **Il Laboratorio del Gelato** for an indulgent scoop. For purchases with a more daily purpose, the **Essex Street Market** houses numerous purveyors of fresh produce, meat, and fish under one roof. The market is truly a gourmet's delight; it features two cheesemongers, a coffee roaster, a chocolatier, and **Shopsin's General Store**, a crazy joint notorious for its encyclopedic menu and cranky owner.

By the 1950s, the melting pot that defined the LES became even more diverse with a new tide of immigrants, this time from Puerto Rico and other parts of Latin America. This population continues to be the dominant force today. For a sampling of home-style Latino fare, like *mofongo* and *pernil*, try **El Castillo de Jagua** on the corner of Essex and Rivington streets.

Rivington Street

Rivington Street embodies this area's hybrid of old and

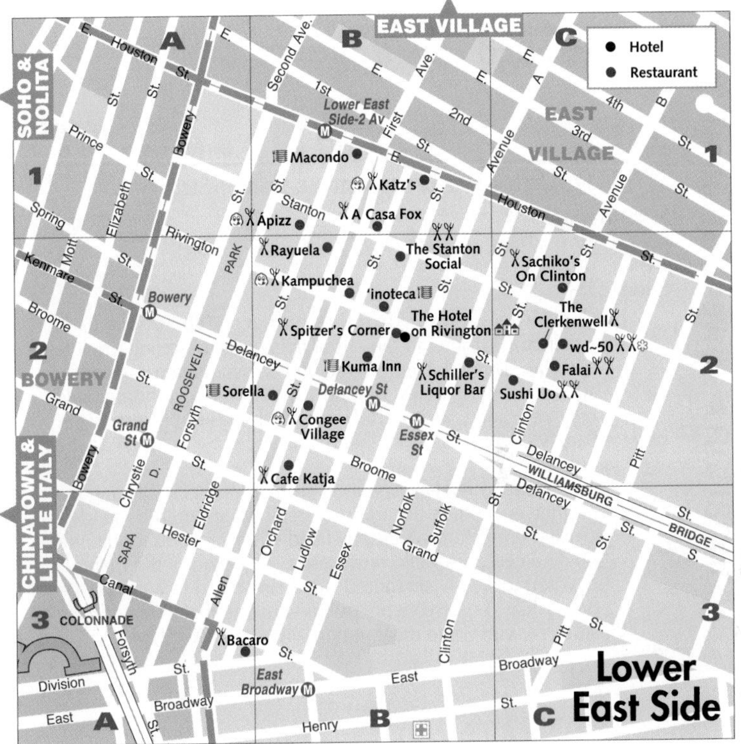

new. Located here is **Streit's Matzo Factory**, in operation since 1925, and **Economy Candy**, an emporium for old-fashioned sweets since 1937. During the day, the mood is pretty chill, perfect for idling in any one of the nearby coffee shops. For a nutritious pick-me-up, **Teany** specializes in vegan vittles served in a café setting. Or, for a helping of what many agree is the city's best stack of pancakes, served all day, stroll over to the always packed **Clinton Street Baking Co.** Come evening, the street fills with meandering groups strolling to and from a number of popular dining spots.

South of Delancey Street, Grand Street is home to well-maintained residential complexes and shops that cater to a cadre of longtime residents. Carb-addicts should be afraid, very afraid; this street is home to **Kossar's Bialys**, several kosher bakeries, and **Doughnut Plant**, where the owner offers an updated take on his grandfather's doughnut recipe in flavors like Valrhona chocolate. For that quintessential deli accent at home, head to **Pickle Guys** on the corner of Essex Street, stocked with barrel upon barrel of ...you guessed it, pickles.

A Casa Fox

B1 **Latin American**

173 Orchard St. (bet. Houston & Stanton Sts.)

Subway: Lower East Side - 2 Av
Lunch & dinner Tue – Sat
Phone: 212-253-1900
Web: www.acasafox.com
Prices: $$

Chef/owner Melissa Fox dishes out savory home-style Latin American cuisine in an attractively rustic setting replete with an open kitchen, gracious service team, variously sized wooden tables topped with bottles of homemade *picante* sauce, exposed brick, and plaster-coated walls. Family keepsakes offer a heartwarming glow by the working fireplace.

The menu reflects inspiration from the chef's Nicaraguan mother and offers an array of small plates such as tender-crusted empanadas, perhaps filled with smoked Gouda and finely diced portobello mushroom. A portion of the menu is devoted to slowly simmered stews presented in a terra cotta bowl, like the arroz con pollo—fluffy tomato-stained rice studded with white meat, green olives, and sweet peas.

Ápizz 

B1 **Italian**

217 Eldridge St. (bet. Rivington & Stanton Sts.)

Subway: Lower East Side - 2 Av
Dinner nightly
Phone: 212-253-9199
Web: www.apizz.com
Prices: $$

In a neighborhood trying to reconcile its past life (think housing projects and homeless shelters) with its glitzy new one (think celebrity sightings and boutique hotels), Ápizz is gloriously above the fray. Why? Because its simple, windowless Lower East Side façade hides the kind of cozy, impossibly quaint New York staple you wish there were more of—with warm, fuzzy lighting, good background music, and a young, sexy crowd.

Okay, there is one diva—the fantastic brick-oven that dominates the room (their motto is "one room, one oven"), but it's earned its girth. Try the plump shrimp, roasted in a casuela, and served in a lemony bath of chorizo, toasted breadcrumbs, and herbs; or a warm risotto, humming with mushrooms and freshly shaved Parmesan.

Bacaro

Italian

A3

136 Division St. (bet. Ludlow & Orchard Sts.)

Subway: East Broadway — Dinner Tue – Sun
Phone: 212-941-5060
Web: www.bacaronyc.com
Prices: $$

From the owners of Peasant comes Bacaro, which takes its name and inspiration from the pub-like wine bars of Venice, and has a warm, inviting glow that sets it apart from its edgier surroundings. The sexy subterranean dining room (a former gambling parlor) evokes an ancient cellar with brick archways, weathered plaster, salvaged ceiling beams, and candlelit alcoves, which are perfect for groups. The marble-topped bar, illuminated by a blown glass chandelier, is a lovely spot to enjoy a *crostini di giorno*, or explore the all-Italian wine list.

The menu highlights Venetian traditions in offerings like tender octopus and cubed potato dressed with olive oil and parsley, or hearty dishes of creamy lasagna Treviso with smoked mozzarella and radicchio.

Cafe Katja

Austrian 

B2

79 Orchard St. (bet. Broome & Grand Sts.)

Subway: Delancey St — Dinner nightly
Phone: 212-219-9545
Web: www.cafe-katja.com
Prices: $$

Cozy in scale yet big in spirit, Cafe Katja turns out an impressive rendition of genuine old-world specialties focusing on the owner's native Austria. The candlelit brick and tan room casts a welcoming glow and is intimately furnished with a mere row of tables supplemented by a bar set adjacent to the tiny back kitchen.

The crock of homemade liverwurst, dense and silky, is accompanied by an array of house-pickled vegetables and thick slices of whole-grain bread, making a fine bar meal, especially when washed down by a well-chosen selection of beers and Austrian wines. Heartier plates feature the likes of homemade Emmentaler sausage—coarse ground, filled with hollows of melted cheese and accompanied by ethereal quark cheese dumplings.

The Clerkenwell

C2 — Gastropub 

49 Clinton St. (bet. Rivington & Stanton Sts.)

Subway: Delancey St — Lunch Sat – Sun
Phone: 212-614-3234 — Dinner Tue – Sun
Web: www.clerkenwellnyc.com
Prices: $$

The Clerkenwell brings the pub-inspired world of beef pie and mushy peas to Clinton Street's already diverse diningscape. Emanating a warm and comfortable vibe to complement its cuisine, the pint-sized space features button-tufted banquettes, a visible kitchen in back that provides diners with a bit of a show, and a comfortable, graciously-tended bar. A wine list is offered but a crisp, cold lager on tap is a much more appropriate way to wash down the contemporary pub grub. Offerings include the likes of a pea and leek tart with poached egg; slow-roasted pork belly with parsnip purée; or plump sausages cradled in Yorkshire pudding and topped with red onion marmalade.

The scattering of tables set out front make a great spot to people watch.

Congee Village

B2 — Chinese

100 Allen St. (at Delancey St.)

Subway: Delancey St — Lunch & dinner daily
Phone: 212-941-1818
Web: www.congeevillagerestaurants.com
Prices: 

Porridge for dinner may not tempt at first, but with more than 25 varieties of *congee*, this attractive spot specializing in Cantonese cuisine is sure to win over even the most wary. This soothing specialty, popular throughout China, is served bubbling hot in an earthenware pot, ready to be seasoned with an assortment of tableside condiments. Besides the namesake signature, sample hard-to-find dishes like pan-fried egg with silver fish, cold jellyfish, and rice baked with meat and vegetables in a bamboo vessel.

Located on the fringe of Chinatown, the well-maintained, multilevel space covered in bamboo and stone has a warm ambience. Large tables, a buzzing bar area, and a host of private rooms fill the space with all the revelry of a town square.

Falai

Italian XX

C2

68 Clinton St. (bet. Rivington & Stanton Sts.)

Subway: Lower East Side - 2 Av
Dinner nightly
Phone: 212-253-1960
Web: www.falainyc.com
Prices: $$

With its sleek décor, sharp service, and ambitious contemporary Italian creations, Falai succeeds in standing above Clinton Street's myriad eating and drinking options. The white-on-white dining room is a sexy, polished sliver of flattering lights, marble counters, and close tables around an open kitchen.

Chef/owner Iacopo Falai started his career as a pastry chef and this foundation is shrewdly applied to his stimulating and streamlined menu. A meal here may include silky strands of red wine stained tagliatelle with crumbles of cinnamon-spiked sausage and braised radicchio, or seared lamb atop toothsome *fregola* with bright arugula purée and warmed goat's milk cream. Meals are enhanced by excellent bread service and petite sweets to finish.

'inoteca

Italian 

B2

98 Rivington St. (at Ludlow St.)

Subway: Delancey St
Lunch & dinner daily
Phone: 212-614-0473
Web: www.inotecanyc.com
Prices: ⊜

This charmingly rustic wine bar adorned with knobby wood furnishings and wrap-around sidewalk seating has come to be a foodie favorite, and perhaps the definitive dining destination of the Lower East Side. Open all day long, 'inoteca continuously tempts with a menu of lovingly simple yet sophisticated Italian fare in an ambience that beckons guests to stop by anytime.

The offerings may include a quick lunchtime salad of grilled mushrooms with watercress and *Piave vecchio*; an after work respite in a glass of chilled lambrusco and a few slices of *coppa*; or a dinnertime sampling of panini and small plates. The *porchetta*-stuffed *ciabatta* garnished with freshly grated horseradish or polenta with charred ramps and poached egg are all worthy favorites.

Katz's 

B1 Deli

205 E. Houston St. (at Ludlow St.)

Subway: Lower East Side - 2 Av
Lunch & dinner daily
Phone: 212-254-2246
Web: www.katzdeli.com
Prices: ⊜

Mercifully, some things never go out of style. Established in 1888, Katz's is as much a New York institution as the Statue of Liberty. One of the few original eastern European vestiges of the Lower East Side, Katz's attracts tourists, residents, and celebrities alike. In the never-ending debate over who serves the best pastrami in the city, Katz's often tops the list.

For an authentic experience, queue up in front of the salty countermen, collect your meal, and score a table. Matzo ball soup and a legendary corned beef on rye (not toasted) with a sour pickle are all unadorned, delicious perfection.

Do not lose the ticket you got upon entering: this is your ticket out. Without it, such a fuss will be made that you'll want to hide under a table.

Your opinions are important to us. Please write to us at: michelin.guides@us.michelin.com

Kuma Inn

Asian

113 Ludlow St. (bet. Delancey & Rivington Sts.)

Subway: Delancey St
Phone: 212-353-8866
Web: www.kumainn.com
Prices:

Dinner nightly

Pan-Asian tapas are the theme at this second floor dining room not much bigger than some of the chic boutiques found in this exciting neighborhood. A veteran of Daniel and Jean Georges, New York City-born Chef/owner King Phojanakong offers well prepared, flavor-packed fare that reflects the multicultural influences of his Thai-Filipino background. The menu is best suited for grazing so bring reinforcements to ensure you hit all the chef's specialties that include sautéed Chinese sausage with Thai chili-lime sauce; sake-braised beef with Asian root vegetables; and *arroz Valenciana* with chicken, seafood, and sausage.

Genteel service and a background soundtrack of the chef's favorite tracks add to the ambience of the minimally decorated room.

Macondo

Latin American

157 E. Houston St. (bet. Allen & Eldridge Sts.)

Subway: Lower East Side - 2 Av
Phone: 212-473-9900
Web: www.macondonyc.com
Prices: $$

Lunch Sat – Sun
Dinner nightly

The vibe at this fun spot from the owners of Rayuela matches that of its high-traffic location. Weather permitting, the front bar opens onto the street and is abuzz with thirty-somethings sipping *mojitos* sweetened with pure sugarcane juice. Inside, the long, narrow space is accented by shelves of Latin provisions, an open kitchen, rows of communal tables, and low, lounge-like booths towards the back.

Crowds come here to linger over the array of Latin-flavored small plates. Perfect for a group, the menu is divided into a large selection of snacks designed for sharing, such as ceviche, arepas, and empanadas. Their toasty, warm *bocadillos* are popular—the pork, ham, Manchego, and pickle stuffed Cubano is an especially tasty treat.

Rayuela

B2

Latin American

165 Allen St. (bet. Rivington & Stanton Sts.)

Subway: Lower East Side - 2 Av

Dinner nightly

Phone: 212-253-8840

Web: www.rayuelanyc.com

Prices: $$

This inspired "freestyle Latin" cuisine expresses an uninhibited journey through South America and beyond. Paella infused with coconut milk, lemongrass, and ginger oil; or pan-roasted pork loin with soy-tamarind sauce are delicious stops along the way. A fine prelude to your meal is a selection from the lengthy ceviche list—each combines traditional, quality ingredients and bracing flavors in unique ways. The cocktail menu is comprised of quenching libations, including a range of sangria.

A slate-tiled bar, exposed brick walls, and iron grating filled with river rock fashion the contemporary interior. Warm candlelight, gauzy fabric panels, a hip crowd, and a majestic olive tree stretching up through the mezzanine soften the sleek space.

Sachiko's On Clinton

C2

Japanese

25 Clinton St. (bet. Houston & Stanton Sts.)

Subway: Delancey St

Dinner Tue – Sun

Phone: 212-253-2900

Web: www.sachikosonclinton.com

Prices: $$

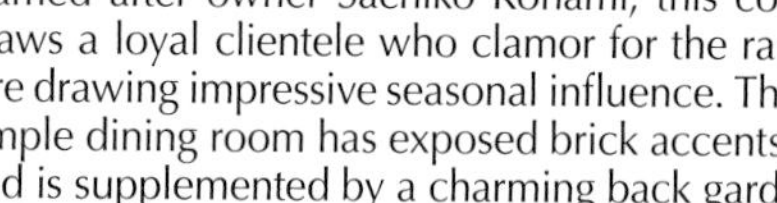

Named after owner Sachiko Konami, this comfortable spot draws a loyal clientele who clamor for the range of creative fare drawing impressive seasonal influence. The attractive but simple dining room has exposed brick accents, orange walls, and is supplemented by a charming back garden. In addition to the rich, tender, and consistently fresh raw offerings neatly arranged at the intimate sushi counter, the kitchen team also displays skill in their cooked items.

The very popular house specialty, *kushiage*, features morsels of beef, chicken, or vegetables threaded on bamboo sticks, breaded in homemade *panko*, and deep fried. The cocktail menu boasts a Japanese focus from the Pink Lady made with plum wine and passion fruit juice to the sake margarita.

Schiller's Liquor Bar

European

131 Rivington St. (at Norfolk St.)

Subway: Delancey St — Lunch & dinner daily
Phone: 212-260-4555
Web: www.schillersny.com
Prices: $$

Schiller's, like Keith McNally's wildly successful Balthazar and Pastis, touts a magical mix—like the most popular girl in high school, it has just the right combination to pop in a crowd. However, its components are breezy retro-bistro good looks, solid (if not inventive) brassiere fare, and a prime location straddling a sunny corner of the Lower East Side. The straightforward menu may not require much contemplation, but be sure to remember a side of their perfect *frites*.

As to how best to describe the atmosphere that draws locals, day trippers, and low-key celebrities alike, we direct you to the cheeky house wine list, categorized into *cheap*, *decent*, or *good*. A terrific cocktail selection rounds out the drink list, including a spot-on Pimm's Cup.

Sorella

Italian 

95 Allen St. (bet. Broome & Delancey Sts.)

Subway: Delancey St — Dinner Tue – Sun
Phone: 212-274-9595
Web: www.sorellanyc.com
Prices: $$

Easily identified by its bulky façade dotted with peepholes, step inside Sorella for a leisurely yet serious offering of small plates.

Seating is available at counters in the narrow, white-washed brick dining area, or at tables in a glass-enclosed back room. The Northern Italian menu is broken down to offer a selection of cheeses, meats, and *qualcosina*, which translates as "a little something." Plates such as marinated anchovies with lemon butter atop richly flavored flatbread, and Salvatore ricotta *gnudi* with basil and sunflower seed pesto are both delicious and impressive.

Complement a meal here with a tempting selection from their expansive list of wines by the glass; Sorella's features twenty-five choices, each priced under $15.

Spitzer's Corner

B2 Gastropub 

101 Rivington St. (at Ludlow St.)

Subway: Delancey St — Lunch & dinner daily
Phone: 212-228-0027
Web: www.spitzerscorner.com
Prices: ⊜

The intentionally grungy gastropub motif gets a slick and modern makeover at the Lower East Side's Spitzer's Corner, where a trendy young crowd piles in despite the no-reservations policy—happy to chill at the bar or settle into a long, sleek waiting bench as long as they can nurse one of the 40 available draft selections, or a glass of wine from the small, but studied, by-the-glass list.

The menu offers a host of delicious salads and sandwiches, but those looking for a proper meal can up the ante with a plate of Spitzer's beef sliders; cedar plank-grilled Salmon; or slow-cooked duck confit salad in passion fruit vinaigrette, paired with foie gras butter-smeared toast.

The Stanton Social

B2 Fusion 

99 Stanton St. (bet. Ludlow & Orchard Sts.)

Subway: Lower East Side - 2 Av — Lunch Sat – Sun, Dinner nightly
Phone: 212-995-0099
Web: www.thestantonsocial.com
Prices: $$

The Stanton Social has a finely tailored décor that pays homage to the haberdashers and seamstress shops that once dotted this trendy neighborhood. Vintage hand mirrors, woven leather straps, and wine shelves laid out in a herringbone pattern outfit the low-lit, dark-wood furnished space.

Choosing from the generous list of ambitious, globally inspired preparations executed by Chef/owner Chris Santos is difficult—bring friends to ensure a wholehearted run of the menu. The signature sliders, charred squid lettuce wraps, and potato and goat cheese pierogies all deserve consideration. This entertaining fare is well-paired with a finely crafted cocktail or selection from the well-chosen wine list. The second floor lounge offers the same menu.

Sushi Uo

Japanese XX

C2

151 Rivington St. (bet. Clinton & Suffolk Sts.)

Subway: Delancey St
Dinner Tue – Sun
Phone: 212-677-5470
Web: N/A
Prices: **$$**

Tucked behind an unmarked door that leads to an intimate second floor dining space along Rivington Street, Sushi Uo is that rare combination of two great things: low-lit, impress-your-date, speakeasy ambience with first-rate Japanese fare. The name is Japanese slang for "fish", and the menu—deftly prepared by two new Japanese chefs (one who worked at the lauded 15 East)—features a contemporary spin on dishes like a miso consommé with heirloom tomatoes and homemade tofu; uni carbonara with homemade pasta; and hanger steak *tataki* with tomato-shiso marmalade. Sushi arrives like a dream: tender room-temperature balls of rice, perfectly packed and sporting bright, bursting piles of roe; rich, ruby-red tuna; and sweet, melt-in-your-mouth scallop.

Look for our new category, small plates.

wd~50 ✿

Contemporary 

C2

50 Clinton St. (bet. Rivington & Stanton Sts.)

Subway: Delancey St — Dinner Wed – Sun
Phone: 212-477-2900
Web: www.wd-50.com
Prices: **$$$**

Robert Polidori

Chef Wylie Dufresne earned his culinary stripes retooling New York's vision of molecular gastronomy with his strange and wonderful concoctions, spinning out dishes that challenge our preconceptions of texture, association, and taste. And like a mad scientist who never tires of his own inventions, Clinton Street's resident genius flips yet another year on his wildly successful Lower East Side restaurant, wd~50—and still doesn't miss a beat.

Kick things off with a glass of wine from a small, but intense list. Better yet, ask the sommelier about any of the small, but intriguing lineup of producers and you'll probably get a story to accompany them—all the more reason to linger in the dining room, a simple, clean-lined space broken up by bright splashes of color.

Witness a smooth, light-as-air tomatillo and pine gazpacho garnished with crunchy little falafel balls, tender rings of octopus, and cucumber noodles; or juicy fans of cider-braised Iberico pork neck served with buckwheat crackers and pilaf, then finished with a creamy brown butter reduction. Dining at this *bijou* is a nice way to unwind after hitting the neighborhood's hipper-than-thou boutiques.

Peter L. Wrenn/MICHELIN

Midtown East & Murray Hill

Started by the Vanderbilts in the 19th century, then saved from the wrecking ball with the help of Jacqueline Kennedy Onassis in the 20th century, Grand Central Terminal has somehow become a 21st century foodie haven.

Grand Central Terminal

A perfect day at the world's largest train station begins with a coffee amid the work-bound masses from **Joe's**. Lunch options range from the multi-ethnic food court offerings (**Café Spice** for Indian, **Mendy's** for kosher, **Zocalo** for Mexican), to the prized concourse restaurants situated beneath the celestial ceiling murals. Nonetheless, one of Manhattan's most beloved icons, the **Oyster Bar**, has been tucked into the cavernous lower level since 1913. Be sure to first visit the "whispering gallery" located near its entrance, where low, ceramic arches allow whispers to sound like shouts.

Come happy hour, Grand Central continues to inspire with **Campbell Apartment**—for those who meet the dress code. This 1920s office of railroad mogul John W. Campbell was restored and re-opened as one of the area's swankier stops for a famously dry martini. Those seeking a quiet night of home cooking can simply walk across the concourse to visit the market, for a stunning array of gourmet treats. Fishmongers, produce stands, butchers, bakeries, and possibly the best spices in the city are all found here.

Local Spots

Grand Central is a perfect microcosm of its eastern midtown home, because stretching through this neighborhood is the same diversity of shopping and dining. Residents of Beekman and Sutton boast their very own top fishmonger (**Piscayne**), cheese shop (**Ideal Cheese**), butcher (**L. Simchik**), bagel and lox shop (**Tal**), and to complete any dinner party, florist (**Zeze**). One of the area's better-kept secrets is **Dessert Delivery**, specializing in delivering expertly baked treats. Luckily, it is free from the ongoing cupcake war between **Buttercup** and **Bruce's**, with **Magnolia** and **Crumbs**' arrival and following. Also find some of the best chocolate in town, from **Richart** to **Teuscher** and **Pierre Marolini**. While **Dag Hammarskjold Greenmarket** may by dwarfed by Union Square, it has just the right amount of everything to satisfy its neighbors.

Japantown

Within these distinctly commuter, residential, and internationally focused midtown nooks, is a very sophisticated Japantown, with casual *izakayas* and secreted-away

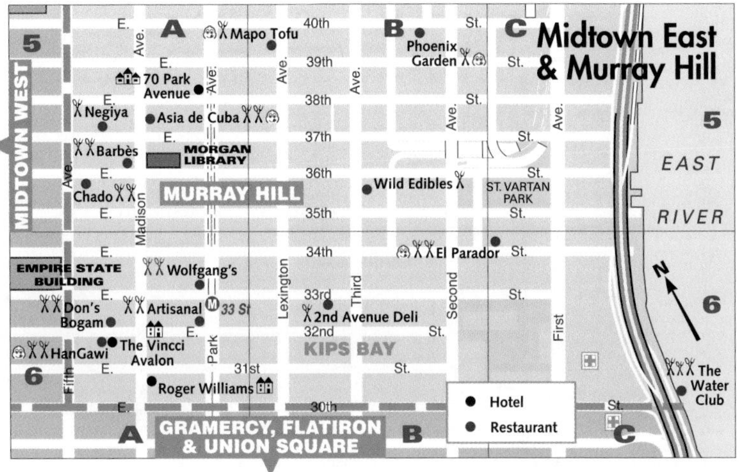

hostess clubs lining the area east of Lexington. For a light lunch or snack, sample *onigiri* at **Oms/b**, or try the modern takeout yakitori, **Kushi-Q**. True Japanophiles should visit the **Japanese Culinary Center** filled with shiny knives and imported delicacies.

United Nations

Along the neighborhood's eastern border is the United Nations. In the spirit of this landmark, the **Delegates Dining Room** at the UN sponsors food festivals that spotlight a different cuisine each month. Just remember to make a reservation for this buffet lunch and arrive early, allowing extra time to clear security.

Murray Hill

Younger and quieter than its northern neighbor, Murray Hill has its own distinct restaurant vibe. Here, faster and casual finds thrive, populated by hungry twenty-somethings seeking a slice of pizza or hearty cheesesteak. Afterwards, they move on to their favored Third Avenue watering holes to hoot and holler with college buddies over Bud Lights while catching the snowboarding championships. This is the Murray Hill of recent college grads spilling out onto sidewalks of **Bar 515** or perhaps **Third and Long**. However, this is only one Murray Hill.

The other Murray Hill rises with the sun over pristine brownstones and apartment towers, awakening young families who gather amid blooming flowers at St. Vartan Park or chat with neighbors over omelets at **Sarge's Deli**. These are the (slightly) senior locals of Murray Hill—they love it here and will remain faithful residents until well-after the frat party has ended.

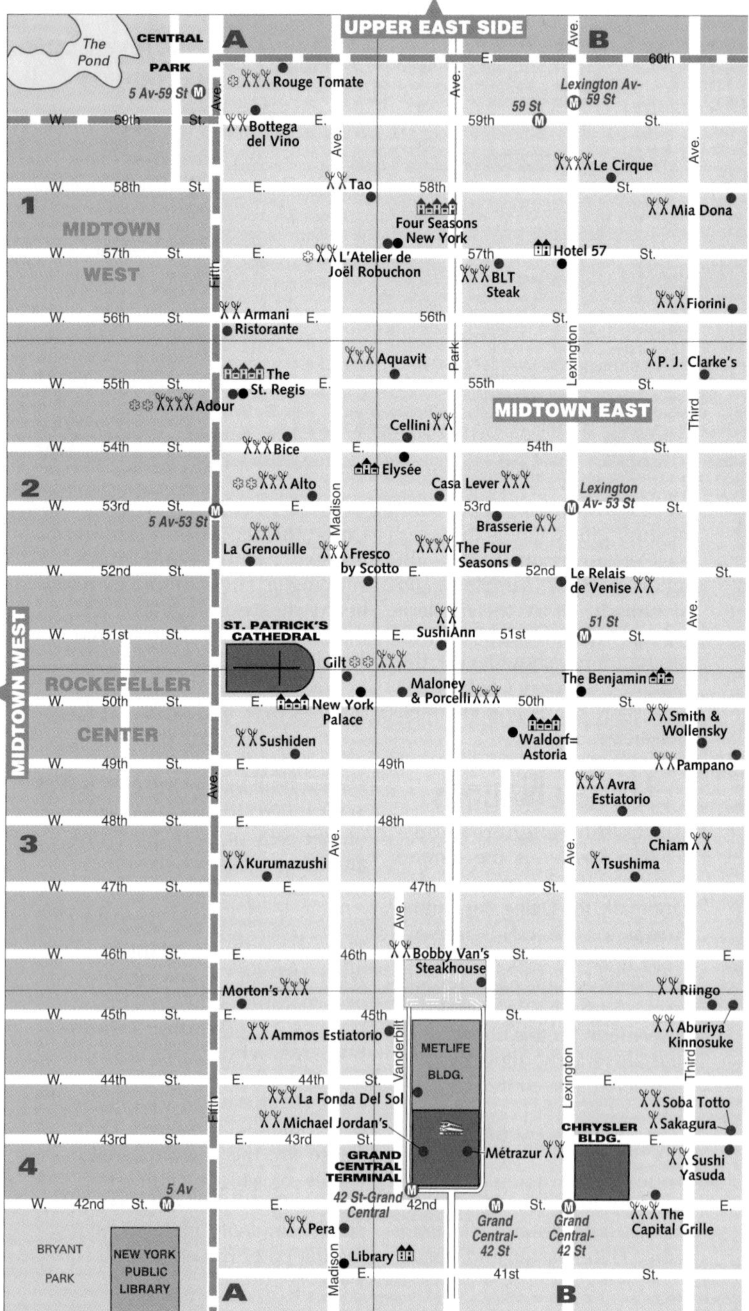

UPPER EAST SIDE
MIDTOWN WEST
MIDTOWN EAST
ROCKEFELLER CENTER
CENTRAL PARK
The Pond
Rouge Tomate
Bottega del Vino
Tao
Le Cirque
Mia Dona
Four Seasons New York
L'Atelier de Joël Robuchon
Hotel 57
BLT Steak
Fiorini
Armani Ristorante
Aquavit
P. J. Clarke's
The St. Regis
Adour
Cellini
Bice
Elysée
Alto
Casa Lever
Brasserie
La Grenouille
Fresco by Scotto
The Four Seasons
Le Relais de Venise
SushiAnn
ST. PATRICK'S CATHEDRAL
Gilt
The Benjamin
Maloney & Porcelli
New York Palace
Smith & Wollensky
Sushiden
Waldorf=Astoria
Pampano
Avra Estiatorio
Chiam
Kurumazushi
Tsushima
Bobby Van's Steakhouse
Morton's
Riingo
Ammos Estiatorio
Aburiya Kinnosuke
METLIFE BLDG.
La Fonda Del Sol
Soba Totto
Michael Jordan's
Sakagura
CHRYSLER BLDG.
GRAND CENTRAL TERMINAL
Métrazur
Sushi Yasuda
The Capital Grille
Pera
Library
BRYANT PARK
NEW YORK PUBLIC LIBRARY
5 Av-59 St
59 St
Lexington Av-59 St
5 Av-53 St
Lexington Av-53 St
51 St
5 Av
42 St-Grand Central
Grand Central-42 St
Grand Central-42 St
Fifth Ave.
Madison Ave.
Park Ave.
Lexington Ave.
Third Ave.
Vanderbilt Ave.
60th
59th St.
58th St.
57th St.
56th St.
55th St.
54th St.
53rd St.
52nd St.
51st St.
50th St.
49th St.
48th St.
47th St.
46th St.
45th St.
44th St.
43rd St.
42nd St.
41st St.
A
B
1
2
3
4

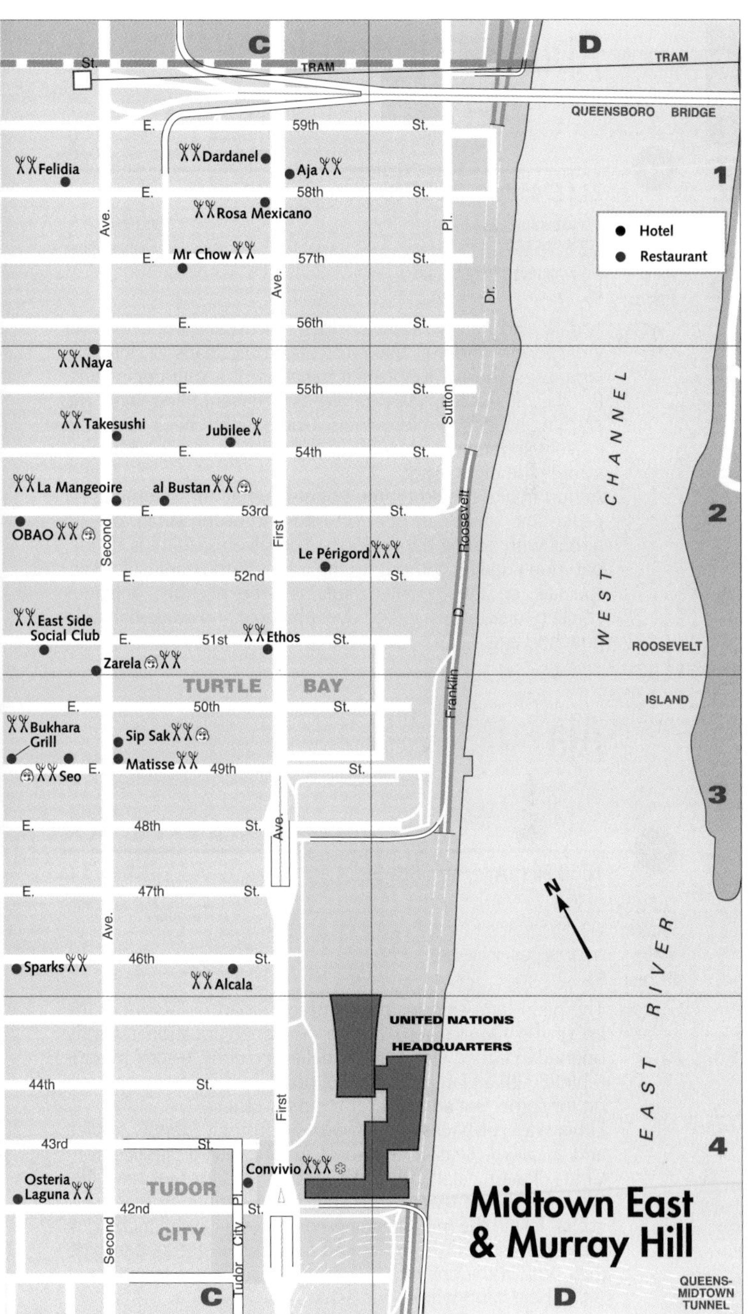
Midtown East & Murray Hill
Hotel
Restaurant
TRAM
QUEENSBORO BRIDGE
Felidia
Dardanel
Aja
Rosa Mexicano
Mr Chow
Naya
Takesushi
Jubilee
La Mangeoire
al Bustan
OBAO
Le Périgord
East Side Social Club
Ethos
Zarela
TURTLE BAY
Bukhara Grill
Sip Sak
Matisse
Seo
Sparks
Alcala
UNITED NATIONS HEADQUARTERS
Convivio
Osteria Laguna
TUDOR CITY
WEST CHANNEL
ROOSEVELT ISLAND
EAST RIVER
QUEENS-MIDTOWN TUNNEL
E. 59th St.
E. 58th St.
E. 57th St.
E. 56th St.
E. 55th St.
E. 54th St.
E. 53rd St.
E. 52nd St.
E. 51st St.
E. 50th St.
E. 49th St.
E. 48th St.
E. 47th St.
46th St.
44th St.
43rd St.
42nd St.
Second Ave.
First Ave.
Sutton Pl.
Roosevelt Dr.
Franklin D. Roosevelt Dr.
Tudor City Pl.

Aburiya Kinnosuke

B4 — Japanese XX

213 E. 45th St. (bet. Second & Third Aves.)

Subway: Grand Central - 42 St — Lunch Mon – Fri
Phone: 212-867-5454 — Dinner nightly
Web: www.aburiyakinnosuke.com
Prices: $$

A dark and narrow hallway does not usually bode well for great food—and yet, this particular route leads to delicious Japanese. Aburiya Kinnosuke has a bit of a split personality. By day, it's an upscale bento box haven filled with the chirping sounds of midtowners. Come nighttime, it turns into a lively, intimate *izakaya* to sip Japanese cocktails while you sample the night away.

Action freaks should hit the counter, while those looking for peace and quiet can peel off into one of the small, private nooks with sliding paper doors. The silken sashimi is divine, but don't leave without trying one of the fantastic daily specials or the popular *tsukune*—inexplicably delicious chicken meatloaves, grilled over charcoal and dunked in cold poached egg.

Aja

C1 — Asian XX

1068 First Ave. (at 58th St.)

Subway: 59 St — Dinner nightly
Phone: 212-888-8008
Web: www.ajaasiancuisine.com
Prices: $$

The plain-Jane exterior of this fusion Asian restaurant at the lip of the Queensboro Bridge (a second location recently opened in Greenwich Village) belies a clubby, trendy interior replete with a giant Buddha, koi pond, and fountain—a turn-on for some, but a bit over-the-top for others.

Either way, Aja packs them in with surprisingly friendly service and a crowd-pleasing lineup of Americanized classics from China, Japan, Thailand, India, and Singapore that read like an Asian dream team. And while the authenticity may have gotten lost in the mix, great ingredients and careful technique make up for it. If there's a wait for a table, guests can bide their time in the tiny lounge which houses a nice selection of Asian beers and wines.

Adour 

Contemporary XXXX

A2

2 E. 55th St. (at Fifth Ave.)

Subway: 5 Av - 53 St

Dinner nightly

Phone: 212-710-2277

Web: www.adour-stregis.com

Prices: $$$$

Bruce Buck

Tucked behind exquisite wooden doors in the elegant St. Regis New York, this Alain Ducasse stunner is a culinary temple of old-school luxury. So what kind of food lives in a house as graceful as this? Incoming chef, Didier Elena's primarily French menu draws droves, and does it quite well, in fact. Millions were poured into the restaurant's design and every last penny shows—from the exquisitely detailed mouldings and delicate archways to the luxurious banquettes and sparkling glass wine cases illuminating the walls.

It's enough to make you feel like a princess for the night, and the pampering hardly stops there. The all-male service staff, immaculately clad in crisp black suits, is incredibly polished, attending to your every need; the sommelier graciously recommends bottles and glasses, then doubles back to make sure each selection worked out.

Chef Elena's fabulous menu might turn out homemade tagliatelle perfectly crafted with pristine sea urchin fillets swimming in a dreamy sea urchin sauce kissed with fennel and peppercorn; or a moist round of veal doused in a rich demi-glace sauce and plated with sautéed wild mushrooms, wilted baby spinach, and soft pillows of potato gnocchi.

al Bustan

C2

Lebanese XX

319 E. 53rd St. (bet. First & Second Aves.)

Subway: Lexington Av - 53 St Lunch & dinner daily
Phone: 212-759-5933
Web: www.albustanny.com
Prices: $$

With a fresh location comes a whole new outlook on food, service and ambience, and suddenly this tired Lebanese favorite—a longtime staple among the United Nations power crowds—is turning heads again.

They didn't physically move far: al Bustan now resides along a sleepy patch of 53rd Street, just a few blocks from the old digs—but the new home is stunning, with a lofty, brick-walled space featuring enormous crystal chandeliers, white leather chairs, and handsome dark wood accents. And the food, which used to go through the motions, now seems to leap off the plate: gorgeous Lebanese meze like *fattoush, hommos bi lahmeh,* and *foul medamas* are not to be missed; and prix-fixe options at $45 or $50 a head offer a nice way to sample from the menu.

Alcala

C3

Spanish XX

342 E. 46th St. (bet. First & Second Aves.)

Subway: Grand Central - 42 St Lunch Mon – Fri
Phone: 212-370-1866 Dinner nightly
Web: www.alcalarestaurant.com
Prices: $$$

You won't find a lot of the garlic-heavy Spanish staples that Americans have come to know so well at this charming little neighborhood restaurant, located across the street from the United Nations headquarters. Instead, you'll find the rustic, often simple, cuisine found throughout Northern Spain and the Basque region, with a kitchen that is not afraid to bring the pork.

Businessmen, United Nations tourists, and Spanish ex-pats alike pile into Alcala for its cozy-as-home vibe, it's pretty, enclosed garden, and friendly, welcoming staff. Try the *espinacas,* a delicious baked casserole with spinach, pine nuts, raisins, onions, and sheep's milk cheese; or a creamy, decadent *arroz con leche*; and don't leave without sampling one of the mean house sangrias.

Alto ✿✿

Italian XXX

A2

11 E. 53rd St. (bet. Fifth & Madison Aves.)

Subway: 5 Av - 53 St
Phone: 212-308-1099
Web: www.altorestaurant.com
Prices: $$$$

Lunch Mon – Fri
Dinner Mon – Sat

Melissa Hom

An authentic piece of the Berlin Wall marks the entrance to this elegant Midtown restaurant, whose name pays homage to Alto Adige, a region on the fringe of Italy and Austria. The gorgeous decor is sophisticated and contemporary boasting an elegant-but-hip business palette of muted browns and lime green; and the marvelously exquisite cuisine has throngs flocking back for more.

It's not that strudel and schnitzel doesn't have its place—its just that Chef Michael White's straightforward Northern Italian food, carefully executed at Alto by Chef de Cuisine Gordon Finn, temporarily erases other cuisines from the picture.

The seasonal, rotating menu happily zigzags between pasta, meat, and seafood, and might even reveal a country-style oxtail and foie gras terrine served with pear *mostarda* and pickled chanterelles; a gorgeous tangle of fresh spaghetti lying amidst sea urchin, sweet dungeness crab, and smoky pancetta; or silky poached halibut dressed in a creamy purée of fresh chickpeas, artichokes, and a drizzle of lemon oil. Grape hounds cannot miss the Italian wine list, which offers a healthy by-the-glass selection as well as an impressive display of vintages.

Ammos Estiatorio

B4 **Greek** XX

52 Vanderbilt Ave. (at 45th St.)

Subway: Grand Central - 42 St — Lunch Mon – Fri
Phone: 212-922-9999 — Dinner Mon – Sat
Web: www.ammosnewyork.com
Prices: $$$

Duck into sunny and sophisticated Ammos, right across from Grand Central station, and leave gray skies behind. Favoring a certain modern Mediterranean-meets-Manhattan elegance, this upscale Greek brightens the midtown lunch crowds with white market umbrellas hanging from the ceiling, warm yet efficient service, and a well-run kitchen serving time-honored favorites with contemporary flair.

The fresh and modern boosts are clear in *spanikopita*, prepared with well-flavored feta and spinach between two crisp, golden layers of phyllo, jazzed up with light tomato sauce and mint olive oil. Salads, the Ammos fries, and a three-course prix-fixe are most popular at lunch, while quieter dinners feature a large selection of entrées and fresh fish by-the-pound.

Aquavit

B2 **Scandinavian** XXX

65 E. 55th St. (bet. Madison & Park Aves.)

Subway: 5 Av - 53 St — Lunch & dinner daily
Phone: 212-307-7311
Web: www.aquavit.org
Prices: $$$

Former second-in-command, Marcus Jernmark, now takes the wheel at New York's most famous Swedish restaurant, and the results are delicious, right down to the house-infused namesake drink.

The elegant, Scandinavian-styled restaurant offers a serene café with an elegant menu and a mod bar outfitted with clever Arne Jacobson egg swivel chairs and a carte of lighter offerings. Those looking for the most ambitious menu can head back to the formal dining room (you may want to don a jacket), where the polished staff walks guests through delicious fare like a duck sausage pâté with pickled root vegetables, fried shallots, and a quenelle of coarse-grained mustard; or tender, perfectly poached cod served with *ängamat*, blanched carrots, snap peas, and fresh dill.

Armani Ristorante

Italian XX

A1

717 Fifth Ave. (at 56th St.)

Subway: 5 Av - 59 St — Lunch daily
Phone: 212-207-1902 — Dinner Mon – Sat
Web: www.armani5thavenue.com
Prices: $$$

Ascend the three-story spiral staircase, past elegant floors of the eponymous clothing line, to arrive in a stunning space cloaked in dramatic, high-design spectacle. Perched above posh 5th Avenue over the Armani store, this dining room is styled with floor-to-ceiling windows bedecked in twinkling strands of fiber-optic lights, round futuristic furniture, and black ceilings and floors.

While its impressive design may align well with haute couture, the well-groomed (yet ill-informed) service staff falls short, and the food itself can be pedestrian; still, dishes do satisfy. Expect the likes of excellent quality veal filet, Parmesan-encrusted sea bass, or crispy meringue stacked with nutty praline *semifreddo,* topped with sticky-sweet *amarena* cherries.

Artisanal

French XX

A6

2 Park Ave. (entrance on 32nd St.)

Subway: 33 St — Lunch & dinner daily
Phone: 212-725-8585
Web: www.artisanalbistro.com
Prices: $$

Terrance Brennan's much-loved restaurant serves a whole roster of bistro delights (think chicken paillard, tuna niçoise, and steamed mussels) but the real fans of Artisanal treat the place like their own private cheese club. Brennan has a passion for the stuff, and the restaurant has oodles of varieties as well as an on-site cheese cave—that you can enjoy it in a lively, upscale brasserie only makes it even more fun.

Choose a glass of wine from the extensive list, and get to work on a perfectly prepared basket of *gougères,* savory little fried cheese pastries paired with fruit chutney; or an irresistible croque monsieur, sporting tender prosciutto, soft Gruyere, and a delicious lick of browned béchamel, paired with a crunchy stack of house-made chips.

Asia de Cuba 

A5 — Fusion XX

237 Madison Ave. (bet. 37th & 38th Sts.)

Subway: Grand Central - 42 St — Lunch Mon – Fri
Phone: 212-726-7755 — Dinner nightly
Web: www.chinagrillmgt.com
Prices: $$

Think Asian-Latin fusion is played out? Welcome to the restaurant that wrote the book on it—and every time you find yourself wandering back into this Manhattan staple, you're once again blown away by the glam crowds; contagious happy hour buzz (don't miss the house cocktails); and mouth-watering fusion fare. Asia De Cuba still nails it.

Philippe Starck designed the space—a sultry, bi-level affair tucked inside the Morgans Hotel in Murray Hill—which features, among other things, a huge waterfall hologram and 50-foot community table. Tuck into dishes like the Thai-spiced salad with chili-rubbed avocado, shredded coconut, and orange; or a honey-and-rum glazed pot roast of pork, paired with sautéed Shanghai bok choy, fried plantains, and enoki mushrooms.

Avra Estiatorio

B3 — Greek 

141 E. 48th St. (bet. Lexington & Third Aves.)

Subway: 51 St — Lunch & dinner daily
Phone: 212-759-8550
Web: www.avrany.com
Prices: $$$

Inviting, from its outdoor terrace to it cavernous dining room, Avra sparkles as a true gem in the heart of midtown. Limestone floors, arched doorways, and colorful crockery suggest a Greek tavern in this always lively space. Billowing fabric laced through the wood ceiling beams brings to mind sailing and the sea, and sets the tone for the seafood-centric menu.

Check out the day's fresh catch, laid out on ice in the front dining room. Fish are grilled whole over charcoal, then drizzled with olive oil and a squeeze of lemon, yielding simple but delicious results. If you go this route—there are other selections on the menu as well—note that your choice of fish will be priced per pound, so keep this in mind if your eyes are bigger than your budget.

Barbès

Mediterranean

21 E. 36th St. (bet. Fifth & Madison Aves.)

Subway: 33 St — Lunch & dinner daily
Phone: 212-684-0215
Web: www.barbesrestaurantnyc.com
Prices: $$

Named for a North African neighborhood near Montmartre, this sultry French-Moroccan restaurant draws hustling city slickers in from the dreary gray streets of midtown with its warm, rustic good looks. Duck past the elaborately carved wooden façade that marks the entrance and you'll find a handsome dining room bathed in burnt orange walls and exposed brick, with a lovely beamed ceiling overhead.

Guests keep sated with zesty, if simple fare, like a smoky, creamy eggplant purée served with toasted pita bread; and tender, charred lamb kebabs paired with a scoop of tangy yogurt sauce. And while the food surely hits the spot, the real draw at Barbès might be the service, which manages to be as warm and polished as the restaurant itself.

Bice

Italian

7 E. 54th St. (bet. Fifth & Madison Aves.)

Subway: 5 Av - 53 St — Lunch & dinner daily
Phone: 212-688-1999
Web: www.bicenewyork.com
Prices: $$$

In a neighborhood teeming with subdued, upscale façades, Bice cuts a cheerful figure with its bright canopies and stream of people walking to and fro. Perhaps it can't help but give off some of that upbeat Milan bustle—the restaurant, which now boasts 40 locations world-wide, began in Italy's most fashionable city.

Judging from the longevity of this location, the formula—solid upscale Northern Italian cuisine in unique city-specific settings—works. Open for lunch and dinner, Bice stays thumping day and night with fashionable diners tucking into tender tagliolini with lobster, shiitake mushrooms, blistered tomatoes, chunky tomato sauce, and a float of basil chiffonade; or crispy *cantuccini*, laced with roasted almonds or chocolate biscotti.

BLT Steak

Steakhouse XXX

B1

106 E. 57th St. (bet. Lexington & Park Aves.)

Subway: 59 St
Phone: 212-752-7470
Web: www.bltrestaurants.com
Prices: $$$$

Lunch Mon – Fri
Dinner Mon – Sat

The en masse belt-tightening hasn't hit BLT Steak—an unexampled and global version of an American steakhouse—which still packs them shoulder-to-shoulder despite the crummy economy. Likely because it's easy to forget your troubles in this lively, elegant steakhouse, which not only dishes up beautifully-executed classic cuts alongside Kobe and Wagyu, but a heady dose of daily specials, fresh fish, and exquisite side dishes as well.

Adding to the abundant spirit are a bunch of delicious, unfussy sides, like towering stacks of crunchy onion rings; clever little complimentary extras like duck mousse; and enormous desserts, big enough to split. Watch for sticker shock on the wine list, though—a better deal can be found glass-by-glass.

Bobby Van's Steakhouse

Steakhouse XX

B3

230 Park Ave. (at 46th St.)

Subway: Grand Central - 42 St
Phone: 212-867-5490
Web: www.bobbyvans.com
Prices: $$$$

Lunch Mon – Sat
Dinner Mon – Sat

This scene is so powerful that it intoxicates. A regular flock of bankers and brokers (entering through the passageway beneath the Helmsley Building at 46th and Park) seek this clubby and boisterous favorite for its scene, pricey wines, and those towering shellfish platters, served with flourish and perhaps a gruff edge.

After starters like the popular steakhouse wedge salad with fried onions and bacon, arrives the meaty main attraction. These steaks are cooked exactly as ordered and carved tableside, with sides like fried zucchini served family-style.

After work, the bar is adorned with addictive house-made potato chips and offers a lighter menu as it comes alive with well-shaken martinis.

Note that Bobby Van's has four other locations in Manhattan.

Bottega del Vino

Italian XX

7 E. 59th St. (bet. Fifth & Madison Aves.)

Subway: 5 Av - 59 St — Lunch & dinner daily
Phone: 212-223-2724
Web: www.bottegadelvinonyc.com
Prices: $$$$

Owner Severino Barzan picked a primo location just off Fifth Avenue for this charmingly rustic wine tavern. In the alluring sun-colored space, adorned with painted columns, carved dark-wood walls, cozy banquettes, and shelves of wine bottles, a stylish and loyal Euro-crowd gathers to sip wine and revel in authentic Northern Italian fare.

Pasta dishes and house specialties best display the kitchen's talent. Elegant and delicate, house-made ravioli filled with velvety Gorgonzola *dolce*, paired with a nutty pistachio sauce is nothing short of amazing.

Serious contenders from the Veneto and Piemonte regions of Italy are highlights of the blockbuster wine list. Wines are served in hand-blown, lead-free glassware that was custom-made for the restaurant.

Brasserie

Contemporary XX

100 E. 53rd St. (bet. Lexington & Park Aves.)

Subway: Lexington Av - 53 St — Lunch & dinner daily
Phone: 212-751-4840
Web: www.rapatina.com/brasserie
Prices: $$$

As it toasts its 50th anniversary with vintage cocktails, Brasserie somehow creates a 21st century vision of its French counterpart with a retro-modern design and interpreted standards. This dovetails nicely with its location in the basement of Ludwig Mies van der Rohe's 1958 Seagram Building. Cameras at the catwalk entry feed the TV screens above the bar, displaying your arrival to the dining room of people-watchers.

The focus is on French classics reinvented with American flair, as in the frisée salad with lardons and Roquefort cheese. The largely corporate-crowd-pleasing offerings may include rotisserie chicken or côte-du-bœuf for two. Skip the mediocre pommes frites to save room for the decadent yet light and sugary chocolate beignets.

Bukhara Grill

Indian

217 E. 49th St. (bet. Second & Third Aves.)

Subway: 51 St — Lunch & dinner daily
Phone: 212-888-2839
Web: www.bukharany.com
Prices: **$$**

Blazing Bukhara Grill's dusky space exudes sophistication, drama, and a dash of kitsch. The upper level leans contemporary; while the rustic and timbered dining room is dressed in tables carved from tree-trunks, Indian artwork, and stoneware. Sink into a lush booth and gaze at imposing masters manning fiery tandoors.

Waiters in traditional garb present upscale diners with foods from India's Northwest Frontier region. Bite into juicy chicken *malai kebab* marinated in ginger, garlic, and spices; *aloo bukhara korma* starring saucy lamb chunks dancing with apricots and potatoes; and the forever beloved *kurkuri bindi*—crispy okra tossed with onions, spices, and coriander. Piles of puffy bread, straight out of the oven, reveal a committed chef and kitchen.

The Capital Grille

Steakhouse

B4

155 E. 42nd St. (bet. Lexington & Third Aves.)

Subway: Grand Central - 42 St — Lunch Mon – Fri
Phone: 212-953-2000 — Dinner nightly
Web: www.thecapitalgrille.com
Prices: **$$$$**

East of Grand Central Terminal, clubby Capital Grille occupies the ground floor of the Chrysler Building complex. The large space harmonizes with leather chairs, mahogany paneling, and gold-framed paintings.

Dry-aged sirloins and tender veal chops arrive perfectly grilled to your requested temperature, with sides like Parmesan-truffle fries that are sure to exceed your calorie count. Entrée-sized chopped salads with citrus-grilled shrimp or classic burgers are popular at lunch.

Let its central location be a reminder to book ahead; the full menu is also available at the long bar, a choice post-work perch. While the professional staff ensures that any wait will be made comfortable, nothing may dampen the blow of the bill, besides an expense-account.

Casa Lever

Italian XXX

B2

390 Park Ave. (entrance on 53rd St.)

Subway: Lexington Av - 53 St — Lunch & dinner daily
Phone: 212-888-2700
Web: www.casalever.com
Prices: $$$

What used to be the Lever House is now the new restaurant, Casa Lever, and though the general scene hasn't changed too much—a unique, retro-modern dining room shaped like a hexagon, where well-heeled Upper East Siders clink glasses in slick, elevated booths—the elegant Italian dishes seem to have taken a step in a very delicious direction.

Kick things off with a plate of nicely seared calamari, served with fresh spring peas, sautéed baby carrots, and rendered pieces of *guanciale*; and then move on to perfectly al dente pockets of homemade ravioli filled with braised duck and laced with brown butter and mushrooms. Finish with a fresh square of moist tiramisu that arrives plated with lovely *langue du chat* and *palmier* cookies. *Perfetto.*

Cellini

Italian XX

B2

65 E. 54th St. (bet. Madison & Park Aves.)

Subway: Lexington Av - 53 St — Lunch Mon – Fri
Phone: 212-751-1555 — Dinner nightly
Web: www.cellinirestaurant.com
Prices: $$$

With its pleasant informality, lively atmosphere, efficient service, and high quality selection of deliciously simple Italian classics, Cellini appeals to all. Even old-school Italian-American standards, like grilled Atlantic calamari, are served with the care and culinary attention often reserved for fancier food. Good flavors and skill are demonstrated in pasta offerings, like their signature spaghetti and meatballs or seafood risotto, brimming with shellfish, roasted artichokes, and shallots in a white wine-lobster broth.

A concise, well-chosen wine list featuring Italian labels plus crowd-pleasers from around the world, a polite waitstaff well-versed in the menu, and undeniable warmth justify Cellini's popularity among locals and tourists alike.

Chado

Japanese XX

A5

4 E. 36th St. (bet. Fifth & Madison Aves.)

Subway: 34 St - Herald Sq
Phone: 212-532-2210
Web: www.chadonyc.com
Prices: $$

Lunch Mon – Fri
Dinner nightly

This new upscale sushi restaurant arrives courtesy of a newfound partnership between Omar Balouma, of Barbès (located across the street) and Babouche (in Brooklyn), and Sushi of Gari's executive chef, Mike Lim. The space is sleek, pale, and pretty—with exposed brick walls, creamy white walls, and hardwood floors. Throw in a handful of chefs trained under the legendary sushi chef, Masatoshi "Gari" Sugio, and you've got yourself a heck of a new place to throw down a few rolls.

The menu rounds the usual sushi bases—and it is lovely sushi indeed—but also offers appetizers like sautéed oysters with garlic-chive sauce and organic egg; and dinner options like pistachio shrimp with crab roe, or sea bass with sake-infused roasted seaweed sauce.

Chiam

Chinese XX

B3

160 E. 48th St. (bet. Lexington & Third Aves.)

Subway: 51 St
Phone: 212-371-2323
Web: www.chiamnyc.com
Prices: $$

Lunch Sun – Fri
Dinner nightly

Don't confuse Chiam with the neighboring noodle joints. Chiam may not have the neighborhood authenticity of Chinatown, or the star appeal of Mr Chow, but it continues to win diners over with its serious Chinese cuisine and top-notch service. Think of this place, with its elegant dining room, quality wine list, and well-heeled clientele, as a choice for a special-occasion feast or an expense-account dinner.

Presenting Cantonese preparations with flair, the kitchen staff uses excellent products and a refined technique that yields consistently good and well-balanced fare. Dishes, such as the rich Grand Marnier prawns, are intended to be shared; order some steamed or sautéed vegetables to round out the mix.

Convivio ✿

Italian XXX

C4

45 Tudor City Pl. (bet. 42nd & 43rd Sts.)

Subway: Grand Central - 42 St
Phone: 212-599-5045
Web: www.convivionyc.com
Prices: $$$

Lunch Mon – Fri
Dinner nightly

Melissa Hom

Partners Michael White and Chris Cannon dropped the curtain on L'Impero to bestow this beautiful surprise on New York City, and the city's high-end Italian food scene hasn't been the same since.

First, there's the whodathunkit location in Tudor City, a lovely little residential nook overlooking the United Nations that's flown under the radar about as long as it can. Then there's the unendingly-elegant space, which offers a small, intimate lounge to kick off your evening; and a gorgeously-appointed dining room, decked out in luxurious silk drapes, smooth sienna banquettes, and a slick, lacquered ceiling, to finish it in.

But the real star of this show is Chef Michael White's Southern Italian menu, backed by a great Italian wine list and a recession-proof $62 four-course prix-fixe option. Dinner spins to the season, but might reveal homemade tomato and *guanciale* confit tortelli pooled in a creamy *cacio e pepe* sauce; succulent lobster meat, served with *fregola sarda* and baby fennel in a spicy *acqua pazza* broth; crispy, roasted baby potatoes showered in soft pecorino; or a dark chocolate ganache and caramel tart, studded with sea salt and paired with soft vanilla gelato.

Dardanel

Turkish XX

C1

1071 First Ave. (bet. 58th & 59th Sts.)

Subway: 59 St — Lunch & dinner daily
Phone: 212-888-0809
Web: www.dardanelnyc.com
Prices: $$

A recent arrival, Dardanel's bright ocean-themed exterior stands out against the rather bleak block on which it sits. Inside, low lighting, mellow tunes, exposed brick, and colorful walls create a lovely atmosphere where a warm and welcoming vibe complement the Mediterranean and Turkish fare.

The house *manti* are reason alone for a visit; these divine micro-versions of the Turkish dumplings are tenderly soaked in a yogurt-garlic sauce. Otherwise, house specialties and starters are the way to go—try the flavorful zucchini pancakes, or shrimp casserole (brick-oven baked with tomatoes, peppers, and mushrooms in a creamy tomato sauce, topped with *kasserie* cheese).

The place hums with a mix of neighborhood locals—a cozy spot for a casual dinner or date.

Don's Bogam

Korean XX

A6

17 E. 32nd St. (bet. Fifth & Madison Aves.)

Subway: 33 St — Lunch & dinner daily
Phone: 212-683-2200
Web: www.donsbogam.com
Prices: $$

K-town gets a kick in the pants from this exciting, group-friendly newcomer. The pretty, contemporary room features a few different seating options, but big parties will want to head for the sleek, modern floor-level tables fitted out with private tabletop grills and specially designed cavities for dangling your feet.

The menu is typically massive—with a bevy of lunch and dinner specials (served both à la carte and as sampler barbecue combos) and *banchan* accompanying most dishes. The atypical thing is the quality and freshness arriving in plates like *mandu*, traditional Korean pork and vegetable dumplings; grilled and marinated barbecue shrimp; or barbecue *bulgogi*, a heavenly pile of tissue-thin beef flash-cooked with cabbage, sprouts, and noodles.

East Side Social Club

Italian XX

C2

230 E. 51st St. (bet. Second & Third Aves.)

Subway: 51 St
Phone: 212-355-9442
Web: www.esscnyc.com
Prices: $$$

Lunch Mon – Sat
Dinner nightly

The name offers the first hint: East Side Social Club is way more downtown speakeasy than earnest midtown. But here it resides nonetheless, housed in a large, cavernous space along East 51st Street, where a big lounge area gives way to a dining room that's part supper club and part Italian bistro; and spacey waitresses hustle to and fro in cocktail outfits.

P.J. Clarke's, this ain't—but the place stays hopping all day and night with an interesting mix of corporate and scenesters, likely because despite the darkness, the food is surprisingly good and the cocktails seriously well made. Try the juicy free range chicken, perfectly cooked "under a brick" and paired with panzanella; or the steak fries saltimbocca draped with prosciutto and Parmesean.

El Parador

Mexican XX

B6

325 E. 34th St. (bet. First & Second Aves.)

Subway: 33 St
Phone: 212-679-6812
Web: www.elparadorcafe.com
Prices: $$

Lunch & dinner daily

For 50 years, El Parador has been pleasing generations of New Yorkers with killer margaritas, tasty Mexican food, accommodating staff, and its "you want it, you got it" ethos (don't hesitate to order something not found on the menu).

Also, do not be deterred by its Midtown Tunnel location or façade that suggests it is a spot where real drinkers drink. Its warm interior offers some of the best tasting Mexican-influenced food around, as in the taco tray—spilling with savories from beef *picadillo* to chorizo, it is as fun and satisfying to prepare as to eat. Equally tasty are the nachos: crisp tortillas spread evenly with toppings and cleanly sliced for easy eating. Wash it down with a sip (or several) of their excellent tequila and perfect margaritas.

Ethos

Greek XX

905 First Ave. (at 51st St.)

Subway: 51 St — Lunch & dinner daily
Phone: 212-888-4060
Web: www.ethosrestaurants.com
Prices: $$

The Murray Hill locals may have hated to part with the beloved, but shabby, Meltemi that used to rent here, but what's emerged in its place might be even better. At once bright, modern and elegant, the stylish new Ethos is bathed in natural light by day; by night, the lights dim and the room fills up with a lively, well-dressed crowd.

The food is solid, not extraordinary, with a menu filled with impossibly lengthy Greek names that evolve into dishes like a smoky roasted eggplant spread with garlic, parsley, olive oil, oregano, and lemon; a country salad with tangy feta, bright red tomatoes, and kalamata olives dancing in a light lemon-olive oil dressing; or a decidedly decadent chicken, baked in a casserole with orzo, tomato, and feta.

Felidia

C1

Italian XX

243 E. 58th St. (bet. Second & Third Aves.)

Subway: Lexington Av - 59 St — Lunch Mon – Fri
Phone: 212-758-1479 — Dinner nightly
Web: www.lidiasitaly.com
Prices: $$$

For the past 25 years, Felidia has attracted a huge, loyal, and diverse following of well-heeled regulars. TV personality and cookbook author Lidia Bastianich's flagship is housed in a cozy brownstone with a copper-topped bar, warm colors, polished wood, and seating on two levels. Wine racks prominently showcase the restaurant's vast, mostly Italian, and very impressive list.

While Lidia is no stranger here, Sicilian-born Chef Fortunato Nicotra skillfully mans the stoves, where for more than a decade he has turned out tempting pastas like spinach tagliatelle with braised Hudson Valley duck and mushrooms; or pear and fresh pecorino-filled ravioli; as well as regional fare and tasting menus. Many dishes are elegantly finished in the dining room.

Fiorini

Italian 

B1

209 E. 56th St. (bet. Second & Third Aves.)

Subway: Lexington Av - 53 St — Lunch Mon – Fri
Phone: 212-308-0830 — Dinner Mon – Sat
Web: www.fiorinirestaurant.com
Prices: $$$

Lello Arpaia and his son, Dino, are masters at the hospitality trade, and they run their Italian eatery, Fiorini, (which translates to little flower) so tightly that you can't help but leave with a special fondness for the place. Make your way past the elegant front bar, and you'll find an intimate, honey-toned dining room aglow in warm pastels and buzzing with a quietly professional service staff.

Modern, straightforward Italian best describes the menu, where you'll find any number of comfort classics along with a lineup of fresh, silky pastas like a perfectly luscious al dente spaghettini *alla carbonara*, tossed with organic egg, fresh Pecorino Romano, cracked pepper, and sweet crumbles of bacon. Polished off with the house espresso? Perfect!

The Four Seasons

American 

B2

99 E. 52nd St. (bet. Lexington & Park Aves.)

Subway: 51 St — Lunch Mon – Fri
Phone: 212-754-9494 — Dinner Mon – Sat
Web: www.fourseasonsrestaurant.com
Prices: $$$$

There is nothing like a night in the pool room, known as the erstwhile country club of New York's elite. The décor—like the crowd—remains stunningly elegant. With monumental floral arrangements that change with the seasons, the entrance to this landmark building will take your breath away.

The food may be on par with a fancy wedding banquet and the service barely adequate for the undistinguished guest, but a quick glimpse at Henry Kissinger and cronies is worth the staggering price tag for one night among the powerful.

The Grill Room is the spot for lunch, where regulars have had their tables long-assigned on the legendary seating chart, while the bar is an impressive place for a cocktail, and surely worth an early arrival to absorb the scene.

Fresco by Scotto

Italian 

34 E. 52nd St. (bet. Madison & Park Aves.)

Subway: 5 Av - 53 St — Lunch Mon – Fri
Phone: 212-935-3434 — Dinner Mon – Sat
Web: www.frescobyscotto.com
Prices: $$$

Despite a location near Rockefeller Center that draws on expense accounts and nearby NBC executives (perhaps the same ones who just produced the Scotto family recipe demonstrations on The Today Show), Fresco by Scotto exudes a comfortable yet cosmopolitan aura. Unobtrusive service and sound Italian-American cuisine enhance the dining room's simple elegance.

Lunch and dinner menus list rustic and robust dishes, including "Fresco Originals" like penne gratin, a hearty pasta with julienned prosciutto di Parma, peas, fontina, provolone, parmigiano, finished with cream and cracked pepper. Equally enticing are their grilled sweet sausages, seasoned with cheese and parsley, in roasted pepper and onion ragù.

Try Fresco on the go for a quick lunch fix.

HanGawi

Korean 

12 E. 32nd St. (bet. Fifth & Madison Aves.)

Subway: 33 St — Lunch & dinner daily
Phone: 212-213-0077
Web: www.hangawirestaurant.com
Prices: $$

Don't worry about wearing your best shoes to HanGawi; you'll have to take them off at the door before settling in at one of the restaurant's low tables. In the serene space, decorated with Korean artifacts and soothed by meditative music, it's easy to forget you're in Manhattan.

The menu is all vegetarian, in keeping with the philosophy of healthy cooking to balance the *um* and *yang*. You can quite literally eat like a king here starting with vermicelli delight (sweet potato noodles), perfectly crisp kimchi and mushroom pancakes, devastatingly delicious tofu clay pot in ginger sauce, and the regal kimchi stone bowl rice made fragrant with fresh veggies. Of course, you'll have to rejoin the crowds outside. Still, it's nice to get away... now and Zen.

Gilt ✿✿

Contemporary

A3

455 Madison Ave. (bet. 50th & 51st Sts.)

Subway: 51 St — Dinner Tue – Sat
Phone: 212-891-8100
Web: www.giltnewyork.com
Prices: **$$$$**

The New York Palace

It's tough to do Gilt's "wow factor" justice by words alone, but let's give it a go. Imagine strolling past a beautiful, iron-gated courtyard and gliding up the New York Palace Hotel's historic Villard Mansion's sweeping staircase. Inside, you feast your eyes on Gilt's ornate, renaissance-styled dining room—impossibly opulent, with sparkling mosaic floors, soaring, mile-high ceilings, and a glossy marble fireplace.

And still the best is yet to come, for Gilt's real gimme is that the food actually stacks up to all that grandeur thanks to Chef Justin Bogle. Dinner might begin with a plate of tender, perfectly caramelized diver scallops garnished with puréed pumpkin, crispy baby Brussels sprouts, and a drizzle of root beer sauce; and then move on to juicy, rosy-pink ribeye, topped with golden breadcrumbs and Manchego and paired with velvety dots of arugula purée and quince paste.

Guests can put together their own 3-course menu from a list of options for $89, or scale up to the 5-course chef's tasting or the 7-course grand tasting menu, which clocks in at $140 without wine. Going without the grape is a shame, though, for Gilt has a great collection; not to mention a fabulous tea list.

Jubilee

French 

347 E. 54th St. (bet. First & Second Aves.)

Subway: Lexington Av - 53 St
Phone: 212-888-3569
Web: www.jubileeny.net
Prices: **$$**

Lunch Sun – Fri
Dinner nightly

Don't tell Turtle Bay, but the secret is out on their beloved neighborhood bistro. With its charming, Old Europe ambience and cozy, close-knit tables, Jubilee was securing two-tops for locals long before the rest of Manhattan decided to horn in on the action. No wonder—the French-Belgian menu is a heady lineup of bistro comfort classics like duck leg confit, escargots, profiteroles, and Prince Edward Island mussels (the house specialty) prepared five different ways.

A warm goat cheese salad arrives brimming with roasted tomatoes and drizzled in a honey and sherry vinaigrette; while a plate of tender mussels is broiled up Provençale-style in garlic and parsley butter, and paired with an addictive stack of crispy frites and a vibrant green salad.

Kurumazushi

Japanese 

A3

7 E. 47th St. (bet. Fifth & Madison Aves.)

Subway: 47-50 Sts - Rockefeller Ctr
Phone: 212-317-2802
Web: www.kurumazushi.com
Prices: **$$$$**

Lunch & dinner Mon – Sat

Hidden in the second story of a bland office building, Kurumazushi is marked by little more than a few plain letters on a nondescript door. Push past this red herring and head upstairs to find impeccable service and a small room dressed in red, white, and black.

This is the house of Toshihiro Uezu, an omakase master of the first order—trust in this chef's choice succession of outstanding sushi (best toro in town), which seems to have swam here from the Tokyo market before its expert preparation. Some loyalists might argue that behind the counter the deft touch of the chef has become inconsistent, yet a dinner here will nonetheless blow your socks off for quality of fish. Of course, so might the hefty bill—a price likely overshadowed by that creamy toro.

La Fonda Del Sol

Spanish XXX

B4

200 Park Ave. (entrance on Vanderbilt Ave.)

Subway: Grand Central - 42 St
Lunch & dinner Mon – Sat
Phone: 212-867-6767
Web: www.patinagroup.com
Prices: $$$

The requisite bullfighter photographs hang on the walls of La Fonda Del Sol, but little else is typical in this Patina Group establishment located in the MetLife building. It has a bit of a split personality; downstairs is a sleek tapas bar and lounge popular with the after-work crowd, while the upstairs is home to a shimmering, gold-accented Adam Tihany-designed dining room.

Latin flavors and ingredients are boldly paired in ways that would make your *abuela* blush. The chef employs a creative take on Spanish cuisine, working like a mad scientist on adventurous dishes such as delicate fresh halibut topped in a "salsa verde" highlighting powdered Padrón peppers, or pumpkin-seed tacos with ribbons of sushi-grade tuna, finished with creamy avocado mousse.

La Grenouille

French XXX

A2

3 E. 52nd St. (bet. Fifth & Madison Aves.)

Subway: 5 Av - 53 St
Lunch Tue – Fri
Phone: 212-752-1495
Dinner Mon ––Sat
Web: www.la-grenouille.com
Prices: $$$$

Like the Judi Dench of French dining, La Grenouille is a respected holdout from another era in Manhattan's fine dining scene—one where white-coated servers fussed over you in a setting fit for royalty. But as over-the-top as the dining room might appear nowadays—think high coffered ceilings, plush red banquettes, and opulent flower arrangements—there is something comforting for the well-heeled regulars who have been calling this Masson family mainstay its second home (one where you're required to wear jackets) since 1962.

Quickly disappearing old-world dishes like *quenelles* and *rognons* share menu space with dishes like duck confit, served over warm green lentils; and tender chicken paillard, paired with crispy sage and tender squash gnocchi.

La Mangeoire

C2 French XX

1008 Second Ave. (bet. 53rd & 54th Aves.)

Subway: Lexington Av - 53 St
Phone: 212-759-7086
Web: www.lamangeoire.com
Prices: **$$**

Lunch Sun – Fri
Dinner nightly

Gorgeous, top-notch ingredients; simple, lovely, and authentic Provençal preparations by a critically-acclaimed chef; a sunny ambience that transports you up and out of midtown and into the South of France—what's not to love here? La Mangeoire may have been around for a while, but incoming chef, Christian Delouvrier, who leaves a trail of starred restaurants in his wake, just gave this neighborhood favorite the booster shot it richly deserves. The dust has been wiped, and underneath lays a very bright gem indeed.

Try the delicious *pizzette antiboise*, topped with caramelized onions, anchovies, and black olives; the wickedly fresh *moules*; or the irresistible blueberry clafoutis tart paired with crème anglaise, red fruit coulis, and whipped cream.

Le Cirque

B1 

151 E. 58th St. (bet. Lexington & Third Aves.)

Subway: 59 St
Phone: 212-644-0202
Web: www.lecirque.com
Prices: **$$$$**

Lunch Mon – Fri
Dinner Mon – Sat

Nestled into One Beacon Court, this legendary restaurant remains dramatic with huge curving windows, billowing tents draped above the main dining room, and circus motifs gracing the walls. As popular as the décor is the ever-charming host, Sirio, who famously tends to this loyal, old-money clientele, who come here as much for the memories as for the lovely contemporary cuisine.

Offerings may include sautéed Gulf shrimp with kaffir lime, hearts of palm, and carrot confit; or pavé of veal with pear, pecorino, and coffee-cardamom jus. Impressive desserts may include sweet, green pistachio macaroons topped with pistachio paste and fresh raspberries, plated tableside.

The café is another popular dining option, offering a focused menu and excellent value.

L'Atelier de Joël Robuchon ✿

Contemporary XX

B1

57 E. 57th St. (bet. Madison & Park Aves.)

Subway: 5 Av - 59 St — Dinner nightly
Phone: 212-829-3844
Web: www.fourseasons.com/newyork
Prices: $$$$

Durston Saylor Photography

Expect nothing less than impeccable service and scrumptious haute cuisine dished up in a luxurious atmosphere at acclaimed French Chef Joël Robuchon's globe-spanning namesake restaurant.

Located in the mezzanine of the tony Four Seasons Hotel, the Manhattan outpost cuts a slightly more relaxed figure than its sister spaces (there are six locations worldwide), but the power crowd still comes in droves, so dress to impress. While those looking for intimate conversation can always huddle in the soothing blonde woods that frame the main dining room, those looking for a little more action should hit the beautiful pearwood counter, where they can watch the open kitchen work their culinary magic from a cozy perch at the large, u-shaped bar.

Chef Xavier Boyer's menu changes seasonally but might include tender little pouches of foie gras ravioli, bobbing in a delicate broth laced with a chiffonade of Asian herbs; perfectly caramelized quail, laced with luscious foie gras and garnished with a pristine little bundle of herb salad and dense, buttery potato purée; or a fluffy, perfectly cooked yuzu soufflé dusted with powdered sugar and served with a creamy quenelle of Okinawa sugar ice cream.

Le Périgord

C2 **French** XXX

405 E. 52nd St. (off First Ave.)

Subway: 51 St
Phone: 212-755-6244
Web: www.leperigord.com
Prices: $$$

Lunch Mon – Fri
Dinner nightly

With a nostalgic feel that dates back to the 1960s, Le Périgord is a beloved period piece that cossets diners at lavish tables with hand-painted Limoges and fresh roses. Adding further elegance are the tuxedo-clad waiters who proffer formal service to diplomats from the nearby United Nations. This is one of the few places in New York where one still dresses for dinner and bears witness to the beauty in tradition.

The time-honored menu is likewise a classic, celebrating French culinary traditions in an outstanding preparation of foie gras, as well as nearly forgotten favorites, like *île flottante*. Offerings go on to include dishes so perfectly suited to this suddenly unique ambience that they are difficult to find in other NYC restaurants.

Le Relais de Venise

B2 **Steakhouse** XX

590 Lexington Ave. (at 52nd St.)

Subway: 51 St
Phone: 212-758-3989
Web: www.relaisdevenise.com
Prices: $$

Lunch & dinner daily

There is no menu at Le Relais de Venise L'Entrecôte, a Parisian restaurant with a new location set along thumping Lexington Avenue. There is only one $24 option, but it is a delightful option indeed—green salad with tangy mustard vinaigrette and walnuts, followed by juicy steak served in two parts (because you wouldn't want the rest of it to get cold, would you?) laced in the house's mouthwatering secret sauce, with all the crunchy frites you can eat.

With a Parisian décor and waitresses darting around in saucy French maid get-ups, this is a lively joint—all the more reason to pluck a glass of *vino* off the extremely affordable list, sit back and relax. By the time the dessert menu rolls around, you'll have forgotten how stressful decisions can be.

Maloney & Porcelli

American XXX

B3

37 E. 50th St. (bet. Madison & Park Aves.)

Subway: 51 St
Phone: 212-750-2233
Web: www.maloneyandporcelli.com
Prices: $$$

Lunch Mon – Fri
Dinner nightly

Much more than a steakhouse, this upbeat and versatile spot is sure to exceed expectations. Note that the first sign of this excess is clear in portion control, with entrée-sized starters, and a Flintstone-sized Porterhouse that has you bringing the bone home for Dino. Pleasant surprises are equally evident in crowd-pleasing offerings like tuna and avocado tartare or the outrageous house signature, crackling pork shank with firecracker applesauce.

Wine glasses and peppermills are also enormous, supplementing the philosophy that more is more. Unfortunately, this also extends to the check—a reminder that these big meals carry big prices. Nonetheless, it is appropriately jammed with an expense-account crowd, and the bar remains very popular post-work.

Métrazur

American XX

B4

Grand Central Terminal

Subway: Grand Central - 42 St
Phone: 212-687-4600
Web: www.charliepalmer.com
Prices: $$$

Lunch Mon – Fri
Dinner Mon – Sat

This serene perch (named for a bygone train that traveled the Côte d'Azur) shows the other side of Grand Central Terminal, best seen from this enviable east balcony setting. Transporting diners from the hubbub below, it commands spectacular views of the station's cavernous main concourse and celestial ceiling.

Charlie Palmer's signature American cuisine enhances the ambience with a variety of contemporary dishes incorporating premium seasonal ingredients, such as tarte flambé with ewe's blue cheese, caramelized onions, and roasted pears; or "10 hour" veal pappardelle with caramelized porcini, fava beans, and Parmesan foam.

Lunches offer salads, and sandwiches to business crowds, while the bar is a primo spot for post-work, pre-train cocktails.

Mapo Tofu

B5

Chinese

338 Lexington Ave. (bet. 39th & 40th Sts.)

Subway: Grand Central - 42 St
Phone: 212-867-8118
Web: N/A
Prices:

Lunch & dinner daily

Just when you think you're sated, this Sichuan Shangri-la bestows you with another boon. At Mapo Tofu it's not just about tofu, but their sumptuous Sichuan; it's not about spicy, but the expert marriage of spices; and it's not about ambience—a slim room with tables and slapdash servers—but the genius locale and superior spread that hoists it into a league of its own.

Start this Sichuan safari with sliced conch steeping in roasted chili vinaigrette; string beans with bamboo shoots and pork are an incredible item; and braised fish, tofu, and cellophane noodles carry a fiercely flavorful chili broth. Camphor tea-smoked duck; *dan dan* noodles with pork; and wok-tossed prawns with spiced salt and Sichuan peppercorns are stunning, flavor-ridden plates.

Matisse

C3

French

924 Second Ave. (at 49th St.)

Subway: 51 St
Phone: 212-546-9300
Web: www.matissenyc.com
Prices: **$$**

Lunch & dinner daily

Matisse might be smack dab in midtown, but this tightly packed, sun-filled bistro looks and feels more downtown. Informal without being casual, this single room restaurant with a front row seat to the action of Second Avenue has that typical New York lack of elbow room, but forever lively and whizzing spirit.

Young and old area denizens are lured by the simple and classic French cooking with a reasonable price tag. The menu presents an appealing range of comfort foods, such as caramelized onion tarte and *croque monsieur*. Sunday brunch delivers the goods with omelets and French toast alongside other usual suspects. Some of the dishes are presented on delightfully rustic wooden boards and exude charm thereby displaying Matisse's stylish flair.

Mia Dona

Italian XX

B1

206 E. 58th St. (bet. Second & Third Aves.)

Subway: 59 St
Phone: 212-750-8170
Web: www.miadona.com
Prices: $$$

Lunch Mon – Fri
Dinner nightly

Donatella Arpaia may have dumped Michael Psilakis but Mia Dona is none the lesser for it. In fact, the divorce allowed Arpaia to revamp the menu here to focus on the *cucina povera* she grew up eating in Puglia. It's a family affair with recipes donated by her mother and aunts for comforting dishes of rustic cuisine. It feels like home in plates of Zia Rosa's *orecchiette con ragù,* little pasta ears catching the rich sauce topped with shaved *ricotta salata,* or Mama Maria's *polpette* in a tomato sauce with savory richness from the simmering meatballs. *Trippa al pomodoro* is a standout accompanied by nutty grilled garlic toast.

Still comfortable and stylish, the interior is sunny, bright, and replete with personable service as well as a well-heeled crowd.

Michael Jordan's

Steakhouse XX

B4

Grand Central Terminal

Subway: Grand Central - 42 St
Phone: 212-655-2300
Web: www.theglaziergroup.com
Prices: $$$

Lunch & dinner daily

Beneath Grand Central Terminal's painstakingly restored celestial mural, Michael Jordan's always offers dining under the stars. Wood paneling and photos of sleek locomotives bring art deco glamour to the lofty mezzanine.

At dinner, expect generous filets, ribeye, and Porterhouse (for two) cuts of well-prepared prime Angus beef and traditional steakhouse sides—be sure to try the Jordan family's macaroni and cheese. Golden beet carpaccio with grilled asparagus and goat cheese is a nice alternative to the ever-decadent warm garlic bread with gorgonzola fondue. Lunch adds lighter fare and a reasonable prix-fixe menu.

The elliptical mahogany bar is an agreeable setting for a happy-hour beverage; while the wine salon is great for a cocktail party.

Morton's

A4 **Steakhouse** XXX

551 Fifth Ave. (entrance on 45th St.)

Subway: 5 Av
Phone: 212-972-3315
Web: www.mortons.com
Prices: $$$

Lunch Mon – Fri
Dinner nightly

Part of a Chicago-born chain with outposts across the country, Morton's understands exactly how to empower the weekday corporate crowds and charm weekend tourists with its fun, formulaic experience.

It all starts with a cart: as the servers recite and explain the menu, a cart is rolled to your table, bearing plastic-wrapped samples of the exact cuts of Prime, aged beef, which will be prepared exactly to your liking. Alongside these meats are virtually every raw ingredient used to round out the menu, from massive potatoes to live lobsters. Gimmicks aside, the food here is high quality and delicious.

As one of the older siblings, this midtown Morton's embraces a clubby décor of mahogany paneling and jewel tones that sets the steakhouse standard.

Mr Chow

C1 **Chinese** XX

324 E. 57th St. (bet. First & Second Aves.)

Subway: 59 St
Phone: 212-751-9030
Web: www.mrchow.com
Prices: $$$$

Dinner nightly

This Mr Chow dates back to 1979 but still lures nightly the Who's Who of Manhattan. Actor, artist, restaurateur, and Renaissance man Michael Chow added interior design to his talents in creating this chic black-and-white dining room draped with a red fabric mobile. The team of white-jacketed servers may lack warmth, but makes packed-in diners feel posh and pampered.

Regulars and cognoscenti do not request the menu; have your waiter order for you (though do ask for the fried seaweed), and don't be shy about dislikes. Find yourself distracted from your meal when the oft-performed noodle-making demonstration begins. It's impressive, as will be the rapidly mounting check. Note the other high-profile, international outposts, as well as a TriBeCa sibling.

Naya

Lebanese XX

C2

1057 Second Ave. (bet. 55th & 56th Sts.)

Subway: Lexington Av - 53 St
Lunch & dinner daily
Phone: 212-319-7777
Web: www.nayarestaurants.com
Prices: $$

In a city starved for good Lebanese food, Naya is a sight for sore eyes. Owner Hady Kfoury, who runs a few restaurants back in Beirut, worked the front-of-house at both Daniel and Payard before bringing in Lebanese chef, Rafic Nehme, to open this tiny, but impeccably sleek space, with its mod, all-white décor and a narrow lineup of glossy, angular booths.

The modern Lebanese menu rounds the usual meze bases before introducing a handful of entrées and a small, but tempting, Lebanese wine list. Try the well-seasoned, crunchy *fattoush*, served with toasted pita; a savory, mint-seasoned kebab of ground lamb, paired with a fluffy stack of Lebanese rice pilaf and grilled vegetables; or a glistening, golden tower of flaky baklava cigars, drizzled with honey.

Negiya

Japanese 

A5

9 E. 37th St. (bet. Fifth & Madison Aves.)

Subway: 34 St - Herald Sq
Lunch Mon – Fri
Dinner Mon – Sat
Phone: 212-686-2233
Web: N/A
Prices: ⊜

Housed in the old Washoku Cafe space, this casual new Japanese joint is a solid bet if you're wandering through bustling Herald Square. Inside the simple, but tastefully decorated space, you'll find a small counter where patrons can grab pre-packaged maki to-go; and an ample dining room featuring clean wood floors and a blackboard menu displaying the day's selection of *donburi*, Japanese-style curry, and udon.

Open for lunch and dinner, the restaurant offers dishes like *tonkotsu* ramen, a fragrant broth bobbing with ramen noodles, hard boiled eggs, Berkshire pork, green onion, bamboo shoots, pickled ginger, and bean sprouts; juicy fried chicken, served freshly chilled; and smooth, creamy flan paired with a tender cake drizzled in caramel syrup.

OBAO

C2 — Asian

222 E. 53rd St. (bet. Second & Third Aves.)

Subway: Lexington Av - 53 St — Lunch & dinner daily
Phone: 212-308-5588
Web: www.obaonyc.com
Prices:

Who knows what possessed Michael Huynh to drop this fantastic new Vietnamese restaurant in Midtown East, but anyone tired of slogging to Chinatown is in for one heck of a treat.

The restaurant has a contemporary urban feel, with a smattering of booths and a communal table toward the center of the room; and while the Vietnamese dishes are the strongest (especially the *pho*), the menu also dabbles in cuisine from Laos and Singapore, adding creative touches that truly work. Don't miss the crispy boneless spare rib, glazed in spicy honey mustard and wrapped around a sugar cane skewer; the Laos beef salad tossed with pineapple, shallots, and mint; or the fried banana spring roll, washed down with Vietnamese coffee or coconut juice straight from the shell.

Osteria Laguna

C4 — Italian

209 E. 42nd St. (bet. Second & Third Aves.)

Subway: Grand Central - 42 St — Lunch Mon – Fri, Dinner nightly
Phone: 212-557-0001
Web: www.osteria-laguna.com
Prices: $$

A primo place for a midtown lunch, Osteria Laguna does a booming midday business and the kitchen fields the crowds with aplomb. Office types and tourists alike appreciate the inviting atmosphere, especially in the rustic front room, which overlooks the street through floor-to-ceiling windows that open onto the sidewalk in summer.

Pizza is a hit any time of day, and if you choose a seat in the back room, you can watch the pies being shoveled in and out of the brick oven. These pizzas are individual size and ring true with Italian ingredients—perhaps prosciutto, artichokes, and black olives; or sweet sausage ragú and porcini. Pasta dishes satisfy too, as in a traditional lasagna Bolognese, baked until it is bubbly and has a crusty layer on top.

Pampano

Mexican XX

B3

209 E. 49th St. (bet. Second & Third Aves.)

Lunch Mon – Fri
Dinner nightly

Subway: 51 St
Phone: 212-751-4545
Web: www.modernmexican.com/pampano
Prices: $$$

This vivid Mexican restaurant is a duet between Mexicateur, Richard Sandoval (who owns sister restaurant, Maya), and legendary tenor, Placido Domingo. The combination hits all the right notes—think coastal Mexican cuisine meets an elegant eastside setting, and you're getting warm. The chic interior, drawn in ivory tones and green palm trees, renders the two-level space open and airy; and there's a great terrace upstairs when the weather plays nice.

The menu's favorites include bowls of ceviche or the *empanadas de camaron* dressed with vibrant salsas, followed by deep entrées like the *pez espada mérida*, a thick fillet of swordfish atop a potato-caper fondue with a fresh pea shoot and Asian pear salad all swimming in a smooth achiote-habañero sauce.

Pera

Turkish XX

A4

303 Madison Ave. (bet. 41st & 42nd Sts.)

Lunch & dinner daily

Subway: Grand Central - 42 St
Phone: 212-878-6301
Web: www.peranyc.com
Prices: $$

Named for an upscale neighborhood in Istanbul, this perennially-packed brasserie pulls in boisterous office groups by day as easily as it does intimate duos come nightfall. No wonder, with Pera's consistently solid kitchen turning out lip-smacking good Turkish fare, like a smoky bowl of whipped, roasted eggplant; or crispy phyllo rolls, stuffed with Turkish cheese and paired with a delicious dunk of *cacik*; or the savory lamb *adana*.

Should the crowds add up to a wait for a table, you can always hang in the lovely lounge area up front, or check out the restaurant's seasoned meats collection, cleverly packaged for takeaway. They cook up almost as well at home—though minus the yummy dipping sauces, they're not nearly as fun.

Phoenix Garden

B5 — Chinese

242 E. 40th St. (bet. Second & Third Aves.)

Subway: Grand Central - 42 St — Lunch & dinner daily
Phone: 212-983-6666
Web: www.thephoenixgarden.com
Prices:

You can take the restaurant out of Chinatown, but you can't take the Cantonese out of this midtown favorite—which serves up authentic dishes at a great value. By day, the office suits set pours in for quick lunches; by dinner, Phoenix Garden lights up with a fun, diverse crowd looking to check out the mouthwatering daily specials.

While the house's tasty Peking duck is not always on the menu, you can certainly try to request it—a deliciously crispy affair that gets rolled into neat little pancakes with hoisin, scallion, and cucumber. Meanwhile, don't miss the steamed chive dumplings, plump with tender shrimp; the succulent pepper and salty shrimp; or the sautéed snow pea shoots in a lovely crabmeat sauce, with tender mushrooms and snow peas.

P.J. Clarke's

B2 — Gastropub

915 Third Ave. (at 55th St.)

Subway: Lexington Av - 53 St — Lunch & dinner daily
Phone: 212-317-1616
Web: www.pjclarkes.com
Prices:

Named for Patrick Joseph Clarke, who purchased the place in 1904, this saloon remains a slice of old New York. Pub fare still reigns at this former haunt of Frank Sinatra and Jackie O: big burgers, hearty sandwiches, crispy shoestring fries, a full rawbar, and a long list of beers on tap. The bar scene, usually packed four deep with an agency crowd, is one of the city's best happy hours. Often the throngs of good-looking young professionals there to meet and greet overshadow the charismatic dining room beyond the bar, with its red checkered tablecloths, worn wood walls, and genial service. Through a separate, marked entrance on 55th Street, Sidecar offers a more conversation-friendly dining experience in a speakeasy-like, brick-walled setting.

Riingo

Fusion XX

B4

205 E. 45th St. (bet. Second & Third Aves.)

Subway: Grand Central - 42 St — Lunch & dinner daily
Phone: 212-867-4200
Web: www.riingo.com
Prices: $$

From the Japanese word for "apple" (as in the Big Apple), this is a stylish, contemporary space just off the Alex Hotel lobby, incorporating ebony, bamboo, and accents like custom-made ceramic sake sets. The day-long menu thoughtfully reinterprets Japanese and American cuisines, going well beyond typical hotel dining. At the front of the restaurant, a small bar and lounge with a few sidewalk tables offer a pleasant, quiet terrace for an innovative cocktail or choice of light snacks, like cassava chips with yuzu sour cream.

The very creative kitchen menu features the likes of duck dumplings in five-spice consommé, near-perfect tuna sandwiches, and an extensive raw-bar selection. Riingo also offers a full range of sushi and maki of impressive quality.

Rosa Mexicano

Mexican XX

C1

1063 First Ave. (at 58th St.)

Subway: 59 St — Dinner nightly
Phone: 212-753-7407
Web: www.rosamexicano.com
Prices: $$

This oldie but goody is why the brand name is now found throughout the country, but this original location is by far the best. The dining room's Mexican hacienda style is cozy; its tightly packed tables only add to the lively ambience. Rosa Mexicano strikes a rare balance with its broad appeal: find young professionals downing pomegranate margaritas alongside couples with children perusing the "Young Amigos" menu.

Specialties like *queso fundido* (cheese casserole with chorizo) and *alambre de camarones* (jumbo shrimp grilled with veggies and served aside *pico de gallo*) pack a flavorful punch. There is nothing gimmicky about the tableside guacamole—it may be the city's best and is a worthy accompaniment to the homemade tortillas and excellent salsa.

Rouge Tomate ✿

A1 **Contemporary** XXX

10 E. 60th St. (bet. Fifth & Madison Aves.)

Subway: 5 Av — Lunch & dinner Mon – Sat
Phone: 646-237-8977
Web: www.rougetomatenyc.com
Prices: **$$$**

Katie Sokoler

Being green has never been easier. This gustatory temple of healthy living makes green living and eating so simple–and still so good. Rouge Tomate uses exclusively eco-friendly fabrics, oak and walnut hardwoods (approved by the Forest Stewardship Council), and other sustainable materials to fashion a sleek, Scandinavian look. Elegant enough for the ladies-who-lunch, this is also a perfect place to duck in for a break from business or shopping.

Blending the healthy know-how of a nutritionist with masterful techniques and talent, Rouge Tomate serves a tasty farm-to-table cuisine that is driven by a commendable philosophy. Dedicated Chef Jeremy Bearman crafts elegant dishes from Hawaiian *walu* ceviche with lemongrass-ginger oil to succulent Long Island duck with pistachio-rhubarb vinaigrette; this healthful cuisine is quietly calorie-conscious and infinitely enjoyable. You can even order that warm cobbler with oatmeal ice cream, but without a side of guilt.

To drink, get your daily greens from a freshly squeezed juice, sample a signature cocktail like the rhubarb spring fling, or perhaps sip a biodynamic wine. Downstairs, a stylish lounge has a view of the gorgeous kitchen.

Sakagura

Japanese

B4

211 E. 43rd St. (bet. Second & Third Aves.)

Subway: Grand Central - 42 St
Phone: 212-953-7253
Web: www.sakagura.com
Prices: $$$

Lunch Mon – Fri
Dinner nightly

With its killer sake list and delicious small plates, this unassuming sake den has gotten deservedly popular in the last few years. For those who can find it (hint: it's in the basement by way of the back stairs), plan for a swinging night out in Tokyo by way of midtown. Grab a seat at the long counter to amp up the fun and watch the libations flow.

Though the menu is built to compliment the sake, the food more than merits its own applause. A soft boiled egg bobs alongside fresh uni and salmon roe in a lovely dashi (*onsen tamago*); while grilled eel is layered with Japanese cucumber and seaweed in a light rice wine vinegar vinaigrette (*uzaku*); and chicken is marinated in sake and ginger-infused soy sauce, then fried to sweet perfection (*tori karaage*).

2nd Avenue Deli

Deli

B6

162 E. 33rd St. (bet. Lexington & Third Aves.)

Subway: 33 St
Phone: 212-689-9000
Web: www.2ndavedeli.com
Prices:

Lunch & dinner daily

While the décor may be more deli-meets-deco and there's a tad less attitude, this food is every bit as good as it was on Second Avenue. Ignore the kvetching and know that this is still a true Jewish deli filled with personality, and one of the best around by far.

The menu remains unchanged: it is still Kosher meat-loving and non-dairy, with phenomenal pastrami, pillowy rye, tangy mustard, perfect potato pancakes, and fluffy matzoh balls in comforting broth. Have the best of both worlds with the soup and half-sandwich combination.

Carve a nook during midday rush, when in pour the crowds. The deli also does takeout (popular with the midtown lunch bunch), and delivery (grandma's pancakes at your door). Giant platters go equally well to a bris or brunch.

Seo

C3

Japanese XX

249 E. 49th St. (bet. Second & Third Aves.)

Subway: 51 St
Lunch & dinner daily
Phone: 212-355-7722
Web: N/A
Prices: $$

This is not your average neighborhood standby, and yet Seo—tucked into a residential street in midtown's booming Japanese culinary scene—draws as many faithful locals as it does weekend adventurers looking for the real deal. Thus, it's best to make reservations early.

The secret lies in Seo's one-two punch of pairing a tranquil dining room and long dining counter with a kitchen staff dedicated to the acumen of traditional Japanese food. Witness a wildly fresh eel and cucumber salad, tossed in a feather-light vinegar sauce; or a perfectly broiled cod, glazed in a spot-on miso sauce, and flanked by Japanese plum and ginger root. Keep an eye out for the popular *chawanmushi*—a silky egg custard that should not be missed if it appears on the daily specials.

Sip Sak

C3

Turkish XX

928 Second Ave. (bet. 49th & 50th Sts.)

Subway: 51 St
Lunch & dinner daily
Phone: 212-583-1900
Web: www.sip-sak.com
Prices: $$

An NY personality and maestro of Turkish cuisine, Orhan Yegen has been at it again. After a drastic face-lift including a pressed tin ceiling and marble-topped tables, Sip Sak is now the very picture of a Parisian bistro. This mad Turk may dance around his tables (and staff), but his is top-notch, classic Turkish food, perhaps the best in the city.

The U.N. posse and locals convene to devour Yegen's diligent crafting of simple and sumptuous flavors. Daily specials abound but taste his terrific Turkish in an appetizing assortment of cold spreads, *borek*, spinach, and eggplant; flaky *pacangas* rolled with spiced beef and fried cheese; *manti* in a yogurt puddle; lamb *adana* atop fried pita with a dollop of *cacik*; and pumpkin soaked in rosewater and honey.

Smith & Wollensky

Steakhouse XX

B3

797 Third Ave. (at 49th St.)

Subway: 51 St
Phone: 212-753-1530
Web: www.smithandwollensky.com
Prices: $$$$

Lunch Mon – Fri
Dinner nightly

Long before Manhattan's steakhouse craze reached epic proportions, there was Smith & Wollensky. The New York flagship opened in 1977, and over 30 years later, the restaurant is still jumping most nights of the week—it's historic green and white façade a welcome beacon to neighborhood power players, families, and tourists alike.

The owners may have plucked the names Smith & Wollensky out of a phone directory, but they were considerably more careful choosing their USDA prime beef, which they dry-age and hand-butcher on premises. The result, paired with heartbreakingly good mashed potatoes or decadent truffled macaroni and cheese, is steakhouse nirvana. Wollensky's Grill serves a late-night menu until 2:00 A.M. to sate the lively bar crowd.

Soba Totto

Japanese XX

B4

211 E. 43rd St. (bet. Second & Third Aves.)

Subway: Grand Central - 42 St
Phone: 212-557-8200
Web: www.sobatotto.com
Prices: $$

Lunch Mon – Fri
Dinner nightly

This fairly young Japanese restaurant arrives courtesy of the family behind the popular Aburiya Kinnosuke, Yakitori Totto, and Totto Ramen. Like their other ventures, Soba Totto offers incredibly fresh, authentically prepared Japanese specialties in a stylishly-appointed, low-lit dining room. There's a bar where you can watch the chefs go to town, and lots of nooks and crannies for private dinners.

At lunch, midtowners flood in for piping hot soba noodles and traditional Japanese lunch sets; come nightfall, the menu expands to include small plates, starters, and a wide selection of yakitori—the remarkable little chicken skewers, featuring unique parts like liver, soft knee bone, and tail, which put them on the map at some of their other venues.

Sparks

Steakhouse XX

C3

210 E. 46th St. (bet. Second & Third Aves.)

Subway: Grand Central - 42 St
Phone: 212-687-4855
Web: www.sparksnyc.com
Prices: $$$$

Lunch Mon – Fri
Dinner Mon – Sat

Phenomenal steaks, exceptional Scotch, frosty martinis, big expense accounts, seating for nearly 700, and carnivorous crowds exuding a raucous, masculine vibe are the fundamentals of Sparks. Service is speedy and efficient, if rough around the edges, throughout the gigantic, bi-level dining space. This is enhanced by large tables and 19th century landscapes of the Hudson River Valley that line the wainscoted walls. There will be time to appreciate the ambience while inevitably waiting for your table among the masses at the bar.

On the menu, go straight to the flavorful, buttery, and perfectly cooked prime sirloin, accompanied by unbeatable creamed spinach. Complete this consistently excellent, powerhouse experience with a bottle of big red wine.

SushiAnn

Japanese XX

B2

38 E. 51st St. (bet. Madison & Park Aves.)

Subway: 51 St
Phone: 212-755-1780
Web: www.sushiann.com
Prices: $$

Lunch Mon – Fri
Dinner Mon – Sat

Lucky are those who accidentally wander into this midtown sushi den. Nestled into a corporate no man's land along 51st Street, it's hard from the outset to see what separates SushiAnn from the pack of smooth-blonde-wood-and-black-lacquered-tray sushi joints that line this pocket of Manhattan.

Take a seat at the sushi bar (where there is a $30 minimum required to sit down), order the omakase, and wait—incredibly fresh mackerel served with ponzu and minced ginger sauce; fatty blue fin fanned over *shiso* leaf and kelp; smoky, chewy slices of grilled giant clam; rich torched sardine—all of it carefully explained by the attentive, knowledgeable staff. Sure, you can also sit at a table and order à la carte, but where's the fun in that?

Sushiden

A3 Japanese XX

19 E. 49th St. (bet. Fifth & Madison Aves.)

Subway: 5 Av - 53 St
Phone: 212-758-2700
Web: www.sushiden.com
Prices: $$$

Lunch Mon – Fri
Dinner Sun – Fri

Close your eyes to the California rolls, forget everything you've heard from the gaijin crowds, and open yourself to experience this classic, skillfully prepared, very authentic sushi-ya. These chefs are no mere amateurs—best to order omakase, allowing the talented professionals to create a delicious parade of seasonal, simply adorned, outrageously fresh fish.

Regardless of recent competition in the form of more modern and stylish spots, Sushiden is more subtly elegant, and remains popular for its traditional food and excellent service. It is an especially big hit with the business lunch crowd that jams the place at midday, so be sure to make reservations.

Another Sushiden location feeds the westside business crowd in a larger but less warm setting.

Sushi Yasuda

B4 Japanese XX

204 E. 43rd St. (bet. Second & Third Aves.)

Subway: Grand Central - 42 St
Phone: 212-972-1001
Web: www.sushiyasuda.com
Prices: $$$$

Lunch Mon – Fri
Dinner Mon – Sat

Start the clock: once you have taken a seat at this gorgeously modern, blond-wood sushi counter, you will have exactly 90 minutes to enjoy your meal—no worries if you lose track of time, as the efficient staff will be sure to remind you of the countdown. Nonetheless, meals here begin with a fantastic variety of some of the freshest fish in town, best appreciated in Chef Yasuda's omakase menu.

Focused preparations limit extraneous embellishments or garnishes to detract from the pristine flavors; however, a tendency to overseason, cuts made in advance, and inconsistent rice do sometimes lead to sloppy mistakes that preclude this from being an authentic sushi experience.

Note that if you arrive more than 10 minutes late, your reservation is forfeited.

Takesushi

Japanese XX

1026 Second Ave. (bet. 54th & 55th Sts.)

Subway: Lexington Av - 53 St
Phone: 212-355-3557
Web: www.takesushi.com
Prices: **$$**

Lunch Mon – Fri
Dinner Mon – Sat

Despite the fact that this place seems to change its name, decor, and concept on a regular basis, it has consistently offered good Japanese cuisine. Obviously, a talented team and a well-trained Japanese chef still hold sway here, no matter what they call it.

Takesushi gets jam-packed for weekday lunch, likely due to the restaurant's proximity to the U.N., as well as its new lunch-menu options. As appealing as they are a good value, set sushi menus and bento box samplers make the best bargains; and though a bit more pricey, the lunchtime omakase will net you some fine fare. Dinner showcases splendid vegetable, fish, and meat dishes.

Kimono-clad and sweet as pie, waitresses perform their jobs with genuine hospitality in the small well-maintained space.

Tao

A1

Asian XX

42 E. 58th St. (bet. Madison & Park Aves.)

Subway: 59 St
Phone: 212-888-2288
Web: www.taorestaurant.com
Prices: **$$$**

Lunch Mon – Fri
Dinner nightly

This former cinema is now (literally) a lively, massive, and über-popular temple of all foods pan-Asian, dramatically outfitted with a Chinese scroll draped across the ceiling and 16-foot statue of Buddha towering over a reflecting pool. The theater's former balconies remain packed, accommodating 300 diners on three levels. The fusion cuisine has a crowd-pleasing combination of Hong Kong, Chinese, Thai, and Japanese dishes, including sushi and sashimi. Perfect for sharing, the well-prepared menu offers everything from small plates of shrimp tempura with garlic-chili sauce or squab lettuce wraps to wasabi-crusted filet mignon.

The loyal after-work business crowd turns younger and trendier on weekends, ordering hip libations like the lychee martini.

Tsushima

Japanese

B3

141 E. 47th St. (bet. Lexington & Third Aves.)

Subway: Grand Central - 42 St
Phone: 212-207-1938
Web: N/A
Prices: $$

Lunch Mon – Fri
Dinner Mon – Sat

There are few restaurant secrets left in New York, but Tsushima is one of them. Chances are, you haven't heard of it, but this place stands out among the competition in the thin slice of midtown jammed with restaurants straight out of Tokyo. It's easy to walk right by Tsushima (it's located a few steps below street level), but once inside, you'll find a sultry décor that contrasts black wood with white leather seating.

Skilled chefs seamlessly juggle the standard table orders with the omakase offerings at the sushi bar, and the kitchen plays backup with an assortment of cooked courses. Though spicy tuna can be had, the chef's choice is the way to go, as Tsushima nets fantastic quality and interesting varieties of fish—all elegantly presented.

The Water Club

Seafood

C6

E. 30th St. (at the East River)

Subway: 33 St
Phone: 212-683-3333
Web: www.thewaterclub.com
Prices: $$$

Lunch & dinner daily

Located on a barge in the East River, it's easy to see why The Water Club is a natural go-to for weddings, birthdays, and anniversaries. Floor-to-ceiling windows offer every table a great view of the water; and servers dressed as a ship's crew give the place a fun, whimsical vibe you don't find in the serious, low-lit restaurants that usually define Manhattan dining.

By day, The Water Club's dining room fills up with power lunchers; but come nightfall, the celebrations begin. The mostly seafood menu is boring and predictable, featuring oysters, crab cakes, and entrées like grilled salmon with artichoke hearts and carrots in tomato broth. The upstairs bar—called the Crow's Nest—makes a great place to catch a happy hour drink when the weather's right.

Wild Edibles

Seafood 

535 Third Ave. (bet. 35th & 36th Sts.)

Subway: 33 St
Lunch & dinner daily
Phone: 212-213-8552
Web: www.wildedibles.com
Prices: $$

It's a fish market. It's a restaurant. It's an oyster bar. Wild Edibles is all those places rolled into one.

With four other markets in New York, including one in Grand Central Station, Wild Edibles prides itself on netting line-caught fish and organic produce from small farms. In the Third Avenue locale, a retail counter displays the day's catch, while a small bar and a few tables provide seating. A vast array of seafood fills the menu with an appealing mix of light fare and entrées—everything from oyster "flights," (with white wine or beer pairings) to fish cooked your way and accompanied with a choice of seasonings. Cheesecake is the only dessert option, and they don't serve coffee.

At lunch, it feels like you're eating in a fish store, but in the evening candlelight kicks in more atmosphere.

Wolfgang's

A6
Steakhouse 

4 Park Ave. (at 33rd St.)

Subway: 33 St
Lunch & dinner daily
Phone: 212-889-3369
Web: www.wolfgangssteakhouse.com
Prices: $$$$

After 40 years at the esteemed Peter Luger, former headwaiter Wolfgang Zwiener ditched retirement to strike out on his own across the river—a decision that has yielded mouthwatering results. Located in the former Vanderbilt Hotel dining room, this 1912 landmark space showcases a vaulted terra-cotta ceiling by famed architect Rafael Guastavino. The setting is handsome, but the steak's arrival refocuses all attention on the strapping portions of Porterhouse, hand-selected and dry-aged in house. Once the meat is basted with some of its sizzling juices, the feast will begin.

Classic starters and scrumptious sides like shrimp cocktail and creamed spinach are delightful distractions. Be sure to hit the bar for a perfect martini.

Zarela

Mexican

953 Second Ave. (bet. 50th & 51st Sts.)

Subway: 51 St
Phone: 212-644-6740
Web: www.zarela.com
Prices: $$

Lunch Mon – Fri
Dinner nightly

Is Zarela Martinez the unsung hero of the city's blazing Mexican food scene? Those who remember Manhattan's tortilla wasteland of ten years ago would argue yes, because this talented chef and food scholar—who can still be found holding court at her favorite corner table most nights—has been dishing up authentic Mexican fare since the late eighties.

Happy hour finds the bar flooded with a young, spirited crowd chucking back the insane margaritas, most of them oblivious to the culinary brilliance passing under their noses. Try the *cochinita pibíl*, a tender, slow-cooked pork shoulder or the *camarones con coco* showered in shredded coconut. And eat whatever the daily specials are, as her regionally-focused recipes are always a slam dunk.

Look out for red symbols, indicating a particularly pleasant ambiance.

Midtown West

New York is a city of incomparable diversity, evident in every quiet, tree-lined neighborhood, ethnic enclave, and luxury high-rise. The truth remains, however, that there is only one street in all five boroughs to be boldly hailed Restaurant Row. Consider that its famed location—where celebrity chefs prepare all-you-can-eat pasta alongside promising sushi bars—is in a neighborhood named Hell's Kitchen is further testament to its dedication to great food.

Everything to Eat

Still, this is an area that insists on reinvention. Hence, Restaurant Row (perhaps due to its uneven reputation) is becoming known as Little Brazil near Sixth Avenue, where samba and street food are celebrated late summer each year on Brazilian Day. A few steps farther west and the city's eclectic identity comes to life again, where a walk down Ninth Avenue offers a world of goods. A wonderful start (or finale) can be found at **Amy's Bread**, whose crusty baguettes supply countless restaurant kitchens, while colorful cakes or cookies tempt passersby. Meanwhile across the avenue, **Poseidon Bakery** is rumored to be the very last place in America to still make its own phyllo dough by hand; a taste of the *spanakopita* will prove it. Regardless of its name, **Sullivan Street Bakery**'s one and only retail outlet is actually on 47th, between 10th and 11th (a location so perilously far west in the Manhattan mindset that its success proves its worth in gold). Absolutely anything artisanal and delicious can be found nearby at the **Amish Market**, filled with fresh produce, meats, and an array of specialty items. A sweet side-trip is the **Little Pie Company**, whose beloved wares are rolled, filled, and baked in its glass-paneled display kitchen.

While this stretch of Hell's Kitchen is rich with markets and restaurants, those highlights are familiar to any theater-going tourist or Lincoln Tunnel-bound commuter who has been stuck in its traffic, yearning for a burger from the **Film Center Café**. To unearth its hidden treasures, travel south of Port Authority Bus Terminal and visit a string of unassuming storefronts, starting with **Ninth Avenue International Foods**. These olives, spices, and spreads are a serious business, but it is the renowned *taramosalata* (as if prepared by the gods atop Mount Olympus) that finds its way into restaurants throughout the city. Stop by **Giovanni Esposito and Son's** meat market for a sampling of their Italian sausages. For sandwiches, **Manganaro's** is the true inventor of the original six-foot Italian-American "hero." These are among the family-owned landmark businesses that have quietly been shaping New York's food scene for the better part of a century. For your Asian sandwich fix, drop by the original **Xie Xie** for their tangy delights.

Street Eats

While this is an area often choked by traffic and overpopulated with hungry office workers, New Yorkers demand outstanding food, no matter the venue. Under the guidance of the Vendy Awards and the blog midtownlunch.com, discover a moveable feast of fast, satisfying street-food vendors. Highlights include sausage and schnitzel from **Hallo German Food Stand** and the **Treats Truck** (check the web or follow on Twitter for upcoming locales). Those seeking a more stable location to grab a fantastic burger, fries, or milkshake will not be disappointed at Le Parker Meridien's **burger joint**. Foodies in need of a rarer treat know to head south to K-town—the type of New York neighborhood that sneaks up and floors you. Its instant, unmistakable Asian vibe owes largely to the prominence of karaoke bars, authentic grocers, and countless spots for fresh tofu or handmade dumplings.

Shopping and Style

Throughout Midtown West, it is clear that equal attention is paid to cuisine as to arranging storybook holiday mannequins behind the velvet ropes of Saks Fifth Avenue. As if to illustrate the point, the Japanese bakery, **Minamoto Kitchoan**, channels elegance and subtlety in its impossibly beautiful rice cakes, bejeweled with plum wine gelée or golden sprinkles. The exquisite packaging makes these the penultimate hostess gift for any uptown dinner party.

On the other end of the spectrum, **AQ Café** puts every effort into serving three outstanding meals a day to its throngs of midtown devotees (four, if counting the fabulous pastries). In the same vein, French-influenced **Petrossian Boutique** offers fine caviar and delectable croissants to their parade of patrons. **Marketa** is great for Greek food fanatics, after which a shot of espresso at **FIKA** (where the Swedes display their passion and skill for the Italian elixir) tastes divine. Wind up the affair with a stirring cocktail at the chic **Empire Room** housed in the Empire State Building.

Time Warner Center

No visit here is complete without tribute to the gargantuan feat that is the AOL Time Warner Center, presiding over Columbus Circle. Here, world-renowned chefs indulge both themselves and their patrons with earth-shaking success. The good news is that the economic downturn has eased demands for reservations (the bad news is the price tag). Still, a range of pleasures can be found here, from **Bouchon Bakery**'s classic French *macaroons*, to the eye-popping style and sass of **Clo** Wine Bar.

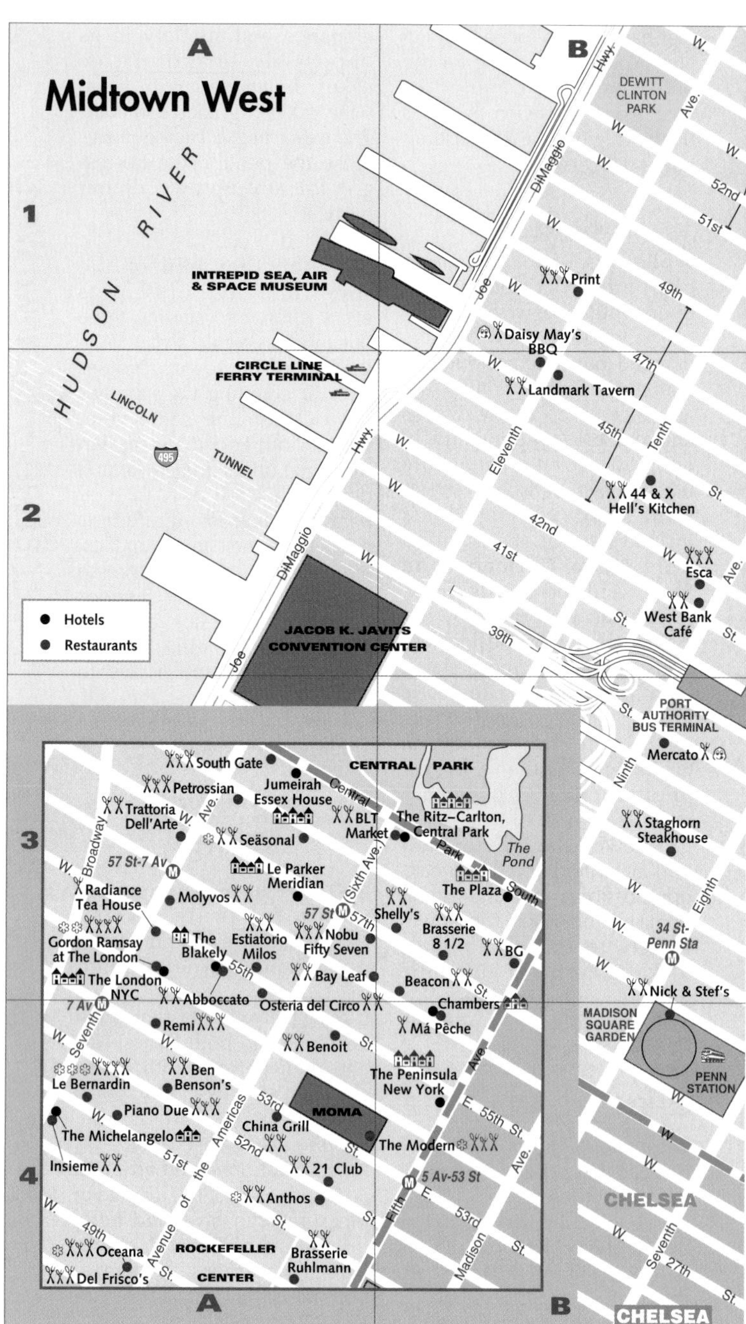
Midtown West
A
B
1
2
3
4
HUDSON RIVER
INTREPID SEA, AIR & SPACE MUSEUM
CIRCLE LINE FERRY TERMINAL
LINCOLN TUNNEL
495
JACOB K. JAVITS CONVENTION CENTER
Hotels
Restaurants
DEWITT CLINTON PARK
Joe DiMaggio Hwy.
Print
Daisy May's BBQ
Landmark Tavern
44 & X Hell's Kitchen
Esca
West Bank Café
PORT AUTHORITY BUS TERMINAL
Mercato
Staghorn Steakhouse
34 St-Penn Sta
Nick & Stef's
MADISON SQUARE GARDEN
PENN STATION
CHELSEA
CENTRAL PARK
The Pond
South Gate
Petrossian
Jumeirah Essex House
Trattoria Dell'Arte
BLT Market
The Ritz–Carlton, Central Park
Seäsonal
57 St-7 Av
Le Parker Meridien
Radiance Tea House
Molyvos
The Plaza
57 St
Shelly's
Brasserie 8 1/2
Gordon Ramsay at The London
The Blakely
Estiatorio Milos
Nobu Fifty Seven
BG
The London NYC
Bay Leaf
Beacon
7 Av
Abboccato
Osteria del Circo
Chambers
Remi
Má Pêche
Benoit
The Peninsula New York
Le Bernardin
Ben Benson's
MOMA
Piano Due
China Grill
The Michelangelo
The Modern
Insieme
21 Club
5 Av-53 St
Anthos
Oceana
Brasserie Ruhlmann
Del Frisco's
ROCKEFELLER CENTER
Avenue of the Americas
Broadway
Seventh
Fifth Ave.
Madison Ave.
Eighth Ave.
Ninth
Tenth Ave.
Eleventh
CHELSEA

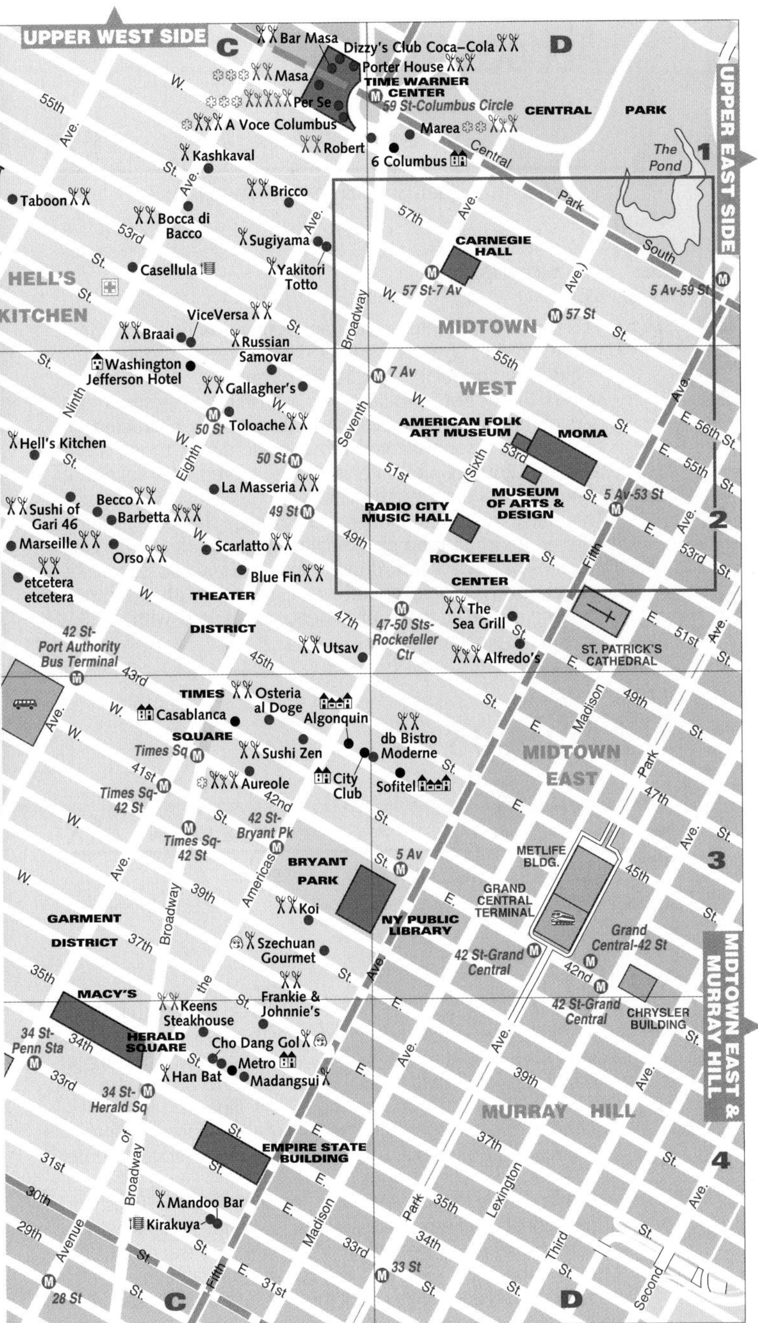
UPPER WEST SIDE
UPPER EAST SIDE
MIDTOWN EAST & MURRAY HILL
Bar Masa
Dizzy's Club Coca-Cola
Porter House
Masa
TIME WARNER CENTER
Per Se
59 St-Columbus Circle
A Voce Columbus
CENTRAL PARK
Marea
Robert
6 Columbus
Kashkaval
The Pond
Taboon
Bricco
Bocca di Bacco
Sugiyama
CARNEGIE HALL
Casellula
Yakitori Totto
HELL'S KITCHEN
57 St-7 Av
5 Av-59 St
57 St
MIDTOWN
ViceVersa
Braai
Russian Samovar
Washington Jefferson Hotel
7 Av
WEST
Gallagher's
50 St
Toloache
AMERICAN FOLK ART MUSEUM
MOMA
Hell's Kitchen
50 St
La Masseria
MUSEUM OF ARTS & DESIGN
5 Av-53 St
Sushi of Gari 46
Becco
Barbetta
49 St
RADIO CITY MUSIC HALL
Marseille
Orso
Scarlatto
ROCKEFELLER CENTER
etcetera etcetera
Blue Fin
THEATER DISTRICT
The Sea Grill
47-50 Sts-Rockefeller Ctr
42 St-Port Authority Bus Terminal
Utsav
Alfredo's
ST. PATRICK'S CATHEDRAL
TIMES SQUARE
Osteria al Doge
Casablanca
Algonquin
db Bistro Moderne
Times Sq
Sushi Zen
MIDTOWN EAST
Times Sq-42 St
Aureole
City Club
Sofitel
42 St-Bryant Pk
Times Sq-42 St
BRYANT PARK
5 Av
METLIFE BLDG.
GRAND CENTRAL TERMINAL
Koi
GARMENT DISTRICT
NY PUBLIC LIBRARY
Szechuan Gourmet
42 St-Grand Central
Grand Central-42 St
MACY'S
Frankie & Johnnie's
Keens Steakhouse
HERALD SQUARE
42 St-Grand Central
CHRYSLER BUILDING
34 St-Penn Sta
Cho Dang Gol
Metro
Han Bat
Madangsui
34 St-Herald Sq
MURRAY HILL
EMPIRE STATE BUILDING
Mandoo Bar
Kirakuya
28 St
33 St

Abboccato

Italian XX

136 W. 55th St. (bet. Sixth & Seventh Aves.)

Subway: 57 St
Phone: 212-265-4000
Web: www.abboccato.com
Prices: **$$$**

Lunch Mon – Sat
Dinner nightly

This smartly appointed restaurant operates under the careful watch of the Livanos family—the seasoned restaurateurs behind the popular Oceana and Molyvos. Abboccato, a stone's throw from the latter, on a bustling cross street and part of the Blakely Hotel, boasts the family's characteristic style—with a sophisticated urban-rustic dining room, a bar area ripe for people watching, and a pretty *terrazza* that almost swings out onto the sidewalk.

The Italian menu meanders all through the old country, offering a virtual map of specialties like a perfectly cooked *bucatini all'amatriciana* doused in a rich, rustic sauce; or a deceptively simple grilled *orata*, topped with a lemony *salmoriglio* and a shake of capers, and paired with a silky mound of spinach.

Alfredo's

D2

Italian XXX

4 W. 49th St. (bet. Fifth & Sixth Aves.)

Subway: 47-50 Sts - Rockefeller Ctr
Phone: 212-397-0100
Web: www.alfredos.com
Prices: **$$$**

Lunch & dinner daily

Make your way past the hungry 30 Rock tourists that mob Alfredo's, and you'll be rewarded with pizza and pasta so delicious it would make your *nonna* blush. How can simple lasagna, layered with pasta, ragù, and béchamel, be so heavenly? How can an enormous Valtellina pizza pie—it's perfectly crispy, paper-thin crust bursting with fresh toppings like creamy gorgonzola, soft mozzarella, ripe pear, and truffle oil—seem like a revelation?

With a whole lot of love and attention from a polished, professional kitchen—an asset Alfredo's has in spades, no matter how busy it gets. It's a philosophy that extends to the front-of-house as well, with a crackerjack waitstaff familiar with the menu and passionate about the ever-rotating daily specials.

Anthos ✿

Greek ✗✗

A4

36 W. 52nd St. (bet. Fifth & Sixth Aves.)

Subway: 47-50 Sts - Rockefeller Ctr
Phone: 212-582-6900
Web: www.anthosnyc.com
Prices: **$$$**

Lunch Mon – Fri
Dinner Mon – Sat

Battman

A tree might grow in Brooklyn, but something else entirely is blossoming in midtown. Set on a bustling block amid the maze of office buildings, serene Anthos, which means "to blossom" in Greek, takes its name quite literally, as cherry blossom branches are a defining element of its design. This world of hushed calm, in a sophisticated palette of dark brown and soft pink, is a sleek step away from the fray and a perfect match for the elite clientele who make this their dining room of choice.

Donatella Arpaia runs a tight ship and despite the departure of Chef Michael Psilakis, nothing is missing from this top spot where gourmet, re-imagined Greek cuisine reigns with creativity and unique personality. The menu leans heavily toward seafood, but a superb roast chicken atop artichoke-yogurt purée, or perfectly grilled pork loin with pistachio-currant caponata and a quenelle of *skordalia* prove the kitchen's skill and range. Also find delicate fish preparations, as in the yellowfin tuna, its crimson flesh barely cooked, with a complex emulsion of lemon yogurt.

Clever and playful ambition shines in desserts like beet and yogurt cannoli or strawberry shortcake artistically paired with dill.

Aureole ✿

Contemporary 

C3

135 W. 42nd St. (bet. Broadway & Sixth Ave.)

Subway: 42 St - Bryant Pk
Phone: 212-319-1660
Web: www.charliepalmer.com
Prices: $$$$

Lunch Mon – Sat
Dinner nightly

Eric Laignel

Having once called the Upper East Side home, Charlie Palmer's beloved Aureole can now be found in the Bank of America Tower—the building rising up above Bryant Park.

The Adam Tihany-designed restaurant is really a tale of two dining rooms (each has their own menu): the casual front bar room, a roomy dining area in its own right, with towering ceilings and handsome detailing; and the more intimate (and formal) glass-enclosed back room, featuring an eye-catching catwalk lined with wine bottles and an elaborate menu. Grapehounds should kick things off with a sip from the excellent, thorough, and unique wine selection, and perhaps a chat with the sommelier who might know why one pinot is better suited for milk-fed as opposed to grass-fed veal.

Back in the kitchen, Chef Christopher Lee oversees Palmer's vision while bringing his own formidable skills to a seasonal, contemporary menu that includes fresh John Dory wrapped in tasty country bacon and paired with black beluga lentils, creamy turnip purée, and salsify dotted with drops of tangy L8 harvest ice wine sauce; or delicate pillows of chestnut ravioli laced with brown butter, shaved pecorino, fried sage, and pomegranate seeds.

A Voce Columbus ✿

Italian 

C1

10 Columbus Circle (in the Time Warner Center)

Subway: 59 St - Columbus Circle
Phone: 212-823-2523
Web: www.avocerestaurant.com
Prices: **$$$**

Lunch Sun – Fri
Dinner nightly

Bruce Buck

The Time Warner Center may literally be a mall, and this third-floor spot (and sibling of beloved A Voce on Madison Square Park) may literally serve rustic Italian, but both concepts are elevated here on Columbus Circle. The look of this chic brasserie is similar to its downtown locale though Columbus sexes it up with rich, dark woods and ivory leather and chrome chairs filling the sunken room gazing over Central Park. It's not the spot for a tête-à-tête since it gets noisy, but the decibel level is just another part of the scene.

The dining room dazzles, and the kitchen sizzles. The menu spotlights jazzed up Italian food, Missy Robbins style. Start with a half portion of pasta like pappardelle spiraled around morsels of meaty rabbit sausage and chanterelles or squid ink tagliatelle swimming in San Marzano tomato-braised *seppie*. Some dishes lean toward the traditional side but these stylish comfort-food classics are flavorful and unexpected, as in the signature dish of fennel and chili-marinated chicken cooked under a brick with Tuscan greens and *gigante* beans.

As might be expected, the impressive and equally approachable wine list slants heavily toward Italian regions.

Barbetta

Italian 

321 W. 46th St. (bet. Eighth & Ninth Aves.)

Subway: 50 St (Eighth Ave.) Lunch & dinner Tue – Sat
Phone: 212-246-9171
Web: www.barbettarestaurant.com
Prices: **$$$**

Standing proud since its 1906 opening, Barbetta proves that the "new" in New York need not be taken literally. From its gilded furnishings to its candelabra and crystal chandeliers, this dining room celebrates an old-world aesthetic. At the ornate tables, find true-blue New Yorkers who, as regulars, have been treated like family here for more than century (though outsiders may detect a hint of indifference from the service staff).

Consistency is the theme here, and some of the menu items, such as *minestrone giardiniera,* have been served since the very beginning. Good, traditional Italian food with a few throwbacks—capped off by a selection from the dessert trolley—prove that this just might be your grandfather's favorite Italian restaurant.

Bar Masa

Japanese 

10 Columbus Circle (in the Time Warner Center)

Subway: 59 St - Columbus Circle Lunch & dinner Mon – Sat
Phone: 212-823-9800
Web: www.masanyc.com
Prices: **$$$**

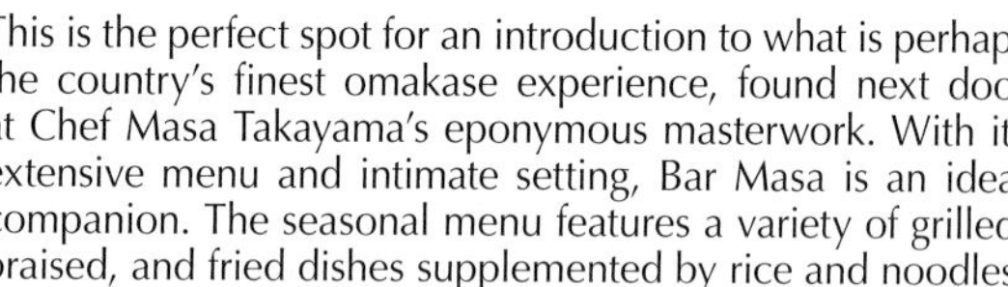

This is the perfect spot for an introduction to what is perhaps the country's finest omakase experience, found next door at Chef Masa Takayama's eponymous masterwork. With its extensive menu and intimate setting, Bar Masa is an ideal companion. The seasonal menu features a variety of grilled, braised, and fried dishes supplemented by rice and noodles, in addition to sushi à la carte.

Despite the cacophony and rather mall-like experience of entering the Time Warner Center, Bar Masa is an immediate respite, promising a relaxed and peaceful meal. The slender room is earthy yet refined with Japanese limestone and wood furnishings that fashion a genuine, Tokyo-like experience.

The popular bar area offers well-chosen wines and creative cocktails.

Bay Leaf

Indian XX

49 W. 56th St. (bet. Fifth & Sixth Aves.)

Subway: 57 St — Lunch & dinner daily
Phone: 212-957-1818
Web: www.bayleafnyc.com
Prices: $$

As every Manhattan office bee knows, appearances can be deceiving in midtown. The clichéd Indian font that marks Bay Leaf's façade belies a lovely little Indian restaurant, with a sunlight-soaked dining room and a pretty outdoor patio overlooking 56th Street.

While the business crowd flocks to its ample buffet come lunch hour, nighttime finds a more languid crowd dabbling in Bay Leaf's classic, understated à la carte items, including a wealth of traditional curries and tandoori dishes. Try the smoky, green chili and chicken, laced with curry leaves; the spicy creamed spinach, studded with chickpeas and fragrant with cardamom; or feather-light cheese and semolina fritters, poached in sweetened milk and dusted with pistachio and green cardamom.

Beacon

American 

25 W. 56th St. (bet. Fifth & Sixth Aves.)

Subway: 57 St — Lunch Sun – Fri
Phone: 212-332-0500 — Dinner nightly
Web: www.beaconnyc.com
Prices: $$$

Everything—even the succulent little oysters—gets the grill treatment at Chef Waldy Malouf's Beacon. If you don't believe it, you can see for yourself at Beacon's Kitchen Counter, a communal, 6-man table set up to face the kitchen's grill, pizza oven, and rotisserie.

By night, diners can watch everything from suckling pig to rotisserie chicken hit the open flames. But come weekday lunches, the table morphs into the Burger Bar, where Malouf includes a delicious tuna burger made from rough-cut chunks of fresh ruby-red tuna, tucked between two slices of grilled tender bread. Paired with a crispy tangle of shoestring fries and a few other inventive sides, the only thing missing is one of those generous cocktails Beacon is known for.

Becco

Italian XX

C2

355 W. 46th St. (bet. Eighth & Ninth Aves.)

Subway: 42 St - Port Authority Bus Terminal — Lunch & dinner daily
Phone: 212-397-7597
Web: www.becco-nyc.com
Prices: **$$**

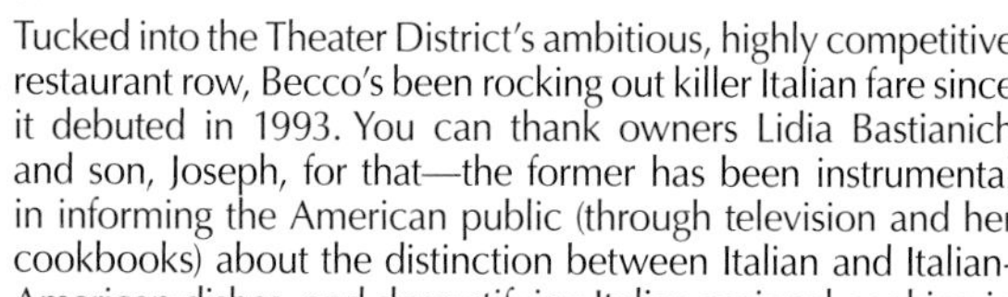

Tucked into the Theater District's ambitious, highly competitive restaurant row, Becco's been rocking out killer Italian fare since it debuted in 1993. You can thank owners Lidia Bastianich and son, Joseph, for that—the former has been instrumental in informing the American public (through television and her cookbooks) about the distinction between Italian and Italian-American dishes, and demystifying Italian regional cooking in general.

How this translates to your plate is a culinary delight—dishes like creamy polenta wrapped in a crispy jacket of *Montasio* cheese arrive with scrumptious slices of speck; while grilled swordfish is laced with pumpkin seed oil and paired with spaghetti squash, stewed cherry tomatoes, and roasted pumpkin seeds.

Ben Benson's

Steakhouse XX

A4

123 W. 52nd St. (bet. Sixth & Seventh Aves.)

Subway: 5 Av - 53 St — Lunch Mon – Fri
Phone: 212-581-8888 — Dinner nightly
Web: www.benbensons.com
Prices: **$$$**

From this office building ground floor, Ben Benson's has spent over 25 years serving prime cuts of USDA meats and other classic American fare to contented power brokers and politicians (regulars' names are engraved on brass plaques). The huge, rotating menu features perfectly cooked steaks and chops, but remembers to include something for everyone, as in the selection of salads or even chicken Parmigiana. Seafood fans will be happy to find shrimp scampi; and the cold poached salmon is a rare find. Oenophiles rejoice in the impressive wine list.

The high-ceilinged dining room, expertly staffed by smartly attired servers, is airier than many of the steakhouses in town. For pleasant alfresco dining, head to the spacious sidewalk terrace in warmer weather.

Benoit

French XX

60 W. 55th St. (bet. Fifth & Sixth Aves.)

Subway: 57 St — Lunch & dinner Mon – Sat
Phone: 646-943-7373
Web: www.benoitny.com
Prices: $$

After opening a New York branch of his beloved bistro, Benoit, to a somewhat lukewarm critical reception, renowned Chef Alain Ducasse shuffled his kitchen lineup and reappeared with a new executive chef and partner—Le Cirque veteran, Pierre Schaedelin.

Together, they've reinvented the menu, introducing a host of new items as well as a daily specials list that pulls from Schaedelin's Alsatian origins. Perhaps as a nod to the economy, they've even dropped their prices a bit—all the more reason to dig into tender pig cheeks, served over a frisée and lentil salad laced with mustard-cumin vinaigrette; or a crispy Chatham cod casserole, dusted with fennel pollen and sea salt, and flanked by a bright mix of vegetables and olives.

BG

American XX

754 Fifth Ave. (at 58th St.)

Subway: 5 Av - 59 St — Lunch & dinner daily
Phone: 212-872-8977
Web: www.bergdorfgoodman.com
Prices: $$$

How many Burnettes does it take to feed a group of Bergdorf Blondes? Just one if it's the talented Darryl Burnette—the chef hired by the luxury department store to create an inviting seventh-floor menu for their discerning clientele. Luckily, Burnette comes armed with a heavy-hitting resume (Spice Market and Métrazur, just to name a few), and a knack for spinning out delicate luncheon goodies like tender coins of ahi tuna tartare, layered with ripe avocado and crunchy *tobiko*.

The afternoon tea, served daily, is a perfect fit for the Parisian-styled salon, with its hand-painted wallpaper and 18th century chairs. Those looking for a soup or sandwich, minus the pomp, might want to wander over to Bar III, located in the men's store across the street.

BLT Market

American XX

B3

1430 Sixth Ave. (at 59th St.)

Subway: 5 Av - 59 St — Dinner Tue – Sat
Phone: 212-521-6125
Web: www.bltrestaurants.com
Prices: $$$

Tucked into the ground floor of the historic Ritz-Carlton Central Park, BLT Market, Laurent Tourondel's market-themed dining hall is a stylish affair with floor-to-ceiling windows flooding light into a big, open room dressed in wood-sculpted credenzas.

With Tourondel's credentials at the helm, this market fare doesn't come cheap, but you'll find only the finest ingredients in the rotating menus that might feature tender pigs in a blanket, slathered in an herby garlic oil and excellent Dijon mustard; spice-crusted yellowfin tuna set atop a purée of a creamy aïoli and paired with roasted beets in vinaigrette and frisée salad; or glazed Long Island duck and Hudson Valley foie gras with Bosc pear-ginger compote and wild mushrooms.

Blue Fin

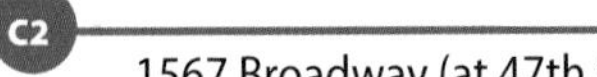

Seafood XX

C2

1567 Broadway (at 47th St.)

Subway: 49 St — Lunch & dinner daily
Phone: 212-918-1400
Web: www.brguestrestaurants.com
Prices: $$$

At first blush, the glass-walled bar that straddles this lively corner of Broadway and 47th Street looks like any other bustling midtown bar—albeit one hip enough to serve time in the W Times Square Hotel. But hidden behind all that happy hour chatter is the impressive Blue Fin—a two-story restaurant with a winding staircase that leads to a beautiful, serene upstairs dining room filled with soft jazz from the live piano.

The menu tackles seafood and sushi with grace—a slender column of ruby-red tuna is piped with creamy avocado, and capped with wonton crackers and a little spicy *sriracha*; while a sesame-crusted bigeye tuna gets some oomph from shiitake mushrooms, a scoop of fragrant jasmine rice, and a tangle of carrots and snow peas.

Bocca di Bacco

Italian 

828 Ninth Ave. (bet. 54th & 55th Sts.)

Subway: 50 St (Eighth Ave.) — Lunch Sat – Sun
Phone: 212-265-8828 — Dinner nightly
Web: www.boccadibacconyc.com
Prices: $$

Nestled into the theater district, rustic yet sultry Bocca di Bacco is a consummate favorite for its great selection of wines, appealing nibbles, and décor that harks back to the *cantine* of Italy with NYC art gallery accents. Solo diners seek the front bar—a sexy perch to snack, sip, and savor.

Through its wine bar identity, the menu spotlights pristine ingredients and products. The array of easy-going dishes may include grilled octopus with a well-dressed potato salad; juicy and tender *fegatini di pollo* (sautéed chicken livers) floating in a sweet onion and port wine reduction; or penne with gorgonzola, green peas, and walnuts that are all sweetness and crunch.

Although nights can get busy and boisterous, the kitchen remains skilled and competent.

Braai

South African 

329 W. 51st St. (bet. Eighth & Ninth Aves.)

Subway: 50 St (Eighth Ave.) — Lunch Tue – Sun
Phone: 212-315-3315 — Dinner nightly
Web: www.braainyc.com
Prices: $$

With a menu that includes ostrich, deviled chicken livers, and African road runner, it didn't take long for this South African restaurant to create a buzz. Opened in 2008, Braai has a few service kinks to iron out if it wants to match the popularity of its sister bar, Xai Xai (a South African wine bar located a few hundred feet away). But for now, the sultry décor—think sexy arched ceilings and gnarled, dark wooden beams—and creative fare more than compensate.

Save room to linger over your wine with a classic South African dessert like the Malva pudding—a soft, springy bread pudding dish of Dutch origin, with caramelized banana and creamy vanilla ice cream that arrives on a thin bed of fragrant *granadilla-amarula* custard.

Brasserie 8 1/2

Contemporary XXX

9 W. 57th St. (bet. Fifth & Sixth Aves.)

Subway: 57 St — Lunch Sun – Fri
Phone: 212-829-0812 — Dinner nightly
Web: www.brasserie8andahalf.com
Prices: $$$

The sweeping, tangerine-colored staircase that delivers you into Brasserie 8 1/2 is probably a bit more theatrical than the restaurant's menu is prepared to live up to, but this Patina Group restaurant has a few tricks up its sleeve. Settle into the main dining room—with its eye-popping hues and unique artwork—and you'll find a solid contemporary French menu, with prettily plated items like yellowfin and mackerel tartare, topped with crème fraîche and passion fruit; or a light and springy trio of fruit sorbets.

Though it's clearly designed to impress company, the restaurant also caters well to solo guests, who can head to the handsome, elevated mezzanine for a quick bite; or hunker down at one of the two sleek, sexy bars that anchor the dining room.

Brasserie Ruhlmann

French XX

A4

45 Rockefeller Plaza (bet. Fifth & Sixth Aves.)

Subway: 47-50 Sts - Rockefeller Ctr — Lunch daily
Phone: 212-974-2020 — Dinner Mon – Sat
Web: www.brasserieruhlmann.com
Prices: $$$

Named for the French designer, Emile-Jacques Ruhlmann, this midtown brasserie—with its dark panels, red velvet, and sexy sconces—sweeps you out of touristy Rockefeller Center and into a heady vision of old-school Paris.

A solid and commendable team heads the kitchen, spinning otherwise staid bistro classics into delicious artistry. A poached artichoke vinaigrette arrives tender and succulent, a rémoulade topped with black olive tapenade spooned into its center; while a pristine Dover Sole Meunière is served whole, beautifully browned, and sided with *pommes fondant* and a bright bundle of sautéed spinach. A decadent cookie plate, filled with creamy lemon squares and rich chocolate triangles, almost prepares you for the outside world again.

Bricco

Italian

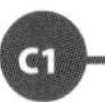
C1

304 W. 56th St. (bet. Eighth & Ninth Aves.)

Subway: 57 St - 7 Av
Phone: 212-245-7160
Web: www.bricconyc.com
Prices: $$

Lunch Mon – Fri
Dinner nightly

It's a bit of a challenge to spot this cozy space in the swirling hubbub of nearby Columbus Circle, but its well worth keeping your eyes peeled. Romantic little nooks like Bricco don't come easy in this neck of the woods, and smooth-talking owner, Nino Catuogno, knows it—he's got the autographed lipstick kisses that line the ceiling to prove it, not to mention a bevy of female fans who line the wooden bar every evening. Couples can head back to the intimate main room for delicious pizzas (made to order in the dining room); fat ribbons of whole wheat pasta in meaty ragù; or tender filet mignon dancing in brandy and cream, and sprinkled with crunchy peppercorns. Save room for a fragrant dessert of deep purple pears, poached in wine and liqueur.

Casellula

American

C1

401 W. 52nd St. (bet. Ninth & Tenth Aves.)

Subway: 50 St (Eighth Ave.)
Phone: 212-247-8137
Web: www.casellula.com
Prices:

Dinner nightly

After running the cheese program at The Modern, Brian Keyser partnered with Joe Farrell to open this simple but charming cheese and wine café off of Ninth Avenue. Inside, a wonderfully attentive staff tends the small bar and handful of wood tables, set against simply adorned brick walls and rustic rows of wine bottles.

With over 30 varieties of excellent cheese, each is clearly organized from fresh to bloomy and beyond. The kitchen's offerings may include delights like a crisp "pig's ass" panini made from a crusty baguette, moist, sweet slices of roast pork, and drizzled with a thick chipotle aïoli; goose-breast reuben with *Fontina Val d'Aosta*, house slaw, and creamy horseradish; or a decadent chocolate cake, with each layer soaked in fresh cream.

China Grill

A4 — Asian XX

60 W. 53rd St. (bet. Fifth & Sixth Aves.)

Subway: 5 Av - 53 St — Lunch Mon – Fri
Phone: 212-333-7788 — Dinner nightly
Web: www.chinagrillmgt.com
Prices: $$$

Opened more than 20 years ago, this first China Grill continues to be a perennial favorite and serves as the flagship of Jeffrey Chodorow's international restaurant organization. The sprawling interior, designed by Jeffrey Beers, is housed on the ground floor of the CBS building and features a multi-level dining room of soaring 30-foot ceilings accented with white canopy light fixtures. The long bar area is a popular spot to unwind after a long day at the office.

Large tables provide the perfect spot to dine with a group; the food is good, fun, and is best enjoyed when shared. Served family style, the Asian-influenced menu may include perfectly fried rice topped with creamy, diced avocado, or delicate pancakes generously filled with tender lobster.

Cho Dang Gol

C4 — Korean

55 W. 35th St. (bet. Fifth & Sixth Aves.)

Subway: 34 St - Herald Sq — Lunch & dinner daily
Phone: 212-695-8222
Web: www.chodanggolny.com
Prices:

Let K-town have its barbecue joints. Cho Dang Gol has its own thing going on—namely tofu, that creamy little bean curd that sets hearts a-jumping. The restaurant is named for a South Korean village that's famous for the stuff, and one imagines the locals would stand by this fresh, silky house-made version, which finds its way into menu items like hot and crispy pancakes, filled with ground pork, vegetables, and scallions; or a cast iron pot, loaded with sweet and spicy octopus, oyster mushrooms, and steamed rice.

Looks-wise, Cho Dang Gol cuts a warm and fuzzy figure with its cute Korean artifacts and rustic wooden tables—but don't expect like-minded service. When the house gets packed, servers respond with brusque efficiency.

Daisy May's BBQ

Barbecue

623 Eleventh Ave. (at 46th St.)

Subway: 50 St (Eighth Ave.) — Lunch & dinner daily
Phone: 212-977-1500
Web: www.daisymaysbbq.com
Prices:

Inside this home-style spot (something between a barn and cafeteria) find classically trained Chef Adam Perry Lang, whose chili vending cart may have brought his first fame, but celebrity appearances (think Oprah) and opening one of the city's best barbeque joints have kept him in the spotlight. The midtown lunch crowds are equally pleased that he maintains his thriving vending cart business (weather permitting).

Everyone from bankers to bike messengers frequent Daisy May's for its fantastic food and friendly aura. Be sure to try the genuine, spicy chili, teeming with chunks of juicy chuck simmered in chilies. With enough friends and planning, indulge in the Big Pig Gig, smoked for eight hours (remember to order this two days in advance).

db Bistro Moderne

Contemporary

55 W. 44th St. (bet. Fifth & Sixth Aves.)

Subway: 5 Av — Lunch Mon – Sat
Phone: 212-391-2400 — Dinner nightly
Web: www.danielnyc.com
Prices: $$$

This stylish Daniel Boulud bistro is an ideal upscale spot for drinking and dining pre- or post-theater. Its moneyed clientele looks perfectly at home in the sophisticated space, which is divided into a lively, red-accented front room and a much quieter, comfortable, more refined elevated back room.

Boulud's French-inflected menu showcases the chef's consistency and formidable skills in dishes like country duck pâté that somehow become richer and more decadent with each bite. The lovely chocolate clafouti is garnished with outstanding vanilla ice cream and chocolate sorbet. Yet most famously, the humble burger is recreated with foie gras, black truffles, and short ribs—a monument that helped ignite New York's gourmet burger renaissance.

Del Frisco's

1221 Sixth Ave. (at 49th St.)

Subway: 47-50 Sts - Rockefeller Ctr — Lunch Mon – Fri
Phone: 212-575-5129 — Dinner nightly
Web: www.delfriscos.com
Prices: **$$$**

Prime, aged, corn-fed beef is the main attraction at this sprawling outpost of the Dallas-based steakhouse chain. Portions range from a six-ounce filet to the 24-ounce Porterhouse to make any Texan proud.

The menu may begin with a suitably rich feast of turtle soup or caviar, but then does an about face with offerings of angel hair pasta or creamed corn. This may be as much a testament to its dedication to please every palate as it is to the fact of its outrageous financial success. Complementing its midtown locale in the McGraw-Hill Building, Del Frisco's showcases a large L-shaped bar, linen-covered tables, and window panels stretching to the second floor. The mezzanine dining area, accessible by a sweeping staircase, enjoys a quieter ambience.

Dizzy's Club Coca-Cola

Southern XX

C1

10 Columbus Circle (in the Time Warner Center)

Subway: 59 St - Columbus Circle — Dinner nightly
Phone: 212-258-9595
Web: www.jalc.org
Prices: **$$**

It took legendary jazz man, Wynton Marsalis, plenty of smooth-talking to convince the myriad city officials and developers that the Time Warner Building should permanently house Jazz at Lincoln Center—but the terrific Dizzy's Club Coca-Cola, a jazz hall-cum-restaurant is all the proof needed to greenlight this project.

Housed on the 5th floor of the North tower, at the Frederick P. Rose Hall, this swanky little gem has glossy windows overlooking Central Park, and grub as delicious as the rotating lineup of performers are talented. Dress loosely—the menu features a naughty lineup of southern staples like succulent fried chicken served with creamy mashed potatoes and tender collard greens; and velvety grits studded with plump shrimp.

Esca

B2

Seafood XXX

402 W. 43rd St. (bet. Ninth & Tenth Aves.)

Subway: 42 St - Port Authority Bus Terminal — Lunch Mon – Sat
Phone: 212-564-7272 — Dinner nightly
Web: www.esca-nyc.com
Prices: $$$

With Mario Batali, Joseph Bastianich, and David Pasternack at the helm, it is no wonder that New Yorkers were introduced to something new when Esca first opened its doors. This is the spot that first put *crudi*, a sort of Italian sashimi, on the culinary map, though they may lie a bit off the well-worn midtown path.

On occasion, this estimable seafood restaurant misses its mark and leaves some to wonder who is steering the ship. But when it's good, it's fantastic—from the table of Italian-style vegetables to the bluefish trio.

The talented staff seems to have a gift for patiently steering newcomers to the perfect Italian wine. Bathed in those creamy yellow walls, dark timbers and soft light, Esca's rustic charms are undeniable.

Estiatorio Milos

A3

Greek XXX

125 W. 55th St. (bet. Sixth & Seventh Aves.)

Subway: 57 St — Lunch Mon – Fri
Phone: 212-245-7400 — Dinner nightly
Web: www.milos.ca
Prices: $$$

It's mod meets the Med in midtown at Estiatorio Milos. This sleek space has cornered the market on industrial chic with its light-filled, atrium-style dining room, raw cement columns and walls, and exposed ducts. Antiqued flooring and decorative objects add a Greek aspect to this otherwise New York-centric space.

Hugely patronized by local businesses and corporate casts, the food here is as polished as the crowd. The kitchen's signature is its simple, yet elegant, preparations of incredibly fresh fish, filleted or left whole. Silky tender and perfectly grilled octopus transports diners straight to the Cyclades, while the meze platter brings together the flavors of Greece with roasted stuffed peppers, olives, tzatziki, *taramasalata*, and fava bean purée.

etcetera etcetera

Italian 

352 W. 44th St. (bet. Eighth & Ninth Aves.)

Subway: 42 St - Port Authority Bus Terminal — Lunch Wed & Sun
Phone: 212-399-4141 — Dinner Tue – Sun
Web: www.etcrestaurant.com
Prices: $$

Hip and modern, etcetera etcetera is a breath of fresh air in the often staid Theater District. The modern and contemporary design punctuated by pops of bright orange has a Milan-meets-Miami sensibility, but the crowd is never too cool for school.

The kitchen turns out seriously solid and well-prepared dishes. Pasta and risotto dishes, such as the homemade basil spaghetti with jumbo lump crab meat and sweet roasted peppers, can be halved and served as appetizers. The entrées (crispy Cornish hen, braised lamb shank) are hearty and offer beautifully balanced flavors and textures. Etcetera etcetera proves that looking good does not always mean spending a fortune—the $35 prix-fixe three-course dinner is an exceptional value.

44 & X Hell's Kitchen

American 

622 Tenth Ave. (at 44th St.)

Subway: 42 St - Port Authority Bus Terminal — Lunch & dinner daily
Phone: 212-977-1170
Web: www.44andx.com
Prices: $$

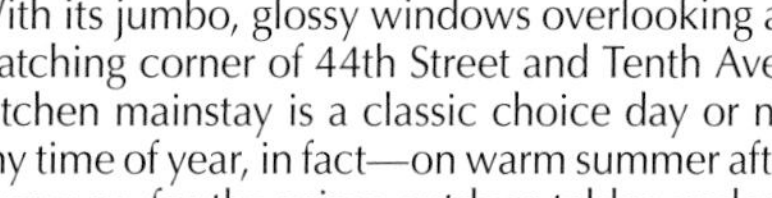

With its jumbo, glossy windows overlooking a prime people-watching corner of 44th Street and Tenth Avenue, this Hell's Kitchen mainstay is a classic choice day or night. Make that any time of year, in fact—on warm summer afternoons, guests queue up for the prime outdoor tables under the big striped awning out front, and come wintertime, the sophisticated, carved wooden bar beckons.

The service staff can read a little flaky on occasion, though it's probably par for the course with waiters sporting cheeky "Heaven" and "Hell" t-shirts. Best to belly up and join the fun, digging into inventive American fare like stacked roasted beets, piped with tangy goat cheese; or moist turkey meat loaf, studded with oyster mushrooms and wrapped in smoky bacon.

Frankie & Johnnie's

Steakhouse XX

32 W. 37th St. (bet. Fifth & Sixth Aves.)

Subway: 34 St - Herald Sq
Phone: 212-947-8940
Web: www.frankieandjohnnies.com
Prices: $$$

Lunch Mon – Fri
Dinner Mon – Sat

You get a slice of history with your perfectly-seared ribeye at this storied Garment District steakhouse. The renovated townhouse—with its masculine sensibility and cozy wood-paneled library-turned upstairs dining room—used to belong to the actor John Drew Barrymore, and it is the second of three sibling restaurants that began in 1926 (the first restaurant is a stone's throw away and the third location resides in Rye, New York).

Served by a professional, all-male brigade, the food is pure steakhouse bliss: think silky Clams Casino, topped with crispy bacon and scallions; tender, bone-on ribeye, seared to perfection; irresistibly crunchy hash browns; and buttery, flaky apple strudel, delivered with a side of fresh whipped cream and mint sprig.

Gallagher's

Steakhouse XX

228 W. 52nd St. (bet. Broadway & Eighth Ave.)

Subway: 50 St (Broadway)
Phone: 212-245-5336
Web: www.gallaghersnysteakhouse.com
Prices: $$$

Lunch & dinner daily

Established in 1927 next to what is now the Neil Simon Theater, this culinary character and true New Yorker (with outposts in New Jersey and Florida) satisfies carnivores with beef grilled over hickory coals. This focus is clear upon entering to face rows of assorted cuts hanging, patiently aging, in the glass-enclosed meat locker. Inside the wood-paneled dining room, charmingly gruff waiters in gold-trimmed blazers efficiently tend red-checked tables, alongside walls lined with nostalgic photographs of Broadway stars, politicians, and athletes.

While meals are not cheap, the quality shines. Classic salads and creamy desserts are delicious bookends to any meal here. The $30 prix-fixe lunch is an excellent option for the budget conscious.

Gordon Ramsay at The London ✿✿

A3 **Contemporary** XXXX

151 W. 54th St. (bet. Sixth & Seventh Aves.)

Subway: 57 St — Dinner Tue – Sat
Phone: 212-468-8888
Web: www.gordonramsay.com
Prices: **$$$$**

Tom Shelby

Despite the power of association, there is nothing Hellish about this kitchen. Namesake Gordon Ramsay may be as famous for his outbursts as he is for this talent, but this chef knows how to ignite passion, and so does this new team. Ramsay opened this restaurant to rave reviews, and while he no longer mans the stoves here, his expertly trained chefs live up to his (culinary) reputation.

With just 45 seats, the elegant dining room feels posh and privileged. Its mid-century modern style, monochromatic color, and chrome fixtures give the impression that Bogey and Bacall would fit right in with this sophisticated, international crowd. The classically prepared contemporary menu displays seasonal products, global accents, and artistry, and is available as a three-course prix-fixe or a seven-course feast.

The food delights the senses with its delicate preparations and dramatic flavors. Expect the likes of grilled rabbit loin with white bean cassoulet and Madeira sauce, hazelnut-crusted Maine diver scallops, and sea bass with tomato and gin consommé. Even if you know your Lafite from a Latour, have the supremely knowledgeable sommelier handpick your selection from the well-chosen list.

Han Bat

Korean

53 W. 35th St. (bet. Fifth & Sixth Aves.)

Subway: 34 St - Herald Sq
Phone: 212-629-5588
Web: N/A
Prices:

Lunch & dinner daily

Pop into this 24-hour K-Town spot for traditional, tasty Korean comfort food. Unlike the surrounding mega-BBQ joints, Han Bat favors a cozy, familial vibe and belly-warming specialties. In place of in-table grills, find *dol sot bi bim bap* (sizzling clay pots of crisp-seared rice topped with beef, pickles, eggs, and condiments); plates of uniquely light *mandoo* (Korean-style dumplings stuffed with pork and vegetables); savory bowls of *sul rung tang* (sliced beef in a milky beef broth); and a spicy stew of kimchi and tofu. Whether stopping in for a lunch special or late-night post-karaoke snack, there is something for everyone on the ample, well-organized menu.

Authentic and intrepid foodies should sample the *u jok sara moo chim*—"jello" from ox legs.

Hell's Kitchen

Mexican

679 Ninth Ave. (bet. 46th & 47th Sts.)

Subway: 50 St (Eighth Ave.)
Phone: 212-977-1588
Web: www.hellskitchen-nyc.com
Prices: **$$**

Lunch Tue – Fri
Dinner nightly

Upscale Mexican food might finally be enjoying its heyday on the city's culinary scene, but Hell's Kitchen was way ahead of the curve. Named for the western midtown neighborhood it calls home, this restaurant has been packing them in from day one—and for good reason. Think delicious, complex Mexican food—spiced to order and lovingly prepared—in a hip, lively, progressive eatery, with great service to boot.

Kick things off with a heaping plate of tender, shredded pork, braised to juicy perfection and folded into soft, warm tortillas, then laced with crème fraîche and chunky guacamole; and wind down with a wickedly good empanada stuffed with warm, gooey sweet banana, and topped with a caramelized bittersweet chocolate sauce.

Insieme

A4 — **Italian** XX

777 Seventh Ave. (at 51st St.)

Subway: 50 St (Broadway) — Lunch Mon – Fri
Phone: 212-582-1310 — Dinner Mon – Sat
Web: www.restaurantinsieme.com
Prices: $$$

Pronounced in-see-em-eh, Insieme means "together" in Italian—a good way to describe the talented team at the heels of the kitchen, the friendly sommelier, and the swift waitstaff. Also, working in striking uniformity is the restaurant's competing menu, which lists contemporary Italian fare beside more traditional Old Country plates (the multi-course tasting menu offers a little of both).

Tucked into the Michelangelo hotel, and cut into clean, Scandinavian lines with a soothing, earthy palette, Insieme's food is just as artfully rendered: a bowl of chewy cavatelli is tossed with caper berries, olives, raisins, pine nuts, and toasty breadcrumbs; while a juicy grilled skirt steak is amped up with arugula, Parmesan and, tangy salsa verde.

Kashkaval

Mediterranean

856 Ninth Ave. (bet. 55th & 56th Sts.)

Subway: 50 St (Eighth Ave.) — Lunch & dinner daily
Phone: 212-581-8282
Web: www.kashkavalfoods.com
Prices: $$

More often than not, there's a long line to get into this charming little Middle Eastern restaurant, tucked into a food-deprived patch of bustling 9th Avenue. The good news is that there's plenty to busy yourself with while you wait, for the front of house doubles as a grocery store stocked with all kinds of mouthwatering goodies like garlicky spreads, delicious cheeses, and exotic oils.

You're also likely to forget all sense of time when you finally do snag a seat in the rustic little back café, and the delicious food starts hitting the table. Try the *muhammara*, a delicious, peppery Lebanese walnut spread; or flaky little cigars stuffed with spinach and feta and rolled into crispy, spiraled buns; or moist turkey meatballs glistening with tomato.

Keens Steakhouse

Steakhouse XX

72 W. 36th St. (bet. Fifth & Sixth Aves.)

Subway: 34 St - Herald Sq
Phone: 212-947-3636
Web: www.keens.com
Prices: **$$$**

Lunch Mon – Fri
Dinner nightly

A survivor of the erstwhile Herald Square Theater District, this palace of steaks, single-malt, and bygone pipe smoke has been thriving since 1885. A sense of history pervades the restaurant, which once enforced a strict men-only rule. The restaurant has an impressive collection of long-stemmed clay churchwarden pipes in racks lining the ceiling, a vestige of its men's-club days; and a sublime whiff of smoke imbues the space that seems to conjure an old English inn.

Fresh oysters; iced trays of seafood; and hearty steaks or chops come in portions—and prices—hefty enough to please the hungriest carnivores. A lighter pub menu of salads, burgers, and sandwiches is also available. Deep earthenware dishes of crème brûlée are perfectly crusted and satisfying.

Kirakuya

Japanese 

2 W. 32n St. (bet. Fifth & Sixth Aves.)

Subway: 34 St - Herald Sq
Phone: 212-695-7272
Web: www.kirakuya-nyc.com
Prices: **$$**

Lunch & dinner Mon – Sat

Though it resides in K-town, this new sake bar and restaurant is Japanese to the hilt. On the second floor of a nondescript building overlooking jumbled 32nd Street, the sultry Kirakuya starts to soothe your nerves long before your first gulp of sake: the spacious room, divided by deep mahogany wood accents, features an elegant bar and high-backed wood banquettes.

Chef Michihiro Kumagai meanders from traditional *izakaya* offerings, fusing Italian ingredients (think anchovy sauce and prosciutto) with classic Japanese technique. At lunch soba and udon are stellar, but don't miss dinner delights like the *unagi don*, a dish of sweetly-glazed, grilled eel, paired with rice, shredded egg, and miso soup; or juicy pork tempura wrapped around okra pods.

Koi

Fusion

C3

40 W. 40th St. (bet. Fifth & Sixth Aves.)

Subway: 42 St - Bryant Pk
Phone: 212-921-3330
Web: www.koirestaurant.com
Prices: **$$$**

Lunch Mon – Fri
Dinner nightly

This stunning, über-trendy New York offshoot of the West Hollywood flagship, with siblings in Las Vegas and Bangkok, is aptly located among the young and affluent in the Bryant Park Hotel. An enormous canopy dominates the dining room; underneath it, elements of feng shui dictate the eye-popping design, in spite of the pulsating music.

The easygoing pan-Asian menu leans toward Japan, with an array of sushi, sashimi, and maki. More original fare may include *sansho*-rubbed hangar steak with *aji-amarillo* sauce, or bowls of creamy, coconut-rice pudding crème brûlée.

From the black-clad waitstaff and attractive plating, to the A-list crowd, cool is the operative word at Koi—perhaps replacing warmth from the staff. The Cellar Bar is equally chic.

La Masseria

Italian

C2

235 W. 48th St. (bet. Broadway & Eighth Ave.)

Subway: 50 St (Eighth Ave.)
Phone: 212-582-2111
Web: www.lamasserianyc.com
Prices: **$$**

Lunch & dinner daily

This Theater District favorite takes your average red-sauce Italian joint, and—like the better Broadway shows outside its door—heightens the everyday into true art. Dressed to look like a Puglian farmhouse, guests are greeted by stone and stucco walls, exposed wood beams, and great old photos; not to mention a few benevolent rounds of cheek-kissing and hand shaking from the chic regulars flocking in.

And yet when it comes to the food, La Masseria leaves the theatrics at the door. You'll find no silly distractions on a plate of tender, grilled artichoke hearts topped with buttery Taleggio; a spot-on penne in a light tomato sauce with bacon, radicchio, and smoked mozzarella; or silky grilled salmon fillet in creamy Dijon mustard sauce.

Landmark Tavern

American XX

B2

626 Eleventh Ave. (at 46th St.)

Subway: 50 St (Eighth Ave.) Lunch & dinner daily
Phone: 212-247-2562
Web: www.thelandmarktavern.org
Prices: $$

Originally opened in 1868, this old cat has had more than a few lives. First it was an Irish saloon that catered to local dock workers; and later, a mediocre restaurant in desperate need of repairs. Finally, in 2005, the space received its long overdue mending and was transformed into the handsome new Landmark Tavern, replete with carved mahogany paneling, shiny beveled mirrors, and a clever new menu to match.

While the tavern isn't quite the ambitious foodie operation it was a few years ago, Landmark's commitment to high-minded pub fare is still very much intact with solid specialties like the juicy cheeseburger laced with a thick slice of grilled Canadian bacon; or the warm, buttery tart, stuffed with tangy raspberry and crunchy walnuts.

Madangsui

Korean 

C4

35 W. 35th St. (bet. Fifth & Sixth Aves.)

Subway: 34 St - Herald Sq Lunch & dinner daily
Phone: 212-564-9333
Web: www.madangsui.com
Prices: $$

If the Korean-speaking waitstaff doesn't tip you off to this K-town joint's authenticity, then perhaps the mind-blowing barbecue, cooked directly at your table, will. Located about a block north of midtown's Korean restaurant hub, Madangsui's clean, glass-fronted façade offers a reprieve from the flurry outside. Inside, soothing leather banquettes and cream colored walls promise more sanity, but the excited hum toward the kitchen reveals a restaurant that is getting its (much deserved) fifteen minutes.

Don't miss the short beef ribs bobbing in a hot beef broth laced with cellophane noodles; spot-on oyster pancakes, studded with green scallions; or the Metropolitan beef and pork combo, which gives delicious new meaning to dinner theater.

Le Bernardin ✿✿✿

A4 Seafood

155 W. 51st St. (bet. Sixth & Seventh Aves.)

Subway: 50 St (Broadway)
Phone: 212-554-1515
Web: www.le-bernardin.com
Prices: **$$$$**

Lunch Mon – Fri
Dinner Mon – Sat

Lyn Hughes Photography

It's one of those strange American restaurant truths that nobody likes to root for the heavily lauded, French-born chef—the back draft, perhaps, for asking folks to shell out so much dough, or an adult extension of rolling one's eyes at the cheerleading captain.

And yet everyone seems to dig Le Bernardin's Eric Ripert, who cut his teeth with Joël Robuchon so many years ago. Probably because he's what you might call a chef's chef—a humble, super-talented guy who prefers manning his own kitchen to celebrity guest spots. It's an authenticity that trickles down to his staff, which is as on-point as any orchestrated ballet, effortlessly winding through the elegant dining room, tending to the mix of old money clientele and splurging food geeks.

Ripert is a master of seafood, and his understanding of fish combined with his French technique makes for an unforgettable meal. The deceptively simple menu is divvied up into three sections—almost raw, barely touched, and lightly cooked—and might include luscious, perfectly grilled escolar, paired with chayote, fried lotus root chips, and a creamy shrimp *sambal* sauce; or sweet, impossibly tender baked lobster with truffled foie gras stuffing.

Mandoo Bar

Korean

2 W. 32nd St. (at Fifth Ave.)

Subway: 34 St - Herald Sq
Phone: 212-279-3075
Web: N/A
Prices:

Lunch & dinner daily

Mandoo is Korean for "dumpling", though you'll find more than that at this K-town favorite. Despite its postage stamp dimensions, Mandoo Bar burns through massive amounts of happy customers a day—most likely due to the fresh, unassuming Korean fare, dished out fast enough to keep weekend shoppers on the move.

The bar serves every kind of dumpling you can dream up, along with a host of Korean specialties like *bulgogi dolsot bibimbob*, rice with marinated beef and vegetables in a hot stone pot; or *yuk kae jang*, spicy beef soup with green onion and egg. Noodle lovers will rejoice in countless options, including the spicy, chewy *joll* noodle with carrots and boiled egg; or the sautéed clear sweet potato noodles that make up the *japchae*.

Má Pêche

Fusion

15 West 56th St. (bet. Fifth & Sixth Aves.)

Subway: 57 St
Phone: 212-777-7773
Web: www.momofuku.com
Prices: $$

Lunch Mon – Sat
Dinner nightly

Tucked into the hip and hot Chambers hotel is David Chang's Má Pêche. Once home to Town, the space wreaks classic Chang and is sparingly dressed in peach walls and blonde wood tables. The staff may be too-cool-for-school, but his is a name and fame that runs far, and fans are happy to make the pilgrimage.

Whether at the plush mezzanine or raucous dining room, this downtown master offers a full menu at his midtown mecca. *Goi calamar*, squid tossed with scallions and peanuts; *mang tay gribiche*, asparagus atop *gribiche* with fish sauce and crab; *xa lach* friseé rolling with tripe, jowl croutons, and egg; and *oc sen sauvage*, wild Burgundy snails and sausage perfectly guarded by a garlic puddle are petite samples of his Asian affair swept with French flair.

Marea ✿✿

D1 — Seafood XXX

240 Central Park South (bet. Broadway & Seventh Ave.)

Subway: 59 St - Columbus Circle — Lunch & dinner Mon – Sat
Phone: 212-582-5100
Web: www.marea-nyc.com
Prices: **$$$$**

Daniel Krieger

Strike while the iron's hot might be what Michael White and Chris Cannon had in mind when they opened this gorgeous Italian seafood venture back in May of 2009. Most folks would have been happy just to sit back and lap up the praise being heaped on the partners' other two fine dining ventures, Alto and Convivio.

Not these two, and thank the stars above—for the city's eating all the better for it. With a fantastic location, steps from the southwest corner of Central Park and Manhattan's elite crowd dining here, Marea is a flat-out stunner, with beautiful back-lit walls, impossibly glossy striped wood panels, and beet red chandeliers.

Chef Michael White hits his wheelhouse with this coastal Italian seafood menu, where a healthy list of *crudo*, pasta, and meat (hand-picked by Pat La Frieda) round out the menu. Dinner might include a plate of perfectly grilled octopus paired with tender, buttery smoked potato, pickled red onion, and a drizzle of chili oil over frisée and baby greens; soft little pillows of *gnocchetti* tossed with ruby red shrimp, Controne bean purée, and rosemary; or sautéed branzino over a sweet, creamy smear of walnut *agrodolce* and tender roasted *radicchio di Treviso*.

Marseille

French XX

630 Ninth Ave. (at 44th St.)

Subway: 42 St - Port Authority Bus Terminal — Lunch & dinner daily
Phone: 212-333-2323
Web: www.marseillenyc.com
Prices: $$

Marseille marries the charm of a classic French bistro with the inimitable style of New York City. The sexy, soft golden glow, convivial spirit, and superlative Theater District location make it a popular choice for everyone from tourists craving a taste of Broadway to colleagues cooling off after a day's work.

The skilled and truly professional kitchen prepares an impressive cuisine bursting with pronounced, balanced flavors. From salads and seasonal specials to more French-formed entrées like steak frites, there is something for everyone. Hungry diners appreciate that the portions lean toward American sensibilities; and the budget-conscious value the prix-fixe lunch and dinner menus. Don't skip out without the frites—they may be the best in the city.

Mercato

Italian 

352 W. 39th St. (bet. Eighth & Ninth Aves.)

Subway: 42 St - Port Authority Bus Terminal — Lunch & dinner daily
Phone: 212-643-2000
Web: www.mercatonyc.com
Prices: $$

This newly minted Italian trattoria in Hell's Kitchen arrives courtesy of Puglian-born Fabio Camardi, a onetime partner at Cacio e Vino. With a charming décor featuring weathered farm tools; vintage signs; a small back-lit wooden bar; and a walk-in wine room, the vibe is decidedly rustic, almost cave-like, at Mercato.

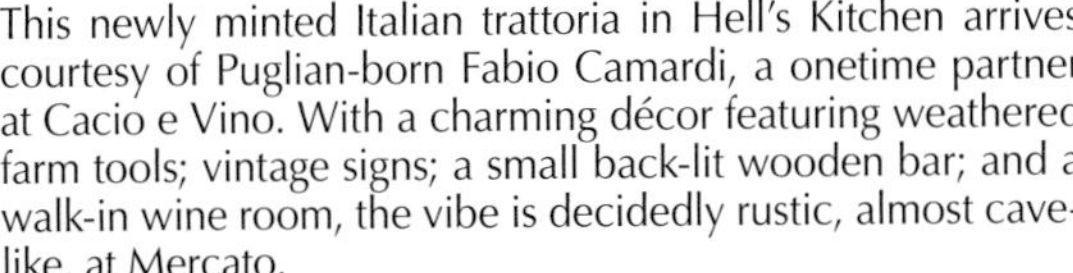

All the better to settle in for a luscious glass of red wine and get things started with a plate of plump, wickedly fresh sardines, grilled to perfection and coated with a lip-smacking *salmoriglio*; and then move on to a heaping *tiella* chock-a-block with mussels, cherry tomatoes, fluffy rice, and potatoes, served tableside from the cast iron skillet; and finish with a silky panna cotta drizzled with aged balsamic vinegar.

Masa ✿✿✿

C1 — Japanese XX

10 Columbus Circle (in the Time Warner Center)

Subway: 59 St - Columbus Circle — Lunch Tue – Fri
Phone: 212-823-9800 — Dinner Mon – Sat
Web: www.masanyc.com
Prices: **$$$$**

Masa

Welcome to the game changer. From the pristine sushi to the perfectly positioned foot rest under the sushi counter, not a single detail is left to chance at legendary sushi chef, Masa Takayama's namesake restaurant. That you may end up shelling out four c-notes for such an otherworldly experience—well, we can only tell you that many would argue that you'll never look at Japanese cuisine the same way again.

Make your way up to the 4th floor of the Time Warner Center, and you'll find a beautiful, soothing Zen-like temple of blonde wood and stone, where a smart, but completely unhurried staff sets the tone for the brilliant parade of fish and extraordinary ingredients to come.

The omakase menu changes nightly, but a night in Takayama's (or one of his talented *itamae's*) hands may reveal impossibly tender Japanese hairy crab strewn with yellow flower petals; pristine toro tartare with caviar, chives, and yuzu; a tangle of needle-thin carrots with micro-herbs and ponzu sauce; deep-fried blowfish head; sea urchin risotto laced with fragrant white truffle; or tender, just-seared Ohmi beef with seaweed, Himalayan salts, and shaved white truffle. And that's before the sushi hits the table.

The Modern 

Contemporary XXX

A4

9 W. 53rd St. (bet. Fifth & Sixth Aves.)

Subway: 5 Av - 53 St
Phone: 212-333-1220
Web: www.themodernnyc.com
Prices: **$$$**

Lunch daily
Dinner Mon – Sat

Ellen Silverman

The Modern proves that art does not simply hang on walls. Much more than a museum cafeteria, this is a destination of its own right, drawing a well-dressed crowd of international sophisticates who come as much for its sleek design as they do for the French-accented American cuisine.

Floor-to-ceiling glass walls overlooking the renowned Abby Aldrich Rockefeller Sculpture Garden and a verdant, wall-sized photograph set a quiet and soothing tone, but its unparalleled modern design is enough to make décor enthusiasts weep with joy. (And if you love that glass you're drinking from, pick it up at the MoMA gift shop.) Alsatian-born chef, Gabriel Kreuther paints an inventive picture of perfection in his kitchen, where everything is at its height of flavor and freshness. Among the masterpieces are dishes like *morcilla* sausage risotto with tart green apple and silky Maine lobster, or buttery slow-baked Scottish salmon with tantalizing horseradish and pickled ramps. Flawless, well-orchestrated servers (and a tempting chocolate trolley) complete the picture.

The stylish and perpetually hopping bar room offers a wide offering of European-influenced small plates from the chef.

Molyvos

A3 Greek XX

871 Seventh Ave. (bet. 55th & 56th Sts.)

Subway: 57 St - 7 Av
Phone: 212-582-7500
Web: www.molyvos.com
Prices: $$

Lunch Mon – Sat
Dinner nightly

Part of the Livanos family restaurant empire, which boasts Oceana as its crown jewel, Molyvos (named for the owner's birthplace on the island of Lesvos) brings the home-style dishes of Greece to midtown.

Chef/partner (and cookbook author) Jim Botsacos can claim his fair share of the restaurant's success. Dishes highlight the freshest fish, whether grilled whole or skewered with marinated Gulf shrimp and summer vegetables. Equally enticing is the Greek-style hamburger, perhaps best enjoyed with a glass of Greek wine.

A block south of Carnegie Hall, Molyvos is well situated for those attending a performance. Order the modestly priced pre- and post-theater menu and the attentive staff will be sure to pace your meal in time with the performance.

Nick & Stef's

B4 Steakhouse XX

9 Penn Plaza (bet. Seventh & Eighth Aves.)

Subway: 34 St - Penn Station
Phone: 212-563-4444
Web: www.nickandstefs.com
Prices: $$$

Lunch Mon – Fri
Dinner Mon – Sat

Adjacent to Madison Square Garden and Penn Station is one of the neighborhood's better dining options: Nick & Stef's (named for partner Chef Joachim Splichal's twin sons). As part of the Patina Restaurant Group, this steakhouse is known for serving consistently good food.

The menu balances its list of broiled steaks with a variety of entrées including Nova Scotia lobster stuffed with crabmeat and organic roasted chicken. Meats are served unadorned, so make sure you order some glorious sides like herbed shoestring fries or garlicky sautéed spinach. Lunchtime also highlights salads, sandwiches, and embellished steakhouse burgers.

A suited clientele regularly fills this contemporary space, featuring warm tones and angled pine ceilings.

Nobu Fifty Seven

Japanese XXX

A3

40 W. 57th St. (bet. Fifth & Sixth Aves.)

Subway: 57 St
Phone: 212-757-3000
Web: www.noburestaurants.com
Prices: $$$$

Lunch Mon – Fri
Dinner nightly

Chef Nobu Matsuhisa continues to succeed with his upscale chain that has expanded into midtown. The entrance feels removed from the bustle of 57th Street, while David Rockwell's sleek interior uses sake jugs, exotic woods, and rattan walls to fashion a sultry mood—a feat for this large and busy space.

The restaurant attracts a cosmopolitan crowd whose expense accounts can handle the hefty prices. Creative à la carte offerings are a highlight, with a variety of fresh, beautifully prepared fish and signature specialties like black cod with miso or rock shrimp tempura with creamy chili sauce. However, the uninhibited gourmand should simply order the omakase, attractively presented in lacquered bento boxes with a guarantee of genuine Nobu quality.

Orso

Italian XX

C2

322 W. 46th St. (bet. Eighth & Ninth Aves.)

Subway: 42 St - Port Authority Bus Terminal
Phone: 212-489-7212
Web: www.orsorestaurant.com
Prices: $$

Lunch & dinner daily

This intimate little restaurant—with its friendly staff and antique photos—is the late-night haunt of Broadway players in search of a post-show meal. It shows off their good taste too, for the food at this Restaurant Row darling rises well above the competition.

Occupying the ground floor of a charming brownstone, Orso offers simple, delicious Italian classics including a very nice selection of pizzas. The 20-dollar selection of five vegetable dishes, like sautéed chickpeas, spinach, and tomatoes with Parmesan, can turn into a meal in itself. From the moment they set the fresh and flavorful white bean dip and bread upon the table, the charming and knowledgeable staff is happy to help. Be sure to call ahead, as pre-theater reservations book quickly.

Oceana ✿

Seafood 

A4

1221 Sixth Ave. (at 49th St.)

Subway: 47-50 Sts - Rockefeller Ctr

Lunch & dinner daily

Phone: 212-759-5941

Web: www.livanosrestaurantgroup.com

Prices: $$$

Paul Johnson

Oceana, one of New York's revered seafood houses (operated by the Livanos family, the group behind Molyvos and Abboccato), gets a new home, a heck of a face-lift, and the buzz begins.

The old Oceana (on East 54th Street) had a quiet, clubby feel. The revamped version is tucked into the ground floor of the McGraw-Hill office tower and is decidedly glossier—with a big marble dining counter-cum-raw bar and an elegant dining room fitted out with dark wood floors and pretty pale walls broken up by pops of color from deep blue hydrangeas. Possibly feeding off their slick new digs, the service staff doesn't miss a beat, pacing the meal with the exacting precision of a well-tuned orchestra.

Seafood still reigns supreme, but fans of the old Oceana will note more options on Chef Ben Pollinger's dinner menu. Fresh snapper ceviche is studded with blood orange, chopped pistachios, and diced red chilies, then topped with micro pea shoots and paper thin slices of hearts of palm; while golden, pan-seared calamari is stuffed with an exquisite seafood sausage, set over sautéed Swiss chard and laced with a creamy lemon dressing; and creamy green apple risotto is flecked with Parmigiano Reggiano.

Osteria al Doge

Italian

C3

142 W. 44th St. (bet. Broadway & Sixth Ave.)

Subway: Times Sq - 42 St
Phone: 212-944-3643
Web: www.osteria-doge.com
Prices: $$

Lunch Mon – Fri
Dinner nightly

Tucked into one of those theater-dominated cross streets that define this jumbled area of Times Square, the first thing Osteria al Doge has on the competition is its good looks: think sunny yellow walls, wrought iron chandeliers, and bright Italian ceramic plates. Not to mention a long marble and wood bar where solo diners can settle into a comfortable padded stool and enjoy a little people-watching before the real show.

Back on the plates it's delicious Italian food tended to with love, like a plump tangle of fettuccine verdi in a silky lamb ragù dotted with lemon rind and pitted black picholine olives; thin slices of tuna carpaccio drizzled with citrus olive oil, a dash of crunchy sea salt, and herbs; or a fresh lemon tart topped with strawberries.

Osteria del Circo

Italian

A3

120 W. 55th St. (bet. Sixth & Seventh Aves.)

Subway: 57 St
Phone: 212-265-3636
Web: www.osteriadelcirco.com
Prices: $$$

Lunch Mon – Fri
Dinner nightly

Ever fantasized about running away to join the circus? Fulfill that dream without all of the acrobatics at Osteria del Circo. This restaurant, run by the Maccioni clan of Le Cirque fame, offers a tasteful take on the Big Top. Its tent-like ceiling is complete with streaming fabric in a riot of colors and is punctuated by spinning circus performers and animal sculptures. There is a palpable buzz here—just one of the reasons there are so many regulars.

However, this menu isn't about peanuts and popcorn. Instead, look forward to deftly prepared Italian dishes like grilled branzino and milk-fed veal chops from the professional kitchen. The staff is warm and engaging—not surprising given the Maccionis reputation for throwing open their arms to guests.

Per Se ✿✿✿

Contemporary

C1

10 Columbus Circle (in the Time Warner Center)

Subway: 59 St - Columbus Circle
Phone: 212-823-9335
Web: www.perseny.com
Prices: $$$$

Lunch Fri – Sun
Dinner nightly

Deborah Jones

It's the culinary million dollar question—or in this case, the $275 question. You're looking to drop some dough on a once-in-a-lifetime meal, and you expect to be blown away. Not mildly impressed or pleasantly surprised; but tears-wetting-your-cheeks-as-you-shake-your-friend's-shoulders blown away.

Chef Thomas Keller has your back. Having risen to international fame with his Napa Valley restaurant, The French Laundry, Keller is what you might call a foodie's foodie. There's no razzmatazz at Per Se to distract you from the divinity on your plate; only pitch-perfect service and a classically beautiful dining room overlooking Central Park.

Three tasting menus are offered nightly, each one a mind-blowing affair that might lead down any number of delicious avenues. Yours might detour into plump Salvatore Bklyn ricotta *agnolotti* with Oregon morels and English peas in a creamy *mousseline de pain au lait*; tender Elysian Fields Farm lamb chop with new potatoes and glazed heirloom radishes in a charred shishito pepper vinaigrette; or butter-poached Nova Scotia lobster mitts paired with San Marzano tomato marmalade, *cipollini* tempura, and baby romaine drizzled in a stunning bacon vinaigrette.

Petrossian

French XXX

A3

182 W. 58th St. (at Seventh Ave.)

Subway: 57 St - 7 Av
Phone: 212-245-2214
Web: www.petrossian.com
Prices: $$$

Lunch & dinner daily

Housed along a tourist-filled stretch near Carnegie Hall in the ornate, Renaissance-style Alwyn Court building dating back to 1907, Petrossian makes no apologies for its old-world bourgeois indulgence. And why should it? Its pedigree speaks for itself: this is the baby sister to Petrossian Paris, a French mainstay that's been going strong since the 1920's.

The original location, opened by two Armenian brothers, put caviar on the map, and the company remains the premier importer of Russian caviar. Not surprisingly, the New York branch specializes in the inky stuff—all the more reason to linger among the Lalique crystal sconces and etched Erté mirrors, and indulge in the house tasting, filled with ace caviar, foie gras, and delicious smoked fish.

Piano Due

Italian XXX

A4

151 W. 51st St. (bet. Sixth & Seventh Aves.)

Subway: 49 St
Phone: 212-399-9400
Web: www.pianoduenyc.net
Prices: $$$

Lunch Mon – Fri
Dinner Mon – Sat

With neighbors like critically-acclaimed Le Bernardin in your hood, there's not a lot of wiggle room for area restaurants to mail it in when it comes to food and ambience. Piano Due has both in spades—but you'll have to find it first.

Duck into always-hopping Palio Bar and make your way up (via an elevator) to this second-floor den, romantically dressed in antique mirrors, silk fabrics, and plush red chairs. Dinner might include a fresh tangle of tagliatelle tossed with Maryland lump crabmeat and *pepperoncini*; or tender braised chicken with Italian sausage in white wine. From the service to the cutlery, Piano Due is all grace and elegance—but not so much so that the restaurant doesn't know a good deal. The $30 lunch prix-fixe is a steal.

Porter House

C1 — Steakhouse XXX

10 Columbus Circle (in the Time Warner Center)

Subway: 59 St - Columbus Circle — Lunch & dinner daily
Phone: 212-823-9500
Web: www.porterhousenewyork.com
Prices: **$$$$**

The name says it all at Porter House, part of the Time Warner Center's elite restaurant collection. Beef is the theme of this modern steakhouse, where the 28-day dry-aged namesake cut is the signature dish.

In a location convenient for business people as well as tourists, and designed with a wall of windows overlooking Columbus Circle and Central Park South, its setting is as prime as its cuts of beef. The dining room takes the clubby elements of a traditional steakhouse and updates them with a clean-lined approach that does not disturb its masculine chi.

Steeped in well-prepared classics like clams casino, T-bones, and coconut cake, the menu also displays a contemporary, if somewhat indulgent, pizzazz (think bacon-studded creamed spinach).

Print

B1 — American XXX

653 Eleventh Ave. (at 48th St.)

Subway: 50 St (Eighth Ave.) — Lunch & dinner daily
Phone: 212-757-2224
Web: www.printrestaurant.com
Prices: **$$**

Set among the car dealerships and new residential units that flank this lonesome section of Midtown West, Print may prove to be a pioneer in this burgeoning hood. As it is, anyone driving up the West Side Highway suddenly has a darn good reason to pull off the 42nd Street exit.

Set just off the lobby of the Kimpton Hotel Group's Ink48, Print is downright lovely, with stunning, mesh-covered windows, copper-topped tables, and rustic ceramics. The food, prepared by the talented husband-wife duo, Charles Rodriguez and Heather Carlucci-Rodriguez, is fresh, seasonal, and unapologetically simple—think juicy, slow-roasted pork sandwiches stuffed with sautéed broccoli rabe and fontina; or lip-smacking chocolate bread with raw honey and ricotta.

Radiance Tea House

Asian

A3

158 W. 55th St. (bet. Sixth & Seventh Aves.)

Subway: 57 St - 7 Av — Lunch & dinner daily
Phone: 212-217-0442
Web: www.radiancetea.com
Prices: 🙾

In frenetic, fast-paced midtown, this serene oasis is a welcome relief. Beautifully carved mahogany tables sit atop natural wooden floors, while exotic teas line the shelves and infuse the air with their delicate fragrances. The space also accommodates a lovely gift and book store where tea is the principal subject.

The pan-Asian menu focuses on delicious soups, cold noodles, rice-flour rolls, and rice bowls. The handmade soupy-pork dumplings are a must—its tender wrappers are stuffed with ground pork and ginger-garlic swimming in savory pork both. Tea lovers rejoice: an international selection of over 150 varieties is available for your sipping pleasure, including the signature blend of green and black teas with rose, jasmine, and sunflowers.

Remi

Italian

A4

145 W. 53rd St. (bet. Sixth & Seventh Aves.)

Subway: 7 Av — Lunch & dinner daily
Phone: 212-581-4242
Web: www.remi-ny.com
Prices: **$$**

There's always a convivial buzz winding through the various rooms of this Italian restaurant, from the thumping party room in back to its atrium-enclosed shop, pushing out gourmet food to-go. At the center of the party is Remi's main room—with its whimsical flying buttress archways, murals and mirrors, and Venetian glass chandeliers.

It's hard to remember the place has a delicious menu in this well-orchestrated production, but indeed it does—grabbing specialties from the Veneto region and coupling them with easygoing, rustic Italian basics. Try the fresh pasta, in a rich lamb ragù studded with meatballs and Parmesan; or a coffee-flavored panna cotta, laced with a supple hazelnut salsa, and carrying hints of vanilla bean.

Robert

Contemporary XX

D1

2 Columbus Circle (bet. Broadway & Eighth Ave.)

Subway: 59 St - Columbus Circle Lunch & dinner daily
Phone: 212-299-7730
Web: www.arkrestaurants.com
Prices: $$

The booming restaurant scene growing around Columbus Circle (nearby Time Warner Center is a hotbed of high-end restaurants) gets another notch on its belt with the Museum of Arts & Design's new restaurant, Robert.

Named for famous party planner Robert Isabell, who unexpectedly passed in 2009, the L-shaped restaurant resides on the ninth floor (request a north-facing table for good views), and its super-modern design—which boasts blush and orange light boxes and video-art installations—leaves you wondering if the food will get any attention. A rich, smoky tomato soup licked with a whirl of cream; and wickedly fresh wild mushroom cavatelli brimming spicy pork sausage, earthy Tuscan kale, and sweet cubes of pumpkin supplies the answer.

Russian Samovar

Russian 

C2

256 W. 52nd St. (bet. Broadway & Eighth Ave.)

Subway: 50 St (Broadway) Dinner nightly
Phone: 212-757-0168
Web: www.russiansamovar.com
Prices: $$

This restaurant's flashy mix of Russian celebrities and hockey players provides enough entertainment to rival Broadway, making it perfectly at home in the Theater District. The outstanding vodka selection, house-infused and available by the shot, carafe, or bottle, has been enlivening this crowd since well before the craze spread to the rest of the city. Though the décor is one part Old World and one part Russian grandmother, no one seems to mind.

The brisk but helpful staff serves authentic favorites, like the house-made *pelmeni*, filled with ground veal and beef, served in a subtle chicken broth with sour cream. Warm blini with vibrant caviar or silky salmon may be deliciously paired with their own horseradish-infused vodka for a memorable kick.

Scarlatto

C2 **Italian** XX

250 W. 47th St. (bet. Broadway & Eighth Ave.)

Subway: 50 St (Eighth Ave.) Lunch & dinner daily
Phone: 212-730-4535
Web: www.scarlattonyc.com
Prices: $$

Step down from the neon lights of Broadway and into the winsome world of Scarlatto. Set below street level, this restaurant pours on the charm in its warm and inviting dining room where exposed brick walls are lined with wine bottles, mirrors, and stills of Audrey Hepburn from the film *Roman Holiday*.

The restaurant caters to theater-lovers who relish classics like veal saltimbocca—pan-seared cutlets strewn with cheese, sage, and prosciutto—served upon garlicky spinach. For interesting departures from the usual, the daily specials should not be missed. A pre-theater menu sprinkles favorites among its three courses while keeping an eye on the clock. Scarlatto's desserts are heavenly, and the delicate tiramisu, made in-house, is a crowd pleaser.

The Sea Grill

D2 **Seafood** XX

19 W. 49 St. (bet. Fifth & Sixth Aves.)

Subway: 47-50 Sts - Rockefeller Ctr Lunch Mon – Fri
Phone: 212-332-7610 Dinner Mon – Sat
Web: www.patinagroup.com
Prices: $$$

This seafood grill overlooking Rockefeller Center's ice skating rink boasts one of the city's most famed locations. As expected, winter bookings start early at The Sea Grill, especially near the holidays, when skaters whizz by your windows filled with the best (and warmest) view of the Christmas tree. However, summertime is likewise charming, when the doors swing open and diners can enjoy an alfresco feel overlooking the Rink Bar.

Perhaps due to its tourist-driven locale, the fare is solid, rather than terrifically surprising. Offerings may include platters of chilled shellfish, teeming with lobster, crab meat, shrimp, and ceviche; Sea Grill chowder; or grilled specialties, like East Coast halibut. Save room for the memorable desserts.

Seäsonal ✿

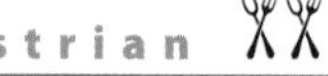

A3 Austrian

132 W. 58th St. (bet. Sixth & Seventh Aves.)

Subway: 57 St - 7 Av — Lunch & dinner Mon – Sat
Phone: 212-957-5550
Web: www.seasonalnyc.com
Prices: $$$

Seäsonal

When Wolfgang Ban and Eduard Frauneder met at the Vienna Culinary Institute, it was a match made in culinary heaven. The chefs share a common taste for turning staid German-Austrian food on its conventional little bum, and this food-starved strip of midtown couldn't be more thankful for it.

Located just behind the Jumeirah Essex House, the restaurant is simply dressed in a sophisticated neutral palette dotted with elegant table settings. The service is impressive and adds a layer of formality to the arena. Settle in and let the warm, polished staff walk you through serious dishes that may include refined classics such as *wiener schnitzel* served with potato, cucumber, and lignonberry.

Dinner turns to the season but might unveil bright orange, smoked ocean trout, served chilled and paired with a smear of smooth cauliflower purée, pickled sweet and sour cabbage, and silky caviar; or *kaisergulasch*, a rich, sienna-hued veal cheek goulash garnished with a fresh dollop of sour cream and a side of tender spätzle. The bar menu offers a great small plates menu—the perfect place to nurse a glass of wine from the restaurant's impressive by-the-glass selection of Austrian vintages.

Shelly's

Italian XX

B3

41 W. 57th St. (bet. Fifth & Sixth Aves.)

Subway: 57 St — Lunch & dinner Mon – Sat
Phone: 212-245-2422
Web: www.shellysnewyork.com
Prices: **$$**

This modern, buzzing neighborhood favorite has all the charm of a coastal trattoria, conveniently located in midtown. Nonetheless, the Italian menu offers something for everyone, perhaps including thin crust pizzas (with some made of whole grains for the health conscious), a sizeable selection of entrée salads, prime steaks dry-aged for 28 days, and, of course, *pesce* flown in daily from the Mediterranean. The raw bar displays sparkling offerings, such as East and West Coast oyster varieties or clams on the half shell, and is cleverly set up near the entrance to tempt arriving diners and passersby alike.

The amiable staff ensures a fulfilling experience in this slender, attractive room featuring burgundy banquettes and polished wood accents.

South Gate

Contemporary XXX

A3

154 Central Park South (bet. Sixth & Seventh Aves.)

Subway: 57 St — Lunch & dinner daily
Phone: 212-484-5120
Web: www.jumeirah.com
Prices: **$$$**

Tucked into the first floor of the Jumeirah Essex House, South Gate is downright splendid in its sophistication. Designed by Tony Chi, the room owns a singular light and airy sexiness, with padded leather tables, creamy swivel chairs, and mirrored glass walls.

Chef Kerry Heffernan's modern American menu elevates contemporary classics to current heights. Don't miss the creamy fried macaroni and cheese, crunchy with breadcrumbs and sporting a bright, perfectly smoked tomato coulis; or the delicately poached lobster salad with ripe avocado and shaved fennel ribbons, beautifully tied together with a lemon emulsion. Spotty service can sometimes put a dent in an otherwise lovely evening, but a seat at the welcoming bar will certainly remedy the situation.

Staghorn Steakhouse

B3 Steakhouse XX

315 W. 36th St. (bet. Eighth & Ninth Aves.)

Subway: 34 St - Penn Station — Lunch Mon – Fri
Phone: 212-239-4390 — Dinner Mon – Sat
Web: www.staghornsteakhouse.com
Prices: $$$

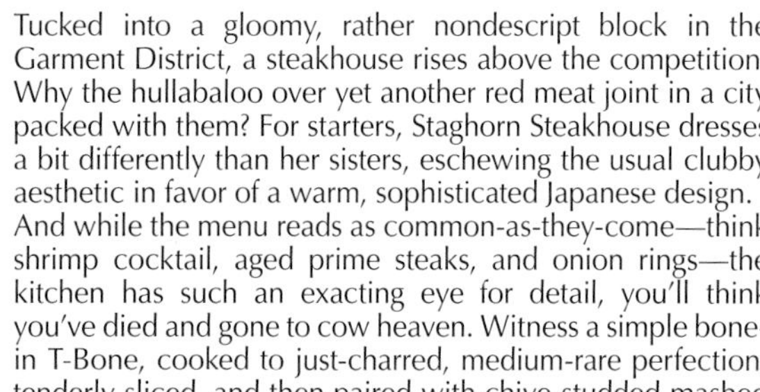

Tucked into a gloomy, rather nondescript block in the Garment District, a steakhouse rises above the competition. Why the hullabaloo over yet another red meat joint in a city packed with them? For starters, Staghorn Steakhouse dresses a bit differently than her sisters, eschewing the usual clubby aesthetic in favor of a warm, sophisticated Japanese design.

And while the menu reads as common-as-they-come—think shrimp cocktail, aged prime steaks, and onion rings—the kitchen has such an exacting eye for detail, you'll think you've died and gone to cow heaven. Witness a simple bone-in T-Bone, cooked to just-charred, medium-rare perfection, tenderly sliced, and then paired with chive-studded mashed potatoes and a silky scoop of creamed spinach.

Sugiyama

C1 Japanese X

251 W. 55th St. (bet. Broadway & Eighth Ave.)

Subway: 57 St - 7 Av — Dinner Tue – Sat
Phone: 212-956-0670
Web: www.sugiyama-nyc.com
Prices: $$$

Remember when hosts and servers actually seemed (gulp) happy to see you? When chefs were honored to have you choose their restaurant, and took the time to tell you so? Seems like a very long time ago to most jaded Manhattan eaters, but the lovely Sugiyama—a little Japanese superstar that looks, at first blush, like so many other kids in its class—offers hope that true hospitality exists.

That—and the *kaiseki* is off the hizzay. It might start with silky monkfish liver blended with fresh, custardy tofu, and paired with grated radish and ponzu sauce; and then move on to a spread of sashimi so bright it could rival a crayon box; tender braised octopus; crab wrapped in whisper-thin white radish; and glazed sea bass, grilled to smoky-sweet perfection.

Sushi of Gari 46

Japanese XX

C2

347 W. 46th St. (bet. Eighth & Ninth Aves.)

Subway: Times Sq - 42 St — Lunch Mon – Fri
Phone: 212-957-0046 — Dinner nightly
Web: www.sushiofgari.com
Prices: $$$$

This outpost of Chef Masatoshi "Gari" Sugio's much-loved sushi trifecta doesn't quite stack up to the near-surreal omakase experience that shot the original Upper East Side prodigy to fame, but coming this close to sushi perfection in the increasingly commercial Theater District is good enough. The pay-per-piece omakase show will put a sizable, albeit worthy, dent in your wallet, but those on a budget can always hit the reasonably-priced regular menu. The place to sit is at the action-packed bar, where you can watch the staff slice and dice their way through Japanese fare like a nori-wrapped bundle of warm rice topped with sweet King crab meat; or gorgeous ruby red tuna, brushed with soy and topped with creamy tofu sauce and freshly grated wasabi.

Sushi Zen

Japanese XX

C3

108 W. 44th St. (bet. Broadway & Sixth Ave.)

Subway: 42 St - Bryant Pk — Lunch Mon – Fri
Phone: 212-302-0707 — Dinner Mon – Sat
Web: www.sushizen-ny.com
Prices: $$$

Nestled among midtown's high-rises, this jewel of a sushi restaurant is a nice respite from the Bryant Park hustle and bustle—with soothing swaths of natural light flooding a small dining room with high ceilings, and a sidewalk seating section protected by fabric panels and potted green plants.

Chef Toshio Suzuki's team doles out a host of rolls, many of them going beyond the conventional preparations to employ seasonal fish and vegetables. Kick things off with a smoky white miso soup bobbing with Asari clams; and then move on to the Bara Chirashi Sushi, or sushi Zen style. "Bara" means little things, and here that translates to a neverending style of fish, sashimi, and vegetables served over rice. Save room for the *yokan*, a sweet, jellied dessert.

Szechuan Gourmet 

Chinese 

C3

21 W. 39th St. (bet. Fifth & Sixth Aves.)

Subway: 42 St - Bryant Pk — Lunch & dinner daily
Phone: 212-921-0233
Web: www.szechuangourmetnyc.com
Prices: $$

Despite the exquisite pain inflicted by their wok tossed green chilies, legions line up for more of Szechuan Gourmet's spicy, tasty, and authentic delicacies. Away from the usual lunch bustle, hordes hustle at this midtown haven for their devilishly delicious repertoire of Sichuan specialties.

The attempt at ambience—dim lighting and walls decked in red Chinese lanterns—is a touch clichéd, but the kitchen's masterful marriage of ingredients amply atones with specialties like tofu crêpes stuffed with shiitakes; crispy lamb dusted with cumin and chilies; and bass fillets swimming in a smoky soup of cabbage and cellophane noodles. Also faithfully flavorful are rabbit pieces glazed with a sweet, spicy oil and conch slivers in roasted chili vinaigrette.

Taboon

Middle Eastern 

C1

773 Tenth Ave. (at 52nd St.)

Subway: 50 St (Eighth Ave.) — Lunch Sun
Phone: 212-713-0271 — Dinner nightly
Web: N/A
Prices: $$

At the far west side of Gotham, amid car dealerships, industrial spaces, and recording studios is the Middle Eastern sanctum —Taboon—where the vibe is pleasant and the aroma enticing. Enter and be greeted by a brick-walled wood-burning oven (*taboon*), whose crackling logs exude an air of rusticity that fuses deftly with the food and philosophy.

Fresh from *taboon* to table, rip into fluffy flatbreads and slather with dollops of *tzatziki*. Linger abroad with the likes of sautéed calamari beside ribbons of fennel, sage, and mint; or fragrant lamb kebabs, grilled to tender perfection, set atop a mélange of eggplant, onion, tomato, cumin, and yogurt. A solid dining feat, Taboon is a pioneer of sorts in merging Middle Eastern and Mediterranean flavors.

Toloache

Mexican XX

251 W. 50th St. (bet. Broadway & Eighth Ave.)

Subway: 50 St (Broadway) Lunch & dinner daily
Phone: 212-581-1818
Web: www.toloachenyc.com
Prices: $$

Mexican dining is at its hottest in New York, and is further elevated at Toloache, a sophisticated yet festive two-story restaurant decked out in brightly painted tiles, tawny wood-beam ceilings, and punched-metal chandeliers.

A pleasure from start to finish, try the *tacos de pastor*, tender *guajillo*-marinated pork tacos stuffed with grilled pineapple salsa, white onion, and bright green cilantro; or the wonderfully smoky house chicken served over boldly flavored corn *pico de gallo* with a fried cheese-and-pinto bean dumpling. A spongy Meyer lemon *tres leches* cake is perfectly paired with deeply floral hibiscus coulis.

A serious list of tequilas is on offer and a worthy follow-up to one of the eight refreshing margaritas poured nightly.

Trattoria Dell'Arte

Italian XX

A3

900 Seventh Ave. (bet. 56th & 57th Sts.)

Subway: 57 St - 7 Av Lunch & dinner daily
Phone: 212-245-9800
Web: www.trattoriadellarte.com
Prices: $$$

There's a downright contagious exuberance to Shelly Firemen's always-packed Carnegie Hall classic, Trattoria Dell'Arte. It might be the smart, confident service staff, or the overflowing, recession-be-damned antipasto bar. Maybe it's the cheeky welcome motto ("What's Italian for Carnegie Hall? Trattoria Dell'Arte."), or the pretty Tuscan-villa styled rooms, lined with mahogany wine racks and dripping candles.

You'll have to pay—perhaps a bit too steeply—for this kind of *io non lo so*, but the flaky, thin crust pizzas and heady dishes of finely-sauced pastas won't leave anyone disappointed. Don't miss the irresistible Italian desserts, like an airy cheesecake wrapped in chocolate sponge cake, then shot with piping-hot chocolate ganache.

21 Club

American XX

A4

21 W. 52nd St. (bet. Fifth & Sixth Aves.)

Subway: 5 Av - 53 St — Lunch Mon – Fri
Phone: 212-582-7200 — Dinner Mon – Sat
Web: www.21club.com
Prices: **$$$**

Now in its 70th year, 21 Club (of the Orient-Express group) remains in the pantheon of restaurants and an inherent part of the NYC experience. Its unique history and speakeasy ambience are loved by glitterati and former presidents alike. Gentleman, embrace the classics and don your finest, though ties are no longer required.

Lantern-holding jockeys and bronze double doors lead back in time, into the old Manhattan world of wealth and tradition still celebrated over dry martinis and oysters, beneath the dining room's low canopy of vintage model toys.

The experienced staff serves a solid American menu that may include creamy cauliflower soup with mushrooms, lobster, and apples; perfectly fresh, grilled Dover sole; or gargantuan wedges of apple-crumb pie.

Utsav

Indian XX

C2

1185 Sixth Ave. (enter on 46th St.)

Subway: 47-50 Sts - Rockefeller Ctr — Lunch & dinner daily
Phone: 212-575-2525
Web: www.utsavny.com
Prices: $$

Push past the humdrum bar seating downstairs, and make your way up the carpeted steps for a lovely surprise. This is Utsav—a unique, upscale little hideaway perched high above the hustle and bustle of 46th Street, on an elevated bridge between two midtown office buildings. Besides the killer views, the restaurant has a light, simple air to it—with billowing fabrics and leafy green plants.

The gorgeous, overflowing lunch buffet brings office workers in by the droves, but the à la carte and evening menus are can't-miss as well, with soft piles of blistered, piping hot naan; plump, juicy garlic chicken, slathered in a tangy chili sauce, paired with a bright green salad; and spicy, tender lamb stir-fried with coconut and curry leaves.

ViceVersa

Italian XX

C1

325 W. 51st St. (bet. Eighth & Ninth Aves.)

Subway: 50 St (Eighth Ave.) Lunch Mon – Fri
Phone: 212-399-9291 Dinner Mon – Sat
Web: www.viceversarestaurant.com
Prices: $$

This urbane, sophisticated restaurant is the brainchild of three Italian gentlemen who met while working at the legendary (now closed) San Domenico on Central Park South. Lucky for us, all that elegant taste rubbed off on them, because ViceVersa (pronounced VEE-chay versa) is one classy joint, with a haze of muted earth tones throughout the dining room, a long, wide bar that begs to be lingered at, and a pretty enclosed garden area that opens up in back when the weather's right.

Though presented artfully, the menu is as Italian as they come, with bold, saucy plates of pasta like creamy fusilli, pocked with smoky chunks of speck and dotted with bright green peas; or plump pockets of veal, tossed with nut-brown butter, sage, and pancetta.

West Bank Café

American XX

B2

407 W. 42nd St. (bet. Ninth & Tenth Aves.)

Subway: 42 St - Port Authority Bus Terminal Lunch & dinner daily
Phone: 212-695-6909
Web: www.westbankcafe.com
Prices: $$

This beloved Theater District mainstay has kept its head above the all-too-choppy waters of Manhattan's dining scene since 1978 by offering delicious, progressive American food at honest prices. To prove it, you'll have to elbow out the flock of regulars that squeeze into this simply adorned bistro most nights of the week.

The vibe is always right on cue at the West Bank Café, so settle into one of the leather banquettes, let the pleasant hum of jazz music fill your senses, and allow yourself to soak in the energy of the lively crowd. If on the menu, try the creamy puréed carrot-ginger soup, sweetened by a dash of rich coconut milk; followed by a tender skirt steak, charred just so, and flanked by a salty tower of beer-battered onion rings.

Yakitori Totto

Japanese 

C1

251 W. 55th St. (bet. Broadway & Eighth Ave.)

Subway: 57 St - 7 Av — Dinner nightly
Phone: 212-245-4555
Web: www.tottonyc.com
Prices: $$

Annoying foodie friend won't stop talking about their trip to Tokyo? Get a pen out. Some argue that Yakitori Totto's is amongst the best Japanese in the city; but we agree they are in the top two at yakitori—those tasty skewers of chicken, meats, vegetables, and other goodies, perfectly seasoned and cooked on a smoky charcoal grill. It's one of Japan's most popular street foods and this lively little den, tucked up a flight of stairs, elevates it to new heights.

House specialties like the chicken hearts, knees and necks are not to be missed, but even finicky eaters will find plenty to devour with dreamy little *tskune* (get them with the sauce); *teba*, so lovingly grilled you'll swear off buffalo sauce; and *nasu*, best enjoyed with miso paste.

Your opinions are important to us. Please write to us at: michelin.guides@us.michelin.com

Peter L. Wrenn/MICHELIN

SoHo & Nolita

SoHo (South of Houston) and Nolita (North of Little Italy) prove not only that New York has a penchant for portmanteaus, but that the downtown "scene" lives on now more than ever. What remains new and ever-changing are the subtle transformations that redefine these neighborhoods block by block.

Despite the retail invasion that has taken over some of SoHo's eastern corners, it remains true to its promise of sun-drenched restaurants and open-air cafés filled with European sophisticates of a certain age and supermodels lingering over salads. There are also plenty of tourists to admire them.

Shopping in SoHo

Those fortunate enough to live in what were once artists' lofts (now multimillion dollar condos) know that there are still a few foodie gems in this area heavily focused on restaurant dining. For your at-home tapas needs, **Despana** offers Spanish foods and ingredients from oil-packed tuna to mouthwatering *bocadillos*; they will even prepare a traditional tortilla Española with advance notice. A visit to the original **Dean and Deluca**, filled with some of the cities favorite cakes and coffees, is another gourmet treat, but be forewarned that its steep prices match the sleek location. Less retouched and perhaps more focused is **Joe's Dairy**; this tiny storefront overflows with SoHo history and arguably the best Italian cheeses in town (their smoked mozzarella is to die for).

Sleepy Nolita

Farther east is Nolita—a neighborhood as cool as its name. This is where a slightly hipper and hungrier downtown set flock (judging by its many offerings). These locals aren't living the typical midtown nine-to-five life and shun the *je ne sais quoi* of SoHo in favor of smallish spots that begin with the word "café."

At the top of this list is **Café Habana**, offering its casual crowds a gritty diner vibe and amazing Mexico City-style corn on the cob (also available for take-out next door at **Café Habana To Go**). Equally hip hangouts can be found at **Café Gitane**, serving French-Moroccan or **Café Colonial** for Brazilian food.

The ethos in Nolita is focused: Do a single thing very well. This may have been inspired by **Lombardi's**, which claims to be America's very first pizzeria (founded in 1905) and still has lines out the door. **Hoomos Asli** may not be attractive and its service is "brisk," but they clearly put effort into the outstanding hummus, fluffy pitas, and falafels to accompany those tart, fresh lemonades whose memory will keep you cool for summers to come. For the best fish tacos this side of California, head to **Pinche**

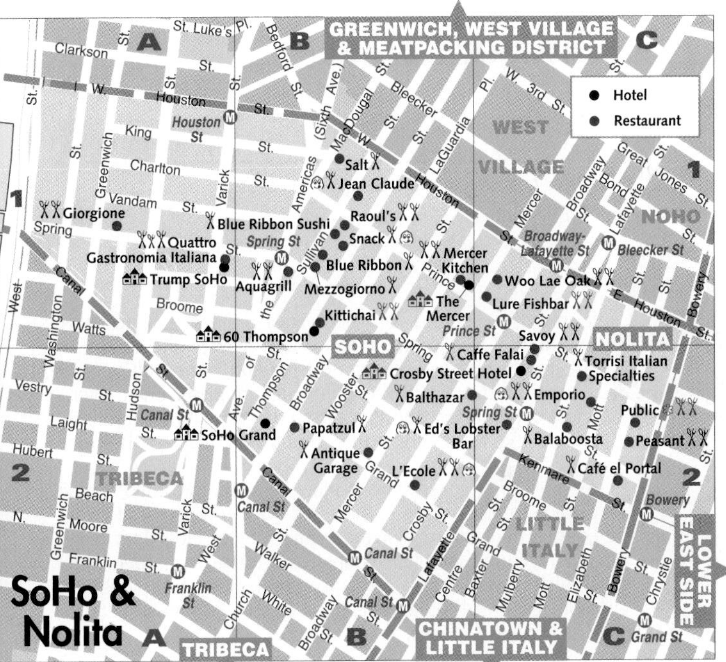

Taqueria. However, if whiling away the afternoon in one of Manhattan's most idyllic outdoor gardens suits your mood, then visit **Le Jardin Bistro**.

Even satisfying a sweet tooth is done with elevated style at **Pappabubble**, whose candies are crafted with an eye-popping sense of design. With equal ingenuity and old-school flair, **Rice to Riches** serves its celebrated bowls of rice pudding with creatively named toppings, like "Mischief" (buttery graham crackers) or "Nudge" (chilled espresso and cocoa). Cheesecake connoisseurs take note that **Eileen's Cheesecake** and its mind-boggling array of flavors has been chasing those Junior's fanatics back to Brooklyn.

Even between feedings, this area promises to nurture your inner epicurean with a visit to the Bowery. The unrefined kitchen supply stores that line the neighborhood's eastern border are technically wholesale only, but some still sell for cash. Come here to stock up on sheet pans, rubber spatulas, and *pu pu* platters. One of the greater challenges Nolita poses is the decision of where to end the day. Tucked into these streets are cozy bars, each with its own stylish, NY feel, sans the masses besetting other neighborhoods. Dark and date-like places, such as **Pravda** with its assortment of vodkas or **Sweet and Vicious** for expert cocktails, are a fitting finale.

Antique Garage

B2 **Turkish** 

41 Mercer St. (bet. Broome & Grand Sts.)

Subway: Canal St (Broadway) Lunch & dinner daily
Phone: 212-219-1019
Web: www.antiquegaragesoho.com
Prices: $$

It sounds ridiculous, but here goes: Imagine an adorable restaurant tucked into a renovated auto repair garage in SoHo. It's homey, *how-did-we-not-know-about-this-place?* vibe is fitted out with beautiful rugs, dripping chandeliers, and a bunch of cool antiques that you can actually purchase. As for the food, how does mouthwatering, off-the-hook Turkish meze sound?

As the saying goes: Only in New York. By day, the Antique Garage offers a quiet reprieve for SoHo shoppers; at night, couples pile in to revel in the intimacy of the close-knit tables and flickering candles. Though the menu leans decidedly Turkish—think eggplant salads and chicken shish kebabs—more general Mediterranean influences rear their head in desserts like a creamy tiramisu.

Aquagrill

B1 **Seafood** XX

210 Spring St. (at Sixth Ave.)

Subway: Spring St (Sixth Ave.) Lunch & dinner daily
Phone: 212-274-0505
Web: www.aquagrill.com
Prices: $$

If only Cheers had such good food! Much-loved Aquagrill is the kind of restaurant where everyone knows your name—well, at least the staff knows the names of the regulars who flank the front bar. The difference, of course, is the quality of seafood at Jeremy and Jennifer Marshall's seafood house, where the husband-and-wife duo divvy up responsibilities: she works the front of house, while he mans the kitchen.

Like any good chef with a fresh piece of fish, Marshall employs a light touch in dishes like his velvety soup loaded with plump, briny mussels; or the Maine lobster salad, laced with creamy avocado, zebra beets, and ruby-red grapefruit. Don't miss a few fresh oysters off the gorgeous raw bar, or the decadent handmade chocolate sampler.

Balaboosta

 **Middle Eastern**

214 Mulberry St. (at Spring St.)

Subway: Spring St (Lafayette St.) — Lunch Sat – Sun
Phone: 212-966-7366 — Dinner nightly
Web: N/A
Prices: $$

Downtown foodies are already well aware of Israeli-born Chef Einat Admony thanks to her popular Taïm, located in the West Village and clearly marked by its lines out the door. Here at the chef's latest in Nolita, Balaboosta (a Yiddish expression meaning the perfect housewife) features a full-service dining experience in an attractively spare room with a petite bar area and a menu of expectedly enjoyable Middle Eastern cuisine.

A listing of small plates includes the crowd-pleasing hummus presented in a mortar and pestle, as well as falafel-wrapped meatballs served with herbed tahini sauce. Entrées display a contemporary sensibility as in the lamb three ways: a seared chop, a cut of loin wrapped in Swiss chard; and kibbeh on a pool of cool *tzatziki*.

Balthazar

 **French**

80 Spring St. (bet. Broadway & Crosby St.)

Subway: Spring St (Lafayette St.) — Lunch & dinner daily
Phone: 212-965-1414
Web: www.balthazarny.com
Prices: $$$

Has an aging downtown darling ever held onto her crown as successfully as Balthazar? Nope—for this Keith McNally bistro, with its legendary red awning and brassy bistro good looks, has been a joyous zoo ever since it opened its doors in 1997.

All of which means you'll need reservations, though there are a few ways to dodge the busy bullet: The bar tables are open to walk-ins; the breakfast hours are lovely; and the bakery next door serves scrumptious salads, sandwiches, and pastries to go (not to mention a killer hot chocolate). Back at the restaurant, you'll want to ride the coattails of Balthazar's steadies, like heaping towers of glistening shellfish; and perfectly-charred steak, laid to rest under a golden stack of crunchy, salty frites.

Blue Ribbon

B1 **Contemporary**

97 Sullivan St. (bet. Prince & Spring Sts.)

Subway: Spring St (Sixth Ave.) — Dinner nightly
Phone: 212-274-0404
Web: www.blueribbonrestaurants.com
Prices: $$$

It's for good reason that the Blue Ribbon family is now liberally fanned out across the city. Meet the catalyst for it all—Blue Ribbon brasserie, a New York classic tucked into Sullivan Street. The restaurant's welcoming and engaging staff is a luxury in a neighborhood more inclined to make you feel plain than cherished—which is quite interesting, considering Blue Ribbon has its own celebrity following.

Namely, the city's chef circuit, that regularly swings through the doors post-shift (the kitchen serves until 4:00 A.M.) come to indulge in a a selection of rawbar delights, and flavor-rich comfort classics like the playful *pu pu* platter of gourmet fried chicken, or the decadent bone marrow with oxtail marmalade.

Blue Ribbon Sushi

B1 **Japanese** 

119 Sullivan St. (bet. Prince & Spring Sts.)

Subway: Spring St (Sixth Ave.) — Lunch & dinner daily
Phone: 212-343-0404
Web: www.blueribbonrestaurants.com
Prices: $$$

There's a reason you keep bumping into Blue Ribbon joints all across this city. Those Bromberg brothers sprinkle their fairy dust, and poof—delicious, casually hip eateries appear. As the name of this discrete little sushi den implies, the restaurateurs here turn their attention to the sea, where the talented Chef Toshi Ueki has one all-important question for his customers: Are you a Pacific or Atlantic man?

That's how he likes to divvy up his killer sashimi and fresh-off-the-boat (or plane) daily specials, although the spicy tuna set can tread safer waters with dishes like the crispy rock shrimp tempura. They don't take reservations and the space is itty-bitty, so aim for off-hours or lunchtime, when you can command a booth for an afternoon feast.

Café el Portal

Mexican

174 Elizabeth St. (bet. Kenmare & Spring Sts.)

Subway: Spring St (Lafayette St.) — Lunch & dinner Mon – Sat
Phone: 212-226-4642
Web: N/A
Prices:

In an area that has recently been attracting newcomers in large, hip spaces, Café el Portal defies this trend with its low-key design, casual ambience, and family-run feel. Despite its less than impressive digs, this restaurant serves some of the most authentic Mexican dishes in the city, such as the classic *pastel con tres leches*, made with fantastic vanilla sponge cake soaked in condensed milk. Everything is made in-house, from the fresh tortillas to the Mexican hot chocolate.

The tiny bar boasts a tequila collection with more bottles than the restaurant has seats, and the cocktail menu goes well beyond margaritas to include many non-alcoholic options. Reasonable prices and flavorful, fun food keep el Portal buzzing with locals and regulars.

Caffe Falai

Italian 

265 Lafayette St. (bet. Prince & Spring Sts.)

Subway: Spring St (Lafayette St.) — Lunch & dinner daily
Phone: 212-274-8615
Web: www.falainyc.com
Prices: $$

The elements come together to make for a delicious meal in Caffe Falai's delicate little jewel box interior, where white-framed mirrors hang from pure white walls, and the pretty round mosaic floor tiles light up under ornate glass chandeliers. All the more reason to linger over one—or two—of former Le Cirque pastry chef, Iacopo Falai's, to-die-for pastries, lovingly displayed in the glass counter by his kitchen.

The dinner menu entices just as much, with a comforting lineup of oldies but goodies from all over Italy, like a gorgeously authentic bowl of minestrone, its heavenly scent delivering all the freshness of spring; or the quickly-becoming-legendary *gnudi*; or a spot-on risotto dancing in a mushroom purée laced with aromatic truffle.

Ed's Lobster Bar 

Seafood 

C2

222 Lafayette St. (bet. Kenmare & Spring Sts.)

Subway: Spring St (Lafayette St.) Lunch & dinner daily
Phone: 212-343-3236
Web: www.lobsterbarnyc.com
Prices: $$

The delicacy and purity of seafood is epitomized in cute and convivial Ed's Lobster Bar. A sunny yet cool space with a good mix of food-savvy NYers, Ed's is that ideal sanctum for anyone who wishes to escape to New England for an hour.

As if to ease the no-reservations policy, this saltwater gem offers a fine choice of seafood-friendly wines and beers that go down as smoothly as the oysters. The narrow space is dotted with tables, but true cheer is found at the marble bar. While side dishes are all enticing, faves like perfectly fried calamari; creamy and luscious chowder with succulent clams; and the stellar buttery lobster roll (piled with juicy meat tossed in mayo, celery, and dill) aside crispy fries and Ed's homemade pickles are sheer decadence.

Emporio 

Italian XX

C2

231 Mott St. (bet. Prince & Spring Sts.)

Subway: Spring St (Lafayette St.) Lunch & dinner daily
Phone: 212-966-1234
Web: www.aurorariStorante.com
Prices: $$

Having charmed Manhattan and Brooklyn with his Aurora restaurants, famed Riccardo Buitoni decided to try an even warmer, more cheery concept on the narrow streets of Nolita with Roman-inspired trattoria, Emporio.

Like his other ventures, this idyllic Italian eatery has loads of rustic appeal. The interior space feels close-knit and is meant to invoke a twenties-era grocery. Usually swarming with crowds on weekends, the menu epitomizes fresh ingredients in tasty preparations. Start with a mouthwatering plate of cured meats presented with grilled, olive oil-brushed bread before digging into dishes like squash blossoms, stuffed with cheese and anchovies; pizza laced with buffalo mozzarella, zucchini, and ricotta; and juicy, oven-roasted rabbit.

Giorgione

A1 — Italian XX

307 Spring St. (bet. Greenwich & Hudson Sts.)

Subway: Spring St (Sixth Ave.) — Lunch Mon – Fri
Phone: 212-352-2269 — Dinner nightly
Web: www.giorgionenyc.com
Prices: $$

Tucked down a nondescript street on the Western reaches of SoHo, Giorgione walks softly but carries a big stick. Owned and founded by Giorgio Deluca (of Dean & Deluca), the restaurant first gathered a following for its octopus salad—these days, it stays packed for its honest Italian fare.

Inside the narrow dining room you'll find sleek chrome tables, cool white leather seats, and icy blue walls—all the better to let one of ace pizzas from the wood-burning oven warm you up. Specials rotate daily, but you might find a *rigatoni alla Norma* tossed with a judicious amount of silky eggplant, ripe tomatoes, and milky ricotta; or a flaky *crostata*, glazed with red currant and topped with mission figs, lemon rind, and a smear of mascarpone cheese.

Jean Claude

B1 — French X

137 Sullivan St. (bet. Houston & Prince Sts.)

Subway: Spring St (Sixth Ave.) — Dinner nightly
Phone: 212-475-9232
Web: www.jeanclauderestaurant.com
Prices: $$

With its tight-knit tables, lived-in good looks, and soft French music quietly thrumming in the background, this romantic little bistro could be straight off of Paris' Left Bank. Luckily for Manhattan, though, the infinitely charming Jean Claude is smack in the middle of SoHo.

In winter, the room is decidedly cozy; while summer finds the front windows thrown open and couples lingering over the reasonably-priced wine list, which boasts a nice carafe and half-carafe list. The French cooking is straightforward and delicious, with a solid lineup of bistro staples like tender *moules marinieres* and frites; seared hangar steak in a thyme, red wine and shallot reduction, paired with a sinful *gratin dauphinois*; and a spot-on rendition of crème brûlée.

Kittichai

Thai XX

B1

60 Thompson St. (bet. Broome & Spring Sts.)

Subway: Spring St (Sixth Ave.) — Lunch & dinner daily
Phone: 212-219-2000
Web: www.kittichairestaurant.com
Prices: $$$

Bangkok has never looked so sexy. Dark and sultry restaurants in trendy urban hotels abound these days, but Kittichai is the real deal—with a jaw-dropping interior (replete with silk swaths, suspended orchids, and floating candles) fit to woo the beautiful people checking into the 60 Thompson hotel that houses it.

There are more authentic Thai places in the city, but Kittichai romances you with its setting and elegant cuisine that sings as much European as Thai. Try the crispy whole fish, laced with a sweet ginger curry; or pineapple-braised short ribs in green curry, paired with baby eggplant. The best route here is to try one of the chefs tasting menus, where you get a sampling of the signature dishes at terrific value, served family style.

L'Ecole

French XX

B2

462 Broadway (at Grand St.)

Subway: Canal St (Broadway) — Lunch daily
Phone: 212-219-3300 — Dinner Mon – Sat
Web: www.frenchculinary.com
Prices: $$

This fun, virtual classroom (courtesy of the French Culinary Institute) provides students their first opportunity to show their expertise, love, and respect for the art of traditional French cooking. However, this is a "learning experience" so there may be a few mistakes alongside a treasured moment of brilliance. Regardless, it is clear these students have mastered the use of top ingredients, where they shine in simple preparations like country pâté or roasted duck.

The classic French menu changes every six weeks, offering four- or five-course dinners as well as an inexpensive prix-fixe lunch.

Conscientious student servers cater to guests in an ambient "SoHo" space with images of a bustling restaurant kitchen and lofty windows overlooking Broadway.

Lure Fishbar

Seafood

142 Mercer St. (bet. Houston & Prince Sts.)

Subway: Prince St — Lunch & dinner daily
Phone: 212-431-7676
Web: www.lurefishbar.com
Prices: $$$

Housed in the basement of the popular Prada showroom, Lure Fishbar easily has some of the best digs in town. Outside, SoHo's streets might be covered in beautiful old-school cobblestones and teeming with young gorgeous gazelles, but down here a tiki-trendy-meets-maritime motif (think tropical prints, angular porthole windows, and cozy booths) and fat seafood plates reign supreme.

A mean-looking sushi-counter and raw bar lets you know how seriously they take the food, though. A plate of yellowtail carpaccio arrives fresh as can be, topped with garlic-chili sauce, sesame oil, thin slices of avocado, and crispy, deep-fried shallots; while a wickedly fresh branzino is served whole, perfectly de-boned and laced with pesto, scallions, and crunchy shallots.

Mercer Kitchen

Contemporary

99 Prince St. (at Mercer St.)

Subway: Prince St — Lunch & dinner daily
Phone: 212-966-5454
Web: www.jean-georges.com
Prices: $$

If svelte had a home, it would be at Jean-Georges' magical Mercer Kitchen. Despite age and its location—in SoHo's swank Mercer Hotel—this star shines bright in the city. Below the sidewalks of Prince Street, Mercer Kitchen opens its drapery-lined doors to stylish and stunning globe trotters. Roost over an aperitif at the sterling bar as you wait—hopefully for a date.

As the hostess slinks your way, make your entrée into a dark and sultry dining room. Allured by the aura, throngs chatter over the kitchen's contemporary (though not always exemplary) affair like crab cakes aside avocado, cucumber, and crystallized ginger; silky salmon matched with Brussels sprouts and truffle vinaigrette; and a light, bright carrot cake kissed with mango soufflé.

Mezzogiorno

B1

Italian 

195 Spring St. (at Sullivan St.)

Subway: Spring St (Sixth Ave.) Lunch & dinner daily
Phone: 212-334-2112
Web: www.mezzogiorno.com
Prices: **$$**

The big, bright blue awnings of this Italian veteran are a fixture on the SoHo scene, and its 100 interior collages by local artists (each one a unique interpretation of the restaurant's logo) a lovely reminder of when the neighborhood was more artists than agents.

The real star of the show, of course, is the beautiful wood-burning oven, which pushes out delicious, thin-crust pies. If you're not in the mood for pizza, no problem—the pasta list goes on for days and there's an extensive list of seasonal Italian specialties like the *carciofi saltati*, a plate of tender artichoke hearts paired with crunchy pistachio, and laced with lemon and parsley—the perfect thing to pick on when spring hits and the raised terrace opens up for people watching.

Papatzul

B2

Mexican 

55 Grand St. (bet. West Broadway & Wooster St.)

Subway: Canal St (Sixth Ave.) Lunch & dinner daily
Phone: 212-274-8225
Web: www.papatzul.com
Prices: **$$**

This tiny, mouthwatering Mexican restaurant is a refreshing find in the model-festooned neighborhood. Its ambience is festive yet comfortable enough for lingering over conversations and effortlessly cool yet welcoming. Beyond the lively bar find closely-spaced tables with couples enjoying pitchers of margaritas. Laid-back service and genial prices add to the warmth, while the relaxed (*un*-Manhattan) pacing may add to its authenticity.

An outstanding start to any meal here is the house ceviche, bright with the flavors of lime, cilantro, and the freshest fish. The ample listing of *platos fuertes* may include the *budin al pasilla*, layered with chili sauce, shredded chicken, cheese, beans, and cream—totally decadent and rich with melted flavors.

Peasant

Italian

194 Elizabeth St. (bet. Prince & Spring Sts.)

Subway: Spring St (Lafayette St.) — Dinner Tue – Sun
Phone: 212-965-9511
Web: www.peasantnyc.com
Prices: $$

The emphasis at this beautiful little Nolita restaurant is honest Italian country fare—more often than not, carefully sourced and expertly prepared dishes that find their way into Chef Frank DeCarlo's beloved wood-burning brick oven.

Dimly lit and romantic, with lots of exposed brick walls and flickering candles, Peasant practically purrs date night. And a more languorous evening could not be found than one spent dawdling over a melt-in-your-mouth pizza pie, or lovely rustic dishes like four plump sardines, baked head-on in a terra-cotta clay pot and dusted with toasted breadcrumbs and a shake of grated lemon zest; or perfectly al dente, hand-cut *malfatti* in a hearty lamb ragù; or tender slices of lamb, dancing in a fluffy, delicate polenta.

Quattro Gastronomia Italiana

Italian

246 Spring St. (at Varick St.)

Subway: Spring St (Sixth Ave.) — Lunch & dinner daily
Phone: 212-842-4500
Web: www.trumpsohohotel.com
Prices: $$

Located at the base of the Trump Soho, Quattro Gastronomia Italiana might be a mouthful to pronounce but it's likely to be on everyone's lips this year just the same. For starters, the design is really something to see—a bi-level space fitted out with custom-made Murano glass chandeliers, mirrored and deep green tiles, and beautiful terrazzo floors.

But the food is equally compelling, thanks to talented Piemontese chef, Fabrizio Carro (his twin brother, Nicola, runs the original restaurant in Miami), who dishes up homemade agnolotti with braised beef; a version of *vitello tonnato* (chilled veal in a tuna-caper sauce) that would make *la signora* weep; and perfectly poached Mediterranean sea bream with Taggiasche olives, capers, and squash filled with *caponata*.

Public ✿

Fusion XX

C2

210 Elizabeth St. (bet. Prince & Spring Sts.)

Subway: Spring St (Lafayette St.) — Lunch Sat – Sun
Phone: 212-343-7011 — Dinner nightly
Web: www.public-nyc.com
Prices: **$$$**

Michael Weber

Public is the quintessential neighborhood restaurant and very definition of casual chic. It reflects Nolita to a tee–with garage door-style windows, tables set atop a loading dock, and that uniquely inviting yet urban NYC vibe. Warm and welcoming, this is a favorite of neighborhood denizens and tourists alike.

Perfectly matching its laid-back looks, the food is simple, unfussy, and fabulous. The menu finds inspiration in every corner of the world and stirs together a veritable melting pot of tastes. Whether he's blending Asian and Continental flavors, adding a dash of Middle Eastern za'tar, or highlighting hard-to-find ingredients, Chef Brad Farmerie earns high marks for his distinctive dishes. Entrées tease and tantalize the taste buds, as in scallops with sweet chili sauce and crème fraîche; or swordfish with eggplant-pine nut relish, and tarragon-citrus salad. Seafood is the spoiled kid here, as are more unusual products, like kangaroo, venison, and wild boar. Desserts can be as adventurous as they are delicious.

Duck into Public's Monday Room to sip wine (there are 60 from Australia and New Zealand available by the glass) while savoring their scrumptious small plates.

Raoul's

French

180 Prince St. (bet. Sullivan & Thompson Sts.)

Subway: Spring St (Sixth Ave.) Dinner nightly
Phone: 212-966-3518
Web: www.raouls.com
Prices: $$$

Whether by charms or talent, this beloved bistro has survived 30-plus years in one of the fussiest parts of town, somehow remaining popular, sophisticated, and stylishly unpretentious. The authentic French fare is prepared simply, but remains impressive with top ingredients and delicious flavors—as in the steak tartare with quail egg, or seared foie gras with Concord grape purée. The menu, exquisitely handwritten on chalkboards and presented by the amiable waitstaff, still appeals to savvy diners and connoisseurs hungry for meaty steaks and fries made crisp with duck fat.

The energetic atmosphere in the dimly lit main room is intoxicating, but those seeking a calmer spot for quiet conversation should try the bright upstairs space or tiny covered garden.

Salt

American 

58 MacDougal St. (bet. Houston & Prince Sts.)

Subway: Spring St (Sixth Ave.) Lunch & dinner daily
Phone: 212-674-4968
Web: www.saltnyc.com
Prices: $$

The expression "neighborhood restaurant" is bandied about on a too casual basis nowadays, but Salt genuinely deserves the moniker. Diners are invited to sit at one of three communal tables in the middle of the simply furnished dining room. Here, you can rub elbows with other locals and catch up on some gossip. Or sit at a table near the large shop front windows.

Long Island duck breast, Alaskan King salmon, and New Zealand rack of lamb are some of the highlights from the brief menu that is a showcase in modern cuisine. Under the section "Protein + 2," select any two sides to accompany the main dish—a classic American mealtime formula. The menu makes fair use of fresh and flavorful combinations, incorporating seasonal and local meats and produce.

Savoy

American XX

C1

70 Prince St. (at Crosby St.)

Subway: Prince St — Lunch Mon – Sat
Phone: 212-219-8570 — Dinner nightly
Web: www.savoynyc.com
Prices: $$

Savoy puts the sexy back in being nice—with a rustic upstairs dining room (replete with crackling fireplace) so steeped in country charm it could convince a city slicker to settle down for good. But that fuzzy-sweater interior belies a menu that's always been way ahead of its time, where the chefs let the exceptional ingredients do the work, focusing on pure flavors and seasonal ingredients from local growers.

Savoy's genius lies both in its good value as well as in its parade of scrumptious dishes like a bright dandelion salad, laced with lemon-anchovy vinaigrette and topped with a breadcrumb-crusted fried egg; or a lovely seasonal chilled nettle soup kissed with yogurt; or a smooth lemon tart topped with fluffy meringue and a dollop of lemon sorbet.

Snack 

Greek X

B1

105 Thompson St. (bet. Prince & Spring Sts.)

Subway: Spring St (Sixth Ave.) — Lunch & dinner daily
Phone: 212-925-1040
Web: N/A
Prices: 

Quaint, laid-back Santorini taverna, Snack is not. But you'll find so much to love in this bustling slip of a restaurant tucked into SoHo's quiet, leafy Thompson Street, you'll hardly mind the slightly clinical interior—for though the old black and white photos and selection of Greek grocery items only hint at far-off lands, those lucky enough to snag one of the four dining room tables will find Hellenic fare authentic enough to transport them at first bite.

Despite the moniker, most of the portions here are hearty, including a generously-sized shredded lamb sandwich, laced with ripe tomatoes, roasted red onions, a smear of aïoli, and a shake of fresh arugula; or a Greek salad bursting with creamy feta, kalamata olives, and fresh oregano.

Torrisi Italian Specialties

Italian

250 Mulberry St. (at Prince St.)

Subway: Spring St (Lafayette St.) — Lunch & dinner Tue – Sun
Phone: 212-965-0955
Web: www.piginahat.com
Prices: $$

Everyone is buzzing about this new Italian restaurant from seasoned chefs, Mario Carbone and Rich Torrisi. At lunch, the two sling heroes that would make a *nonna* blush, with thick, silky meats, fragrant jus, and spicy broccoli rabe. By night, the crowds gather, praying for a seat (no reservations accepted) in the charming space, replete with white penny tile floor, red brick walls, and wooden banquettes.

The nightly dinner is fixed, no substitutions allowed: 5 small *antipasti* followed by pasta, choice of entrée, Italian ice, and dessert divinity via a fab cookie plate. Fresh mozzarella made with milk thistle cream, and served with out-of-this-world garlic toast, might be followed by devil's chicken in a brick-red chile sauce, paired with creamy yogurt.

Woo Lae Oak

Korean

148 Mercer St. (bet. Houston & Prince Sts.)

Subway: Prince St — Lunch & dinner daily
Phone: 212-925-8200
Web: www.woolaeoaksoho.com
Prices: $$

In design, temperament, and palate, this sleek, upscale Korean restaurant is a perfect match for the ultra swank set that frequents it. Step inside the wide subterranean dining room, and you'll find a sexy, highly designed room lined in chrome and granite, an open kitchen and long, sleek banquettes featuring private table grills.

The Korean dishes are elegantly prepared and fairly straightforward in terms of flavor, and those nervous about venturing into foreign territory will find solace in the never-ending options. Try the steak tartare, tossed with sesame, garlic, and soy sauce and served over Asian pear; perfectly gooey *pa jun*, the traditional pancakes studded with scallion, shrimp, and squid; or silky tofu braised in a spicy chili pepper broth.

TriBeCa

Catering to its local clientele of creative types, trendy TriBeCa is, quite simply, a cool place to eat. Here, splurge on meals in pricey restaurants whose reputations and namesake celebrity chefs precede them, or go for more modest gastropub fare. On sunny days, snag an umbrella-shaded table outside—TriBeCa's wide sidewalks are famously accommodating and among the city's top spots for star-gazing.

This wedge of cobblestoned streets, galleries, design stores, and historic warehouses converted to multi-million-dollar lofts was named in the 1970s by a real-estate agent hoping to create a hip identity for the area. The acronym—which stands for Triangle Below Canal—describes an area that is not a triangle at all, but a trapezoid bounded by Canal Street, Broadway, Murray Street, and the Hudson River. Greenwich and Hudson streets are its main thoroughfares for dining and nightlife.

In keeping with its independence and artistry, TriBeCa offers a gourmet experience for any palate (or pricetag). On Hudson Square, **City Winery** gives urban wine enthusiasts a place to make their own private-label wine by providing the grapes (a selection of varietals from international vineyards), the barrels, the storage, and the expertise. Those looking for something to enjoy with their wine will rejoice in the monthly events sponsored by **New York Vintners**, which may include free cheese tastings or lessons on making mozzarella.

The neighborhood is loaded with wonderful bakeries, the most popular of which include the **Duane Park Patisserie** for pastries, and seasonal specialties; or **Tribeca Treats** for scrumptious chocolates. Since 1886, venerable **Bazzini** has occupied the building where company founder, Anthony Bazzini, first opened the business in 1886. Drop by to pick up some gourmet groceries or prepared foods for dinner, and don't leave without a bag of nuts or a jar of their old-fashioned cashew butter.

Puffy's Tavern is a friendly neighborhood bar boasting five plasma-screen TVs for sports fans, happy-hour drinks, and hearty lunchtime signature Italian sandwiches. Speaking of local faves, **Bubby's** will cater to your homestyle food cravings.

Like every New York neighborhood, TriBeCa claims its own great pizza joints, as in the Roman-style *pizza al taglio* at newcomer **Farinella**. Owner Alberto Polo Cretara is a Neapolitan hip-hop artist who honed his pizza-making skills at the legendary Il Forno in Rome. Round up some friends to sample his tasty four-foot-long pies.

Under the "dinner and a movie" category, the 2001 film

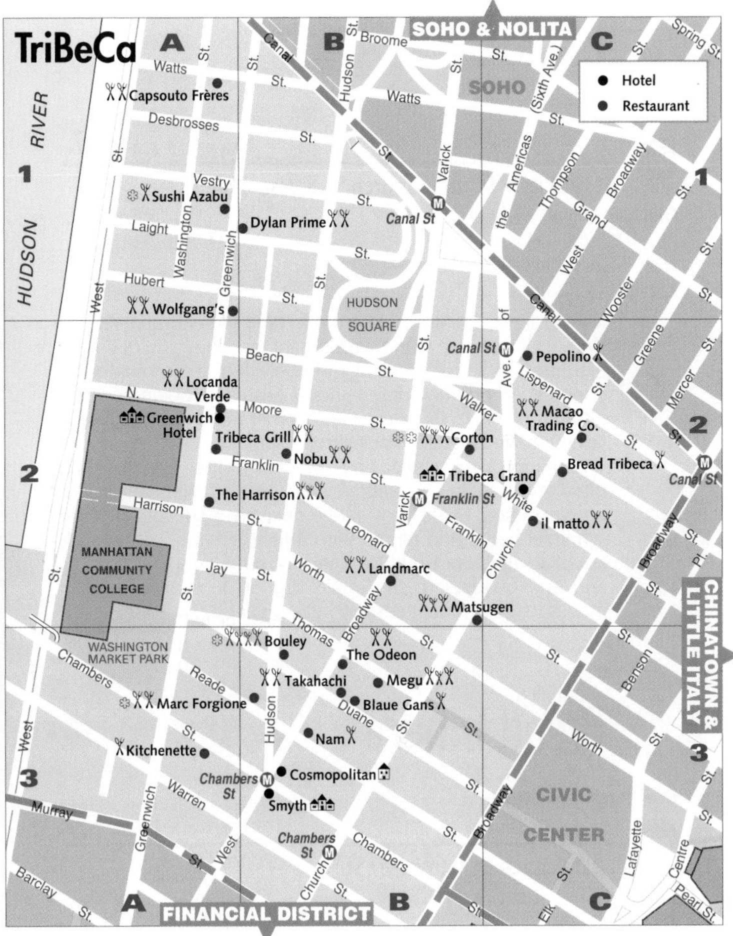

Dinner Rush used TriBeCa as a stage. In fact, director Bob Giraldi shot this Mafia- and food-themed movie at one of his famed eateries, **Gigino Trattoria**. The plot tells the story of a night in the life of a chic TriBeCa restaurant, delving into sidelines such as food critics and ambitious chefs.

Today this area is still associated with films of many stripes, thanks to the annual Tribeca Film Festival, created in 2002 by Robert DeNiro and others to revitalize the area after 9/11. This world-famous springtime event hosts twelve days of great films, special events, and community camaraderie. Throngs of locals and tourists alike flock here during this time to see the movies and experience TriBeCa's many wonderful restaurants.

Blaue Gans

Austrian 

B3

139 Duane St. (bet. Church St. & West Broadway)

Subway: Chambers St (West Broadway) Lunch & dinner daily
Phone: 212-571-8880
Web: www.wallse.com
Prices: $$

It's hard not to fall in love with Kurt Gutenbrunner's (of Wallsé fame) Blaue Gans, a restaurant that does a lot of things extremely well, while making the whole thing look completely effortless: modern, unpretentious Austrian cooking; cozy, urban ambience; excellent German beer and Austrian wine selection; and a crackerjack service staff. Need we go on?

The menu offers regular and seasonal dishes, and none of them miss—pillowy quark ravioli, sautéed with mint and brown butter; tender free range chicken, perfectly fried in schnitzel batter and paired with a light, creamy potato and arugula salad. Start with a platter of schnitzels and wursts, and end on dessert (the apple strudel does nicely)—two moves that seem unnecessary but deliver big.

Bread Tribeca

Italian 

C2

301 Church St. (at Walker St.)

Subway: Canal St (Sixth Ave.) Lunch & dinner daily
Phone: 212-334-8282
Web: www.breadtribeca.com
Prices: $$

Still trendy among locals, celebrities, and corporate casts, this TriBeCa treasure is graced by large windows, soaring ceilings, creaky floors, and iron columns. The bar upfront is beloved by businessmen seeking happy-hour drinks and nibbles, while an assembly line in the open kitchen routinely dispatches panini, pasta, pizza, and myriad entrées.

The menu goes on to include simple preparations that rise to the sublime through skill and quality of ingredients, as in the excellent *caprese* salad. Italian cravings are further indulged in rich saffron linguine twirled with shrimp, roasted tomatoes, and parsley; or pizza *carciofi* topped with artichokes, prosciutto, and Parmigiano Reggiano. A wonderfully fresh and creamy ricotta cheesecake is a fine finale.

Bouley ✿

Contemporary 

163 Duane St. (at Hudson St.)

Subway: Chambers St (West Broadway) — Lunch & dinner daily
Phone: 212-964-2525
Web: www.davidbouley.com
Prices: $$$$

Nicole Bartelme

One well-shod step inside Bouley and you'll quickly feel that you're not in TriBeCa anymore. There's not an exposed duct in sight; instead, find the Old World and Old Money. The opulent space is like a French chateau with vaulted, gold-leaf ceilings, hand-painted floral walls, and velour seating. Even the stone floors were sourced from a quarry that supplied Versailles.

David Bouley rules over a culinary empire and this eponymous restaurant is his flagship property. He is more than just the name on the door—he is actually at the stove on a regular basis.

The elegant cuisine is as French as it is decidedly contemporary, influenced by global accents, deftly prepared, and presented with aplomb. On occasion, some dishes do sacrifice success for ambitious flavor combinations, but they do reflect skill and talent. The four-course lunch and five-course dinner tasting menus offer a gourmet spectrum of the kitchen's range, from the perfectly crisp skin of a roasted Long Island duck sprinkled with crushed buckwheat to the pleasingly tart taste of grapefruit-accented salmon to the assortment of chocolate desserts. Ever the mad scientist, Bouley's cuisine is as dizzying as it is delicious.

Capsouto Frères

A1 French XX

451 Washington St. (at Watts St.)

Subway: Canal St (Sixth Ave.) Lunch Tue – Sun
Phone: 212-966-4900 Dinner nightly
Web: www.capsoutofreres.com
Prices: $$

This family-owned French institution has been going strong since 1980—step inside this gorgeous landmark building, which dates all the way back to 1891, and you'll find howling steam pipes echoing against carved wainscoting, dark wooden floors, and large jacquard curtain-lined windows.

The menu is honest and focused, though quality slips in and out with different dishes: a foie gras terrine is not particularly good; but a *Saucisson de Lyon en croute* with Madeira sauce delights. Don't miss the wine list—a unique, hand-chosen list by Jacques Capsouto (who leads the New York chapter of Compagnons du Beaujolais with wine tastings and monthly meals) carefully selected from all over the world, including unique lifts from countries like Israel.

Dylan Prime

B1 Contemporary XX

62 Laight St. (at Greenwich St.)

Subway: Franklin St Lunch Mon – Fri
Phone: 212-334-4783 Dinner nightly
Web: www.dylanprime.com
Prices: $$$

With a menu that boasts a parade of cuts like Porterhouse, filet mignon, or aged prime rib, Dylan Prime is undeniably a steakhouse. However, unlike many in this category, this menu boldly and deftly expands to offer very enjoyable American fare. Still, anyone considering a steak should try adding a chapeau—savory crust made with the likes of Maytag blue cheese and chives or mushroom and truffles. Featured on the separate lounge menu or at lunchtime, great value is served in the $14 Dylan Prime Burger, thick and juicy on a warm brioche.

The service is swift, but relaxed in this spacious setting located along a quieter strip of TriBeCa.

Inside, the mood is dark, sultry, and romantic, thanks to low lighting, cozy banquettes, and flickering votives.

Corton ✿✿

Contemporary XXX

B2

239 West Broadway (bet. Walker & White Sts.)

Subway: Franklin St — Dinner Mon – Sat
Phone: 212-219-2777
Web: www.cortonnyc.com
Prices: $$$$

Richard Pare

It's been over two years since Drew Nieporent and Paul Liebrandt's opened Corton to a thunderclap of critical praise in the fall of 2008—no small feat considering the country's economy was in the tank—and it would appear that the boys plan to keep the streak alive. The good just keeps getting better.

You could give some of the credit to the restaurant's sleek TriBeCa charms, with its effortlessly elegant downtown vibe; soft, everyone-looks-gorgeous lighting; and perfectly warm and polished staff. But good looks aside, what really sets the foodies' hearts afire is Liebrandt's irresistibly modern French fare, which sounds simple on the menu and is anything but.

The prix-fixe and multi-course tasting menus rotate daily, but might reveal a velvety piece of John Dory with finely grated black truffle, dressed tableside with coconut milk and lemongrass sauce and paired with a silky pile of spinach wrapped in tender sorrel leaves; soft, butter-poached lobster presented three ways, each more otherworldly than the next; or a creamy chocolate tart enrobed in thread-bare pastry crust, surrounded by dots of toasted, candied hazelnuts, rose grapefruit sorbet and mini-segments, and anise foam.

The Harrison

American

355 Greenwich St. (at Harrison St.)

Subway: Franklin St — Dinner nightly
Phone: 212-274-9310
Web: www.theharrison.com
Prices: $$

Almost a decade into its tenure, The Harrison is still getting it right. It's cool, but not too cool. It's casual, but not too casual. Much of the credit goes to Chef/owner Jimmy Bradley, a seasoned master of downtown hip and homey who doesn't stop at the surface goods, but digs deeper to bring in talented chefs like Amanda Freitag to seal the deal.

Grab a seat in the sexy, amber-soaked dining room and treat yourself to a spread of Freitag's seasonal fare, like fresh arctic char spooned with lemon gastrique, and laid over tender slices of cauliflower and earthy chanterelles; or jumbo crispy shrimp, served with a lemon-caper aïoli; or pan-seared hake, served in a summer corn ragout studded with favas, pearl onions, saffron, and chervil.

il matto

Italian

281 Church St. (at White St.)

Subway: Canal St (Sixth Ave.) — Dinner nightly
Phone: 212-226-1607
Web: www.ilmattonyc.com
Prices: $$$

This sophisticated new Italian restaurant arrives courtesy of Chef Matteo Boglione and partner Gian Perugini. The name means "the mad man" in Italian, and one gets the feeling Don Draper might have enjoyed the downright wicked cocktails going on compliments of Christina Bini, an Italian mixologist with a flair for the truly unique.

The space is super-modern, with whites and mirrors doing the heavy lifting in a room featuring a string of Christmas lights. The party line for the menu is "sophisticated Italian fare with an eccentric twist", and the focused menu offers up a delicious handful of pastas, meats, and fishes. Don't miss the baby artichoke croquettes, laced with saffron sauce and paired with creamy *burrata*, and shaved black summer truffles.

Kitchenette

A3

156 Chambers St. (bet. Greenwich St. & West Broadway)

Subway: Chambers St (West Broadway) Lunch & dinner daily
Phone: 212-267-6740
Web: www.kitchenetterestaurant.com
Prices:

Styled after an old-school luncheonette with black-and-white floor tiles, swiveling barstools and a long formica-topped counter, Kitchenette stops just sort of kitsch when it comes to the food. This ain't your Momma's Betty Crocker, but delicious, real-deal home cooking—think freshly baked cornbread, decadent four-cheese macaroni, and silky turkey meatloaf. Washed down with a Boylan's bottled soda, a meal at Kitchenette could put a smile on the grumpiest man's face.
The desserts are all made in-house and should not be missed: try the lemon and poppy seed layered cake, a fresh, mile-high slice of crumbly, buttery divinity laced with cream cheese frosting. For the Columbia University crowd, Kitchenette has a sister location in Morningside Heights.

Landmarc

B2

179 West Broadway (bet. Leonard & Worth Sts.)

Subway: Franklin St Lunch & dinner daily
Phone: 212-343-3883
Web: www.landmarc-restaurant.com
Prices: $$

Rustic yet modern French bistro fare is made with flair here, largely thanks to the open grill, boldly placed just a few feet from the bar, bustling with patrons and cheery servers. This not only acts as a festive focal point for the room, but also transforms straightforward dishes like roast chicken into expertly charred, juicy centerpieces. Plated alongside mustardy French beans, the result is abundantly rich in flavor.
The easy space (another location is in the Time Warner Center) is relaxed but trendy, featuring exposed brick walls and a narrow second-floor balcony that opens to the street in warm weather. The frugal oenophile will be happy to know that Landmarc's famed half-bottle list is still well-chosen, and gloriously within budget.

Locanda Verde

Italian 

379 Greenwich St. (at N. Moore St.)

Subway: Franklin St
Phone: 212-925-3797
Web: www.locandaverdenyc.com
Prices: $$$

Lunch & dinner daily

It may be located inside the trendy Greenwich Hotel, but Locanda Verde feels more like a hip neighborhood hang out than a hotel restaurant. While this rustic Italian remains casual with more jeans than suits, the star power of owner Robert DeNiro and Chef Andrew Carmellini brings an upscale bent and downtown vibe to the crowd who looks as good as the space.

The comfort food-style menu headlines simple dishes like fire-roasted garlic chicken and porchetta sandwiches. Exemplary focaccia and blockbuster pastas can display an incredible brilliance and unique talent, as in the house-made penne with lamb Bolognese, topped with ricotta and just the right touch of mint. Perfectly executed in every way, this dish is some of the kitchen's best work.

Macao Trading Co.

Portuguese 

311 Church St. (bet. Lispenard & Walker Sts.)

Subway: Canal St (Sixth Ave.)
Phone: 212-431-8642
Web: www.macaonyc.com
Prices: $$$

Lunch Sat – Sun
Dinner nightly

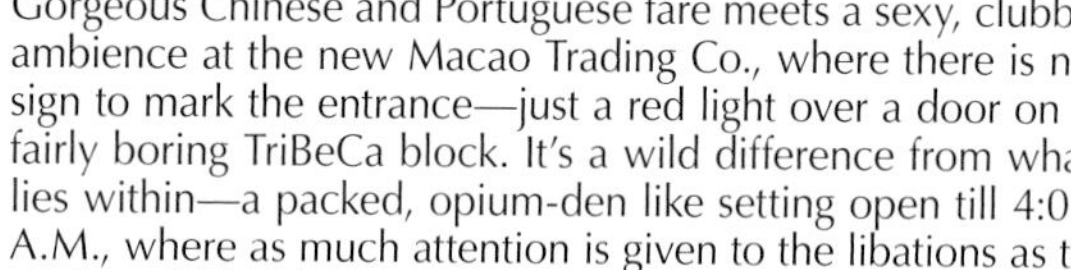

Gorgeous Chinese and Portuguese fare meets a sexy, clubby ambience at the new Macao Trading Co., where there is no sign to mark the entrance—just a red light over a door on a fairly boring TriBeCa block. It's a wild difference from what lies within—a packed, opium-den like setting open till 4:00 A.M., where as much attention is given to the libations as to the beautiful dishes.

The region of Macao (often spelled Macau) belonged to the Portuguese before they handed the island over to the Chinese in 1999, and the two cultures are given equal play time, but never fused, on the restaurant's menu. Save room for a mind-blowing trio of silky flans—including mandarin, *dulce de leche*, and espresso—all topped in a decadent layer of caramel.

Marc Forgione ✿

American XX

B3

134 Reade St. (bet. Greenwich & Hudson Sts.)

Subway: Chambers St (West Broadway)
Phone: 212-941-9401
Web: www.marcforgione.com
Prices: $$$

Lunch Sun
Dinner nightly

Daniel Krieger

Like father, like son. It's not uncommon for children to follow in their parent's footsteps. But when the father is Larry Forgione (New American chef extraordinaire) and the son is rising star Marc Forgione, you need to stop and take notice. Marc earned his chops early—first with his father and then with celebrity chefs like Laurent Tourondel—but this whiz kid has forged his own path.

His eponymous TriBeCa restaurant proves that Forgione stands in no shadows. Inside, it's the perfect representation of countrified chic. Stripped down, with exposed brick and reclaimed cedar from a 1900s sawmill, the restaurant looks a bit like the inside of a barn. A golden glow comes from the flickering candles set in custom-made glass lanterns strung along elevator cables. It's all very laid back in that sophisticated and studied way.

With a nod to Dad, Forgione ramps up modern American cuisine. Influenced by the market, the menu changes constantly, but it's all top-notch. Suckling pig with perfectly crispy crackled skin and served with green apple risotto; strips of sweet cuttlefish cosseted in pesto atop pasta; it's like poetry on the plate. Even the freshly baked potato rolls are sensational.

Matsugen

B2 — Japanese XXX

241 Church St. (at Leonard St.)

Subway: Chambers St (Church St.) — Lunch & dinner daily
Phone: 212-925-0202
Web: www.jean-georges.com
Prices: $$$

Gorgeous, spectacularly beautiful (if expensive) bowls of soba—thin, silky buckwheat flour noodles—star at Matsugen. These are rivaled only by the stunningly sexy, mammoth space, the brainchild of Jean-Georges Vongerichten and Japanese restaurateurs, the Matsushita brothers.

Some may claim that comparable noodles can be found for less, but the experience of settling into a black Eames chair along a runway-length communal table and plucking a sweet, crisp slice of duck from a steaming bowl of soba is both chic and deeply satisfying. Another highlight is the chef's omakase, perhaps featuring eel so perfectly steamed that it verges on creamy. Dining here reflects the high quality, skilled kitchen, and passion that the owners bring to their cuisine.

Megu

B3 — Japanese XXX

62 Thomas St. (bet. Church St. & West Broadway)

Subway: Chambers St (West Broadway) — Dinner Mon – Sat
Phone: 212-964-7777
Web: www.megurestaurants.com
Prices: $$$

Sleek, gorgeous, and sexy Megu takes good advantage of this lofty, subterranean setting that has the heart of the Euro-scene thumping, while a midtown location provides Zen elegance for the diplomat crowd.

After a short descent down a row of stairs, visitors discover this jaw-dropping décor, replete with a carved ice Buddha hovering over a pool strewn with rose petals, all beneath a dramatic replica of a Japanese temple bell. Nevertheless, Megu's kitchen lives up to this grand-scale design, sourcing only the highest-quality ingredients, and turning out plates of bright, inventive Japanese delicacies, touched with influences farther afield. Extensive offerings may include inventive salads, fresh sushi, and desserts that verge on the ethereal.

Nam

B3

Vietnamese

110 Reade St. (bet. Church St. & West Broadway)

Subway: Chambers St (West Broadway)
Phone: 212-267-1777
Web: www.namnyc.com
Prices: $$

Lunch Mon – Fri
Dinner nightly

Nam strives to please—and it does, bringing diners bounding back for the attentive service and alluring ambience. Slowly turning ceiling fans, backlit Vietnamese portraits, a wall lined with bamboo reeds, and natural light pouring in through the generously sized front windows all add to the appeal of this small, charming restaurant.

The menu certainly contains no surprises and the food here may appear a bit scripted or inauthentic, but there's something to be said for tried and true. Vietnamese standards such as *ca hap* made with perfectly steamed sea bass, bean-thread noodles, earthy yet sweet shiitake mushrooms, ginger, and scallions are rendered with good quality ingredients and a careful, if somewhat restrained, hand in the kitchen.

Nobu

B2

Japanese

105 Hudson St. (at Franklin St.)

Subway: Franklin St
Phone: 212-219-0500
Web: www.myriadrestaurantgroup.com
Prices: $$$$

Lunch Mon – Fri
Dinner nightly

The exemplary care, skill, and excellence of celebrity chef, Nobu Matsuhisa and partner, Drew Nieporent, have made Nobu a wildly popular formula for success.

Since 1994, lines out the door and demand for reservations have been testament to this contemporary Japanese fusion cuisine (also try Nobu's other NY location). Inside this former bank, which now uses its vault for wine storage, architect David Rockwell virtually started a movement in recreating the Japanese countryside with stylized birch trees and black river stones.

The talented kitchen serves creative and delicious specialties like fresh yellowtail sashimi with jalapeño and squid "pasta" with garlic sauce. Sharing multiple dishes may provide the most authentic "Nobu" experience.

The Odeon

American

145 West Broadway (at Thomas St.)

Subway: Chambers St (West Broadway) Lunch & dinner daily
Phone: 212-233-0507
Web: www.theodeonrestaurant.com
Prices: **$$**

Occupying a prime piece of real estate smack in the middle of TriBeCa, The Odeon has been going strong since the 1980's—go at the right hour these days, and you're still likely to find the lawyers and City Hall types who put the place on the map perched on their bar stools.

Between the art deco architecture, wood framed-windows, and the lazy fans slowly rotating overhead, you'll feel like you've walked into a lovely brasserie in Lyon. The food matches the atmosphere—charming and noisy, laid-back but never absent-minded. Try the heirloom beet salad with silky shaved fennel, aged goat cheese and blood orange vinaigrette; or a sushi-grade yellowfin tuna burger licked with wasabi mayonnaise and tucked between a toasted sesame seed bun.

Pepolino

281 West Broadway (bet. Canal & Lispenard Sts.)

Subway: Canal St (Sixth Ave.) Lunch & dinner daily
Phone: 212-966-9983
Web: www.pepolino.com
Prices: **$$**

Simple Tuscan fare, neither reimagined nor stripped down, is the recipe for success at this institution, where the two-floor dining space fills up nightly with neighborhood regulars. Named for a variety of wild thyme found in the Northern Italian region, Pepolino has been going strong since 1999—no easy feat in a town where restaurants measure their anniversaries like cat years.

You can thank original (and current) chef, Enzo Pezone, for steadily guiding diners through dishes like crispy pork feet terrine, donning a sinfully creamy inside and topped with sharp mustard and a flutter of Italian greens; or a light polenta soufflé paired with savory venison ragù. Don't miss the tomato-basil pâté, an opener guaranteed to please the whole table.

Sushi Azabu ✿

Japanese

A1

428 Greenwich St. (at Laight St.)

Subway: Franklin St
Phone: 212-274-0428
Web: www.greenwichgrill.com
Prices: $$$

Lunch Sun – Fri
Dinner nightly

Greenwich Grill

There's a sexy speakeasy vibe to Sushi Azabu, where there is no outside sign to mark the restaurant, and you have to make your way through bustling Greenwich Grill (a restaurant owned by the same group) to get to the basement location. Once inside, you'll find a lovely sushi den fitted out in classic Japanese décor and a smattering of contemporary round booths. It's a particularly pleasing aesthetic to enjoy early in the evening, before the see-and-be-seen crowd descends on the place.

There are three different omakase styles to choose from: sushi, sashimi-and-sushi, or one including hot dishes. And while the hot dishes are far from disappointing, there's no contest which two reign supreme given the title of the restaurant.

The menu changes, but a typical omakase might kick off with creamy monkfish liver, and then move onto an endless parade of colorful fish over perfectly nutty balls of sticky rice. Think silky, buttery toro; creamy sea eel with vibrant lemon zest and a touch of sweet soy; or super-fresh beads of unctuous salmon roe. Finished with a small bowl of miso soup flavored with a bobbing shrimp head and a bit of fresh scallion, this is pure sushi nirvana.

Takahachi

B3 — Japanese XX

145 Duane St. (bet. Church St. & West Broadway)

Subway: Chambers St (West Broadway)
Phone: 212-571-1830
Web: www.takahachi.net
Prices: $$

Lunch Mon – Fri
Dinner nightly

In a neighborhood dominated by Japanese behemoths like Nobu, Megu, and Matsugen, the unassuming Takahachi is a welcome reprieve for nouveau Japanese fare in TriBeCa—minus the fuss, high-flying theatrics, and exorbitant price tags. And for those willing to forgo the sexy ambience, there's even a little romantic lighting from the skylights in Takahachi's dining room come sunset.

The menu is a mish-mash of the country's offerings, with a lineup that might include a bright, velvety plate of sashimi; a fresh tangle of sesame-dressed buckwheat soba noodles studded with shiitake mushrooms and avocado; or a hot appetizer of creamy black cod marinated in miso so nutty and irresistible it might give the young Mr. Naoto Kan himself pause.

Tribeca Grill

A2 — Contemporary XX

375 Greenwich St. (at Franklin St.)

Subway: Franklin St
Phone: 212-941-3900
Web: www.myriadrestaurantgroup.com
Prices: $$$

Lunch Sun – Fri
Dinner nightly

Two decades ago, Drew Neiporent and Robert DeNiro turned a 1905 warehouse into a New York classic. Exposed pipes and brick walls preserved the past and set an architectural standard for many modern TriBeCa eateries.

Celebrity investors (from Barishnikov to Sean Penn), moneyed locals, and many more of the city's beautiful and powerful people comprise a large part of the clientele. The contemporary menu highlights dishes using well-sourced ingredients, such as roasted Denver leg of venison.

The staff is efficient, well paced, and happy to bring the sommelier if guests have questions on the very impressive wine list. For a savory after-dinner treat, sample the extensive selection of artisanal cheeses with quince paste, fig jam, and walnut bread.

Wolfgang's

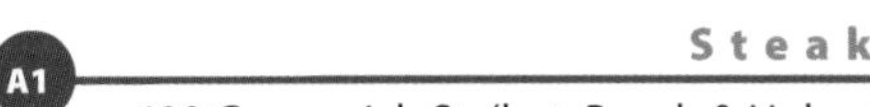

A1 **Steakhouse** XX

409 Greenwich St. (bet. Beach & Hubert Sts.)

Subway: Franklin St — Lunch Mon – Fri
Phone: 212-925-0350 — Dinner nightly
Web: www.wolfgangssteakhouse.com
Prices: **$$$$**

Wolfgang Zwiener clocked in four decades waiting tables at Brooklyn's esteemed Peter Luger before venturing across the bridge with wacky ideas about improving the legendary steakhouse's recipe. A bold move, but it worked so well he now has five self-titled locations across the world.

The TriBeCa outpost is a bit more chill than its uptown sisters (the waiters seem to have picked up a taste for Luger's blasé service style as well) but the beautifully aged steak—cooked to crispy-outside-rosy-pink-inside perfection and ladled with decadent, lip-smacking drippings—seems to taste even better at this location. Starters like tender, chilled lobster cocktail are worth springing for, but sides of sautéed spinach seem to be there solely to round out the menu.

Couverts (X... XXXXX) indicate the level of comfort found at a restaurant. The more X's, the more upscale a restaurant will be.

Upper East Side

The Upper East Side is a vast, mainly residential neighborhood with many faces ranging from prominent New York families to fresh from college prepsters.

Closest to the park are posh spots catering to the Euro crowd and ladies who lunch. Walk further east to find young families filling the latest, casual sushi-ya or artisanal pizzeria. Along First and Second avenues, pubs are packed with raucous post-grads keeping the party alive.

The most upper and eastern reaches were originally developed by renowned families of German descent who built country estates in what has become Yorkville. **Schaller & Weber** is one of the few remaining butchers carrying traditional Austro-German products including fantastic wursts for winter steaming or summer grilling, and the pungent mustards to accompany them.

The Upper East Side has a greater concentration of gourmet markets than any other neighborhood in the city, most with a European feel. Each shop may be more packed than the next, yet has made processing long lines an art of inspired efficiency. **Agata & Valentina** specializes in everything Italian with a considerable regional cheese selection. **Citarella** pumps its mouthwatering aroma of rotisserie chickens out the storefront to entice passersby, but the seafood selection is where they find nirvana. **Grace's Marketplace** is a longtime favorite, loved for its cramped corners and cascading displays. Insiders frequent their trattoria, showcasing quality ingredients carried in the store. However, the true champion of everything uptown and gourmet, is Eli Zabar and his ever-expanding empire. **E.A.T.** has been a Madison Avenue darling since 1973, selling baked goods and takeout foods alongside its casual café. Later branches include his **Vinegar Factory** and newer mega-mart **Eli's**.

Still, there are plenty of smaller purveyors to patronize. **Lobel's** and **Ottomanelli** are among the cities best remaining classic butcher shops, both offering the best meats and pragmatic cooking advice. **William Greenberg Jr.** bakes New York's favorite cookie, the black-and-white, along with to-die-for *babka*. **Glaser's** looks and tastes of everything Old World. On the high end, **Lady M's** boutique and couture cakes blend right in with its chic Madison Avenue neighbors.

For any foodie, Kitchen Arts & Letters has the largest stock of food and wine publications in the country...and owner Nach Waxman is as good a source of industry insight as any book or blog.

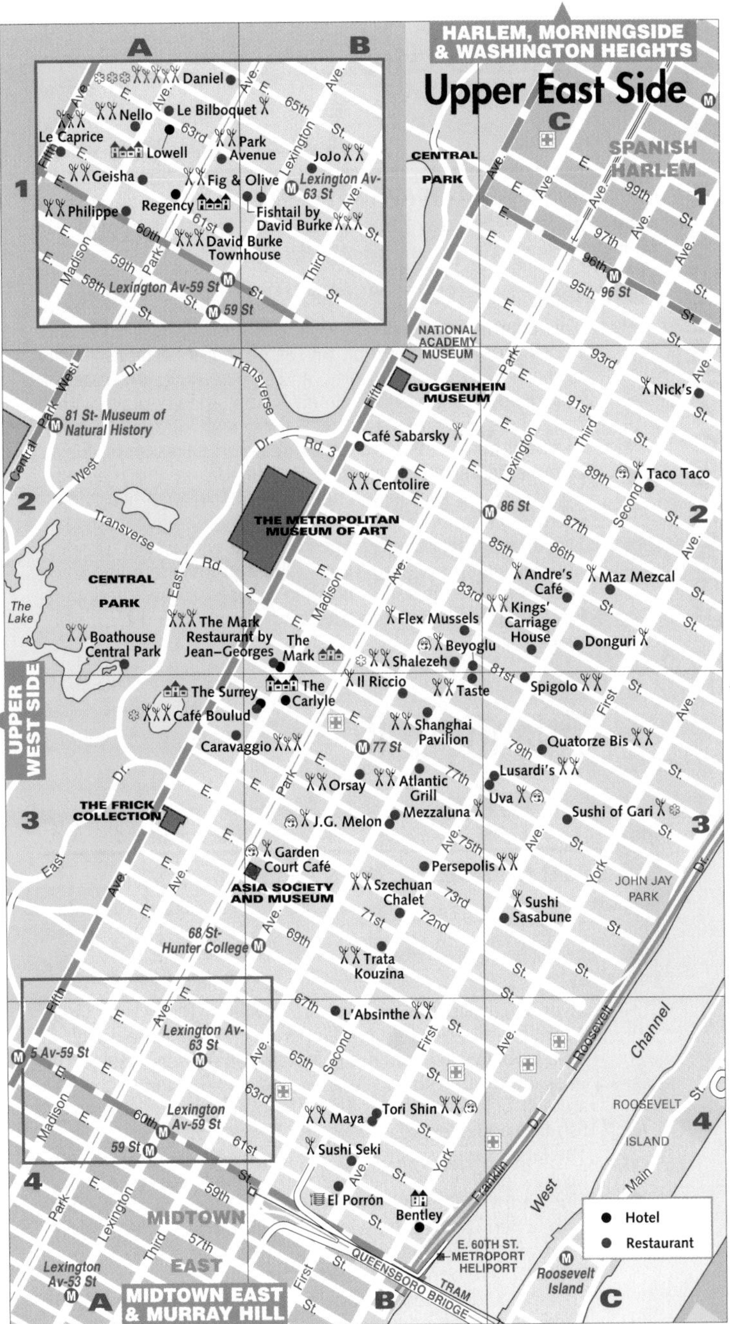
Upper East Side
HARLEM, MORNINGSIDE & WASHINGTON HEIGHTS
UPPER WEST SIDE
MIDTOWN EAST & MURRAY HILL
SPANISH HARLEM
CENTRAL PARK
NATIONAL ACADEMY MUSEUM
GUGGENHEIN MUSEUM
THE METROPOLITAN MUSEUM OF ART
THE FRICK COLLECTION
ASIA SOCIETY AND MUSEUM
JOHN JAY PARK
ROOSEVELT ISLAND
MIDTOWN EAST
E. 60TH ST. METROPORT HELIPORT
QUEENSBORO BRIDGE
TRAM
The Lake
Daniel
Le Bilboquet
Nello
Le Caprice
Lowell
Park Avenue
JoJo
Geisha
Fig & Olive
Philippe
Regency
Fishtail by David Burke
David Burke Townhouse
Lexington Av-63 St
Lexington Av-59 St
59 St
81 St- Museum of Natural History
96 St
86 St
77 St
68 St-Hunter College
5 Av-59 St
Lexington Av-53 St
Roosevelt Island
Nick's
Café Sabarsky
Centolire
Taco Taco
Andre's Café
Maz Mezcal
Kings' Carriage House
Flex Mussels
Beyoglu
Donguri
Boathouse Central Park
The Mark Restaurant by Jean-Georges
The Mark
Shalezeh
Il Riccio
Taste
Spigolo
The Surrey
The Carlyle
Café Boulud
Shanghai Pavilion
Caravaggio
Quatorze Bis
Lusardi's
Orsay
Atlantic Grill
Uva
Mezzaluna
Sushi of Gari
J.G. Melon
Garden Court Café
Persepolis
Szechuan Chalet
Sushi Sasabune
Trata Kouzina
L'Absinthe
Tori Shin
Maya
Sushi Seki
El Porrón
Bentley
Hotel
Restaurant

Andre's Café

Eastern European 

1631 Second Ave. (bet. 84th & 85th Sts.)

Subway: 86 St (Lexington Ave.) — Lunch & dinner daily
Phone: 212-327-1105
Web: www.andrescafeny.com
Prices: ⊜

This charming café details deliciously old fashioned baked goods from a bakery of the same name established in Queen's in 1976. Tiny, tidy, and welcoming, the exterior proudly boasts this establishment's Hungarian heritage with a red, white, and green awning. A temptingly-arranged display of sweet and savory strudels, tortes, and cakes greet guests upon entering. Table service is available in the rear, and before delving into dessert, there is a full menu of hearty old-world fare offered daily.

Weekday meal specials come complete with a salad or soup and a selected yet sinful pastry, and can include home spun traditional favorites like chicken *paprikash,* swathed in a luscious paprika cream sauce and accompanied by freshly made *nokedli.*

Atlantic Grill

B3

Seafood

1341 Third Ave. (bet. 76th & 77th Sts.)

Subway: 77 St — Lunch & dinner daily
Phone: 212-988-9200
Web: www.brguestrestaurants.com
Prices: $$

Swimmingly similar to its downtown sibling Blue Water Grill, Atlantic Grill hooks a very Upper East Side clientele with a vast, globally-accented menu focused on the sea. A selection of sushi (from both the Atlantic and Pacific) and a raw bar are still beloved, while other offerings remember to satisfy fish-free appetites.

The large, luring space is frequented by a well-dressed, fun-loving crowd occupying two rooms—one features a nautical blue and white theme; and the other has a sunny disposition with a terrazzo floor, wicker seating, and potted palms. Sidewalk seating is in high demand when the sun comes out, and the place booms at weekend brunch.

The splendidly intent service team perfectly completes the offerings at this long-time crowd-pleaser.

Beyoglu

Turkish

B2

1431 Third Ave. (at 81st St.)

Subway: 77 St — Lunch & dinner daily
Phone: 212-650-0850
Web: N/A
Prices: $$

Sharing may not come naturally to everyone; but when dining at Beyoglu, it is the best course of action. This way, one can fully experience the delicious range of Mediterranean meze that earns this establishment praise. Most of the recipes—and some wine and beer offerings—come from Turkey, though Greek and Lebanese accents can be found throughout. Warm and tender pita bread makes a delightful accompaniment to anything on the menu. Thick homemade yogurt with spinach and garlic; pan-fried cubes of eggplant with sautéed fresh tomato; grilled shrimp; and marinated octopus are a short sampling of the wide selection.

If grazing doesn't satisfy, choose from a list of larger daily specials, including meat kebabs and grilled fish.

Boathouse Central Park

American

A2

The Lake at Central Park (E. 72nd St. & Park Dr. North)

Subway: 68 St - Hunter College — Lunch & dinner daily
Phone: 212-517-2233
Web: www.thecentralparkboathouse.com
Prices: $$

This unique locale offers Manhattan's only lakeside dining experience. Built in 1954, Loeb Boathouse is a pleasant multi-venue operation that includes a charming outdoor bar perched along the water and a lovely glass-walled dining room offering views of the lake, greenery, and skyline beyond—there isn't a bad seat in the house.

Highlighting American ingredients and sensibilities, the menu features an updated approach with items such as beef carpaccio dressed with syrupy balsamic and a parmesan *frico*; braised chicken thighs with plumped prunes and glazed endive; and a brownie-dense chocolate tart capped with ginger ice cream.

While lunch and brunch are served year-round, note that dinner is only offered during warmer months (April through November).

Café Boulud ✿

French XXX

B3

20 E. 76th St. (bet. Fifth & Madison Aves.)

Subway: 77 St

Lunch & dinner daily

Phone: 212-772-2600

Web: www.danielnyc.com

Prices: **$$$$**

Bill Milne

Tucked into the first floor of the elegant Surrey Hotel, the inspiration for Daniel Boulud's upscale café was the Boulud family's old farm restaurant back in France, located just outside of Lyon, in Saint-Pierre de Chandieu. Duck through the hotel's main entrance and you'll find the elegant dining room, where a clutch of white-clothed tables and bright poppy paintings break up the elegantly renovated dining room.

It's on the plate that things get really vibrant. Rising chef and all-around dreamy new it-boy, Gavin Kaysen, offers four roads to travel down the Café Boulud menu: *la tradition, la saison, le potager*, and *le voyage*. The good news is that at this stylish café, there are no roads too traveled by—each and every lane of this mix-and-match menu offers up delicious possibility.

Diners can opt for the seasonal prix-fixe or float between the menu's columns, where you might find a tangle of black squid ink *spaghetti nero* in a *fra diavolo* choc-a-block with fresh mussels, succulent prawns, and tender baby squid; or wildly fresh *loup de mer* in a buttery brioche crust, garnished with watercress leaves, fluffy gnocchi, braised pearl onion petals, and a creamy sauce *ravigote*.

Café Sabarsky

B2 — **Austrian** X

1048 Fifth Ave. (at 86th St.)

Subway: 86 St (Lexington Ave.)
Phone: 212-288-0665
Web: www.wallse.com
Prices: $$

Lunch Wed – Mon
Dinner Thu – Sun

In addition to the renowned art displayed at the intimately scaled Neue Galerie, find Chef Kurt Gutenbrunner's charming café modeled after a late 19th century Viennese *kaffehause*, complete with dark-wood-paneled walls and formally attired servers. The museum, housed in a 1914 Beaux-Arts mansion, was conceived by cosmetic mogul Ronald Lauder and art dealer Serge Sabarsky to display their collections of early 20th century Austrian and German art.

The traditional menu features savory fare like sautéed bratwurst over riesling sauerkraut, along with an indulgent listing of classic sweets like apple strudel. Beverages include a very nice selection of German and Austrian wines by the glass, tremendous coffee offerings, and divine hot chocolate.

Caravaggio

A3 — **Italian** XXX

23 E. 74th St. (bet. Fifth & Madison Aves.)

Subway: 77 St
Phone: 212-288-1004
Web: N/A
Prices: $$$

Lunch & dinner Mon – Sat

This ambitious newcomer adds a dose of elegance to the city's Italian dining scene. Caravaggio's slender dining room, decorated with silk covered walls, sleek leather seating, and evocative, original artwork exudes a cool palette that, at times, mirrors the disposition of the formally attired waitstaff.

The menu is enhanced by a lengthy list of daily specials that is verbally recited in minute detail. Be sure to pay attention, because you wouldn't want to miss out on the likes of *Amarone* risotto—a magenta-hued mound of starchy perfection piled with taleggio cheese, and drizzled with syrupy balsamic vinegar. But fret not, because the printed menu offers other gems as well, like monkfish osso buco dressed with braised fennel, *garganelli*, and paprika jus.

Centolire

Italian XX

B2

1167 Madison Ave. (bet. 85th & 86th Sts.)

Subway: 86 St (Lexington Ave.) Lunch & dinner daily
Phone: 212-734-7711
Web: www.pinoluongo.com
Prices: $$$

Tuscan-born restaurateur, Pino Luongo, opened Centolire to honor those Italians who, like himself, came to America to start a new life. This establishment has a pleasantly elegant air to its second floor dining room accessed via glass enclosed elevator. The spacious setting is sunlit by large windows overlooking Madison Avenue and is attractively appointed with colorful fabrics and antique kitchen tools. The smartly attired service team graciously attends to diners and prepares Caesar salad tableside—a luscious starting point from which to enjoy the classically infused menu of house-made pastas and entrées that include farm-raised rabbit *"cacciatora."*
Centolire's ground floor dining room features an all-day café menu of salads and panini.

David Burke Townhouse

Contemporary XXX

A1

133 E. 61st St. (bet. Lexington & Park Aves.)

Subway: Lexington Av - 59 St Lunch & dinner daily
Phone: 212-813-2121
Web: www.davidburketownhouse.com
Prices: $$$

On the heels of a 2008 split from partner Donatella Arpaia, Chef/owner David Burke has redesigned his beloved Upper East Side restaurant. Housed in a quaint, red-bricked building with a white-furnished lounge, the renovated dining room features an elegantly appointed room dressed with handsome red banquettes amidst tall white walls featuring Roman shaded mirrors and bright artwork.
An immaculately attired service staff might kick things off with a warm gruyere and poppy seed popover, and then move on to Burke's signature brand of bold, contemporary cuisine (carefully executed by Executive Chef Sylvain Delpique) like crisp and angry lobster; tender rack of lamb with roasted octopus; or "Bronx-style" filet mignon of veal with veal cheeks.

Daniel ✿✿✿

French

A1

60 E. 65th St. (bet. Madison & Park Aves.)

Subway: 68 St - Hunter College

Dinner Mon – Sat

Phone: 212-288-0033

Web: www.danielnyc.com

Prices: $$$$

Eric Laignel

Ask any self-respecting New Yorker what's topping their restaurant bucket list, and you'll hear Daniel time and time again. It's worth the hype—Chef Daniel Boulud's critically-acclaimed flagship is an effortless example of fine dining done right, with its precise, smooth-as-roller-balls service, impeccable attention to detail, and otherworldly French fare.

A face-lift in 2008 by designer Adam D. Tihany gave the dining room a fresh, contemporary look (though jackets are still required, thank you very much), with lots of warm creamy whites broken up by bright Manolo Valdez paintings and custom-made chandeliers sporting beautiful Limoge porcelain tiles.

The ethereal food remains mercifully the same—unapologetically French, and carefully executed by Chef Jean-François Bruel. Dinner spins to the season but may include a silky Meyer lemon royale with plump oysters, North Star caviar, juicy beads of finger lime and a tapioca vinaigrette; silky, slow-baked artic char paired with Maine shrimp, glazed salsify, *cipollini* marmalade, and a Dijon mustard-chicken jus; or soft pillows of artichoke *raviolini* in saffron sauce, pocked with fresh littleneck clams, plump bay scallops, and tender squid.

Donguri

Japanese

309 E. 83rd St. (bet. First & Second Aves.)

Subway: 86 St (Lexington Ave.) Dinner Tue – Sun
Phone: 212-737-5656
Web: www.donguriny c.com
Prices: $$$

The ongoing construction of the Second Avenue subway may have obscured Donguri's already unassuming location, but this demure Japanese still draws a devout following. Its steady clientele of high-powered international bankers, neighborhood couples, and Japanese ex-pats longing for a taste of home speaks to its sophistication and authenticity.

With just 24 seats, Donguri has a minimalist décor and is lovingly attended by a polite team. Deliciously straightforward preparations may include wonderfully fresh sashimi (though no sushi); flash-fried and sublimely crunchy sweet-corn tempura; rice bowls of grated mountain yam, luscious sea urchin from Maine, and yuzu zest; or a refreshing finale of delicate grapefruit gelée, honey-sweet and blushing pink.

El Porrón

Spanish

1123 First Ave. (bet. 61st & 62nd Sts.)

Subway: Lexington Av - 59 St Lunch & dinner daily
Phone: 212-207-8349
Web: www.elporronnyc.com
Prices: $$

The tapas movement shows no signs of ceasing anytime soon, but this still-blushing new restaurant, opened just over a year ago, more than does the small plate craze justice with its energetic ambience featuring upbeat Spanish tunes; a lively crowd chugging down delicious sangria come nighttime; and finger-licking authentic Spanish cuisine.

Chef Gonzalo Bermeo's menu is as playful as the room, gracefully dancing between traditional entrées and scrumptious paellas made to order; classic tapas like tender chicken with ratatouille or a sizzling *cazuela* filled with garlic shrimp, white wine, and olive oil; and original creations like tender veal meatballs, slow-cooked in a fragrant leek and tomato stew then finished with toasted sliced almonds.

Fig & Olive

Mediterranean XX

B1

808 Lexington Ave. (bet. 62nd & 63rd Sts.)

Subway: Lexington Av - 63 St — Lunch & dinner daily
Phone: 212-207-4555
Web: www.figandolive.com
Prices: $$$

The bounty of the Mediterranean's olive groves is not only featured on the menu of this casually elegant Upper East spot (with midtown and Meatpacking locations), but is also available for purchase in gift-worthy packaging. Each dish—from salad Niçoise to grilled *branzino*—is accented with a specific extra virgin oil, carefully selected to highlight their extensive stock. Dinners begin with an olive oil trio to sample (though your server will choose which ones you try).

Inside the bright, sunny space, shoppers find a soothing respite in light Mediterranean plates of ceviche, a sampling of crostini, or pastas and grilled fare. The wine list echoes the same regions of origin as the fragrant oils, with many selections available by the glass.

Fishtail by David Burke

Seafood XXX

B1

135 E. 62nd St. (bet. Lexington & Park Aves.)

Subway: Lexington Av - 63 St — Lunch Sun – Fri
Phone: 212-754-1300 — Dinner nightly
Web: www.fishtaildb.com
Prices: $$$

This fitting addition to Chef David Burke's oeuvre features a sophisticated setting throughout two levels of a cozy townhouse. The first floor is an oyster bar and lounge popular with the after-work crowds, while the upstairs dining room is wrapped in deep red and bedecked with accents that colorfully convey the ocean theme.

The menu focuses on seafood, of which 80% is caught through sustainable fishing methods—perhaps from the chef's own boat. The preparations are stamped with the chef's unique touch, whether simply prepared as a whole, roasted striped bass, or more creatively interpreted in the pan-roasted Atlantic salmon with braised bok choy and two curries. Regardless of your selection, these dishes show the hand of a skilled kitchen.

Flex Mussels

Seafood 

B2

174 E. 82nd St. (bet. Lexington & Third Aves.)

Subway: 86 St (Lexington Ave.) Dinner nightly
Phone: 212-717-7772
Web: www.flexmusselsny.com
Prices: **$$**

Despite its strong name, Flex Mussels is actually a fun, casual, and intimate seafood shack with uptown polish. Usually packed to the gills, the slim bar area features pretty touches like flowers, slender mirrors, and long-legged aluminum chairs against a dining counter. The back dining room is spare, contemporary, and more subdued.

The menu features the namesake bi-valve, hailing from Prince Edward Island, steamed in more than twenty globally-inspired guises, like the "Tokyo" with miso and seaweed. The mussels are priced by the pound and are best accompanied by sides of piping-hot, hand-cut skinny fries. The menu also features non-mussel options such as an impressive lobster roll, the likes of which would normally require a trip downtown.

Garden Court Café

Asian 

B3

725 Park Ave. (at 70th St.)

Subway: 68 St - Hunter College Lunch Tue – Sun
Phone: 212-570-5202
Web: www.asiasociety.org
Prices: **$$**

Flooded by natural light in the glass-enclosed, plant-filled lobby of the Asia Society, this café is a far cry from your garden-variety museum restaurant. Though it doesn't generate much fanfare, it is worth seeking out, not only for its quiet ambience, but for the Asian dishes that expertly fuse east and west.

Serving lunch Tuesday through Sunday, the menu draws inspiration from the east in its offerings that may include roasted chicken glazed with sweet chili sauce and black bean cakes with mango chutney. The bento box features two chef selections along with rice and salad.

It's a quality show, right down to the careful presentation and good service—and the museum's entry fee is not required. Don't miss the museum gift shop for its wonderful wares.

Geisha

33 E. 61st St. (bet. Madison & Park Aves.)

Subway: Lexington Av - 59 St — Lunch Mon – Fri
Phone: 212-813-1112 — Dinner Mon – Sat
Web: www.geisharestaurant.com
Prices: $$$

The duo that brought Serafina to the Upper East Side, Vittorio Assaf and Fabio Granato, succeed again—though this geisha prefers polished cool to bowing modesty. Decked in origami and cherry blossom light fixtures, this vibrant two-floor space fills with a lively, socially minded, and sophisticated Euro-crowd that pours in nightly, as much for the well-rounded cocktail list as for the cuisine.

Originally developed by Chef Eric Ripert of Le Bernardin, the crowd-pleasing menu features ample sushi bar offerings as well as creative salads and cooked entrées that display modern Asian influence and a skillful hand. The fine quality of ingredients may be highlighted in fresh sea urchin roe sushi or the wonderfully conceived flavors of Peking duck salad.

Il Riccio

152 E. 79th St. (bet. Lexington & Third Aves.)

Subway: 77 St — Lunch & dinner daily
Phone: 212-639-9111
Web: N/A
Prices: $$

This low-key Italian, and its smiling cadre of charming staff, is just the right spot to recharge after an afternoon perusing the fabulous neighborhood boutiques or meandering through the nearby Metropolitan Museum of Art.

The likes of a refreshing arugula and roasted red pepper salad with marinated fresh anchovies; grilled grouper dressed simply with olive oil and fresh lemon; and a straightforward selection of dessert pastries indicates the fuss-free approach to cooking offered at Il Riccio, which focuses on the cuisine of the Amalfi coast. Regulars know to enjoy these dishes in the back, enclosed garden.

Inside, the space offers a cozy feel with warm ochre walls, simple furnishings, and an assemblage of photographs strewn throughout.

J.G. Melon

B3

American

1291 Third Ave. (at 74th St.)

Subway: 77 St
Lunch & dinner daily
Phone: 212-744-0585
Web: N/A
Prices:

J.G. Melon is the kind of place parents tell their children they used to frequent when they were young in the city. In fact in many cases, this is still the norm. It's a multi-generational watering hole for the masses, feeding Upper East Siders burgers and beers in a convivial setting that hasn't changed over the generations.

The key here is the burger. Griddled and served on a toasted bun with or without cheese, it's one of the best in the city. Add a bowl of the crispy round fries, a cool draft, and a savory chili or spinach salad starter and you've got the essence of what's been packing this place all these years.

Sure tables are tight and the waits can be long, but the service is jovial and it's come-as-you-are and, did we mention the burger?

JoJo

B1

Contemporary

160 E. 64th St. (bet. Lexington & Third Aves.)

Subway: Lexington Av - 63 St
Lunch & dinner daily
Phone: 212-223-5656
Web: www.jean-georges.com
Prices: $$$

With its snug velvet banquettes; romantic, tapestry-framed archways; and seductive, bordello-low lighting, Jean-Georges Vongerichten's first-born New York restaurant (at last count, the maestro had no less than eight Manhattan establishments) is a welcome reprieve from its stuffy Upper East Side cousins, earning the little red townhouse a special place on the neighborhood scene. The sophisticated locals still come in droves.

Given the tony 10021 address, the compact à la carte menu is surprisingly reasonable, and might include a crispy, pan-fried terrine filled with a soft pocket of warm Coach Farms goat cheese; tart lemon späetzle choc-a-block with fresh, roasted lobster; or apple *pain perdu* paired with a smooth scoop of green apple sorbet.

Kings' Carriage House

Contemporary XX

251 E. 82nd St. (bet. Second & Third Aves.)

Subway: 86 St (Lexington Ave.) Lunch & dinner daily
Phone: 212-734-5490
Web: www.kingscarriagehouse.com
Prices: $$

Picture the mist rolling in when dining at this bona fide facsimile of an Irish manor. The elegantly countrified setting, warmly run by Elizabeth King and husband Paul Farrell (of Dublin), features creaky wooden floors and goldenrod walls mounted with a plethora of crockery, chinoiserie, and framed portraits. White-linen tables are draped with lacy overlays and set with vintage silverware. A collection of china teapots is even available for purchase.

The nightly prix-fixe menu offers an updated take on classically prepared cuisine with items like grilled quail with carrot and parsnip hashbrowns; potato-crusted halibut with tomato-caper butter; and crème brûlée with caramelized banana. Afternoon tea is quite popular, so be sure to reserve in advance.

L'Absinthe

French XX

227 E. 67th St. (bet. Second & Third Aves.)

Subway: 68 St - Hunter College Lunch & dinner daily
Phone: 212-794-4950
Web: www.labsinthe.com
Prices: $$$

A true charmer, L'Absinthe is a uniquely enjoyable classic neighborhood bistro that can claim few peers. The warm and amiable setting boasts an authentically continental elegance that is enhanced by an understated, sophisticated clientele.

The flawless menu offers a culling of preparations that are seasonal and contemporary in theme, but the real draw here are Chef Jean-Michel Bergougnoux's "brasserie classics" like the *choucroute royale Alsacienne*, presented as a heaping platter of expertly prepared pork: garlicky sausage, *boudin blanc*, belly, and ham; also await caraway-spiced braised cabbage and boiled potatoes. Another classic, the *baba au rhum* is deliciously done—a boozy moist cake slathered with *crème pâtissière* and *brunoise* of tropical fruits.

Le Bilboquet

French

A1

25 E. 63rd St. (bet. Madison & Park Aves.)

Subway: Lexington Av - 63 St — Lunch & dinner daily
Phone: 212-751-3036
Web: N/A
Prices: **$$**

This Upper East Side institution still draws a chic and pampered crowd to its attractive but minuscule setting that is part bistro and part Euro-social club. Named for a 16th century game, scoring a table in this butter-yellow room can be quite challenging. But once past the door and settled into a plush banquette, consider yourself among the in-crowd; enjoy the scene, brightened by bold artwork and vivid flowers. The support staff is as well dressed as the clientele and politely speed things along.

The pleasant cooking here is solid throughout the classic menu that may offer the likes of country pâté made of duck and served with perfectly toasted baguette, cornichons, and ground Dijon mustard; or a pan-seared, crispy skin fillet of sea bass.

Le Caprice

Contemporary 

A1

795 Fifth Ave. (bet. 60th & 61st Sts.)

Subway: 5 Av - 59 St — Lunch & dinner daily
Phone: 212-940-8195
Web: www.capriceny.com
Prices: **$$$**

Taking up residence in the extensively renovated Pierre, this London export has elicited a faithful following among the city's elite. The cutting-edge brasserie setting renders a bar area that is generous in length and comfort; and an art deco dining room, that is at once resplendent and dramatic with sparkling chrome fixtures, and encased in gleaming black and white marble.

The menu offers straightforward cuisine marked by excellent product, and even a few of the English classics manage to shine through. Fish and chips, a tough find in this town, is made exquisite and upscale with pristine cod fillets cloaked in a featherlight golden batter and accompanied by mint-flecked mushy peas, decadent tartar sauce, and a side of excellent fries (chips).

Lusardi's

Italian

1494 Second Ave. (bet. 77th & 78th Sts.)

Subway: 77 St — Lunch Mon – Fri
Phone: 212-249-2020 — Dinner nightly
Web: www.lusardis.com
Prices: $$$

A neighborhood mainstay since 1982, brothers Luigi and Mauro Lusardi continue to run an impressive operation. Tastefully appointed with pumpkin-colored walls and deep-toned woodwork, the dining room is warmly attended by a beaming staff that suits Lusardi's comfortable elegance and old-world vibe.

Fresh ingredients and careful preparation go into the Northern Italian fare such as *crespelle Fiorentina*, a cylinder of pan fried eggplant filled with a fluffy blend of spinach and ricotta then bathed in bright and creamy tomato sauce. Many of the preparations feature an appetizingly rustic presentation as in the *fegato alla Veneziana*—chunks of chicken liver sautéed with sweet onions and white wine, then piled onto a nest of coarse ground polenta.

The Mark Restaurant by Jean-Georges

Contemporary

25 E. 77th St. (at Madison Ave.)

Subway: 77 St — Lunch & dinner daily
Phone: 212-606-3030
Web: www.themarkrestaurantnyc.com
Prices: $$$

You'll find a straightforward but beautifully executed menu at this new Jean-Georges Vongerichten restaurant, where a raw bar and a selection of pizzas, pastas, and entrées won't move you to tears, but is guaranteed to please a crowd. Housed in the newly renovated Mark Hotel, the restaurant was designed by legendary French designer Jacques Grange, and the result is a chic dining space featuring high ceilings, plush ivory banquettes and warm, sexy lighting.

Chef de Cuisine Pierre Schutz oversees a menu that might feature homemade cheese ravioli garnished with fresh sweet peas, julienned pea pods, wilted baby spinach, and basil; or tender branzino with slow-roasted tomatoes, paired with a fluffy pile of couscous studded with Swiss chard.

Maya

Mexican XX

B4

1191 First Ave. (bet. 64th & 65th Sts.)

Subway: 68 St - Hunter College — Dinner nightly
Phone: 212-585-1818
Web: www.modernmexican.com
Prices: $$

Maya continues to impress as one of the city's finest examples of upscale Mexican cuisine. To add to the spark, it now offers increased accommodations with their recently redone bar and lounge, that serves divine mango margaritas—still perfect after all these years. Service may lag a bit but the kitchen excels, serving up a contemporary version of Mexican classics in a colorful and chic dining room.

Here, Mexican flavors are captured with modern style, combining seamlessly and deliciously in *entradas* such as *quesadillas surtidas*, fried masa dough filled with Oaxaca cheese, chile poblano *rajas*, and doubly dressed with salsas. Creative and classic *platos fuertes* may include tequila-flambéed shrimp paired with decadent black bean and *Gouda huarache*.

Maz Mezcal

Mexican 

C2

316 E. 86th St. (bet. First & Second Aves.)

Subway: 86 St (Lexington Ave.) — Lunch Sat – Sun
Phone: 212-472-1599 — Dinner nightly
Web: www.mazmezcal.com
Prices: $$

Simple, bountiful Mexican food leaves locals and families eager to return to Maz Mezcal, located on a busy stretch of 86th Street. Eduardo Silva (who has long been a part of Mexican dining on the Upper East) hosts his family's eastside stalwart, where a low-key party begins almost every night, spilling into the street in warm weather.

The flavorful fare includes an assortment of enchiladas, flautas, tostadas, and burritos to create your own Tex-Mex-style platter, or choose from the house combinations named for Mexican beach towns. Specialties may include traditional mole poblano made with seven distinct chile varieties and bittersweet chocolate.

Dishes are tailored to mild palates, but the kitchen is happy to accommodate those who prefer food *picante*.

Mezzaluna

Italian

1295 Third Ave. (bet. 74th & 75th Sts.)

Subway: 77 St — Lunch & dinner daily
Phone: 212-535-9600
Web: www.mezzalunany.com
Prices: **$$**

Named after the crescent-shaped chopping knife, Mezzaluna's walls are decorated with 77 depictions of the kitchen tool created by artists, who were paid with fine Italian meals.
The dining room feels timeless with its terra-cotta floor, pink marble-topped tables, and yellow painted walls hung with rustic crockery. A wood-burning pizza oven beckons from the cozy space. The fact that Mezzaluna uses ingredients such as flour, tomatoes, and mozzarella that are only imported from Italy, make them a beloved destination for pizza. Delicately fried vegetable croquettes; homemade black linguini with shrimp and spicy tomato sauce; and pistachio semifreddo with bittersweet chocolate sauce are a few examples of why this institution has been going strong since 1984.

Nello

Italian

696 Madison Ave. (bet. 62nd & 63rd Sts.)

Subway: 5 Av - 59 St — Lunch & dinner daily
Phone: 212-980-9099
Web: N/A
Prices: **$$$$**

Nello offers a chic and polished yet satisfying Italian dining experience, fashionably perched among pricy boutiques and astronomical real estate. The bright and airy room—resplendent with marble, ivory walls hung with black-and-white safari scenes, and thick linen-covered tables dressed with white flowers—is overseen by a well-orchestrated, suit-clad service team. Everything here radiates privilege and optimism. Even the menu's typeface appears elegant... and expensive.
While high prices and celebrity sightings do not ensure an enjoyable meal, the flavorful offerings like San Daniele prosciutto and melon, neat mounds of perfectly prepared pasta, or hearty entrées of *osso buco* should bring enough pleasure to help ease the potential sticker shock.

Nick's

 Pizza 

1814 Second Ave. (at 94th St.)

Subway: 96 St (Lexington Ave.) — Lunch & dinner daily
Phone: 212-987-5700
Web: www.nicksnyc.com
Prices: ⊜

Due to a blockade of equipment needed for the ongoing construction of the Second Avenue subway line, Nick's may be a bit harder to spot but still ranks highly on Upper East Siders' short list of pizza favorites. This Manhattan location of the Forest Hills original, named for owner Nick Angelis, has cozy surroundings with tables overlooking the dough-tossing *pizzaiolos* and jovial service.

In addition to the excellent, bronzed, crackling thin-crust pizzas, a variety of Italian-American pastas (referred to as "macaroni") and entrées are available as full or half portions for family-friendly dining. Offerings may include veal scaloppini with lemon and butter or an enjoyable tangle of linguini with white clam sauce infused with roasted garlic cloves.

Orsay

French XX

1057 Lexington Ave. (at 75th St.)

Subway: 77 St — Lunch & dinner daily
Phone: 212-517-6400
Web: www.orsayrestaurant.com
Prices: $$

Commanding a prime corner of *cher* Manhattan real estate, Orsay is fronted with elegant wood paneling and crowned with a deep awning to protect its well-dressed clientele as they sip, sup, and socialize on this fashionable stretch of Lexington Ave. Inside, the art nouveau dining room has an impressive air of authenticity accented by a mosaic-tiled floor, lacy café curtains, and a zinc-topped bar.

Orsay's French-accented staff underscores the richly atmospheric setting. Though French at heart, the menu displays the intriguing elements of a creative kitchen. Escargots with parsley and garlic butter, or truffle-scented cheese soufflé may be offered alongside lobster ravioli made with vanilla pasta, or barbecued lamb shank with chorizo risotto.

Park Avenue

A1 **Contemporary** XX

100 E. 63rd St. (at Park Ave.)

Subway: 59 St — Lunch & dinner daily
Phone: 212-644-1900
Web: www.parkavenyc.com
Prices: $$$

While many restaurants pay the utmost attention to seasonality on the plate, Park Avenue extends it to the décor. Every three months, it shutters for 48 hours to re-emerge as a celebration of spring, summer, fall, or winter. In a sort of architectural trompe l'oeil, a series of panels were devised to frame the dining room and create a fresh backdrop that changes throughout the year.

The beautifully prepared menu displays the same determined playfulness with boosts from ingredients such as fig carpaccio with goat cheese in autumn, or wintertime plates of stout-braised lamb shank with aged-cheddar polenta and green apples. The cocktail menu is likewise enticing.

One constant: the decadent and shareable "chocolate cube" is a dessert menu fixture.

Persepolis

B3 **Persian** XX

1407 Second Ave. (bet. 73rd & 74th Sts.)

Subway: 77 St — Lunch & dinner daily
Phone: 212-535-1100
Web: www.persepolisnyc.com
Prices: $$

This savory Persian cuisine piques both interest and appetite, offering alluring dishes fragrant with parsley, lemon, and saffron served graciously in an attractive setting. The large selection of salads and appetizers may include tabouli: a finely chopped salad of bulgar, bright with the flavors of fresh herbs and citrus. After a medley of starters, move on to flavorful marinated meats such as rack of lamb or beautifully presented kebabs of chicken, delicately flavored and yellow with saffron. In lieu of the meat-focused entrées, there is a mildly spiced, satisfying vegetarian stew. Each entrée is accompanied by your choice of sour cherry-studded, almond-flecked, or dill-flavored rice.

Takeout and delivery are popular options for locals.

Philippe

A1 **Chinese** XX

33 E. 60th St. (bet. Madison & Park Aves.)

Subway: Lexington Av - 59 St — Lunch Mon – Sat
Phone: 212-644-8885 — Dinner nightly
Web: www.philippechow.com
Prices: $$$

This luxe Chinese from former Mr Chow chef, Philippe Chow (no relation), showcases linen-draped tables set with Wedgwood flatware, chopsticks neatly stored in wooden boxes, and celebrity sightings. The support staff pairs white jackets and mandarin collar uniforms with red canvas sneakers—this whimsical departure from formality is juxtaposed by the stately monochromatic color scheme of deep brown with light accents that flows throughout the multi-room space.

The satisfying menu carries dumplings, satays, and lettuce wraps, alongside main courses such as Beijing chicken dressed with walnuts and sweet brown sauce, that are sized for sharing. Lunchtime is a good chance to experience Philippe solo, when the popular prix-fixe is available.

Quatorze Bis

C3 **French** 

323 E. 79th St. (bet. First & Second Aves.)

Subway: 77 St — Lunch Tue – Sun
Phone: 212-535-1414 — Dinner nightly
Web: N/A
Prices: $$

With its lipstick-red façade and sunny yellow awning, Quatorze Bis easily stands out along this high-rise stretch of the Upper East. The pleasant interior, frequented by a mature, well-dressed crowd, displays a continental flair with framed vintage posters, mirrored panels painted with the wine list, and comfortable red-velvet banquettes. The friendly waitstaff greets patrons with a small blackboard to present the day's specials.

The menu's roster of satisfying French classics is executed with savoir faire, as in the terrine *maison* and a savory tart of bacon, leek, and Gruyère. Grilled sirloin with light and crispy frites and decadent sauce béarnaise followed by the excellent hot apple tart is testament to the timelessness of true bistro cooking.

Shalezeh ✿

Persian XX

B2

1420 Third Ave. (bet. 80th & 81st Sts.)

Subway: 77 St

Lunch & dinner daily

Phone: 212-288-0012

Web: www.shalezeh.com

Prices: $$

Shalezeh

The name of Shalezeh (née Shalizar) has changed, but most else remains blissfully the same. Head here on a summer night and you'll still find those lovely French doors flung open and think—this is not bustling Third Avenue in Manhattan's Upper East Side, but a relaxing mini-vacation to Persia. Now, if only Shalezeh's sometimes harried staff would get the memo.

The space has a lovely minimalist appeal, with light wood floors and pale walls accented with exposed brick—up front tends to read bright and sassy, while couples retreat to the back for more intimate conversation. You'll need it to comb through the menu's impossibly long dish titles, but the good news is all of them translate deliciously.

Kick things off with a colorful plate of spreads boasting all kinds of goodies like *dolmas* stuffed with tender rice and fragrant herbs, *baba* with Persian goat cheese, walnuts, and onions, and homemade yogurt done three ways (each more irresistible than the next); and then move on to an entrée called *koofteh tabrizi*, a gorgeous, herb-flecked meatball stuffed with tender stewed prunes and fava beans, then pooled in a lip-smacking stew of tomatoes, sweet peas, turmeric, curry, and saffron.

Shanghai Pavilion

B3 — Chinese XX

1378 Third Ave. (bet. 78th & 79th Sts.)

Subway: 77 St — Lunch & dinner daily
Phone: 212-585-3388
Web: N/A
Prices:

Service with a smile by a smartly attired staff, an attractively appointed dining room with silk curtains and apricot walls, and a menu that features a list of celebration-worthy, order-in-advance specialties give Shanghai Pavilion an upscale ambience that continually attracts a devoted following of well-heeled neighborhood residents.

Shanghai and Cantonese specialties abound, as with the slurp-inducing steamed juicy buns. While enjoying these toothsome treats, the efficient servers stealthily restock your soup spoon with the next bun from the tabletop bamboo steamer. Velvet sea bass, Grand Marnier lobster, and crispy baby chicken with bronzed skin, glazed with sweet and spicy brown sauce, are just a few of the chef's tempting specialties.

Spigolo

C3 — Italian XX

1561 Second Ave. (at 81st St.)

Subway: 86 St (Lexington Ave.) — Lunch Sat – Sun
Phone: 212-744-1100 — Dinner nightly
Web: N/A
Prices: $$

With less than 25 seats, a copper-topped bar, an adeptly contrived menu marked by bold flavors, and siren service, Spigolo is a place wistfully wished to be a trusted secret. However, crowds hungry for a sophisticated meal know all to well of this impressive Italian, owned and operated by husband-and-wife team Scott and Heather Fratangelo.

Clams and oysters on the half shell, or fresh Arctic char tartare studded with capers and roasted tomato, make for a bracing start; perhaps followed by excellent pastas or rustic entrées of roasted halibut with *cipollini* marmalade and Tuscan-style grilled strip steak.

The dessert selection may prove irresistible, especially when faced with divine choices like warm quince pound cake with cream cheese gelato.

Sushi of Gari ✿

Japanese

C3

402 E. 78th St. (bet. First & York Aves.)

Subway: 77 St Dinner nightly
Phone: 212-517-5340
Web: www.sushiofgari.com
Prices: **$$$**

Sushi of Gari

Omakase, please: such a simple pair of words, and yet they begin a most extraordinary odyssey into the world of avant sushi chef, Masatoshi "Gari" Sugio. His mastery of the craft is the reason sushiphiles across the city are willing to trek to this otherwise food-starved strip of Yorkville; knowing no matter who is behind the counter that night they'll have trained with the best.

Once inside, you'll find a warm reception from a staff happy to attend to your every need in the contemporary restaurant. With such a simple décor, regulars jockey for a seat at the sushi bar, where a culinary walk with the masters might kick off with slices of luminescent red snapper seasoned with grated wasabi root and paired with glistening mesclun, fried lotus root chips, and pine nuts; and then move on to ruby-red tuna laced with whipped tofu; melt-in-your-mouth toro topped with a soy-drenched dollop of grated daikon; or smoky barbecued eel bound to ripe avocado with a nori ribbon.

The simplicity of the restaurant won't alert you to the cost, so be prepared to pay a bit for paradise. The good news is that in Gari's house, you call the shots—and the chefs won't stop serving until you buckle.

Sushi Sasabune

C3 **Japanese**

401 E. 73rd St. (at First Ave.)

Subway: 77 St
Phone: 212-249-8583
Web: N/A
Prices: $$$

Lunch Tue – Fri
Dinner Tue – Sat

Nestled in the Upper East Side, this third outpost of the Sasabune family is paradise for devoted followers who appreciate premium quality fish and palatable price tag. The style of rice preparation is likewise a draw here, with more assertive vinegar and a warmer temperature.

Since Sasabune only serves sushi and sashimi omakase, this is no place for newbies or picky eaters. In fact, the restaurants motto clearly states: "No Spicy Tuna. No California Roll. TRUST ME." So, those hankering for tempura should steer clear.

Aficionados or anyone sincerely seeking outstanding fish will find a home here, amid the parade of butterfish, stuffed squid, and local oysters. This wholly gratifying experience justifies the cult status of this modest spot.

Sushi Seki

B4 **Japanese** 

1143 First Ave. (bet. 62nd & 63rd Sts.)

Subway: Lexington Av - 59 St
Phone: 212-371-0238
Web: N/A
Prices: $$$

Dinner Mon – Sat

Seki is all about sushi and the impressive quality has anchored its popularity among the devoted neighborhood regulars. It can be tough to get a reservation at this casual establishment, so it's best to book in advance to sample creations of the namesake chef, who once worked in the kitchen of the esteemed Sushi of Gari.

In the modest dining nooks, the waitstaff keeps up a steady tempo, while at the cramped counter, chef's craft fresh-from-the-boat products into tasty morsels. Those in the know will ask about the chef's signature sushi and daily specials that aren't written on the menu, but even the spicy tuna set is well-fed here.

Late hours are a plus for night-owls, and Seki's first-rate sushi is available for takeout.

Szechuan Chalet

Chinese

B3

1395 Second Ave. (bet. 72nd & 73rd Sts.)

Subway: 68 St - Hunter College — Lunch & dinner daily
Phone: 212-737-1838
Web: www.szechuanchaletnyc.com
Prices: $$

Uptown dwellers rejoice at the opening of this new Chinese standout. Spicier fare prevails, but the kitchen shows a talent for balancing flavors and offering quality. The menu is large, so focus on the chef's specials and regionally specific dishes that include Sichuan pork dumplings red with chili-spiked oil or shredded chicken in a fiery vinaigrette, served chilled and doused with a creamy sesame sauce. The "chili fish pond" (mind the pun) is a red chili-oil based broth brimming with fish and vegetables, capped by a flotilla of Sichuan peppercorns and dried red chilies.

Graciously attended by professional staff, the fresh and contemporary space is adorned with red upholstery, pale walls, inked landscapes, and a sparkly blue-accented ceiling.

Taco Taco

Mexican

C2

1726 Second Ave. (bet. 89th & 90th Sts.)

Subway: 86 St (Lexington Ave.) — Lunch Tue – Sun
Phone: 212-289-8226 — Dinner nightly
Web: N/A
Prices: $$

With prices as palatable as the food, the reputation of this neighborhood darling extends far beyond its Upper East enclave. The tacos alone are worth a visit—picture soft corn tortillas abundantly filled with the likes of *puerco enchilado* or *pollo asado,* simply adorned with chopped onion and cilantro. Tacos aside, this colorful spot offers much more than its namesake. The authentically Mexican and Tex-Mex menu also offers burritos, *tortas,* and house specials like *chiles rellenos,* or sautéed shrimp with lemon and garlic.

The bar stocks a full variety of tequilas, but a *michelada* (beer seasoned with lime and Tabasco, served on the rocks with a salted rim) makes for a refreshing thirst quencher.

Downtown sister Mole shares a similar menu.

Taste

American XX

B3

1411 Third Ave. (at 80th St.)

Subway: 77 St — Lunch & dinner daily
Phone: 212-717-9798
Web: www.elizabar.com
Prices: $$

Located on what may as well be known as "Eli's block," Taste is part of Eli Zabar's vast operation that includes a sprawling market, wine store, flower shop, and even an ice-cream stand. This attractive dining room is appointed with a striking inlaid tile floor, tobacco-brown walls, and mocha-hued furnishings. At night, the rich colors are lightened by tables dressed in orange Frette linens.

The impressive menu focuses on seasonality and simplicity in offerings like peekytoe crab salad with honeydew purée; olive-oil poached salmon with greenmarket string beans; and for dessert, peach and fig tart baked in the wood-burning oven, served with vanilla ice cream.

Breakfast and lunch is self-service, with a wide variety of items priced by the pound.

Tori Shin

Japanese XX

B4

1193 First Ave. (bet. 64th & 65th Sts.)

Subway: 68 St - Hunter College — Lunch & dinner Mon – Sat
Phone: 212-988-8408
Web: www.torishinny.com
Prices: $$

127 million Japanese people can't be wrong. It's what you'll need to remind yourself if you're new to yakitori—a Japanese dish where chicken offal like heart, liver, and soft knee bone are skewered and grilled, usually over charcoal.

This is absolutely the place to try it—from its unassuming façade to its mostly Japanese clientele, Tori Shin might feel like a downtown speakeasy but this is top-flight Japanese fare. Grab a seat at the counter, where you can watch the chefs work the grill (shipped in from Tokyo), skewering the fresh, organic chicken (raised especially for Tori Shin by a local farm in Pennsylvania) into mouthwatering concoctions laced with the restaurant's inimitable sauce. Omakase starts at $65; the skewers-only option even less.

Trata Kouzina

Greek XX

B3

1331 Second Ave. (bet. 70th & 71st Sts.)

Subway: 68 St - Hunter College — Lunch & dinner daily
Phone: 212-535-3800
Web: N/A
Prices: $$$

In spring 2010, popular Trata Estiatorio received a face-lift and now fronts a more casual home-style approach to Greek cuisine. The space is light and airy done in bright white with pale blue accents and oodles of outdoor seating for when the weather behaves.

The menu is rooted in a selection of meze and traditional entrées which include tempting rotiserrie prepared meats and whole fish. Small plates include a luscious assortment of bites such as amazingly tender octopus, grilled and served with a salad of tomatoes and white beans; and *kolokithokeftedes,* fluffy zucchini fritters served with cool and creamy *tzatziki.* The wine list also merits attention—the all-Greek selection is bolstered by Greek beers and aperitifs.

Uva

Italian 

C3

1486 Second Ave. (bet. 77th & 78th Sts.)

Subway: 77 St — Lunch Sat – Sun
Phone: 212-472-4552 — Dinner nightly
Web: www.uvawinebar.com
Prices: $$

Bathed in an amber glow, this rustic wine bar features brick wall mounted sconces, votive-topped wooden tables, and a copper clad bar. The lived-in décor is complemented by an upbeat vibe, especially when dining in the charming back garden, weather permitting.

The well selected wine list includes more than 30 wines by the glass; while the substantial menu teases with Emilian-style focaccia, Sardinian flatbread, and heaping cheeses and cured meats. The kitchen is equally adept in preparing more elegant edibles, as in *polenta tartufata*—soft polenta stuffed with robiola cheese and sauced with black truffle cream. Desserts are wonderfully simple and include a special composition of orange pound cake with vanilla ice cream and dark caramel sauce.

Upper West Side

Proudly situated between two of Manhattan's most celebrated parks, home to venerable Lincoln Center, and the beloved Natural History Museum, the family-friendly Upper West Side is one of this city's most distinct neighborhoods. It has a near-cultish belief in its own way of doing things—whether this is because they boast the world's best bagels at **H&H** or that life here means constantly tripping through the set of *Law and Order*—these residents cannot imagine being elsewhere.

Hollywood's New York

First and foremost, the Upper West is a neighborhood for strolling. Its sidewalks are lined with quaint brownstones, as well as more daunting architectural feats, like the Dakota (where *Rosemary's Baby* was filmed). Imagine rambling apartments filled with bookish locals arguing with equal gusto over the future of opera, or whether the best sturgeon is at **Murray's** or **Barney Greengrass**. If a scene from *Hannah and Her Sisters* comes to mind, you are beginning to understand this neighborhood.

Medley of Markets

This enthusiasm extends to all aspects of life—particularly food. For shopping, the **Tucker Square Greenmarket** is popular and anchored on West 66th Street ("Peter Jennings Way"). Equally celebrated is the original **Fairway**, filled with reasonably priced gourmet treats. Intrepid shoppers should brave its famously cramped elevator to visit the exclusively organic second floor.

No visit to the Upper West is complete without **Zabar's**—home of all things gourmet and kosher—to ogle the barrels of olives and grab a few knishes. If planning an Italian themed evening, visit Cesare Casella's stellar **Salumeria Rosi**. This neighborhood jewel proffers an excellent and enormous selection of cured meats, while their selection of small plates will leave you hungering for more.

A Spread of Sweet and Savory

If in need of refreshment, stop by **Soutine Bakery**, a quiet little storefront with jaw-dropping cakes; or opt for the legendary chocolate chip cookies from **Levain**. Of course, **Magnolia's** newest outpost is sure to gain a quick cupcake following. For a more savory snack, grab a "Recession Special" at **Gray's Papaya**—the politically outspoken (check the window slogans) and quintessentially Upper West hot dog chain.

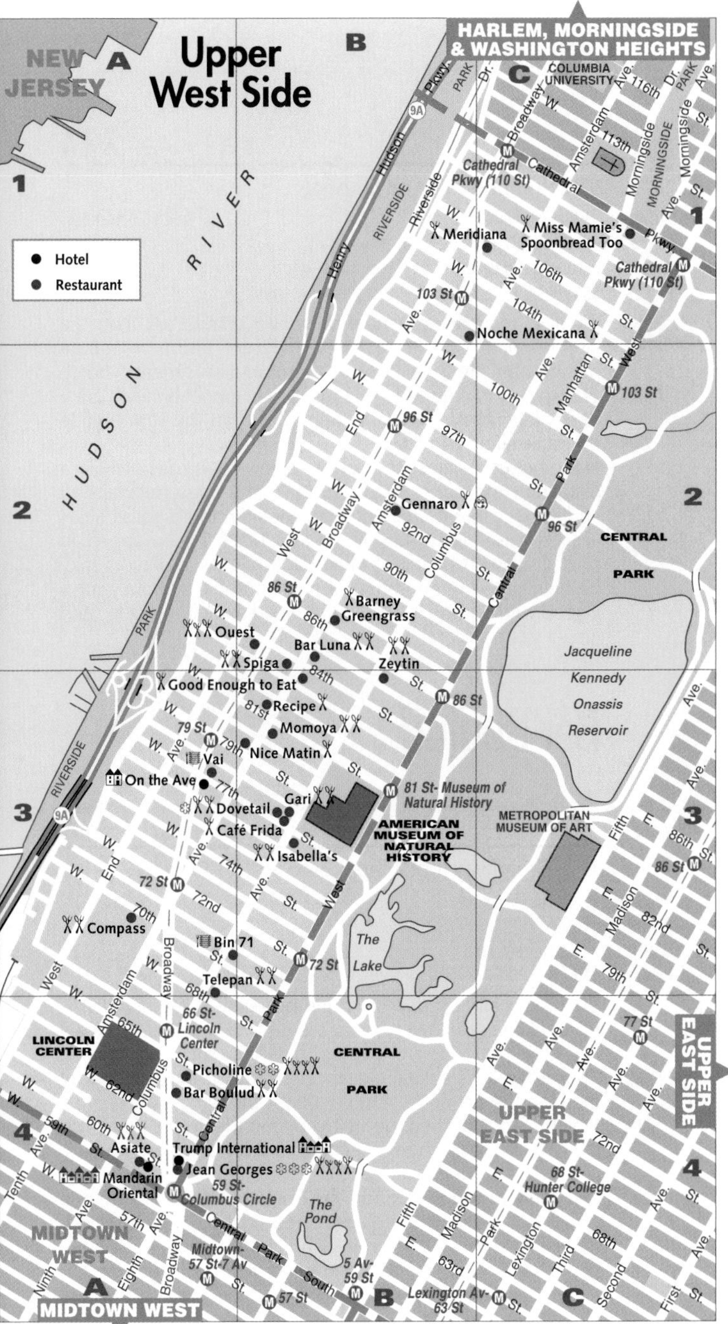

Upper West Side
Hotel
Restaurant
HARLEM, MORNINGSIDE & WASHINGTON HEIGHTS
NEW JERSEY
HUDSON RIVER
COLUMBIA UNIVERSITY
Meridiana
Miss Mamie's Spoonbread Too
Noche Mexicana
Gennaro
CENTRAL PARK
Jacqueline Kennedy Onassis Reservoir
Barney Greengrass
Ouest
Bar Luna
Zeytin
Spiga
Good Enough to Eat
Recipe
Momoya
Nice Matin
Vai
On the Ave
Gari
Dovetail
Café Frida
Isabella's
AMERICAN MUSEUM OF NATURAL HISTORY
81 St- Museum of Natural History
METROPOLITAN MUSEUM OF ART
Compass
Bin 71
Telepan
The Lake
LINCOLN CENTER
66 St- Lincoln Center
Picholine
Bar Boulud
Asiate
Trump International
Jean Georges
Mandarin Oriental
59 St- Columbus Circle
The Pond
UPPER EAST SIDE
68 St- Hunter College
MIDTOWN WEST
Midtown- 57 St-7 Av
5 Av- 59 St
Lexington Av- 63 St

Asiate

Fusion 

80 Columbus Circle (at 60th St.)

Subway: 59 St - Columbus Circle — Lunch & dinner daily
Phone: 212-805-8881
Web: www.mandarinoriental.com
Prices: **$$$$**

It's hard to imagine a finer view of Central Park than the jaw-dropping one at Asiate, an elegant fusion restaurant perched on the 35th floor of the Mandarin Oriental hotel. This splendor, unfurled like a lush green carpet beneath New York's legendary skyline, is displayed from the surrounding floor-to-ceiling windows.

Nonetheless, Asiate recognizes that views alone do not make a restaurant and proves its own worth with a masterful waitstaff and impeccably trained kitchen. Mediterranean sensibilities are expressed in dishes like warm black figs wrapped in prosciutto with beads of olive oil, while Asian flavors may be highlighted in an entrée of moist and flakey honey-miso glazed wild salmon, served with spiced mandarin orange and ginger gastrique.

Bar Boulud

French XX

A4

1900 Broadway (bet. 63rd & 64th Sts.)

Subway: 66 St - Lincoln Center — Lunch & dinner daily
Phone: 212-595-0303
Web: www.danielnyc.com
Prices: **$$$**

Bright and airy by day, sexy and booming come nightfall—Chef Daniel Boulud's young, unfussy Bar Boulud wears two different, albeit charming, hats for lunch and dinner. The restaurant's casual elegance starts with the wine barrel marking the entrance, and continues through to the service which reads polished, but relaxed, and the ample grape list, divided into four whimsical categories: Discoveries, Classics, Legends, and Heartthrobs.

The food doesn't stray too far from the classically-trained Boulud's wheelhouse but airs on the simple side, with wine-friendly plates of pâté, terrine, and charcuterie (a must-do—specific team members trained under the legendary Parisian charcutier, Gilles Vérot) doing some heavy lifting on a terrific French comfort menu.

Bar Luna

Italian

B2

511 Amsterdam Ave. (bet. 84th & 85th Sts.)

Subway: 86 St (Broadway) — Lunch Sat – Sun
Phone: 212-362-1098 — Dinner nightly
Web: www.barlunanyc.com
Prices: $$

Long-time restaurateur Turgut Balikci illuminates the Amsterdam Avenue dining scene with this sexy newcomer, while ex-West Branch talent runs the kitchen. The stylish interior sports bare-wood tables and striped banquets against weathered brick walls donning fuchsia-framed mirrors and stunning glossy photos. Bursts of yellow bring warmth to the space, softly lit by hanging lamps and fairy lights.

Nurse a pre-dinner cocktail at the spacious, friendly bar before tackling the sublime menu offerings, such as the spoon-tender rabbit richly braised with white wine, anise, and green olives. Pair the meal with a carafe of rosé, and perhaps finish it with a juicy cube of brioche bread pudding, studded with poached black cherries and doused in caramel.

Barney Greengrass

Deli

B2

541 Amsterdam Ave. (at 86th St.)

Subway: 86 St (Broadway) — Lunch Tue – Sun
Phone: 212-724-4707
Web: www.barneygreengrass.com
Prices:

New York's venerable "Sturgeon King" has earned its title and position as an Upper West Side institution.

In addition to serving breakfast and lunch until 5:00 P.M., they do double duty as a vibrant carry-out business and now take internet orders. The place is darling, whether eating in or taking out; the deli sandwiches—piled high with pastrami or homemade egg salad, and served with a big, bright, crunchy pickle—are among the best in the city.

Order a heaping plate of sturgeon, house-cured gravlax, or clear, flavorful bowl of matzoh ball soup at this formica-clad jewel and take a trip back in time; this food is the real thing. Service without ceremony but unique NY attitude makes a trip to Barney Greengrass an authentic and essential experience.

Bin 71

Italian

A3

237 Columbus Ave. (at 71st St.)

Subway: 72 St
Phone: 212-362-5446
Web: www.bin71.com
Prices: $$

Lunch Wed – Sun
Dinner nightly

With its low-slung ceiling and pretty marble bar packed with an endless stream of happy, buzzing patrons, this charming Italian wine and tapas bar is still going strong. With over thirty wine varieties available by the glass, and bottles from as far-reaching places as Slovenia, there's a vinoversity to be had here.

Choose from a delicious roster of small plates, all quick and easy enough to get you in and out in time to make a show at nearby Lincoln Center: plump, juicy meatballs puddled in a lip-smacking lemon-and-white wine broth; fresh, oven-roasted oysters laced with thin ribbons of fennel, sweet butter, and salty capers; or moist olive oil cake, paired with tender braised apples and a smooth dollop of whipped cream.

Café Frida

Mexican

B3

368 Columbus Ave. (bet. 77th & 78th Sts.)

Subway: 81 St - Museum of Natural History
Phone: 212-712-2929
Web: www.cafefrida.com
Prices: $$

Lunch & dinner daily

This Mexican enchantress may have undergone a recent face-lift, but continues to exude much charm. Inviting Café Frida aims to elevate your notions of authentic Mexican cooking straight out of the gate. The menu is vast and features handmade tortillas; bright, organic produce; and intricate specialties—the food matches this prettified little hacienda to a tee.

Set sail with one of Mixologist Junior Merino's mouthwatering margaritas, or pluck a gorgeous tequila off the comprehensive tequila menu, then sink your teeth into pan-seared *tacos al pastor* laced with cool cilantro and freshly chopped onions; or a soft, fragrant shank of lamb, marinated in *guajill*o sauce, avocado leaf, and green olives, then cooked in parchment paper until it's fork-tender.

Compass

Seafood XX

A3

208 W. 70th St. (bet. Amsterdam & West End Aves.)

Subway: 72 St (Broadway) — Lunch Sun
Phone: 212-875-8600 — Dinner nightly
Web: www.compassrestaurant.com
Prices: $$$

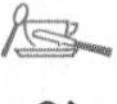

The Upper West Side is bursting with high-profile eateries, and yet the local urbanista-sophisticate set still crowds Compass most nights of the week, gliding between the lovely lounge, with its high-backed booths and back-lit bar; the sleek dining room underneath its mosaic-patched ceiling; and the elevated café, perfect for a quick bite and people-watching.

Seafood is the name of the game at Compass, with a menu divvied up into categories like *shellfish, classic* and *not fish*; and an inventive cocktail list and well-chosen wine selection to match. Try the tender, wild stripped bass with eggplant caviar, stewed lentils, lardoons, and parsley beurre blanc; or a sinfully dense chocolate cheesecake streaked with an Earl Grey-caramel sauce.

Gari

Japanese XX

B3

370 Columbus Ave. (bet. 77th & 78th Sts.)

Subway: 81 St - Museum of Natural History — Lunch Sat – Sun
Phone: 212-362-4816 — Dinner nightly
Web: N/A
Prices: $$$

The Columbus Avenue outpost of Sushi of Gari (there are three in Manhattan) fashions a hip aesthetic with contemporary Asian décor and large glass windows facing the sidewalk.

While ingredients are top quality and everything is made to order, there is strong focus on mass appeal here, as more guests order à la carte rather than put themselves in the skillful hands of the sushi chefs and try the highly recommended omakase, where the true beauty of Gari lies. A fine mix of sushi, including signatures by Chef Masatoshi "Gari" Sugio, and cooked dishes are all prepared with a modern touch. European influences are evident in items like duck and lamb chops.

Offering a well-chosen list of sake and wine, plus professional service, Gari is packed nightly.

Dovetail ✿

B3 **Contemporary** XX

103 W. 77th St. (at Columbus Ave.)

Subway: 81 St - Museum of Natural History — Lunch Wed – Sun
Phone: 212-362-3800 — Dinner nightly
Web: www.dovetailnyc.com
Prices: $$$

Emilie Baltz

If there was a sneaking suspicion that the Upper West Side was closing in on the city's food party, Dovetail stamped the memo: *case closed*, because this is the kind of place you actually travel uptown to hit—a cozy, exposed brick charmer gussied up in serene hues, intimate tables, and a sexy little alcove bar. Add a couple points for the impeccable service staff—polished, friendly, and always informative—and then let the food seal the deal.

The man behind the curtain is Chef John Fraser, who honed his craft at some of the most venerable restaurants in the world—The French Laundry in Napa Valley, and Taillevent in Paris—before packing up his suitcase for Manhattan.

With Dovetail, the talented chef has hit his wheelhouse, deftly spinning ingredients into dishes like a bowl of almond gazpacho bobbing with fresh cucumber, red grapes, and micro greens; potato gnocchi pooled in a creamy sauce studded with sweet corn, apple cider-soaked blueberries, and shaved summer truffles; perfectly seared rainbow trout fillet laced with creamy lemon beurre blanc, warm cucumbers, haricots verts, and wax beans; or a wickedly good brioche bread pudding sporting bananas, bacon brittle, and rum ice cream.

Gennaro

Italian

665 Amsterdam Ave. (bet. 92nd & 93rd Sts.)

Subway: 96 St (Broadway) — Dinner nightly
Phone: 212-665-5348
Web: N/A
Prices: ⊜

There might be a wait at this bright, boisterous trattoria, because the throngs of regulars who flood the place know that it can't be beat for a delicious neighborhood Italian meal. The lovely, unpretentious space, filled with colorful hanging ceramic plates, helps to pass the time until you can settle into one of the snug tables (the roomy ones seem to go to the regulars), but the food payout is worth it.

Try the perfectly tender *bucatini*, dusted with fresh cracked pepper and cheese; or a tender-to-the-fork pair of monkfish fillets licked with lemon, oregano, and capers. The daily specials list is nearly as long as the regular menu and filled with goodies; but be sure to ask about prices, which can be considerably steeper than their everyday offerings.

Good Enough to Eat

American 

483 Amsterdam Ave. (bet. 83rd & 84th Sts.)

Subway: 79 St — Lunch & dinner daily
Phone: 212-496-0163
Web: www.goodenoughtoeat.com
Prices: $$

Serving breakfast, lunch, dinner, and takeout, Good Enough to Eat is an affordable neighborhood gem in an area quickly pricing such establishments out of reach. The décor is oddly endearing with its kitschy folk art, countrified quirky décor, and cows, cows, everywhere.

Chef/owner Carrie Levin has been serving a solid (if uninventive) menu of crispy buttermilk onion rings or meatloaf with mashed potatoes to repeat audiences since opening in 1981. Other creations may include a moist and buttery fish and chips or chili of the day.

The children's menu has been taste-tested by young and picky palates, so even if greeted by long lines at brunch or other peak times, join the masses in bringing the whole family for a perfectly divine affair.

Isabella's

Mediterranean 

B3

359 Columbus Ave. (at 77th St.)

Subway: 81 St - Museum of Natural History — Lunch & dinner daily
Phone: 212-724-2100
Web: www.brguestrestaurants.com
Prices: **$$**

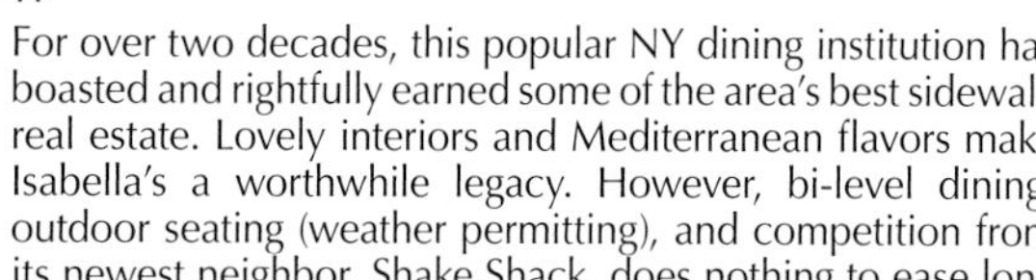

For over two decades, this popular NY dining institution has boasted and rightfully earned some of the area's best sidewalk real estate. Lovely interiors and Mediterranean flavors make Isabella's a worthwhile legacy. However, bi-level dining, outdoor seating (weather permitting), and competition from its newest neighbor, Shake Shack, does nothing to ease long waits for tables, especially during weekend brunch which features a variety of Benedicts, from eggs to filet mignon.

Music keeps tempo with the bustling activity, while the charming and professional staff tends to diners relishing the likes of roasted chicken cassoulet. Regulars know two things: for a small corkage fee, they may BYO; and always save room for the generous desserts.

Meridiana

Italian 

C1

2756 Broadway (bet. 105th & 106th Sts.)

Subway: 103 St (Broadway) — Dinner nightly
Phone: 212-222-4453
Web: N/A
Prices: **$$**

With its rhythmic ceiling fans, a long bar stretching the length of the room, and towering palm trees, Meridiana's airy dining room begs you to relax, take your coat off, and stay a while. And stay they do—a loyal following having kept this mainstay going strong for over 16 years in an otherwise fickle food hood.

Much of the restaurant's ongoing success can be attributed to Chef/owner Gianni "Johnny" Nicolosi and his wife, Pilar, who know how to keep the food straightforward and delicious. Grilled *orata* fillets are kissed with lemon, garlic, and parsley, then paired with tender, thyme-dusted, glazed carrots and crispy roasted potatoes flecked with sea salt; while a wickedly smooth ricotta cheesecake arrives fragrant with vanilla.

Jean Georges ✿✿✿

Contemporary XXXX

A4

1 Central Park West (bet. 60th & 61st Sts.)

Subway: 59 St - Columbus Circle — Lunch & dinner Mon – Sat
Phone: 212-299-3900
Web: www.jean-georges.com
Prices: $$$$

Thomas Loof

With a lovely geometric motif sculpted by design guru, Adam Tihany, soft chandelier light dancing off cream walls, and luxurious ivory leather chairs, Jean-Georges Vongerichten's cherished flagship looks every bit the part—this is New York fine dining at its grandest.

Located just off the ground floor lobby of the Trump International Hotel, guests pass through the casual Nougatine (which serves breakfast, lunch, and dinner without the pomp or price tag), before finding their way into this sophisticated lair—where Chef Mark Lapico deftly marries Vongerichten's passion for flavor and texture into dishes, and a service staff sent from the gods seamlessly delivers each plate to your table.

Lapico's menu rotates constantly, but some treasures include pristine sea urchin flown in from Santa Barbara, paired with toasted black bread, freshly flavorful yuzu, and thin slices of jalapeño; fluffy sweetbreads fried to golden perfection, and matched with an irresistible Alsatian potato salad studded with diced onion and bright slivers of radish; or gorgeously seared duck breast cloaked in crushed Jordan almonds, and laced with an inky amaretto jus poured tableside.

Miss Mamie's Spoonbread Too

C1 — Southern

366 W. 110th St./Cathedral Pkwy. (bet. Columbus & Manhattan Aves.)

Subway: Cathedral Pkwy/110 St (Central Park West) — Lunch & dinner daily
Phone: 212-865-6744
Web: www.spoonbreadinc.com
Prices: ⊜

The warm, welcoming atmosphere and service evokes an easygoing country setting—smack dab in the middle of the city. Homey, rustic touches, like kitchen implements hanging on the walls, mix well with retro red and yellow tile floors and formica-top tables. The dining room floods with natural light, while pure, raw soul music plays in the background.
The menu is a celebration of Southern classics and does not veer much from this trajectory. However, this should not stop anyone from reviewing the daily boards for specials. Food this appealing, genuine, and satisfying can only be topped with perfectly sweet homemade ice tea and red velvet cake (a dark, moist, indulgent specimen of this classic dessert). Finish with the best coffee a dollar can buy.

Momoya

B3 — Japanese

427 Amsterdam Ave. (bet. 80th & 81st Sts.)

Subway: 79 St — Lunch Sat – Sun
Phone: 212-580-0007 — Dinner nightly
Web: www.themomoya.com
Prices: $$$

It's a bit more sophisticated than its Chelsea sister (think curvy wood and painted brick walls, slate floors, and cream leather booths), but there's nothing pretentious or fussy about Momoya. Instead, this sushi restaurant with its swift service, consistently good sushi, and fair prices, has won the hearts of Upper West Siders.
The sleek setting doesn't hurt either. Given the location, Momoya's menu isn't altogether a surprise, so await familiar favorites like spicy tuna rolls and sashimi platters with eel, toro, Spanish mackerel, and sea urchin. Dessert is often an after-thought at Japanese restaurants, but the delicious *mille crêpes* with green tea and crème anglaise is perfectly delicate and provides a cool and light finish to a satisfying meal.

Nice Matin

Mediterranean

201 W. 79th St. (at Amsterdam Ave.)

Subway: 79 St
Lunch & dinner daily
Phone: 212-873-6423
Web: www.nicematinnyc.com
Prices: $$

Named after the daily newspaper published in a major city on France's Côte d'Azur, Nice Matin transports diners to the sun-drenched Mediterranean coast.

Niçoise dishes here exhibit as many vibrant flavors and colors as appear in the room's luminous décor. Fashioned as a coastal brasserie, Nice Matin asserts its unique personality by avoiding all the decorative clichés found in many Gallic-style restaurants; lights dangle from the tops of high pillars that spread umbrella-like against the ceiling, and tables are topped in Formica.

Starting with their wonderful breakfasts of poached eggs Provençal or fresh scones, the menu finds inspiration in wandering the wider Mediterranean region, from a perfectly cooked risotto to a traditional bouillabaisse.

Noche Mexicana

Mexican

852 Amsterdam Ave. (bet. 101st & 102nd Sts.)

Subway: 103 St (Broadway)
Lunch & dinner daily
Phone: 212-662-6900
Web: www.noche-mexicana.com
Prices: ⓢ

Squeezed between a bunch of no-name cafés and run-down bodegas on a grungy strip of Amsterdam Avenue, Noche Mexicana certainly doesn't woo its regulars with fancy digs. Rather, it's the friendly staff and deliciously authentic Mexican fare that keep this little hole-in-the-wall jumping.

Though the menu is teeming with real-deal enchiladas and *chile rellenos*, Noche's star ticket is undoubtedly the house made tamales, which you can see being made by hand if you score a seat toward the back of the house. The soft green tamale arrives tenderly wrapped in a banana leaf, packed with sweet shredded pork and a smoky, tart green mole sauce. It's enough to make you order a second one for dessert, but a smooth caramel and vanilla-scented flan draws you back.

Ouest

B2 **Contemporary** XXX

2315 Broadway (bet. 83rd & 84th Sts.)

Subway: 86 St (Broadway) — Lunch Sun
Phone: 212-580-8700 — Dinner nightly
Web: www.ouestny.com
Prices: $$$

The last decade saw a slew of serious eateries marching into the Upper West—notably this popular outpost from the trailblazing Chef/owner Tom Valenti.

As with his other ventures, Chef Valenti's top priorities are both hospitality and his kitchen, where nothing is overlooked and everything is delicious. Expect edgy riffs on American comfort foods like plump, house-made potato gnocchi with short-rib ragout and herbed ricotta or pan-roasted rack of lamb with chickpea purée.

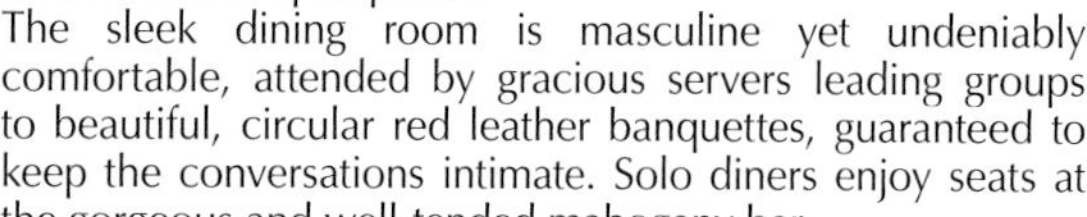

The sleek dining room is masculine yet undeniably comfortable, attended by gracious servers leading groups to beautiful, circular red leather banquettes, guaranteed to keep the conversations intimate. Solo diners enjoy seats at the gorgeous and well-tended mahogany bar.

Recipe

B3 **American** X

452 Amsterdam Ave. (bet. 81st & 82nd Sts.)

Subway: 79 St — Lunch & dinner daily
Phone: 212-501-7755
Web: www.recipenyc.com
Prices: $$

This sweet little sliver of a restaurant arrives courtesy of the team behind Land, a beloved Thai restaurant located merely steps away. With Recipe, they turn their well-focused attention to contemporary American fare—and the result is yet another reason to deem the Upper West Side the city's fastest rising food corridor.

In a simple space dressed in white-washed walls, reclaimed knick-knacks, and industrial light fixtures, you'll find a straightforward menu touting a rustic lineup that might include an exceptionally fresh pike mackerel, grilled whole and topped with a lively caper radish; a fresh tangle of pappardelle primavera studded with plump Gulf shrimp; or a downright sultry chocolate pignoli tart, topped with creamy caramel.

Picholine ✿✿

Mediterranean XXXX

A4

35 W. 64th St. (bet. Broadway & Central Park West)

Subway: 66 St - Lincoln Center | Dinner Tue – Sat

Phone: 212-724-8585

Web: www.picholinenyc.com

Prices: $$$$

Picholine

Located opposite Lincoln Center, in the middle of a quiet, residential street, Terrance Brennan's elegant Picholine is nearing the end of its second decade on the New York fine dining scene. It couldn't have been easy when the restaurant first swung open its doors back in 1993—the city, faced with a recent recession, had just begun to question the validity of fine dining. Would Picholine have the goods to back up her price tag?

The answer then, and remains in these financially turbulent times, most decidedly *oui*. If you're going to splurge, this is a great place to do it.

These days you'll find Brennan's Provençal touches informing a simple, seasonal menu carefully executed by chef de cuisine, Carmine DiGiovanni. The seasonal menu is tantalizing and may reveal gems like a bright pile of baby arugula dotted with tender fava beans, shards of nutty, aged pecorino, and acorn-fed Spanish ham, piled over a crunchy croquette filled with creamy béchamel; a deceptively simple rabbit loin in a wickedly good reduction, paired with roasted *cipollini* onions and tender spätzle; or flaky, paper-thin cannoli filled with silky passion fruit and served over coconut tapioca and tropical fruit jus.

Spiga

Italian XX

B2

200 W. 84th St. (bet. Amsterdam Ave. & Broadway)

Subway: 86 St (Broadway)
Phone: 212-362-5506
Web: www.spiganyc.com
Prices: $$$

Dinner nightly

Follow a set of wide plank steps into this postage stamp-sized restaurant and you're in for a treat. Spiga might sneak tables into every cranny, but the space is well-designed with high ceilings, handsome dark wood and pillow-strewn banquettes lining jumbo windows looking onto the street. Toss in an electric atmosphere, a creative kitchen, and a polished, professional waitstaff—and you have the makings of a truly memorable neighborhood meal.

Kick things off with a lovely bowl of *pasta e fagioli* laced with exquisite olive oil; and then move on to fresh Chatham cod set atop tender lentil stew. Finish with a fresh trio of cannolis, stuffed with chocolate mousse, zabaglione, and ricotta, and topped with Grand Marnier cream sauce and fresh berries.

Telepan

American XX

A3

72 W. 69th St. (bet. Central Park West & Columbus Ave.)

Subway: 66 St - Lincoln Center
Phone: 212-580-4300
Web: www.telepan-ny.com
Prices: $$$

Lunch Wed – Sun
Dinner nightly

Tucked behind a simple green awning near bustling Lincoln Center, Telepan—with its pretty, pecan-wood interior and crackling fireplaces—opened with a loyal following firmly in place thanks to Chef/owner Bill Telepan's popular former restaurant, JUdson Grill.

The locavore chef is dedicated to sustainability and organic products both inside his restaurants, and out (he even cooks healthy meals for school children in Washington Heights). The result is deliciously evident in dishes like the house-smoked trout, laid over a fluffy corn blini and laced with springy green onion and sour cream; a wildly fresh preserved tuna and arugula salad, paired with chickpea-rosemary crostini; or the rich house-made s'more, sporting a beautiful, crackling golden crown.

Vai

Italian 

A3

225 W. 77th St. (bet. Amsterdam Ave. & Broadway)

Subway: 79 St — Dinner nightly
Phone: 212-362-4500
Web: www.vairestaurant.com
Prices: $$

Vai means "go" in Italian, and go they do—this small plate charmer is packed most nights with a loyal neighborhood crowd. Marked by fresh green plants and a pair of benches, Vai resides on an otherwise non-descript stretch of 77th Street; inside, guests are greeted with a sexy, low-lit space dressed in dark wood tables, flickering votive candles, and a long communal table.

Daily specials rotate but dinner might include a plate of beautifully-marbled porchetta carpaccio laced with caper-garlic sauce, Fuji apple purée, and baby greens; a prosciutto, fig, and brie *pizzetta* baked like Sardinian bread; al dente rigatoni, dancing with spicy sausage and ricotta salata; or crêpes filled with hazelnut-chocolate and topped with orange zest marmalade.

Zeytin

Turkish XX

B3

519 Columbus Ave. (at 85th St.)

Subway: 86 St (Central Park West) — Lunch & dinner daily
Phone: 212-579-1145
Web: www.zeytinny.com
Prices: $$

Visitors making their way from the Museum of Natural History would do well to bypass the turn-and-burn restaurants that plague this bustling section of Columbus Avenue, and set their sights on the more exotic offerings scattered around the hood. Namely Zeytin—a lovely, upscale Turkish restaurant with supple leather chairs, polished slate floors, and great big people-watching windows.

The restaurant's name means "olive" in Turkish, but the menu easily surpasses the implied simplicity. Elaborate dishes like *harem sarmasi* and *hünkâr begendi* share menu space with simple kebab fare; and the traditional, but mouthwatering, baklava dessert—perfectly rendered with tissue-thin sheets of phyllo dough, soft golden honey and crushed, syrup-soaked pistachios.

John Peden/The New York Botanical Garden

The Bronx

The Bronx

The only borough attached to the mainland, the Bronx is marked by contrasts. Although abandoned apartment buildings and massive housing projects once overran the borough's south section, private foundations and grassroots movements are successfully revitalizing these areas. As always, grand mansions and lush gardens still characterize the northern areas of Riverdale and Fieldston.

Wealth of Variety

Hispanics, African-Americans, Irish-Americans, West Indians, and Albanians comprise much of the current population. Though a host of Italians once settled in the Belmont area, today they only reside as proprietors of shops.

Thanks to 19th century journalist John Mullaly, who led a movement in the late 1800s to buy and preserve inexpensive parcels of land, 25 percent of the Bronx today consists of parkland. This includes Pelham Bay Park, with its sandy Orchard Beach. Here, step into pizza paradise—**Louie and Ernie's**—for a slice of heaven.

Beyond, City Island is a gem of a coastal community, much like New England with its charming inns and seafood spots. During the summer, stroll down City Island Ave., and into **Lickety Split** for a scoop of divine ice cream.

Belmont's most renowned street and Italian food mecca, Arthur Avenue, lures from far and wide. Tear into warm, freshly baked breads from **Terranova**, **Madonia**, or **Addeo**—the choices are plenty. Dive into a ball of warm and creamy mozzarella at **Joe's Deli** (open on Sundays!). The pistachio-studded mortadella from **Teitel Brothers** or *salumi* from **Calabria Pork Store** are perfect salt licks for tigers on the prowl.

Check out **The Arthur Avenue Retail Market**, a covered oasis built by Mayor LaGuardia to prevent pushcart vendors from crowding busy streets. The dwindling vendors inside sell quality Italian pasta, homemade sausage, olive oil, notorious heroes, heirloom seeds, and hand-rolled cigars.

Although the Belmont section is now mainly known as Little Mexico and Ecuador, it has a world of Eastern European offerings. Visit **Tony & Tina's** Pizza, but skip the Italian stuff. Instead, devour Albanian or Kosovar *burek*—these flaky rolls are packed with pumpkin purée and are *sine qua non.* **Gustiamo**'s warehouse, now open to retail will delight your palate with well-chosen Italian specialties. Bronxite's will revel in the heart-satisfying *chicharron de cerdo* at **El Bohio Lechonera** in nearby Crotona Park.

Take yourself out to a ball game at the new Yankee Stadium and snack from the **Lobel's** cart or if you're lucky enough to have premium seats, enjoy one of their expertly dry aged steaks.

Caribbean Comfort

The Eastchester, Wakefield, and Williamsbridge sections of the Bronx cradle a number of communities and their tasty eats. The spicy, smoky tidbits of the Caribbean have become a local staple. Visit Vernon's **New Jerk House** for mouthwatering jerk chicken, and end with something sweet from **Kingston Tropical Bakery**.

Or for Italian, drop by **G & R Deli** on Williamsbridge Road for big flavors in their homemade sausages or rich meaty sauce sold by the quart. End at **Sal & Dom's** for some *sfogliatelle*.

Asian Treats

Asia comes alive at **Pho Saigon No.1**; peek in and discover that authentic Vietnamese food has officially arrived in the Bronx. For a flurry of Cambodian delights, step into the **Phnom Penh-Nha Trang Market** across the street. The hamburger craze continues uptown with newcomer **Bronx Ale House** and the established **Bruckner Bar & Grill**.

A Latin Affair

A unique blend of Latin American spots populates the South Bronx, with the largest concentration hailing from Puerto Rico. On Willis Avenue, Mott Haven's main drag, bright awnings designate Honduran diners, Mexican bodegas, and Puerto Rican takeout; fenced off empty lots allow for older folks to chat, play cards, and linger over authentic dishes from their homeland.

Plethora of Produce

Vital to New York's food business is the **Hunts Point Food Distribution Center**, a 329-acre complex containing a mass of food wholesalers, distributors, and food processing businesses. The mega complex includes **The Hunts Point Meat Market**, **Hunts Point Terminal Produce Market**, and **The Fulton Fish Market**, a wholesale triumvirate where the city's restaurateurs and market owners come to pick their goods.

Riverdale's Treasure Trove

Riverdale may not be widely known for its dining culture and culinary treasures, but **Liebman's** is still considered one of the finest kosher delis in the Bronx. They comfort local masses with dishes like steamy soups, hot dogs, and brisket. At the primped **Mother's Bake Shop**, stop to savor the traditional *babkas* and challahs; and **Skyview Wines** carries a unique selection of Kosher wines, completing your culinary journey with a touch of meat, sweet, and spirit. Hop, skip, and a jump from the last stop on the 1 line, follow your nose (cause it always knows!) to **Lloyd's Carrot Cake** for one or several slices of their sinfully divine carrot cake and the like.

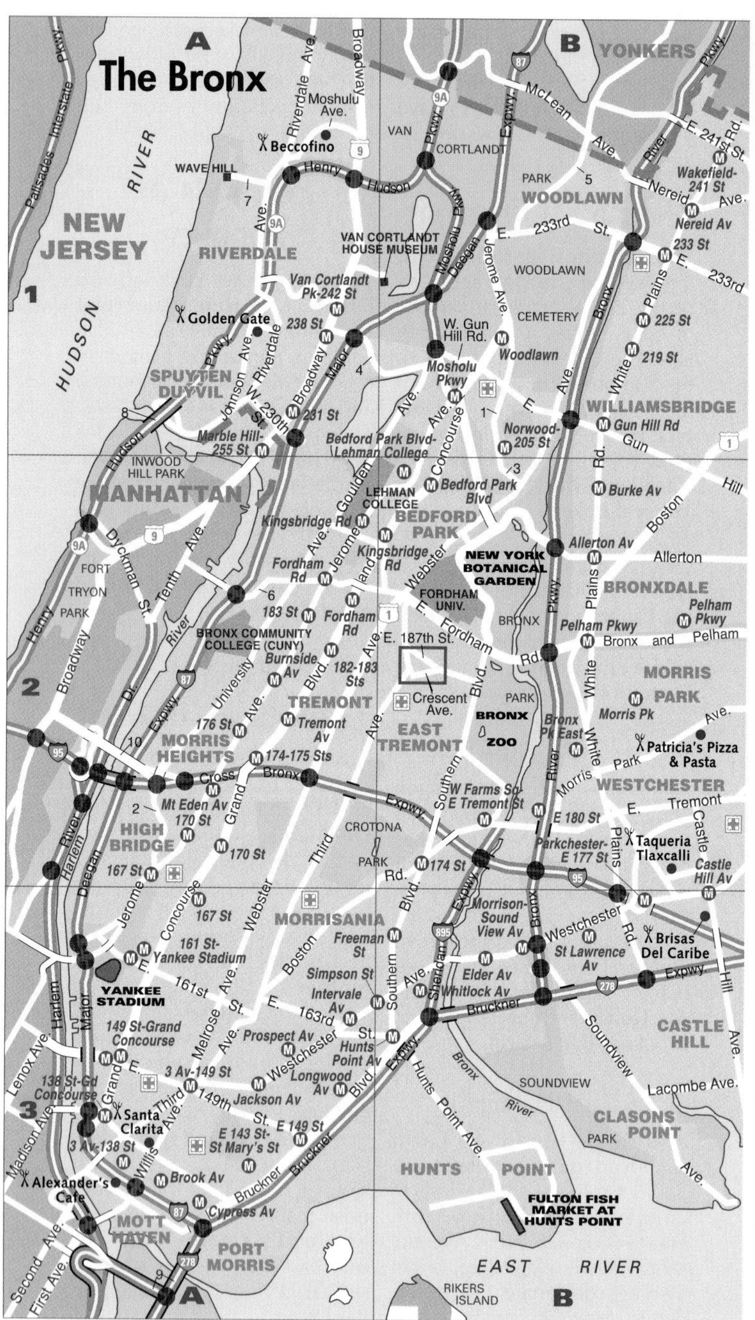

The Bronx
A
B
1
2
3
NEW JERSEY
HUDSON
RIVER
Palisades Interstate Pkwy.
YONKERS
RIVERDALE
WAVE HILL
Beccofino
Moshulu Ave.
Riverdale Ave.
Broadway
VAN CORTLANDT
Henry Hudson
VAN CORTLANDT HOUSE MUSEUM
Van Cortlandt Pk-242 St
Golden Gate
238 St
SPUYTEN DUYVIL
Johnson Ave.
Riverdale
W. 230th St.
231 St
Marble Hill-255 St
INWOOD HILL PARK
MANHATTAN
McLean Ave.
E. 241st St.
Wakefield-241 St
Nereid Ave.
Nereid Av
WOODLAWN
E. 233rd St.
233 St
WOODLAWN CEMETERY
225 St
219 St
Mosholu Pkwy
W. Gun Hill Rd.
Woodlawn
Jerome Ave.
Deegan
Major
Bronx River Pkwy.
White Plains Rd.
WILLIAMSBRIDGE
Gun Hill Rd
Norwood-205 St
Bedford Park Blvd-Lehman College
Bedford Park Blvd
LEHMAN COLLEGE
BEDFORD PARK
Burke Av
Boston
Allerton Av
Allerton
NEW YORK BOTANICAL GARDEN
BRONXDALE
Kingsbridge Rd
Fordham Rd
Goulden Ave.
Webster
FORDHAM UNIV.
Dyckman St.
Tenth Ave.
FORT TRYON PARK
Henry Hudson
Broadway
Harlem River Dr.
183 St
Fordham Rd
E. Fordham Rd.
E. 187th St.
BRONX COMMUNITY COLLEGE (CUNY)
Burnside Av
182-183 Sts
Crescent Ave.
Pelham Pkwy
Bronx and Pelham
MORRIS PARK
Morris Pk
TREMONT
Tremont Av
EAST TREMONT
BRONX PARK
BRONX ZOO
Bronx Pk East
176 St
MORRIS HEIGHTS
University Ave.
174-175 Sts
Cross Bronx Expwy.
Patricia's Pizza & Pasta
Morris Park Ave.
WESTCHESTER
W Farms Sq-E Tremont St
E 180 St
E. Tremont
Mt Eden Av
170 St
HIGH BRIDGE
Grand
CROTONA PARK
Third
Southern
Parkchester-E 177 St
Taqueria Tlaxcalli
Castle Hill Av
167 St
174 St
Concourse
MORRISANIA
Morrison-Sound View Av
Westchester Ave.
St Lawrence Av
Brisas Del Caribe
161 St-Yankee Stadium
Freeman St
YANKEE STADIUM
E. 161st St.
Simpson St
Elder Av
Whitlock Av
Bruckner Expwy
Intervale Av
E. 163rd St.
149 St-Grand Concourse
Prospect Av
Hunts Point Av
CASTLE HILL
Soundview
3 Av-149 St
Longwood Av
Melrose Ave.
Lenox Ave.
Harlem
138 St-Gd Concourse
Santa Clarita
Jackson Av
E. 149th St.
E 149 St
E 143 St-St Mary's St
3 Av-138 St
Willis Ave.
Madison Ave.
Alexander's Cafe
Brook Av
Cypress Av
MOTT HAVEN
PORT MORRIS
Second Ave.
First Ave.
Hunts Point Ave.
Bronx River
SOUNDVIEW
Lacombe Ave.
CLASONS POINT PARK
HUNTS POINT
FULTON FISH MARKET AT HUNTS POINT
EAST RIVER
RIKERS ISLAND

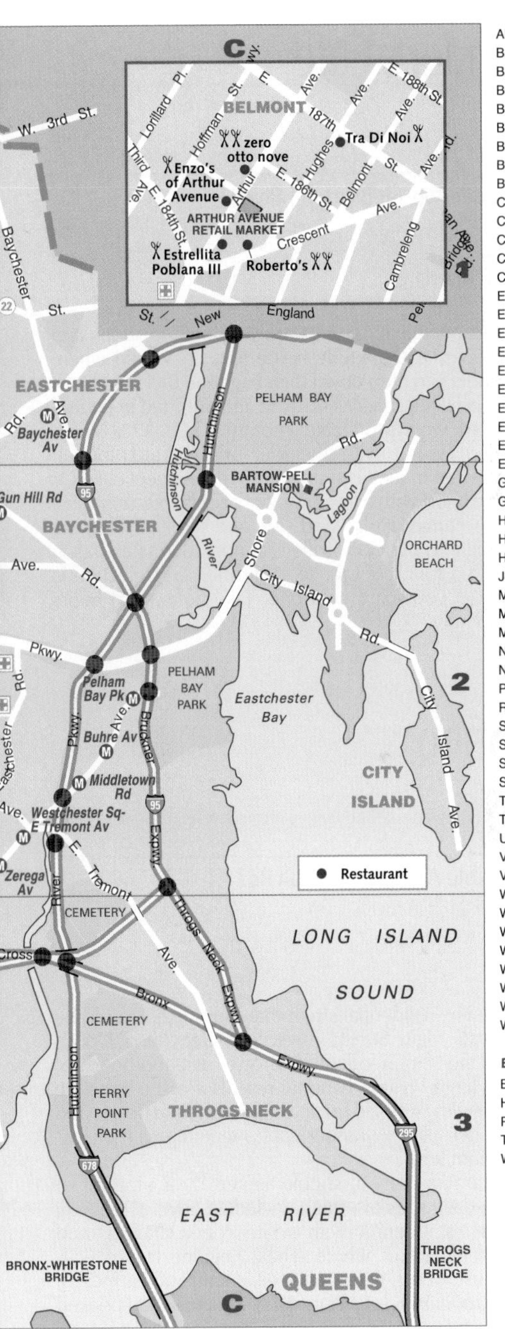

Allerton Ave.	BC2
Bainbridge Ave.	1 B1
Baychester Ave.	C1
Boston Rd.	A3C1
Broadway	A1
Bronx and Pelham Pkwy.	BC2
Bronx River Pkwy.	B1 3
Bruckner Blvd.	A3
Bruckner Expwy.	A3C2
Castle Hill Ave.	B2 3
City Island Ave.	C2
City Island Rd.	C2
Crescent Ave.	B2
Cross Bronx Expwy.	A2C3
Edward L. Grant Hwy.	2 A2
E. Gun Hill Rd.	B1C2
E. Fordham Rd.	AB2
E. Tremont Ave.	B2C3
E. 149th St.	A3
E. 161st St.	A3
E. 163rd St.	A3
E. 204th St.	3 B2
E. 233rd St.	BC1
E. 241st St.	B1
Goulden Ave.	A2B1
Grand Blvd. and Concourse	A1B3
Henry Hudson Pkwy.	A1B2
Hunts Point Ave.	B3
Hutchinson River Pkwy.	C1 3
Jerome Ave.	A3B1
Major Deegan Expwy.	A3B1
Melrose Ave.	A3
Mosholu Pkwy.	B1
Nereid Ave.	B1
New England Thruway	C1
Pelham Bridge Rd.	C1
Riverdale Ave.	A1
Sheridan Expwy.	B3 2
Shore Rd.	C1 2
Soundview Ave.	B 3
Southern Blvd.	B2 3
Third Ave.	A2B3
Throgs Neck Expwy.	C3
University Ave.	A2
Van Cortlandt Park South	4 AB1
Van Cortlandt Park East	5 B1
Webster Ave.	A1B3
Westchester Ave.	A3C2
W. Fordham Rd.	6 A2
W. 230th St.	A1
W.252nd St.	7 A1
W. Gun Hill Rd.	B1
White Plains Rd.	BX3
Willis Ave.	A3

BRIDGES

Bronx-Whitestone Bridge	C3
Henry Hudson Bridge	8 A1
Robert F. Kennedy Bridge	9 A3
Throgs Neck Bridge	C3
Washington Bridge	10 A2

Alexander's Cafe

A3

129 Alexander Ave. (at Bruckner Blvd.)

Subway: 3 Av - 138 St
Phone: 718-993-5281
Web: www.alexanderstogo.com
Prices: 

Lunch daily
Dinner Fri – Sat

Bustling Bruckner Blvd., with its army of antique shops and fruit juice trucks, is thankfully home to a cozy café where weary shoppers can plop down their bags and tuck into tasty, fresh food. The sleek space is softly lit and outfitted in neutral colors and dark woods to create a comfy aura.

You can't go wrong with the well-priced lunch buffet: succulent chicken in lemon sauce, BBQ ribs, or beef chili. Or take a seat and start with a lemony plate of delicious hummus, flavored with cumin, garlic, and chili and served with fresh pita. Next, dig into perfectly grilled salmon, marinated in soy and lime with a touch of orange. A terrific beer selection is on offer, so get yourself a cold one. Take note, meal hours change frequently.

Beccofino

Italian

A1

5704 Mosholu Ave. (at Fieldston Rd.)

Subway: Van Cortlandt Park-242 St (& bus BX9)
Phone: 718-432-2604
Web: N/A
Prices: $$

Dinner nightly

Set along a leafy, residential street that looks like it could be plucked out of Main Street, Anywhere, Beccofino blends nicely into the family-oriented Bronx neighborhood of Riverdale. A large inviting window reveals a rustic brassiere motif, replete with exposed brick walls, terra-cotta floors, and a handful of deli-paper wrapped tables teeming with chatty, well-heeled families.

The Italian comfort menu, supplemented by a nice list of hand-written daily specials, might include a bowl of tenderly sautéed mussels, fragrant with white wine, shallots, and cream; a soft tangle of whole wheat linguine tossed with peas, wild mushrooms, garlic, olive oil, cream and Parmesan; or salmon *Napolitano*, set atop a spicy tomato sauce pocked with cherry peppers.

Brisas Del Caribe

Puerto Rican

B3

1207 Castle Hill Ave. (bet. Ellis & Gleason Aves.)

Subway: Castle Hill Av — Lunch & dinner daily
Phone: 718-794-9710
Web: N/A
Prices: ◎◎

This popular eatery stays packed to the rim day and night with those looking for solid Puerto Rican fare at bargain basement prices. Tucked into a multi-ethnic enclave of the Bronx dotted with 99 Cent stores, 1950s coffee houses, and Korean grocers, Brisas Del Caribe's waiters bounce around the bright, airy room at a good clip and seem to like it when you can woo them with a bit of Spanish. But don't be dissuaded if you don't talk the talk—anyone and everyone is welcome here. It just might take a little longer to order is all. Don't miss the spot-on *mofongo*, a crispy, delicious mountain of plantain studded with tender shredded chicken; or the killer Cubano sandwich, stuffed with sweet and salty shredded pork, cheese, sliced pickles, and mayo.

Enzo's of Arthur Ave

Italian 

C1

2339 Arthur Ave. (bet. Crescent Ave. & 187th St.)

Subway: Fordham Rd (Grand Concourse) — Lunch Mon – Sat
Phone: 718-733-4455 — Dinner nightly
Web: N/A
Prices: $$

With its old-fashioned tiled floors, bistro tables, and pressed-tin ceiling, this offshoot of the original Enzo's (located at 1998 Williamsbridge Rd.) might look like your average red-sauce joint, but Enzo's takes *nonna's* spaghetti-and-meatballs to a new level.

Yes, it's super informal and the menu is best shared with a gaggle of friends, but owner Enzo DiRende (whose father co-founded Arthur Ave.'s legendary Dominick's) kicks the standbys up a notch with his devotion to sourcing local vendors—a smart thing when your hood is teeming with killer Italian markets. The fresh, crusty baguettes are baked across the street; the delicious cured meats are sourced from a local pork store; and the vanilla-scented cheesecake is baked around the corner.

Estrellita Poblana III

Mexican 

2328 Arthur Ave. (bet. Crescent Ave. & 186th St.)

Subway: Fordham Rd (Grand Concourse) Lunch & dinner daily
Phone: 718-220-7641
Web: N/A
Prices: ⓢⓢ

The smallest of its brethren, this adorable Arthur Ave spot serves up the same mouthwatering Mexican as the other two, but in sweeter surroundings. The sparkling room is like a tiny, immaculate jewel box with powder blue walls, wood wainscoting, and purple hand-cut flowers atop each table.

At the heart of this local favorite is the food—homemade, fresh, honest, and satisfying. Though the friendly staff speaks little English, the menu is clear and the specials delicious. Start with the likes of *budin Azteca*, corn tortillas with layers of shredded chicken, cheese, and chile with a spicy-nutty mole sauce. Specials punctuating the menu may include their fantastic *pozole* of tender hominy and pork.

Take note: tamales are available on weekends only.

Golden Gate

Chinese 

3550 Johnson Ave. (bet. 235th & 236th Sts.)

Subway: 231 St (& bus BX 7, 10, 20) Lunch & dinner daily
Phone: 718-549-6206
Web: www.goldengateriverdale.com
Prices: $$

The recent expansion of this beloved 50 year-old Bronx mainstay marks the enduring popularity of a certain kind of Chinese-American restaurant—one where New Yorkers of all ages rub elbows over exotic Chinese cocktails and safe, no-miss fare like chop suey, egg foo young, and *pu pu* platters. Those lucky enough to call Golden Gate their local Chinese joint have seen the place morph into a large, deep space with new trimmings, lots of leg room, and a big, welcoming bar area that fills up most nights with loyal regulars.

Don't miss the surprisingly tender lobster with (intentionally) burnt pork; crispy barbecued spareribs, slathered with a finger-licking sweet-and-salty coating; or an old-school chicken chow mein that manages to raise the bar.

Patricia's Pizza & Pasta

Italian

B2

1082 Morris Park Ave. (bet. Haight & Lurting Aves.)

Subway: Morris Park (& bus BX8) — Lunch & dinner daily
Phone: 718-409-9069
Web: N/A
Prices: $$

You know there's something good inside when people are willing to wait outside. That was then, but now after an expansion, Patricia's is the very picture of a restaurant. French doors frame a comfy new wing where people clamor for a taste of the irresistible pizzas and pastas. This reliable Italian spot knows how to make guests feel welcome.

Oven-baked goodness arrives in the form of addictive *focaccia*; if you can, resist the urge to down the whole thing and save room for what's ahead. Crispy pizzas baked in the real wood-burning oven are a highlight, as are the rustic Italian dishes (slow-cooked lamb chops with broccoli rabe, pasta specials) featured on the daily menu. If you're not stuffed to the gills, savor a slice of the house-made tiramisu.

Roberto's

C1

603 Crescent Ave. (at Hughes Ave.)

Subway: Fordham Rd (Grand Concourse) — Lunch Mon – Fri
Phone: 718-733-9503 — Dinner Mon – Sat
Web: www.robertobronx.com
Prices: $$

Widely recognized as one of the best in the Bronx, this Southern Italian institution has more than earned its red, white, and green stripes. All that's left to do is not muck up the hype—something owner Roberto Paciullo is unlikely to let happen with his keen attention to décor (think rustic farmhouse tables and marvelous ceramic urns), detail-oriented service staff, and sigh-inducing fare.

Tuck into soft, plump pillows of *agnolotti*, filled with tender, braised short ribs and folded into a creamy sauce of sweet corn-butter and sage; or indulge in a traditional Neapolitan *pastiera*, lovingly crafted with a perfect little lattice hat. The daily specials are divine, but those on a budget should ask about prices—which can climb steeply when no one's looking.

Santa Clarita

Mexican 

A3

237 Willis Ave. (bet. 138th & 139th Sts.)

Subway: 3 Av - 138 St
Lunch & dinner daily
Phone: 718-292-9399
Web: N/A
Prices: 

Make your way past the Honduran and Puerto Rican restaurants that flank Willis Avenue in the Mott Haven section of the Bronx, and you'll find a lovely little taste of Mexico. Santa Clarita's theatrical façade (replete with a rosary-draped statue of the restaurant's namesake) belies a charming interior with small wooden tables, a visible kitchen where women tend to smoking stoves, and a jukebox stocked with vibrant music.

Chef/owner Conrado Ramos (affectionately known as El Chile) likes to cue it up himself on occasion. Don't miss the appetizers like the *carnitas estilo Michoacán*, a small tortilla triple-stacked with tender, juicy *carnita*; or a soft quesadilla filled with fragrant mushrooms, zucchini flowers, and a creamy Mexican cheese.

Taqueria Tlaxcalli

Mexican 

B2

2103 Starling Ave. (bet. Odell St. & Olmstead Ave.)

Subway: Castle Hill Av
Lunch & dinner daily
Phone: 347-851-3085
Web: N/A
Prices: 

It's the little touches at Taqueria Tlaxcalli—the fuchsia ribbon tied around the cutlery, the tortilla basket topped with a colorful painted lid, the myriad sauces served for each and every taco ordered—that make a visit up to this new Parkchester taqueria worth the hike. That the food is complex, authentic, and lip-smacking good is just the icing on the cake.

Locals and day-trippers pour into the tiny, crayola-bright space to pop open a beer to the strum of contemporary Mexican music, and tuck into *sopas del dia* blooming with smoky chipotle and bobbing with plump *camarones*, tender yucca, and bright carrots; tender tacos stuffed with chewy tripe; or a *molcajete* filled with fragrant beef, sautéed onions, Mexican sausage, and grilled cactus.

Tra Di Noi

Italian

622 E. 187th St. (bet. Belmont & Hughes Aves.)

Subway: Fordham Rd (Grand Concourse) Lunch & dinner Tue – Sun
Phone: 718-295-1784
Web: N/A
Prices: $$

Standing proudly amid the Italian markets and delis where shopkeepers have been selling their goods for generations, Tra Di Noi radiates the kind of nostalgic warmth found only in the most authentic places. Loyal locals flock to this beloved eatery where Chef Marco Coletta turns out delicious Italian-American favorites, while his wife showers patrons with generous doses of Abbruzzi-style hospitality.

The lasagna and *pizzaiola* alone are reason enough to dine here, but food lovers from across the tri-state area return for a mouthwatering plate of pasta *carbonara*, pounded veal chop, or fresh swordfish Siciliana. The jovial atmosphere hums with bits of bilingual banter rising from the tables—further evidence of a true Italian-American experience.

zero otto nove

Italian

2357 Arthur Ave. (at 186th St.)

Subway: Fordham Rd (Grand Concourse) Lunch & dinner Tue – Sun
Phone: 718-220-1027
Web: www.roberto089.com
Prices: $$

The smiles here begin with a glimpse of the retro, aqua-blue Fiat 500 with Salerno plates parked inches from the sidewalk entrance, as if just driven up from the Amalfi coast. Inside, the décor recreates scenes of old Italy, with brick archways, colorful frescoes, and high ceilings rising into skylights. A second-floor mezzanine mimics a warm residential terrace overlooking this "piazza."

An attractive wood-burning oven crafted in mosaics and marble anchors the space and turns out Salerno-style specialties, enhancing each dish that passes through its flames. Divinely prepared pastas and perfectly charred pizzas reign at Roberto Pacuillo's beloved trattoria. Although service can be hurried (pray for a senior waiter), the food seriously satisfies.

Peter L. Wrenn/MICHELIN

Brooklyn

Brooklyn

Forage Brooklyn's trellis of neighborhoods and discover an exciting dining destination characterized by mom and pop stores, ethnic eateries, and trendy hotspots. Credit the influx of enterprising young chefs—many trained at Manhattan's top restaurants—for ushering in a new level of dining, while sedate establishments maintain the borough's rugged authenticity.

The sustainable food movement has taken root as eco-conscious communities expand, and local artisans gain popularity for their high quality, handcrafted goods. Locavores, want to support your neighbor's garden? Check out the handy website (www.eatwellguide.org) which offers a citywide directory of "green" gastronomy—family farms, farmers' markets, et al.

Warehouse Meets Elegant Eats

Williamsburg, traditionally an Italian, Hispanic, and Hasidic neighborhood, is now home to hipsters and artists. Here in "Billyburg," artistic food endeavors abound: find upscale eateries in former factories, an artisan chocolate line handcrafted from bean to bar (**Mast Brothers Chocolate**), and an online cooking show dedicated to making meals and mates (*Feed Me: The Brooklyn Cooking Dating Show*). If interested in learning how to pickle, bake a great pie, or ferment kombucha, sign up for a cooking class at the **Brooklyn Kitchen**. For a caffeine fix, head to **Blue Bottle Coffee Co.** on Berry Street. Over on Metropolitan Avenue, cute take-out shop **Saltie** offers a short list of tempting sandwiches and sweets; and **Fette Sau** stokes legions of fans with its dry-rubbed smoked meats and sides. **Pie 'n' Thighs** has returned to comfort with heaps of down-home goodness.

Besides DUMBO's breathtaking views, stroll down cobblestoned Water Street and into **Jacques Torres** for a taste of chocolate heaven. Bordering Prospect Park, verdant Park Slope boasts blocks of tony trattorias, catering to an army of stroller-rolling parents. The **Park Slope Food Coop** is a member operated and owned cooperative selling locally farmed produce, fair trade products, grass-fed meat, free-range poultry, and more. It is the largest of its kind in the country, and membership is offered to anyone willing to pay a small fee and work a shift of less than three hours each month.

All in the Family

Carroll Gardens, a historically Italian neighborhood, offers shoppers a bevy of family-owned butchers and bakeries along Court Street. **Da'Mico** is coffee-lovers' nirvana, while **Caputo's** has sandwiches worth the wait and...don't forget to grab a ball of their incredible mozzarella. As Court Street blends into family-friendly Cobble Hill, find **Staubitz Market**, the friendliest butcher around. Continue the stroll to Atlantic Avenue with its Middle Eastern goodies at **Sahadi's** and **Damascus Bakery**.

Revel in Red Hook

On Brooklyn's waterfront rests Red Hook, attracting action with its large spaces and low rents. Industrious residents are transforming the neighborhood's aged piers and warehouses into cool breweries, bakeries, and bistros. Royalty reigns with the Queen Mary 2 docked here. In the mood for a sweet treat? Head to **Baked**; or follow the signs to **Steve's Authentic Key Lime Pie**.

The **Red Hook Farmer's Market** features produce grown on Red Hook Community Farm. Both ventures are operated by Added Value, a mentoring organization that teaches urban youth how to till, sow, and harvest. On weekends from May through October, the ever-popular trucks and tents that line the Red Hook Ball Fields cater to hordes of New Yorkers in the know with their array of homemade Latin American and Caribbean street foods.

The International Expressway

Saunter to Fort Greene for a taste of African delicacies: Ethiopian at **Bati's** and South African at **Madiba**, where the sidewalk offers some great alfresco dining. Land at Sunset Park, and the vivid Mexican foods and flavors will tantalize your senses. Throw caution to the wind and bite into a *pambazo* from **Tacos Xochimilco**. Rows of grocery stores carry authentic ingredients; butcher shops offer unique meats; whilst bakeries carry sweets 'n treats. Slightly south, Mexico meets China, and this fusion is best expressed in unique culinary offerings.

Sidewalks teem with vendors steaming fresh tofu and fishmongers selling offbeat eats...bullfrog anyone? Chinatown encroaches into Bay Ridge where dim sum is delicious and Asian markets aplenty.

In a flock of Kosher restaurants, **Di Fara** is an unorthodox pizzeria and has called Midwood home for decades. And at the end of Brooklyn, Brighton Beach is best known for its borscht and blintzes; **Café Ghechik** is a Ukranian *bijou*. There is no confusing the Chesapeake with Sheepshead Bay, but **Clemente's Maryland Crab House** will provide you with a similar seafood experience.

Brooklyn
Hotel
Restaurant
Inset I
Miranda
Zenkichi
Osteria il Paiolo
Sea
An Nhau
Egg
Bedford Av
El Almacen
Baci & Abracci
Sui Ren
1 or 8
La Superior
Vutera
Marlow & Sons
Rye
Fatty 'Cue
Dressler
Diner
Peter Luger
MANHATTAN
Paulie Gee's
Karczma
GREENPOINT
Nassau St
See inset I
Marcy Av
Hewes St
See inset II
LIBERTY STATE PARK
BATTERY PARK
ELLIS ISLAND
UPPER NEW YORK BAY
LIBERTY ISLAND
GOVERNORS ISLAND
BROOKLYN HEIGHTS
Umi Nom
Classon Av
Franklin Av
Park Pl
RED HOOK
RED HOOK RECREATION AREA
PARK SLOPE
BROOKLYN MUSEUM
Botanic Garden
Gowanus Bay
Fonda
Applewood
Beer Table
Thistle Hill Taven
25 St
15 St-Prospect Pk
PROSPECT PARK
Prospect Pk
LOWER NEW YORK BAY
36 St
GREENWOOD CEMETERY
Maria's Bistro Mexicano
Parkside Av
Fort Hamilton Pkwy
Church Av
45 St
53 St
9 Av
SUNSET PARK
Beverly Rd
Cortelyou Rd
59 St
Lucky Eight
44 St
Mimi's Hummus
Purple Yam
Pacificana
The Farm on Adderly
Picket Fence
Bay Ridge Av
8 Av
BAY RIDGE
50 St
Ditmas Av
Newkirk Av
Bamboo Garden
East Harbor Seafood
Tanoreen
55 St
Island of Taiwan
Fort Hamilton Pkwy
BROOKLYN COLLEGE
77 St
18 Av
Av H
The Pearl Room
BOROUGH PARK
62 St
New Utrecht Av
Av I
86 St
World Tong
Av J
Tuscany Grill
Eliá
18 Av
71 St
Bay Pkwy
20 Av
Av M
95 St
Bamboo Pavilion

Atlantic Ave.	B2
Bay Pkwy.	B4
Bay Ridge Pkwy.	A4
Bedford Ave.	B1C4
Broadway	B1C2
Brooklyn-Queens Expwy.	B2C1
Caton Ave.	B3
Church Ave.	B3 4
Coney Island Ave.	B4
Cortelyou Rd.	B4
Court St.	B2 3
DeGraw St.	AB2
Ditmas Ave.	B4
Driggs Ave.	BC1
Eastern Pkwy.	B3
Flatbush Ave.	B2 4
Flushing Ave.	B2C1
Fort Hamilton Pkwy.	A4B3
Franklin St.	B1
Fulton St.	B2
Gates Ave.	BC2
Gowanus Expwy.	A4B2
Graham Ave.	C1 2
Grand St.	BC1
Greenpoint Ave.	BC1
Hamilton Ave.	B2 3
Humboldt St.	C1 2
Kent Ave.	B1 2
Lafayette Ave.	BC2
McDonald Ave.	B3 4
McGuinness Blvd.	C1
Metropolitan Ave.	BC1
Moore St.	C2
Morgan Ave.	C1
Myrtle Ave.	B2C2
New Utrecht Ave.	B4
Nostrand Ave.	C2
Ocean Ave.	B3 4
Ocean Pkwy.	B4
Prospect Expwy.	B3
Putman Ave.	BC2
Shore Pkwy.	A4
Smith St.	B2
Tompkins Ave.	C2
Union Ave.	C1
Van Brunt St.	A2
Washington Ave.	B2 3
3rd Ave.	A4
4th Ave.	A4B2
5th Ave.	A4B2
7th Ave.	A4, B2 3
8th Ave.	A4B3
9th St.	B3
11th St.	B3
14th Ave.	AB3
15th St.	B3
18th Ave.	B4
23rd St.	B3
39th St.	A3B4
47th St.	A3B4
55th St.	A3B4
65th St.	AB4
86th St.	A4

BRIDGES AND TUNNELS

Brooklyn-Battery Tunnel	1 A2
Brooklyn Bridge	2 B1 2
Manhattan Bridge	3 B1 2
Williamsburg Bridge	4 B1

Inset II

Al di Là

Italian

D4

248 Fifth Ave. (at Carroll St.)

Subway: Union St — Lunch Wed – Mon
Phone: 718-783-4565 — Dinner nightly
Web: www.aldilatrattoria.com
Prices: $$

With its mouthwatering Northern Italian cuisine and a charming atmosphere, it's no wonder this neighborhood fixture run by husband-and-wife team Emiliano Coppa and Anna Klinger continues to be a first choice dining option for both nearby residents and foodies from afar.

The high-ceilinged room boasts a faded chic, with its church-pew seats, and eccentric touches, such as coffee pots hanging from the wall and a blown glass chandelier.

Al di La also serves a lunch menu, which is pared down from the evening offerings. The perfect seasonal salad of young spinach with favas, fennel, and pecorino; and lasagna *al forno*, richly layered with meat and tomato ragù and béchamel are not only delicious, but priced at what can simply be called "a great deal."

Aliseo Osteria del Borgo

Italian

D4

665 Vanderbilt Ave. (bet. Park & Prospect Pls.)

Subway: 7 Av (Flatbush Ave.) — Dinner Tue – Sun
Phone: 718-783-3400
Web: N/A
Prices: $$

Just a few blocks north of Prospect Park, a tiny sliver of a restaurant pokes a delightful hole in the fabric of low-end joints that line the neighborhood. The quaint interior of Aliseo Osteria del Borgo is decidedly romantic, from the rustic tables to the porcelain lights to the cute garden out back. And if you sidle up to the counter with a minute to spare, the charming owner will tell you all about his labor of love.

Mercifully, the food is just as lovely, with a scrumptious lineup of Italian specialties that might include a zippy plate of baby beef meatballs; juicy, pan-roasted *trota di mare*, laid over a bundle of mushrooms in spring onion sauce; or a wicked dark chocolate tart laced with orange sauce and a lick of sweet and salty caramel.

Alma

Mexican

C3

187 Columbia St. (at Degraw St.)

Subway: Carroll St — Lunch Sat – Sun
Phone: 718-643-5400 — Dinner nightly
Web: www.almarestaurant.com
Prices: $$

It might be a hassle to get to Alma via public transportation, but this contemporary Mexican charmer is well worth the hike to the outskirts of Brooklyn, where it sits overlooking the ship yards, right around the point where the neighborhoods of Carroll Gardens and Red Hook connect.

Duck into the Degraw St. entrance (the Columbia St. entrance takes you through the rollicking bar), and head up the stairs. There, you can choose from a whimsically-appointed dining room or an enormous rooftop dining area (that gets covered in winter) offering up gorgeous spreads of lower Manhattan. Don't miss the guacamole, chock-a-block with fresh avocado; or the fragrantly spiced Anaheim rellenos, stuffed with cheese, butternut squash, and cactus leaves.

An Nhau

Vietnamese

A1

172 Bedford Ave. (bet. N. 7th & N. 8th Sts.)

Subway: Bedford Av — Lunch & dinner daily
Phone: 718-384-0001
Web: N/A
Prices: 

Set along busy Bedford Avenue, this everyday Vietnamese restaurant is located alongside sister spot Banh Mi, a take out shop specializing in the famed namesake sandwich. An Nhau offers table service in a room outfitted by wooden shutters, mirrors, and a wall decked with a big, delightful mural of a Vietnamese street scene.

Begin the affair with rolls and salads and make your way through the menu's home-style cooking featuring enjoyably aromatic preparations as well as myriad variations of the classic *pho*. Other delectable entrées include *bun*—lemongrass, garlic, and mint scented meats served over cool rice vermicelli; and pork belly braised in a sweet and savory coconut water-based broth, served with a hard boiled egg and pickled mustard greens.

Applewood

Contemporary

501 11th St. (bet. Seventh & Eighth Aves.)

Subway: 7 Av (9th St.)
Phone: 718-788-1810
Web: www.applewoodny.com
Prices: $$

Lunch Sat – Sun
Dinner Tue – Sat

Skillfully prepared cuisine and a dainty setting reflect the seriousness of Applewood's owners David and Laura Shea. The pair is committed to promoting the work of organic and local farmers in a changing menu of small plates and entrées dedicated to reflecting the seasons.

The spare yet comfortable dining room, set in a century-old townhouse on a tree-lined street, is furnished with honey-toned wood tables and spindle-back chairs. When in use, a working fireplace warms the light-colored room, accented by the work of local artists.

Thick slices of fresh bread set the tone for an enjoyable meal of wild fish and hormone-free meats in delectable offerings such as lobster risotto with mascarpone and chili oil, or pan-seared bass with tomatillo jam.

Baci & Abbracci

Italian

204 Grand St. (bet. Bedford & Driggs Sts.)

Subway: Bedford Av
Phone: 718-599-6599
Web: www.baciny.com
Prices: $$

Lunch Sat – Sun
Dinner nightly

This popular, upbeat Williamsburg eatery features Italian cuisine with a wholehearted emphasis on pizza. With more than twenty permutations of wood-oven baked pies, these smoky-chewy crusts are the foundation for toppings that may begin with just the right amount of sauce and creamy-luscious globs of freshly made mozzarella. Beyond this, the adept kitchen also boasts its own house-made bread and enjoyable pastas, as well as impressive *secondi* like lamb chops, charred and juicy, sauced with a bold reduction of balsamic and fresh mint.

The intimate space sports a contemporary design framed by a concrete floor, sleek furnishings, and glazed-tile accents. A charming little patch of backyard makes an especially popular setting for weekend brunch.

Bamboo Garden

Chinese 

A4

6409 Eighth Ave. (at 64th St.)

Subway: 8 Av — Lunch & dinner daily
Phone: 718-238-1122
Web: N/A
Prices: 

This bustling establishment proves that there is impressive dim sum to be found in the borough of Brooklyn. The large setting may look a bit tattered but it is clean and boasts a generous number of large round, linen draped tables; during the day the space is jam-packed with a gregarious flock of local residents.

The tables are attended to by Cantonese-speaking ladies, cheerfully dressed in fuchsia blouses and red vests, pushing cart after cart of steaming treats through the hungry hordes. Resist the urge to stock your table all at once; survey the delicacies and pace yourself for a spectrum of fresh, delish dumplings, buns, and pastries. The feast also includes some refreshingly unique preparations that steer away from the standard dim sum lineup.

Bamboo Pavilion

Chinese 

6920 Eighteenth Ave. (bet. Bay Ridge Ave. & 70th St.)

Subway: 18 Av — Lunch & dinner Mon – Sat
Phone: 718-236-8088
Web: N/A
Prices: $$

How did this hot pot joint find its way onto Bensonhurst's predominantly Sicilian 18th Avenue, the one made famous by the movie Saturday Night Fever? The times they are a' changin'—for this area is now home to a growing Chinese population and enough authentic Sichuan joints to warrant some critics stating it has become the city's most recent Chinatown.

A meal at Bamboo Pavilion might convince you, for these fiery delights don't fool around. The restaurant itself is nondescript, with bamboo-etched wallpapered walls, bright lighting, and jumbo round tables for big parties. All the more reason to set your eyes to the center of each table—where piles of soft noodles, succulent raw meats, and leafy vegetables surround fragrant pots of bubbling broth.

Barrio

Mexican

210 Seventh Ave. (at 3rd St.)

Subway: 7 Av (9th St.)
Phone: 718-965-4000
Web: www.barriofoods.com
Prices: $$

Lunch Thu – Sun
Dinner nightly

This cozy new neighborhood fave doubles its capacity in warmer weather with a covered outdoor dining space cheerfully decorated with strings of colored lights overhead. The blithe yet beautiful spot displays a glazed ceramic tile floor, with pink and orange embellishments.

Even beyond this setting is the impressive cooking of Mexico City native and Chef/partner Adrian Leon, whose skills have been honed in some of Manhattan's most popular Mexican kitchens. Excellent tortilla chips accompanied by red and green salsa begin what is sure to be an enjoyable meal.

Parents take note: the assortment of soft *taquitos*, enticing entrées, and *"platos del dia"* is accompanied by a kid's menu offering tidbits such as miniature short rib soft tacos and the like.

Beer Table

Gastropub

B3

427 B Seventh Ave. (bet. 14th & 15th Sts.)

Subway: 7 Av (9th St.)
Phone: 718-965-1196
Web: www.beertable.com
Prices:

Lunch Sun
Dinner nightly

With a listing of more than 25 bottled beers, some priced on par with fine wine, Beer Table gives the typical neighborhood pub a sophisticated new angle. Three communal tables are tucked into a pleasant setting accented with shelves of sparkling stemware and jars of house-made pickles.

Snacks like ricotta on toast with black mission figs are offered to accompany their artisanal beer selections; but there is also a not-to-be-missed prix-fixe menu offered nightly alongside optional beer pairings. Seasonal ingredients are showcased in meals that may feature baby arugula and cucumber salad with herbed yogurt; striped bass on a bed of *fregola* spiked with roasted garlic and preserved lemon; or warm strawberry *amaretti* crumble.

Belleville 

French

330 5th St. (at Fifth Ave.)

Subway: 4 Av - 9 St — Lunch Sat – Sun
Phone: 718-832-9777 — Dinner nightly
Web: www.bellevillebistro.com
Prices: $$

From décor to ambience to food, Belleville (named for the Parisian neighborhood) fashions the perfectly French bistro here in Park Slope. Designed to appear lovingly well-worn, Belleville is at once comfortable, with mosaic floors, mirrored walls displaying the wine list, rows of wood-paneled banquettes, and tables nuzzled close together. In fair weather, windows open out onto Brooklyn's bustling Fifth Avenue and sidewalk seating.

The reasonably priced menu features very good bistro fare from *croques madames* to steak frites. There's even a kids menu for little gourmands-in-training. This is a welcoming neighborhood place for a romantic dinner, weekend brunch, or small bites and a glass of wine in the warm and toasty lounge.

Blue Ribbon Sushi

Japanese

278 Fifth Ave. (bet. 1st St. & Garfield Pl.)

Subway: Union St — Dinner nightly
Phone: 718-840-0408
Web: www.blueribbonrestaurants.com
Prices: $$

Consistent excellence has made this Brooklyn location of the Bromberg brother's notable restaurant line-up worthy of bearing the Blue Ribbon name. Slats of warmly polished wood and a cool grey palette lends a chic finish to this popular spot—filled with Park Slope parents towing along the next generation of sushi connoisseurs.

Classified according to ocean of origin (Atlantic or Pacific), the sushi here is delightful and is shored up by a creative menu of maki, such as the Blue Ribbon roll which lavishly combines lobster, caviar, and *shiso*. The lengthy list of appetizers and salads may include *yasei kinoko* (broiled wild mushrooms with tamari butter).

Complement your meal with a selection from the well chosen sake list or a Japanese boutique beer.

Brooklyn Fish Camp

D4 — Seafood

162 Fifth Ave. (bet. De Graw & Douglass Sts.)

Subway: Union St — Lunch & dinner Mon – Sat
Phone: 718-783-3264
Web: www.brooklynfishcamp.com
Prices: $$

Inspired by the simplicity of rural Southern fish shacks, the menu at this Brooklyn offshoot of Mary's Fish Camp displays a reverence for seriously prepared seafood.

The welcoming bar upfront leads to a simple dining room furnished with warm-hued wood tables, topped with brown paper mats and bags of oyster crackers. Out back, picnic tables and folding chairs make a fine setting for a summertime meal, accompanied by movies shown on a whitewashed wall.

The excellent lobster roll, oyster Po' boy, and shrimp tacos are all fun favorites; but do not overlook more inspired entrées like roasted monkfish with horseradish-bacon beurre blanc. Tempting home-style desserts, like banana pudding and peach cobbler, are listed on the wall-mounted blackboard.

Buttermilk Channel

C4 — American

524 Court St. (at Huntington St.)

Subway: Smith - 9 Sts. — Lunch Sat – Sun
Phone: 718-852-8490 — Dinner nightly
Web: www.buttermilkchannelnyc.com
Prices: $$

A fresh coat of glossy, dark paint and large windows emanating a warm glow give this establishment an inviting, turn-of-the-century maritime feel. This befits its name, which references the (once crossable) strait separating Brooklyn from Governor's Island. The butter-yellow dining room attracts a lively and diverse crowd; regardless of one's tastes, the menu is bound to please.

A listing of small bites like house-made pickles, charcuterie, and greenmarket cheeses are perfect to nibble along with a local brew and make a lovely prelude. The full offering of seasonal comfort food may include winter squash tart with homemade buttermilk ricotta; or duck meatloaf with creamy spinach purée, with a separate (equally impressive) menu devoted to vegetarians.

Chance

C4

Asian

223 Smith St. (bet. Baltic & Butler Sts.)

Subway: Bergen St (Smith St.) — Lunch & dinner daily
Phone: 718-242-1515
Web: www.chancecuisine.com
Prices:

Sporting a freshened décor, Chance continues to beautifully present a luscious, unique selection of Pan-Asian delights. The menu celebrates these varied influences, and even includes an occasional nod to France. Inside, ivory leather seating and dark glossy tables give the space a modern look, and attractive red lanterns suspended over the bar allude to the Asian theme.

The dim sum assortment makes a fine starting point, followed by impressive and enjoyable dishes like black pepper chicken, coated in crisp *panko* and topped with flavorful ground pork. While the carte du jour is reasonably priced, quality is not sacrificed. Savor the dinner prixe-fixe for less than $20, with decadent dessert choices such as smooth and rich vanilla ice cream brûlée.

Char No. 4

C3

Gastropub

196 Smith St. (bet. Baltic & Warren Sts.)

Subway: Bergen St (Smith St.) — Lunch Fri – Sun
Phone: 718-643-2106 — Dinner nightly
Web: www.charno4.com
Prices: $$

More shrine than pub, this Smith Street watering hole offers an encyclopedic listing of whiskey, half of which are devoted to bourbon and all are available in one or two ounce pours—allowing for a civilized examination of the elixir's varied styles.

The comfortable front bar radiates warmth with its wall of amber-filled bottles; the slender dining room in the back is decorated in shades of brown.

The Southern-inspired menu of crispy cheddar nuggets with pimento sauce; shrimp and grits; and smoked honey-glazed chicken accentuates the sweet, spicy, and charred essences, which in turn marry well with the stack of smoky bourbons. Finish it all with a lick of house-made butter pecan ice cream, drizzled with a shot of bourbon, of course.

Chef Table at Brooklyn Fare 

Contemporary

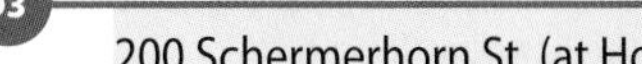

200 Schermerhorn St. (at Hoyt St.)

Subway: Hoyt-Schermerhorn

Dinner Tue – Sat

Phone: 718-243-0050

Web: www.brooklynfare.com

Prices: **$$$$**

Douglas Kim

It's the kind of experience that epitomizes Brooklyn's blazing new culinary scene. By day, Brooklyn Fare operates as a gourmet grocery tucked away on a somewhat desolate strip of downtown Brooklyn. By night, owner Moe Issa flings open the doors on a nearby space dubbed "The Kitchen" for 18 guests.

What's the hubbub? Late in the spring of 2009, Chef César Ramirez (formerly of Bouley and Bar Blanc) packed up his wares and crossed the river to host incredible nightly dinners in this gleaming, intimate workspace, which reveals a stainless steel counter, polished copperware, and a smattering of seats where guests can watch the action up close.

No tasting menu is repeated twice; and dishes described simply on the menu translate to culinary genius on the plate. An evening spent with Ramirez might unveil crispy black bass in a shallow pool of mouthwatering dashi featuring foie gras, sweet peas, fava beans, and fresh squid, laced with summer truffle shavings and foam; or slow-cooked pork loin and belly, plated with a strip of crispy, rendered skin and served with a smooth mushroom purée, sweated sweet onions, a dab of apricot purée, wilted pea tendrils, and a cloud of walnut froth.

Chestnut

Contemporary

C4

271 Smith St. (bet. De Graw & Sackett Sts.)

Subway: Carroll St — Lunch Sun
Phone: 718-243-0049 — Dinner Tue – Sun
Web: www.chestnutonsmith.com
Prices: $$

This Carroll Gardens eatery is the kind of place every neighborhood should have. Like its moniker, the philosophy here is comforting and seasonal. Chestnut's farm-reared chef spends time sourcing the best ingredients and then lets them shine in a menu reminding diners that the best supermarket is nature itself. The simple décor has just the right amount of personality, and the laid-back staff delivers genuinely warm service, starting your meal with fresh-baked bread and homemade pickles.

Come on Tuesday or Wednesday nights to take advantage of the three-course, prix-fixe value menus. Or, order à la carte any night to dine on skillfully-prepared items that may include salt cod *brandade*, roasted chicken breast with sausage filling, or chocolate *budino*.

Clover Club

American

C3-4

210 Smith St. (bet. Baltic & Butler Sts.)

Subway: Bergen St (Smith St.) — Lunch Sat – Sun
Phone: 718-855-7939 — Dinner nightly
Web: www.cloverclubny.com
Prices: $$

A former shoe store is now an atmospheric Smith Street watering hole that fashions a spot-on vintage vibe with mosaic tiled floors, glove-soft leather banquettes, and pressed-tin ceilings dangling with etched-glass pendants that create a glow warmer than single malt. The rear mahogany bar is overseen by a skillful, natty bartender vigorously shaking and artfully pouring a noteworthy selection of libations, like the "improved whiskey cocktail" (rye whiskey, maraschino, absinthe, and bitters served in a frosted glass with a single block of ice).

An excellent menu of savory bites is just as impressively prepared and includes treats such as deviled eggs four ways; shrimp roll sliders; and brioche bread pudding with bourbon caramel sauce.

Diner

American

A1

85 Broadway (at Berry St.)

Subway: Marcy Av — Lunch & dinner daily
Phone: 718-486-3077
Web: www.dinernyc.com
Prices: $$

Do not let Diner's impossibly hip crowd and rather ramshackle setting deter you. Beneath all that plaid are ordinary folk who appreciate the renovated 1920s Kulman Diner setting and an impressively unfussy kitchen that knows how to make a perfect block of head cheese. Pioneering restaurateurs and publishers of *Diner Journal*, Mark Firth and Andrew Tarlow have run this establishment with heart and personality since 1998.

The kitchen uses spot-on technique in preparing specials that highlight seasonality, such as a Portuguese-inspired seafood stew. This neat pile of plump, tender mussels, sweet clams, cubes of firm fish, and thin slices of linguiça is served atop an olive oil-brushed crouton so a drop of brilliant sauce won't go to waste.

DuMont

American

C1

432 Union Ave. (bet. Devoe St. & Metropolitan Ave.)

Subway: Lorimer St - Metropolitan Av — Lunch & dinner daily
Phone: 718-486-7717
Web: www.dumontrestaurant.com
Prices: $$

DuMont espouses its neighborhood's relaxed, edgy, and creative vibe. The multi-room space is warm and comfortably worn, furnished with dark-wood tables topped in brown paper, vintage tile floor, and cool leather seating handmade by the owner. There is also a lovely backyard with elevated seating called "the treehouse."

Executive Chef Polo Dobkin fuels local crowds of Billyburg hipsters who clamor for his near-addictive comfort food menu. Favorites may include crispy artichokes with creamy garlic dressing; N.Y. strip steak with Bordelaise sauce; and of course, the DuMac and cheese (with *radiatore* pasta, richly coated in béchamel, under a molten blend of cheeses). Brunch keeps weekends groovy.

For a quick burger and a beer, try nearby DuMont Burger.

Dressler ✿

American XX

149 Broadway (bet. Bedford & Driggs Aves.)

Subway: Marcy Av — Lunch Sun
Phone: 718-384-6343 — Dinner nightly
Web: www.dresslernyc.com
Prices: $$

Stephanie Lemper

You can't wave a stick in Williamsburg without hitting a hip, buzzed-about eatery specializing in a unique, Brooklyn-style cuisine, but Colin Devlin's critically-acclaimed Dressler is the one that raised the bar—and kept it there.

A sophisticated sibling to Devlin's more casual neighborhood staples, DuMont and DuMont Burger, Dressler occupies the same hallowed area as legendary steakhouse, Peter Luger's—a truck-rumbling street that, despite its growing list of big name eateries, has a quiet, pre-boom Meatpacking District feel. Thankfully, it's a mood that the sleek, polished Dressler—a cavernous old printer's shop redesigned with mosaic tiles, polished mahogany, and a zinc-topped bar—manages to wash away with its devotion to detail.

Chef Polo Dobkin has an eye for minutia, and his finely-tuned American cuisine gets a contemporary polish in dishes like a warm artichoke heart salad with plump cranberry beans, a neat bundle of arugula, delicate shards of fine Parmesan, and a touch of salsa verde; or deceptively simple pan-roasted Hudson Valley chicken, presented over a fluffy cloud of white polenta and bright green escarole, with an irresistible brown jus laced around its edges.

East Harbor Seafood Palace

Chinese

A4

714-726 65th St. (bet. Seventh & Eighth Aves.)

Subway: 8 Av
Lunch & dinner daily
Phone: 718-765-0098
Web: N/A
Prices: $$

East Harbor Seafood Palace is a haven for authentic dim sum devotees. Favored by Chinese locals, this behemoth presides over a commercial area that chronically rumbles with forklifts and foot-traffic—though closer scrutiny reveals tidy row houses and supermarkets. These residents are among the first to know that Brooklyn's N and D lines are coming to rival the foodie thrills found along the 7 through Queens.

Inside the lofty room flanked by fish tanks, the kindly staff circulates with steaming carts offering the likes of *cha siu bao* (barbecue pork buns); *cha siu soh* (barbecue pork puff pastry); and *zha liang* (a fried dough stick wrapped with cheung fun skin). Chef's specials like pan-fried mei fun with frogs legs and celery will leave you smitten.

Egg

American

135 N. 5th St. (bet. Bedford Ave. & Berry St.)

Subway: Bedford Av
Lunch daily
Phone: 718-302-5151
Dinner Thu – Sun
Web: www.pigandegg.com
Prices: $$

Offering daily breakfast well into the afternoon, Egg's slender dining room seems to serve as a remote office for Williamsburg's work-from-home set. We may never know how many bestsellers were conceived here, while downing cups of sustainably-grown coffee or doodling with crayons provided on the paper-topped tables. On weekends, the wait for a table can be lengthy—jot your name on the flipchart stationed outside and be patient.

Southern-accented preparations like fresh-baked buttermilk biscuits layered with country ham, cheddar, and fig jam are popular, but also find homemade granola served with local yogurt and griddle fare accompanied by Vermont maple syrup. Dinner hour brings the likes of deviled eggs and fried chicken with collard greens.

El Almacen

Argentinian

557 Driggs Ave. (bet. N. 6th & N. 7th Sts.)

Subway: Bedford Av
Phone: 718-218-7284
Web: N/A
Prices: $$

Lunch Sat – Sun
Dinner nightly

This Argentinian grill is a carnivore's delight with its menu of meats prepared *de la parilla*: grass-fed cuts of beef, corn-fed pork, homemade chorizo, and *morcilla* (blood sausage). Tender empanadas, vibrant ceviches, and entrées like *Milanesa de pollo* or pappardelle with coffee-braised oxtail ragù are among the hearty offerings best followed by *dulce de leche* in one of its several guises.

El Almacen, which means general store in Spanish, boasts a dark and rustic interior and atmospheric setting replete with creaking wood furnishings, shelves filled with bric-a-brac, and cast iron skillets mounted on a brick wall. The inviting bar is amply stocked with bottles of wine and set against a backdrop of creamy white tile warmed by the candlelit room.

Eliá

8611 Third Ave. (bet. 86th & 87th Sts.)

Subway: 86 St
Phone: 718-748-9891
Web: www.eliarestaurant.org
Prices: $$

Dinner Tue – Sun

Long known to Bay Ridge residents, this little gem is no longer a secret. Now, regulars share their favorite Greek restaurant with diners from Manhattan. That said, everyone is treated like family at this affable and spotless taverna.

The chef sometimes steers the menu into uncharted waters with elaborate creations and mixed results. Hold steady with the simple, traditional dishes at which the kitchen excels, like classic *spanakopita* of spinach, leeks, and feta cheese layered in flakey, buttery phyllo dough, or baklava topped with nuts and a spiced citrus-infused syrup. Generous portions assure value for money.

In the dining room, white-washed brick walls and marine blues evoke sun-washed stucco buildings and the color of the Aegean Sea.

Fanny

Mediterranean

C1

425 Graham Ave. (bet. Frost & Withers Sts.)

Subway: Graham Av — Lunch & dinner daily
Phone: 718-389-2060
Web: www.fannyfood.com
Prices: $$

Building the perfect neighborhood bistro is a delicate thing. It should be intimate and cozy, but lively when the mood fits; it should traffic in the kind of delicious, straightforward fare regulars won't tire of easily; and the owners ought to be the kind of folks you'd want to share a drink with.

Fanny, a romantic, low-lit charmer tucked into East Williamsburg's Graham Avenue, has the formula in spades—with rustic country house good looks, two French ex-pat owners, Julie Eck and Stephane Alix, who know all their regulars' names, and a spot-on Southern French menu featuring mussels in white wine; juicy rack of lamb; silky lavender blancmange; and that final test of any bistro worth its salt—a perfect stack of crunchy frites with garlicky aïoli.

The Farm on Adderley

American

B4

1108 Cortelyou Rd. (bet. 12th St. & Stratford Rd.)

Subway: Cortelyou Rd — Lunch & dinner daily
Phone: 718-287-3101
Web: www.thefarmonadderley.com
Prices: $$

Tom Kearney, who earned his culinary stripes at Blue Hill and Jean Georges before crossing the river, doesn't need to bend over backward to expand his fan base—he has a plenty captive audience in the incoming mix of bright young professionals gentrifying Ditmas Park, a quickly-evolving neighborhood south of Prospect Park.

And yet he delivers sweet perfection with each dish, plying newcomers who make their way into his softly lit dining room with simple, seasonal fare like kale soup, bobbing with poached egg and brown lentils; arctic char, grilled with roasted beets, green lentils, and pickled garlic; or a tender buttermilk tart, paired with irresistible blueberry compote. Morning commuters, rejoice: the restaurant recently added breakfast.

Fatty 'Cue

Asian

91 S. 6th St. (bet. Bedford Ave. & Berry St.)

Subway: Marcy Av — Dinner nightly
Phone: 718-599-3090
Web: www.fattycue.com
Prices: $$

Chef Zakary Pelaccio, of Fatty Crab fame, and pit master Robbie Richter, formerly of Hill Country fame, join forces for a lip-smacking mash-up of Southeast Asian influenced barbecue. Perched virtually underneath the Williamsburg Bridge, the roadhouse-looking space features a bar-dominated dining room supplemented by an alleyway used for outdoor seating.

Exotic and creative, Fatty 'Cue's menu boasts preparations like *ikan baker*, a smoky, banana leaf-seared mackerel seasoned with tumeric salt. Beef brisket brings deliciously hands-on eating—thin slices of lean meat and pieces of glazed fat arrive with chili jam, aïoli, and steamed buns for filling.

The cocktail list and unique drink specials perfectly complement this spirited, Brooklyn-soigné setting.

Fonda

Mexican 

434 Seventh Ave. (bet. 14th & 15th Sts.)

Subway: 7 Av (9th St.) — Lunch Sat – Sun
Phone: 718-369-3144 — Dinner Tue – Sun
Web: www.fondarestaurant.com
Prices: $$

Chef Robert Santibañez, a Le Cordon Bleu graduate and former culinary director of Rosa Mexicano, offers an updated take on Mexican cuisine at this cheerful Park Slope newcomer. Bright colors and bold artwork decorate the petite dining room, which is supplemented by warm-weather seating on the back patio.

Fonda's menu is endowed with a creative spin, evident in preparations such as fish *salpicon*—finely chopped with plenty of white onion, cilantro, and green chiles, then brightened with fresh lime juice and accompanied by warm hand-pressed tortillas. The banana leaf-wrapped *marco pollo* comes dressed with a crimson hued sauce of achiote and roasted tomato, while desserts offer a home-style touch as in the softly set, citrus-scented *natillas*.

Frankies 457 Spuntino

Italian

457 Court St. (bet. 4th Pl. & Luquer St.)

Subway: Smith - 9 Sts — Lunch & dinner daily
Phone: 718-403-0033
Web: www.frankiesspuntino.com
Prices: 

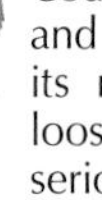

Courtesy of the Franks (Castronovo and Falcinelli) is this rustic and deliciously homestyle Italian that strives to highlight its relationship with local producers. Although *spuntino* loosely translates as "snack," this menu richly satisfies both serious foodies and old-school Brooklynites in a cozy setting. While preparation is initially done in the basement kitchen, dishes are assembled in the casual dining room, behind a counter stacked with charcuterie and crusty breads. This practice entices guests with mouthwatering aromas of tender homemade *pappardelle* with braised lamb; or visions of cured meats and *formaggio*.

Weather permitting, dine in the inviting back garden, illuminated by strings of tiny lights. Also try the Lower East Side location.

Franny's

Italian

295 Flatbush Ave. (bet. Prospect Pl. & St. Marks Ave.)

Subway: Bergen St (Flatbush Ave.) — Lunch Sat – Sun
Phone: 718-230-0221 — Dinner nightly
Web: www.frannysbrooklyn.com
Prices: $$

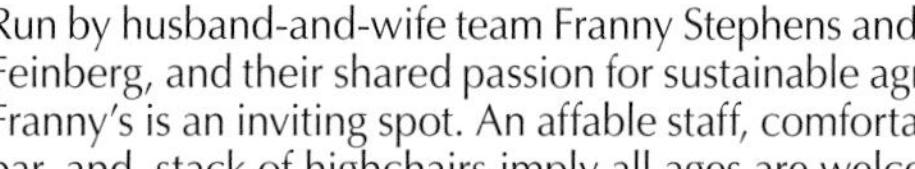

Run by husband-and-wife team Franny Stephens and Andrew Feinberg, and their shared passion for sustainable agriculture, Franny's is an inviting spot. An affable staff, comfortable front bar, and stack of highchairs imply all ages are welcome.

The open kitchen's centerpiece is a wood-burning brick oven from which individual-size pizzas emerge puffed and crispy; their notable clam pie is a much-craved specialty. While daily specials are tempting, remember that the chef's selection of house-cured meats and small plates is also worth considering.

Decorated with greenery, strings of white lights, and a neat wood pile to feed the pizza oven, the back patio is perfect for warm evenings. Be sure to visit their neighboring food boutique, Brooklyn Larder.

The General Greene

American 

D3

229 DeKalb Ave. (at Clermont Ave.)

Subway: Lafayette Av — Lunch & dinner daily
Phone: 718-222-1510
Web: www.thegeneralgreene.com
Prices: $$

The rustic American revolution marches on with The General Greene, a solidly ensconced Fort Greene restaurant that taps the talents of acclaimed city boy chef, Nicholas Morgenstern and his accomplished staff. Together, they have cooked up a creative Southern-inflected menu guaranteed to steal the hearts of the upscale bohemian crowd that floods this neighborhood—its simple diner good looks and coolio waitstaff only seal the deal.

The seasonal menu may include a silky chicken liver pâté, dusted with sea salt; or grilled prawns, licked with an herb-infused olive oil. Save room for one of their more clever savory dishes like a thick slab of moist bread pudding, loaded with ham and Gruyere, and paired with a tangle of pig's feet-studded collard greens.

Get Fresh Table and Market

American 

D4

370 Fifth Ave. (bet. 5th & 6th Sts.)

Subway: 4 Av - 9 St — Lunch daily
Phone: 718-360-8469 — Dinner Tue – Sun
Web: www.getfreshnyc.com
Prices: ⊜

This minimally embellished space operates as a combination restaurant, take-out shop, and market—shelves and refrigerator cases stocked with artisanal ingredients offer a glimpse of what inspires the impressive product-driven menu.

Brunch is served daily and includes eye-openers such as house-made granola and cage-free truffled eggs; while heartier preparations have included *garam* masala-spiced lentil soup and a burrito filled with chunks of heritage pork, tender heirloom beans, cheese, and annatto-tinged rice. A blackboard displays daily specials and a nightly market-influenced prix-fixe dinner menu.

The light, airy room offers small marble-topped tables and communal seating along a large wooden plank; an outdoor area extends seating in fine weather.

The Good Fork 

Contemporary

391 Van Brunt St. (bet. Coffey & Van Dyke Sts.)

Subway: Smith - 9 Sts (& bus B77) Dinner Tue – Sun
Phone: 718-643-6636
Web: www.goodfork.com
Prices: $$

It's literally a pain in the neck to get to The Good Fork's far-flung Red Hook location (even if you spring for a cab, the potholes will kill you), but this is one little restaurant worth the hump. Guests can either duck into the quaint dining room, reminiscent of a train car from a bygone era, or head back to a small patio surrounded by an iron gazebo and trees wrapped in twinkling lights.

Storybook, yes—but the lovingly prepared dishes seal the deal. Run by Ben Schneider and his classically-trained Korean-American wife, Sohui Kim, The Good Fork's menu gleefully trots the globe, showcasing Kim's ethnic background—try the Korean-style steak and eggs over kimchi rice—and then switching gears to bang out a spot-on burger and salty stack of onion rings.

The Grocery

Contemporary

288 Smith St. (bet. Sackett & Union Sts.)

Subway: Carroll St Lunch Thu – Sat
Phone: 718-596-3335 Dinner Tue – Sat
Web: www.thegroceryrestaurant.com
Prices: $$

Opened in 1999, this Smith Street charmer helped put fine dining on the Brooklyn map. Today it continues to please a devoted following in a quaint space simply furnished with white paper-topped tables, whimsically accented with seasonal fruit. The verdant backyard is prized on warmer evenings, but be aware that these precious tables are offered as first-come first-served. Chefs and co-owners Sharon Pachter and Charles Kiely run their operation with passion and a genuine regard for their guests satisfaction.

The concise menu lists items that reflect the best of the season and local farmers' markets, such as roasted beets with goat cheese ravioli, stuffed whole boneless trout, and steamed spicy-sweet gingerbread pudding with roasted pineapple.

Island of Taiwan

Chinese

6817 Eighth Ave. (bet. 68th St. & Bay Ridge Ave.)

Subway: 8 Av — Lunch & dinner daily
Phone: 718-680-0033
Web: N/A
Prices: ⊝

Located in Dyker Heights, this inviting restaurant is a standout among a burgeoning strip of Chinese dining and markets and offers diners tasty insight into the regionally unique preparations specific to this island. The space is well kept, and the room's sunny disposition—decorated with splashes of orange and blue—matches the service.

The food is always freshly prepared and enticingly aromatic; and specialties include chicken soup enriched with toasted sesame oil and rice wine; preserved radish studded egg pancake; mildly spicy minced pork tossed with Chinese chives, chopped chilies, and slicked with a rich, slightly sweet dark sauce; and clay pot baked "three cup" chicken—sauced with soy sauce, rice wine, and a fresh, sweet touch of basil.

Jack the Horse

American

66 Hicks St. (at Cranberrry St.)

Subway: High St — Lunch Sun
Phone: 718-852-5084 — Dinner nightly
Web: www.jackthehorse.com
Prices: **$$**

For all its upscale bohemian charm and perfect little brownstones, the picture-book neighborhood of Brooklyn Heights could use a few more restaurants like Jack the Horse—a homey, exposed brick tavern that's been kept under wraps by the locals who frequent it.

Who would want to share this gem? With its bright, window-lined walls and impossibly delicious cocktail list, this place would be a destination spot even without Tim Oltmans' gorgeous American fare like a savory artichoke, pancetta cheesecake starter topped with tomato-caper relish and crispy greens; creamy pan-seared hake with sweet red peppers, zucchini, chorizo, and plantains, dancing in a tomato cilantro-lime broth; or silky coconut panna cotta studded with crunchy sesame seeds.

James

Contemporary XX

605 Carlton Ave. (at St. Marks Ave.)

Subway: 7 Av (Flatbush Ave.) — Lunch Sun
Phone: 718-942-4255 — Dinner nightly
Web: www.jamesrestaurantny.com
Prices: $$

The concise menu at James first may appear simple and straightforward, like the establishment's moniker. However, plump, roasted quail stuffed with homemade duck sausage; crispy, seared salmon served on a bed of leek stew; and grilled lemon-almond pound cake accompanied by a scoop of blueberry-streaked ice cream, are all the proof one needs to see the level of sophistication and skill at work in the kitchen.

Likewise, the dining room housed on a tree-lined corner of Prospect Heights displays signs of refinement with a space accented in whitewashed brick walls and espresso-dark leather and wood furnishings. Warm lighting adds a flattering glow throughout, and the comfortable bar is nicely appointed by a vintage mirror and floral arrangements.

Jolie

French XX

320 Atlantic Ave. (bet. Smith & Hoyt Sts.)

Subway: Bergen St (Smith St.) — Lunch & dinner daily
Phone: 718-488-0777
Web: www.jolierestaurant.com
Prices: $$

Jolie, indeed. With its lovely, curved marble bar; elegant, rotating art collection gracing clean walls; and shady back garden laced in flowery vines, Jolie is probably the prettiest restaurant gracing this lonely stretch of Atlantic Avenue in Brooklyn's Boerum Hill.

Jolie does the whole relaxed-neighborhood-French-restaurant thing just right, with a menu care of Chef/owner Michel Pombet (who also owns Parigot, in Little Italy) that rounds the usual bistro bases with panache. Dinner might include a plate of bacon-wrapped scallops, paired with eggplant purée, tomato cumin coulis, and brioche toast; or a soft bowl of lobster risotto, laced with truffle butter, freshly-shelled fava beans, tender mushrooms, sundried tomatoes, and cracked pepper.

Karczma

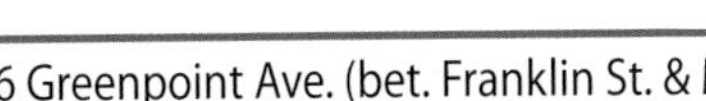

B1

136 Greenpoint Ave. (bet. Franklin St. & Manhattan

Subway: Greenpoint Av — Lunch & dinner daily
Phone: 718-349-1744
Web: www.karczmabrooklyn.com
Prices: ⊜

Located in a section of Greenpoint that still boasts a sizeable Polish population, Karczma offers a lovely old-world ambience that fits perfectly with its lengthy menu boasting hearty servings of traditional specialties. The pierogis, offered in three varieties, can be steamed but are even better fried, topped with sliced onions and drizzled with butter—the lean, chopped-meat filling is ethereal. A generous listing of main courses feature grilled platters for two or three; soul-satisfying stews; and an excellent (if outrageously large) paprika-dusted pork shank braised in beer, with fluffy mashed potatoes and caraway-scented cabbage.

The charmingly rustic space is efficiently staffed by smiling servers in floral skirts and embroidered vests.

Kif

Moroccan

D3

219 DeKalb Ave. (bet. Adelphi St.& Clermont Ave.)

Subway: Lafayette Av — Lunch Sat – Sun
Phone: 718-852-7273 — Dinner nightly
Web: N/A
Prices: $$

Wanted: adorable bohemian spot in Brooklyn with sexy velvet banquettes, billowing linens draped from the ceiling, and a leafy outdoor garden. Food should be creative, exotic, and fresh—authenticity a plus.

Kif, a clever new Moroccan spot in Fort Greene, fits the bill perfectly—mostly because the Algerian owner keeps his standards a mile high by having a completely open kitchen, where diners can watch the chefs work delicious amounts of imported spices and oils into lip-smacking good small plates like a spot-on *zaalouk*; a plate of smoky roasted eggplant purée with roasted red peppers and flecks of bright green parsley; or a plate of moist, tender grilled merguez sausages dusted with cumin and chili, and set atop a thick and smoky *harissa* sauce.

Ki Sushi

Japanese

122 Smith St. (bet. Dean & Pacific Sts.)

Subway: Bergen St (Smith St.)
Phone: 718-935-0575
Web: www.ki-sushi.com
Prices: $$

Lunch Mon – Sat
Dinner nightly

Count sushi among Smith Street's wealth of dining options. At Ki, the impressive quality and talent continue to satisfy a devoted clientele relishing the raw and the cooked in a Zen-chic space complete with a gently flowing wall of water and potted flowers.

The smiling sushi team works from a long counter stocked with a tempting array of pristine fish. The sushi and sashimi are excellent, as is the whimsical and visually appealing maki, like the Fashion Roll of chopped tuna, jalapeño, and yuzu *tobiko* wrapped in slices of raw scallop. Preparations such as rock shrimp tempura drizzled with spiced mayonnaise emerge from the small kitchen located in back.

The genuinely friendly and attentive service adds to the charm of this Cobble Hill favorite.

La Superior

Mexican 

295 Berry St. (bet. S. 2nd & S. 3rd Sts.)

Subway: Bedford Av
Phone: 718-388-5988
Web: www.lasuperiornyc.com
Prices: 

Lunch & dinner daily

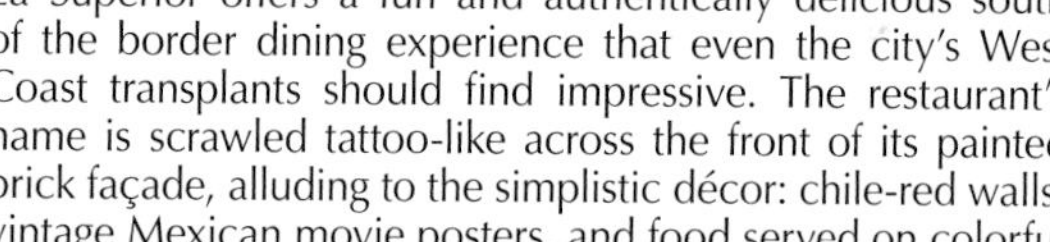

La Superior offers a fun and authentically delicious south of the border dining experience that even the city's West Coast transplants should find impressive. The restaurant's name is scrawled tattoo-like across the front of its painted brick façade, alluding to the simplistic décor: chile-red walls, vintage Mexican movie posters, and food served on colorful plastic plates.

Liquor is not available, but Mexican sodas and *aguas frescas* are offered to wash down the inexpensive fare. Highlights may include crispy flautas dressed with excellent salsa verde; *panuchos de cochinita* (slow cooked pork and mashed black beans atop a thick tortilla); and tacos like the surprisingly decadent *rajas*, filled with strips of roasted poblanos and tangy *crema*.

Locanda Vini & Olii

Italian

D3

129 Gates Ave. (at Cambridge Pl.)

Subway: Clinton - Washington Avs — Dinner Tue – Sun
Phone: 718-622-9202
Web: www.locandany.com
Prices: $$

With its enchanting atmosphere, well-prepared rustic Italian cuisine, and personalized service, Locanda Vini & Olii merits a trip out to Brooklyn. François Louy, who owns the restaurant with his wife, Catherine, warmly greets guests to this Clinton Hill eatery. Housed in a century-old drugstore, the cozy dining room employs the former apothecary shelves and drawers to display cookbooks, wine bottles, and vintage kitchen equipment.

The cuisine, deeply rooted in Tuscan tradition, is often reinterpreted. Thus mildly sweet chestnut-flavored lasagna noodles might be layered with ground pork sausage, caramelized onions, and chickpeas; and grilled duck breast served simply with pan juices and a dollop of shallot marmalade.

If you're dining with a party of four or more, call ahead to request a tasting menu.

Lucky Eight

Chinese

5204 Eighth Ave. (bet. 52nd & 53rd Sts.)

Subway: 8 Av — Lunch & dinner daily
Phone: 718-851-8862
Web: N/A
Prices:

With its plethora of dim sum spots, Chinese bakeries, and markets hawking everything from live bull frogs to fresh silky tofu, Sunset Park has emerged as Brooklyn's prominent Chinatown. From this, Lucky Eight's excellent food, good service, and pristine setting is an authentic and rewarding find.

Until late afternoon, pick from a list of some 40 items priced at 80 cents each. The laminated dinner menu is crammed with pages illustrating unique, regional Chinese fare. The aptly named signature dish, Pride of Lucky Eight, offers a sumptuous stir-fry of chives, celery, shiitake, and meaty abalone.

The highlight of the no-frills décor is the red-lacquer case at the back of the room, displaying shark fins and other artifacts.

Maria's Bistro Mexicano

B3 **Mexican** 

886 Fifth Ave. (bet. 37th & 38th Sts.)

Subway: 36 St — Lunch & dinner daily
Phone: 718-438-1608
Web: www.mariasbistromexicano.com
Prices: $$

A sunny streak of yellow signage sweeps along the storefront, name emblazoned across it, cheerfully beckoning diners into the lovely quarters. Inside, the narrow dining space is flanked by exposed brick on one side, and brightly painted walls on the other, and trimmed with foliage and colorful knick-knacks. Here at Maria's Bistro, food is as fresh and tasty as the staff is warm and helpful.

Get things going with guac—perfectly made to order and served up in a lava rock mortar with homemade tortilla chips. Dive into the *barbacoa de Borrego*: lip smacking lamb, swathed in banana and avocado leaves, stewed in its own flavorful juices to tender perfection. Short on cash? Check out the website for specials like Unemployed Mondays and Ceviche Thursdays.

Marlow & Sons

A1 **Gastropub** 

81 Broadway (bet. Berry St. & Wythe Ave.)

Subway: Marcy Av — Lunch & dinner daily
Phone: 718-384-1441
Web: www.marlowandsons.com
Prices: $$

By day, Marlow & Sons offers sandwiches and pastries in a store lined with shelves chock-full of boutique provisions. But at night, the atmosphere takes on the role of packed to the rafters foodie pleasure den replete with shabby-chic furnishings and dusky lighting.

The concise menu is all about quality not quantity, features a pastoral tone and oft-changing list of specials that include homemade spaghetti with wilted mustard greens, toasted walnuts, and white beans, all slicked with a luscious and buttery Parmesan sauce. The brick chicken, a menu mainstay, is a gorgeously bronzed, flattened whole bird; and for dessert, maple custard may sound mundane but is anything but—silky smooth, darkly sweet, and matched with crumbly-as-sand shortbread.

Mesa Coyoacan

Mexican

C1

372 Graham Ave. (bet. Conselyea St. & Skillman Ave.)

Subway: Graham Av
Phone: 718-782-8171
Web: www.mesacoyoacan.com
Prices: $$

Lunch Sat – Sun
Dinner nightly

Who knows what possessed the talented Ivan Garcia, the Mexican-born chef who banged out menus for Barrio Chino and Mercadito, to cross the bridge and set up his first solo venture in East Williamsburg's infamous glass tower—but every Brooklynite within spitting distance of this sexy new joint is thanking their sweet fedoras he did.

It's not just the swank interior, fitted out in richly-patterned wallpapers, snug banquettes, and two long communal tables, but the mouthwatering Mexican food: tender little tacos stuffed with tender *suadero*; chicken enchiladas in Garcia's family's *mole poblano* recipe; or *chiles en nogada*, a roasted poblano pepper stuffed with shredded pork, almonds, and fruit, laced with creamy walnut sauce and pomegranate seeds.

Mimi's Hummus

Mediterranean

B4

1209 Cortelyou Rd. (at 12th St.)

Subway: Cortelyou Rd
Phone: 718-284-4444
Web: www.mimishummus.com
Prices: 

Lunch & dinner daily

Think snack taverna and you have the right idea about this adorable newcomer to Brooklyn's ever-changing Ditmas Park. Though the space is teeny-tiny, excellent design and wise use of space give Mimi's a modern holistic feel—with large windows ferrying swaths of natural light into the dining room by day, and an open kitchen adding cheerful ambience come nightfall.

The menu is simple but scrumptious, with super-fresh ingredients and spot-on spices doing the work in dishes like silky fava bean hummus, served with fresh pita; chunky tomato stew paired with plump poached egg and Israeli salad; or irresistibly thick and creamy *labane*, laced with fragrant herbs. At dinner, the menu opens up to include several entrées and take-out is available.

Miranda

A1 — **Fusion** XX

80 Berry St. (at N. 9th St.)

Subway: Bedford Av
Phone: 718-387-0711
Web: www.mirandarestaurant.com
Prices: $$

Lunch Sat – Sun
Dinner Wed – Mon

Run by husband and wife team Mauricio Miranda and Sasha Rodriquez, this welcoming establishment located in Williamsburg has a lovely rustic charm accentuated by straw seat chairs, vintage crockery, and exposed brick walls. The duo has an impressive resume between them that includes work as such esteemed establishments as Spigolo and Alto.

The cuisine here weds the sunny flavors of Italy and Latin America for a menu of creative and vibrant treats. Small plate starters include *arancini* and empanadas; the pastas are made in house as in the perfectly delicious *garganelli*—embellished with sweet peas, fresh mozzarella, and diced *longaniza* (a chewy and slightly spiced sausage); and entrées include roasted pork tenderloin with tomatillo-fresh *mole verde*.

Moim

D4 — **Korean** X

206 Garfield Pl. (at Seventh Ave.)

Subway: 7 Av (Flatbush Ave.)
Phone: 718-499-8092
Web: www.moimrestaurant.com
Prices: $$

Dinner Tue – Sun

Well-known for its dining diversity, Park Slope can add Korean as one more worldly option with Moim, tucked away on a charming brownstone-lined street. The slender space mixes a chic palette of dark wood, cement gray, and green apple, with a small front bar where guests wait for tables while sipping ginger *soju-tinis*.

Moim translates as "gathering," and the sizeable tables encourage sharing of the menu's polished yet inspired takes on Korean classics. The Korean "tapas" are a fine start, followed by delish *pa jun*—thick, smooth-textured pancakes copiously filled with tender scallion greens, squid, and shrimp; while hearty portions of meaty spare ribs in sweet-smoky sauce are creatively accompanied by caramelized chunks of diced sweet potatoes.

Motorino

Pizza

319 Graham Ave. (at Devoe St.)

Subway: Graham Av
Phone: 718-599-8899
Web: www.motorinopizza.com
Prices:

Lunch & dinner daily

This upscale pizzeria draws in a steady flow of passers-by with its seductive aroma of wood-oven baked pies. Embracing Neapolitan tradition, Motorino's Belgian-born Chef/owner Mathieu Palombino is trained in Italy and officially certified by the *Verace Pizza Napoletana*. These impressive pizzas feature San Marzano tomatoes, *mozzarella di bufala*, and often unexpected toppings that highlight the seasons, as in squash with pancetta and sage. A simple selection of antipasti such as imported octopus or roasted beet salad and delicious *dolci* like tiramisu complete the menu.

The pleasant space is furnished with white marble-topped tables, pressed-tin ceilings, and an open kitchen in back. Note the new East Village outpost.

Noodle Pudding

Italian

C3

38 Henry St. (bet. Cranberry & Middagh Sts.)

Subway: High St
Phone: 718-625-3737
Web: N/A
Prices: $$

Dinner Tue – Sun

The mood is perfectly relaxed at this Brooklyn Heights restaurant, where old jazz tunes ooze from the speakers and the friendly waitstaff doles out killer Italian fare (pay attention to those daily specials). In warm weather, the windows fly open and the space has an indoor garden vibe, but you'll want to beat the crowds by arriving early: this neighborhood favorite doesn't take reservations.

Named for a savory pudding baked with noodles and traditionally served on the Sabbath, Noodle Pudding hits its wheelhouse with savory dishes. Dip into a soft bowl of rigatoni *arrabiata* studded with sweet onions and pecorino; or succulent rabbit, braised in red wine with tomatoes, garlic, and fresh herbs, then paired with a fluffy side of polenta.

No. 7

D3 Contemporary

7 Greene Ave. (bet. Cumberland & Fulton Sts.)

Subway: Lafayette Av
Phone: 718-522-6370
Web: www.no7restaurant.com
Prices: $$

Lunch Sat – Sun
Dinner Tue – Sun

Fort Greene gets a significant notch on its foodie belt with No. 7 (an offshot No. 7 Sub is now at the Ace Hotel). This unique, sunken space is anchored by an energetic bar scene up front; and a clean, white-washed dining room in back, that dims into a lovely muted palette with candles.

Chef Tyler Kord, who used to work at Jean-Georges Vongerichten's Perry Street, heads up the talented young team—and the limited, but well-executed, menu reflects his former boss' eye for detail. Try the soft, melt-in-your-mouth, crimson-red lamb carpaccio; or a tight *ballotine* of succulent roasted chicken. And save room for one of the surprising desserts, like an apple tart kicked up with a smear of goat cheese mousse and drops of heat-spiked honey.

1 or 8

A1 Japanese

66 S. 2nd St. (at Wythe Ave.)

Subway: Bedford Av
Phone: 718-384-2152
Web: www.oneoreightbk.com
Prices: $$

Dinner Tue – Sun

Taking its moniker from a Japanese gambling expression that means all or nothing, this atelier of food is a sure thing for a truly creative meal. The lofty space boldly features a blank-canvas décor of monochromatic white, accentuated by an open kitchen.

A comfortable sushi counter indicates the kitchen's serious sushi offerings, while a menu of cooked preparations offers a unique take on Japanese cuisine. Dishes may include octopus ceviche, tender and refreshing, studded with green grapes and a gelée of bonito-infused vinegar; a terrine of beef sukiyaki stacking flavorful rib eye with carrots and shiitakes, with a soft-cooked egg; or a delicate fillet of tilefish grilled in phyllo, dressed with dashi-poached vegetables and classic sauce Américaine.

Osteria il Paiolo

Italian XX

A1

106 N. 6th St. (bet. Berry & Wythe Sts.)

Subway: Bedford Av
Phone: 718-218-7080
Web: www.ilpaiolonyc.com
Prices: **$$**

Lunch Sat – Sun
Dinner nightly

Housed in a raw space of brick and concrete that is prettied by linen-draped, flower-topped tables and serviced by a team of natty veterans, Williamsburg's Osteria il Pailo rocks a slick vibe that is decidedly urbane for this hipster enclave.

The impressive Northern Italian cuisine features an ingredient-driven menu incorporating several daily specials, such as shaved fennel salad studded with bits of oxtail and brightly dressed with fresh herbs. Also on offer is a listing of heirloom polenta and house-made pastas—the *maccheroncini alla crudaiola* combines rigatoni with blistered cherry tomatoes, a slab of cool imported *burrata*, and fresh basil that pools into a creamy pink sauce. Desserts include a rich vanilla bean-flecked panna cotta.

Pacificana

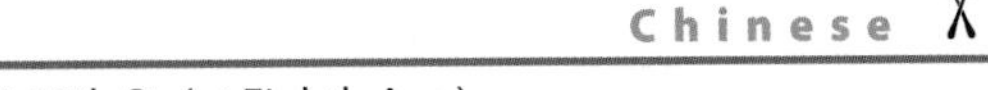

Chinese XX

A4

813 55th St. (at Eighth Ave.)

Subway: 8 Av
Phone: 718-871-2880
Web: N/A
Prices: **$$**

Lunch & dinner daily

You can thank Sunset Park's growing Asian population for the influx of excellent Chinese restaurants into this far-flung pocket of Brooklyn. Among the best of the lot is Pacificana, a bright, airy restaurant—think vaulted ceilings, jumbo windows, and an open kitchen sporting floor-to-ceiling fish tanks—tucked into a second floor space off bustling Eighth Avenue.

Dim sum carts packed to the gills with dishes like crispy pork over jelly fish, and tender shrimp dumplings, roll by like temptations-on-wheels, as dinner guests tuck into traditional fare like the rich, fragrant South China duck casserole; or chicken with crunchy, pale green preserved mustard greens, paired with preserved black beans and a steaming bowl of fluffy white rice.

Brooklyn

Paulie Gee's

Pizza

B1

60 Greenpoint Ave. (bet. Franklin & West Sts.)

Subway: Greenpoint Av
Dinner Tue – Sun
Phone: 347-987-3747
Web: www.pauliegee.com
Prices: 

Owner Paul Gianonne, aka Paulie Gee, channeled a lifelong love of pizza into this charmingly delicious newcomer that feels as if it has been around forever. Rustic in appearance, the room's cool concrete and brick elements are warmed by the glow of the wood-burning pizza oven imported from Naples. It's from here that Gianonne and son work their magic.

The addictive crust is beguilingly moist and chewy, perfumed with smoke, and adroitly salted. Pizza dominates the menu with tempting combinations, excellent ingredients, and whimsical titles. Offerings may include the Arugula Shmoogala topped with baby arugula and Parmigiano Reggiano; and the Baconmarmalade Picante slathered with *fior di latte*, dollops of spiced bacon marmalade, and red onion.

The Pearl Room

Contemporary

A4

8201 Third Ave. (at 82nd St.)

Subway: 86 St
Lunch & dinner daily
Phone: 718-833-6666
Web: www.thepearlroom.net
Prices: $$

With its jumbo garden and bright, sun-streaked dining room, this Brooklyn steady is a solid choice year-round. Most days, you'll catch a glimpse of the charming Chef/owner Anthony Rinaldi floating around, working his magic back in the kitchen and out in the dining room.

The Pearl Room is known for its vast seafood spread, and Rinaldi's wheelhouse is intricately designed fish plates like a lemon sole, coated in golden breading and pine nuts, and then tossed in a perfectly balanced lemongrass-kiwi sauce. But don't discount his other offerings—the menu boasts a wealth of vegetarian and meat dishes, many of them ample enough to split, as well as a few tongue-wagging desserts like a trio of luscious chocolate truffles rolled in bright green pistachios.

Peter Luger ✿

Steakhouse

A1

178 Broadway (at Driggs Ave.)

Lunch & dinner daily

Subway: Marcy Av
Phone: 718-387-7400
Web: www.peterluger.com
Prices: $$$

Peter Luger

Is there anything left to be said about this iconic Brooklyn steakhouse that hasn't been said before? Well, one: a recent face-lift has one of the dining rooms looking uncharacteristically sparkly and new. Otherwise, the rest of this beloved restaurant, that sits beside the Williamsburg Bridge since 1887, is mercifully the same.

Crack the menu at Luger's and you'll find some worthy things in there to divert your attention, like a freshly ground burger (served at lunch only) or soft cheesecake sporting whipped *schlag*—but the indisputable star of this show is the mouthwatering Porterhouse. The regulars order it by number for the table ("Porterhouse for 2, 3, or 4"), assign a temperature to the dry-aged beauty, and then tack on a few delicious sides like crispy hash browns, garlicky creamed spinach, or thick, scrumptious slabs of bacon.

If it seems like you have to flag down the somewhat indifferent all-male waitstaff—well, try to take it as a natural extension of the clanking beer hall atmosphere. The steak is well worth it, and you can always remind them it's a woman—not a man—who holds Luger's illustrious buyer position, choosing the steaks fit to be served in this den of macho.

Picket Fence

B4 **American**

1310 Cortelyou Rd. (at Argyle Rd.)

Subway: Cortelyou Rd
Phone: 718-282-6661
Web: www.picketfencebrooklyn.com
Prices: $$

Lunch & dinner daily

Nestled into Ditmas Park, a slowly gentrifying Brooklyn neighborhood lined with Victorian homes and (gasp) real live trees, Picket Fence is pure comfort. In spring, the wide doors swing open to the sidewalk, flooding light into the beautiful, sunny dining room, lined with rattan chairs and cozy banquettes. Out back, a cheerful little garden offers waddle space for the hood's growing baby scene.

The no-fuss food does what it does simply and deliciously—with a broad menu that might include a scrumptious turkey meatloaf sandwich, the tender slices of meat studded with carrots, onions, and spices, and loaded onto a brioche bun with gravy, caramelized onions, and cheddar cheese; or a walnut-crusted sliver of cheesecake laced with strawberry compote.

Prime Meats

C4 **Gastropub**

465 Court St. (at Luquer St.)

Subway: Smith - 9 Sts.
Phone: 718-254-0327
Web: www.frankspm.com
Prices: $$

Lunch & dinner daily

From the Franks (of Frankies 457 Spuntino) comes this neighborhood darling inspired by a vintage sign purchased prior to the restaurant's inception. Exposed brick, dark woods, and filament-bulbs set an almost too perfect scene for throngs of Brooklyn foodies lining the seat-less bar, sipping expertly crafted libations.

Once seated, the personable staff and friendly vibe relegates any memory of a wait to the past, especially once the hearty, old-world selection of small plates and house specials arrives. Simplicity reigns supreme here, with dry-aged steaks or dishes of *weisswurst*, a traditional German white sausage, served with sweet mustard, and a pretzel roll. Complete meals with selections of American farmstead cheese with bread, nuts, and honey.

Purple Yam

Asian

1314 Cortelyou Rd. (at Rugby Rd.)

Subway: Cortelyou Rd
Phone: 718-940-8188
Web: www.purpleyamnyc.com
Prices: $$

Lunch Mon – Fri
Dinner nightly

What could be just another hip neighborhood restaurant gets elevated to destination restaurant heights in the hands of talented chef, Romy Dorotan, and his wife, Amy Besa. After losing their lease at Cendrillon, the Filipino restaurant they ran in SoHo, the pair relocated to Ditmas Park's Cortelyou Road, a Victorian-strewn street that's become a sort of restaurant row for the ever-gentrifying neighborhood.

With the new menu, Dorotan ventures into even more parts of Asia, most notably toward Korea, then ties the dishes together with a European sensibility. Don't miss the outstanding duck leg *betutu* with taro leaves, slow-cooked in Balinese spices, and coconut milk to such silky perfection, so good, they should bottle the sauce and sell it.

Quercy

French 

242 Court St. (bet. Baltic & Kane Sts.)

Subway: Bergen St (Smith St.)
Phone: 718-243-2151
Web: N/A
Prices: $$

Lunch Sat – Sun
Dinner nightly

Named for the chef's hometown in Southern France, Quercy is a truly satisfying destination for authentic bistro fare. With its cobalt blue façade, checkerboard-tile floor, and a chalkboard scrawled *carte*, this Cobble Hill charmer emanates a comforting aura. The blue and white color scheme is nicely accented with touches of red, and the small art deco bar is a cozy spot to sip an aperitif prior to sitting at one of the dining room's white-paper-topped tables, tended by a cordial staff.

As one would hope and expect, the menu serves up heartwarming classics like *escargot au Cognac*; fork-tender bœuf Bourguignon; and tarte Tatin dressed with a dollop of crème fraîche, along with a wine list that highlights the varietals of Southwestern France.

River Café ✿

C2 **Contemporary** XXX

1 Water St. (bet. Furman & Old Fulton Sts.)

Subway: High St — Lunch & dinner daily
Phone: 718-522-5200
Web: www.rivercafe.com
Prices: $$$$

The River Cafe

Talk about finder's keepers. It has been more than thirty years since Michael "Buzzy" O'Keefe first swung open the doors to the celebrated River Café, and boy has the neighborhood changed. The choice of location—tucked into a sketchy slice of abandoned waterfront underneath the towering Brooklyn Bridge—probably struck people as odd back in 1977.

But now that the area is gorgeously restored, a history-filled walk across the bridge and into this Brooklyn neighborhood, with its cobblestoned streets, stunning views of Manhattan, and small-town vibe, is a must-do afternoon for any self-respecting tourist.

Resting along the water, you'll find a perfect cap to the day in River Café—where guests (hopefully in jackets after 5:00 P.M.) can meander through gardens, soak in mind-boggling views of the Manhattan skyline and bridge, and dig into delicious contemporary fare like a soup bobbing with poached Maine peekytoe crab and humming with notes of chili, coconut, and lemongrass; or delicate branzino laced with warm lemon juice and paired with al dente zucchini, blistered cherry tomatoes, and an irresistibly delicious and crunchy stuffing choc-a-block with tender shrimp and savory chorizo.

Roberta's

Pizza

261 Moore St. (bet. Bogart & White Sts.)

Subway: Morgan Av — Lunch & dinner daily
Phone: 718-417-1118
Web: www.robertaspizza.com
Prices: $$

To really understand Brooklyn's new food guard, you'll want to start in one of its more challenged hoods. Surrounded by industrial warehouses and deserted lots, there's not a lot to welcome you into this Bushwick trailblazer, but its what's inside that counts—a big, cozy room filled with wooden tables and a laid-back bar; a roaring brick oven; and a rooftop farm that Alice Waters herself helped fund.

Roberta's may have first caught buzz for their bubbling pizzas, but the real stars are tucked into the dinner menu, which may disclose honeycomb tripe braised in sweet tomato sauce with pecorino; near-translucent ribbons of *lardo* over freshly grilled sourdough bread; or perfectly chewy orecchiette in a spicy pork ragù studded with crispy *guanciale*.

Roman's

Italian 

243 DeKalb Ave. (bet. Clermont & Vanderbilt Aves.)

Subway: Lafayette Av — Dinner Tue – Sun
Phone: 718-622-5300
Web: www.romansnyc.com
Prices: $$

Your *mamma* didn't give you much of a choice for dinner, and neither will Andrew Tarlow and Mark Firth—at least not on the menu at their newest restaurant. But have faith, young Brooklyn—for this is the brilliant duo behind Diner and Marlow & Sons, two wildly successful Williamsburg restaurants that helped put a distinct Brooklyn cuisine on the map.

Housed in the duo's old Bonita space, Roman's is small and warm, with candlelight bouncing off white tiled walls, and blazing color mosaic tiles dotting the room. The menu offers a handful of simple, but delicious dishes that might include sweet, grassy carrot ribbons tossed with raisins, nuts, and parsley; tender pasta rings stuffed with fresh ricotta over chunky tomato sauce; or creamy chocolate gelato.

Rye

American 

A1

247 S. 1st St. (bet. Havemeyer and Roebling Sts.)

Subway: Marcy Av
Phone: 718-218-8047
Web: www.ryerestaurant.com
Prices: $$

Lunch Sun
Dinner nightly

Chef/owner Cal Elliott's solo venture is housed in a non-descript section of south Williamsburg that coolly lacks any signage to promote its existence. The former bodega is outfitted with rough hewn wood flooring, zinc-topped tables, and exposed filament bulbs. The hefty bar, restored by the chef, dominates the intimate room; and arched, mirror-backed shelving is stocked with a collection of brown liquors.

The succinct menu of snacks and grilled items boasts classic touches that reflect the kitchen's talents and skill. Offerings may include house-made gnocchi, topped with shreds of meltingly tender duck confit; golden and crisp, pan-roasted halibut drizzled with herb-flecked beurre blanc; or warm and fudgy chocolate cake with vanilla ice cream.

Savoia

Italian 

C4

277 Smith St. (bet. De Graw & Sackett Sts.)

Subway: Carroll St
Phone: 718-797-2727
Web: N/A
Prices: $$

Lunch & dinner daily

Whether young at-home moms, lunching construction crews, or savvy foreign visitors, all walks of life are drawn to this Smith Street charmer, pastorally furnished with wooden tables and straw-seat chairs. Exposed brick and colorful tiles complement the two-room setting, equipped with a wood-burning pizza oven. Fittingly, Savoia devotes a large portion of its menu to manifold pizza offerings made in the Neopolitan tradition. Not in the mood for pizza? There is also an ample selection of gratifying pastas, like the linguini with clams (heightened here with ground *soppressata*); as well as heartier items like the roasted pork chop with eggplant caponata and grilled *orata* with sun dried tomatoes.

Affable service adds to Savoia's casual vibe.

Saul 

Contemporary XX

C3

140 Smith St. (bet. Bergen & Dean Sts.)

Subway: Bergen St (Smith St.) — Dinner nightly
Phone: 718-935-9844
Web: www.saulrestaurant.com
Prices: $$$

Daniel Krieger

With a seemingly endless row of cafés and hip boutiques, there's a lot to fill an afternoon along Brooklyn's Smith Street, a popular thoroughfare tucked into quaint, yuppified Boerum Hill. But no matter where your day leads you, be sure to set aside a few hours for a meal at Saul, a charming, brick-lined restaurant with pressed-tin ceilings and hardwood floors.

Co-owner and chef, Saul Bolton, cut his teeth with Le Bernardin's Eric Ripert, and clearly brought his master's penchant for intricate technique and pristine seafood across the river with him. Look for plump, pan-seared sardines, paired with eggplant caponata, sweet pine nuts, and crispy candied lemon; succulent Giannone Farms chicken, roasted to juicy perfection and stuffed with spinach, butternut squash, and shallots, then fanned over a riot of seasonal vegetables; and moist apple cake, fragrant with crisp apples, brown sugar, cinnamon, apple cider, cloves, and a hint of lemon juice.

Saul's considerable charms don't stop at the food. The precise, oh-so-warm staff nails the timing of each dish; and the good vibes set forth by the happy buzz of friends catching up after a hard day in the city are positively contagious.

Sea

Thai

A1

114 N. 6th St. (bet. Berry St. & Wythe Ave.)

Subway: Bedford Av
Lunch & dinner daily
Phone: 718-384-8850
Web: www.spicethainyc.com
Prices: ⊖⊖

Resembling a trendy Manhattan lounge yet serving fresh, well-made Asian cuisine, Sea is an exotic bird among the small hipster bars of Williamsburg. The cavernous space pulsates with energy, and its popularity is enjoyed by a diverse clientele, from young families to large after-work groups. The dining room, flanked by two bars, has an industrial-chic vibe with its concrete floor and cement walls complemented by a section of seating around a reflecting pool crowned by a life-size Buddha.

Considering the festive environs, the staff is impressively gracious and attentive.

The Thai-focused menu may lack authenticity but is reasonably priced and extensive in its offerings of dumplings, spring rolls, and salads, along with curries and sautéed dishes.

Sette Enoteca & Cucina

Italian

D4

207 Seventh Ave. (at 3rd St.)

Subway: 7 Av (9th St.)
Lunch & dinner daily
Phone: 718-499-7767
Web: www.setteparkslope.com
Prices: $$

This consistently excellent Park Slope Italian gem is popular with most everyone—from cool couples lingering over shared plates of light, crispy *fritto misto*, to hip moms twirling pappardelle with braised lamb and shaved Parmesan, alongside their offspring sharing pizzas. Rustic entrées offer the likes of grilled salmon with arugula and fresh orange salad; these skillful preparations can be observed from the open kitchen.

Complement meals with selections from the inexpensive Italian wine list, offering a range of bottles under $20, and many available by the glass or *quartino*.

This bustling corner location features covered outdoor dining, a bar, and a contemporary dining room with chunky, blonde wooden tables, and metallic-fabric-covered banquettes.

Stone Park Cafe

Contemporary

324 Fifth Ave. (at 3rd St.)

Subway: Union St
Phone: 718-369-0082
Web: www.stoneparkcafe.com
Prices: $$

Lunch Tue – Sun
Dinner nightly

At this corner location, large windows peer onto Park Slope's vibrant Fifth Avenue thoroughfare and small park namesake. Opened in 2004, Stone Park Cafe remains popular with neighborhood couples and families seeking seasonally inspired, creative fare. Offerings may range from smoked salmon cheesecake to lamb cassoulet. The $30 prix-fixe menu option is a very good value for such quality.

The light and airy interior is simply accented with exposed brick, light wood, and pale sage walls. A long bar near the entrance is a welcome spot for a pre-dinner cocktail. In the sunken dining room, tables are covered with white linens, brown paper, and clear glass votives. Weather permitting, alfresco sidewalk seating is available.

Sui Ren

Japanese

302 Metropolitan Ave. (bet. Driggs Ave. & Roebling St.)

Subway: Bedford Av
Phone: 718-218-7878
Web: www.suirennyc.com
Prices:

Dinner Tue – Sun

Helmed by a team of Kai and Bond Street alumni, this Williamsburg *izakaya* (Japanese pub) offers an extensive listing of cold and hot small plates, fire-kissed skewers of *yakitori*, deep fried *kushiage*, and daily specials. Whittling the menu down to just a few choices is challenging, so bring friends for a tour that includes such *oishii* preparations as lusciously tender grilled octopus with yuzu salt, ramen embellished with poached tuna belly and tuna jerky, and *okonomiyaki*—a Jackson Pollack-looking pancake filled with cabbage and squid (or pork) and drizzled with sweet-dark sauce and mayonnaise.

The chic spot has an earthy aesthetic with dark-wood furnishings and artist-made pendant lighting; the spacious backyard offers a pleasant warm-weather seat.

The Smoke Joint

Barbecue

87 S. Elliot Pl. (bet. Fulton St & Lafayette Ave.)

Subway: Lafayette Av — Lunch & dinner daily
Phone: 718-797-1011
Web: www.thesmokejoint.com
Prices: ◎◎

Just steps away from the Brooklyn Academy of Music (BAM), harmonic barbecue bliss awaits courtesy of pedigreed restaurateurs, Craig Samuel (of City Hall) and Ben Grossman (of Picholine and La Grenouille).

Unlike some of its too-cool-for-school Brooklyn cousins, Fort Greene is hip but playfully unpretentious—and those tired of the servers who skulk around Williamsburg will eat up the waitstaff's terrific energy. An irresistible combination when paired with lip-smacking fare like the tender, house-smoked chicken; meltingly good pulled pork; meaty, dry-rubbed ribs; or creamy macaroni and cheese, arguably some of the best in the city. Bourbon freaks should make their way to the adjoined Pig Bar, where brown liquor gets top shelf treatment.

Tanoreen

Middle Eastern

7523 Third Ave. (at 76th St.)

Subway: 77 St — Lunch & dinner Tue – Sun
Phone: 718-748-5600
Web: www.tanoreen.com
Prices: ◎◎

In a roomy new setting with glassed-in sidewalk dining and jewel-toned sconces, Tanoreen continues to impress with its extensive menu of Middle Eastern home-style specialties. Chef/owner Rawia Bishara may have started her career by feeding friends and families at countless dinner parties, but today she runs this popular operation with her daughter for the city's eager destination-driven foodies.

Meals graciously commence with house-pickled vegetables and warm breads, prepping the way for an array of exotic delights such as: *makdous*—pickled baby eggplant stuffed with walnuts; *sujok*—thin slices of Armenian dried beef in a crimson sauce of red pepper, garlic, and olive oil; and *musakhan*—grilled flatbread topped with sumac-seasoned chicken.

Thistle Hill Tavern

Contemporary

B3

441 Seventh Ave. (at 15th St.)

Subway: 15 St - Prospect Park — Lunch & dinner daily
Phone: 347-599-1262
Web: www.thistlehillbrooklyn.com
Prices: $$

This South Slope newbie conjures a classic tavern ambience usually found in a longtime neighborhood favorite. The corner location is flanked by sidewalk seating for a leisurely al fresco lunch; inside, exposed brick and chocolate–brown wainscoting paint a warm and inviting scene.

Light fare is on order for lunch, as in the market-fresh chopped salad of heirloom tomatoes, corn sliced off the cob, bacon, and ricotta salata; sandwiches may include a grilled mushroom panino stuffed with goat cheese and basil alongside fries paired with homemade ketchup. Dinner offerings are a hearty expansion of the seasonal, locally sourced dishes, while desserts feature the likes of an espresso semifreddo showered with dark cherries, Marcona almonds, and chocolate.

Tuscany Grill

Italian 

A4

8620 Third Ave. (bet. 86th & 87th Sts.)

Subway: 86 St — Dinner nightly
Phone: 718-921-5633
Web: N/A
Prices: $$

Bay Ridge's ever-changing demographic does not deter this charismatic, quintessential neighborhood restaurant from serving Italian-American favorites to a loyal cadre of locals who come for dishes that burst with flavor as well as to share their latest adventures with the waitstaff.

The menu offers hefty portions of honest, good food, such as homey Hunter-style *farfalle* pasta baked in tomatoes, mushrooms, and cheese, with sweet and hot sausage. Crostini of fresh, milky ricotta, roasted red bell pepper, and basil leaf over toast brushed with quality olive oil makes a wonderful prelude to any meal. Save room for decadent house-made desserts such as the pignoli tart—lemony and piney—served in a crust that is truly worth every buttery calorie.

Umi Nom

B2

Asian

433 DeKalb Ave. (bet. Classon Ave. & Taaffe Pl.)

Subway: Classon Av

Lunch & dinner Mon – Sat

Phone: 718-789-8806

Web: www.uminom.com

Prices: $$

You'll have to travel deep into Pratt's somewhat dodgy backyard for this one, but this popular new Southeast Asian charmer is well worth the adventure to Bed Stuy. The restaurant arrives courtesy of King Phojanakong, the man behind the Lower East Side's Kuma Inn, and owns a pretty, minimalist design fitted out with wooden pews, sultry lighting slung from brick walls, and a half-open kitchen emitting heavenly drafts from the wok.

Small plates abound on the menu, which might offer tender, market-fresh baby bok choy simmered with garlic and creamy butter; a plate of gorgeous prawns, served head-on in a devilishly spicy, lip-smacking chili sauce; or mackerel, grilled to a lovely char and paired with bright strips of pickled carrots and cool cucumber.

The Vanderbilt

D4

Contemporary

570 Vanderbilt Ave. (at Bergen St.)

Subway: Bergen St (Flatbush Ave.)

Lunch Sat – Sun
Dinner nightly

Phone: 718-623-0570

Web: www.thevanderbiltnyc.com

Prices: $$

Chef Saul Bolton's new venture, opened in partnership with Ben Daitz, is the perfect contrast to his beloved namesake dining room on Smith Street. This lively, loud, and packed Prospect Heights spot, clad in reclaimed wood and marble-topped communal tables, is great for boisterous groups or a quick solo bite at the bar offering a worldly assemblage of mouthwatering small plates.

The fuss-free and fun fare may include the likes of caramelized Brussels sprouts tossed with lime, honey, and *sriracha* sauce; a rich, luscious block of crispy pig's feet draped with tart and creamy sauce *gribiche*; or delicately fried spiced-apple turnover for dessert. A blackboard list of thirst-quenching spirits adds to the Vanderbilt's casually sophisticated appeal.

Vinegar Hill House

American

D2

72 Hudson Ave. (near Water St.)

Subway: York St — Dinner Tue – Sun
Phone: 718-522-1018
Web: www.vinegarhillhouse.com
Prices: $$

Sam Buffa and Jean Adamson's cozy little spot couldn't have arrived at this up-and-coming neighborhood at a more ideal moment. Its isolated, restaurant-starved locale between DUMBO and the Brooklyn Navy Yards leaves Vinegar Hill packed nightly. That the owners live over the space adds to the homey warmth; this is their labor of love.

Those familiar with Brooklyn's latest trends will recognize the hodge-podge interior and claims of sustainable fish. What sets this place apart is its wood-burning oven, which might produce perfectly-charred sourdough bread or a wood-fired tart with collard greens and pork belly. Straightforward preparations may include roasted pollock with Brussel sprouts or braised beef cheeks with celeriac and chestnut honey.

Vutera

Mediterranean

A1

345 Grand St. (bet. Havemeyer St. & Marcy Ave.)

Subway: Bedford Av — Dinner nightly
Phone: 718-388-8451
Web: N/A
Prices: $$

Head to the Rose Live Music performance space, bypass the lounge's tattooed bartender, and descend a small flight of stairs to reach this basement restaurant replete with a charmingly rough-hewn cellar look that will have you wondering if you've fallen down a rabbit hole. Bathed in candlelight, the setting is cloaked in exposed brick and stone, and furnished with flower-topped tables set with a mix-and-match collection of chairs.

The menu's sunny flavors are abundant in small plates like the fresh Spanish mackerel *escabeche* with ruby grapefruit; or entrées of tender, pan-fried parsnip gnocchi with a pesto of beet greens and blue cheese sauce. The honey-drizzled cannoli filled with Salvatore Brooklyn ricotta thinks globally and acts locally.

Waterfalls Café

Middle Eastern

144 Atlantic Ave. (bet. Clinton & Henry Sts.)

Subway: Borough Hall — Lunch & dinner daily
Phone: 718-488-8886
Web: www.waterfallscafe.com
Prices: ⓈⓈ

Deliciously uncompromised, made-to-order Middle Eastern food: what's not to love at the Waterfalls Café, a little café that rises above the rush of Arabic joints that cluster along this stretch of Atlantic Avenue? Perhaps the service, which can be a bit stilted and off-the-mark from time to time—that said, you'll soon realize that patience is a mighty big virtue here.

The reward is in the spectacularly creamy hummus; light-as-air falafel, fresh and crackling from the fryer; moist stuffed grape leaves; perfectly-spiced *moujadarra*, spiked with tender caramelized onions; and supremely tender chunks of lamb *shawarma*, served with fresh pita. No alcohol is served, but fragrant teas and Arabic coffee finish the meal; and takeout is available.

World Tong

Chinese

6202 Eighteenth Ave. (at 62nd St.)

Subway: 18 Av — Lunch & dinner daily
Phone: 718-236-8118
Web: N/A
Prices: ⓈⓈ

With its bland dining room and unadorned interior, this monochromatic Bensonhurst gem gets right down to business by putting its money where its customers mouths would like to be—wrapped around some killer dim sum. And judging from the flood of locals who patron the joint, this no-nonsense approach appears to be right on cue.

Dreamy carts wheeling past showcase an endless array of tiny delights, like sticky-rice dumplings wrapped in lotus leaves; golden shrimp balls; or spare ribs with black bean sauce and taro. Don't miss the phenomenal parade of tender soup dumplings, a variety of soft pouches bursting with spice-infused broths, including star anise, clove, and ginger; or the strange-smelling, but oddly addictive, durian pastries.

Zenkichi

Japanese

A1

77 N. 6th St. (at Wythe Ave.)

Subway: Bedford Av

Dinner Wed – Sun

Phone: 718-388-8985

Web: www.zenkichi.com

Prices: $$

Beyond a rather daunting wood-armored exterior, Zenkichi's small entryway is practically camouflaged. Once inside however, warm greetings ensue as groups small and large are escorted through the dim, three-level space to private dining booths. Service is serious here; when ready to order, summon the staff with the tabletop button.

The *izakaya* menu features an assortment of snacks designed to be enjoyed with sake. Ordering à la carte is fine, but more impressive is the well-priced omakase: an eight-course seasonal feast that may feature chilled plates of Kumamoto oysters; winter salad topped with grilled scallops; roasted honey-soy duck; or rice flavored with free-range chicken and mushrooms.

Return visits are inevitable—just remember to reserve.

Bib Gourmand ☺ indicates our inspectors' favorites for good value.

Jeanine C. Hart/MICHELIN

Queens

Queens

Nearly as large as Manhattan, the Bronx, and Staten Island combined, the borough of Queens covers 120 square miles on the western end of Long Island. Thousands of immigrants arriving here each year make Queens the most culturally diverse county in the country. They are drawn to the relatively affordable housing, a familial quality of life, and the tight-knit cultural communities formed by extended immigrant families. Such a unique convergence results in the borough's international flavor, drawing throngs of New Yorkers eager to dine on affordable, ethnic eats.

Global Buffet

Stroll through Astoria, a charming quarter of brick row houses and Mediterranean groceries. Discover grilled octopus and baklava at one of the many terrific Greek restaurants; make your way to Little Egypt on Steinway Street for a juicy kebab; or chow on Czech kielbasas at the local *biergarten*. Along global lines, the **Hot Bread Kitchen** project is introducing NYers to a selection of traditional breads from around the world. Beer-lovers, on any lazy day, should frequent Astoria's newest beer havens.

For an intimate setting with a serious selection head to **Sweet Afton**; and for the ultimate alfresco experience, **Studio Square** is THE place! Entertain the crowds with a night of karaoke and peruse the unique beer offerings at **Mingle Beer House**.

Pan-Asian

Flushing still reigns as Queens' most vibrant Asian neighborhood; drop in for dim sum or slurp an avocado shake and a savory bowl of hot *pho* like you'd find street side in Saigon. Food vendors at Flushing's mini-malls offer a feast for the ravenous that's light on pockets with delights from every corner of China. You'll find anything at these stalls including hand pulled noodles, fiery Sichuan chili-oil dishes, peking duck pancakes, *bings*, and buns in a bustling setting that's right out of a Hong Kong alley. And the Chinese offerings don't stop here! If in the mood for vegetarian kosher Chinese delights, forge ahead on Main Street to **Buddha Bodai**. En-route to JFK, stop by **Warung Kario** on Liberty Avenue for unique Indonesian-Surinamese cuisine.

Traveling east is the **Queens Country Farm Museum**. Considered one of the largest working farms in the city, it supports sustainable farming, offers farm-to-table meals, and is replete with livestock, a greenhouse complex, and educational programs.

Eating in Elmhurst

Vivacity and diversity personify Elmhurst, the thriving hearth to immigrants primarily from China, Southeast Asia, and Latin America. The Royal Kathin, a celebration that occurs at the end of Thailand's rainy season, pays homage to the spirit of the monks. The Elmhurst adaptation may lack the floods, but offers a bounty of faithful Thai foods. Whitney Avenue hosts a restaurant row with a range of tiny Southeast Asian storefronts. Indulge your *gado gado* craving at **Minangasli** or **Upi Jaya** and get your *laksa* on at **Taste Good**. Elmhurst spans the globe so if the powerful and pungent flavors of Southeast Asia aren't your thing, dive into an Argentinean *parilla* for a shift from Asia to the Americas.

A Marriage of Cultures

Jackson Heights is home to a distinct South Asian community. Take in the *bhangra* beats blaring from cars rolling along 74th Street, a dynamic commercial stretch of Indian markets, Bengali sweet shops, and Himalayan-style eateries. Some faves include Indian *tandoor* specialties and Tibetan *momos* (beef dumplings). Latin Americans from Colombia, Ecuador, Argentina, Uruguay, Peru, and Mexico also make up a large part of the demographic here.

Catering to their tastes, Roosevelt Avenue sizzles with a sampling of taquerias, Colombian coffee shops, and Argentinean bakeries. The bustling thoroughfare connects several neighborhoods, shape shifting from country to country.

Follow the Avenue west to Woodside, where Irish bars commingle with fiery Thai spots. Once home to a large Irish population Woodside now shares its blocks with a small Thai and Filipino population. The kelly green awnings of decade-old pubs dot the streets and clover-covered doors advertise in Gaelic. Here **Donovan's** has one of the best burgers in all the five boroughs. Alongside is Little Manila, an eight-block stretch of Roosevelt Avenue, where you can find Filipino groceries and restaurants galore. The recent opening of **Jollibee**, the ultra-popular fast-food chain, has folks lined up for a taste of home.

On Queens Boulevard in Sunnyside (one of the most divergent 'hoods), eat your way through Korea, Columbia, Mexico, Romania, China, and Turkey. Of course, not in one day!

Bites by the Bay

May through October, head over to Water Taxi Beach at Hunters Point to soak in views of the Manhattan skyline over burgers and beers. In late June, check out The New York City Food Film Festival where food and film lovers gather to view screenings of food films while noshing on a range of scrumptious nibbles.

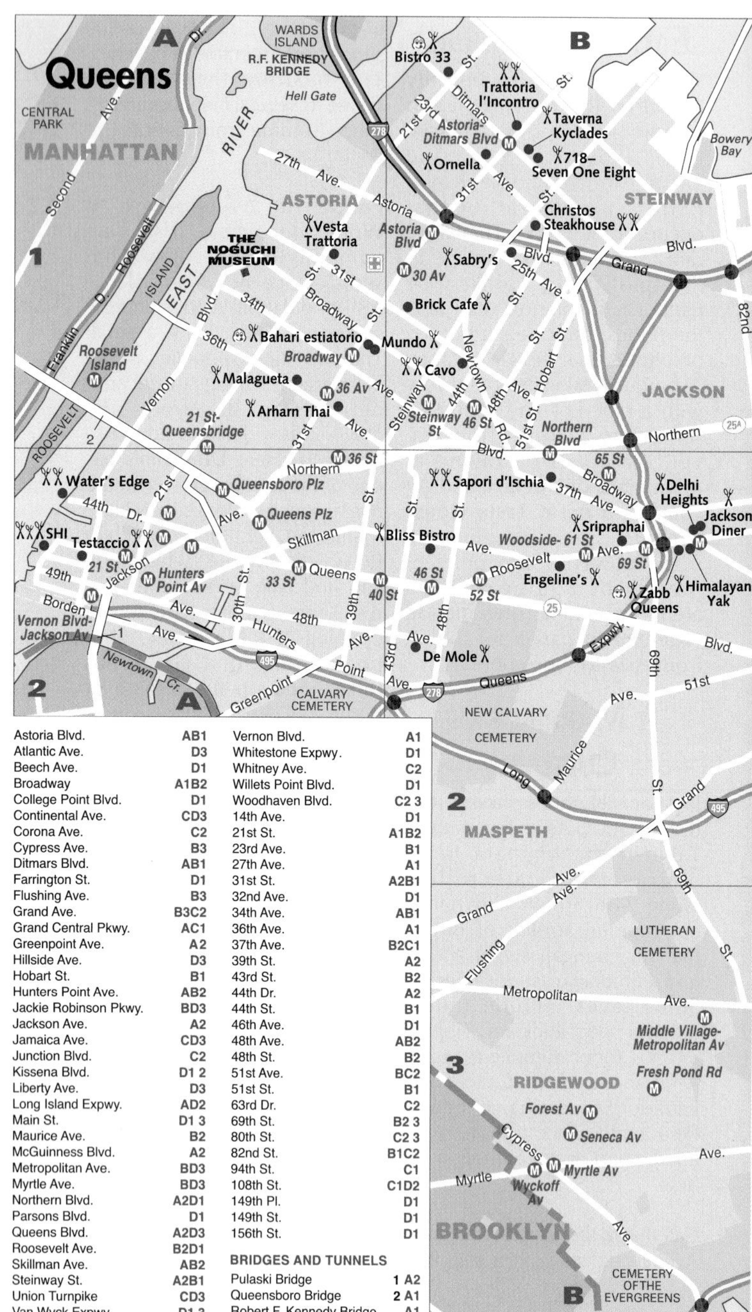

Astoria Blvd.	AB1	Vernon Blvd.	A1
Atlantic Ave.	D3	Whitestone Expwy.	D1
Beech Ave.	D1	Whitney Ave.	C2
Broadway	A1B2	Willets Point Blvd.	D1
College Point Blvd.	D1	Woodhaven Blvd.	C2 3
Continental Ave.	CD3	14th Ave.	D1
Corona Ave.	C2	21st St.	A1B2
Cypress Ave.	B3	23rd Ave.	B1
Ditmars Blvd.	AB1	27th Ave.	A1
Farrington St.	D1	31st St.	A2B1
Flushing Ave.	B3	32nd Ave.	D1
Grand Ave.	B3C2	34th Ave.	AB1
Grand Central Pkwy.	AC1	36th Ave.	A1
Greenpoint Ave.	A2	37th Ave.	B2C1
Hillside Ave.	D3	39th St.	A2
Hobart St.	B1	43rd St.	B2
Hunters Point Ave.	AB2	44th Dr.	A2
Jackie Robinson Pkwy.	BD3	44th St.	B1
Jackson Ave.	A2	46th Ave.	D1
Jamaica Ave.	CD3	48th Ave.	AB2
Junction Blvd.	C2	48th St.	B2
Kissena Blvd.	D1 2	51st Ave.	BC2
Liberty Ave.	D3	51st St.	B1
Long Island Expwy.	AD2	63rd Dr.	C2
Main St.	D1 3	69th St.	B2 3
Maurice Ave.	B2	80th St.	C2 3
McGuinness Blvd.	A2	82nd St.	B1C2
Metropolitan Ave.	BD3	94th St.	C1
Myrtle Ave.	BD3	108th St.	C1D2
Northern Blvd.	A2D1	149th Pl.	D1
Parsons Blvd.	D1	149th St.	D1
Queens Blvd.	A2D3	156th St.	D1
Roosevelt Ave.	B2D1		
Skillman Ave.	AB2	**BRIDGES AND TUNNELS**	
Steinway St.	A2B1	Pulaski Bridge	1 A2
Union Turnpike	CD3	Queensboro Bridge	2 A1
Van Wyck Expwy.	D1 3	Robert F. Kennedy Bridge	A1

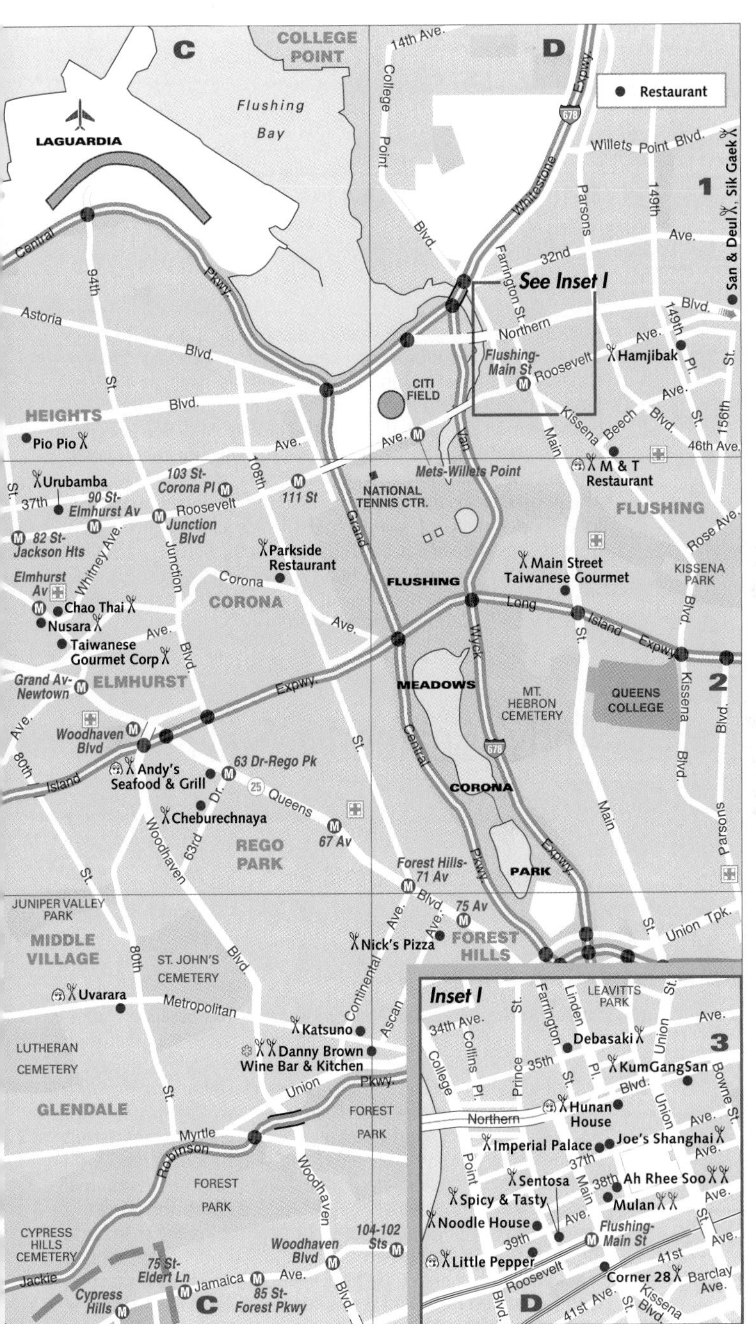

COLLEGE POINT
C
D
Restaurant
LAGUARDIA
Flushing Bay
Pio Pio
Urubamba
Parkside Restaurant
Chao Thai
Nusara
Taiwanese Gourmet Corp
Andy's Seafood & Grill
Cheburechnaya
Main Street Taiwanese Gourmet
M & T Restaurant
Hamjibak
San & Deul, Sik Gaek
See Inset I
CITI FIELD
NATIONAL TENNIS CTR.
FLUSHING
MEADOWS
CORONA
PARK
MT. HEBRON CEMETERY
QUEENS COLLEGE
KISSENA PARK
HEIGHTS
CORONA
ELMHURST
REGO PARK
FOREST HILLS
MIDDLE VILLAGE
JUNIPER VALLEY PARK
ST. JOHN'S CEMETERY
LUTHERAN CEMETERY
GLENDALE
FOREST PARK
CYPRESS HILLS CEMETERY
Nick's Pizza
Uvarara
Katsuno
Danny Brown Wine Bar & Kitchen
Inset I
LEAVITTS PARK
Debasaki
KumGangSan
Hunan House
Imperial Palace
Joe's Shanghai
Sentosa
Ah Rhee Soo
Spicy & Tasty
Mulan
Noodle House
Little Pepper
Corner 28
Flushing-Main St
1
2
3

Ah Rhee Soo

Korean XX

D3

38-10 138th St. (at 38th Ave.)

Subway: Flushing - Main St — Lunch & dinner daily
Phone: 718-713-0308
Web: www.ahrheesoo.com
Prices: $$

Korean barbecue gets a sweep of sophistication at this slick and spacious restaurant tucked into the upscale Queens Crossing mall in Flushing. The place bills itself as Korean-Japanese, but only a complete sushiphile could resist the call of those multiple grills flanking the tables: Ah Rhee Soo was built for barbecue and big parties. (In fact, the menu offers four set menus for just such occasions, starting at $500.)

The good news is that you only need bring yourself to indulge in a tender plate of sweet beef ribs, freckled with radish, mushrooms, chestnuts, and jujubes; baby octopus, sautéed with tender pork belly in a hearty red sauce; or a soft tangle of cold buckwheat noodles in a heat-packing garlic sauce, spiked with boiled egg and pressed pork.

Andy's Seafood & Grill

Chinese X

95-26 Queens Blvd. (bet. 63rd Ave. & 63rd Dr.)

Subway: 63 Dr - Rego Park — Lunch & dinner daily
Phone: 718-275-2388
Web: N/A
Prices: ⊜

Smack in the center of Queens Boulevard in bustling, multi-cultural Rego Park, is this new seafood-focused spot featuring mouth-watering Taiwanese and Sichuan specialties.

Offerings may seem infinite, so start by asking for the *non*-American menu—yes, there are two—to focus your selections and heighten authenticity. Dishes may range from the fantastic "smelly tofu," aged and deep fried, served with crunchy-sweet diakon and chili paste, to the restorative *hakku*-style soup, with chewy rice balls bobbing in a beautifully clarified, flavorful pork broth. Highlights include the über-fresh, steamed whole sea bass topped with ginger, scallions, and cilantro, bathed in a delicate broth, finished with fermented beans for a quintessential taste of umami.

Arharn Thai

Thai

32-05 36th Ave. (bet. 32nd & 33rd Sts.)

Subway: 36 Av
Phone: 718-728-5563
Web: N/A
Prices: ⊜

Lunch & dinner daily

Astoria takes a break from its usual souvlaki scene to dabble with Thai food—and the results are delicious. Just a block off the N train, Arharn Thai is a fairly non-descript operation, with clean, minimally-dressed tables and a couple of Thai-inspired artifacts dotting the walls.

Breaking up the blandness of the room are the vibrant Thai specialties—each dish deftly incorporating the contradictory sweet, salty, and sour elements that define the country's cuisine. The only thing missing is the heat—which is given the usual Western taming—but you won't miss it too much in plates like *yum ma kear yao,* a silky white eggplant salad with roasted vegetables and dried shrimp; or *gaeng ped yen,* a roasted duck dish in red curry and sweet, cool coconut milk.

Bahari estiatorio 

Greek

31-14 Broadway (bet. 31st & 32nd Sts.)

Subway: Broadway
Phone: 718-204-8968
Web: www.bahariestiatorio.com
Prices: $$

Lunch & dinner daily

Old, beloved Stamatis on Broadway got itself a hip makeover. Gone are the kitschy seafaring murals, usurped by the likes of exposed brick walls, an artsy display of window shutters, and wooden beams planking the ceiling. But don't fret, Astorians, though the name's different, this spruced-up replacement still has the same owners, same scrumptious menu, and same loving family feel.

So get in here, find your old favorite table, and get eating. *Kriya pikilia* is a fine way to start: a tasty assortment of traditional Greek spreads, from *skordalia* to *tzatziki,* with warm pita for dipping. Next, sink your chops into the succulent *hirines brizoles*—lightly seasoned, tender pork chops with rice and fresh veggies. Or stick to a classic—melt-in-your mouth *mousakas.*

Bistro 33 ☺

Fusion

B1

19-33 Ditmars Blvd. (at 21st St.)

Subway: Astoria - Ditmars Blvd
Phone: 718-721-1933
Web: www.lilbistro33.com
Prices: $$

Lunch Sat – Sun
Dinner nightly

French Culinary Institute alumnus and all-around sushi guru, Gary Anza, knifed the maki at prestigious Bond Street and Bao 111, before crossing the river to open this fantastic French-Asian fusion bistro in Astoria. Located a few blocks from scenic Shore Blvd., Bistro 33's menu effortlessly combines Anza's classical training with a bevy of Asian-influenced dishes, not to mention a foray into the deep South with alligator fritters and New Orleans gumbo.

Don't miss a dish of cool, perfectly-seared yellowfin tuna, set atop a sweet Asian pear chutney, and paired with a pristine lobe of seared Hudson Valley foie gras, sour cherries, spicy cashews, and wildflower honey. Washed down with one of Anza's seasonal, fruit-infused sakes, this is fusion done right.

Bliss Bistro

French

B2

45-20 Skillman Ave. (at 46th (Bliss) St.)

Subway: 46 St - Bliss St
Phone: 718-729-0778
Web: www.blissbistro.com
Prices: $$

Lunch Sun
Dinner nightly

Just a fifteen minute subway ride from midtown Manhattan, Sunnyside Gardens is a pretty little pocket of Queens with shady residential streets and lush courtyards. The commute must have looked pretty good to Alim Maruf, who packed his bags at Manhattan's Park Bistro in order to transform the old American Bliss restaurant into this upscale bistro.

With its lovely garden and intimate dining room dressed in creamy whites and tables set for two, Bliss Bistro is as romantic as they come. The food matches, with glorious dishes like a frisée salad, tossed with silky duck confit and crunchy bacon; or fork-tender coq au vin, paired with a fluffy stack of mashed potatoes; or pillowy profiteroles, stuffed with vanilla ice cream bathed in rich chocolate.

Brick Cafe

Mediterranean

30-95 33rd St. (at 31st Ave.)

Subway: Broadway
Phone: 718-267-2735
Web: www.brickcafe.com
Prices: $$

Lunch Sat – Sun
Dinner nightly

The food is simple and the service sweet at Brick Cafe, where locals rave about the brunch and the outdoor area is flooded come summer. With its chunky wood tables, reclaimed flooring, and farm bric-a-brac, the interior will transport you straight back to that little restaurant you can never remember the name of in Montmartre—and who couldn't use a little rustic romance on a corner of Queens usually reserved for Greek diners and thumping Euro clubs?

Best not to fight this kind of momentum and join the crowds digging into Southern French-and-Italian style dishes like grilled Maya shrimp, zucchini, and Portobello mushroom caps tossed in a cilantro-garlic olive oil. The brunch menu carries the usual omelets and French toast, but also octopus carpaccio.

Cavo

Mediterranean

42-18 31st Ave. (bet. 42nd & 43rd Sts.)

Subway: Steinway St
Phone: 718-721-1001
Web: www.cavoastoria.com
Prices: $$$

Dinner Tue – Sun

Nightlife in Astoria? It's happening, and the stunning Cavo—fitted out with soaring, triple-high ceilings, a beautiful second floor balcony, and a garden that rivals the city's best outdoor spaces—is even more surprising tucked into a workaday strip of 31st Avenue, with only a pizza joint and laundromat to call its neighbors.

Even better news—in between the belly dancing and requisite Euro scene, you'll also find a few exceptional dishes courtesy of Chef Richard Farnabe, formerly of Picholine. The starters and sides are better than the entrées: try the sushi grade tuna Napoleon with olive tapenade, crispy pork rinds, micro greens, and feta mousse; or crispy, corn meal-dusted mussels, paired with deep-fried artichokes and almond tahini.

Chao Thai

Thai

85-03 Whitney Ave. (at Broadway)

Subway: Elmhurst Av — Lunch & dinner daily
Phone: 718-424-4999
Web: N/A
Prices: ⊜

Tiny Chao Thai is not only a friendly lull from the cacophony of the LIRR, but a lovely culinary gem. Teeming with Asian diners, Chao Thai rises above its competition with earnest authenticity. The menu is manifold with classics, but most dishes hail from the North like *moo pad phrik ging,* juicy pork and crisp string beans stir-fried in a fragrant curry paste. It would be remiss to skip the daily specials (in Thai), so ask a waiter to explain.

All tables are dotted with complex, richly scented sauces that blend sublimely with classics like *massaman* curry (chicken and potatoes in a pungent coconut gravy); and grilled eggplant salad with ground pork and shrimp. The "potato chip bags" with deep-fried salted fish are a thrilling countertop takeaway.

Cheburechnaya

Uzbek 

92-09 63rd Dr. (at Austin St.)

Subway: 63 Dr - Rego Park — Lunch Sun – Fri
Phone: 718-897-9080 — Dinner Sat – Thu
Web: www.cheburechnaya.com
Prices: ⊜

Make no mistake: the service can be halting, the halogen lighting is brutal, and the blaring Russian music videos don't exactly scream date night. But this boisterous Rego Park restaurant's inconveniences fade when the dining room's open grill lights up—crackling and sizzling with succulent kebabs—and gorgeous plates of food start flying out of the kitchen (sometimes all at once).

It's hard to miss with Cheburechnaya's gorgeous kosher food, which caters to the neighborhood's Bukharan Jewish population, but keep an eye peeled for the carrot salad, cut into noodle-thin strips and humming with chili, paprika, and cilantro; and the *noni toki* bread, a charred beauty that reads something like a cross between cumin seed-studded flat bread and matzo.

Christos Steakhouse

Steakhouse XX

B1

41-08 23rd Ave. (at 41st St.)

Subway: Ditmars Blvd — Dinner nightly
Phone: 718-777-8400
Web: www.christossteakhouse.com
Prices: $$$

A dark red awning dips down over windows promising hearty portions of dry-aged beef while neat hedges line the entrance to this beloved Astoria institution. Inside, a front area serves as both bar and butcher shop, beautifully displaying their range of house-aged chops. Hardwood floors, warm tones, and mahogany tables draped in white linens complete the traditional setting.

But what sets Christos apart from its chophouse brethren is the uniquely Greek influence of the food: *taramosalata* and salads of Greek sausage over *gigante* beans share the menu with standards like roast chicken, lobster, and ribeye. Expertly prepared sides like tart and tender dandelion greens (*horta*) tossed in lemon juice and olive oil bring fresh flavors to steakhouse dining.

Corner 28

Chinese 

40-28 Main St. (at 40th Rd.)

Subway: Flushing - Main St — Lunch & dinner daily
Phone: 718-886-6628
Web: N/A
Prices: $$

Straddling a busy corner of Flushing is the bright, double-decker goliath, Corner 28. Choose from two entrances for different—albeit tasty—experiences. The left door leads to a chaotic take-out joint, where you can score a 75¢ Peking duck from early morning until 2:00 A.M. The right door leads guests up to the second floor, where a sunlight-flooded room finds diners flipping through glossy menus while friendly servers hustle to and fro with heaping plates of Chinese food.

The space can get crowded quickly and the Chinese music can jangle the nerves, but oh-how-soothing it is to finally tuck your chopsticks into a heat-packing dish of soft, shredded pork, bathed in ruby-colored garlic sauce; or meltingly tender lamb chops, fragrant with herbs and spices.

Danny Brown Wine Bar & Kitchen

Mediterranean

104-02 Metropolitan Ave. (at 71st Dr.)

Subway: Forest Hills - 71 Av Dinner Tue – Sun
Phone: 718-261-2144
Web: www.dannybrownwinekitchen.com
Prices: $$

Gaetano Salvadore

Long stuck in the shadow of neighboring culinary giants, Manhattan and Brooklyn, Queens gets a big old notch on its foodie belt with this Forest Hills gem. You can thank Chef Danny Brown, who packed up a suitcase of style from his days cooking in SoHo and headed across the river to risk this new self-titled venture in 2006.

Part French wine bar; Spanish tapas joint; and Italian *enoteca*, it's tough to jam this square peg into a round hole, but suffice to say the result is pure magic: a warm, sophisticated restaurant that comes alive at night with sultry music; a polished, buzzing waitstaff; and locals grateful not to have to even look at the subway.

The menu features cured meats and cheeses; small and big plates; sides and desserts. Guests are encouraged to share—not the worst idea when you're staring down the barrel of your dining companion's crispy Serrano ham and cheese croquettes, laced with saffron aïoli and garlic-cilantro-parsley pesto; succulent prawns served over a creamy sunchoke purée with grilled scallion, seared Serrano ham, and citrus-chive aïoli; or a pile of soft ricotta gnocchi with fresh English peas, bright mint, Niçoise olives, and garlicky basil pesto.

De Mole

Mexican

45-02 48th Ave. (at 45th St.)

Subway: 46 St — Lunch & dinner daily
Phone: 718-392-2161
Web: N/A
Prices:

Straddling a corner of Sunnyside dominated by Columbian bakeries, taco joints, and residential buildings, tiny, immaculate De Mole takes its namesake dish—and a wealth of other Mexican standbys—to new heights.

The flavors start rolling out at breakfast, which offers heavy hitters like *huevos rancheros* and De Mole buffalo burger. The pace marches on to a lunch and dinner menu that might include tender *chuleta*, a grilled pork chop smothered in caramelized onions and served with red rice, beans, and a fluffy stack of steaming corn tortillas; a spot-on torta boasting juicy strips of tender carne asada; or melt-in-your mouth coconut flan. Less adventurous eaters will find solace in Tex-Mex standbys like fajitas, nachos, and taco salads.

Debasaki

Japanese

33-67 Farrington St. (bet. 33rd & 35th Aves.)

Subway: Flushing - Main St — Dinner nightly
Phone: 718-886-6878
Web: N/A
Prices: $$

Surrounded by chop-shops and industrial outlets, this sexy, intimate Korean chicken joint in Flushing gets a bit isolated after 8:00 P.M., though those who know where they're headed are in for a treat. Inside, you'll find a slick, stylish interior fitted out with cushy, high-backed striped booths, thumping Korean pop beats, and an intimate back bar that manages to be even darker than the restaurant.

The soups are notable at Debaski, but it's the chicken that keeps this restaurant packed all hours of the night (the place stays open until 2:00 A.M.). Don't miss the *gyoza* of fried chicken wings stuffed with shrimp, corn, cheese, hot peppers, and corn kimchi; boneless barbecue chicken topped with crunchy fish eggs; or the tart kimchi-fried rice with cheese.

Delhi Heights

Indian 

B2

37-66 74th St. (at 37th Rd.)

Subway: Jackson Hts - Roosevelt Av
Lunch & dinner Tue – Sun
Phone: 718-507-1111
Web: www.delhiheights.us
Prices: $$

Gone are the ticky-tacky Christmas lights and reclaimed banquet chairs that afflict so many Indian restaurants—succulent Delhi Heights, which occupies a prominent corner near Queens' bustling Roosevelt Avenue, aims to be a cut above, with a modern, good-looking interior and a clever menu divided into three sections: South Indian, Indian, and Indian-Chinese.

The kitchen, which offers dozens of breads, noodles, and vegetarian options, isn't afraid to kick the heat up in dishes like *keema mutter*, spicy ground lamb in a fragrant, tomato-based sauce with onions and shelled peas; and then cool you down with dishes like the *dahi vada*, a cluster of crispy lentil flour doughnuts smothered in a thick, tangy yogurt and studded with crunchy cardamom seeds.

Engeline's

Filipino 

58-28 Roosevelt Ave. (bet. 58th & 59th Sts.)

Subway: Woodside - 61 St
Lunch & dinner daily
Phone: 718-898-7878
Web: N/A
Prices: ⊜

Sometimes you wake up and think—man, I would love some deep fried pork knuckles for breakfast. The good people at Engeline's won't judge you. In fact, this sweet little bakery-cum-restaurant, which doubles as a local hangout for the neighborhood's Filipino ex-pat scene, will serve it to you with a smile.

The bakery makes a mean pastry any way you slice it, but it's worth grabbing a seat at one of the simple wooden tables and plunking down some change for a full meal, for this kind of authentic Filipino comfort food doesn't come easy—try the *kare-kare*, a sweet, peanut-butter stew of oxtail and tender honeycomb tripe, kicked up with a pungent, salty fish sauce; or *menudo*, a traditional peasant stew with addictive little cubes of spicy, perfumed pork.

Hamjibak

Korean

41-08 149th Pl. (bet. Barclay & 41st Aves.)

Subway: Flushing - Main St — Lunch & dinner daily
Phone: 718-460-9289
Web: N/A
Prices: $$

A healthy assortment of *banchan* (small plates, such as kimchi or spicy mackerel) is usually a good indicator of a serious Korean restaurant, and you'll find no shortage of them at Hamjibak—a delicious Korean barbecue restaurant buried down a nondescript side street in the blossoming K-town that's sprung up near Queens' Murray Hill LIRR station.

The unassuming Hamjibak won't woo you with it's plain-Jane décor, but scores major points for the patient, oh-so-knowledgable waitstaff service, and masterful Korean specialties like *daeji bulgogi,* a plate of marinated pork ribs in chili-garlic sauce sprinkled with bright green scallions; or *boyang jeongol,* a traditional hot pot of lamb, dumplings, and vegetables swimming in a rich, spicy beef broth.

Himalayan Yak

Tibetan

72-20 Roosevelt Ave. (bet. 72nd & 73rd Sts.)

Subway: 74 St - Broadway — Lunch & dinner daily
Phone: 718-779-1119
Web: www.himalayanyakrestaurant.com
Prices: 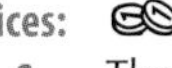

The slick, revamped Himalayan Yak is not too far from its former digs, but a change of scenery has served it well. The new location boasts sultry sienna walls and handsome exposed brick, lined with carved masks and little black and white Yaks.

The food, on the other hand, remains deliciously the same. Perhaps best described as Indian light, this hybrid restaurant draws specialties from several cuisines, including Nepali, Tibetan, Himalayan, and Indian. Take a culinary tour with *tsam thuk,* a thick, porridge-like soup served at room temperature, and bobbing with yak milk; or gigantic beef dumplings in a rich, savory soup of tender greens and diced carrots; or a vegetarian tray which includes pickled mango strips and Indian pepper paper bread.

Hunan House

Chinese

D3

137-40 Northern Blvd. (bet. Main & Union Sts.)

Subway: Flushing - Main St — Lunch & dinner daily
Phone: 718-353-1808
Web: N/A
Prices: ㊂

Sweet Flushing! Does New York's rising (and slowly reigning) Chinatown ever cease to delight those willing to trek out to its far-flung environs? Not if Hunan House has anything to say about it—a plain, but tidy, little joint pushing out authentic, hard-to-find Hunanese fare.

The province's name means "south of the lake," and Hunan kitchens typically use more seafood than those of neighboring Sichuan—though they certainly share their neighbor's affinity for chili peppers. Witness a braised fish head in a spicy broth, topped with pickled chilies and cool cilantro; a fragrant, delicately preserved beef with pickled peppers and "white chili" (which turns out to be fried bean curd skin); or Hunan-style spare ribs laced with red chili sauce.

Imperial Palace

Chinese

D3

136-13 37th Ave. (bet. Main & Union Sts.)

Subway: Flushing - Main St — Lunch & dinner daily
Phone: 718-939-3501
Web: N/A
Prices: $$

Grab a group of your fellow chowhounds and hop the 7 train to Flushing for plates of scrumptious classic Chinese cuisine. You'll be needing your nosh buddies to help you tackle the ample menu, which is jam packed with delectable offerings like crunchy snow pea shoots with garlic, flavorful squid with chives, and fragrant preserved meat (sausage) with tart mounds of spinach. But the claim to fame at this locally frequented spot is the sticky rice and crab...did we say Dungeness? Oh, yes. Juicy, plump, sweet crabmeat served in a leaf-lined steamer with sublime bits of crisp, golden rice, along with black mushrooms, ginger, scallions, and dried shrimp.

Large, banquet style tables dot the dining space where the lively atmosphere brims with a prominently Asian crowd.

Jackson Diner

Indian

B2

37-47 74th St. (bet. Roosevelt & 37th Aves.)

Subway: Jackson Hts - Roosevelt Av — Lunch & dinner daily
Phone: 718-672-1232
Web: www.jacksondiner.com
Prices:

Gone are Jackson Diner's budget chandeliers and gaudy seating—thoughtful sconces now grace the wall, and the tables sparkle in clean, tidy little rows. What hasn't changed, thank goodness, is the fragrant and tasty Indian food. This Queens steady bills itself as "A Culinary Passage to India"—a promise it delivers on, though it has lost some substantial heat with the arrival of more and more Western faces.

Easy enough to get over when you sink your teeth into crispy samosas filled with spicy peas and potatoes; tangy lamb vindaloo simmered in a thick ginger and tamarind-chili sauce; or jumbo dumplings served with three bright dipping sauces of creamy burnt-orange tamarind, chunky coconut and black mustard seed, and bright green coriander.

Joe's Shanghai

136-21 37th Ave. (bet. Main & Union Sts.)

Subway: Flushing - Main St — Lunch & dinner daily
Phone: 718-539-3838
Web: www.joeshanghairestaurants.com
Prices: $$

City kids that have given up on the banal kitchen at the Pell Street outpost of this popular soup dumpling house ought to take a little jaunt out to the original in Flushing, Queens. Because the doughy little pouches sure earn their pleated stripes at this location, thank you very much.

Kick things off with an order of the pork and crab soup dumplings—for the uninitiated, these are thin, soft purses of dough filled with a rich, lip-smacking-good hot broth. If you don't end up ordering back-to-back rounds of these heavenly dumplings, you might try any number of dishes like a trio of sweet and salty wine chicken, jellyfish strips, and duck's web feet; or tender sautéed pork, diced with minced jalapeño, diced squid, and dried tofu.

Katsuno

Japanese

103-01 Metropolitan Ave. (at 71st Rd.)

Subway: Forest Hills - 71 Av — Lunch Tue – Fri
Phone: 718-575-4033 — Dinner Tue – Sun
Web: www.katsunorestaurant.com
Prices: $$

Authentic Japanese food has finally crossed the bridge to Queens, and not a moment too soon, but blink and you'll miss this ever popular gem. There is no sign to mark the entrance, only a small white lantern and the traditional Japanese *noren* curtains to usher you into a beautiful little space with a smattering of tables. While his wife runs the front room, the talented Katsuyuki Seo crafts every plate, and the chef's flawless technique is evident right from the first slice.
The seasonal menu employs fish flown in from Japan daily, and might include a translucent tangle of fresh squid noodles, topped with needle-thin yuzu zest; or a bowl of toothsome soba, bobbing in a fragrant broth with grilled scallion, silky tofu, and tender slices of duck breast.

KumGangSan

138-28 Northern Blvd. (bet. Bowne & Union Sts.)

Subway: Flushing - Main St — Lunch & dinner daily
Phone: 718-461-0909
Web: www.kumgangsan.net
Prices: $$

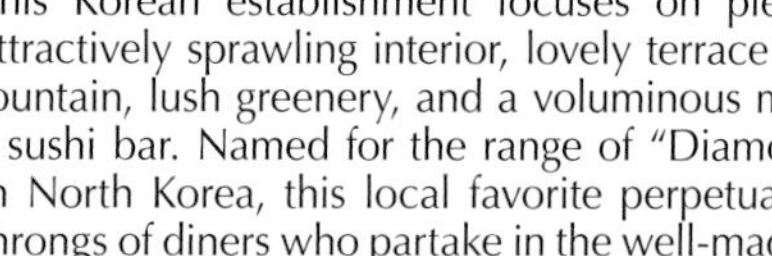

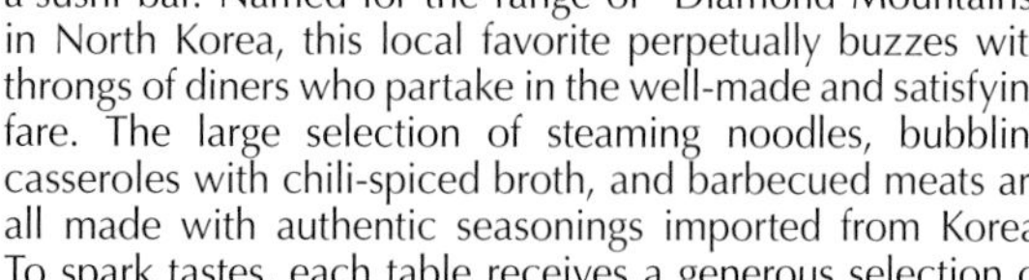

This Korean establishment focuses on pleasure, with an attractively sprawling interior, lovely terrace with a burbling fountain, lush greenery, and a voluminous menu, as well as a sushi bar. Named for the range of "Diamond Mountains" in North Korea, this local favorite perpetually buzzes with throngs of diners who partake in the well-made and satisfying fare. The large selection of steaming noodles, bubbling casseroles with chili-spiced broth, and barbecued meats are all made with authentic seasonings imported from Korea. To spark tastes, each table receives a generous selection of fresh, attractive small plates (*banchan*), from sliced abalone to wilted water spinach, at the start of the meal.
Another location in Midtown West is open 24/7 as well.

Little Pepper

Chinese

133-43 Roosevelt Ave. (bet. Main & Prince Sts.)

Subway: Flushing - Main St — Lunch & dinner daily
Phone: 718-939-7788
Web: www.little-pepper.com
Prices: ⊜

Adorable name aside, you don't go to Little Pepper for the ambience. With only a handful of clean tables and a small fridge stacked with beer and soda to call décor, this Flushing restaurant is all about Sichuan food and—as one might gather from the peppers gracing the walls, a sign outside the restaurant, and almost every item on the menu—chili peppers.

As it turns out, this is a very good thing indeed: tuck into thin strips of ox tripe tossed in a riot of chili, scallions, sprouts, and cilantro; spicy chicken stewed with chili and peanuts; tender lamb, wok-seared to perfection and tossed with cumin, chili, and a shake of bright green cilantro; or a light fish soup, bobbing with sprouts, bamboo shoots, and scallions.

Main Street Taiwanese Gourmet

Chinese

D2

59-14 Main St. (bet. 59th & 60th Aves.)

Subway: Flushing - Main St — Lunch & dinner daily
Phone: 718-886-8788
Web: N/A
Prices: ⊜

With its impossibly long name and simple, Zen-like interior, Main Street Taiwanese Gourmet isn't trying to woo anyone out to Flushing for ambience. You can find that anywhere, after all. It's all about the food at this new gem—and you'll have to take a subway ride and a bus to get there.

Rest assured it's worth it for the stinky tofu alone. The staff speaks little English, but with a dash of ingenuity you'll soon be on your way to exquisite delights like bamboo pork, served together in a hot cast iron vessel with scallions and a mouthwatering sauce; wildly fresh oyster pancakes sporting caramelized edges and a tantalizingly sweet sauce; and tender cuttlefish tossed with minced pork, crunchy Chinese celery, and seared green peppers.

Malagueta

25-35 36th Ave. (at 28th St.)

Subway: 36 Av — Lunch Sat – Sun
Phone: 718-937-4821 — Dinner Tue – Sun
Web: www.malaguetany.com
Prices: $$

Just when it seemed like all of Brazil was on the Atkins diet, along comes this sweet little number where dinner is not dominated by stupefying amounts of meat. Not that there's anything wrong with getting your beef on—it's just that Herbet Gomes, Malagueta's Chef/owner, and his wife, Alda, prefer to run their place with an eye towards Brazil's diverse culinary offerings.

Set along a fairly residential street, Malagueta's parcel of tables fills up fast with neighborhood regulars and city slickers willing to hop the short train ride out to Long Island City.

Try the tender black-eyed pea fritters laced with *vatapá*, a creamy shrimp and coconut milk sauce; or the pork tenderloin, marinated and cooked to fork-tender perfection, then laced in dill sauce.

M & T Restaurant

44-09 Kissena Blvd. (bet. Cherry St. & 45th Ave.)

Subway: Flushing - Main St — Lunch & dinner daily
Phone: 718-539-4100
Web: N/A
Prices:

The décor—Spartan. The menu—vast and confusing. The cuisine—oh the cuisine—outstanding. Rejoice, residents of Flushing! The good folks at M & T Restaurant have brought you the cuisine of Qingdao, a seaside city in China's northeastern Shandong province, known for the popular beer Tsingtao.

Offerings are wildly, wonderfully exciting which may leave you a bit overwhelmed. Our advice? Skip straight to the terrific specials like succulent, sautéed kidney with veggies and crunchy slices of red jelly fish. Or the mouthwatering marriage of fragrant beef tendons with juicy shrimp. Though the sweet staff speaks little English, they're eager to help navigate the menu. If all else fails, point to a delicious looking dish on a neighboring table, and order that.

Mulan

Asian

D3

136-17 39th Ave. (at Main St.)

Subway: Flushing - Main St
Phone: 718-886-8526
Web: www.mulan-restaurant.com
Prices: $$$

Lunch & dinner daily

Just a short walk from Flushing's bustling main drag, sits the Queens Crossing mall—a Time Warner Center for the borough's Chinatown, if you will. And like its Manhattan counterpart, there are a few upscale restaurants worth checking out, should you find yourself in this neck of the woods.

One of them is the gorgeous Mulan—a modern Asian restaurant filled with cherry blossom silk panels and creamy leather chairs that's making a quick name for itself with polished service and a respectable wine list (for Flushing, that is). Not to mention continental Cantonese fare like the char-grilled salmon, varnished with a honey-tinged miso sauce and topped with sweet mango; or bone-in chicken, puddled in a dark, aromatic sauce pocked with creamy whole chestnuts.

Mundo

31-18 Broadway (at 32nd St.)

Subway: Broadway
Phone: 718-777-2829
Web: www.mundoastoria.com
Prices: $$

Dinner nightly

Like the eclectic neighborhood it resides in, this Astoria charmer traffics in a unique mix of global fare. The locals respond with unflagging loyalty, and anyone who is lucky enough to accidentally wander in will find a bustling dining room filled with regulars lapping up the gracious and funny hospitality of Mundo's spirited host, Willy.

Kick things off with a Red Sonja, a cold starter of hand-formed red lentil and chickpea patties that allegedly count Donatella Versace as a fan; and then move on to plates like the creamy artichokes filled with diced carrots and peas, paired with braised fresh fava beans; moist, feather-light Turkish meatballs; or warm semolina cake soaked in mouthwatering syrup and stuffed with a cool lobe of vanilla ice cream.

Nick's Pizza

Pizza 

D3

108-26 Ascan Ave. (off Austin St.)

Subway: 75 Av — Lunch & dinner daily
Phone: 718-263-1126
Web: N/A
Prices: $$

Pizza couldn't be hotter in New York right now, but this quiet little Forest Hills pie joint was kicking it long before the recent influx of newcomers. Located a stone's throw from the legendary Forest Hills Gardens, a lovely neighborhood featuring stunning Tudor homes, the pizzeria boasts a Norman Rockwell charm, with big glossy windows, a marble pizza counter, and cushy soda shop booths made for dinner with the family.

The menu is straightforward, with pizza, calzones, and a near-perfect cannoli, but don't be fooled by the simplicity—this is some of the city's finest pizza, its perfectly pliant crust lightly charred and laced with a lick-your-fingers red sauce, then loaded with toppings like crumbly sausage, fresh prosciutto, or tart anchovies.

Noodle House

Chinese 

D3

38-12 Prince St. (bet. 38th & 39th Aves.)

Subway: Flushing - Main St — Lunch & dinner daily
Phone: 718-321-3838
Web: N/A
Prices: $$

Also known as Nan Shian Dumpling House, it is easily found among a strip of restaurants reflecting the diversity of Flushing's dominant Asian population. Simply decorated, the comfortable dining room features rows of closely set tables and a mirrored wall that successfully gives the illusion of space.

This enjoyable and interesting menu focuses on noodle-filled soups, toothsome stir-fried rice cakes, and the house specialty, steamed pork buns. These are made in-house and have a delicate, silky wrapper encasing a flavorful meatball of ground pork or crab and rich tasting broth. Eating these may take some practice, but take your cue from the slurping crowd: puncture the casing on your spoon to cool the dumplings and avoid burning your mouth.

Nusara

Thai

82-80 Broadway (at Whitney Ave.)

Subway: Elmhurst Av
Phone: 718-898-7996
Web: www.nusarathaikitchen.com
Prices: $$

Lunch & dinner daily

Tucked into an Elmhurst strip mall teeming with enough Asian food to send Asiaphiles into a coma, Nusara is indisputably the belle of the ball. Its edge? Ace Thai food, a pretty, softly lit dining room, and a staff willing to bend over backwards for their customers.

Newbies to authentic Thai will rejoice in Nusara's snappy, well-organized menu with its detailed explanations, but the spice-shy should proceed slowly. For all the sweetness of the staff, Nusara isn't afraid to bring the heat in dishes like whole red snapper, tossed in garlic and pepper; or mouthwatering, seasonal Chinese watercress, sautéed with ginger, red chili, and garlic. Cool your heels with a roasted duck salad, loaded with pineapple and cashews in a chili and lime vinaigrette.

Ornella

29-17 23rd Ave. (bet. 29th & 31st Sts.)

Subway: Ditmars Blvd
Phone: 718-777-9477
Web: www.ornellatrattoria.com
Prices: $$

Lunch & dinner daily

All hands are on deck at Ornella and Giuseppe Viterale's fantastic new trattoria, where the husband and wife proprietors are always on hand to ensure smooth sailing. A cheery striped awning welcomes you into an intimate, narrow room fitted out with sunset-colored walls, but the real draw at this Astoria restaurant is the food—where a passion for homegrown veggies, fresh ingredients, and inspired sauces elevate otherwise rote Italian-American dishes to hubba-hubba homemade fare.

Dinner may begin with fluffy potato-and-ricotta gnocchi tossed with sweet gorgonzola cheese and cream, then baked into heaven on earth; and then move on to *pollo alla Scarpariello,* an otherwise pedestrian chicken dish that graduates to excellence with a gorgeous reduction sauce.

Parkside Restaurant

Italian

C2

107-01 Corona Ave. (bet. 108th St. & 51st Ave.)

Subway: 103 St - Corona Plaza — Lunch & dinner daily
Phone: 718-271-9871
Web: N/A
Prices: $$$

Enter this warm, convivial Corona landmark and immediately feel welcomed by all—from hostess and bartender, to server and chef. A contagious, celebratory spirit fills the enthusiastic diners enjoying old-fashioned, Italian-American dishes in a perennially packed, multi-room space. Its brick arches, twinkling white lights, wicker chairs, and hanging foliage conjure an upscale greenhouse, staffed by tuxedo-clad waiters.

Take a seat among the family-friendly patrons and order a plate of perfectly prepared *rigatoni all'amatriciana*, served in a fresh tomato sauce with pancetta and basil; or thin cutlets of *veal piccata*, glazed in a luscious lemon-caper sauce. When the dessert tray rolls by, make sure you've saved room for biscotti or the beloved cannoli.

Pio Pio

Peruvian 

84-02 Northern Blvd. (at 84th St.)

Subway: 82 St - Jackson Hts — Lunch & dinner daily
Phone: 718-426-4900
Web: www.piopionyc.com
Prices: ⊜

The Peruvian rotisserie chicken joint that spawned a mini-empire (at last count, there were 8 locations) recently moved from its colorful, exposed brick digs in Queens, but they didn't go far. Located just across the street from the old spot, the new Pio Pio is a sprawling, street level operation featuring a pleasant little garden and jumbo photos of the mother land.

The menu remains blissfully similar, with Peruvian goodies like crispy empanadas stuffed with sweet, fragrant chicken and a wicked salsa *criolla* (a house specialty that, when it appears on the menu accompanying any dish, should scream "order me"); or the *arroz con mariscos*, a Peruvian paella chock-a-block with fresh scallops, octopus, mussels, shrimp, and squid in a terrific red sauce.

Sabry's

B1

24-25 Steinway St. (bet. Astoria Blvd. & 25th Ave.)

Subway: Astoria Blvd — Lunch & dinner daily
Phone: 718-721-9010
Web: N/A
Prices: **$$**

Located in an area of Astoria now known as Little Egypt, Sabry's uses Egyptian accents in preparing an array of well-priced, pristine seafood—a large ice-filled case displays the day's fresh catch at the entrance. In the style of many Mediterranean eateries, fish from this case are grilled or baked whole, permeated with Middle Eastern flavorings like garlic, cumin, cardamom, and red pepper. Aromatic *taogines*, including a shellfish version in rich and heady tomato sauce, are equally delicious. Smoky baba ghanoush is packed with flavor, especially when accompanied by fantastic pita bread, made fresh to order.

Be aware that the restaurant does not serve alcohol, nor is BYO permitted. However, other interesting options include a tasty mint tea.

San & Deul

Korean

D1

251-05 Northern Blvd. (bet. 251st St & Browvale Ln.)

Subway: Flushing - Main St (& bus Q12) — Lunch & dinner daily
Phone: 718-281-0218
Web: N/A
Prices: **$$**

At the edge of the Queen's border, where the borough starts to meet Long Island, along a wide boulevard known as 25A, sits San & Deul—a Korean restaurant where the cooking is done table-top with real wood, the *panchan* is delightful, and the service is lovely.

If the décor—a clean, bright room with large windows overlooking the street—is a little on the functional end, you can probably look the other way. Food like this is ambience enough: a mashed soybean casserole is dotted with veggies and fresh clams; deep-fried dumplings are stuffed with pork, shiitake mushrooms, fish sauce, and tofu; and tender prime beef short ribs are cooked over a wood burning grill, then served with red rice, kimchi, and red-leaf lettuce for wrapping.

Queens

Sapori d'Ischia

B2 — Italian XX

55-15 37th Ave. (at 56th St.)

Subway: Northern Blvd — Lunch & dinner Tue – Sun
Phone: 718-446-1500
Web: N/A
Prices: $$

If you're looking for red-checkered tablecloth Italian-American, its best to keep on trucking past this little Woodside gem, because the house rules posted at the bar spell it out clear as mud—they don't grate cheese on seafood, they don't serve butter, and you can forget the lemon peel in your espresso.

So what do Frank and Antonio Galano, the father-son team who runs this adorable little restaurant and grocery, do? How about flat-out delicious Southern Italian seafood, a little live piano on occasion, and darn reasonable prices. Don't miss the killer house-made black linguini in an intricate white wine sauce pocked with juicy clams, *peperoncino*, and roasted garlic; or a delicate chocolate and hazelnut torte paired with a scoop of pistachio ice cream.

Sentosa

D3 — Malaysian X

39-07 Prince St. (at 39th Ave.)

Subway: Flushing - Main St — Lunch & dinner daily
Phone: 718-886-6331
Web: N/A
Prices:

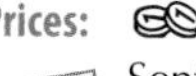

Sentosa, the Malay word for tranquility, celebrates an agreeable intermingling of the mainly Chinese and Indian influences of Malaysia's multi-ethnic descendants. This very enjoyable restaurant features a contemporary setting with warm lighting, polished teak, and stone tiles.

Meals here may include *mee siam* rice noodles, stir-fried with a sweet chili sauce, fried tofu, bean sprouts, and fresh shrimp. Other flavorful offerings may include *rendang*, a rich stew of tender beef simmered in coconut milk, perfectly heated with chili paste; alongside a large selection of rice and noodle dishes. Remember to save room for your vegetables here, which may highlight the alluring flavors of *belacan* (ground, fermented shrimp) sautéed with halved okra.

718 - Seven One Eight

Mediterranean ✗

35-01 Ditmars Blvd. (at 35th St.)

Subway: Astoria - Ditmars Blvd — Lunch & dinner daily
Phone: 718-204-5553
Web: www.718restaurant.com
Prices: $$

With its lovely sienna hues, silky fabrics, and flickering red votive candles, this elegant little Astoria charmer brings a dose of warmth to this section of Astoria. Named for the Queens area code it resides in, 718's menu fiddles with Mediterranean fare quite deftly—dinner might include a tender roasted duck with crispy skin, lovingly fanned out over a fluffy potato purée studded with earthy mushrooms and a lick of tart passion-coriander sauce; or a decadent molten chocolate cake that turns sinful and oozing when the fork delivers the first blow.

The regularly packed happy hour bar is a fantastic place to take a peek at the restaurant's ample tapas menu, and on Friday nights you may soak up the *caliente* Latin beats to your hearts content.

SHI

Asian ✗✗✗

47-20 Center Blvd. (bet. 47th & 48th Aves.)

Subway: Vernon Blvd - Jackson Av — Dinner nightly
Phone: 347-242-2450
Web: www.shilic.com
Prices: $$

Tucked into the base of a gorgeous high-rise building along the East River, SHI is the stamp Long Island City's been waiting for: Consider this upscale hipster hub signed, sealed, and delivered.

Developers have poured millions into the new buildings that dot this area of the waterfront, and SHI is appropriately stunning—with floor-to-ceiling windows offering breathtaking views of the Manhattan skyline; sexy white leather plush chairs flanking the beautiful bar area; and a dining room dripping in crystal chandeliers.

So how does the food fit into all this? Solidly, with simple, well-crafted Chinese-American and Japanese specialties like tender shrimp, wrapped in smoky bacon; and crispy popcorn beef, topped with chilies and bright cilantro.

Sik Gaek

D1 Korean

161-29 Crocheron Ave. (bet. 161st & 162nd Sts.)

Subway: Flushing - Main St (& bus Q12) Dinner nightly
Phone: 718-321-7770
Web: N/A
Prices: $$

When David Chang and Anthony Bourdain have sunk their pincers into some far-flung outer borough joint, you know you're in for a treat. Sik Gaek, a Korean restaurant in Auburndale, is a riot of a place: think corrugated metal roofs, blaring rock music, neon aquariums, and flashing traffic lights, and you only start to get a picture.

But the fun atmosphere is only the beginning. Kick things off with a piping hot bowl of fish broth bobbing with thin noodles, fish cake, vegetables, boiled egg, and scallions; and then move on to the money shot: an enormous paella-style pan heaped with fresh vegetables, loads of shellfish, and a live—yes, live—octopus, which will probably try to make a run for it. Thankfully, there's not a yellow cab in sight.

Spicy & Tasty

D3 Chinese

39-07 Prince St. (at 39th Ave.)

Subway: Flushing - Main St Lunch & dinner daily
Phone: 718-359-1601
Web: N/A
Prices: ㊂

Spicy & Tasty has found its home in this bustling pocket of Queens, where a dizzying array of restaurants, bakeries, and stores jockey to win the favor of Flushing's booming Asian population. Its local love is clear in the diverse ethnicities scattered across the clean, contemporary, and spacious dining room, as well as in the cuisine—though it does seem to restrain its punchy Sichuan heat for fear of scaring the newbies.

Nonethess, this food is thoroughly enjoyable. It is likewise fun to watch the warm, knowledgeable staff walk first-timers through steaming plates of dumplings, plump with a spicy red chili sauce and minced meat; broad noodles in a powerful, rich, meaty sauce dancing with scallions and peppers; or tender and fiery cold tripe salad.

Sripraphai

Thai

64-13 39th Ave. (bet. 64th & 65th Sts.)

Subway: Woodside - 61 St
Phone: 718-899-9599
Web: www.sripraphairestaurant.com
Prices: $$

Lunch & dinner Thu – Tue

A few years ago, this local favorite set off a critical firestorm for delivering killer, authentic-as-it-gets Thai food, then smartly expanded into roomier digs. In the current space, you'll find a large, elegant dining room with an enormous backyard garden, replete with gurgling fountain.

But with the flood of Westerners hovering like wolves outside the front door, has this beloved Woodside restaurant tamed her fiery ways? She has, but the bland food still remains quite popular regardless of diminished quality. The menu may feature bright green papaya salads; tender roasted duck over a bed of greens; fluffy Thai-style frittatas studded with ground pork; or fresh soft shell crab, lightly fried and pooled in delicious coconut-laced green curry.

Taiwanese Gourmet Corp

Chinese 

84-02 Broadway (at St. James Ave.)

Subway: Elmhurst Av
Phone: 718-429-4818
Web: N/A
Prices: $$

Lunch & dinner daily

A spotless semi-open kitchen is one of the first signs that this Taiwanese restaurant is just a little bit different than the other kids. Straddling a corner of Elmhurst, Taiwanese Gourmet is a bright spot on Queens' Chinatown circuit, with jumbo windows flooding the dining room with daylight and beautifully framed ancient warrior gear flanking the walls.

The menu reads minimalist, but the staff can be quite helpful if you approach them with questions. Skip the unimpressive oyster pancakes, and dive into dishes like shredded beef and dried tofu, stir-fried in a complex, dark sauce; a delicate, beer-infused duck hot pot teeming with juju beans and Chinese herbs; or a scrumptious clam and chicken hotpot bursting with flavor from smoky *bonito* flakes.

Taverna Kyclades

Greek 

B1

33-07 Ditmars Blvd. (bet. 33rd & 35th Sts.)

Subway: Astoria - Ditmars Blvd
Phone: 718-545-8666
Web: www.tavernakyclades.com
Prices:

Lunch & dinner daily

This traditional and beloved Greek taverna, headed by a dedicated chef/owner and staff, continues to serve fresh fish daily, grilled or fried (note the showcase refrigerator in the semi-open kitchen), along with perfect portions tzatziki or *tarmosalata*.

Years of non-stop service to a loyal and diverse clientele has not diminished the classic patina of the small, but warm and boisterous dining room. The setting here is no frills; this is a perfect spot to dine family style, elbow-to-elbow at simple wood chairs, on solid food with ambience to match. Meals can also be enjoyed year-round in the enclosed garden area. The surrounding space is crowded with back-to-back stores and restaurants. Service here is cool, helpful, and without attitude. *Opa*!

Testaccio

Italian

A2

47-30 Vernon Blvd. (at 47th Rd.)

Subway: Vernon Blvd - Jackson Av
Phone: 718-937-2900
Web: Vernon Blvd - Jackson Av
Prices: $$

Lunch & dinner daily

This new Italian gem arrives courtesy of one of the early owners behind TriBeCa's Pepolino, and those making their way to Long Island City's Vernon Blvd. will find a sexy, contemporary dining room fitted out in leather banquettes, votive candles, and white-washed exposed brick walls.

Excellent pizza and homemade pastas round out the dinner menu, and the latter should not be missed—the more traditional (think *bucatini all'amatriciana, fettuccine alla ciociara,* and *spaghetti alla carbonara*), the better. Dinner might kick off with delicately fried baby risotto balls or a fresh tangle of tagliolini with pecorino romano, black truffle, and cracked pepper; before moving onto velvety oxtail braised in red wine with roasted vegetables and caramelized onions.

Trattoria l'Incontro

Italian XX

B1

21-76 31st St. (at Ditmars Blvd.)

Subway: Astoria - Ditmars Blvd
Lunch & dinner Tue – Sun
Phone: 718-721-3532
Web: www.trattorialincontro.com
Prices: $$

Take the N train to the last stop to track down this feel-good Italian mainstay. The expansion and wine bar still might not offer enough room to hold the throngs of serious foodies that flood this local favorite nightly. Yet no matter how busy they get, Abruzzi native Tina Sacramone and her son, Rocco, always find time to pour on the hospitality.

In the back, a brick oven churns out a host of savory pies (including a chocolate-stuffed one for dessert), as endearing (if gushy) servers circulate the tranquil, well-appointed dining room, reciting a dizzying array of daily specials. Outrageously generous pasta dishes highlight Italian-American sensibilities, with hearty amounts of everything from black linguini with seafood to gnocchi with rabbit ragù.

Urubamba

Peruvian X

C2

86-20 37th Ave. (at 86th St.)

Subway: 82 St - Jackson Hts
Dinner nightly
Phone: 718-672-2224
Web: www.urubambarestaurant.com
Prices: $$

This new Jackson Heights restaurant claims it has been serving traditional Peruvian food since 1976, albeit not at this location. The owner used to run Inti Raymi, a restaurant up the street, but closed it to open the handsome little Urubamba—a long, narrow space lined with Peruvian artifacts, indigenous paintings, and brick-lined walls.

Don't miss the proper Peruvian breakfast served on weekends, where diners can feast on *chanfainita*, a mouthwatering traditional beef stew, or *sopa de gallina*, a fragrant chicken noodle soup. At night, diners tuck into moist, golden tamales filled with chicken, hard boiled eggs, and black olives; light-as-air shrimp chowders, topped with bright green cilantro; and towering platters of fresh, lime-poached ceviche.

Uvarara 

C3

79-28 Metropolitan Ave. (at 80th St.)

Subway: Middle Village - Metropolitan Av (& bus Q54)
Lunch & dinner Tue – Sun
Phone: 718-894-0052
Web: www.uvararany.com
Prices: $$

The "location is everything" memo must have missed the convivial Italian family behind Uvarara, who plunked down their new Italian wine bar between two cemeteries on a gloomy stretch of Metropolitan Avenue. But thank goodness, because this kind of cozy bohemian charmer—with its killer wine list and deliciously honest cooking—wouldn't be nearly as cool in the city.

Housed in what was once a showroom for headstones, the sultry interior is all sex appeal now, with low, flickering candles, mismatched chairs, and beaded curtains made of wine bottle corks. The menu rolls with the seasons, but might include a puffy Naples-style *pizzetta* stuffed with creamy buffalo mozzarella, ripe tomatoes, and basil; or baked gnocchi, tossed in butter and fresh sage.

Vesta Trattoria

A1

21-02 30th Ave. (at 21st St.)

Subway: 30 Av
Lunch & dinner daily
Phone: 718-545-5550
Web: www.vestavino.com
Prices: $$

Named for the virgin god of the hearth in Roman mythology, the adorable Vesta continues to be popular with the local Astoria set. You can blame the low-lit, brick-lined interior, which offers the kind of easygoing weeknight meal the neighborhood was begging for, but our money's on the greenmarket-inspired Italian menu—where it's as easy to indulge in celebrated old-world steadies as it is to head into more intricate culinary territory. Add to that a slew of vegetarian options, and a small, but clever, wine list—and you've got a sleeper.

Don't miss the delicious *minestra* soup; the fresh, hand-rolled pastas; or the Baby Jesus cake, a fluffy spice cake with a crispy, toffee-like crust covered in a caramel sauce and a fluffy dollop of whip cream.

Water's Edge

American XX

A2

4-01 44th Dr. (at the East River)

Subway: 23 St - Ely Av
Phone: 718-482-0033
Web: www.watersedgenyc.com
Prices: $$$

Lunch Mon – Sat
Dinner nightly

If New York is famous for blowing its use of waterfront land, Water's Edge didn't get the memo. A complimentary boat shuttles guests with reservations from Manhattan's 35th street pier to this time-honored Queens fine dining institution, where a wall of windows offers breathtaking views of the East River and Manhattan skyline.

A recent facelift has served the restaurant well, and the new interior is contemporary and stylish, fitted out in steely greys and ebony-rimmed chairs. Guests relax to live piano music and dip their forks into classic upscale fare like a plate of grilled lobster with roasted tomato hollandaise, leek fondue, and soft pillows of tarragon gnocchi; or cheesecake mousse, paired with almond crumble and blueberry compote.

Zabb Queens

Thai X

B2

71-28 Roosevelt Ave. (bet. 70th & 72nd Sts.)

Subway: 74 St - Broadway
Phone: 718-426-7992
Web: N/A
Prices:

Lunch & dinner daily

You don't come for the décor, you come for the food: Northeastern Thai cooking that is not afraid to bring the heat. Not to say the dining room at Zabb is unpleasant—just a bit boring with its clean metal tables, cream colored walls, and flat screen televisions. Of course, maybe that's what makes the delightful service and authentic fare stand out even more.

Thailand's Isaan region is the culinary focus here, and dinner might include a fragrant pork spare rib soup bobbing with dried Chinese wood mushrooms, tomatoes, and basil in a spicy lemongrass broth; a delicious sour sausage salad, chock-a-block with vegetables, herbs, and tamarind sauce; or small plates of spice-laden meats like barbecue pork neck, chicken gizzards, and Thai meatballs.

Jeanine C. Hart/MICHELIN

Staten Island

Staten Island

Unless you live there, chances are that Staten Island is different from the perception. Think of ports, shores, and waterfronts perched at the gateway to New York Harbor. Then, consider that, in some ways, much of what enters the city has first passed through this most secluded borough.

It is only fitting that the bridge which opened it up and may have ended its previously bucolic existence be named for Giovanni da Verrazano, the Italian explorer who first arrived here in 1524. This is particularly apt, because one of the strongest and most accurate generalizations of Staten Island is that it is home to a large Italian-American population. No self-respecting foodie would consider a visit here without picking up a scungilli pizza from **Joe and Pat's**, or at least a slice from **Nunzio**...and maybe **Denino's**, too.

Display of Deliciousness

Beyond this, Staten Island continues to surprise with its ethnically diverse neighborhoods. Take a virtual tour of the eastern Mediterranean at **Dinora** or **Nova's** food market for imported olives, cheeses, and freshly butchered meat. Or, visit the old-world Polish delis, many of which seem to comfortably survive based on their large take-out business...and those delicious homemade jams. Sri Lankan devotees can rejoice in the area surrounding Victory Boulevard for its storefront eateries and restaurants serving a range of this spicy and fragrant cuisine, with perhaps a stop at **Lakruwana** or **Lakshmi's**. Close by these newcomers are a few authentic taquerias as well as the **St. George Greemarket**, where one can find produce grown locally on Staten Island's own Decker Farm. Historic Richmond Town also organizes the family-focused festival *Uncorked!*, featuring the best in professional and homemade wine and food, offering recipes of traditional favorites. For rare and mature wines, visit **Mission Fine Wines**.

Food, Fun & Frolic

With all this in mind, it should be no surprise to learn that the Staten Island of the future includes plans for a floating farmer's market, aquarium, and revamped waterfronts. So sit back and have a drink at one of the vibrant bars along Bay Street, and lament the world's myopic view of this much maligned borough. Drive through some of the city's wealthiest zip codes, boasting superb views of Manhattan and beyond.

Whether here for the Sri Lankan fish buns from **New Asha**; to glimpse the world's only complete collection of rattlesnakes at the S.I. Zoo; or to seek out the birthplaces of Christina Aguilera and Joan Baez, a visit to Staten Island is sure to surprise.

Amboy Rd	AB2
Arthur Kill Rd.	A2
Bay St.	B1
Bloomingdale Rd.	A2
Clarke Ave.	1 B2
Clove Rd.	2 B1
Dr. M.L. King Jr. Expwy.	B1
Father Capodanno Blvd.	B1 2
Forest Ave.	AB1
Forest Hill Rd.	B1
Huguenot Ave.	A2
Hylan Blvd.	A2B1
Jewett Ave.	B1
Korean War Vet. Pkwy.	A2
Lily Pond Ave.	3 B1
Manor Rd.	B1
Ocean Terrace	4 B1
Page Ave.	5 A2
Richmond Ave.	A1 2
Richmond Hill Rd.	6 A1
Richmond Rd.	7 B2
Richmond Ter.	B1
School Rd.	8 B1
South Ave.	A1
Staten Island Expwy.	AB1
Todt Hill Rd.	B1
Vanderbilt Ave.	9 B1
Victory Blvd.	AB1
West Shore Expwy.	A1 2

BRIDGES

Bayonne Bridge	B1
Goethals Bridge	A1
Outerbridge Crossing	10 A2
Verrazano-Narrows Bridge	B1

Angelina's

A3 **Italian** XX

399 Ellis St.

Bus: N/A Lunch & dinner Tue – Sun
Phone: 718-227-2900
Web: www.angelinasristorante.com
Prices: $$$

Getting here requires perseverance and an excellent sense of direction: expect lefts, rights, and u-turns alongside smoke-stacks and tug boats before Angelina's emerges like a mirage before glistening water and a heart-stopping sunset at the tip of Staten Island. Your arrival, completed by uniformed valets, is transporting in itself.

Now occupying a gorgeous multi-level Victorian home, the beloved restaurant stuns with original woodwork, wide windows, and scene-stealing views. Loyal locals arrive in droves to savor the vast Italian offerings such as *linguini alle vongole* served al dente in garlic, parsley, and wine sauce with tender clams, topped with red pepper flakes; or a Fontina-stuffed veal chop with mushroom-Marsala sauce. A trek, but worth it.

Bayou Restaurant

B2 **Cajun** 

1072 Bay St. (bet. Chestnut & St. Marys Aves.)

Bus: 51, 81 Lunch & dinner daily
Phone: 718-273-4383
Web: www.bayoustatenisland.com
Prices: $$

Just a ferry hop from Manhattan and you are on your way to Cajun Country. Make sure you land at Bayou Restaurant, Staten Island's very own slice of the French Quarter. Despite its location in a somewhat nondescript neighborhood, close your eyes, prepare your palate, and step inside this faithfully recreated New Orleans bistro. Exposed brick walls make a gallery for trumpets, banjos, Mardi Gras beads, and portraits of Louisiana's favorite son, Louie Armstrong.

Here, the menu showcases the delicious basics of what N'awlins does best, offering red beans and rice, simmered in beer with just the right splash of heat; or skillets generously filled with seafood jambalaya in rich, spicy sauce. For dessert, the very popular fried cheesecake with raspberry sauce deserves every mouthful of praise it receives.

Beso

Spanish 

B1

11 Schuyler St. (bet. Richmond Terrace & Stuyvesant Pl.)

Lunch & dinner daily

Bus: N/A
Phone: 718-816-8162
Web: www.besonyc.com
Prices: $$

A free ride on the Staten Island Ferry from Manhattan will deliver you right across the street from this tasty addition to the island's dining lineup. Bring some friends to Beso ("kiss" in Spanish) to enjoy a fun night out without spending a fortune. Inside this lovely space, shawls double as window treatments, an antique Spanish sideboard forms part of the bar, and a white adobe fireplace is studded with colorful tiles. Locals love the grazing menu of vibrant tapas, which can include anything from *guajillo*-crusted tuna to *fundito* (broiled chorizo served in a green-chile and tomatillo sauce topped with melted Mahon cheese). And that's not all: entrées will pique your interest with the likes of a grilled ancho-crusted salmon fillet and a roasted duck breast glazed with honey and smoked chile.

Cafe Luna

Italian 

A3

31 Page Ave. (bet. Boscombe Ave. & Richmond Valley Rd.)

Lunch & dinner daily

Bus: 74
Phone: 718-227-8582
Web: www.cafelunanyc.com
Prices: $$

When the moon hits your eye, it's amore at Cafe Luna. Staten Islanders have been fans of the Hyland Blvd original for years, but this new sister restaurant takes the cake for its more upscale, fresh, and contemporary setting. There's even ample parking—something of a rarity in this neck of the woods. Bright yellow and blue walls studded with sparkling star light fixtures lift your spirits, while a warm staff makes you feel like part of the *famiglia*.

From lasagna to linguine, the food is Italian-American to its core. Sicilian in spirit, the kitchen doles out the standards with favorites like chicken parmigiana and veal Marsala. Homemade pastas, crispy pizzas, creamy cheesecake—it's all enough to make "The Chairman" proud.

Carol's Cafe

B2 American

1571 Richmond Rd. (at Four Corners Rd. & Seaview Ave.)

Bus: 74, 76, 84, 86 Dinner Wed – Sat
Phone: 718-979-5600
Web: www.carolscafe.com
Prices: $$$

Chef/owner Carol Frazzetta knows her way around a kitchen. In fact, she even teaches these talents at the cooking school located through the rear of the main dining room, with classes like "My Sicilian Family Recipes."

Those seeking a less hands-on experience choose to relax in the wonderfully homey dining space and tear into the piping-hot basket of fresh breads. However, save room for the deep fried pizza—a crispy wedge of dough topped with fresh tomato, mozzarella, and basil. Other dishes offer refined sensibilities such as the sautéed salmon nestled against divine cinnamon-glazed carrots. End with a fantastic apple-cranberry-pecan crisp.

Pacing is challenged with courses arriving all at once, though you can request to have dishes staggered.

Fushimi

B2 Fusion 

2110 Richmond Rd. (bet. Colfax & Lincoln Aves.)

Bus: 51, 81 Lunch & dinner daily
Phone: 718-980-5300
Web: www.fushimi-us.com
Prices: $$$

This local favorite remains in a league of its own as one of the better Japanese-leaning restaurants on Staten Island, serving an imaginative fare inclined towards fusion. While the ingredients may not be blue-ribbon, the presentation is nonetheless alluring, with large white platters elaborately decorated with fronds and bamboo tepees.

Despite its strip-mall location, the expansive outdoor seating and festive bar fashion a convivial mood, and is an ideal setting for the local crowd. Inside the more subdued yet busy dining room—accented with red lacquer, river stones, and autumnal branches—diners gather at brown banquettes and dark-wood tables to enjoy innovative maki, sushi, and entrées that boast surprising elements and perfectly balanced sauces.

Giuliana's

Italian XX

B2

4105 Hylan Blvd. (at Osborn Ave.)

Bus: 54, 78, 79 — Lunch & dinner Tue – Sun
Phone: 718-317-8507
Web: www.giulianasrestaurant.com
Prices: **$$**

Hylan Boulevard's bakeries, cafés, grocers, and bridal shops paint the perfect picture of Italian-American culture, Staten Island's largest demographic. On this corner, framed in twinkling lights, is a lovely spot known for fresh-made mozzarella and toothsome Italian specialties.

Inside, framed photos of local diners, sports legends, and cast members of the Sopranos line the walls, setting an "everybody knows your name" kind of vibe. White linens drape wooden tables and walls are painted in warm golden hues. For a taste of a tried-and-true Sicilian dish, dig into the exquisite and authentically made *perciatelle con sarde*—piping hot pasta topped with flaky sardines, tender fennel, golden raisins, a touch of saffron, and crispy toasted breadcrumbs.

The Indian Clove

Indian XX

B2

1180 Victory Blvd. (at Clove Rd.)

Bus: 61, 62, 66 — Lunch & dinner daily
Phone: 718-442-5100
Web: www.indianclove.com
Prices: **$$**

Poor Staten Island. With its spaghetti-and-meatballs reputation, New York City's oft-ignored borough has always been treated like a bit of a culinary stepchild. But change is in the air with The Indian Clove, a clever new Indian restaurant with a fresh, modern interior soaked in beautiful, natural light, and a serious talent for Indian fare.

Try the orange and fig salad, a gorgeous minimalist number with skinless orange segments and crispy greens; or the *tandoori jhinga,* a perfectly-cooked plate of plump, tender shrimp in fragrant spices; or a silky, bone-in lamb chop curry, spiked with chili and garlic, then carpeted in fresh coriander. Non-meat eaters should head next door to Victory Bhavan—a vegetarian, kosher restaurant by the same owners.

Nurnberger Bierhaus

B1 German

817 Castleton Ave. (at Davis Ave.)

Bus: 46, 96
Phone: 718-816-7461
Web: www.nurnbergerbierhaus.com
Prices: $$

Lunch & dinner daily

A warm *willkomen* awaits patrons at this cozy Bavarian *biergarten* in the mostly residential neighborhood of West Brighton. The comfy, kitschy surroundings summon an old-world charm: waitresses don traditional frocks, peppy German folksongs pipe through the air, steins and knickknacks line shelves, and a suit of armor stands at the door.

A dark-wood bar with well-worn spouts supplies guests with a splendid, albeit dizzying, selection of imported brews; while the kitchen cooks up an authentic array of rich regional specials, like wursts and schnitzels alongside sauerkraut and mashed potatoes. The Black Forest Cake—moist and chocolaty, studded with black cherries tucked in layers of light buttercream—is the perfect end to a day of unabashed comfort seeking.

Vida

B1 American

381 Van Duzer St. (bet. Beach & Wright Sts.)

Bus: 78
Phone: 718-720-1501
Web: N/A
Prices: $$

Lunch Fri – Sat
Dinner Tue – Sat

Festooned with dried poblano braids, this entryway opens to a luminous, immaculate, sun-yellow room, warmly serving food that further brightens this Staten Island find. Vida indeed breathes life into its excellent dishes, many of which tip their hats to a Southwestern culinary heritage, like the hefty Mexican duo of corn tortillas filled with flavorful Chimayo chicken or juicy pulled pork.

Accompaniments are also perfectly cooked, as in the black beans that arrive heady with thyme and fiery chili, or earthy mushroom bisque, rich with sour cream and a touch of brandy. Tempting as the menu is, innovative daily specials display the chef/owner's genuine dedication, care, creativity, and are not to be missed. Desserts showcase the best of each season.

Zest

French XX

977 Bay St. (bet. Lynhurst & Willow Sts.)

Bus: 51, 81
Phone: 718-390-8477
Web: www.zestsiny.com
Prices: $$

Lunch Tue – Fri
Dinner Tue – Sun

Inside this area's new and welcome French bistro, dark wood paneling, handsome wainscoting, and jazzy red portraits reinforce a "supper club meets the Mediterranean" aura. Lighting emits a romantic golden hue to warm the cozy dining room, where close tables are set with clean, crisp linens, and topped with a votive candle and fresh flowers. A semi-private room is a great option for larger parties. The restaurant also offers outdoor seating (weather permitting) and a top-floor lounge.

The French menu features familiar favorites such as hearty and aromatic cassoulet of white beans, tender lamb, and rich duck sausage, or a traditional tarte Tatin. Though prices may be pricey by neighborhood standards, the dishes are of surprisingly fine quality.

Do not confuse X with ✿! X defines comfort, while ✿ are awarded for the best cuisine. Stars are awarded across all categories of comfort.

Where to Stay

The Maritime

363 W. 16th St. (at Ninth Ave.)

Subway: 14 St - 8 Av
Phone: 212-242-4300 or 800-466-9092
Web: www.themaritimehotel.com
Prices: **$$$**

123 Rooms

3 Suites

The Maritime Hotel

Polka-dotted with porthole windows, The Maritime Hotel is a 2003 reincarnation of the truly unique, 12-story white-tile edifice designed by Albert C. Ledner in 1966 to house the National Maritime Union. The location, amid Chelsea's art galleries and the Meatpacking District's hip nightlife, assures the property a clientele encompassing artists and fashionistas as well as business travelers.

A complimentary bottle of wine and a personalized note welcome guests to the cabin-like rooms, each echoing the nautical feel with its five-foot porthole window and palette of sea blues and greens. All include a CD player and a flat-screen LCD TV. Marble baths and 500-thread-count bed linens add the luxury of an ocean-liner state room. A warning to guests seeking peace and quiet: request a room on a higher floor rather than try and engineer the noise-reducing "window plugs" in the middle of the night.

Dining options include La Bottega, an Italian trattoria with a large outdoor terrace; and chic Matsuri for Japanese cuisine. Between Cabanas rooftop bar and Hiro Ballroom, opportunities abound to drink in the Chelsea scene.

The Bowery Hotel

A2

335 Bowery (at 3rd St.)

Subway: Astor Pl
Phone: 212-505-9100 or 866-726-9379
Web: www.theboweryhotel.com
Prices: **$$$$**

128 Rooms
7 Suites

Gregory Goode

This nondescript block of what was once known as Skid Row might seem an unlikely location for a trendy boutique hotel, but Eric Goode and Sean MacPherson (who brought you the Maritime in Chelsea) are betting that their East Village property will draw hordes of hipsters and Europeans. Though the block can be dodgy late at night, it's within easy walking distance of New York's coolest 'hoods (East Village, SoHo, Nolita, Greenwich Village, Lower East Side).

From the outside, the hotel's new redbrick façade towers castle-like above neighboring structures. Giant black-paned windows give the building a pre-war charm. Step inside and you'll be engulfed in the dim, sultry lobby, where dark woods, fireplaces, velvet couches and mosaic mirrors create a distinctly old-world air.

Those huge, sound-proofed windows afford great city views, and paired with whitewashed brick walls, make the rooms seem larger. A mix of period and contemporary pieces add to the art deco-meets-21st century design, while 500-thread-count bed linens, hi-def TV, and rainfall showerheads add luxury.

The outdoor courtyard bar and restaurant Gemma are popular with the in-crowd.

Cooper Square Hotel

A2

25 Cooper Square (bet. 4th & 5th Sts.)

Subway: Astor Pl
Phone: 212-475-5700 or 888-251-7979
Web: www.thecoopersquarehotel.com
Prices: **$$$$**

139 Rooms

6 Suites

The Cooper Square Hotel

What's different about the Bowery these days? Well, besides the appearance of chic boutiques and restaurants, the curving 21-story glass and aluminum tower that rises above Cooper Square. Designed by Carlos Zapata Studio and opened in fall 2008, this hotel adds a sleek note to a once-gritty East Village neighborhood.

Unlike its façade, the lodging's intimate interior spaces take their cues from the 19th century tenement building around which the hotel is built. Check-in is not your standard experience. When guests walk through the huge wooden doors, they are escorted not to the front desk (there isn't one), but to the Library, a book-lined lounge area set up with an honor bar and warmed by a fireplace in winter. Here room keys are issued and a more personalized version of the check-in process is accomplished.

Guests are escorted to rooms that command striking views of the city and feature a warm minimalist décor courtesy of furnishings by B & B Italia. An eclectic collection of books is on hand in each room.

Downstairs, Faustina restaurant brings the contemporary Italian cuisine of Chef Scott Conant to the East Village.

Andaz Wall Street

75 Wall St. (at Water St.)

Subway: Wall St (William St)
Phone: 212-590-1234
Web: www.andaz.com
Prices: $$$

249 Rooms
4 Suites

Andaz Wall Street

Take what you know about Hyatt Hotels and toss it out the window before entering Andaz. This designer hotel, steps away from the Stock Exchange, is part of Hyatt's international empire, but it rips the rug out from the traditional hotel experience right from the beginning. Instead of a reception desk, arriving guests relax with drink in hand while hosts provide check-in services via handheld computers (or skip it altogether– they'll check you in while you ride the elevator).

Andaz is Urdu for "however you want to express yourself," but this hotel knows exactly who it is with its chic, modern sensibility. Clean, uncluttered lines, exquisite fabrics, and distinct architectural touches define the public and private spaces. The rooms are exceedingly spacious and capped off with 11-foot ceilings. Gadget geeks drool over the technological touches, such as the bedside lighting controls and tastefully disguised data ports. Fear the fridge? Not here, where mini bars are stocked with complimentary snacks and beverages.

There is 24-hour room service for the time-starved, while others can kick back at Bar Seven Five or dine at the elegant Wall & Water restaurant.

Best Western Seaport Inn

33 Peck Slip (at Front St.)

Subway: Fulton St
Phone: 212-766-6600 or 800-937-8376
Web: www.seaportinn.com
Prices: $$

72 Rooms

Best Western Seaport Inn

This pleasant and welcoming Best Western hotel in Manhattan's Financial District is the perfect perch for history buffs seeking old New York with modern amenities to make any guest feel at home while traveling. Cobblestoned streets and Federal-style structures on the surrounding blocks transport visitors back in time to the 17th century, when the settlement known as Nieuw Amsterdam was taking shape. This hotel is steps from the historic ships docked at South Street Seaport.

Tidy, well-kept rooms have recently been refreshed; all come equipped with comforts including a safe and complimentary WiFi access (available throughout the hotel). Rooms on the 6th and 7th floors offer private balconies overlooking the Brooklyn Bridge—a glittering sight after dark. The upgraded chambers also offer flat-screen TVs and whirlpool soaking tubs. Other perks include a complimentary continental breakfast each morning and fresh-baked cookies in the afternoon.

For shoppers, the mall at Pier 17 is a short walk away (where one can also catch a water taxi to Brooklyn). Also nearby are the skyscrapers of Wall Street and the greensward of Battery Park, which borders New York Harbor.

Gild Hall

B2

15 Gold St. (enter on Platt St.)

Subway: Fulton St
Phone: 212-232-7700 or 800-268-0700
Web: www.thompsonhotels.com
Prices: **$$$**

116 Rooms
10 Suites

Thompson Hotels

A magnet for a young, hip, moneyed crowd, Gild Hall is an important member and integral part of the Thompson Hotel group. Located just steps from Wall Street, South Street Seaport, and some of downtown's best bars, this fashionable roost was conceived by interior-design guru Jim Walrod. The boutique property's style brings to mind a European gentlemen's club in the wood paneling, leather furniture, antler-shaped chandeliers, and shelves of fine literature. Yet there's nothing stodgy here; the leather furnishings sport sleek modern lines, and the chandeliers are crafted of chrome.

This clubby feel continues down the cranberry-colored hallways to the tranquil masculine-style guestrooms, where oversize leather-covered headboards, custom designed wood furnishings, and plaid throw blankets team with contemporary touches such as Sferra linens, mini-bar selections courtesy of Dean & DeLuca, and tinted glass tiles in the baths.

On the ground floor, Libertine does an ultra-modern take on an English tavern, spotlighting pub fare. Visit the Library Bar upstairs (2nd floor) if you're looking to sip on drinks and pump up the party vibe.

The Ritz-Carlton, Battery Park

2 West St. (at Battery Pl.)

Subway: Bowling Green
Phone: 212-344-0800 or 800-241-3333
Web: www.ritzcarlton.com
Prices: **$$$$**

259 Rooms
39 Suites

The Ritz-Carlton New York, Battery Park

If unique art deco furnishings, top-notch service, and stunning views of New York Harbor, the Statue of Liberty, and Ellis Island sound like your idea of a hotel, put on this Ritz. Occupying floors 3 to 14 of a 39-story glass and brick tower, the Ritz-Carlton, Battery Park lords it over a neighborhood that includes several museums as well as the greensward that defines the southwestern tip of Manhattan.

Guests nest here in spacious rooms and suites outfitted with Frette linens, featherbeds, and down duvets and pillows. Accommodations with harbor views have telescopes for checking out the dramatic waterscapes. All rooms provide classic Ritz luxury enhanced by plush robes, Bulgari bath amenities, and deep soaking tubs.

Of course, the hotel offers 24-hour room service, but you can dine on prime Angus beef on-site at 2 West; or lull over some classic cocktails in the lounge before retiring to your glorious room. Before you turn in, hand over your city-worn shoes for a complimentary overnight shine.

After a day of high-end shopping and sightseeing, return for a solid workout at the fitenss center, followed by luxurious pampering at their top-of-the-line spa.

Wall Street Inn

9 S. William St. (bet. Beaver & Broad Sts.)

Subway: Wall St (William St.)
Phone: 212-747-1500 or 877-747-1500
Web: www.thewallstreetinn.com
Prices: $$

46 Rooms

The Wall Street Inn

Although it's not actually on the street that traces the wood-plank wall erected by Dutch colonists in 1653, this charming inn is nonetheless a good option for travelers with business on Wall Street. Tucked away off William Street, the Wall Street Inn fills two landmark buildings that date back to 1895 and 1920.

Early American period reproductions, floral prints, and marble baths decorate the two classes (superior and deluxe) of tasteful rooms; and with in-room refrigerators, high-speed Internet access, a small basement exercise room, and complimentary continental breakfast, this low-key hotel offers good value for money. A small business center offers a full range of services. The back of the inn overlooks cobbled Stone Street, one of the narrow 17th century byways, which boasts some of the city's more renowned watering holes, namely Ulysses and Brouwers.

While party-loving guests appreciate the ability to stumble back to the hotel, there is a downside. Despite the soundproofed windows, lower rooms on this side of the property are privy to the noise made by other revelers on a nightly basis.

Ace Hotel New York

B1

20 W. 29th St. (at Broadway)

Subway: 28 St (Sixth Ave.)
Phone: 212-679-2222
Web: www.acehotel.com/newyork
Prices: **$$$**

262 Rooms
3 Suites

Douglas Lyle Thompson

You don't need to be an artist to stay at the Ace Hotel, but you'll certainly feel like one. Formerly known as the historic Breslin Hotel, which was once home to artists and personalities like "Diamond Jim" Brady, the design firm of Roman and Williams has completely redone the space, injecting it with an upscale bohemian flavor.

The rooms have an undeniably hip dorm room feel. The furnishings include vintage steamer trunks and other reclaimed items that give the rooms a certain thrift shop chic, while industrial furnishings (bent plumbing pipe clothes racks), plant the rooms firmly in the 21st century. Even the amenities play off the funky feel—instant ramen noodle soup sits next to the fridge, blank music sheets fill the bedside table, and the specially commissioned "bathrobes" are really more like hooded gray sweatshirts.

Ban the phrase "starving artist" from this hotel, since foodie-minded establishments are all the rage. Portland's famed Stumptown Coffee Shop has set up its first East Coast spot here, while Fort Greene's hip No. 7 has opened No. 7 Sub. The piece de resistance is The Breslin Bar and Dining Room, headed by Ken Friedman and April Bloomfield of Spotted Pig fame.

The Carlton

B1

88 Madison Ave. (at 29th St.)

Subway: 28 St (Park Ave. South)
Phone: 212-532-4100 or 800-601-8500
Web: www.carltonhotelny.com
Prices: **$$$**

294 Rooms

23 Suites

The Carlton Hotel

New and old dovetail seamlessly in this Beaux-Arts property, which premiered in 1904 as the Hotel Seville. The attractive property has gracefully entered the 21st century courtesty of a $60 million renovation led by starchitect, David Rockwell. The project's showpiece is the grand three-story lobby. With its new entrance on Madison Avenue, this space synthesizes early-20th century style with sleek seating and crystal chandeliers shrouded in cylindrical metal-mesh covers—a Rockwell signature. A sepia-toned portrait of the Hotel Seville, the lobby's focal point, glitters like a rainy scene through the three-story waterfall that envelops it.

All 317 rooms have a modern aspect and include geometric-print fabrics, 42-inch flat-screen TVs, and large work desks. Streamlined furnishings now complement such amenities as Frette linens, in-room wireless Internet access, plush robes, and Apple iHome sound systems.

Off the lobby, the Café and Dining Room are slated to receive a much-anticipated makeover in the near future.

Gramercy Park Hotel

2 Lexington Ave. (at 21st St.)

Subway: 23 St (Park Ave. South)
Phone: 212-920-3300 or 866-784-1300
Web: www.gramercyparkhotel.com
Prices: **$$$$**

140 Rooms
45 Suites

Gramercy Park Hotel

Reinvented by hip hotelier Ian Schrager and artist Julian Schnabel, the lobby of this 1925 Renaissance revival-style edifice could be an artist's home with its juxtaposition of true antiques and contemporary pieces. A custom-made Venetian glass chandelier hangs from the coffered ceiling, illuminating periodically changing works by modern masters such as Andy Warhol, Keith Haring, and Schnabel himself.

Velvet draperies in deep-rose hues with royal blue accents, tapestry-print fabrics, and louvered wood blinds lend a masculine feel to the rooms. Original photography and paintings adorn the walls. In keeping with its history of hosting artists, actors, and other glitterati, the hotel still pampers its guests. A landscaped private rooftop garden for dining (accessible only via a special key); a key to adjacent Gramercy Park—impossible to access unless you live on the square overlooking the gated greensward; personal trainers at the on-site Aerospace gym; and a "best of" room-service menu from famous area restaurants will give you the idea. Meanwhile, the celebutante scene at the Rose and Jade bars begs you to don your best Manolos.

Inn at Irving Place

56 Irving Pl. (bet 17th & 18th Sts.)

Subway: 14 St - Union Sq
Phone: 212-533-4600 or 800-685-1447
Web: www.innatirving.com
Prices: $$$$

12 Rooms

Roy Wright/The Inn at Irving Place

Infused with a 19th century charm not often found in Manhattan hotels, this inn takes up two single-family brownstones built in 1834. To find it, look for the street number; the inn is unmarked. Walk inside and you'll be enveloped in a cozy parlor furnished with antique settees and armchairs covered in floral-patterned silk. If it's cold out, chances are the fireplace will be roaring.

A glass of champagne and a plate of cookies welcome you to your room. Decked out with hardwood floors and period furniture, each of the 12 guestrooms offers a work desk, a well-stocked minibar and a Sony CD/radio. Pedestal sinks, antique mirrors, and black and white tile decorate the large bathrooms.

In the morning, a continental breakfast including fresh-baked croissants and sliced fruit is served in the parlor or delivered to your room—whichever you prefer. For a civilized afternoon break, make reservations for the five-course high tea at Lady Mendl's tea salon. Cibar Lounge, also on-site, is a clubby place for a martini and light fare.

One caveat: If you're traveling with heavy luggage in tow, note that there's a steep flight of stairs at the inn's entrance.

W - Union Square

B3

201 Park Ave. South (at 17th St.)

Subway: 14 St - Union Sq
Phone: 212-253-9119 or 877-782-0027
Web: www.whotels.com
Prices: **$$$$**

270 Rooms

18 Suites

W-New York

Since its launch in New York City in 1998, the W brand has come to signify sophistication in its minimalist contemporary design and stylish comfort. This member of the Starwood group is no exception. Designed by David Rockwell, it recalls the grand gathering places of the early 20th century inside the landmark 1911 granite and limestone Guardian Life Building, but with a modern twist. In the two-story lobby, the Living Room provides a chic place to meet and greet under tall arched windows, while up the striking staircase, the beaux arts-style Great Room preserves the past. Now used for conferences, this grand chamber is framed by splendid marble columns and original plasterwork on the coffered ceiling.

Rooms and suites each come in three sizes and even the least-expensive rooms are large by New York City standards. All see to your comfort with luxurious velvet armchairs, massive work desks, goose-down duvets and pillows, and beaming windows with an incredible view of Union Square.

The neighborhood's hip frequent the swank basement club, Underbar; while Olives caters to gourmands with a Mediterranean menu designed by Chef Todd English.

Gansevoort

18 Ninth Ave. (at 13th St.)

Subway: 14 St - 8 Av
Phone: 212-206-6700 or 877-462-7386
Web: www.hotelgansevoort.com
Prices: **$$$$**

166 Rooms
21 Suites

Hotel Gansevoort

In the Dutch language, the name "Gansevoort" refers to the goose (*gans*) at the head (*voort*) of a flock of geese, and indeed, this swanky hotel rises above; its 14 stories tower over the burgeoning hip-dom of the Meatpacking District.

As you step into the ultra-chic lobby, you'll be launched into the 21st century through a 14-foot-high revolving door. Inside, the building seems to be supported by light, thanks to internally illuminated glass columns. Lofty rooms with 9-foot ceilings dress in dusky hues with splashes of blackberry; beds wear 400-thread-count Egyptian cotton sheets, and large lavish bathrooms are equipped with sleek steel sinks. On the high floors, huge windows command fabulous views of the Hudson River and surrounding city. Downstairs, Tanuki Tavern seats 100 for Japanese food.

Speaking of views, check out the hotel's rooftop. The neighborhood hot spot and the Gansevoort's signature, the rooftop holds the hip Plunge Bar and a heated swimming pool that pipes in underwater music. Special events are made even more so in the rooftop loft, where a landscaped garden can't quite compete with the 360-degree cityscape.

The Standard

848 Washington St. (at 13th St.)

Subway: 14 St - 8 Av
Phone: 212-645-4646
Web: www.standardhotels.com
Prices: $$$

337 Rooms

The Standard, New York

Setting the standard for accommodations in the Meatpacking District, this modern slab of concrete and glass stands on concrete stilts above an area filled with low-rise warehouses. The structure's lofty position insures that the hotel lords it over the neighborhood, drinking in every inch of this spectacular city. As if that weren't enough, the building is literally suspended above the High Line, the city's newest greensward that has revamped an abandoned freight railway into a public park.

The lobby sets the sexy tone with its mirrored ceiling, sleek furnishings, and light-diffusing walls. Rooms are small, the décor funky and retro. Baths are open to the rest of the space, so privacy is in short supply. Hands-down, the floor-to-ceiling windows win the prize for their breathtaking panoramas of the Hudson River and the Manhattan skyline. Ask for a corner room to optimize your view.

Off the lobby, the Living Room cocktail lounge overlooks the grand plaza and spins tunes by live DJs on Friday and Saturday nights. But the fun doesn't stop there. The Standard is also outfitted with the outdoor Biergarten as well as Le Bain, a rooftop lounge.

The Hotel on Rivington

107 Rivington St. (bet. Essex & Ludlow Sts.)

Subway: Delancey St
Phone: 212-475-2600 or 800-915-1537
Web: www.hotelonrivington.com
Prices: **$$$**

89 Rooms

21 Suites

Hotel on Rivington

Grit and glamour collide on the Lower East Side, a neighborhood that has come into its own while retaining its diversity and refreshing lack of attitude. A great example of the area's newfound glamour, The Hotel on Rivington towers 21 stories above low-rise brick buildings. Floor-to-ceiling glass walls offer magnificent unobstructed views of Manhattan.

The remarkable result of a collaboration of cutting-edge architects, designers, decorators, and artists from around the world, this hotel combines sleek minimalist décor with ultramodern amenities, and, yes, comfort. If you notice anything else besides the view, you'll appreciate the Swedish sleep system that conforms to your every curve by sensing your body temperature and weight, as well as the Italian mosaic bathrooms decked out with heated floors, steam showers, and two-person Japanese-style soaking tubs. An on-site fitness facility, a DVD library of rare films, and a restaurant serving global fare round out the amenities.

Largely populated by guests who work in the fashion, music, and media industries, The Rivington appeals to an artsy clientele who prefer not to stay in mainstream midtown.

The Benjamin

125 E. 50th St. (bet. Lexington & Third Aves.)

Subway: 51 St
Phone: 212-715-2500 or 866-222-2365
Web: www.thebenjamin.com
Prices: **$$$$**

112 Rooms
97 Suites

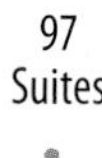

The Benjamin

From its ECOTEL certification to the cheerful and efficient staff who greet guests by name and care for them, The Benjamin ensures the comfort of its visitors. Before you arrive, just call the Sleep Concierge, who will help outfit your room with your preferred pillow (from a menu of 12 different types), aromatherapy fragrance, and relaxing lullaby. Then settle into the custom-designed mattress, wrap yourself in the fluffy duvet, and drift off to sleep. Argon-gas-filled windows should filter out any unwanted sounds. Canine guests can expect equally sweet dreams thanks to customized pet beds, puppy bathrobes, and gourmet food.

Rooms are designed as executive suites, encompassing all the technological amenities to facilitate working on-site. Many of the accommodations also have galley kitchens with state-of-the-art appliances. Given advance notice, the hotel will even stock your fridge with your favorite foods and beverages. Don't care to cook? The Restaurant at The Benjamin and the Emery Bar are right downstairs.

In the public spaces, marble floors, upholstered walls, and Venetian mirrors reflect the spirit of this 1927 structure, which owes its elegant style to architect Emery Roth.

Elysée

60 E. 54th St. (bet. Madison & Park Aves.)

Subway: 5 Av - 53 St
Phone: 212-753-1066 or 800-535-9733
Web: www.elyseehotel.com
Prices: $$$

90 Rooms

13 Suites

Hotel Elysée

Low-key, intimate, and discreet, the Elysée has weathered the decades with grace since its opening in 1926. A timeless quality pervades the black and white marble flooring and gold-fabric-covered walls of the lobby, as well as the French-influenced old-world style in the guestrooms where cut-glass and polished brass sconces cast a warm glow. In its early days, this hotel was a haven for writers, actors, and musicians. Vladimir Horowitz once lived in the suite where his piano still stands; Tennessee Williams lived and died here (in the Sunset Suite); and Ava Gardner once made this her New York home.

The property's soft residential ambience appeals to a range of patrons. Moneyed or not, they appreciate the complimentary breakfast and evening wine and hors d'oeuvres, served in the second-floor Club Room; as well as the computer located there for guest use. Guests may also request a complimentary pass for nearby NY Sports Club including their daily fitness classes.

The Elysée is known and loved for its premier location, just steps away from 5th Avenue with its shopping galore, MoMA, St. Patrick's, Rockefeller Center, and many other midtown gems.

Four Seasons New York

B1

57 E. 57th St. (bet. Madison & Park Aves.)

Subway: 59 St
Phone: 212-758-5700 or 800-487-3769
Web: www.fourseasons.com
Prices: $$$$

305 Rooms

63 Suites

Durston Saylor

In the heart of it all, New York's Four Seasons Hotel continues to have its finger on the pulse of this energetic city. Designed by renowned architect I.M Pei, the Four Seasons chooses not to wow from the outside—it looks like any other non-descript midtown building—but step inside and you'll feel that you've been transported to an oasis of peace. There is an instant hush as you glide past the doors into this temple of luxury where French limestone columns, low lighting, and gleaming floors create a sophisticated, yet soothing, atmosphere.

The guest rooms and suites manage to feel luxurious while remaining exceedingly comfortable. Deep-soaking bathtubs that fill in just 60 seconds? Check. And jaw-dropping views? Check. Four Seasons' legendary white-glove service is just another part of the "standard" offerings at this posh hotel.

It doesn't stop there. Fine dining? It's here. From caviar (Calvisius Caviar Lounge) to Chablis (Garden Wine Bar), the hotel offers a variety of settings for wining and dining. Serious foodies save their appetite for dinner at the stellar, show-stopper L'Atelier de Joël Robuchon, where French and Asian cuisines collide for spectacular results.

Hotel 57

B1

130 E. 57th St. (at Lexington Ave.)

Subway: 59 St
Phone: 212-753-8841
Web: www.marriott.com
Prices: $$

169 Rooms

31 Suites

Chris Molina

It may be owned by mega-chain Marriott, but there's nothing typical about Hotel 57. This boutique-style hotel definitely has a personality all of its own. Situated on 57th street, this hotel has a prime location, but that's not the only reason it is packed with savvy sophisticates. Stylish surroundings, a perennially packed restaurant and bar, and a palatable price point that proves being hip doesn't have to hurt are among the top reasons.

From the intimate lobby dressed in funky furnishings and unique artwork to the chic yet comfortable accommodations, this hotel sports a modern metropolitan flair. The rooms and suites are well designed (spacious, marble bathrooms, ample closet space, convenient built-ins) and complete the urban, contemporary look with neutral colors, birch wood paneling, and sleek furnishings. Exposed brick and features like back-lit headboards lend a unique flavor to the accommodations.

Step outside onto 57th street and a world of dining, shopping, and sightseeing awaits, but you don't need to go far to find a festive spirit. Opia Restaurant and Lounge is always hopping with a chic crowd of hotel guests and New Yorkers who come for the food and fun.

Library

A4

299 Madison Ave. (enter on 41st St.)

Subway: Grand Central - 42 St
Phone: 212-983-4500 or 877-793-7323
Web: www.libraryhotel.com
Prices: **$$$**

60 Rooms

HK Hotels

A welcoming inn well-located in midtown, The Library keeps to a literary theme with its collection of 6,000 volumes (if that's not enough books for you, the New York Public and the Pierpont Morgan libraries are just minutes away). Each floor is numbered after a category in the Dewey Decimal System, and rooms contain books on a particular subject. Math maven? Request a room on the fifth floor. Literature your thing? Head to the 8th floor.

Rooms, though small, are comfortable, and manage to squeeze a basic desk, an all-inclusive entertainment center (containing bookshelves, drawers, a small closet, a mini bar, and a flat-screen TV) into the cramped quarters. Modern bathrooms come equipped with a hairdryer, magnifying mirror, and scale.

On the second floor, the Reading Room is where you'll find the complimentary continental breakfast laid out in the morning, snacks throughout the day, and the wine and cheese reception each evening. The comfy Writer's Den and the terrace Poetry Garden are perfect for—what else?—reading.

When it's warm outside, head up to the rooftop bar—Bookmarks—for a cocktail and snack.

New York Palace

455 Madison Ave. (enter on 50th St.)

Subway: 51 St
Phone: 212-888-7000 or 800-697-2522
Web: www.newyorkpalace.com
Prices: $$$$

808 Rooms

86 Suites

The New York Palace

Best recognized by its lovely gated courtyard—formerly a carriage entrance—on Madison Avenue at 50th Street, The Palace serves up New York City on a silver platter. Enter through these gates and you'll be immersed in the old-world opulence that fills the 1882 Villard Houses, a U-shaped group of brownstones designed in the Italian Renaissance style by the firm of McKim, Mead and White.

Today the property blends the town houses with a 55-story tower added in 1980. Here, you'll find 808 guest rooms, 86 suites, a vast spa and fitness center, and 22,000 square feet of conference facilities. Guests in the modern tower rooms have access to a private lounge and concierge, as well as personal butler services. More modest deluxe rooms feature no less comfort, however, with their warm tones, new bedding, and oversize marble baths.

If you can tear yourself away from this palace be sure to check out the neighboring sights and sounds. Come back for afternoon tea in the lobby, or to experience cutting-edge cuisine in Gilt's sexy walnut-paneled space. Sophisticated cocktails abound in the contemporary Gilt Bar; and during warmer months, the opulent courtyard is home to the Palace Gate lounge.

Roger Williams

131 Madison Ave. (at 31st St.)

Subway: 33 St
Phone: 212-448-7000 or 888-448-7788
Web: www.hotelrogerwilliams.com
Prices: $$$

191 Rooms
2 Suites

Hotel Roger Williams

Just blocks from the Empire State Building, this stylish boutique hotel makes a bright impression with its clean lines and pure colors. The "living room," as the lobby is called, is adorned with light wood paneling, soaring ceilings, and 20-foot-high windows creating an airy, cosmopolitan feel. Comfy contemporary furniture scattered throughout the lobby provide contemporary spaces to meet and greet.

Though on the small side, rooms at "the Roger" all feature flat-screen plasma TVs, mini bars, Aveda bath products, and wireless high-speed Internet access. Splashes of tangerine, lime green, cobalt blue, and red illuminate each room. The peppy colors aren't noisy and neither are the accommodations, thanks to well-insulated windows that help dampen the hustle and bustle of midtown. Japanese-inspired double rooms add shoji screens and sliding-glass bathroom doors, while 15 garden terrace rooms enjoy private patios and stirring cityscapes.

A help-yourself European style breakfast—ranging from fresh croissants, to smoked salmon and prosciutto—is available in the mezzanine lounge each morning, and it's a sunny spot for an afternoon espresso as well.

70 Park Avenue

70 Park Ave. (at 38th St.)

Subway: Grand Central - 42 St
Phone: 212-973-2400 or 877-707-2752
Web: www.70parkave.com
Prices: $$$

201 Rooms
4 Suites

David Phelps

For sophisticated midtown digs located mere minutes away by foot from Grand Central Terminal, 70 Park can't be beat. This Murray Hill property embodies the Kimpton Group's signature elements: care, comfort, style, flavor, and fun.

Care highlights thoughtful amenities such as the pet-friendly policy, and a dedicated yoga channel on your flat-screen TV. In-room comfort surrounds you in the down comforters and pillows, terrycloth robes, and luxury bath products. Designed by Jeffrey Bilhuber in neutral hues of limestone gray, shimming bronze, and light cocoa brown, the hotel's contemporary style speaks for itself. The complimentary wine reception held around the limestone fireplace on weeknights affords guests an opportunity for fun, as does the lively bar scene at the Silverleaf Tavern. You'll taste the 70 Park flavor in the tavern's limited menu of pub fare.

Other reasons to stay here? An easy walk to midtown offices and shopping, 24-hour room service, in-room spa services, and guest privileges at the NY Sports Club—a couple of blocks away. Strollers, cribs, and connecting rooms accommodate families.

The St. Regis

A2

2 E. 55th St. (at Fifth Ave.)

Subway: 5 Av - 53 St
Phone: 212-753-4500 or 800-759-7550
Web: www.stregis.com/newyork
Prices: **$$$$**

164 Rooms
65 Suites

Bruce Buck

Stylish and elegant, and with service close to perfection, the St. Regis reigns among the city's finest hotels. Commissioned by John Jacob Astor in 1904, this Beaux-Arts confection at the corner of Fifth Avenue is located just blocks from Central Park, MoMA, and other midtown attractions. Its public spaces and lobby, from the painted ceilings to the marble staircase, are steeped in Gilded Age opulence.

Rooms fitted with elegant guestrooms are lined with silk wall coverings and custom-made furniture. Guests in the spacious suites (the smallest is 600 square feet and range up to 3,400 square feet) are cosseted with extra luxuries, such as a bouquet of fresh roses delivered daily. Unparalleled service includes a butler you can call on 24 hours a day, an on-site florist, complimentary garment pressing when you arrive, and the exclusive Remède spa. Their signature massage calms jangled nerves with a mix of Shiatsu, Swedish, deep-tissue, and reflexology.

Be sure to stop in the King Cole Bar to peek at Maxfield Parrish's famous mural, and to sip a Bloody Mary, which was introduced here in the 1920s.

The Vincci Avalon

16 E. 32nd St. (bet. Fifth & Madison Aves.)

Subway: 33 St
Phone: 212-299-7000 or 888-442-8256
Web: www.theavalonny.com
Prices: **$$**

80 Rooms

20 Suites

Vincci Avalon

Right around the corner from the Empire State Building, this boutique property indulges business travelers with six meeting rooms and complimentary high-speed Internet access in each guestroom. Leisure travelers and theater lovers profit from The Avalon's setting, a short walk from Times Square and the bright lights of Broadway.

All appreciate large "Superior" rooms, each of which flaunt 27-inch flat-screen TVs, ample closet space, velour robes, and Irish cotton linens. Dark hardwood floors, earth tones (soft green, brown, and rust), and Italian marble baths accentuate the décor. At the top tier of room types, the 20 executive suites average 450 square feet and come with Jacuzzi tubs, fax machines, sofa beds, and Bose Wave radios.

Just off the elegant lobby, which is set about with pillars and paneling, the Library/Club room is a den-like area with free access to WiFi and a personal computer. Guests here will enjoy thoughtful and warm service from the affable staff, as well as discounted passes to the nearby Boom gym. The Serra Mediterranean Bistro serves a scrumptious spread for breakfast every morning and American fare for lunch and dinner.

The Waldorf=Astoria

B3

301 Park Ave. (bet. 49th & 50th Sts.)

Subway: 51 St
Phone: 212-355-3000 or 800-925-3673
Web: www.waldorfastoria.com
Prices: **$$$$**

1085 Rooms

331 Suites

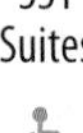

Waldorf=Astoria

Nothing says New York high society like The Waldorf=Astoria. Built in 1931, the hotel blends exquisite art deco ornamentation and lavish Second Empire furnishings. The original Waldorf, built in 1893, was demolished along with its companion, the Astoria, to make room for the Empire State Building. The huge "new" hotel (including its boutique counterpart with a private entrance, the Waldorf Towers) occupies the entire block between Park and Lexington avenues. Its lobby features a striking inlaid-tile mosaic and art deco chandelier, and emanates a generally palatial feel.

A $400-million renovation refreshed the grand dame; and deluxe fabrics as well as classic furniture dress the richly appointed and beautifully maintained rooms and suites, all outfitted with sumptuous marble baths.

Long a midtown power scene, the mahogany-paneled Bull and Bear teems with brokers and finance types who come for the signature martinis, the dry-aged prime Angus beef, and the men's-club ambience. Also among the property's three restaurants, Peacock Alley (in the center of the main lobby) is worth seeking out for its elegant cuisine.

Algonquin

59 W. 44th St. (bet. Fifth & Sixth Aves.)

Subway: 42 St - Bryant Pk
Phone: 212-840-6800
Web: www.algonquinhotel.com
Prices: $$$

150 Rooms

24 Suites

Algonquin Hotel

New York's oldest operating hotel remains true to its classically elegant roots and timeless aura. Best known for the the circle of literati, including Dorothy Parker and Robert Benchley, who lunched in the Round Table Room in the years after World War I, the Algonquin preserves the feel and look of a fine Edwardian club.

Rooms have been smartly upgraded to include all modern amenities (tastefully hidden); top-quality fabrics and fittings lend rich jewel tones to the accommodations. You may not want to rise from your pillow-top mattress, 350-thread-count linen sheets, down pillows, and the famous "Algonquin Bed." (Order one for home, if you like.) Each of the suites adds a fully stocked refrigerator.

For a taste of 1930s café society, step into the Oak Room, the legendary cabaret where famous audiences and performers (crooners Harry Connick Jr. and Diana Krall got their starts here) made merry. The mood lingers, and the shows still go on, with such talent as Andrea Marcovicci and Jack Jones. In the intimate Blue Bar, you'll find artwork by the late Al Hirschfeld, who was a regular.

The Blakely

136 W. 55th St. (bet. Sixth & Seventh Aves.)

Subway: 57 St
Phone: 212-245-1800
Web: www.blakelynewyork.com
Prices: $$

63 Rooms
55 Suites

Blakely New York

Don't expect hipsters lounging in the lobby or rooms designed by the latest "it" decorator at The Blakely. Instead, this comfortable hotel is a perfect home-away-from-home for those looking for a terrific bang for the buck. Its enviable location puts this hotel smack dab in the heart of midtown's action. Business travelers flock here for access to area offices, but it's also a great choice for vacationers who want to traipse over to Central Park or hit up the shops on Fifth Avenue.

Everything about The Blakely feels like a classic New York residence. At first glance, the brick façade and blue awning could easily be mistaken for a private building, but it's the inside where guests feel immediately at home. The hotel shows off its old bones with terrific wood floors and large wood-framed windows.

The intimate English-style lobby is inviting, and the rooms and suites are well-designed to maximize comfort and function. Suites, equipped with kitchenettes and fully stocked pantries, are exceptionally large and are worth the extra bucks. If making your own coffee and snacks just isn't on your agenda, room service is available through the hotel's restaurant, Abboccato.

Casablanca

C3

147 W. 43rd St. (bet. Broadway & Sixth Ave.)

Subway: 42 St - Bryant Pk
Phone: 212-869-1212 or 888-922-7225
Web: www.casablancahotel.com
Prices: $$

43 Rooms

5 Suites

Christopher Ottaunick/HK Hotels

Exotic tilework, warm wood paneling, and wrought-iron details greet guests at this European-style hotel. Convenient to Times Square and its many attractions, the Casablanca takes on the theme of the 1942 film starring Humphrey Bogart and Ingrid Bergman—without being kitschy. All the elements are here, from the pastel mural of the city of Casablanca that decorates the lobby stairway to the second-floor café called—you guessed it—Rick's.

With its tiled fireplace and bentwood chairs, Rick's Café is where you can wake up to a complimentary continental breakfast. In the afternoon, a selection of tea, coffee drinks, and cookies will tide you over until the wine-and-cheese reception at 5:00 P.M. Room service is provided by Tony's di Napoli restaurant, next door to the hotel.

The Moroccan ambience extends to the rooms, furnished with wooden headboards, damask linens, ceiling fans, and bathrobes. Guests enjoy free passes to the New York Sports Club, and a DVD library of films starring New York City.

No matter where you go when you leave this oasis, one thing's for sure: you'll always have Casablanca.

Chambers

15 W. 56th St. (bet. Fifth & Sixth Aves.)

Subway: 57 St
Phone: 212-974-5656 or 866-204-5656
Web: www.chambershotel.com
Prices: **$$$$**

72 Rooms

5 Suites

Scott G. Morris/SGM Photography

Ideal for doing serious business or serious shopping (Bendel's is around the corner; Norma Kamali is next door; Bergdorf's is one block up), Chambers exudes a downtown feel despite its midtown location. It all begins with the two-story lobby where plenty of open space and a flickering fireplace provide a welcome cozy space. Sequestered seating on the mezzanine level above is the place to sneak away to with your laptop or a glass of wine—perhaps both.

The hotel's commitment to contemporary artists shows beautifully in the well-curated collection of more than 500 original pieces of art that is displayed throughout the public spaces, with different installations on each floor. Rooms continue the modern mood in SoHo-like appointments such as a plate-glass desktop balanced on a sawhorse-style base, and a poured concrete floor in the bathroom. Despite the cool aspect of the front-desk staff, service is very warm and accommodating.

Whether you're visiting for business or pleasure, one thing is for sure, the hotel will envelop you with their creativity and luxury.

City Club

55 W. 44th St. (bet. Fifth & Sixth Aves.)

Subway: 42 St - Bryant Pk
Phone: 212-921-5500
Web: www.cityclubhotel.com
Prices: $$$

62 Rooms
3 Suites

Matthew Hranek

Originally conceived as an elite social club opened in 1904, the City Club now opens its doors to all. Located on 44th Street, the intimately scaled hotel is situated among a number of still active private clubs and has a sophisticated and exclusive ambience with a petite lobby that feels more like the entryway of a private residence than a hotel. The rooms are attractively designed to maximize square footage with a handsome beige and brown color scheme dominating. Marble bathrooms are outfitted with bidets and Waterworks showers.

All guests enjoy complimentary high-speed Internet access as well as in-room DVD players, and electronic safe-deposit boxes. In the evening, turndown service includes a plate of freshly baked cookies. Truly spectacular are the hotel's three duplex suites, decked out with private terraces and circular stairways that lead up to the sleeping room from a well-appointed sitting room below. Room Service is provided by Daniel Boulud's db Bistro Moderne which connects to the lobby via a paneled wine bar.

Jumeirah Essex House

160 Central Park South (bet. Sixth & Seventh Aves.)

Subway: 57 St - 7 Av
Phone: 212-247-0300 or 888-645-5697
Web: www.jumeirahessexhouse.com
Prices: $$$$

428 Rooms
81 Suites

Jumeirah Essex House

Operated by the Dubai-based Jumeirah hospitality group, the venerable Essex House flaunts its enviable location at the foot of Central Park, with the shops and restaurants of 5th Avenue and the Time Warner Center right outside its door. This art deco gem, which opened its doors the same year as the Empire State Building (1931), underwent a $90-million face-lift after its new owners took over. Public spaces, outfitted with the likes of Macassar ebony chairs, and red wool carpets hand-knotted in Nepal, now pay homage to the hotel's vintage.

Why wouldn't you feel coddled in a room fitted with custom-designed furnishings, a glass-vessel sink, a touch-screen control pad, and lights underneath the nightstands to prevent stumbling in the dark? Access to the in-house spa and 24-hour health club are added perks.

Newest on the roster of renovations is the 2,500-square-foot two-bedroom Presidential Suite, indeed fit for royalty with magnificent park views, original artwork, sumptuous fabrics, and bathrooms lined in marble and rosewood.

Tony Chi designed the dining room at South Gate, where contemporary cuisine takes on an urbane twist.

Le Parker Meridien

118 W. 57th St. (bet. Sixth & Seventh Aves.)

Subway: 57 St
Phone: 212-245-5000 or 800-543-4300
Web: www.parkermeridien.com
Prices: $$$$

510 Rooms

221 Suites

Le Parker Meridien New York

To reach the lobby here, guests must pass through a columned, two-story lounge lined with marble, which sets the tone for Le Parker Meridien experience. The hotel, just steps away from Carnegie Hall, Central Park, and Fifth Avenue shops, divides its accommodations between the upper and lower tower—each has their own elevator bank.

Expect ergonomically designed rooms and suites to tout contemporary chic with platform beds, warm woods, 32-inch TVs, and CD/DVD players. There's a business center on-site, but if you wish to work in your room, a large desk, high-speed Internet access, and a halogen reading lamp provide all the necessities.

In the morning, fuel up on tasty breakfast dishes at Norma's. Then get in a workout at Gravity—the 15,000-square-foot fitness facility—or take a dip in the enclosed and heated rooftop pool that overlooks Central Park. For dinner, choose between French bistro fare at Seppi's or a simple burger at the rough-and-ready burger joint, arguably the best in the city.

Whimsical touches, like a "do not disturb" sign that reads "fuhgetaboudit," and vintage cartoons broadcast in the guest elevators, set this place apart from your standard midtown business hotel.

The London NYC

151 W. 54th St. (bet. Sixth & Seventh Aves.)

Subway: 57 St
Phone: 212-307-5000 or 866-690-2029
Web: www.thelondonnyc.com
Prices: $$$$

552 Rooms
10 Suites

The London NYC

The London NYC is like a hop across the pond without the guilt of those pesky carbon emissions. Formerly the Righa Royal Hotel, The London with its ivy-covered façade rises a glorious 54 stories above Manhattan's midtown.

Guest suites epitomize modern sophistication with Italian linens, limed oak flooring, sectional sofas, and embossed-leather desks. Tones of soft gray, plum, sky-blue, and crisp white dominate. Styled by Waterworks, bathrooms have the last word in luxury, with white marble mosaic-tile floors, double rain showerheads, and sumptuous towels and bathrobes.

Since service is a hallmark of The London, the expert concierge services of Quintessentially are on hand to assist you with any business or personal requests. Novel extras include complimentary cleaning of your workout wear, and an iPod docking station in each room.

The hotel's elegant dining room, Gordon Ramsay at The London, is no longer home to the cantankerous chef, but continues to impresses with its polished service and contemporary cuisine. For a casual alternative, try boisterous Maze for it's worldly menu of small plates served in a sleek brasserie setting.

Metro

45 W. 35th St. (bet. Fifth & Sixth Aves.)

Subway: 34 St - Herald Sq
Phone: 212-947-2500 or 800-356-3870
Web: www.hotelmetronyc.com
Prices: $$

161 Rooms
18 Suites

Hotel Metro

Though not hip or stylish, the Hotel Metro is nonetheless a good stay for the money. Located in the heart of the Garment District, near Penn Station (light sleepers take note that the hotel's location is not a quiet one), the building was constructed in 1901. An art deco-inspired lobby leads into a spacious breakfast room/lounge where tea and coffee are available throughout the day.

Guest rooms have been recently refurbished and are equipped with mini-bars, and upgraded "plush-top" mattresses. Many of the marble bathrooms benefit from natural light, and the overall standard of housekeeping is good. The hotel offers high-speed wireless Internet access, as well as a small business center. Room rates include a complimentary continental breakfast served in the lounge area.

From the large rooftop bar which has become quite popular, you can enjoy stunning views of the Empire State Building and the surrounding neighborhood, which includes Macy's, for all you hard-core shoppers.

The Michelangelo

152 W. 51st St. (at Seventh Ave.)

Subway: 50 St (Broadway)
Phone: 212-765-1900 or 800-237-0990
Web: www.michelangelohotel.com
Prices: $$$

123 Rooms

55 Suites

James Starkman/Starquest Media LLC

Steps from Times Square, the Theater District, Rockefeller Center, and midtown offices, The Michelangelo caters to both leisure and business travelers. A recent renovation has polished the two-story lobby, regal in its liberal use of marble, rich fabric panels, and crystal chandeliers.

Winding hallways have been freshened with new paint and carpeting; shelves of books add a homey touch. Attractively appointed with marble foyers, small sitting areas, down pillows, and Bose radio/CD players, guest rooms are generous for Manhattan, with a standard king measuring about 325 square feet (upgrades get bigger from there). Marble bathrooms come equipped with hair dryers, make-up mirrors, deep soaking tubs, terrycloth robes, and even a small TV. Part of the Starhotels group, The Michelangelo interprets hospitality with *gusto di vivere italiano*. Turndown service, a complimentary continental breakfast, a small fitness center, and limo service to Wall Street on weekday mornings number among the amenities.

The sophisticated Italian theme carries over to the hotel's dining room, Insieme, which proffers an urbane take on Italian dining.

The Peninsula New York

B4

700 Fifth Ave. (at 55th St.)

Subway: 5 Av - 53 St
Phone: 212-956-2888 or 800-262-9467
Web: www.peninsula.com
Prices: $$$$

185 Rooms

54 Suites

The Peninsula New York

When this magnificent 1905 hotel was built as The Gotham, it was the city's tallest skyscraper, towering 23 stories. Today the property still sparkles as the Peninsula group's U.S. flagship.

Plush rooms exude a timeless elegance, and art nouveau accents complement their rich colors and appointments. Ample in size and well-conceived for business travelers, each guest room provides a silent fax machine, and a bottled-water bar (with a choice of still or sparkling water). Service is a strong suit at The Peninsula, and the smartly liveried staff effortlessly executes your every request.

You could spend hours on the rooftop, site of the new ESPA, the state-of-the-art fitness center, and the glass-enclosed pool. Asian, European, and Ayurvedic philosophies inspire the spa treatments; check in early and relax in the Asian tea lounge, then loosen up those muscles in the steam room or sauna before your massage. Sharing this lofty perch, the new rooftop bar, Salon de Ning, wows patrons with its Fifth Avenue views and vivid Shanghai style. In addition to the interior bar, there are two large outdoor terraces furnished with Chinese-style day beds—perfect for a romantic liaison.

The Plaza

768 Fifth Ave. (at Central Park South)

Subway: 5 Av - 59 St
Phone: 212-759-3000
Web: www.theplaza.com
Prices: **$$$$**

180 Rooms

102 Suites

The Plaza Hotel

This storied Beaux-Arts masterpiece once again ushers the well-heeled and well-traveled through its gilded doors. Opened in 1907 and now managed by Fairmont Hotels & Resorts, this historic landmark has been lavishly renovated to restore the past and embrace the future. The hotel's Fifth Avenue lobby has an ethereal feel with gleaming marble flooring, Baccarat chandeliers, and picture windows framing the Pulitzer fountain in Grand Army Plaza.

Generously sized accommodations mix elegant appointments with a touch-screen monitor that dims the lighting, adjusts the temperature, and contacts guest services. You won't want to leave the mosaic stone-tiled bathroom complete with 24-karat-gold fixtures. And with each guest floor staffed by a team of affable butlers, the service is as impressive as the surroundings.

Purveyors of all things luxurious await the Shops at The Plaza and The Plaza Food Hall by Todd English. For prime pampering, treatments at Caudalíe Vinothérapie Spa use beneficial polyphenols extracted from grapes. End your day with a Manhattan at the Oak Bar followed by a scrumptious dinner at the spiffed-up Oak Room.

The Ritz-Carlton, Central Park

B3

50 Central Park South (at Sixth Ave.)

Subway: 5 Av - 59 St
Phone: 212-308-9100 or 800-826-8129
Web: www.ritzcarlton.com
Prices: $$$$

212 Rooms

47 Suites

The Ritz-Carlton New York, Central Park

Built in 1929 as the St. Moritz, the Ritz holds its place at the vanguard of luxury and graceful service among Manhattan's hotels. While the marble-floored reception lobby remains intimate, it opens into a grand two-story gathering space.

Sumptuous guestrooms are generously sized, beginning at 425 square feet and topping out at 1,900 for the Central Park Suite. Steeped in Old World elegance, rooms dress up in rich fabrics, crisp, white 400-thread-count linens, and a plethora of fluffy pillows. Gleaming, luxurious, and oversized marble baths are stocked with spacious vanities, hairdryers, and Frédéric Fekkai products.

If stress has sapped your energy, a visit to the on-site La Prairie spa is in order. The massage menu tailors treatments to most every ailment of upscale urban life, including jet lag, shopping fatigue, and executive stress.

The addition of BLT Market brings a frequently changing menu of market-fresh breakfast and dinner fare designed by Chef Laurent Tourondel. For afternoon tea or a well-shaken martini, stop by the clubby Star Lounge, or relax in the lobby over an expertly-prepared and served refreshment.

6 Columbus

6 Columbus Circle (at 58th St.)

Subway: 59 St - Columbus Circle
Phone: 212-204-3000
Web: www.sixcolumbus.com
Prices: $$

72 Rooms
16 Suites

6 Columbus

This new addition to the Thompson Hotels collection (which includes 60 Thompson in SoHo) sparkles with a hip vibe. You can't beat the location, across the street from the Time Warner Center and Central Park. Despite its ritzy setting, the urban retreat is casual in style and surprisingly reasonable in price.

Sixties-mod describes the décor, which dresses the public spaces with teak paneling, molded chairs, and leather sofas in a palette of earthy tones. The same spirit—and teak paneling—infuses the sleek rooms, where custom-made furniture and chrome accents abound. Walls are decorated with artwork by fashion photographer Guy Bourdin. Frette linens, soft lighting, iPod docking stations, and complimentary WiFi Internet access round out the amenities. Bath products are by Fresh.

Adjacent to the lobby, Blue Ribbon Sushi Bar and Grill adds a new concept by the well-known Blue Ribbon restaurants group. Japanese fare here runs the gamut from hamachi to hanger steak. As for the young staff, they're friendly and helpful, catering to a clientele largely made up of savvy urban professionals and international visitors.

Sofitel

45 W. 44th St. (bet. Fifth & Sixth Aves.)

Subway: 47-50 Sts - Rockefeller Ctr
Phone: 212-354-8844 or 877-565-9240
Web: www.sofitel-newyork.com
Prices: $$$$

346 Rooms

52 Suites

Sofitel

Located mid-block on 44th Street, this 30-story glass and limestone tower couldn't be more convenient to Fifth Avenue shopping, Times Square, and the Theater District. It's an easy walk from here to Grand Central Station too. Owned by the French hotel group—Accor—the Sofitel New York maintains a European feel throughout.

The art deco-style lobby is as welcoming as it is elegant, set about with blonde wood paneling, green marble, and groups of sleek leather club chairs arranged on a colorful floral-patterned carpet. Off the lobby, Gaby Bar offers a stylish lounge in which to sip a cocktail, while its sister restaurant—also called Gaby—features flavorful French classics along with more contemporary fare for lunch and dinner.

Honey-colored velvet drapes, red chenille armchairs, sumptuous damask linens, and marble baths outfit the attractive and well-maintained guest rooms. The glass-topped blonde wood desk paired with a cushioned leather chair caters to business travelers; WiFi Internet access is available for a fee. A thoughtful touch for European guests, a voltage adaptor is included in each room.

Washington Jefferson Hotel

318 W. 51st St. (bet. Eighth & Ninth Aves.)

Subway: 50 St (Eighth Ave.)
Phone: 212-246-7550 or 888-567-7550
Web: www.wjhotel.com
Prices: $

135 Rooms

The Washington Jefferson Hotel

Fresh, contemporary design at a decent price in Manhattan was once a pipe dream, but the Washington Jefferson Hotel delivers style without a high price tag. Located in the up-and-coming neighborhood of Hell's Kitchen, the hotel is close to the bright lights of the Theater District.

The lobby is warm and welcoming, and the staff ensures that all guests feel at home from the moment they step inside the doors. Rooms are somewhat spartan, with platform beds dressed in crisp white linens, yet provide all the necessary amenities (TV with premium channels, radio/CD player). Clean lines extend to the bathrooms, outfitted with slate flooring and slate-tiled tubs. While standard rooms are on the small side, comfort is never sacrificed. Guests have 24-hour access to a small exercise room on-site, while serious athletes can take advantage of the reduced-price daily pass to Gold's Gym, available at the hotel's front desk.

Although there is no room service, you can enjoy lunch and dinner at the hotel's restaurant, Shimizu. Sushi is a popular component here, but for those who prefer their fish cooked, the restaurant offers a delightful array of traditional Japanese dishes.

Crosby Street Hotel

79 Crosby St. (bet. Prince & Spring Sts.)

Subway: Prince St
Phone: 212-226-6400
Web: www.crosbystreethotel.com
Prices: $$$$

75 Rooms
11 Suites

Firmdale Hotels

Tim and Kit Kemp, the very successful husband- and -wife team behind some of London's hottest properties, have hopped across the Pond for their American debut, and it looks like they've done it again. They picked the right spot—in the heart of SoHo on a charming cobblestoned street—but this hotel's attributes go far beyond location alone.

Kit Kemp has won awards for her inimitable design sense which is equal parts quirky and delightful. Distinctive artwork and objects are littered throughout the public and private spaces and are surefire conversation starters. The guest-only drawing room (perfect for afternoon tea) and its adjacent private garden provide an oasis in the Big City. Amenities include a well-equipped gym, private screening room, and a restaurant/bar.

Interesting patterns and pops of color define the guestrooms, which look and feel like an artist's pied-à-terre. Fabric-covered headboards, silk embroidered pillows, and eclectic decorative items prove that details are big here. Guests may linger at writing desks (turn-down service brings sharpened pencils), or enjoy the unobstructed views (on higher floors) and fresh air (the windows open!) from the lovely window seats.

The Mercer

B1

147 Mercer St. (at Prince St.)

Subway: Prince St
Phone: 212-966-6060
Web: www.mercerhotel.com
Prices: $$$$

67 Rooms
8 Suites

Thomas Loof

Even if your name isn't Leonardo DiCaprio, Cher, or Calvin Klein, you'll be equally welcome at The Mercer. Housed in a striking Romanesque Revival-style building erected in 1890, the hotel caters to the glitterati with discreet, personalized service, and intimate elegance. The modern lobby feels like your stylish friend's living room, complete with comfy seating, appealing coffee-table books, and an Apple for guests' use.

A Zen vibe pervades the guestrooms, fashioned by Parisian interior designer Christian Liaigre with high, loft-like ceilings, large European-style windows, soothing neutral palettes, and Asian decorative touches. Don't fret if you get a room facing the street; soundproofing filters out the noise. You'll find everything you need for business or leisure travel in your room, right down to scented candles and oversize FACE Stockholm bath products. Forgot something? The hotel's warm staff will gladly accommodate you with a laptop, a cell phone, or a fax machine in your room.

Sure, the hotel offers 24-hour room service, but in this case the food comes from downstairs, Chef Jean-Georges Vongerichten's modern Mercer Kitchen.

60 Thompson

B1

60 Thompson St. (bet. Broome & Spring Sts.)

Subway: Spring St (Sixth Ave.)
Phone: 212-431-0400 or 877-431-0400
Web: www.60thompson.com
Prices: $$$$

87 Rooms
10 Suites

60 Thompson

With its spare 1940s look inspired by French designer Jean-Michel Frank, 60 Thompson absolutely oozes SoHo style. The lobby, decorated in gray, brown, and moss-green tones, is accented by bouquets of fresh flowers, and natural light floods in from floor-to-ceiling windows.

Room sizes vary, but all sport a minimalist look, with crisp, white Frette linens standing out against a wall of dark, paneled leather. Business travelers take note that 60 Thompson has replaced the requisite in-room desk with a sitting area in its standard rooms. Bathrooms are tiled with chocolate-colored marble and stocked with spa products by Fresh. For those who don't appreciate the smell of cigarette smoke in their room, the hotel devotes two entire floors to non-smoking chambers.

Check out the rooftop bar on the 12th floor, where you can sip a cocktail and drink in the great city views. In good weather, the rooftop scene is a hot one, whereas the lobby bar bustles year-round with a cool crowd. Downstairs, Kittichai puts out modern Thai cuisine in an Asian-chic setting. The small bar here mixes fantastic and creative cocktails.

Soho Grand

B2

310 West Broadway (bet. Canal & Grand Sts.)

Subway: Canal St (Sixth Ave.)
Phone: 212-965-3000 or 800-965-3000
Web: www.sohogrand.com
Prices: $$$$

361 Rooms

2 Suites

Soho Grand Hotel

Cutting-edge fashion, fine art, and delicious dining beckon in the blocks right outside this hip hotel (whose equally chic sister, the Tribeca Grand, lies a short walk to the south). Inside, designer William Sofield calls to mind the neighborhood's industrial roots in the lobby's clean lines, concrete pillars, and cast-iron details.

Rooms are swathed in neutral tones, with leather headboards, Egyptian cotton sheets, and a host of modern amenities. Bose Wave CD/radios, DVD players, and in-room CD selections come in every room; iPods and docking stations are available on request. For true grandeur, reserve one of the penthouse lofts. In these spacious custom-designed suites, you will have the luxury of two bedrooms, as well as a 1,200-square-foot wraparound furnished terrace on which to entertain or simply to take in the killer view of the Manhattan skyline.

Bicycles are on hand for complimentary guest use when the weather permits; and the hotel's "grandlife" website provides a wealth of information about goings-on in the city. Families are welcomed with signature programs for babies and children, not to mention the hotel's pet-friendly policy. Ain't life grand?

Trump SoHo

246 Spring St. (at Varick St.)

Subway: Spring St (Sixth Ave.)
Phone: 212-842-5500
Web: www.trumpsohohotel.com
Prices: $$$$

245 Rooms
146 Suites

Phillip Ennis Photography

You definitely won't need directions to find this hotel—just look up. Trump SoHo's lanky silver-glass skyscraper dominates the SoHo skyline.

This stylish hotel caters to well-heeled business and leisure travelers who appreciate the convenience of downtown but crave the creature comforts of a serious hotel. Whether it's the personal shopping and other individualized services of the Trump Attache or the 11,000 square-foot spa (the largest in the city!), the amenities are top-notch.

Milan meets Manhattan in the guestrooms and suites. Outfitted in sleek furnishings by Casa Fendi, they are the last word in modern elegance. Chocolate brown tufted leather headboards, curvy benches, chrome fixtures—it's all very glam in a masculine way. Whether it's the tech gadgets or the fluffy bedside rugs, the rooms have it all.

The public spaces are not to be outdone by the fabulous guestrooms, though. Whether you seek quiet reflection and a cappuccino at The Library, dig in to upscale Italian at Quattro Gastronomia, or hit up late-night hot spot Kastel, Trump SoHo has you covered. Feeling competitive? Take the elevator up to Bar d'Eau, the indoor/outdoor pool deck complete with a bocce court.

Cosmopolitan

B3

95 West Broadway (at Chambers St.)

Subway: Chambers St (West Broadway)
Phone: 212-566-1900 or 888-895-9400
Web: www.cosmohotel.com
Prices: $

125 Rooms

Cosmopolitan Hotel

This privately owned seven-story hotel enjoys a valuable location in the heart of TriBeCa, while catering to more budget-conscious visitors to the city. Just a few steps away from Wall Street, SoHo, and Chinatown, the Cosmopolitan pulls in a steady clientele of business travelers and European tourists, who may appreciate the hotel's low prices, convenient setting, and cigarette-friendly policy.

The Cosmopolitan may lack the frills of some grander city hostelries, but guests can use the money saved on a room here to splurge on a show or dinner in a fine restaurant. Basic rooms are well-maintained, fairly spacious, and they all have private baths. Scant in-room amenities include a hair dryer, cable TV, a ceiling fan, and free wireless Internet access. Ask for a room on the back side of the hotel if worried about the street noise. Despite the fact that the entire hotel is smoking-friendly, the halls and the rooms seems absent of cigarettes traces.

The hotel does not offer room service, but the Cosmopolitan Café is right next door. This tiny eatery, with its rustic country style, makes a good spot for a light breakfast or to catch a quick sandwich at midday.

Greenwich Hotel

377 Greenwich St. (at N. Moore St.)

Subway: Franklin St
Phone: 212-941-8900
Web: www.thegreenwichhotel.com
Prices: $$$$

75 Rooms

13 Suites

The Greenwich Hotel

Spanning the worlds of classic elegance and city chic, this TriBeCa stunner was unceremoniously unveiled in spring 2008. Though the hoopla was kept to a minimum—despite the fact that Robert DeNiro and his son are partners—the Greenwich is a hotel to crow about. Attention to detail is evident here from the construction materials to the organic bath amenities, all reflecting au courant Italian sensibilities.

Among the 88 rooms, no two are alike. Carved pine doors open into refined chambers boasting Duxiana beds, custom-designed settees, and hardwood floors. Ten-foot-high ceilings create an airy feel. The same care is taken in the design of the bathrooms, with their brass hardware, Frette towels, and mosaic tiled showers. All the modern electronic amenities apply as well.

An on-site fitness center and a lantern-lit indoor swimming pool will take care of your exercise needs, while the Japanese-inspired Shibui spa spotlights relaxation with a shiatsu room and a room for traditional bathing rituals. Italian fare takes top billing at Locanda Verde by Chef Andrew Carmellini.

Smyth

B3

85 West Broadway (at Chambers St.)

Subway: Chambers St (West Broadway)
Phone: 212-587-7000 or 888-587-6984
Web: www.thompsonhotels.com
Prices: **$$$**

96 Rooms

4 Suites

Michael Weber

The latest in the Thompson Hotel Group's string of boutique properties around Manhattan, the Smyth is a 13-story condominium/hotel hybrid; the top four floors are dedicated to Smyth Upstairs, consisting of 15 luxurious apartments. Designer Yabu Pushelberg decked out the stunning public spaces in a modern mélange of marble, onyx, leather, and textured wall coverings. It all combines to create a playful sense and a sexy vibe—with attitude to spare.

Room décor reflects a mid-20th century sensibility, illustrated by clean lines, white walls, velvet fabrics, Sferra linens, and lots of wood. Despite the hotel's location right off busy Chambers Street, the windows do a surprisingly good job of blocking out noise from the street below. Suite upgrades add the likes of a wet bar, two full bathrooms, and perhaps a terrace with seating for six. In the bathrooms, gray-and-white marble subway tiles create a sparkling facing on the walls.

Plein Sud, the highly anticipated restaurant provides room service; amenities such as in-room massage, valet parking, and a personal shopper are de rigueur. The jury is still out, but the Smyth may be destined as the TriBeCa hot spot for the hip traveling set.

Tribeca Grand

2 Sixth Ave. (at Church St.)

Subway: Canal St (Sixth Ave.)
Phone: 212-519-6600 or 877-519-6600
Web: www.tribecagrand.com
Prices: $$$

186 Rooms

15 Suites

Tribeca Grand

Frequented by celebrities and the oh-so-hip Euro-set, the Tribeca Grand gives every guest the star treatment. Sister to the Soho Grand, this hotel greets guests in its airy, vaulted atrium lobby—often used as a movie backdrop—whose clean lines evoke the Prairie style of architect Frank Lloyd Wright. In the evening, the lobby's swanky Church Lounge becomes a destination in itself, as it fills with the hot and hip music- and film-industry set. In summer, the party spills out to sidewalk seating along Sixth Avenue.

Deep earth tones, with bright sparks of orange and yellow, color the comfortable guest rooms, which are equally well-equipped for business and leisure travelers. Movie mavens may want to reserve an iStudio room, furnished with a video camera and a computer loaded with every program an amateur film buff could want.

Paris Hilton may feel perfectly at home here, but so would her pup. Owned by Leonard and Emanuel Stern, members of the family that founded Hartz Mountain Industries, the Tribeca Grand accommodates pets in equally high style. Had to leave your four-footed friend at home? Request a goldfish to keep you company in your room.

Bentley

B4

500 E. 62nd St. (at York Ave.)

Subway: Lexington Av - 59 St
Phone: 212-644-6000 or 888-664-6835
Web: www.nychotels.com
Prices: **$$**

161 Rooms
36 Suites

The Bentley

It may be a little bit of a walk to the subway, Central Park, and the shops, but sitting on the East River, with easy access to-and-from the airports, it's worth the extra blocks for the value and accessibility. The Bentley may not be new or trendy, but it makes a fashionable first impression. Floor-to-ceiling windows, geometric-patterned carpets, marble flooring, and contemporary furnishings fill the art deco lobby of this 21-story glass-and-steel office building, which was converted into a hotel in 1998.

By New York City standard, rooms are surprisingly spacious. A bit the worse for wear, furnishings and carpeting adhere to a neutral color scheme. Seating nooks by the windows take in views of the East River and Queensboro Bridge. Families favor the extra space offered in the 36 suites, complete with pull-out sofas or futons. Given the location and moderate prices, this hotel is a good find.

The Bentley doesn't serve breakfast, but offers complimentary coffee during the day. If you don't feel up to dining out, the rooftop restaurant boasts panoramic city views with its limited menu. Valet parking, free daily newspapers, and concierge service count among other amenities provided.

The Carlyle

35 E. 76th St. (at Madison Ave.)

Subway: 77 St
Phone: 212-744-1600 or 800-227-5737
Web: www.thecarlyle.com
Prices: **$$$$**

124 Rooms

64 Suites

The Carlyle

Named for British historian Thomas Carlyle, this hotel epitomizes opulence with its fine artwork, Baccarat crystal light fixtures, and marble baths. Individually decorated Classic aka "standard" rooms are dressed in Louis XVI-style with original Audubon prints, 440-thread-count Italian linens, and elegant area rugs over wood floors. A select few of the Carlyle's roomy suites feature a baby-grand piano for the musically inclined.

Since it opened across from Central Park in 1930, The Carlyle has hosted every American president since Truman, along with a roster of foreign dignitaries from Prime Minister Nehru to Princess Diana—how's that for an A-list?

For entertainment, there's Café Carlyle, where Woody Allen regularly jams with the Eddie Davis New Orleans jazz band. Legendary Bemelmans Bar, renowned for its whimsical mural of characters from artist Ludwig Bemelmans' famous Madeline series of children's books, is a popular place for a cocktail.

With a contemporary menu almost as classy as the crowd it draws, the handsome Carlyle Restaurant proves a perfect complement to the hotel's sophistication. The hotel's new Sense Spa offers weary guests 4,000 square feet of soothing indulgence.

The Lowell

28 E. 63rd St. (bet. Madison & Park Aves.)

Subway: Lexington Av - 63 St
Phone: 212-838-1400 or 800-221-4444
Web: www.lowellhotel.com
Prices: **$$$$**

25 Rooms
47 Suites

The Lowell

From the moment you step inside the silk-paneled lobby, you'll sense the European elegance that defines The Lowell. Intimate and sumptuous, this place appeals to those who value discretion, in both the size of the property and the attitude of the staff.

With suites outnumbering rooms 47 to 25, the emphasis here is on residential luxury. Indeed, this art deco brick and glazed terra-cotta structure was completed in 1926 as an apartment hotel. While lavish suites boast wood-burning fireplaces, private terraces, kitchens, and more, all rooms are individually decorated with marble baths and original art and antiques.

The Lowell unveiled new healthful-living options in response to requests from its sophisticated travelers. Guests don't need to forsake their daily exercise routine since the hotel's fully equipped fitness center offers personal trainers and Pilates instructors, in addition to Cybex equipment and free weights. Maps of nearby Central Park are available for those who prefer to exercise outdoors. Come mealtime, menus for the Pembroke Room and in-room dining are now stocked with nutritious, low-calorie, and low-carb choices—so there's no excuse for cheating on your diet.

The Mark

B2

25 E. 77th St. (at Madison Ave.)

Subway: 77 St
Phone: 212-744-4300
Web: www.themarkhotel.com
Prices: $$$$

100 Rooms

50 Suites

Todd Eberle

This landmark hotel, originally opened in 1927, hits all of the right marks. Closed for three years for a top-to-bottom renovation by famed French designer Jacques Grange, The Mark has reopened with a bang. Grange's updates—like the dramatic black-and-white flooring—have given the hotel an incredibly fresh new look.

Set just off Madison Avenue, The Mark has a prime location. Close to it all, yet located on a side street, this hotel feels more like an exclusive private residence than an internationally known hotel. Even the white-glove amenities—Frédéric Fekkai salon, Jean-Georges Vongerichten restaurant, and John Sitaras 24-hour fitness center attest to the residential atmosphere.

Comfortably sized, the rooms and suites deliver top notch accommodations. Creamy coffered ceilings show off a classic style, while polished metal light fixtures, contemporary art, and sleek upholstered furnishings punch up the modern quotient. Creature comforts, including ample closet space that would make any New Yorker green with envy, are abundant. Even the mini bar goes above and beyond with three pullout, refrigerated drawers. Butler services ensure that guests never endure PC-related frustration.

The Regency

540 Park Ave. (at 61st St.)

Subway: Lexington Av - 59 St
Phone: 212-759-4100 or 800-233-2356
Web: www.loewshotels.com
Prices: $$$$

267 Rooms
86 Suites

Thibault Jeanson

Public spaces ooze personality at the Loews flagship, sitting right on Park Avenue. Accommodations are bland in comparison, but large by New York standards, with abundant closet space and enough room to stay comfortably for several days (as long as you don't mind that the mattresses and bathrooms could use upgrading). The pleasant team offers a high level of service, and if your pup is traveling with you, the hotel offers dog-walking services as well as a separate room-service menu for pets.

For good dining and entertainment options, you don't have to leave the hotel. The upscale restaurant, 540 Park, is always packed in the evening, attracting as much of a local following as it does hotel guests. At breakfast, this place shakes with major players brokering deals over bacon and eggs. The Library lounge is a cozy—and popular—spot for a cocktail any night of the week. Its menu runs to comfort food such as chicken pot pie and braised lamb shank.

Last but not least, there's Feinsteins at the Regency, named for its owner—pop vocalist and songwriter Michael Feinstein. This blast from the past still packs 'em in for cabaret headliners six nights a week.

The Surrey

20 E. 76th St. (at Madison Ave.)

Subway: 77 St
Phone: 212-288-3700
Web: www.thesurrey.com
Prices: $$$$

158 Rooms
32 Suites

Tom McWilliam

There is just something debonair about The Surrey. Maybe it's because this former private residence once housed the likes of Claudette Colbert, Bette Davis, and John F. Kennedy. After a $60 million renovation, it looks and feels swanky, suave, and sophisticated. It is the kind of place where the cast of *Mad Men* could easily take up residence.

In keeping with the building's history, the rooms and suites feel wonderfully private. The guestrooms are handsomely decorated in shades of gray and cream with polished wood furnishings. The in-room dining (or drinking) menu would make Don Draper seriously drool—a mixologist is sent up to your room to prepare cocktails with enough for 4-5 drinks.

First-rate amenities, such as the elegant spa and well-appointed 24-hour fitness room, are the calling card of The Surrey. The rooftop terrace is an exceptional private space reserved exclusively for hotel guests. Bar Pleiades, part art deco, part homage to Coco Chanel, personifies the luxury and class of the Upper East Side. Of course, Café Boulud's winning cuisine and elegant atmosphere make it the jewel in the Surrey's crown.

Mandarin Oriental

A4

80 Columbus Circle (at 60th St.)

Subway: 59 St - Columbus Circle
Phone: 212-805-8800 or 866-801-8880
Web: www.mandarinoriental.com
Prices: $$$$

202 Rooms

46 Suites

Mandarin Oriental

Everything you could desire in New York City lies literally at the doorstep of the Mandarin Oriental. Occupying floors 35 to 54 in the north tower of the Time Warner Center, this hotel flaunts its enviable location overlooking Central Park. Also the site of such stellar restaurants as Per Se and Masa, hotel guests have direct access to the shops located inside the Time Warner Center at Columbus Circle. And don't pass up the contemporary Asian cuisine on-site at Asiate.

From the moment you enter to the moment you leave, the hotel's top-drawer service will make you feel like a VIP. Masculine yet delicate, modern yet timeless, guestrooms incorporate soigné touches such as cherry woods, silvery silks, and Fili D'oro linens. The view's the thing here; and the scenery is played up to full advantage with a wall of floor-to-ceiling windows in each room.

No visit to this unforgettable place is complete without a trip to the 36th-floor spa, which offers a customized "journey for the senses," booked in blocks of time rather than by treatment. The lobby lounge is an elegant spot to sip on a modern cocktail while taking in the panoramic view.

On the Ave

2178 Broadway (at 77th St.)

Subway: 79 St
Phone: 212-362-1100 or 800-497-6028
Web: www.ontheave.com
Prices: $$

274 Rooms

8 Suites

On The Ave

Broadway without the buzz is what awaits you On the Ave. Guests here get a respite from the bustle of midtown in this quiet Upper West Side neighborhood, where many of the city's natural and man-made treasures can be found. Fancy a walk in Central Park or a visit to the Museum of Natural History? Both are less than three blocks away. If you wish to explore farther afield, the subway station is just a two-block walk.

Shades of gray, ecru, and pewter color the restrained contemporary room décor, while baths sport brushed stainless-steel sinks and marble tiles. If you're not afraid of heights, rooms on the top three floors boast balconies with panoramas of the Hudson River and Central Park. Don't have a view? Take the elevator to the 16th floor, where you can relax and look out over uptown from the furnished and landscaped balcony. Backlit black-and-white photographs of Gotham City adorn the lobby and hallways of this hotel.

Exhilarated and ravenous after a day flooded with shopping and sightseeing? Step out of your room for a slew of comforting and contemporary American delights from Fatty Crab to Vai.

Trump International Hotel & Tower

1 Central Park West (at Columbus Circle)

Subway: 59 St - Columbus Circle
Phone: 212-299-1000 or 888-448-7867
Web: www.trumpintl.com
Prices: $$$$

38 Rooms

129 Suites

Trump Hotel Collection

An icon for its association with its flamboyant owner, this 52-story tower does Donald Trump proud. The location is ideal, with upscale shopping at the Time Warner Center and the attractions of Central Park right outside the door.

More than two-thirds of the accommodations—located on the 3rd through 17th floors—are spacious one- or two-bedroom suites boasting custom-designed furniture and great city and park views. A blissful night's sleep awaits in lodgings that range from 460 square feet for a junior suite to 1,350 square feet for a two-bedroom unit. All have kitchens stocked with china and crystal; if you don't feel like cooking, you can arrange for a member of the staff from the stellar chef—Jean Georges' restaurant—to prepare a gourmet meal in your room.

The 55-foot-long indoor pool is perfect for swimming laps, and the Techno-Gym equipment at the fitness center supplies a challenging workout (personal training and one-on-one yoga sessions are available).

Offering everything from complimentary business cards to free local phone calls, Trump's signature Attaché service caters to The Donald in everyone.

Nu Hotel

D3

85 Smith St. (bet. Atlantic Ave. & State St.)

Subway: Hoyt - Schermerhorn
Phone: 718-852-8585
Web: www.nuhotelbrooklyn.com
Prices: $

90 Rooms

3 Suites

Gridley & Graves Photography

Housed in a condominium tower near the quaint residential neighborhood of Cobble Hill, Nu Hotel opened in July 2008 and caters to the budget-conscious with contemporary style for reasonable rates. Located steps away from the government offices of downtown Brooklyn, the hotel is as ideally situated for those with business in the area as it is for guests visiting nearby family and friends.

Wide hallways lead to eco-friendly rooms dressed in organic white linens and modern light wood furnishings against a cool palette swathed in lead-free paint. White-tiled bathrooms incorporate a whimsical touch: a chalkboard wall for doodling or leaving messages for housekeeping. Inspired by urban lofts, suites may add a hammock or bunk beds as inventive sleeping spaces for extra guests.

The hotel has no restaurant, but does offer a complimentary daily buffet continental breakfast downstairs at Nu Bar.

And, sure, you can take the subway into Manhattan—there are a multitude of lines nearby—for shopping and dining, but why bother when the chic boutiques and culinary enticements of Smith Street are such an easy walk away?

Where to **Eat**

Where to **Stay**

Alphabetical List of Restaurants

C

D

E

F

G

H

I

N

O

S

T

U

V

W

X

Y

Z

Restaurants by Cuisine

American

Argentinian

Asian

Deli

Eastern European

Ethiopian

European

Filipino

French

Fusion

Gastropub

German

Greek

Indian

International

Italian

Japanese

Korean

Latin American

Lebanese

Malaysian

Mediterranean

Russian

Scandinavian

Seafood

South African

Southern

Southwestern

Spanish

Sri Lankan

Steakhouse

Thai

Tibetan

Turkish

Uzbek

Vegan

Vegetarian

Vietnamese

Cuisines by Neighborhood

MANHATTAN

Chelsea

Chinatown & Little Italy

East Village

Financial District

Gramercy, Flatiron & Union Square

Greenwich, West Village & Meatpacking District

SoHo & Nolita

TriBeCa

Upper East Side

Starred Restaurants

Within the selection we offer you, some restaurants deserve to be highlighted for their particularly good cuisine. When giving one, two, or three Michelin stars, there are a number of elements that we consider including the quality of the ingredients, the technical skill and flair that goes into their preparation, the blend and clarity of flavours, and the balance of the menu. Just as important is the ability to produce excellent cooking time and again. We make as many visits as we need, so that our readers may be assured of quality and consistency.

A two or three-star restaurant has to offer something very special in its cuisine; a real element of creativity, originality, or "personality" that sets it apart from the rest. Three stars – our highest award – are given to the choicest restaurants, where the whole dining experience is superb.

Cuisine in any style, modern or traditional, may be eligible for a star. Due to the fact we apply the same independent standards everywhere, the awards have become benchmarks of reliability and excellence in over 20 countries in Europe and Asia, particularly in France, where we have awarded stars for 100 years, and where the phrase "Now that's real three-star quality!" has entered into the language.

The awarding of a star is based solely on the quality of the cuisine.

✿✿✿

Exceptional cuisine, worth a special journey.

One always eats here extremely well, sometimes superbly. Distinctive dishes are precisely executed, using superlative ingredients.

✿✿

Excellent cuisine, worth a detour.

Skillfully and carefully crafted dishes of outsanding quality.

✿

A very good restaurant in its category.

A place offering cuisine prepared to a consistently high standard.

Bib Gourmand

This symbol indicates our inspector's favorites for good value. For $40 or less, you can enjoy two courses and a glass of wine or a dessert (not including tax or gratuity).

Under $25

Brunch

Late Dining

Where to **eat** ▶ Late Dining

Alphabetical List of Hotels

The world No.1 in tires with 16.3% of the market

A business presence in over 170 countries

A manufacturing footprint at the heart of markets

In 2009 **72** industrial sites in **19** countries produced:

- **150** million tires
- **10** million maps and guides

Highly international teams

Over **109 200** employees* from all cultures on all continents including **6 000** people employed in R&D centers in Europe, the US and Asia.

*102,692 full-time equivalent staff

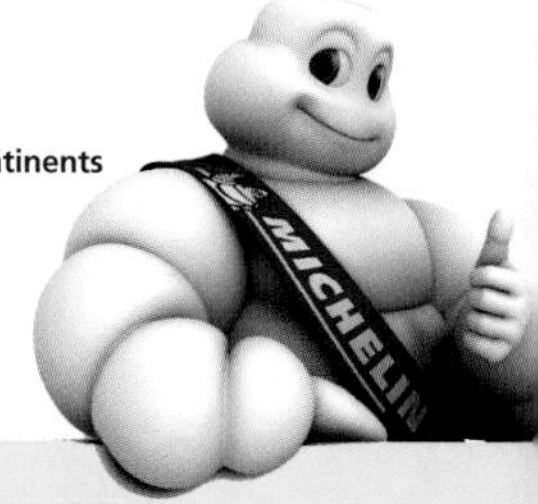

The Michelin Group at a glance

Michelin competes

At the end of 2009

Le Mans 24-hour race
12 consecutive years of victories

Endurance 2008
- 6 victories on 6 stages in Le Mans Series
- 12 victories on 12 stages in American Le Mans Series

Paris-Dakar
Since the beginning of the event, the Michelin group has won in all categories

Moto Endurance
2009 World Champion

Trial
Every World Champion title since 1981 (except 1992)

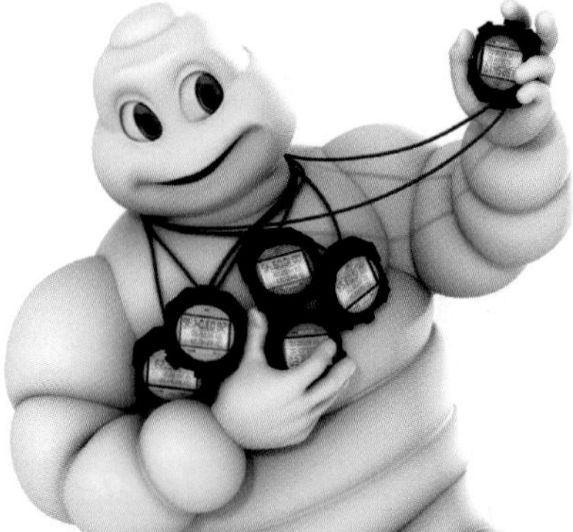

Michelin, established close to its customers

○ **68 plants in 19 countries**

- Algeria
- Brazil
- Canada
- China
- Colombia
- France
- Germany
- Hungary
- Italy
- Japan
- Mexico
- Poland
- Romania
- Russia
- Serbia
- Spain
- Thailand
- UK
- USA

● **A Technology Center spread over 3 continents**

- Asia
- Europe
- North America

● **2 Natural rubber plantations**

- Brazil

Our mission

To make a sustainable contribution to progress in the mobility of goods and people by enhancing freedom of movement, safety, efficiency and pleasure when on the move.

Michelin committed to environmental-friendliness

Michelin, world leader in low rolling resistance tires, actively reduces fuel consumption and vehicle gas emission.

For its products, Michelin develops state-of-the-art technologies in order to:
- Reduce fuel consumption, while improving overall tire performance.
- Increase life cycle to reduce the number of tires to be processed at the end of their useful lives;
- Use raw materials which have a low impact on the environment.

Furthermore, at the end of 2008, 99.5% of tire production in volume was carried out in ISO 14001* certified plants.

Michelin is committed to implementing recycling channels for end-of-life tires.

*environmental certification

Passenger Car
Light Truck

Truck

Michelin
a key mobility enabler

Earthmover

Aircraft

Agricultural

Two-wheel **Distribution**

Partnered with vehicle manufacturers, in tune with users, active in competition and in all the distribution channels, Michelinis continually innovating to promote mobility today and to invent that of tomorrow.

Maps and Guides

ViaMichelin, travel assistance services

Michelin Lifestyle, for your travel accessories

MICHELIN
plays on balanced performance

- **Long tire life**
- **Fuel savings**
- **Safety on the road**

... MICHELIN tires provide you with the best performance, without making a single sacrifice.

The MICHELIN tire pure technology

1 Tread
A thick layer of rubber provides contact with the ground. It has to channel water away and last as long as possible.

2 Crown plies
This double or triple reinforced belt has both vertical flexibility and high lateral rigidity. It provides the steering capacity.

3 Sidewalls
These cover and protect the textile casing whose role is to attach the tire tread to the wheel rim.

4 Bead area for attachment to the rim
Its internal bead wire clamps the tire firmly against the wheel rim.

5 Inner liner
This makes the tire almost totally impermeable and maintains the correct inflation pressure.

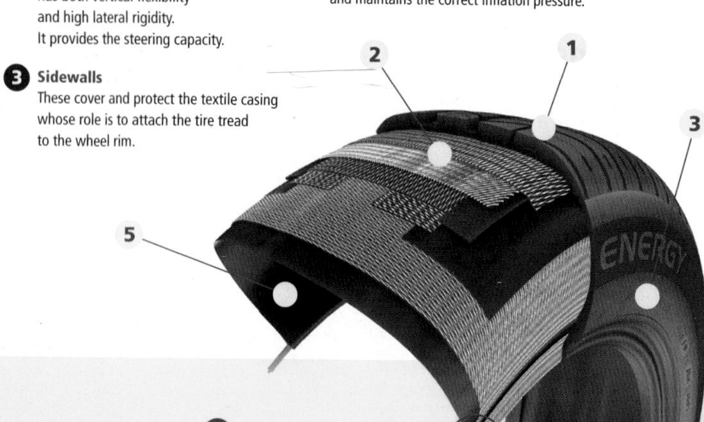